ROUTLEDGE
STUDENT STATUTES

....

European Union Legislation
2010–2011

Designed specifically for students, and responding to current market feedback, Routledge Student Statutes offer a comprehensive collection of statutory provisions un-annotated and therefore ideal for LLB and GDL course and exam use. In addition, an accompanying website offers extensive guidance on how to use and interpret statutes, providing valuable tutorial and exam preparation.

The Routledge Student Statutes series collect together, in each volume, all the legislation students need to pass their exams so it is comprehensive, clearly presented and easy to access.

Routledge Student Statutes provide extensive innovative features, vital in aiding LLB and GDL learning:

- Comprehensive content, with legislation carefully selected to match the common curriculum
- Written by leading experts in each field so students can feel confident in the experience and judgement behind each selection
- Un-annotated, making the series ideal for both course and exam use
- Each title contains alphabetical, chronological and thematic contents listings and is fully indexed making it easy to navigate
- A free Companion Website providing students with extra guidance and testing on how to use and interpret statutes
- Updated annually to incorporate all of the latest legislation covered in UK law syllabi
- Highly competitive price makes Routledge Student Statutes the statutes series of choice

Jeffrey Kenner is Professor of European Law at the University of Nottingham.

ROUTLEDGE STUDENT STATUTES

Titles in the series:

http://cw.routledge.com/textbooks/statutes/

ROUTLEDGE
STUDENT STATUTES

European Union Legislation
2010–2011

JEFFREY KENNER

Professor of European Law at the University of Nottingham

Routledge
Taylor & Francis Group

LONDON AND NEW YORK

First published 2011
by Routledge
2 Park Square, Milton Park, Abingdon, Oxon, OX14 4RN

Simultaneously published in the USA and Canada
by Routledge
270 Madison Avenue, New York, NY 10016

Routledge is an imprint of the Taylor & Francis Group, an informa business

Typeset in Sabon by RefineCatch Limited, Bungay, Suffolk
Printed and bound in Great Britain by MPG Book Group, UK

British Library Cataloguing in Publication Data
A catalogue record for this book is available from the British Library

Parliamentary material is reproduced with the permission of the Controller of HMSO on behalf of Parliament.

ISBN13: 978–0–415–58240–7 (pbk)

Contents

Preface

The purpose of this book is to compile and present in an accessible form the essential European Union legislation that all law students need to have to hand in tutorials, in private study and in the examination hall. EU Treaty and legislation books are the principal tool for instant reference for students on a regular basis throughout the year. My aim has been to produce a book that students can use quickly and effectively whenever and wherever the need arises, whether in parallel to reading from text books, the Internet, or lecture notes, or when seeking to intervene in class, or, ultimately, to search for and speedily identify an elusive point of law in the examination. It is also ideal to use in conjunction with further research into the sources of the law from EUR-Lex, the EU's wonderful online depository of the *acquis communautaire* and the essential source for the material contained within this book.

Having taught European Union law for the best part of the last twenty years I have witnessed an astounding process of legislative change, with at least five attempts – not always successful – at amending the Treaties, not counting the Acts of Accession for new Member States. In whole areas of substantive EU Law, from the completion of the internal market to new or expanded competences in areas such a social policy, the legal framework has been transformed. For an EU legislation book to be effective in the contexts in which it is most needed by students, the selection of laws must be relevant and up to date, the editing concise, and the presentation clear. I have sought to ensure that every editorial decision I make is tested against these criteria.

For the 2010–2011 edition it is a question of out with the old and in with the new. After almost ten years of constitutional ping-pong the European Union's Treaty structure has, at last, been radically reformed with the adoption of the Treaty of Lisbon, effective from 1 December 2009. Lisbon has spawned not one but two treaties which have "the same legal value" – the Treaty on European Union (TEU) and the unfortunately named Treaty on the Functioning of the European Union (TFEU). The former is the successor to the old TEU but it is much broader in scope, setting out the Union's values and principles, its institutional framework, and wide-ranging provisions on external action and the Common Foreign and Security Policy. The latter is a continuation Treaty evolving from the original European Economic Community Treaty signed in Rome in 1957. Both treaties are included in full in Part I of the book followed by a selection of the most important protocols annexed to them. In Part II, the official Tables of Equivalences are reproduced for converting the old Treaty numbers into the new and vice versa. Part III contains the text of the Charter of Fundamental Rights of the European Union of 2000, as adapted in 2007. Following the collapse of the Constitutional Treaty in 2004, the Charter remains constitutionally separate from the Treaties and yet it has, under Article 6 of the TEU, the "same legal value as the Treaties". The Charter's application is subject to a separate Protocol concerning the United Kingdom and Poland, included in the Protocols section of Part I.

Fortunately, the texts of the Treaties, the protocols and the Charter can now be found in a single volume of the *Official Journal of the European Union*. In order to make these documents as accessible and readable as possible in this book it has been necessary to exclude some of the lesser protocols and the other annexes and declarations that accompany the Treaties.

For secondary legislation, I have included, firstly, the essential supplementary rules governing the institutions, law-making and the judicial process – the core constitutional elements of undergraduate law courses – and, secondly, implementing legislation in the substantive areas of internal market and competition law, normally taught in the second semester of whole year EU law courses or as separate subjects on both undergraduate and postgraduate programmes. I have also included the core directives on equal treatment and working conditions as a source for those studying in the broad field of EU social policy.

I have sought to cover these areas as fully as possible in preference to extending the book thinly into other areas. In order to ensure that the book has a readable font size and to start each piece of legislation on a separate page I have sought to eliminate superfluous material by omitting unnecessary footnotes and, in some cases, dispensing with preambles.

For more guidance on how to use this book why not access the additional learning resources online at http://cw.routledge.com/textbooks/statutes? Here you can practice your application of EU legislation in a series of exam-type scenarios. You will find a set of multiple choice questions to test you on your knowledge of both primary and secondary legislation. Finally, there is a guide on how to gain the maximum benefit from an EU legislation book.

The legislation in this book is up-to-date as of 1st June 2010. I am grateful to the Publications Office of the European Union for their kind permission to reproduce the materials from EUR-Lex and Europa used in this volume. In some cases the consolidated form of legislation published in EUR-Lex has been the basis for reproduction and, although wholly accurate, it is not strictly authentic as it is not reproduced in the form published in the *Official Journal of the European Union*

I have been immensely helped in this task by the smooth operation at Routledge, especially from Rebecca Slorach, Lloyd Langman, Holly Davis and Fiona Kinnear. I am also hugely in debt, as ever, to Jacqueline Abbott for her encouragement and support throughout this project.

Jeff Kenner
Nottingham
June 2010

Guide to the Companion Website

....

http://cw.routledge.com/textbooks/statutes

Visit the Companion Website for Routledge Student Statutes in order to:

- Understand how to use a statute book in tutorials and exams;

- Learn how to interpret statutes and other legislation to maximum effect;

- Gain essential practice in statute interpretation prior to your exams, through unique problem-based scenarios;

- Test your understanding of statutes through a set of Multiple Choice Questions for revision or to check your own progress;

- Understand how the law is developing with updates, additional information and links to useful websites.

I Treaties

NOTE TO THE READER ACCOMPANYING THE CONSOLIDATED VERSIONS OF THE TREATY ON EUROPEAN UNION AND THE TREATY ON THE FUNCTIONING OF THE EUROPEAN UNION
OJ C 83, 30.3.2010*

This publication contains the consolidated versions of the Treaty on European Union and of the Treaty on the Functioning of the European Union, together with the annexes and protocols thereto, as they result from the amendments introduced by the Treaty of Lisbon, which was signed on 13 December 2007 in Lisbon and which entered into force on 1 December 2009. It also contains the declarations annexed to the Final Act of the Intergovernmental Conference which adopted the Treaty of Lisbon.

As indicated in the Note to the Reader accompanying the previous issue of the consolidated Treaties (OJ C 115, 9.5.2008, p. 1), the current issue includes those rectifications which were adopted up to the time of publication.

This publication also contains the Charter of Fundamental Rights of the European Union which was proclaimed at Strasbourg on 12 December 2007 by the European Parliament, the Council and the Commission (OJ C 303, 14.12.2007, p. 1). This text repeats and adapts the Charter proclaimed on 7 December 2000, and replaces it with effect from 1 December 2009, the date of entry into force of the Treaty of Lisbon. By virtue of the first subparagraph of Article 6(1) of the Treaty on European Union, the Charter proclaimed in 2007 has the same legal value as the Treaties.

Final paragraph omitted.

---

*   EDITOR'S NOTE: This book reproduces essentially the bulk of the material referred to in the above Note to the Reader accompanying the consolidated Treaties in the edition of the *Official Journal of the European Union* of 30 March 2010, C 83. However, a number of the protocols have been omitted as have the annexes and declarations. For a full set of the Treaties, past and present, including the Treaties of Accession, refer to EUR-Lex at: http://eur-lex.europa.eu/en/treaties/index.htm.

CONSOLIDATED VERSION OF THE TREATY ON EUROPEAN UNION

OJ C 83, 30.3.2010, p. 13*

PREAMBLE

His Majesty the King of the Belgians, Her Majesty the Queen of Denmark, The President of the Federal Republic of Germany, The President of Ireland, The President of the Hellenic Republic, His Majesty the King of Spain, The President of the French Republic, The President of the Italian Republic, His Royal Highness the Grand Duke of Luxembourg, Her Majesty the Queen of the Netherlands, The President of the Portuguese Republic, Her Majesty the Queen of the United Kingdom of Great Britain and Northern Ireland,[1]

RESOLVED to mark a new stage in the process of European integration undertaken with the establishment of the European Communities,

DRAWING INSPIRATION from the cultural, religious and humanist inheritance of Europe, from which have developed the universal values of the inviolable and inalienable rights of the human person, freedom, democracy, equality and the rule of law,

RECALLING the historic importance of the ending of the division of the European continent and the need to create firm bases for the construction of the future Europe,

CONFIRMING their attachment to the principles of liberty, democracy and respect for human rights and fundamental freedoms and of the rule of law,

CONFIRMING their attachment to fundamental social rights as defined in the European Social Charter signed at Turin on 18 October 1961 and in the 1989 Community Charter of the Fundamental Social Rights of Workers,

---

*   EDITOR'S NOTE: Where articles in the Treaty on European Union replace previous Treaty articles, the old article numbers from the previous version of the Treaty on European Union (TEU) and/or the now replaced Treaty establishing the European Community (TEC) are shown in brackets. See the Table of Equivalences for the Treaty on European Union reproduced in Part II of this edition for a complete conversion table from the old to the new article numbers and vice versa.

1   The Republic of Bulgaria, the Czech Republic, the Republic of Estonia, the Republic of Cyprus, the Republic of Latvia, the Republic of Lithuania, the Republic of Hungary, the Republic of Malta, the Republic of Austria, the Republic of Poland, Romania, the Republic of Slovenia, the Slovak Republic, the Republic of Finland and the Kingdom of Sweden have since become members of the European Union.

DESIRING to deepen the solidarity between their peoples while respecting their history, their culture and their traditions,

DESIRING to enhance further the democratic and efficient functioning of the institutions so as to enable them better to carry out, within a single institutional framework, the tasks entrusted to them,

RESOLVED to achieve the strengthening and the convergence of their economies and to establish an economic and monetary union including, in accordance with the provisions of this Treaty and of the Treaty on the Functioning of the European Union, a single and stable currency,

DETERMINED to promote economic and social progress for their peoples, taking into account the principle of sustainable development and within the context of the accomplishment of the internal market and of reinforced cohesion and environmental protection, and to implement policies ensuring that advances in economic integration are accompanied by parallel progress in other fields,

RESOLVED to establish a citizenship common to nationals of their countries,

RESOLVED to implement a common foreign and security policy including the progressive framing of a common defence policy, which might lead to a common defence in accordance with the provisions of Article 42, thereby reinforcing the European identity and its independence in order to promote peace, security and progress in Europe and in the world,

RESOLVED to facilitate the free movement of persons, while ensuring the safety and security of their peoples, by establishing an area of freedom, security and justice, in accordance with the provisions of this Treaty and of the Treaty on the Functioning of the European Union,

RESOLVED to continue the process of creating an ever closer union among the peoples of Europe, in which decisions are taken as closely as possible to the citizen in accordance with the principle of subsidiarity,

IN VIEW of further steps to be taken in order to advance European integration,

HAVE DECIDED to establish a European Union and to this end have designated as their Plenipotentiaries: *(list of plenipotentiaries not reproduced)*

WHO, having exchanged their full powers, found in good and due form, have agreed as follows:

TITLE I
COMMON PROVISIONS

Article 1 (ex Article 1 TEU)
By this Treaty, the HIGH CONTRACTING PARTIES establish among themselves a EUROPEAN UNION, hereinafter called 'the Union', on which the Member States confer competences to attain objectives they have in common.

This Treaty marks a new stage in the process of creating an ever closer union among the peoples of Europe, in which decisions are taken as openly as possible and as closely as possible to the citizen.

The Union shall be founded on the present Treaty and on the Treaty on the Functioning of the European Union (hereinafter referred to as 'the Treaties'). Those two Treaties shall have the same legal value. The Union shall replace and succeed the European Community.

Article 2

The Union is founded on the values of respect for human dignity, freedom, democracy, equality, the rule of law and respect for human rights, including the rights of persons belonging to minorities. These values are common to the Member States in a society in which pluralism, non-discrimination, tolerance, justice, solidarity and equality between women and men prevail.

Article 3 (ex Article 2 TEU)

1. The Union's aim is to promote peace, its values and the well-being of its peoples.

2. The Union shall offer its citizens an area of freedom, security and justice without internal frontiers, in which the free movement of persons is ensured in conjunction with appropriate measures with respect to external border controls, asylum, immigration and the prevention and combating of crime.

3. The Union shall establish an internal market. It shall work for the sustainable development of Europe based on balanced economic growth and price stability, a highly competitive social market economy, aiming at full employment and social progress, and a high level of protection and improvement of the quality of the environment. It shall promote scientific and technological advance.

    It shall combat social exclusion and discrimination, and shall promote social justice and protection, equality between women and men, solidarity between generations and protection of the rights of the child.

    It shall promote economic, social and territorial cohesion, and solidarity among Member States.

    It shall respect its rich cultural and linguistic diversity, and shall ensure that Europe's cultural heritage is safeguarded and enhanced.

4. The Union shall establish an economic and monetary union whose currency is the euro.

5. In its relations with the wider world, the Union shall uphold and promote its values and interests and contribute to the protection of its citizens. It shall contribute to peace, security, the sustainable development of the Earth, solidarity and mutual respect among peoples, free and fair trade, eradication of poverty and the protection of human rights, in particular the rights of the child, as well as to the strict observance and the development of international law, including respect for the principles of the United Nations Charter.

6. The Union shall pursue its objectives by appropriate means commensurate with the competences which are conferred upon it in the Treaties.

Article 4

1. In accordance with Article 5, competences not conferred upon the Union in the Treaties remain with the Member States.

2. The Union shall respect the equality of Member States before the Treaties as well as their national identities, inherent in their fundamental structures, political and constitutional, inclusive of regional and local self-government. It shall respect their essential State functions, including ensuring the territorial integrity of the State, maintaining law and order and safeguarding national security. In particular, national security remains the sole responsibility of each Member State.

3. Pursuant to the principle of sincere cooperation, the Union and the Member States shall, in full mutual respect, assist each other in carrying out tasks which flow from the Treaties.

    The Member States shall take any appropriate measure, general or particular, to ensure fulfilment of the obligations arising out of the Treaties or resulting from the acts of the institutions of the Union.

The Member States shall facilitate the achievement of the Union's tasks and refrain from any measure which could jeopardise the attainment of the Union's objectives.

Article 5 (ex Article 5 TEC)

1. The limits of Union competences are governed by the principle of conferral. The use of Union competences is governed by the principles of subsidiarity and proportionality.

2. Under the principle of conferral, the Union shall act only within the limits of the competences conferred upon it by the Member States in the Treaties to attain the objectives set out therein. Competences not conferred upon the Union in the Treaties remain with the Member States.

3. Under the principle of subsidiarity, in areas which do not fall within its exclusive competence, the Union shall act only if and in so far as the objectives of the proposed action cannot be sufficiently achieved by the Member States, either at central level or at regional and local level, but can rather, by reason of the scale or effects of the proposed action, be better achieved at Union level.

   The institutions of the Union shall apply the principle of subsidiarity as laid down in the Protocol on the application of the principles of subsidiarity and proportionality.

   National Parliaments ensure compliance with the principle of subsidiarity in accordance with the procedure set out in that Protocol.

4. Under the principle of proportionality, the content and form of Union action shall not exceed what is necessary to achieve the objectives of the Treaties.

   The institutions of the Union shall apply the principle of proportionality as laid down in the Protocol on the application of the principles of subsidiarity and proportionality.

Article 6 (ex Article 6 TEU)

1. The Union recognises the rights, freedoms and principles set out in the Charter of Fundamental Rights of the European Union of 7 December 2000, as adapted at Strasbourg, on 12 December 2007, which shall have the same legal value as the Treaties.

   The provisions of the Charter shall not extend in any way the competences of the Union as defined in the Treaties.

   The rights, freedoms and principles in the Charter shall be interpreted in accordance with the general provisions in Title VII of the Charter governing its interpretation and application and with due regard to the explanations referred to in the Charter, that set out the sources of those provisions.

2. The Union shall accede to the European Convention for the Protection of Human Rights and Fundamental Freedoms. Such accession shall not affect the Union's competences as defined in the Treaties.

3. Fundamental rights, as guaranteed by the European Convention for the Protection of Human Rights and Fundamental Freedoms and as they result from the constitutional traditions common to the Member States, shall constitute general principles of the Union's law.

Article 7 (ex Article 7 TEU)

1. On a reasoned proposal by one third of the Member States, by the European Parliament or by the European Commission, the Council, acting by a majority of four fifths of its members after obtaining the consent of the European Parliament, may determine that there is a clear risk of a serious breach by a Member State of the values referred to in Article 2. Before making such a determination, the Council shall hear the Member State in question and may address recommendations to it, acting in accordance with the same procedure.

The Council shall regularly verify that the grounds on which such a determination was made continue to apply.

2. The European Council, acting by unanimity on a proposal by one third of the Member States or by the Commission and after obtaining the consent of the European Parliament, may determine the existence of a serious and persistent breach by a Member State of the values referred to in Article 2, after inviting the Member State in question to submit its observations.

3. Where a determination under paragraph 2 has been made, the Council, acting by a qualified majority, may decide to suspend certain of the rights deriving from the application of the Treaties to the Member State in question, including the voting rights of the representative of the government of that Member State in the Council. In doing so, the Council shall take into account the possible consequences of such a suspension on the rights and obligations of natural and legal persons.

The obligations of the Member State in question under this Treaty shall in any case continue to be binding on that State.

4. The Council, acting by a qualified majority, may decide subsequently to vary or revoke measures taken under paragraph 3 in response to changes in the situation which led to their being imposed.

5. The voting arrangements applying to the European Parliament, the European Council and the Council for the purposes of this Article are laid down in Article 354 of the Treaty on the Functioning of the European Union.

Article 8
1. The Union shall develop a special relationship with neighbouring countries, aiming to establish an area of prosperity and good neighbourliness, founded on the values of the Union and characterised by close and peaceful relations based on cooperation.

2. For the purposes of paragraph 1, the Union may conclude specific agreements with the countries concerned. These agreements may contain reciprocal rights and obligations as well as the possibility of undertaking activities jointly. Their implementation shall be the subject of periodic consultation.

TITLE II
PROVISIONS ON DEMOCRATIC PRINCIPLES

Article 9
In all its activities, the Union shall observe the principle of the equality of its citizens, who shall receive equal attention from its institutions, bodies, offices and agencies. Every national of a Member State shall be a citizen of the Union. Citizenship of the Union shall be additional to and not replace national citizenship.

Article 10
1. The functioning of the Union shall be founded on representative democracy.

2. Citizens are directly represented at Union level in the European Parliament.

Member States are represented in the European Council by their Heads of State or Government and in the Council by their governments, themselves democratically accountable either to their national Parliaments, or to their citizens.

3. Every citizen shall have the right to participate in the democratic life of the Union. Decisions shall be taken as openly and as closely as possible to the citizen.

4.   Political parties at European level contribute to forming European political awareness and to expressing the will of citizens of the Union.

Article 11

1.   The institutions shall, by appropriate means, give citizens and representative associations the opportunity to make known and publicly exchange their views in all areas of Union action.

2.   The institutions shall maintain an open, transparent and regular dialogue with representative associations and civil society.

3.   The European Commission shall carry out broad consultations with parties concerned in order to ensure that the Union's actions are coherent and transparent.

4.   Not less than one million citizens who are nationals of a significant number of Member States may take the initiative of inviting the European Commission, within the framework of its powers, to submit any appropriate proposal on matters where citizens consider that a legal act of the Union is required for the purpose of implementing the Treaties.

The procedures and conditions required for such a citizens' initiative shall be determined in accordance with the first paragraph of Article 24 of the Treaty on the Functioning of the European Union.

Article 12

National Parliaments contribute actively to the good functioning of the Union:

(a)   through being informed by the institutions of the Union and having draft legislative acts of the Union forwarded to them in accordance with the Protocol on the role of national Parliaments in the European Union;

(b)   by seeing to it that the principle of subsidiarity is respected in accordance with the procedures provided for in the Protocol on the application of the principles of subsidiarity and proportionality;

(c)   by taking part, within the framework of the area of freedom, security and justice, in the evaluation mechanisms for the implementation of the Union policies in that area, in accordance with Article 70 of the Treaty on the Functioning of the European Union, and through being involved in the political monitoring of Europol and the evaluation of Eurojust's activities in accordance with Articles 88 and 85 of that Treaty;

(d)   by taking part in the revision procedures of the Treaties, in accordance with Article 48 of this Treaty;

(e)   by being notified of applications for accession to the Union, in accordance with Article 49 of this Treaty;

(f)   by taking part in the inter-parliamentary cooperation between national Parliaments and with the European Parliament, in accordance with the Protocol on the role of national Parliaments in the European Union.

TITLE III
PROVISIONS ON THE INSTITUTIONS

Article 13

1.   The Union shall have an institutional framework which shall aim to promote its values, advance its objectives, serve its interests, those of its citizens and those of the Member States, and ensure the consistency, effectiveness and continuity of its policies and actions.

The Union's institutions shall be:

> — the European Parliament,
> — the European Council,
> — the Council,
> — the European Commission (hereinafter referred to as "the Commission"),
> — the Court of Justice of the European Union,
> — the European Central Bank,
> — the Court of Auditors.

2. Each institution shall act within the limits of the powers conferred on it in the Treaties, and in conformity with the procedures, conditions and objectives set out in them. The institutions shall practice mutual sincere cooperation.

3. The provisions relating to the European Central Bank and the Court of Auditors and detailed provisions on the other institutions are set out in the Treaty on the Functioning of the European Union.

4. The European Parliament, the Council and the Commission shall be assisted by an Economic and Social Committee and a Committee of the Regions acting in an advisory capacity.

Article 14

1. The European Parliament shall, jointly with the Council, exercise legislative and budgetary functions. It shall exercise functions of political control and consultation as laid down in the Treaties. It shall elect the President of the Commission.

2. The European Parliament shall be composed of representatives of the Union's citizens. They shall not exceed seven hundred and fifty in number, plus the President. Representation of citizens shall be degressively proportional, with a minimum threshold of six members per Member State. No Member State shall be allocated more than ninety-six seats.

   The European Council shall adopt by unanimity, on the initiative of the European Parliament and with its consent, a decision establishing the composition of the European Parliament, respecting the principles referred to in the first subparagraph.

3. The members of the European Parliament shall be elected for a term of five years by direct universal suffrage in a free and secret ballot.

4. The European Parliament shall elect its President and its officers from among its members.

Article 15

1. The European Council shall provide the Union with the necessary impetus for its development and shall define the general political directions and priorities thereof. It shall not exercise legislative functions.

2. The European Council shall consist of the Heads of State or Government of the Member States, together with its President and the President of the Commission. The High Representative of the Union for Foreign Affairs and Security Policy shall take part in its work.

3. The European Council shall meet twice every six months, convened by its President. When the agenda so requires, the members of the European Council may decide each to be assisted by a minister and, in the case of the President of the Commission, by a member of the Commission. When the situation so requires, the President shall convene a special meeting of the European Council.

4. Except where the Treaties provide otherwise, decisions of the European Council shall be taken by consensus.

5. The European Council shall elect its President, by a qualified majority, for a term of two and a half years, renewable once. In the event of an impediment or serious misconduct,

the European Council can end the President's term of office in accordance with the same procedure.

6.   The President of the European Council:
   (a) shall chair it and drive forward its work;
   (b) shall ensure the preparation and continuity of the work of the European Council in cooperation with the President of the Commission, and on the basis of the work of the General Affairs Council;
   (c) shall endeavour to facilitate cohesion and consensus within the European Council;
   (d) shall present a report to the European Parliament after each of the meetings of the European Council.
   The President of the European Council shall, at his level and in that capacity, ensure the external representation of the Union on issues concerning its common foreign and security policy, without prejudice to the powers of the High Representative of the Union for Foreign Affairs and Security Policy.

   The President of the European Council shall not hold a national office.

Article 16

1.   The Council shall, jointly with the European Parliament, exercise legislative and budgetary functions. It shall carry out policy-making and coordinating functions as laid down in the Treaties.

2.   The Council shall consist of a representative of each Member State at ministerial level, who may commit the government of the Member State in question and cast its vote.

3.   The Council shall act by a qualified majority except where the Treaties provide otherwise.

4.   As from 1 November 2014, a qualified majority shall be defined as at least 55% of the members of the Council, comprising at least fifteen of them and representing Member States comprising at least 65% of the population of the Union.

   A blocking minority must include at least four Council members, failing which the qualified majority shall be deemed attained.

   The other arrangements governing the qualified majority are laid down in Article 238(2) of the Treaty on the Functioning of the European Union.

5.   The transitional provisions relating to the definition of the qualified majority which shall be applicable until 31 October 2014 and those which shall be applicable from 1 November 2014 to 31 March 2017 are laid down in the Protocol on transitional provisions.

6.   The Council shall meet in different configurations, the list of which shall be adopted in accordance with Article 236 of the Treaty on the Functioning of the European Union.

   The General Affairs Council shall ensure consistency in the work of the different Council configurations. It shall prepare and ensure the follow-up to meetings of the European Council, in liaison with the President of the European Council and the Commission.

   The Foreign Affairs Council shall elaborate the Union's external action on the basis of strategic guidelines laid down by the European Council and ensure that the Union's action is consistent.

7.   A Committee of Permanent Representatives of the Governments of the Member States shall be responsible for preparing the work of the Council.

8. The Council shall meet in public when it deliberates and votes on a draft legislative act. To this end, each Council meeting shall be divided into two parts, dealing respectively with deliberations on Union legislative acts and non-legislative activities.

9. The Presidency of Council configurations, other than that of Foreign Affairs, shall be held by Member State representatives in the Council on the basis of equal rotation, in accordance with the conditions established in accordance with Article 236 of the Treaty on the Functioning of the European Union.

Article 17

1. The Commission shall promote the general interest of the Union and take appropriate initiatives to that end. It shall ensure the application of the Treaties, and of measures adopted by the institutions pursuant to them. It shall oversee the application of Union law under the control of the Court of Justice of the European Union. It shall execute the budget and manage programmes. It shall exercise coordinating, executive and management functions, as laid down in the Treaties. With the exception of the common foreign and security policy, and other cases provided for in the Treaties, it shall ensure the Union's external representation. It shall initiate the Union's annual and multiannual programming with a view to achieving interinstitutional agreements.

2. Union legislative acts may only be adopted on the basis of a Commission proposal, except where the Treaties provide otherwise. Other acts shall be adopted on the basis of a Commission proposal where the Treaties so provide.

3. The Commission's term of office shall be five years.

    The members of the Commission shall be chosen on the ground of their general competence and European commitment from persons whose independence is beyond doubt.

    In carrying out its responsibilities, the Commission shall be completely independent. Without prejudice to Article 18(2), the members of the Commission shall neither seek nor take instructions from any Government or other institution, body, office or entity. They shall refrain from any action incompatible with their duties or the performance of their tasks.

4. The Commission appointed between the date of entry into force of the Treaty of Lisbon and 31 October 2014, shall consist of one national of each Member State, including its President and the High Representative of the Union for Foreign Affairs and Security Policy who shall be one of its Vice- Presidents.

5. As from 1 November 2014, the Commission shall consist of a number of members, including its President and the High Representative of the Union for Foreign Affairs and Security Policy, corresponding to two thirds of the number of Member States, unless the European Council, acting unanimously, decides to alter this number.

    The members of the Commission shall be chosen from among the nationals of the Member States on the basis of a system of strictly equal rotation between the Member States, reflecting the demographic and geographical range of all the Member States. This system shall be established unanimously by the European Council in accordance with Article 244 of the Treaty on the Functioning of the European Union.

6. The President of the Commission shall:
    (a) lay down guidelines within which the Commission is to work;
    (b) decide on the internal organisation of the Commission, ensuring that it acts consistently, efficiently and as a collegiate body;
    (c) appoint Vice-Presidents, other than the High Representative of the Union for Foreign Affairs and Security Policy, from among the members of the Commission.

A member of the Commission shall resign if the President so requests. The High Representative of the Union for Foreign Affairs and Security Policy shall resign, in accordance with the procedure set out in Article 18(1), if the President so requests.

7. Taking into account the elections to the European Parliament and after having held the appropriate consultations, the European Council, acting by a qualified majority, shall propose to the European Parliament a candidate for President of the Commission. This candidate shall be elected by the European Parliament by a majority of its component members. If he does not obtain the required majority, the European Council, acting by a qualified majority, shall within one month propose a new candidate who shall be elected by the European Parliament following the same procedure.

The Council, by common accord with the President-elect, shall adopt the list of the other persons whom it proposes for appointment as members of the Commission. They shall be selected, on the basis of the suggestions made by Member States, in accordance with the criteria set out in paragraph 3, second subparagraph, and paragraph 5, second subparagraph.

The President, the High Representative of the Union for Foreign Affairs and Security Policy and the other members of the Commission shall be subject as a body to a vote of consent by the European Parliament. On the basis of this consent the Commission shall be appointed by the European Council, acting by a qualified majority.

8. The Commission, as a body, shall be responsible to the European Parliament. In accordance with Article 234 of the Treaty on the Functioning of the European Union, the European Parliament may vote on a motion of censure of the Commission. If such a motion is carried, the members of the Commission shall resign as a body and the High Representative of the Union for Foreign Affairs and Security Policy shall resign from the duties that he carries out in the Commission.

Article 18

1. The European Council, acting by a qualified majority, with the agreement of the President of the Commission, shall appoint the High Representative of the Union for Foreign Affairs and Security Policy. The European Council may end his term of office by the same procedure.

2. The High Representative shall conduct the Union's common foreign and security policy. He shall contribute by his proposals to the development of that policy, which he shall carry out as mandated by the Council. The same shall apply to the common security and defence policy.

3. The High Representative shall preside over the Foreign Affairs Council.

4. The High Representative shall be one of the Vice-Presidents of the Commission. He shall ensure the consistency of the Union's external action. He shall be responsible within the Commission for responsibilities incumbent on it in external relations and for coordinating other aspects of the Union's external action. In exercising these responsibilities within the Commission, and only for these responsibilities, the High Representative shall be bound by Commission procedures to the extent that this is consistent with paragraphs 2 and 3.

Article 19

1. The Court of Justice of the European Union shall include the Court of Justice, the General Court and specialised courts. It shall ensure that in the interpretation and application of the Treaties the law is observed.

Member States shall provide remedies sufficient to ensure effective legal protection in the fields covered by Union law.

2. The Court of Justice shall consist of one judge from each Member State. It shall be assisted by Advocates-General.

The General Court shall include at least one judge per Member State.

The Judges and the Advocates-General of the Court of Justice and the Judges of the General Court shall be chosen from persons whose independence is beyond doubt and who satisfy the conditions set out in Articles 253 and 254 of the Treaty on the Functioning of the European Union. They shall be appointed by common accord of the governments of the Member States for six years. Retiring Judges and Advocates-General may be reappointed.

3.   The Court of Justice of the European Union shall, in accordance with the Treaties:
(a)   rule on actions brought by a Member State, an institution or a natural or legal person;
(b)   give preliminary rulings, at the request of courts or tribunals of the Member States, on the interpretation of Union law or the validity of acts adopted by the institutions;
(c)   rule in other cases provided for in the Treaties.

TITLE IV
PROVISIONS ON ENHANCED COOPERATION

Article 20 (ex Articles 27a to 27e, 40 to 40b and 43 to 45 TEU and ex Articles 11 and 11a TEC)
1.   Member States which wish to establish enhanced cooperation between themselves within the framework of the Union's non-exclusive competences may make use of its institutions and exercise those competences by applying the relevant provisions of the Treaties, subject to the limits and in accordance with the detailed arrangements laid down in this Article and in Articles 326 to 334 of the Treaty on the Functioning of the European Union.

Enhanced cooperation shall aim to further the objectives of the Union, protect its interests and reinforce its integration process. Such cooperation shall be open at any time to all Member States, in accordance with Article 328 of the Treaty on the Functioning of the European Union.

2.   The decision authorising enhanced cooperation shall be adopted by the Council as a last resort, when it has established that the objectives of such cooperation cannot be attained within a reasonable period by the Union as a whole, and provided that at least nine Member States participate in it. The Council shall act in accordance with the procedure laid down in Article 329 of the Treaty on the Functioning of the European Union.

3.   All members of the Council may participate in its deliberations, but only members of the Council representing the Member States participating in enhanced cooperation shall take part in the vote. The voting rules are set out in Article 330 of the Treaty on the Functioning of the European Union.

4.   Acts adopted in the framework of enhanced cooperation shall bind only participating Member States. They shall not be regarded as part of the *acquis* which has to be accepted by candidate States for accession to the Union.

TITLE V
GENERAL PROVISIONS ON THE UNION'S EXTERNAL ACTION AND SPECIFIC PROVISIONS ON THE COMMON FOREIGN AND SECURITY POLICY

Chapter 1 GENERAL PROVISIONS ON THE UNION'S EXTERNAL ACTION

Article 21
1.   The Union's action on the international scene shall be guided by the principles which have inspired its own creation, development and enlargement, and which it seeks to advance in

the wider world: democracy, the rule of law, the universality and indivisibility of human rights and fundamental freedoms, respect for human dignity, the principles of equality and solidarity, and respect for the principles of the United Nations Charter and international law.

The Union shall seek to develop relations and build partnerships with third countries, and international, regional or global organisations which share the principles referred to in the first subparagraph. It shall promote multilateral solutions to common problems, in particular in the framework of the United Nations.

2.   The Union shall define and pursue common policies and actions, and shall work for a high degree of cooperation in all fields of international relations, in order to:
   (a) safeguard its values, fundamental interests, security, independence and integrity;
   (b) consolidate and support democracy, the rule of law, human rights and the principles of international law;
   (c) preserve peace, prevent conflicts and strengthen international security, in accordance with the purposes and principles of the United Nations Charter, with the principles of the Helsinki Final Act and with the aims of the Charter of Paris, including those relating to external borders;
   (d) foster the sustainable economic, social and environmental development of developing countries, with the primary aim of eradicating poverty;
   (e) encourage the integration of all countries into the world economy, including through the progressive abolition of restrictions on international trade;
   (f) help develop international measures to preserve and improve the quality of the environment and the sustainable management of global natural resources, in order to ensure sustainable development;
   (g) assist populations, countries and regions confronting natural or man-made disasters; and
   (h) promote an international system based on stronger multilateral cooperation and good global governance.

3.   The Union shall respect the principles and pursue the objectives set out in paragraphs 1 and 2 in the development and implementation of the different areas of the Union's external action covered by this TITLE and by Part Five of the Treaty on the Functioning of the European Union, and of the external aspects of its other policies.

The Union shall ensure consistency between the different areas of its external action and between these and its other policies. The Council and the Commission, assisted by the High Representative of the Union for Foreign Affairs and Security Policy, shall ensure that consistency and shall cooperate to that effect.

Article 22
1.   On the basis of the principles and objectives set out in Article 21, the European Council shall identify the strategic interests and objectives of the Union.

Decisions of the European Council on the strategic interests and objectives of the Union shall relate to the common foreign and security policy and to other areas of the external action of the Union. Such decisions may concern the relations of the Union with a specific country or region or may be thematic in approach. They shall define their duration, and the means to be made available by the Union and the Member States.

The European Council shall act unanimously on a recommendation from the Council, adopted by the latter under the arrangements laid down for each area. Decisions of the European Council shall be implemented in accordance with the procedures provided for in the Treaties.

2.   The High Representative of the Union for Foreign Affairs and Security Policy, for the area of common foreign and security policy, and the Commission, for other areas of external action, may submit joint proposals to the Council.

Chapter 2 SPECIFIC PROVISIONS ON THE COMMON FOREIGN AND SECURITY POLICY

SECTION 1 COMMON PROVISIONS

Article 23
The Union's action on the international scene, pursuant to this Chapter, shall be guided by the principles, shall pursue the objectives of, and be conducted in accordance with, the general provisions laid down in Chapter 1.

Article 24 (ex Article 11 TEU)
1.   The Union's competence in matters of common foreign and security policy shall cover all areas of foreign policy and all questions relating to the Union's security, including the progressive framing of a common defence policy that might lead to a common defence.

The common foreign and security policy is subject to specific rules and procedures. It shall be defined and implemented by the European Council and the Council acting unanimously, except where the Treaties provide otherwise. The adoption of legislative acts shall be excluded. The common foreign and security policy shall be put into effect by the High Representative of the Union for Foreign Affairs and Security Policy and by Member States, in accordance with the Treaties. The specific role of the European Parliament and of the Commission in this area is defined by the Treaties. The Court of Justice of the European Union shall not have jurisdiction with respect to these provisions, with the exception of its jurisdiction to monitor compliance with Article 40 of this Treaty and to review the legality of certain decisions as provided for by the second paragraph of Article 275 of the Treaty on the Functioning of the European Union.

2.   Within the framework of the principles and objectives of its external action, the Union shall conduct, define and implement a common foreign and security policy, based on the development of mutual political solidarity among Member States, the identification of questions of general interest and the achievement of an ever-increasing degree of convergence of Member States' actions.

3.   The Member States shall support the Union's external and security policy actively and unreservedly in a spirit of loyalty and mutual solidarity and shall comply with the Union's action in this area.

The Member States shall work together to enhance and develop their mutual political solidarity. They shall refrain from any action which is contrary to the interests of the Union or likely to impair its effectiveness as a cohesive force in international relations.

The Council and the High Representative shall ensure compliance with these principles.

Article 25 (ex Article 12 TEU)
The Union shall conduct the common foreign and security policy by:
(a)   defining the general guidelines;

(b)   adopting decisions defining:
      (i)   actions to be undertaken by the Union;
      (ii) positions to be taken by the Union;

(iii) arrangements for the implementation of the decisions referred to in points (i) and (ii); and by

(c)   strengthening systematic cooperation between Member States in the conduct of policy.

Article 26 (ex Article 13 TEU)

1.   The European Council shall identify the Union's strategic interests, determine the objectives of and define general guidelines for the common foreign and security policy, including for matters with defence implications. It shall adopt the necessary decisions.

If international developments so require, the President of the European Council shall convene an extraordinary meeting of the European Council in order to define the strategic lines of the Union's policy in the face of such developments.

2.   The Council shall frame the common foreign and security policy and take the decisions necessary for defining and implementing it on the basis of the general guidelines and strategic lines defined by the European Council.

The Council and the High Representative of the Union for Foreign Affairs and Security Policy shall ensure the unity, consistency and effectiveness of action by the Union.

3.   The common foreign and security policy shall be put into effect by the High Representative and by the Member States, using national and Union resources.

Article 27

1.   The High Representative of the Union for Foreign Affairs and Security Policy, who shall chair the Foreign Affairs Council, shall contribute through his proposals to the development of the common foreign and security policy and shall ensure implementation of the decisions adopted by the European Council and the Council.

2.   The High Representative shall represent the Union for matters relating to the common foreign and security policy. He shall conduct political dialogue with third parties on the Union's behalf and shall express the Union's position in international organisations and at international conferences.

3.   In fulfilling his mandate, the High Representative shall be assisted by a European External Action Service. This service shall work in cooperation with the diplomatic services of the Member States and shall comprise officials from relevant departments of the General Secretariat of the Council and of the Commission as well as staff seconded from national diplomatic services of the Member States. The organisation and functioning of the European External Action Service shall be established by a decision of the Council. The Council shall act on a proposal from the High Representative after consulting the European Parliament and after obtaining the consent of the Commission.

Article 28 (ex Article 14 TEU)

1.   Where the international situation requires operational action by the Union, the Council shall adopt the necessary decisions. They shall lay down their objectives, scope, the means to be made available to the Union, if necessary their duration, and the conditions for their implementation.

If there is a change in circumstances having a substantial effect on a question subject to such a decision, the Council shall review the principles and objectives of that decision and take the necessary decisions.

2.   Decisions referred to in paragraph 1 shall commit the Member States in the positions they adopt and in the conduct of their activity.

3.   Whenever there is any plan to adopt a national position or take national action pursuant to a decision as referred to in paragraph 1, information shall be provided by the Member State concerned in time to allow, if necessary, for prior consultations within the Council. The obligation to provide prior information shall not apply to measures which are merely a national transposition of Council decisions.

4.   In cases of imperative need arising from changes in the situation and failing a review of the Council decision as referred to in paragraph 1, Member States may take the necessary measures as a matter of urgency having regard to the general objectives of that decision. The Member State concerned shall inform the Council immediately of any such measures.

5.   Should there be any major difficulties in implementing a decision as referred to in this Article, a Member State shall refer them to the Council which shall discuss them and seek appropriate solutions. Such solutions shall not run counter to the objectives of the decision referred to in paragraph 1 or impair its effectiveness.

Article 29 (ex Article 15 TEU)
The Council shall adopt decisions which shall define the approach of the Union to a particular matter of a geographical or thematic nature. Member States shall ensure that their national policies conform to the Union positions.

Article 30 (ex Article 22 TEU)
1.   Any Member State, the High Representative of the Union for Foreign Affairs and Security Policy, or the High Representative with the Commission's support, may refer any question relating to the common foreign and security policy to the Council and may submit to it, respectively, initiatives or proposals.

2.   In cases requiring a rapid decision, the High Representative, of his own motion, or at the request of a Member State, shall convene an extraordinary Council meeting within 48 hours or, in an emergency, within a shorter period.

Article 31 (ex Article 23 TEU)
1.   Decisions under this Chapter shall be taken by the European Council and the Council acting unanimously, except where this Chapter provides otherwise. The adoption of legislative acts shall be excluded.

When abstaining in a vote, any member of the Council may qualify its abstention by making a formal declaration under the present subparagraph. In that case, it shall not be obliged to apply the decision, but shall accept that the decision commits the Union. In a spirit of mutual solidarity, the Member State concerned shall refrain from any action likely to conflict with or impede Union action based on that decision and the other Member States shall respect its position. If the members of the Council qualifying their abstention in this way represent at least one third of the Member States comprising at least one third of the population of the Union, the decision shall not be adopted.

2.   By derogation from the provisions of paragraph 1, the Council shall act by qualified majority:
      — when adopting a decision defining a Union action or position on the basis of a decision of the European Council relating to the Union's strategic interests and objectives, as referred to in Article 22(1),
      — when adopting a decision defining a Union action or position, on a proposal which the High Representative of the Union for Foreign Affairs and Security Policy has presented following a specific request from the European Council, made on its own initiative or that of the High Representative,

— when adopting any decision implementing a decision defining a Union action or position,
— when appointing a special representative in accordance with Article 33.

If a member of the Council declares that, for vital and stated reasons of national policy, it intends to oppose the adoption of a decision to be taken by qualified majority, a vote shall not be taken. The High Representative will, in close consultation with the Member State involved, search for a solution acceptable to it. If he does not succeed, the Council may, acting by a qualified majority, request that the matter be referred to the European Council for a decision by unanimity.

3.   The European Council may unanimously adopt a decision stipulating that the Council shall act by a qualified majority in cases other than those referred to in paragraph 2.

4.   Paragraphs 2 and 3 shall not apply to decisions having military or defence implications.

5.   For procedural questions, the Council shall act by a majority of its members.

Article 32 (ex Article 16 TEU)

Member States shall consult one another within the European Council and the Council on any matter of foreign and security policy of general interest in order to determine a common approach. Before undertaking any action on the international scene or entering into any commitment which could affect the Union's interests, each Member State shall consult the others within the European Council or the Council. Member States shall ensure, through the convergence of their actions, that the Union is able to assert its interests and values on the international scene. Member States shall show mutual solidarity.

When the European Council or the Council has defined a common approach of the Union within the meaning of the first paragraph, the High Representative of the Union for Foreign Affairs and Security Policy and the Ministers for Foreign Affairs of the Member States shall coordinate their activities within the Council.

The diplomatic missions of the Member States and the Union delegations in third countries and at international organisations shall cooperate and shall contribute to formulating and implementing the common approach.

Article 33 (ex Article 18 TEU)

The Council may, on a proposal from the High Representative of the Union for Foreign Affairs and Security Policy, appoint a special representative with a mandate in relation to particular policy issues. The special representative shall carry out his mandate under the authority of the High Representative.

Article 34 (ex Article 19 TEU)

1.   Member States shall coordinate their action in international organisations and at international conferences. They shall uphold the Union's positions in such forums. The High Representative of the Union for Foreign Affairs and Security Policy shall organise this coordination.

In international organisations and at international conferences where not all the Member States participate, those which do take part shall uphold the Union's positions.

2.   In accordance with Article 24(3), Member States represented in international organisations or international conferences where not all the Member States participate shall keep the other Member States and the High Representative informed of any matter of common interest.

Member States which are also members of the United Nations Security Council will concert and keep the other Member States and the High Representative fully informed. Member States which are members of the Security Council will, in the execution of their functions, defend the positions and the interests of the Union, without prejudice to their responsibilities under the provisions of the United Nations Charter.

When the Union has defined a position on a subject which is on the United Nations Security Council agenda, those Member States which sit on the Security Council shall request that the High Representative be invited to present the Union's position.

Article 35 (ex Article 20 TEU)

The diplomatic and consular missions of the Member States and the Union delegations in third countries and international conferences, and their representations to international organisations, shall cooperate in ensuring that decisions defining Union positions and actions adopted pursuant to this Chapter are complied with and implemented.

They shall step up cooperation by exchanging information and carrying out joint assessments.

They shall contribute to the implementation of the right of citizens of the Union to protection in the territory of third countries as referred to in Article 20(2)(c) of the Treaty on the Functioning of the European Union and of the measures adopted pursuant to Article 23 of that Treaty.

Article 36 (ex Article 21 TEU)

The High Representative of the Union for Foreign Affairs and Security Policy shall regularly consult the European Parliament on the main aspects and the basic choices of the common foreign and security policy and the common security and defence policy and inform it of how those policies evolve. He shall ensure that the views of the European Parliament are duly taken into consideration. Special representatives may be involved in briefing the European Parliament.

The European Parliament may address questions or make recommendations to the Council or the High Representative. Twice a year it shall hold a debate on progress in implementing the common foreign and security policy, including the common security and defence policy.

Article 37 (ex Article 24 TEU)

The Union may conclude agreements with one or more States or international organisations in areas covered by this Chapter.

Article 38 (ex Article 25 TEU)

Without prejudice to Article 240 of the Treaty on the Functioning of the European Union, a Political and Security Committee shall monitor the international situation in the areas covered by the common foreign and security policy and contribute to the definition of policies by delivering opinions to the Council at the request of the Council or of the High Representative of the Union for Foreign Affairs and Security Policy or on its own initiative. It shall also monitor the implementation of agreed policies, without prejudice to the powers of the High Representative.

Within the scope of this Chapter, the Political and Security Committee shall exercise, under the responsibility of the Council and of the High Representative, the political control and strategic direction of the crisis management operations referred to in Article 43.

The Council may authorise the Committee, for the purpose and for the duration of a crisis management operation, as determined by the Council, to take the relevant decisions concerning the political control and strategic direction of the operation.

Article 39

In accordance with Article 16 of the Treaty on the Functioning of the European Union and by way of derogation from paragraph 2 thereof, the Council shall adopt a decision laying down the rules relating to the protection of individuals with regard to the processing of personal data by the Member States when carrying out activities which fall within the scope of this Chapter, and the rules relating to the free movement of such data. Compliance with these rules shall be subject to the control of independent authorities.

Article 40 (ex Article 47 TEU)

The implementation of the common foreign and security policy shall not affect the application of the procedures and the extent of the powers of the institutions laid down by the Treaties for the exercise of the Union competences referred to in Articles 3 to 6 of the Treaty on the Functioning of the European Union.

Similarly, the implementation of the policies listed in those Articles shall not affect the application of the procedures and the extent of the powers of the institutions laid down by the Treaties for the exercise of the Union competences under this Chapter.

Article 41 (ex Article 28 TEU)

1. Administrative expenditure to which the implementation of this Chapter gives rise for the institutions shall be charged to the Union budget.

2. Operating expenditure to which the implementation of this Chapter gives rise shall also be charged to the Union budget, except for such expenditure arising from operations having military or defence implications and cases where the Council acting unanimously decides otherwise.

   In cases where expenditure is not charged to the Union budget, it shall be charged to the Member States in accordance with the gross national product scale, unless the Council acting unanimously decides otherwise. As for expenditure arising from operations having military or defence implications, Member States whose representatives in the Council have made a formal declaration under Article 31(1), second subparagraph, shall not be obliged to contribute to the financing thereof.

3. The Council shall adopt a decision establishing the specific procedures for guaranteeing rapid access to appropriations in the Union budget for urgent financing of initiatives in the framework of the common foreign and security policy, and in particular for preparatory activities for the tasks referred to in Article 42(1) and Article 43. It shall act after consulting the European Parliament.

   Preparatory activities for the tasks referred to in Article 42(1) and Article 43 which are not charged to the Union budget shall be financed by a start-up fund made up of Member States' contributions.

   The Council shall adopt by a qualified majority, on a proposal from the High Representative of the Union for Foreign Affairs and Security Policy, decisions establishing:
   (a) the procedures for setting up and financing the start-up fund, in particular the amounts allocated to the fund;
   (b) the procedures for administering the start-up fund;
   (c) the financial control procedures.
   When the task planned in accordance with Article 42(1) and Article 43 cannot be charged to the Union budget, the Council shall authorise the High Representative to use the fund. The High Representative shall report to the Council on the implementation of this remit.

SECTION 2 PROVISIONS ON THE COMMON SECURITY AND DEFENCE POLICY

Article 42 (ex Article 17 TEU)

1. The common security and defence policy shall be an integral part of the common foreign and security policy. It shall provide the Union with an operational capacity drawing on civilian and military assets. The Union may use them on missions outside the Union for

peace-keeping, conflict prevention and strengthening international security in accordance with the principles of the United Nations Charter. The performance of these tasks shall be undertaken using capabilities provided by the Member States.

2.   The common security and defence policy shall include the progressive framing of a common Union defence policy. This will lead to a common defence, when the European Council, acting unanimously, so decides. It shall in that case recommend to the Member States the adoption of such a decision in accordance with their respective constitutional requirements.

The policy of the Union in accordance with this Section shall not prejudice the specific character of the security and defence policy of certain Member States and shall respect the obligations of certain Member States, which see their common defence realised in the North Atlantic Treaty Organisation (NATO), under the North Atlantic Treaty and be compatible with the common security and defence policy established within that framework.

3.   Member States shall make civilian and military capabilities available to the Union for the implementation of the common security and defence policy, to contribute to the objectives defined by the Council. Those Member States which together establish multinational forces may also make them available to the common security and defence policy.

Member States shall undertake progressively to improve their military capabilities. The Agency in the field of defence capabilities development, research, acquisition and armaments (hereinafter referred to as "the European Defence Agency") shall identify operational requirements, shall promote measures to satisfy those requirements, shall contribute to identifying and, where appropriate, implementing any measure needed to strengthen the industrial and technological base of the defence sector, shall participate in defining a European capabilities and armaments policy, and shall assist the Council in evaluating the improvement of military capabilities.

4.   Decisions relating to the common security and defence policy, including those initiating a mission as referred to in this Article, shall be adopted by the Council acting unanimously on a proposal from the High Representative of the Union for Foreign Affairs and Security Policy or an initiative from a Member State. The High Representative may propose the use of both national resources and Union instruments, together with the Commission where appropriate.

5.   The Council may entrust the execution of a task, within the Union framework, to a group of Member States in order to protect the Union's values and serve its interests. The execution of such a task shall be governed by Article 44.

6.   Those Member States whose military capabilities fulfil higher criteria and which have made more binding commitments to one another in this area with a view to the most demanding missions shall establish permanent structured cooperation within the Union framework. Such cooperation shall be governed by Article 46. It shall not affect the provisions of Article 43.

7.   If a Member State is the victim of armed aggression on its territory, the other Member States shall have towards it an obligation of aid and assistance by all the means in their power, in accordance with Article 51 of the United Nations Charter. This shall not prejudice the specific character of the security and defence policy of certain Member States.

Commitments and cooperation in this area shall be consistent with commitments under the North Atlantic Treaty Organisation, which, for those States which are members of it, remains the foundation of their collective defence and the forum for its implementation.

Article 43
1.   The tasks referred to in Article 42(1), in the course of which the Union may use civilian and military means, shall include joint disarmament operations, humanitarian and rescue

tasks, military advice and assistance tasks, conflict prevention and peace-keeping tasks, tasks of combat forces in crisis management, including peace-making and post-conflict stabilisation. All these tasks may contribute to the fight against terrorism, including by supporting third countries in combating terrorism in their territories.

2.   The Council shall adopt decisions relating to the tasks referred to in paragraph 1, defining their objectives and scope and the general conditions for their implementation. The High Representative of the Union for Foreign Affairs and Security Policy, acting under the authority of the Council and in close and constant contact with the Political and Security Committee, shall ensure coordination of the civilian and military aspects of such tasks.

Article 44

1.   Within the framework of the decisions adopted in accordance with Article 43, the Council may entrust the implementation of a task to a group of Member States which are willing and have the necessary capability for such a task. Those Member States, in association with the High Representative of the Union for Foreign Affairs and Security Policy, shall agree among themselves on the management of the task.

2.   Member States participating in the task shall keep the Council regularly informed of its progress on their own initiative or at the request of another Member State. Those States shall inform the Council immediately should the completion of the task entail major consequences or require amendment of the objective, scope and conditions determined for the task in the decisions referred to in paragraph 1. In such cases, the Council shall adopt the necessary decisions.

Article 45

1.   The European Defence Agency referred to in Article 42(3), subject to the authority of the Council, shall have as its task to:
    (a)   contribute to identifying the Member States' military capability objectives and evaluating observance of the capability commitments given by the Member States;
    (b)   promote harmonisation of operational needs and adoption of effective, compatible procurement methods;
    (c)   propose multilateral projects to fulfil the objectives in terms of military capabilities, ensure coordination of the programmes implemented by the Member States and management of specific cooperation programmes;
    (d)   support defence technology research, and coordinate and plan joint research activities and the study of technical solutions meeting future operational needs;
    (e)   contribute to identifying and, if necessary, implementing any useful measure for strengthening the industrial and technological base of the defence sector and for improving the effectiveness of military expenditure.

2.   The European Defence Agency shall be open to all Member States wishing to be part of it. The Council, acting by a qualified majority, shall adopt a decision defining the Agency's statute, seat and operational rules. That decision should take account of the level of effective participation in the Agency's activities. Specific groups shall be set up within the Agency bringing together Member States engaged in joint projects. The Agency shall carry out its tasks in liaison with the Commission where necessary.

Article 46

1.   Those Member States which wish to participate in the permanent structured cooperation referred to in Article 42(6), which fulfil the criteria and have made the commitments on military capabilities set out in the Protocol on permanent structured cooperation, shall notify their intention to the Council and to the High Representative of the Union for Foreign Affairs and Security Policy.

2. Within three months following the notification referred to in paragraph 1 the Council shall adopt a decision establishing permanent structured cooperation and determining the list of participating Member States. The Council shall act by a qualified majority after consulting the High Representative.

3. Any Member State which, at a later stage, wishes to participate in the permanent structured cooperation shall notify its intention to the Council and to the High Representative.

    The Council shall adopt a decision confirming the participation of the Member State concerned which fulfils the criteria and makes the commitments referred to in Articles 1 and 2 of the Protocol on permanent structured cooperation. The Council shall act by a qualified majority after consulting the High Representative. Only members of the Council representing the participating Member States shall take part in the vote.

    A qualified majority shall be defined in accordance with Article 238(3)(a) of the Treaty on the Functioning of the European Union.

4. If a participating Member State no longer fulfils the criteria or is no longer able to meet the commitments referred to in Articles 1 and 2 of the Protocol on permanent structured cooperation, the Council may adopt a decision suspending the participation of the Member State concerned.

    The Council shall act by a qualified majority. Only members of the Council representing the participating Member States, with the exception of the Member State in question, shall take part in the vote.

    A qualified majority shall be defined in accordance with Article 238(3)(a) of the Treaty on the Functioning of the European Union.

5. Any participating Member State which wishes to withdraw from permanent structured cooperation shall notify its intention to the Council, which shall take note that the Member State in question has ceased to participate.

6. The decisions and recommendations of the Council within the framework of permanent structured cooperation, other than those provided for in paragraphs 2 to 5, shall be adopted by unanimity. For the purposes of this paragraph, unanimity shall be constituted by the votes of the representatives of the participating Member States only.

TITLE VI
FINAL PROVISIONS

Article 47
The Union shall have legal personality.

Article 48 (ex Article 48 TEU)
1. The Treaties may be amended in accordance with an ordinary revision procedure. They may also be amended in accordance with simplified revision procedures.

Ordinary revision procedure
2. The Government of any Member State, the European Parliament or the Commission may submit to the Council proposals for the amendment of the Treaties. These proposals may, inter alia, serve either to increase or to reduce the competences conferred on the Union in the Treaties. These proposals shall be submitted to the European Council by the Council and the national Parliaments shall be notified.

3. If the European Council, after consulting the European Parliament and the Commission, adopts by a simple majority a decision in favour of examining the proposed amendments,

the President of the European Council shall convene a Convention composed of representatives of the national Parliaments, of the Heads of State or Government of the Member States, of the European Parliament and of the Commission. The European Central Bank shall also be consulted in the case of institutional changes in the monetary area. The Convention shall examine the proposals for amendments and shall adopt by consensus a recommendation to a conference of representatives of the governments of the Member States as provided for in paragraph 4.

The European Council may decide by a simple majority, after obtaining the consent of the European Parliament, not to convene a Convention should this not be justified by the extent of the proposed amendments. In the latter case, the European Council shall define the terms of reference for a conference of representatives of the governments of the Member States.

4.   A conference of representatives of the governments of the Member States shall be convened by the President of the Council for the purpose of determining by common accord the amendments to be made to the Treaties.

The amendments shall enter into force after being ratified by all the Member States in accordance with their respective constitutional requirements.

5.   If, two years after the signature of a treaty amending the Treaties, four fifths of the Member States have ratified it and one or more Member States have encountered difficulties in proceeding with ratification, the matter shall be referred to the European Council.

Simplified revision procedures

6.   The Government of any Member State, the European Parliament or the Commission may submit to the European Council proposals for revising all or part of the provisions of Part Three of the Treaty on the Functioning of the European Union relating to the internal policies and action of the Union.

The European Council may adopt a decision amending all or part of the provisions of Part Three of the Treaty on the Functioning of the European Union. The European Council shall act by unanimity after consulting the European Parliament and the Commission, and the European Central Bank in the case of institutional changes in the monetary area. That decision shall not enter into force until it is approved by the Member States in accordance with their respective constitutional requirements.

The decision referred to in the second subparagraph shall not increase the competences conferred on the Union in the Treaties.

7.   Where the Treaty on the Functioning of the European Union or Title V of this Treaty provides for the Council to act by unanimity in a given area or case, the European Council may adopt a decision authorising the Council to act by a qualified majority in that area or in that case. This subparagraph shall not apply to decisions with military implications or those in the area of defence.

Where the Treaty on the Functioning of the European Union provides for legislative acts to be adopted by the Council in accordance with a special legislative procedure, the European Council may adopt a decision allowing for the adoption of such acts in accordance with the ordinary legislative procedure.

Any initiative taken by the European Council on the basis of the first or the second subparagraph shall be notified to the national Parliaments. If a national Parliament makes known its opposition within six months of the date of such notification, the decision referred to in the first or the second subparagraph shall not be adopted. In the absence of opposition, the European Council may adopt the decision.

For the adoption of the decisions referred to in the first and second subparagraphs, the European Council shall act by unanimity after obtaining the consent of the European Parliament, which shall be given by a majority of its component members.

Article 49 (ex Article 49 TEU)

Any European State which respects the values referred to in Article 2 and is committed to promoting them may apply to become a member of the Union. The European Parliament and national Parliaments shall be notified of this application. The applicant State shall address its application to the Council, which shall act unanimously after consulting the Commission and after receiving the consent of the European Parliament, which shall act by a majority of its component members. The conditions of eligibility agreed upon by the European Council shall be taken into account.

The conditions of admission and the adjustments to the Treaties on which the Union is founded, which such admission entails, shall be the subject of an agreement between the Member States and the applicant State. This agreement shall be submitted for ratification by all the contracting States in accordance with their respective constitutional requirements.

Article 50

1.   Any Member State may decide to withdraw from the Union in accordance with its own constitutional requirements.

2.   A Member State which decides to withdraw shall notify the European Council of its intention. In the light of the guidelines provided by the European Council, the Union shall negotiate and conclude an agreement with that State, setting out the arrangements for its withdrawal, taking account of the framework for its future relationship with the Union. That agreement shall be negotiated in accordance with Article 218(3) of the Treaty on the Functioning of the European Union. It shall be concluded on behalf of the Union by the Council, acting by a qualified majority, after obtaining the consent of the European Parliament.

3.   The Treaties shall cease to apply to the State in question from the date of entry into force of the withdrawal agreement or, failing that, two years after the notification referred to in paragraph 2, unless the European Council, in agreement with the Member State concerned, unanimously decides to extend this period.

4.   For the purposes of paragraphs 2 and 3, the member of the European Council or of the Council representing the withdrawing Member State shall not participate in the discussions of the European Council or Council or in decisions concerning it.

      A qualified majority shall be defined in accordance with Article 238(3)(b) of the Treaty on the Functioning of the European Union.

5.   If a State which has withdrawn from the Union asks to rejoin, its request shall be subject to the procedure referred to in Article 49.

Article 51

The Protocols and Annexes to the Treaties shall form an integral part thereof.

Article 52

1.   The Treaties shall apply to the Kingdom of Belgium, the Republic of Bulgaria, the Czech Republic, the Kingdom of Denmark, the Federal Republic of Germany, the Republic of Estonia, Ireland, the Hellenic Republic, the Kingdom of Spain, the French Republic, the Italian Republic, the Republic of Cyprus, the Republic of Latvia, the Republic of Lithuania, the Grand Duchy of Luxembourg, the Republic of Hungary, the Republic of Malta, the Kingdom of the Netherlands, the Republic of Austria, the Republic of Poland,

the Portuguese Republic, Romania, the Republic of Slovenia, the Slovak Republic, the Republic of Finland, the Kingdom of Sweden and the United Kingdom of Great Britain and Northern Ireland.

2.   The territorial scope of the Treaties is specified in Article 355 of the Treaty on the Functioning of the European Union.

Article 53 (ex Article 51 TEU)
This Treaty is concluded for an unlimited period.

Article 54 (ex Article 52 TEU)
1.   This Treaty shall be ratified by the High Contracting Parties in accordance with their respective constitutional requirements. The instruments of ratification shall be deposited with the Government of the Italian Republic.

2.   This Treaty shall enter into force on 1 January 1993, provided that all the Instruments of ratification have been deposited, or, failing that, on the first day of the month following the deposit of the Instrument of ratification by the last signatory State to take this step.

Article 55 (ex Article 53 TEU)
1.   This Treaty, drawn up in a single original in the Bulgarian, Czech, Danish, Dutch, English, Estonian, Finnish, French, German, Greek, Hungarian, Irish, Italian, Latvian, Lithuanian, Maltese, Polish, Portuguese, Romanian, Slovak, Slovenian, Spanish and Swedish languages, the texts in each of these languages being equally authentic, shall be deposited in the archives of the Government of the Italian Republic, which will transmit a certified copy to each of the governments of the other signatory States.

2.   This Treaty may also be translated into any other languages as determined by Member States among those which, in accordance with their constitutional order, enjoy official status in all or part of their territory. A certified copy of such translations shall be provided by the Member States concerned to be deposited in the archives of the Council.

IN WITNESS WHEREOF the undersigned Plenipotentiaries have signed this Treaty.

Done at Maastricht on the seventh day of February in the year one thousand nine hundred and ninety-two.

(List of signatories not reproduced)

CONSOLIDATED VERSION OF THE TREATY ON THE FUNCTIONING OF THE EUROPEAN UNION
OJ C 83, 30.3.2010, p. 47*

....

*   EDITOR'S NOTE: Where articles in the Treaty on the Functioning of the European Union (TFEU) replace previous Treaty articles, the old article numbers from the previous version of the Treaty on European Union (TEU) and/or the now replaced Treaty establishing the European Community (TEC) are shown in brackets. See the Table of Equivalences for the TFEU reproduced in Part II of this edition for a complete conversion table from the old to the new article numbers and vice versa.

Preamble

His Majesty the King of the Belgians, The President of the Federal Republic of Germany, The President of the French Republic, The President of the Italian Republic, Her Royal Highness the Grand Duchess of Luxembourg, Her Majesty the Queen of the Netherlands,[1]

DETERMINED to lay the foundations of an ever closer union among the peoples of Europe,

RESOLVED to ensure the economic and social progress of their States by common action to eliminate the barriers which divide Europe,

AFFIRMING as the essential objective of their efforts the constant improvements of the living and working conditions of their peoples,

RECOGNISING that the removal of existing obstacles calls for concerted action in order to guarantee steady expansion, balanced trade and fair competition,

ANXIOUS to strengthen the unity of their economies and to ensure their harmonious development by reducing the differences existing between the various regions and the backwardness of the less favoured regions,

DESIRING to contribute, by means of a common commercial policy, to the progressive abolition of restrictions on international trade,

INTENDING to confirm the solidarity which binds Europe and the overseas countries and desiring to ensure the development of their prosperity, in accordance with the principles of the Charter of the United Nations,

RESOLVED by thus pooling their resources to preserve and strengthen peace and liberty, and calling upon the other peoples of Europe who share their ideal to join in their efforts,

DETERMINED to promote the development of the highest possible level of knowledge for their peoples through a wide access to education and through its continuous updating, and to this end HAVE DESIGNATED as their Plenipotentiaries:

---

1   The Republic of Bulgaria, the Czech Republic, the Kingdom of Denmark, the Republic of Estonia, Ireland, the Hellenic Republic, the Kingdom of Spain, the Republic of Cyprus, the Republic of Latvia, the Republic of Lithuania, the Republic of Hungary, the Republic of Malta, the Republic of Austria, the Republic of Poland, the Portuguese Republic, Romania, the Republic of Slovenia, the Slovak Republic, the Republic of Finland, the Kingdom of Sweden and the United Kingdom of Great Britain and Northern Ireland have since become members of the European Union.

(List of plenipotentiaries not reproduced)

WHO, having exchanged their full powers, found in good and due form, have agreed as follows.

Part One PRINCIPLES
Article 1
1. This Treaty organises the functioning of the Union and determines the areas of, delimitation of, and arrangements for exercising its competences.

2. This Treaty and the Treaty on European Union constitute the Treaties on which the Union is founded. These two Treaties, which have the same legal value, shall be referred to as 'the Treaties'.

TITLE I
CATEGORIES AND AREAS OF UNION COMPETENCE

Article 2
1. When the Treaties confer on the Union exclusive competence in a specific area, only the Union may legislate and adopt legally binding acts, the Member States being able to do so themselves only if so empowered by the Union or for the implementation of Union acts.

2. When the Treaties confer on the Union a competence shared with the Member States in a specific area, the Union and the Member States may legislate and adopt legally binding acts in that area. The Member States shall exercise their competence to the extent that the Union has not exercised its competence. The Member States shall again exercise their competence to the extent that the Union has decided to cease exercising its competence.

3. The Member States shall coordinate their economic and employment policies within arrangements as determined by this Treaty, which the Union shall have competence to provide.

4. The Union shall have competence, in accordance with the provisions of the Treaty on European Union, to define and implement a common foreign and security policy, including the progressive framing of a common defence policy.

5. In certain areas and under the conditions laid down in the Treaties, the Union shall have competence to carry out actions to support, coordinate or supplement the actions of the Member States, without thereby superseding their competence in these areas.

    Legally binding acts of the Union adopted on the basis of the provisions of the Treaties relating to these areas shall not entail harmonisation of Member States' laws or regulations.

6. The scope of and arrangements for exercising the Union's competences shall be determined by the provisions of the Treaties relating to each area.

Article 3
1. The Union shall have exclusive competence in the following areas:
    (a) customs union;
    (b) the establishing of the competition rules necessary for the functioning of the internal market;
    (c) monetary policy for the Member States whose currency is the euro;
    (d) the conservation of marine biological resources under the common fisheries policy;
    (e) common commercial policy.

2. The Union shall also have exclusive competence for the conclusion of an international agreement when its conclusion is provided for in a legislative act of the Union or is

necessary to enable the Union to exercise its internal competence, or in so far as its conclusion may affect common rules or alter their scope.

Article 4

1. The Union shall share competence with the Member States where the Treaties confer on it a competence which does not relate to the areas referred to in Articles 3 and 6.

2. Shared competence between the Union and the Member States applies in the following principal areas:
    (a) internal market;
    (b) social policy, for the aspects defined in this Treaty;
    (c) economic, social and territorial cohesion;
    (d) agriculture and fisheries, excluding the conservation of marine biological resources;
    (e) environment;
    (f) consumer protection;
    (g) transport;
    (h) trans-European networks;
    (i) energy;
    (j) area of freedom, security and justice;
    (k) common safety concerns in public health matters, for the aspects defined in this Treaty.

3. In the areas of research, technological development and space, the Union shall have competence to carry out activities, in particular to define and implement programmes; however, the exercise of that competence shall not result in Member States being prevented from exercising theirs.

4. In the areas of development cooperation and humanitarian aid, the Union shall have competence to carry out activities and conduct a common policy; however, the exercise of that competence shall not result in Member States being prevented from exercising theirs.

Article 5

1. The Member States shall coordinate their economic policies within the Union. To this end, the Council shall adopt measures, in particular broad guidelines for these policies.

    Specific provisions shall apply to those Member States whose currency is the euro.

2. The Union shall take measures to ensure coordination of the employment policies of the Member States, in particular by defining guidelines for these policies.

3. The Union may take initiatives to ensure coordination of Member States' social policies.

Article 6

The Union shall have competence to carry out actions to support, coordinate or supplement the actions of the Member States. The areas of such action shall, at European level, be:
(a) protection and improvement of human health;

(b) industry;

(c) culture;

(d) tourism;

(e) education, vocational training, youth and sport;

(f) civil protection;

(g) administrative cooperation.

TITLE II
PROVISIONS HAVING GENERAL APPLICATION

Article 7

The Union shall ensure consistency between its policies and activities, taking all of its objectives into account and in accordance with the principle of conferral of powers.

Article 8 (ex Article 3(2) TEC)

In all its activities, the Union shall aim to eliminate inequalities, and to promote equality, between men and women.

Article 9

In defining and implementing its policies and activities, the Union shall take into account requirements linked to the promotion of a high level of employment, the guarantee of adequate social protection, the fight against social exclusion, and a high level of education, training and protection of human health.

Article 10

In defining and implementing its policies and activities, the Union shall aim to combat discrimination based on sex, racial or ethnic origin, religion or belief, disability, age or sexual orientation.

Article 11 (ex Article 6 TEC)

Environmental protection requirements must be integrated into the definition and implementation of the Union's policies and activities, in particular with a view to promoting sustainable development.

Article 12 (ex Article 153(2) TEC)

Consumer protection requirements shall be taken into account in defining and implementing other Union policies and activities.

Article 13

In formulating and implementing the Union's agriculture, fisheries, transport, internal market, research and technological development and space policies, the Union and the Member States shall, since animals are sentient beings, pay full regard to the welfare requirements of animals, while respecting the legislative or administrative provisions and customs of the Member States relating in particular to religious rites, cultural traditions and regional heritage.

Article 14 (ex Article 16 TEC)

Without prejudice to Article 4 of the Treaty on European Union or to Articles 93, 106 and 107 of this Treaty, and given the place occupied by services of general economic interest in the shared values of the Union as well as their role in promoting social and territorial cohesion, the Union and the Member States, each within their respective powers and within the scope of application of the Treaties, shall take care that such services operate on the basis of principles and conditions, particularly economic and financial conditions, which enable them to fulfil their missions. The European Parliament and the Council, acting by means of regulations in accordance with the ordinary legislative procedure, shall establish these principles and set these conditions without prejudice to the competence of Member States, in compliance with the Treaties, to provide, to commission and to fund such services.

Article 15 (ex Article 255 TEC)

1. In order to promote good governance and ensure the participation of civil society, the Union's institutions, bodies, offices and agencies shall conduct their work as openly as possible.

2.   The European Parliament shall meet in public, as shall the Council when considering and voting on a draft legislative act.

3.   Any citizen of the Union, and any natural or legal person residing or having its registered office in a Member State, shall have a right of access to documents of the Union's institutions, bodies, offices and agencies, whatever their medium, subject to the principles and the conditions to be defined in accordance with this paragraph. General principles and limits on grounds of public or private interest governing this right of access to documents shall be determined by the European Parliament and the Council, by means of regulations, acting in accordance with the ordinary legislative procedure.

Each institution, body, office or agency shall ensure that its proceedings are transparent and shall elaborate in its own Rules of Procedure specific provisions regarding access to its documents, in accordance with the regulations referred to in the second subparagraph.

The Court of Justice of the European Union, the European Central Bank and the European Investment Bank shall be subject to this paragraph only when exercising their administrative tasks.

The European Parliament and the Council shall ensure publication of the documents relating to the legislative procedures under the terms laid down by the regulations referred to in the second subparagraph.

Article 16 (ex Article 286 TEC)
1.   Everyone has the right to the protection of personal data concerning them.

2.   The European Parliament and the Council, acting in accordance with the ordinary legislative procedure, shall lay down the rules relating to the protection of individuals with regard to the processing of personal data by Union institutions, bodies, offices and agencies, and by the Member States when carrying out activities which fall within the scope of Union law, and the rules relating to the free movement of such data. Compliance with these rules shall be subject to the control of independent authorities.

The rules adopted on the basis of this Article shall be without prejudice to the specific rules laid down in Article 39 of the Treaty on European Union.

Article 17
1.   The Union respects and does not prejudice the status under national law of churches and religious associations or communities in the Member States.

2.   The Union equally respects the status under national law of philosophical and non-confessional organisations.

3.   Recognising their identity and their specific contribution, the Union shall maintain an open, transparent and regular dialogue with these churches and organisations.

Part Two NON-DISCRIMINATION AND CITIZENSHIP OF THE UNION
Article 18 (ex Article 12 TEC)
Within the scope of application of the Treaties, and without prejudice to any special provisions contained therein, any discrimination on grounds of nationality shall be prohibited.
The European Parliament and the Council, acting in accordance with the ordinary legislative procedure, may adopt rules designed to prohibit such discrimination.

Article 19 (ex Article 13 TEC)
1.   Without prejudice to the other provisions of the Treaties and within the limits of the powers conferred by them upon the Union, the Council, acting unanimously in

accordance with a special legislative procedure and after obtaining the consent of the European Parliament, may take appropriate action to combat discrimination based on sex, racial or ethnic origin, religion or belief, disability, age or sexual orientation.

2.   By way of derogation from paragraph 1, the European Parliament and the Council, acting in accordance with the ordinary legislative procedure, may adopt the basic principles of Union incentive measures, excluding any harmonisation of the laws and regulations of the Member States, to support action taken by the Member States in order to contribute to the achievement of the objectives referred to in paragraph 1.

Article 20 (ex Article 17 TEC)

1.   Citizenship of the Union is hereby established. Every person holding the nationality of a Member State shall be a citizen of the Union. Citizenship of the Union shall be additional to and not replace national citizenship.

2.   Citizens of the Union shall enjoy the rights and be subject to the duties provided for in the Treaties. They shall have, inter alia:
      (a) the right to move and reside freely within the territory of the Member States;
      (b) the right to vote and to stand as candidates in elections to the European Parliament and in municipal elections in their Member State of residence, under the same conditions as nationals of that State;
      (c) the right to enjoy, in the territory of a third country in which the Member State of which they are nationals is not represented, the protection of the diplomatic and consular authorities of any Member State on the same conditions as the nationals of that State;
      (d) the right to petition the European Parliament, to apply to the European Ombudsman, and to address the institutions and advisory bodies of the Union in any of the Treaty languages and to obtain a reply in the same language.
      These rights shall be exercised in accordance with the conditions and limits defined by the Treaties and by the measures adopted thereunder.

Article 21 (ex Article 18 TEC)

1.   Every citizen of the Union shall have the right to move and reside freely within the territory of the Member States, subject to the limitations and conditions laid down in the Treaties and by the measures adopted to give them effect.

2.   If action by the Union should prove necessary to attain this objective and the Treaties have not provided the necessary powers, the European Parliament and the Council, acting in accordance with the ordinary legislative procedure, may adopt provisions with a view to facilitating the exercise of the rights referred to in paragraph 1.

3.   For the same purposes as those referred to in paragraph 1 and if the Treaties have not provided the necessary powers, the Council, acting in accordance with a special legislative procedure, may adopt measures concerning social security or social protection. The Council shall act unanimously after consulting the European Parliament.

Article 22 (ex Article 19 TEC)

1.   Every citizen of the Union residing in a Member State of which he is not a national shall have the right to vote and to stand as a candidate at municipal elections in the Member State in which he resides, under the same conditions as nationals of that State. This right shall be exercised subject to detailed arrangements adopted by the Council, acting unanimously in accordance with a special legislative procedure and after consulting the European Parliament; these arrangements may provide for derogations where warranted by problems specific to a Member State.

2. Without prejudice to Article 223(1) and to the provisions adopted for its implementation, every citizen of the Union residing in a Member State of which he is not a national shall have the right to vote and to stand as a candidate in elections to the European Parliament in the Member State in which he resides, under the same conditions as nationals of that State. This right shall be exercised subject to detailed arrangements adopted by the Council, acting unanimously in accordance with a special legislative procedure and after consulting the European Parliament; these arrangements may provide for derogations where warranted by problems specific to a Member State.

Article 23 (ex Article 20 TEC)

Every citizen of the Union shall, in the territory of a third country in which the Member State of which he is a national is not represented, be entitled to protection by the diplomatic or consular authorities of any Member State, on the same conditions as the nationals of that State. Member States shall adopt the necessary provisions and start the international negotiations required to secure this protection.

The Council, acting in accordance with a special legislative procedure and after consulting the European Parliament, may adopt directives establishing the coordination and cooperation measures necessary to facilitate such protection.

Article 24 (ex Article 21 TEC)

The European Parliament and the Council, acting by means of regulations in accordance with the ordinary legislative procedure, shall adopt the provisions for the procedures and conditions required for a citizens' initiative within the meaning of Article 11 of the Treaty on European Union, including the minimum number of Member States from which such citizens must come.

Every citizen of the Union shall have the right to petition the European Parliament in accordance with Article 227.

Every citizen of the Union may apply to the Ombudsman established in accordance with Article 228.

Every citizen of the Union may write to any of the institutions or bodies referred to in this Article or in Article 13 of the Treaty on European Union in one of the languages mentioned in Article 55(1) of the Treaty on European Union and have an answer in the same language.

Article 25 (ex Article 22 TEC)

The Commission shall report to the European Parliament, to the Council and to the Economic and Social Committee every three years on the application of the provisions of this Part. This report shall take account of the development of the Union.

On this basis, and without prejudice to the other provisions of the Treaties, the Council, acting unanimously in accordance with a special legislative procedure and after obtaining the consent of the European Parliament, may adopt provisions to strengthen or to add to the rights listed in Article 20(2). These provisions shall enter into force after their approval by the Member States in accordance with their respective constitutional requirements.

Part Three UNION POLICIES AND INTERNAL ACTIONS

TITLE I
THE INTERNAL MARKET

Article 26 (ex Article 14 TEC)

1. The Union shall adopt measures with the aim of establishing or ensuring the functioning of the internal market, in accordance with the relevant provisions of the Treaties.

2.   The internal market shall comprise an area without internal frontiers in which the free movement of goods, persons, services and capital is ensured in accordance with the provisions of the Treaties.

3.   The Council, on a proposal from the Commission, shall determine the guidelines and conditions necessary to ensure balanced progress in all the sectors concerned.

Article 27 (ex Article 15 TEC)

When drawing up its proposals with a view to achieving the objectives set out in Article 26, the Commission shall take into account the extent of the effort that certain economies showing differences in development will have to sustain for the establishment of the internal market and it may propose appropriate provisions.

If these provisions take the form of derogations, they must be of a temporary nature and must cause the least possible disturbance to the functioning of the internal market.

TITLE II
FREE MOVEMENT OF GOODS

Article 28 (ex Article 23 TEC)

1.   The Union shall comprise a customs union which shall cover all trade in goods and which shall involve the prohibition between Member States of customs duties on imports and exports and of all charges having equivalent effect, and the adoption of a common customs tariff in their relations with third countries.

2.   The provisions of Article 30 and of Chapter 2 of this Title shall apply to products originating in Member States and to products coming from third countries which are in free circulation in Member States.

Article 29 (ex Article 24 TEC)

Products coming from a third country shall be considered to be in free circulation in a Member State if the import formalities have been complied with and any customs duties or charges having equivalent effect which are payable have been levied in that Member State, and if they have not benefited from a total or partial drawback of such duties or charges.

Chapter 1 THE CUSTOMS UNION

Article 30 (ex Article 25 TEC)

Customs duties on imports and exports and charges having equivalent effect shall be prohibited between Member States. This prohibition shall also apply to customs duties of a fiscal nature.

Article 31 (ex Article 26 TEC)

Common Customs Tariff duties shall be fixed by the Council on a proposal from the Commission.

Article 32 (ex Article 27 TEC)

In carrying out the tasks entrusted to it under this Chapter the Commission shall be guided by:

(a)   the need to promote trade between Member States and third countries;

(b)   developments in conditions of competition within the Union in so far as they lead to an improvement in the competitive capacity of undertakings;

(c)   the requirements of the Union as regards the supply of raw materials and semi-finished goods; in this connection the Commission shall take care to avoid distorting conditions of competition between Member States in respect of finished goods;

(d)   the need to avoid serious disturbances in the economies of Member States and to ensure rational development of production and an expansion of consumption within the Union.

Chapter 2 CUSTOMS COOPERATION

Article 33 (ex Article 135 TEC)

Within the scope of application of the Treaties, the European Parliament and the Council, acting in accordance with the ordinary legislative procedure, shall take measures in order to strengthen customs cooperation between Member States and between the latter and the Commission.

Chapter 3 PROHIBITION OF QUANTITATIVE RESTRICTIONS BETWEEN MEMBER STATES

Article 34 (ex Article 28 TEC)

Quantitative restrictions on imports and all measures having equivalent effect shall be prohibited between Member States.

Article 35 (ex Article 29 TEC)

Quantitative restrictions on exports, and all measures having equivalent effect, shall be prohibited between Member States.

Article 36 (ex Article 30 TEC)

The provisions of Articles 34 and 35 shall not preclude prohibitions or restrictions on imports, exports or goods in transit justified on grounds of public morality, public policy or public security; the protection of health and life of humans, animals or plants; the protection of national treasures possessing artistic, historic or archaeological value; or the protection of industrial and commercial property. Such prohibitions or restrictions shall not, however, constitute a means of arbitrary discrimination or a disguised restriction on trade between Member States.

Article 37 (ex Article 31 TEC)

1.   Member States shall adjust any State monopolies of a commercial character so as to ensure that no discrimination regarding the conditions under which goods are procured and marketed exists between nationals of Member States.

       The provisions of this Article shall apply to any body through which a Member State, in law or in fact, either directly or indirectly supervises, determines or appreciably influences imports or exports between Member States. These provisions shall likewise apply to monopolies delegated by the State to others.

2.   Member States shall refrain from introducing any new measure which is contrary to the principles laid down in paragraph 1 or which restricts the scope of the articles dealing with the prohibition of customs duties and quantitative restrictions between Member States.

3.   If a State monopoly of a commercial character has rules which are designed to make it easier to dispose of agricultural products or obtain for them the best return, steps should be taken in applying the rules contained in this Article to ensure equivalent safeguards for the employment and standard of living of the producers concerned.

TITLE III
AGRICULTURE AND FISHERIES

Article 38 (ex Article 32 TEC)

1.   The Union shall define and implement a common agriculture and fisheries policy.

       The internal market shall extend to agriculture, fisheries and trade in agricultural products. 'Agricultural products' means the products of the soil, of stockfarming and of fisheries and products of first-stage processing directly related to these products.

References to the common agricultural policy or to agriculture, and the use of the term 'agricultural', shall be understood as also referring to fisheries, having regard to the specific characteristics of this sector.

2.   Save as otherwise provided in Articles 39 to 44, the rules laid down for the establishment and functioning of the internal market shall apply to agricultural products.

3.   The products subject to the provisions of Articles 39 to 44 are listed in Annex I.

4.   The operation and development of the internal market for agricultural products must be accompanied by the establishment of a common agricultural policy.

Article 39 (ex Article 33 TEC)

1.   The objectives of the common agricultural policy shall be:
   (a) to increase agricultural productivity by promoting technical progress and by ensuring the rational development of agricultural production and the optimum utilisation of the factors of production, in particular labour;
   (b) thus to ensure a fair standard of living for the agricultural community, in particular by increasing the individual earnings of persons engaged in agriculture;
   (c) to stabilise markets;
   (d) to assure the availability of supplies;
   (e) to ensure that supplies reach consumers at reasonable prices.

2.   In working out the common agricultural policy and the special methods for its application, account shall be taken of:
   (a) the particular nature of agricultural activity, which results from the social structure of agriculture and from structural and natural disparities between the various agricultural regions;
   (b) the need to effect the appropriate adjustments by degrees;
   (c) the fact that in the Member States agriculture constitutes a sector closely linked with the economy as a whole.

Article 40 (ex Article 34 TEC)

1.   In order to attain the objectives set out in Article 39, a common organisation of agricultural markets shall be established.

   This organisation shall take one of the following forms, depending on the product concerned:
   (a) common rules on competition;
   (b) compulsory coordination of the various national market organisations;
   (c) a European market organisation.

2.   The common organisation established in accordance with paragraph 1 may include all measures required to attain the objectives set out in Article 39, in particular regulation of prices, aids for the production and marketing of the various products, storage and carryover arrangements and common machinery for stabilising imports or exports.

   The common organisation shall be limited to pursuit of the objectives set out in Article 39 and shall exclude any discrimination between producers or consumers within the Union.

   Any common price policy shall be based on common criteria and uniform methods of calculation.

3.   In order to enable the common organisation referred to in paragraph 1 to attain its objectives, one or more agricultural guidance and guarantee funds may be set up.

Article 41 (ex Article 35 TEC)

To enable the objectives set out in Article 39 to be attained, provision may be made within the framework of the common agricultural policy for measures such as:

(a) an effective coordination of efforts in the spheres of vocational training, of research and of the dissemination of agricultural knowledge; this may include joint financing of projects or institutions;

(b) joint measures to promote consumption of certain products.

Article 42 (ex Article 36 TEC)

The provisions of the Chapter relating to rules on competition shall apply to production of and trade in agricultural products only to the extent determined by the European Parliament and the Council within the framework of Article 43(2) and in accordance with the procedure laid down therein, account being taken of the objectives set out in Article 39.

The Council, on a proposal from the Commission, may authorise the granting of aid:

(a) for the protection of enterprises handicapped by structural or natural conditions;

(b) within the framework of economic development programmes.

Article 43 (ex Article 37 TEC)

1. The Commission shall submit proposals for working out and implementing the common agricultural policy, including the replacement of the national organisations by one of the forms of common organisation provided for in Article 40(1), and for implementing the measures specified in this Title.

   These proposals shall take account of the interdependence of the agricultural matters mentioned in this Title.

2. The European Parliament and the Council, acting in accordance with the ordinary legislative procedure and after consulting the Economic and Social Committee, shall establish the common organisation of agricultural markets provided for in Article 40(1) and the other provisions necessary for the pursuit of the objectives of the common agricultural policy and the common fisheries policy.

3. The Council, on a proposal from the Commission, shall adopt measures on fixing prices, levies, aid and quantitative limitations and on the fixing and allocation of fishing opportunities.

4. In accordance with paragraph 2, the national market organisations may be replaced by the common organisation provided for in Article 40(1) if:
   (a) the common organisation offers Member States which are opposed to this measure and which have an organisation of their own for the production in question equivalent safeguards for the employment and standard of living of the producers concerned, account being taken of the adjustments that will be possible and the specialisation that will be needed with the passage of time;
   (b) such an organisation ensures conditions for trade within the Union similar to those existing in a national market.

5. If a common organisation for certain raw materials is established before a common organisation exists for the corresponding processed products, such raw materials as are used for processed products intended for export to third countries may be imported from outside the Union.

Article 44 (ex Article 38 TEC)

Where in a Member State a product is subject to a national market organisation or to internal rules having equivalent effect which affect the competitive position of similar production in another Member State, a countervailing charge shall be applied by Member States to imports of this product coming from the Member State where such organisation or rules exist, unless that State applies a countervailing charge on export.

The Commission shall fix the amount of these charges at the level required to redress the balance; it may also authorise other measures, the conditions and details of which it shall determine.

TITLE IV
FREE MOVEMENT OF PERSONS, SERVICES AND CAPITAL

Chapter 1 WORKERS

Article 45 (ex Article 39 TEC)

1.   Freedom of movement for workers shall be secured within the Union.

2.   Such freedom of movement shall entail the abolition of any discrimination based on nationality between workers of the Member States as regards employment, remuneration and other conditions of work and employment.

3.   It shall entail the right, subject to limitations justified on grounds of public policy, public security or public health:
    (a) to accept offers of employment actually made;
    (b) to move freely within the territory of Member States for this purpose;
    (c) to stay in a Member State for the purpose of employment in accordance with the provisions governing the employment of nationals of that State laid down by law, regulation or administrative action;
    (d) to remain in the territory of a Member State after having been employed in that State, subject to conditions which shall be embodied in regulations to be drawn up by the Commission.

4.   The provisions of this Article shall not apply to employment in the public service.

Article 46 (ex Article 40 TEC)

The European Parliament and the Council shall, acting in accordance with the ordinary legislative procedure and after consulting the Economic and Social Committee, issue directives or make regulations setting out the measures required to bring about freedom of movement for workers, as defined in Article 45, in particular:

(a) by ensuring close cooperation between national employment services;

(b) by abolishing those administrative procedures and practices and those qualifying periods in respect of eligibility for available employment, whether resulting from national legislation or from agreements previously concluded between Member States, the maintenance of which would form an obstacle to liberalisation of the movement of workers;

(c) by abolishing all such qualifying periods and other restrictions provided for either under national legislation or under agreements previously concluded between Member States as imposed on workers of other Member States conditions regarding the free choice of employment other than those imposed on workers of the State concerned;

(d) by setting up appropriate machinery to bring offers of employment into touch with applications for employment and to facilitate the achievement of a balance between supply and demand in the employment market in such a way as to avoid serious threats to the standard of living and level of employment in the various regions and industries.

Article 47 (ex Article 41 TEC)

Member States shall, within the framework of a joint programme, encourage the exchange of young workers.

Article 48 (ex Article 42 TEC)

The European Parliament and the Council shall, acting in accordance with the ordinary legislative procedure, adopt such measures in the field of social security as are necessary to provide freedom of movement for workers; to this end, they shall make arrangements to secure for employed and self- employed migrant workers and their dependants:

(a)   aggregation, for the purpose of acquiring and retaining the right to benefit and of calculating the amount of benefit, of all periods taken into account under the laws of the several countries;

(b)   payment of benefits to persons resident in the territories of Member States.

Where a member of the Council declares that a draft legislative act referred to in the first subparagraph would affect important aspects of its social security system, including its scope, cost or financial structure, or would affect the financial balance of that system, it may request that the matter be referred to the European Council. In that case, the ordinary legislative procedure shall be suspended. After discussion, the European Council shall, within four months of this suspension, either:

(a)   refer the draft back to the Council, which shall terminate the suspension of the ordinary legislative procedure; or

(b)   take no action or request the Commission to submit a new proposal; in that case, the act originally proposed shall be deemed not to have been adopted.

Chapter 2 RIGHT OF ESTABLISHMENT

Article 49 (ex Article 43 TEC)

Within the framework of the provisions set out below, restrictions on the freedom of establishment of nationals of a Member State in the territory of another Member State shall be prohibited. Such prohibition shall also apply to restrictions on the setting-up of agencies, branches or subsidiaries by nationals of any Member State established in the territory of any Member State.

Freedom of establishment shall include the right to take up and pursue activities as self-employed persons and to set up and manage undertakings, in particular companies or firms within the meaning of the second paragraph of Article 54, under the conditions laid down for its own nationals by the law of the country where such establishment is effected, subject to the provisions of the Chapter relating to capital.

Article 50 (ex Article 44 TEC)

1.   In order to attain freedom of establishment as regards a particular activity, the European Parliament and the Council, acting in accordance with the ordinary legislative procedure and after consulting the Economic and Social Committee, shall act by means of directives.

2.   The European Parliament, the Council and the Commission shall carry out the duties devolving upon them under the preceding provisions, in particular:

(a)   by according, as a general rule, priority treatment to activities where freedom of establishment makes a particularly valuable contribution to the development of production and trade;

(b)   by ensuring close cooperation between the competent authorities in the Member States in order to ascertain the particular situation within the Union of the various activities concerned;

(c)   by abolishing those administrative procedures and practices, whether resulting from national legislation or from agreements previously concluded between Member States, the maintenance of which would form an obstacle to freedom of establishment;

(d)   by ensuring that workers of one Member State employed in the territory of another Member State may remain in that territory for the purpose of taking up activities therein as self-employed persons, where they satisfy the conditions which they would be required to satisfy if they were entering that State at the time when they intended to take up such activities;

(e) by enabling a national of one Member State to acquire and use land and buildings situated in the territory of another Member State, in so far as this does not conflict with the principles laid down in Article 39(2);

(f) by effecting the progressive abolition of restrictions on freedom of establishment in every branch of activity under consideration, both as regards the conditions for setting up agencies, branches or subsidiaries in the territory of a Member State and as regards the subsidiaries in the territory of a Member State and as regards the conditions governing the entry of personnel belonging to the main establishment into managerial or supervisory posts in such agencies, branches or subsidiaries;

(g) by coordinating to the necessary extent the safeguards which, for the protection of the interests of members and others, are required by Member States of companies or firms within the meaning of the second paragraph of Article 54 with a view to making such safeguards equivalent throughout the Union;

(h) by satisfying themselves that the conditions of establishment are not distorted by aids granted by Member States.

Article 51 (ex Article 45 TEC)

The provisions of this Chapter shall not apply, so far as any given Member State is concerned, to activities which in that State are connected, even occasionally, with the exercise of official authority.

The European Parliament and the Council, acting in accordance with the ordinary legislative procedure, may rule that the provisions of this Chapter shall not apply to certain activities.

Article 52 (ex Article 46 TEC)

1. The provisions of this Chapter and measures taken in pursuance thereof shall not prejudice the applicability of provisions laid down by law, regulation or administrative action providing for special treatment for foreign nationals on grounds of public policy, public security or public health.

2. The European Parliament and the Council shall, acting in accordance with the ordinary legislative procedure, issue directives for the coordination of the abovementioned provisions.

Article 53 (ex Article 47 TEC)

1. In order to make it easier for persons to take up and pursue activities as self-employed persons, the European Parliament and the Council shall, acting in accordance with the ordinary legislative procedure, issue directives for the mutual recognition of diplomas, certificates and other evidence of formal qualifications and for the coordination of the provisions laid down by law, regulation or administrative action in Member States concerning the taking-up and pursuit of activities as self- employed persons.

2. In the case of the medical and allied and pharmaceutical professions, the progressive abolition of restrictions shall be dependent upon coordination of the conditions for their exercise in the various Member States.

Article 54 (ex Article 48 TEC)

Companies or firms formed in accordance with the law of a Member State and having their registered office, central administration or principal place of business within the Union shall, for the purposes of this Chapter, be treated in the same way as natural persons who are nationals of Member States.

'Companies or firms' means companies or firms constituted under civil or commercial law, including cooperative societies, and other legal persons governed by public or private law, save for those which are non-profit-making.

Article 55 (ex Article 294 TEC)

Member States shall accord nationals of the other Member States the same treatment as their own nationals as regards participation in the capital of companies or firms within the meaning of Article 54, without prejudice to the application of the other provisions of the Treaties.

Chapter 3 SERVICES

Article 56 (ex Article 49 TEC)

Within the framework of the provisions set out below, restrictions on freedom to provide services within the Union shall be prohibited in respect of nationals of Member States who are established in a Member State other than that of the person for whom the services are intended.

The European Parliament and the Council, acting in accordance with the ordinary legislative procedure, may extend the provisions of the Chapter to nationals of a third country who provide services and who are established within the Union.

Article 57 (ex Article 50 TEC)

Services shall be considered to be 'services' within the meaning of the Treaties where they are normally provided for remuneration, in so far as they are not governed by the provisions relating to freedom of movement for goods, capital and persons.
'Services' shall in particular include:

(a)   activities of an industrial character;

(b)   activities of a commercial character;

(c)   activities of craftsmen;

(d)   activities of the professions.

Without prejudice to the provisions of the Chapter relating to the right of establishment, the person providing a service may, in order to do so, temporarily pursue his activity in the Member State where the service is provided, under the same conditions as are imposed by that State on its own nationals.

Article 58 (ex Article 51 TEC)

1.   Freedom to provide services in the field of transport shall be governed by the provisions of the Title relating to transport.

2.   The liberalisation of banking and insurance services connected with movements of capital shall be effected in step with the liberalisation of movement of capital.

Article 59 (ex Article 52 TEC)

1.   In order to achieve the liberalisation of a specific service, the European Parliament and the Council, acting in accordance with the ordinary legislative procedure and after consulting the Economic and Social Committee, shall issue directives.

2.   As regards the directives referred to in paragraph 1, priority shall as a general rule be given to those services which directly affect production costs or the liberalisation of which helps to promote trade in goods.

Article 60 (ex Article 53 TEC)

The Member States shall endeavour to undertake the liberalisation of services beyond the extent required by the directives issued pursuant to Article 59(1), if their general economic situation and the situation of the economic sector concerned so permit.

To this end, the Commission shall make recommendations to the Member States concerned.

Article 61 (ex Article 54 TEC)
As long as restrictions on freedom to provide services have not been abolished, each Member State shall apply such restrictions without distinction on grounds of nationality or residence to all persons providing services within the meaning of the first paragraph of Article 56.

Article 62 (ex Article 55 TEC)
The provisions of Articles 51 to 54 shall apply to the matters covered by this Chapter.

Chapter 4 CAPITAL AND PAYMENTS

Article 63 (ex Article 56 TEC)

1.   Within the framework of the provisions set out in this Chapter, all restrictions on the movement of capital between Member States and between Member States and third countries shall be prohibited.

2.   Within the framework of the provisions set out in this Chapter, all restrictions on payments between Member States and between Member States and third countries shall be prohibited.

Article 64 (ex Article 57 TEC)

1.   The provisions of Article 63 shall be without prejudice to the application to third countries of any restrictions which exist on 31 December 1993 under national or Union law adopted in respect of the movement of capital to or from third countries involving direct investment — including in real estate — establishment, the provision of financial services or the admission of securities to capital markets. In respect of restrictions existing under national law in Bulgaria, Estonia and Hungary, the relevant date shall be 31 December 1999.

2.   Whilst endeavouring to achieve the objective of free movement of capital between Member States and third countries to the greatest extent possible and without prejudice to the other Chapters of the Treaties, the European Parliament and the Council, acting in accordance with the ordinary legislative procedure, shall adopt the measures on the movement of capital to or from third countries involving direct investment — including investment in real estate — establishment, the provision of financial services or the admission of securities to capital markets.

3.   Notwithstanding paragraph 2, only the Council, acting in accordance with a special legislative procedure, may unanimously, and after consulting the European Parliament, adopt measures which constitute a step backwards in Union law as regards the liberalisation of the movement of capital to or from third countries.

Article 65 (ex Article 58 TEC)

1.   The provisions of Article 63 shall be without prejudice to the right of Member States:
      (a) to apply the relevant provisions of their tax law which distinguish between taxpayers who are not in the same situation with regard to their place of residence or with regard to the place where their capital is invested;
      (b) to take all requisite measures to prevent infringements of national law and regulations, in particular in the field of taxation and the prudential supervision of financial institutions, or to lay down procedures for the declaration of capital movements for purposes of administrative or statistical information, or to take measures which are justified on grounds of public policy or public security.

2.   The provisions of this Chapter shall be without prejudice to the applicability of restrictions on the right of establishment which are compatible with the Treaties.

3.   The measures and procedures referred to in paragraphs 1 and 2 shall not constitute a means of arbitrary discrimination or a disguised restriction on the free movement of capital and payments as defined in Article 63.

4.   In the absence of measures pursuant to Article 64(3), the Commission or, in the absence of a Commission decision within three months from the request of the Member State concerned, the Council, may adopt a decision stating that restrictive tax measures adopted by a Member State concerning one or more third countries are to be considered compatible with the Treaties in so far as they are justified by one of the objectives of the Union and compatible with the proper functioning of the internal market. The Council shall act unanimously on application by a Member State.

Article 66 (ex Article 59 TEC)

Where, in exceptional circumstances, movements of capital to or from third countries cause, or threaten to cause, serious difficulties for the operation of economic and monetary union, the Council, on a proposal from the Commission and after consulting the European Central Bank, may take safeguard measures with regard to third countries for a period not exceeding six months if such measures are strictly necessary.

TITLE V
AREA OF FREEDOM, SECURITY AND JUSTICE

Chapter 1 GENERAL PROVISIONS

Article 67 (ex Article 61 TEC and ex Article 29 TEU)

1.   The Union shall constitute an area of freedom, security and justice with respect for fundamental rights and the different legal systems and traditions of the Member States.

2.   It shall ensure the absence of internal border controls for persons and shall frame a common policy on asylum, immigration and external border control, based on solidarity between Member States, which is fair towards third-country nationals. For the purpose of this Title, stateless persons shall be treated as third-country nationals.

3.   The Union shall endeavour to ensure a high level of security through measures to prevent and combat crime, racism and xenophobia, and through measures for coordination and cooperation between police and judicial authorities and other competent authorities, as well as through the mutual recognition of judgments in criminal matters and, if necessary, through the approximation of criminal laws.

4.   The Union shall facilitate access to justice, in particular through the principle of mutual recognition of judicial and extrajudicial decisions in civil matters.

Article 68

The European Council shall define the strategic guidelines for legislative and operational planning within the area of freedom, security and justice.

Article 69

National Parliaments ensure that the proposals and legislative initiatives submitted under Chapters 4 and 5 comply with the principle of subsidiarity, in accordance with the arrangements laid down by the Protocol on the application of the principles of subsidiarity and proportionality.

Article 70

Without prejudice to Articles 258, 259 and 260, the Council may, on a proposal from the Commission, adopt measures laying down the arrangements whereby Member States, in collaboration with the Commission, conduct objective and impartial evaluation of the implementation of the Union policies referred to in this Title by Member States' authorities, in particular in order to facilitate full application of the principle of mutual recognition.
The European Parliament and national Parliaments shall be informed of the content and results of the evaluation.

Article 71 (ex Article 36 TEU)

A standing committee shall be set up within the Council in order to ensure that operational cooperation on internal security is promoted and strengthened within the Union. Without prejudice to Article 240, it shall facilitate coordination of the action of Member States' competent authorities. Representatives of the Union bodies, offices and agencies concerned may be involved in the proceedings of this committee. The European Parliament and national Parliaments shall be kept informed of the proceedings.

Article 72 (ex Article 64(1) TEC and ex Article 33 TEU)

This Title shall not affect the exercise of the responsibilities incumbent upon Member States with regard to the maintenance of law and order and the safeguarding of internal security.

Article 73

It shall be open to Member States to organise between themselves and under their responsibility such forms of cooperation and coordination as they deem appropriate between the competent departments of their administrations responsible for safeguarding national security.

Article 74 (ex Article 66 TEC)

The Council shall adopt measures to ensure administrative cooperation between the relevant departments of the Member States in the areas covered by this Title, as well as between those departments and the Commission. It shall act on a Commission proposal, subject to Article 76, and after consulting the European Parliament.

Article 75 (ex Article 60 TEC)

Where necessary to achieve the objectives set out in Article 67, as regards preventing and combating terrorism and related activities, the European Parliament and the Council, acting by means of regulations in accordance with the ordinary legislative procedure, shall define a framework for administrative measures with regard to capital movements and payments, such as the freezing of funds, financial assets or economic gains belonging to, or owned or held by, natural or legal persons, groups or non-State entities.

The Council, on a proposal from the Commission, shall adopt measures to implement the framework referred to in the first paragraph.

The acts referred to in this Article shall include necessary provisions on legal safeguards.

Article 76

The acts referred to in Chapters 4 and 5, together with the measures referred to in Article 74 which ensure administrative cooperation in the areas covered by these Chapters, shall be adopted:

(a)   on a proposal from the Commission, or

(b)   on the initiative of a quarter of the Member States.

Chapter 2 POLICIES ON BORDER CHECKS, ASYLUM AND IMMIGRATION

Article 77 (ex Article 62 TEC)

1.   The Union shall develop a policy with a view to:
  (a) ensuring the absence of any controls on persons, whatever their nationality, when crossing internal borders;
  (b) carrying out checks on persons and efficient monitoring of the crossing of external borders;
  (c) the gradual introduction of an integrated management system for external borders.

2. For the purposes of paragraph 1, the European Parliament and the Council, acting in accordance with the ordinary legislative procedure, shall adopt measures concerning:
    (a) the common policy on visas and other short-stay residence permits;
    (b) the checks to which persons crossing external borders are subject;
    (c) the conditions under which nationals of third countries shall have the freedom to travel within the Union for a short period;
    (d) any measure necessary for the gradual establishment of an integrated management system for external borders;
    (e) the absence of any controls on persons, whatever their nationality, when crossing internal borders.

3. If action by the Union should prove necessary to facilitate the exercise of the right referred to in Article 20(2)(a), and if the Treaties have not provided the necessary powers, the Council, acting in accordance with a special legislative procedure, may adopt provisions concerning passports, identity cards, residence permits or any other such document. The Council shall act unanimously after consulting the European Parliament.

4. This Article shall not affect the competence of the Member States concerning the geographical demarcation of their borders, in accordance with international law.

Article 78 (ex Articles 63, points 1 and 2, and 64(2) TEC)

1. The Union shall develop a common policy on asylum, subsidiary protection and temporary protection with a view to offering appropriate status to any third-country national requiring international protection and ensuring compliance with the principle of non-refoulement. This policy must be in accordance with the Geneva Convention of 28 July 1951 and the Protocol of 31 January 1967 relating to the status of refugees, and other relevant treaties.

2. For the purposes of paragraph 1, the European Parliament and the Council, acting in accordance with the ordinary legislative procedure, shall adopt measures for a common European asylum system comprising:
    (a) a uniform status of asylum for nationals of third countries, valid throughout the Union;
    (b) a uniform status of subsidiary protection for nationals of third countries who, without obtaining European asylum, are in need of international protection;
    (c) a common system of temporary protection for displaced persons in the event of a massive inflow;
    (d) common procedures for the granting and withdrawing of uniform asylum or subsidiary protection status;
    (e) criteria and mechanisms for determining which Member State is responsible for considering an application for asylum or subsidiary protection;
    (f) standards concerning the conditions for the reception of applicants for asylum or subsidiary protection;
    (g) partnership and cooperation with third countries for the purpose of managing inflows of people applying for asylum or subsidiary or temporary protection.

3. In the event of one or more Member States being confronted by an emergency situation characterised by a sudden inflow of nationals of third countries, the Council, on a proposal from the Commission, may adopt provisional measures for the benefit of the Member State(s) concerned. It shall act after consulting the European Parliament.

Article 79 (ex Article 63, points 3 and 4, TEC)

1. The Union shall develop a common immigration policy aimed at ensuring, at all stages, the efficient management of migration flows, fair treatment of third-country nationals

residing legally in Member States, and the prevention of, and enhanced measures to combat, illegal immigration and trafficking in human beings.

2.   For the purposes of paragraph 1, the European Parliament and the Council, acting in accordance with the ordinary legislative procedure, shall adopt measures in the following areas:

(a) the conditions of entry and residence, and standards on the issue by Member States of long-term visas and residence permits, including those for the purpose of family reunification;

(b) the definition of the rights of third-country nationals residing legally in a Member State, including the conditions governing freedom of movement and of residence in other Member States;

(c) illegal immigration and unauthorised residence, including removal and repatriation of persons residing without authorisation;

(d) combating trafficking in persons, in particular women and children.

3.   The Union may conclude agreements with third countries for the readmission to their countries of origin or provenance of third-country nationals who do not or who no longer fulfil the conditions for entry, presence or residence in the territory of one of the Member States.

4.   The European Parliament and the Council, acting in accordance with the ordinary legislative procedure, may establish measures to provide incentives and support for the action of Member States with a view to promoting the integration of third-country nationals residing legally in their territories, excluding any harmonisation of the laws and regulations of the Member States.

5.   This Article shall not affect the right of Member States to determine volumes of admission of third-country nationals coming from third countries to their territory in order to seek work, whether employed or self-employed.

Article 80
The policies of the Union set out in this Chapter and their implementation shall be governed by the principle of solidarity and fair sharing of responsibility, including its financial implications, between the Member States. Whenever necessary, the Union acts adopted pursuant to this Chapter shall contain appropriate measures to give effect to this principle.

Chapter 3 JUDICIAL COOPERATION IN CIVIL MATTERS

Article 81 (ex Article 65 TEC)

1.   The Union shall develop judicial cooperation in civil matters having cross-border implications, based on the principle of mutual recognition of judgments and of decisions in extrajudicial cases. Such cooperation may include the adoption of measures for the approximation of the laws and regulations of the Member States.

2.   For the purposes of paragraph 1, the European Parliament and the Council, acting in accordance with the ordinary legislative procedure, shall adopt measures, particularly when necessary for the proper functioning of the internal market, aimed at ensuring:

(a) the mutual recognition and enforcement between Member States of judgments and of decisions in extrajudicial cases;

(b) the cross-border service of judicial and extrajudicial documents;

(c) the compatibility of the rules applicable in the Member States concerning conflict of laws and of jurisdiction;

(d) cooperation in the taking of evidence;

(e) effective access to justice;

(f) the elimination of obstacles to the proper functioning of civil proceedings, if necessary by promoting the compatibility of the rules on civil procedure applicable in the Member States;

(g) the development of alternative methods of dispute settlement;

(h) support for the training of the judiciary and judicial staff.

3. Notwithstanding paragraph 2, measures concerning family law with cross-border implications shall be established by the Council, acting in accordance with a special legislative procedure. The Council shall act unanimously after consulting the European Parliament.

The Council, on a proposal from the Commission, may adopt a decision determining those aspects of family law with cross-border implications which may be the subject of acts adopted by the ordinary legislative procedure. The Council shall act unanimously after consulting the European Parliament.

The proposal referred to in the second subparagraph shall be notified to the national Parliaments. If a national Parliament makes known its opposition within six months of the date of such notification, the decision shall not be adopted. In the absence of opposition, the Council may adopt the decision.

Chapter 4 JUDICIAL COOPERATION IN CRIMINAL MATTERS

Article 82 (ex Article 31 TEU)

1. Judicial cooperation in criminal matters in the Union shall be based on the principle of mutual recognition of judgments and judicial decisions and shall include the approximation of the laws and regulations of the Member States in the areas referred to in paragraph 2 and in Article 83.

The European Parliament and the Council, acting in accordance with the ordinary legislative procedure, shall adopt measures to:

(a) lay down rules and procedures for ensuring recognition throughout the Union of all forms of judgments and judicial decisions;

(b) prevent and settle conflicts of jurisdiction between Member States;

(c) support the training of the judiciary and judicial staff;

(d) facilitate cooperation between judicial or equivalent authorities of the Member States in relation to proceedings in criminal matters and the enforcement of decisions.

2. To the extent necessary to facilitate mutual recognition of judgments and judicial decisions and police and judicial cooperation in criminal matters having a cross-border dimension, the European Parliament and the Council may, by means of directives adopted in accordance with the ordinary legislative procedure, establish minimum rules. Such rules shall take into account the differences between the legal traditions and systems of the Member States.

They shall concern:

(a) mutual admissibility of evidence between Member States;

(b) the rights of individuals in criminal procedure;

(c) the rights of victims of crime;

(d) any other specific aspects of criminal procedure which the Council has identified in advance by a decision; for the adoption of such a decision, the Council shall act unanimously after obtaining the consent of the European Parliament.

Adoption of the minimum rules referred to in this paragraph shall not prevent Member States from maintaining or introducing a higher level of protection for individuals.

3.   Where a member of the Council considers that a draft directive as referred to in paragraph 2 would affect fundamental aspects of its criminal justice system, it may request that the draft directive be referred to the European Council. In that case, the ordinary legislative procedure shall be suspended. After discussion, and in case of a consensus, the European Council shall, within four months of this suspension, refer the draft back to the Council, which shall terminate the suspension of the ordinary legislative procedure.

Within the same timeframe, in case of disagreement, and if at least nine Member States wish to establish enhanced cooperation on the basis of the draft directive concerned, they shall notify the European Parliament, the Council and the Commission accordingly. In such a case, the authorisation to proceed with enhanced cooperation referred to in Article 20(2) of the Treaty on European Union and Article 329(1) of this Treaty shall be deemed to be granted and the provisions on enhanced cooperation shall apply.

Article 83 (ex Article 31 TEU)

1.   The European Parliament and the Council may, by means of directives adopted in accordance with the ordinary legislative procedure, establish minimum rules concerning the definition of criminal offences and sanctions in the areas of particularly serious crime with a cross-border dimension resulting from the nature or impact of such offences or from a special need to combat them on a common basis. These areas of crime are the following: terrorism, trafficking in human beings and sexual exploitation of women and children, illicit drug trafficking, illicit arms trafficking, money laundering, corruption, counterfeiting of means of payment, computer crime and organised crime.

On the basis of developments in crime, the Council may adopt a decision identifying other areas of crime that meet the criteria specified in this paragraph. It shall act unanimously after obtaining the consent of the European Parliament.

2.   If the approximation of criminal laws and regulations of the Member States proves essential to ensure the effective implementation of a Union policy in an area which has been subject to harmonisation measures, directives may establish minimum rules with regard to the definition of criminal offences and sanctions in the area concerned. Such directives shall be adopted by the same ordinary or special legislative procedure as was followed for the adoption of the harmonisation measures in question, without prejudice to Article 76.

3.   Where a member of the Council considers that a draft directive as referred to in paragraph 1 or 2 would affect fundamental aspects of its criminal justice system, it may request that the draft directive be referred to the European Council. In that case, the ordinary legislative procedure shall be suspended. After discussion, and in case of a consensus, the European Council shall, within four months of this suspension, refer the draft back to the Council, which shall terminate the suspension of the ordinary legislative procedure.

Within the same timeframe, in case of disagreement, and if at least nine Member States wish to establish enhanced cooperation on the basis of the draft directive concerned, they shall notify the European Parliament, the Council and the Commission accordingly. In such a case, the authorisation to proceed with enhanced cooperation referred to in Article 20(2) of the Treaty on European Union and Article 329(1) of this Treaty shall be deemed to be granted and the provisions on enhanced cooperation shall apply.

Article 84

The European Parliament and the Council, acting in accordance with the ordinary legislative procedure, may establish measures to promote and support the action of Member States in the field of crime prevention, excluding any harmonisation of the laws and regulations of the Member States.

Article 85 (ex Article 31 TEU)

1. Eurojust's mission shall be to support and strengthen coordination and cooperation between national investigating and prosecuting authorities in relation to serious crime affecting two or more Member States or requiring a prosecution on common bases, on the basis of operations conducted and information supplied by the Member States' authorities and by Europol.

    In this context, the European Parliament and the Council, by means of regulations adopted in accordance with the ordinary legislative procedure, shall determine Eurojust's structure, operation, field of action and tasks. These tasks may include:
    (a) the initiation of criminal investigations, as well as proposing the initiation of prosecutions conducted by competent national authorities, particularly those relating to offences against the financial interests of the Union;
    (b) the coordination of investigations and prosecutions referred to in point (a);
    (c) the strengthening of judicial cooperation, including by resolution of conflicts of jurisdiction and by close cooperation with the European Judicial Network.

    These regulations shall also determine arrangements for involving the European Parliament and national Parliaments in the evaluation of Eurojust's activities.

2. In the prosecutions referred to in paragraph 1, and without prejudice to Article 86, formal acts of judicial procedure shall be carried out by the competent national officials.

Article 86

1. In order to combat crimes affecting the financial interests of the Union, the Council, by means of regulations adopted in accordance with a special legislative procedure, may establish a European Public Prosecutor's Office from Eurojust. The Council shall act unanimously after obtaining the consent of the European Parliament.

    In the absence of unanimity in the Council, a group of at least nine Member States may request that the draft regulation be referred to the European Council. In that case, the procedure in the Council shall be suspended. After discussion, and in case of a consensus, the European Council shall, within four months of this suspension, refer the draft back to the Council for adoption.

    Within the same timeframe, in case of disagreement, and if at least nine Member States wish to establish enhanced cooperation on the basis of the draft regulation concerned, they shall notify the European Parliament, the Council and the Commission accordingly. In such a case, the authorisation to proceed with enhanced cooperation referred to in Article 20(2) of the Treaty on European Union and Article 329(1) of this Treaty shall be deemed to be granted and the provisions on enhanced cooperation shall apply.

2. The European Public Prosecutor's Office shall be responsible for investigating, prosecuting and bringing to judgment, where appropriate in liaison with Europol, the perpetrators of, and accomplices in, offences against the Union's financial interests, as determined by the regulation provided for in paragraph 1. It shall exercise the functions of prosecutor in the competent courts of the Member States in relation to such offences.

3. The regulations referred to in paragraph 1 shall determine the general rules applicable to the European Public Prosecutor's Office, the conditions governing the performance of its functions, the rules of procedure applicable to its activities, as well as those governing the admissibility of evidence, and the rules applicable to the judicial review of procedural measures taken by it in the performance of its functions.

4. The European Council may, at the same time or subsequently, adopt a decision amending paragraph 1 in order to extend the powers of the European Public Prosecutor's Office to

include serious crime having a cross-border dimension and amending accordingly paragraph 2 as regards the perpetrators of, and accomplices in, serious crimes affecting more than one Member State. The European Council shall act unanimously after obtaining the consent of the European Parliament and after consulting the Commission.

Chapter 5 POLICE COOPERATION

Article 87 (ex Article 30 TEU)

1. The Union shall establish police cooperation involving all the Member States' competent authorities, including police, customs and other specialised law enforcement services in relation to the prevention, detection and investigation of criminal offences.

2. For the purposes of paragraph 1, the European Parliament and the Council, acting in accordance with the ordinary legislative procedure, may establish measures concerning:
    (a) the collection, storage, processing, analysis and exchange of relevant information;
    (b) support for the training of staff, and cooperation on the exchange of staff, on equipment and on research into crime-detection;
    (c) common investigative techniques in relation to the detection of serious forms of organised crime.

3. The Council, acting in accordance with a special legislative procedure, may establish measures concerning operational cooperation between the authorities referred to in this Article. The Council shall act unanimously after consulting the European Parliament.

    In case of the absence of unanimity in the Council, a group of at least nine Member States may request that the draft measures be referred to the European Council. In that case, the procedure in the Council shall be suspended. After discussion, and in case of a consensus, the European Council shall, within four months of this suspension, refer the draft back to the Council for adoption.

    Within the same timeframe, in case of disagreement, and if at least nine Member States wish to establish enhanced cooperation on the basis of the draft measures concerned, they shall notify the European Parliament, the Council and the Commission accordingly. In such a case, the authorisation to proceed with enhanced cooperation referred to in Article 20(2) of the Treaty on European Union and Article 329(1) of this Treaty shall be deemed to be granted and the provisions on enhanced cooperation shall apply.

    The specific procedure provided for in the second and third subparagraphs shall not apply to acts which constitute a development of the Schengen *acquis*.

Article 88 (ex Article 30 TEU)

1. Europol's mission shall be to support and strengthen action by the Member States' police authorities and other law enforcement services and their mutual cooperation in preventing and combating serious crime affecting two or more Member States, terrorism and forms of crime which affect a common interest covered by a Union policy.

2. The European Parliament and the Council, by means of regulations adopted in accordance with the ordinary legislative procedure, shall determine Europol's structure, operation, field of action and tasks. These tasks may include:
    (a) the collection, storage, processing, analysis and exchange of information, in particular that forwarded by the authorities of the Member States or third countries or bodies;
    (b) the coordination, organisation and implementation of investigative and operational action carried out jointly with the Member States' competent authorities or in the context of joint investigative teams, where appropriate in liaison with Eurojust.

These regulations shall also lay down the procedures for scrutiny of Europol's activities by the European Parliament, together with national Parliaments.

3.   Any operational action by Europol must be carried out in liaison and in agreement with the authorities of the Member State or States whose territory is concerned. The application of coercive measures shall be the exclusive responsibility of the competent national authorities.

Article 89 (ex Article 32 TEU)

The Council, acting in accordance with a special legislative procedure, shall lay down the conditions and limitations under which the competent authorities of the Member States referred to in Articles 82 and 87 may operate in the territory of another Member State in liaison and in agreement with the authorities of that State. The Council shall act unanimously after consulting the European Parliament.

TITLE VI
TRANSPORT

Article 90 (ex Article 70 TEC)

The objectives of the Treaties shall, in matters governed by this Title, be pursued within the framework of a common transport policy.

Article 91 (ex Article 71 TEC)

1.   For the purpose of implementing Article 90, and taking into account the distinctive features of transport, the European Parliament and the Council shall, acting in accordance with the ordinary legislative procedure and after consulting the Economic and Social Committee and the Committee of the Regions, lay down:
   (a) common rules applicable to international transport to or from the territory of a Member State or passing across the territory of one or more Member States;
   (b) the conditions under which non-resident carriers may operate transport services within a Member State;
   (c) measures to improve transport safety;
   (d) any other appropriate provisions.

2.   When the measures referred to in paragraph 1 are adopted, account shall be taken of cases where their application might seriously affect the standard of living and level of employment in certain regions, and the operation of transport facilities.

Article 92 (ex Article 72 TEC)

Until the provisions referred to in Article 91(1) have been laid down, no Member State may, unless the Council has unanimously adopted a measure granting a derogation, make the various provisions governing the subject on 1 January 1958 or, for acceding States, the date of their accession less favourable in their direct or indirect effect on carriers of other Member States as compared with carriers who are nationals of that State.

Article 93 (ex Article 73 TEC)

Aids shall be compatible with the Treaties if they meet the needs of coordination of transport or if they represent reimbursement for the discharge of certain obligations inherent in the concept of a public service.

Article 94 (ex Article 74 TEC)

Any measures taken within the framework of the Treaties in respect of transport rates and conditions shall take account of the economic circumstances of carriers.

Article 95 (ex Article 75 TEC)

1. In the case of transport within the Union, discrimination which takes the form of carriers charging different rates and imposing different conditions for the carriage of the same goods over the same transport links on grounds of the country of origin or of destination of the goods in question shall be prohibited.

2. Paragraph 1 shall not prevent the European Parliament and the Council from adopting other measures pursuant to Article 91(1).

3. The Council shall, on a proposal from the Commission and after consulting the European Parliament and the Economic and Social Committee, lay down rules for implementing the provisions of paragraph 1.

    The Council may in particular lay down the provisions needed to enable the institutions of the Union to secure compliance with the rule laid down in paragraph 1 and to ensure that users benefit from it to the full.

4. The Commission shall, acting on its own initiative or on application by a Member State, investigate any cases of discrimination falling within paragraph 1 and, after consulting any Member State concerned, shall take the necessary decisions within the framework of the rules laid down in accordance with the provisions of paragraph 3.

Article 96 (ex Article 76 TEC)

1. The imposition by a Member State, in respect of transport operations carried out within the Union, of rates and conditions involving any element of support or protection in the interest of one or more particular undertakings or industries shall be prohibited, unless authorised by the Commission.

2. The Commission shall, acting on its own initiative or on application by a Member State, examine the rates and conditions referred to in paragraph 1, taking account in particular of the requirements of an appropriate regional economic policy, the needs of underdeveloped areas and the problems of areas seriously affected by political circumstances on the one hand, and of the effects of such rates and conditions on competition between the different modes of transport on the other.

    After consulting each Member State concerned, the Commission shall take the necessary decisions.

3. The prohibition provided for in paragraph 1 shall not apply to tariffs fixed to meet competition.

Article 97 (ex Article 77 TEC)

Charges or dues in respect of the crossing of frontiers which are charged by a carrier in addition to the transport rates shall not exceed a reasonable level after taking the costs actually incurred thereby into account.

Member States shall endeavour to reduce these costs progressively.

The Commission may make recommendations to Member States for the application of this Article.

Article 98 (ex Article 78 TEC)

The provisions of this Title shall not form an obstacle to the application of measures taken in the Federal Republic of Germany to the extent that such measures are required in order to compensate for the economic disadvantages caused by the division of Germany to the economy of certain areas of the Federal Republic affected by that division. Five years after the entry into force of the Treaty of Lisbon, the Council, acting on a proposal from the Commission, may adopt a decision repealing this Article.

Article 99 (ex Article 79 TEC)

An Advisory Committee consisting of experts designated by the governments of Member States shall be attached to the Commission. The Commission, whenever it considers it desirable, shall consult the Committee on transport matters.

Article 100 (ex Article 80 TEC)

1. The provisions of this Title shall apply to transport by rail, road and inland waterway.

2. The European Parliament and the Council, acting in accordance with the ordinary legislative procedure, may lay down appropriate provisions for sea and air transport. They shall act after consulting the Economic and Social Committee and the Committee of the Regions.

TITLE VII
COMMON RULES ON COMPETITION, TAXATION AND APPROXIMATION OF LAWS

Chapter 1 RULES ON COMPETITION

SECTION 1 RULES APPLYING TO UNDERTAKINGS

Article 101 (ex Article 81 TEC)

1. The following shall be prohibited as incompatible with the internal market: all agreements between undertakings, decisions by associations of undertakings and concerted practices which may affect trade between Member States and which have as their object or effect the prevention, restriction or distortion of competition within the internal market, and in particular those which:
    (a) directly or indirectly fix purchase or selling prices or any other trading conditions;
    (b) limit or control production, markets, technical development, or investment;
    (c) share markets or sources of supply;
    (d) apply dissimilar conditions to equivalent transactions with other trading parties, thereby placing them at a competitive disadvantage;
    (e) make the conclusion of contracts subject to acceptance by the other parties of supplementary obligations which, by their nature or according to commercial usage, have no connection with the subject of such contracts.

2. Any agreements or decisions prohibited pursuant to this Article shall be automatically void.

3. The provisions of paragraph 1 may, however, be declared inapplicable in the case of:
    — any agreement or category of agreements between undertakings,
    — any decision or category of decisions by associations of undertakings,
    — any concerted practice or category of concerted practices,

    which contributes to improving the production or distribution of goods or to promoting technical or economic progress, while allowing consumers a fair share of the resulting benefit, and which does not:
    (a) impose on the undertakings concerned restrictions which are not indispensable to the attainment of these objectives;
    (b) afford such undertakings the possibility of eliminating competition in respect of a substantial part of the products in question.

Article 102 (ex Article 82 TEC)

Any abuse by one or more undertakings of a dominant position within the internal market or in a substantial part of it shall be prohibited as incompatible with the internal market in so far as it may affect trade between Member States.

Such abuse may, in particular, consist in:
(a)   directly or indirectly imposing unfair purchase or selling prices or other unfair trading conditions;

(b)   limiting production, markets or technical development to the prejudice of consumers;

(c)   applying dissimilar conditions to equivalent transactions with other trading parties, thereby placing them at a competitive disadvantage;

(d)   making the conclusion of contracts subject to acceptance by the other parties of supplementary obligations which, by their nature or according to commercial usage, have no connection with the subject of such contracts.

Article 103 (ex Article 83 TEC)
1.   The appropriate regulations or directives to give effect to the principles set out in Articles 101 and 102 shall be laid down by the Council, on a proposal from the Commission and after consulting the European Parliament.

2.   The regulations or directives referred to in paragraph 1 shall be designed in particular:
       (a)   to ensure compliance with the prohibitions laid down in Article 101(1) and in Article 102 by making provision for fines and periodic penalty payments;
       (b)   to lay down detailed rules for the application of Article 101(3), taking into account the need to ensure effective supervision on the one hand, and to simplify administration to the greatest possible extent on the other;
       (c)   to define, if need be, in the various branches of the economy, the scope of the provisions of Articles 101 and 102;
       (d)   to define the respective functions of the Commission and of the Court of Justice of the European Union in applying the provisions laid down in this paragraph;
       (e)   to determine the relationship between national laws and the provisions contained in this Section or adopted pursuant to this Article.

Article 104 (ex Article 84 TEC)
Until the entry into force of the provisions adopted in pursuance of Article 103, the authorities in Member States shall rule on the admissibility of agreements, decisions and concerted practices and on abuse of a dominant position in the internal market in accordance with the law of their country and with the provisions of Article 101, in particular paragraph 3, and of Article 102.

Article 105 (ex Article 85 TEC)
1.   Without prejudice to Article 104, the Commission shall ensure the application of the principles laid down in Articles 101 and 102. On application by a Member State or on its own initiative, and in cooperation with the competent authorities in the Member States, which shall give it their assistance, the Commission shall investigate cases of suspected infringement of these principles. If it finds that there has been an infringement, it shall propose appropriate measures to bring it to an end.

2.   If the infringement is not brought to an end, the Commission shall record such infringement of the principles in a reasoned decision. The Commission may publish its decision and authorise Member States to take the measures, the conditions and details of which it shall determine, needed to remedy the situation.

3.   The Commission may adopt regulations relating to the categories of agreement in respect of which the Council has adopted a regulation or a directive pursuant to Article 103(2)(b).

Article 106 (ex Article 86 TEC)

1. In the case of public undertakings and undertakings to which Member States grant special or exclusive rights, Member States shall neither enact nor maintain in force any measure contrary to the rules contained in the Treaties, in particular to those rules provided for in Article 18 and Articles 101 to 109.

2. Undertakings entrusted with the operation of services of general economic interest or having the character of a revenue-producing monopoly shall be subject to the rules contained in the Treaties, in particular to the rules on competition, in so far as the application of such rules does not obstruct the performance, in law or in fact, of the particular tasks assigned to them. The development of trade must not be affected to such an extent as would be contrary to the interests of the Union.

3. The Commission shall ensure the application of the provisions of this Article and shall, where necessary, address appropriate directives or decisions to Member States.

SECTION 2 AIDS GRANTED BY STATES

Article 107 (ex Article 87 TEC)

1. Save as otherwise provided in the Treaties, any aid granted by a Member State or through State resources in any form whatsoever which distorts or threatens to distort competition by favouring certain undertakings or the production of certain goods shall, in so far as it affects trade between Member States, be incompatible with the internal market.

2. The following shall be compatible with the internal market:
    (a) aid having a social character, granted to individual consumers, provided that such aid is granted without discrimination related to the origin of the products concerned;
    (b) aid to make good the damage caused by natural disasters or exceptional occurrences;
    (c) aid granted to the economy of certain areas of the Federal Republic of Germany affected by the division of Germany, in so far as such aid is required in order to compensate for the economic disadvantages caused by that division. Five years after the entry into force of the Treaty of Lisbon, the Council, acting on a proposal from the Commission, may adopt a decision repealing this point.

3. The following may be considered to be compatible with the internal market:
    (a) aid to promote the economic development of areas where the standard of living is abnormally low or where there is serious underemployment, and of the regions referred to in Article 349, in view of their structural, economic and social situation;
    (b) aid to promote the execution of an important project of common European interest or to remedy a serious disturbance in the economy of a Member State;
    (c) aid to facilitate the development of certain economic activities or of certain economic areas, where such aid does not adversely affect trading conditions to an extent contrary to the common interest;
    (d) aid to promote culture and heritage conservation where such aid does not affect trading conditions and competition in the Union to an extent that is contrary to the common interest;
    (e) such other categories of aid as may be specified by decision of the Council on a proposal from the Commission.

Article 108 (ex Article 88 TEC)

1. The Commission shall, in cooperation with Member States, keep under constant review all systems of aid existing in those States. It shall propose to the latter any appropriate measures required by the progressive development or by the functioning of the internal market.

2.   If, after giving notice to the parties concerned to submit their comments, the Commission finds that aid granted by a State or through State resources is not compatible with the internal market having regard to Article 107, or that such aid is being misused, it shall decide that the State concerned shall abolish or alter such aid within a period of time to be determined by the Commission.

If the State concerned does not comply with this decision within the prescribed time, the Commission or any other interested State may, in derogation from the provisions of Articles 258 and 259, refer the matter to the Court of Justice of the European Union direct.

On application by a Member State, the Council may, acting unanimously, decide that aid which that State is granting or intends to grant shall be considered to be compatible with the internal market, in derogation from the provisions of Article 107 or from the regulations provided for in Article 109, if such a decision is justified by exceptional circumstances. If, as regards the aid in question, the Commission has already initiated the procedure provided for in the first subparagraph of this paragraph, the fact that the State concerned has made its application to the Council shall have the effect of suspending that procedure until the Council has made its attitude known.

If, however, the Council has not made its attitude known within three months of the said application being made, the Commission shall give its decision on the case.

3.   The Commission shall be informed, in sufficient time to enable it to submit its comments, of any plans to grant or alter aid. If it considers that any such plan is not compatible with the internal market having regard to Article 107, it shall without delay initiate the procedure provided for in paragraph 2. The Member State concerned shall not put its proposed measures into effect until this procedure has resulted in a final decision.

4.   The Commission may adopt regulations relating to the categories of State aid that the Council has, pursuant to Article 109, determined may be exempted from the procedure provided for by paragraph 3 of this Article.

Article 109 (ex Article 89 TEC)

The Council, on a proposal from the Commission and after consulting the European Parliament, may make any appropriate regulations for the application of Articles 107 and 108 and may in particular determine the conditions in which Article 108(3) shall apply and the categories of aid exempted from this procedure.

Chapter 2 TAX PROVISIONS

Article 110 (ex Article 90 TEC)

No Member State shall impose, directly or indirectly, on the products of other Member States any internal taxation of any kind in excess of that imposed directly or indirectly on similar domestic products.

Furthermore, no Member State shall impose on the products of other Member States any internal taxation of such a nature as to afford indirect protection to other products.

Article 111 (ex Article 91 TEC)

Where products are exported to the territory of any Member State, any repayment of internal taxation shall not exceed the internal taxation imposed on them whether directly or indirectly.

Article 112 (ex Article 92 TEC)

In the case of charges other than turnover taxes, excise duties and other forms of indirect taxation, remissions and repayments in respect of exports to other Member States may not be granted and countervailing charges in respect of imports from Member States may not be imposed unless the measures contemplated have been previously approved for a limited period by the Council on a proposal from the Commission.

Article 113 (ex Article 93 TEC)

The Council shall, acting unanimously in accordance with a special legislative procedure and after consulting the European Parliament and the Economic and Social Committee, adopt provisions for the harmonisation of legislation concerning turnover taxes, excise duties and other forms of indirect taxation to the extent that such harmonisation is necessary to ensure the establishment and the functioning of the internal market and to avoid distortion of competition.

Chapter 3 APPROXIMATION OF LAWS

Article 114 (ex Article 95 TEC)

1. Save where otherwise provided in the Treaties, the following provisions shall apply for the achievement of the objectives set out in Article 26. The European Parliament and the Council shall, acting in accordance with the ordinary legislative procedure and after consulting the Economic and Social Committee, adopt the measures for the approximation of the provisions laid down by law, regulation or administrative action in Member States which have as their object the establishment and functioning of the internal market.

2. Paragraph 1 shall not apply to fiscal provisions, to those relating to the free movement of persons nor to those relating to the rights and interests of employed persons.

3. The Commission, in its proposals envisaged in paragraph 1 concerning health, safety, environmental protection and consumer protection, will take as a base a high level of protection, taking account in particular of any new development based on scientific facts. Within their respective powers, the European Parliament and the Council will also seek to achieve this objective.

4. If, after the adoption of a harmonisation measure by the European Parliament and the Council, by the Council or by the Commission, a Member State deems it necessary to maintain national provisions on grounds of major needs referred to in Article 36, or relating to the protection of the environment or the working environment, it shall notify the Commission of these provisions as well as the grounds for maintaining them.

5. Moreover, without prejudice to paragraph 4, if, after the adoption of a harmonisation measure by the European Parliament and the Council, by the Council or by the Commission, a Member State deems it necessary to introduce national provisions based on new scientific evidence relating to the protection of the environment or the working environment on grounds of a problem specific to that Member State arising after the adoption of the harmonisation measure, it shall notify the Commission of the envisaged provisions as well as the grounds for introducing them.

6. The Commission shall, within six months of the notifications as referred to in paragraphs 4 and 5, approve or reject the national provisions involved after having verified whether or not they are a means of arbitrary discrimination or a disguised restriction on trade between Member States and whether or not they shall constitute an obstacle to the functioning of the internal market.

   In the absence of a decision by the Commission within this period the national provisions referred to in paragraphs 4 and 5 shall be deemed to have been approved.

   When justified by the complexity of the matter and in the absence of danger for human health, the Commission may notify the Member State concerned that the period referred to in this paragraph may be extended for a further period of up to six months.

7.   When, pursuant to paragraph 6, a Member State is authorised to maintain or introduce national provisions derogating from a harmonisation measure, the Commission shall immediately examine whether to propose an adaptation to that measure.

8.   When a Member State raises a specific problem on public health in a field which has been the subject of prior harmonisation measures, it shall bring it to the attention of the Commission which shall immediately examine whether to propose appropriate measures to the Council.

9.   By way of derogation from the procedure laid down in Articles 258 and 259, the Commission and any Member State may bring the matter directly before the Court of Justice of the European Union if it considers that another Member State is making improper use of the powers provided for in this Article.

10.   The harmonisation measures referred to above shall, in appropriate cases, include a safeguard clause authorising the Member States to take, for one or more of the non-economic reasons referred to in Article 36, provisional measures subject to a Union control procedure.

Article 115 (ex Article 94 TEC)
Without prejudice to Article 114, the Council shall, acting unanimously in accordance with a special legislative procedure and after consulting the European Parliament and the Economic and Social Committee, issue directives for the approximation of such laws, regulations or administrative provisions of the Member States as directly affect the establishment or functioning of the internal market.

Article 116 (ex Article 96 TEC)
Where the Commission finds that a difference between the provisions laid down by law, regulation or administrative action in Member States is distorting the conditions of competition in the internal market and that the resultant distortion needs to be eliminated, it shall consult the Member States concerned.

If such consultation does not result in an agreement eliminating the distortion in question, the European, Parliament and the Council, acting in accordance with the ordinary legislative procedure, shall issue the necessary directives. Any other appropriate measures provided for in the Treaties may be adopted.

Article 117 (ex Article 97 TEC)
1.   Where there is a reason to fear that the adoption or amendment of a provision laid down by law, regulation or administrative action may cause distortion within the meaning of Article 116, a Member State desiring to proceed therewith shall consult the Commission. After consulting the Member States, the Commission shall recommend to the States concerned such measures as may be appropriate to avoid the distortion in question.

2.   If a State desiring to introduce or amend its own provisions does not comply with the recommendation addressed to it by the Commission, other Member States shall not be required, pursuant to Article 116, to amend their own provisions in order to eliminate such distortion. If the Member State which has ignored the recommendation of the Commission causes distortion detrimental only to itself, the provisions of Article 116 shall not apply.

Article 118
In the context of the establishment and functioning of the internal market, the European Parliament and the Council, acting in accordance with the ordinary legislative procedure, shall establish measures for the creation of European intellectual property rights to provide uniform

protection of intellectual property rights throughout the Union and for the setting up of centralised Union-wide authorisation, coordination and supervision arrangements.

The Council, acting in accordance with a special legislative procedure, shall by means of regulations establish language arrangements for the European intellectual property rights. The Council shall act unanimously after consulting the European Parliament.

TITLE VIII
ECONOMIC AND MONETARY POLICY

Article 119 (ex Article 4 TEC)

1. For the purposes set out in Article 3 of the Treaty on European Union, the activities of the Member States and the Union shall include, as provided in the Treaties, the adoption of an economic policy which is based on the close coordination of Member States' economic policies, on the internal market and on the definition of common objectives, and conducted in accordance with the principle of an open market economy with free competition.

2. Concurrently with the foregoing, and as provided in the Treaties and in accordance with the procedures set out therein, these activities shall include a single currency, the euro, and the definition and conduct of a single monetary policy and exchange-rate policy the primary objective of both of which shall be to maintain price stability and, without prejudice to this objective, to support the general economic policies in the Union, in accordance with the principle of an open market economy with free competition.

3. These activities of the Member States and the Union shall entail compliance with the following guiding principles: stable prices, sound public finances and monetary conditions and a sustainable balance of payments.

Chapter 1 ECONOMIC POLICY

Article 120 (ex Article 98 TEC)

Member States shall conduct their economic policies with a view to contributing to the achievement of the objectives of the Union, as defined in Article 3 of the Treaty on European Union, and in the context of the broad guidelines referred to in Article 121(2). The Member States and the Union shall act in accordance with the principle of an open market economy with free competition, favouring an efficient allocation of resources, and in compliance with the principles set out in Article 119.

Article 121 (ex Article 99 TEC)

1. Member States shall regard their economic policies as a matter of common concern and shall coordinate them within the Council, in accordance with the provisions of Article 120.

2. The Council shall, on a recommendation from the Commission, formulate a draft for the broad guidelines of the economic policies of the Member States and of the Union, and shall report its findings to the European Council.

   The European Council shall, acting on the basis of the report from the Council, discuss a conclusion on the broad guidelines of the economic policies of the Member States and of the Union.

   On the basis of this conclusion, the Council shall adopt a recommendation setting out these broad guidelines. The Council shall inform the European Parliament of its recommendation.

3. In order to ensure closer coordination of economic policies and sustained convergence of the economic performances of the Member States, the Council shall, on the basis of

reports submitted by the Commission, monitor economic developments in each of the Member States and in the Union as well as the consistency of economic policies with the broad guidelines referred to in paragraph 2, and regularly carry out an overall assessment.

For the purpose of this multilateral surveillance, Member States shall forward information to the Commission about important measures taken by them in the field of their economic policy and such other information as they deem necessary.

4.   Where it is established, under the procedure referred to in paragraph 3, that the economic policies of a Member State are not consistent with the broad guidelines referred to in paragraph 2 or that they risk jeopardising the proper functioning of economic and monetary union, the Commission may address a warning to the Member State concerned. The Council, on a recommendation from the Commission, may address the necessary recommendations to the Member State concerned. The Council may, on a proposal from the Commission, decide to make its recommendations public.

Within the scope of this paragraph, the Council shall act without taking into account the vote of the member of the Council representing the Member State concerned.

A qualified majority of the other members of the Council shall be defined in accordance with Article 238(3)(a).

5.   The President of the Council and the Commission shall report to the European Parliament on the results of multilateral surveillance. The President of the Council may be invited to appear before the competent committee of the European Parliament if the Council has made its recommendations public.

6.   The European Parliament and the Council, acting by means of regulations in accordance with the ordinary legislative procedure, may adopt detailed rules for the multilateral surveillance procedure referred to in paragraphs 3 and 4.

Article 122 (ex Article 100 TEC)

1.   Without prejudice to any other procedures provided for in the Treaties, the Council, on a proposal from the Commission, may decide, in a spirit of solidarity between Member States, upon the measures appropriate to the economic situation, in particular if severe difficulties arise in the supply of certain products, notably in the area of energy.

2.   Where a Member State is in difficulties or is seriously threatened with severe difficulties caused by natural disasters or exceptional occurrences beyond its control, the Council, on a proposal from the Commission, may grant, under certain conditions, Union financial assistance to the Member State concerned. The President of the Council shall inform the European Parliament of the decision taken.

Article 123 (ex Article 101 TEC)

1.   Overdraft facilities or any other type of credit facility with the European Central Bank or with the central banks of the Member States (hereinafter referred to as 'national central banks') in favour of Union institutions, bodies, offices or agencies, central governments, regional, local or other public authorities, other bodies governed by public law, or public undertakings of Member States shall be prohibited, as shall the purchase directly from them by the European Central Bank or national central banks of debt instruments.

2.   Paragraph 1 shall not apply to publicly owned credit institutions which, in the context of the supply of reserves by central banks, shall be given the same treatment by national central banks and the European Central Bank as private credit institutions.

Article 124 (ex Article 102 TEC)

Any measure, not based on prudential considerations, establishing privileged access by Union institutions, bodies, offices or agencies, central governments, regional, local or other public authorities, other bodies governed by public law, or public undertakings of Member States to financial institutions, shall be prohibited.

Article 125 (ex Article 103 TEC)

1. The Union shall not be liable for or assume the commitments of central governments, regional, local or other public authorities, other bodies governed by public law, or public undertakings of any Member State, without prejudice to mutual financial guarantees for the joint execution of a specific project. A Member State shall not be liable for or assume the commitments of central governments, regional, local or other public authorities, other bodies governed by public law, or public undertakings of another Member State, without prejudice to mutual financial guarantees for the joint execution of a specific project.

2. The Council, on a proposal from the Commission and after consulting the European Parliament, may, as required, specify definitions for the application of the prohibitions referred to in Articles 123 and 124 and in this Article.

Article 126 (ex Article 104 TEC)

1. Member States shall avoid excessive government deficits.

2. The Commission shall monitor the development of the budgetary situation and of the stock of government debt in the Member States with a view to identifying gross errors. In particular it shall examine compliance with budgetary discipline on the basis of the following two criteria:
    (a) whether the ratio of the planned or actual government deficit to gross domestic product exceeds a reference value, unless:
        — either the ratio has declined substantially and continuously and reached a level that comes close to the reference value,
        — or, alternatively, the excess over the reference value is only exceptional and temporary and the ratio remains close to the reference value;
    (b) whether the ratio of government debt to gross domestic product exceeds a reference value, unless the ratio is sufficiently diminishing and approaching the reference value at a satisfactory pace.
    The reference values are specified in the Protocol on the excessive deficit procedure annexed to the Treaties.

3. If a Member State does not fulfil the requirements under one or both of these criteria, the Commission shall prepare a report. The report of the Commission shall also take into account whether the government deficit exceeds government investment expenditure and take into account all other relevant factors, including the medium-term economic and budgetary position of the Member State.

    The Commission may also prepare a report if, notwithstanding the fulfilment of the requirements under the criteria, it is of the opinion that there is a risk of an excessive deficit in a Member State.

4. The Economic and Financial Committee shall formulate an opinion on the report of the Commission.

5. If the Commission considers that an excessive deficit in a Member State exists or may occur, it shall address an opinion to the Member State concerned and shall inform the Council accordingly.

6.   The Council shall, on a proposal from the Commission, and having considered any observations which the Member State concerned may wish to make, decide after an overall assessment whether an excessive deficit exists.

7.   Where the Council decides, in accordance with paragraph 6, that an excessive deficit exists, it shall adopt, without undue delay, on a recommendation from the Commission, recommendations addressed to the Member State concerned with a view to bringing that situation to an end within a given period. Subject to the provisions of paragraph 8, these recommendations shall not be made public.

8.   Where it establishes that there has been no effective action in response to its recommendations within the period laid down, the Council may make its recommendations public.

9.   If a Member State persists in failing to put into practice the recommendations of the Council, the Council may decide to give notice to the Member State to take, within a specified time limit, measures for the deficit reduction which is judged necessary by the Council in order to remedy the situation.

      In such a case, the Council may request the Member State concerned to submit reports in accordance with a specific timetable in order to examine the adjustment efforts of that Member State.

10.   The rights to bring actions provided for in Articles 258 and 259 may not be exercised within the framework of paragraphs 1 to 9 of this Article.

11.   As long as a Member State fails to comply with a decision taken in accordance with paragraph 9, the Council may decide to apply or, as the case may be, intensify one or more of the following measures:
      — to require the Member State concerned to publish additional information, to be specified by the Council, before issuing bonds and securities,
      — to invite the European Investment Bank to reconsider its lending policy towards the Member State concerned,
      — to require the Member State concerned to make a non-interest-bearing deposit of an appropriate size with the Union until the excessive deficit has, in the view of the Council, been corrected,
      — to impose fines of an appropriate size.
      The President of the Council shall inform the European Parliament of the decisions taken.

12.   The Council shall abrogate some or all of its decisions or recommendations referred to in paragraphs 6 to 9 and 11 to the extent that the excessive deficit in the Member State concerned has, in the view of the Council, been corrected. If the Council has previously made public recommendations, it shall, as soon as the decision under paragraph 8 has been abrogated, make a public statement that an excessive deficit in the Member State concerned no longer exists.

13.   When taking the decisions or recommendations referred to in paragraphs 8, 9, 11 and 12, the Council shall act on a recommendation from the Commission.

      When the Council adopts the measures referred to in paragraphs 6 to 9, 11 and 12, it shall act without taking into account the vote of the member of the Council representing the Member State concerned.

      A qualified majority of the other members of the Council shall be defined in accordance with Article 238(3)(a).

14.   Further provisions relating to the implementation of the procedure described in this Article are set out in the Protocol on the excessive deficit procedure annexed to the Treaties.

The Council shall, acting unanimously in accordance with a special legislative procedure and after consulting the European Parliament and the European Central Bank, adopt the appropriate provisions which shall then replace the said Protocol.

Subject to the other provisions of this paragraph, the Council shall, on a proposal from the Commission and after consulting the European Parliament, lay down detailed rules and definitions for the application of the provisions of the said Protocol.

Chapter 2 MONETARY POLICY

Article 127 (ex Article 105 TEC)

1. The primary objective of the European System of Central Banks (hereinafter referred to as 'the ESCB') shall be to maintain price stability. Without prejudice to the objective of price stability, the ESCB shall support the general economic policies in the Union with a view to contributing to the achievement of the objectives of the Union as laid down in Article 3 of the Treaty on European Union. The ESCB shall act in accordance with the principle of an open market economy with free competition, favouring an efficient allocation of resources, and in compliance with the principles set out in Article 119.

2. The basic tasks to be carried out through the ESCB shall be:
   — to define and implement the monetary policy of the Union,
   — to conduct foreign-exchange operations consistent with the provisions of Article 219,
   — to hold and manage the official foreign reserves of the Member States,
   — to promote the smooth operation of payment systems.

3. The third indent of paragraph 2 shall be without prejudice to the holding and management by the governments of Member States of foreign-exchange working balances.

4. The European Central Bank shall be consulted:
   — on any proposed Union act in its fields of competence,
   — by national authorities regarding any draft legislative provision in its fields of competence, but within the limits and under the conditions set out by the Council in accordance with the procedure laid down in Article 129(4).

   The European Central Bank may submit opinions to the appropriate Union institutions, bodies, offices or agencies or to national authorities on matters in its fields of competence.

5. The ESCB shall contribute to the smooth conduct of policies pursued by the competent authorities relating to the prudential supervision of credit institutions and the stability of the financial system.

6. The Council, acting by means of regulations in accordance with a special legislative procedure, may unanimously, and after consulting the European Parliament and the European Central Bank, confer specific tasks upon the European Central Bank concerning policies relating to the prudential supervision of credit institutions and other financial institutions with the exception of insurance undertakings.

Article 128 (ex Article 106 TEC)

1. The European Central Bank shall have the exclusive right to authorise the issue of euro banknotes within the Union. The European Central Bank and the national central banks may issue such notes. The banknotes issued by the European Central Bank and the national central banks shall be the only such notes to have the status of legal tender within the Union.

2. Member States may issue euro coins subject to approval by the European Central Bank of the volume of the issue. The Council, on a proposal from the Commission and after

consulting the European Parliament and the European Central Bank, may adopt measures to harmonise the denominations and technical specifications of all coins intended for circulation to the extent necessary to permit their smooth circulation within the Union.

Article 129 (ex Article 107 TEC)

1. The ESCB shall be governed by the decision-making bodies of the European Central Bank which shall be the Governing Council and the Executive Board.

2. The Statute of the European System of Central Banks and of the European Central Bank (hereinafter referred to as 'the Statute of the ESCB and of the ECB') is laid down in a Protocol annexed to the Treaties.

3. Articles 5.1, 5.2, 5.3, 17, 18, 19.1, 22, 23, 24, 26, 32.2, 32.3, 32.4, 32.6, 33.1(a) and 36 of the Statute of the ESCB and of the ECB may be amended by the European Parliament and the Council, acting in accordance with the ordinary legislative procedure. They shall act either on a recommendation from the European Central Bank and after consulting the Commission or on a proposal from the Commission and after consulting the European Central Bank.

4. The Council, either on a proposal from the Commission and after consulting the European Parliament and the European Central Bank or on a recommendation from the European Central Bank and after consulting the European Parliament and the Commission, shall adopt the provisions referred to in Articles 4, 5.4, 19.2, 20, 28.1, 29.2, 30.4 and 34.3 of the Statute of the ESCB and of the ECB.

Article 130 (ex Article 108 TEC)

When exercising the powers and carrying out the tasks and duties conferred upon them by the Treaties and the Statute of the ESCB and of the ECB, neither the European Central Bank, nor a national central bank, nor any member of their decision-making bodies shall seek or take instructions from Union institutions, bodies, offices or agencies, from any government of a Member State or from any other body. The Union institutions, bodies, offices or agencies and the governments of the Member States undertake to respect this principle and not to seek to influence the members of the decision-making bodies of the European Central Bank or of the national central banks in the performance of their tasks.

Article 131 (ex Article 109 TEC)

Each Member State shall ensure that its national legislation including the statutes of its national central bank is compatible with the Treaties and the Statute of the ESCB and of the ECB.

Article 132 (ex Article 110 TEC)

1. In order to carry out the tasks entrusted to the ESCB, the European Central Bank shall, in accordance with the provisions of the Treaties and under the conditions laid down in the Statute of the ESCB and of the ECB:
    — make regulations to the extent necessary to implement the tasks defined in Article 3.1, first indent, Articles 19.1, 22 and 25.2 of the Statute of the ESCB and of the ECB in cases which shall be laid down in the acts of the Council referred to in Article 129(4),
    — take decisions necessary for carrying out the tasks entrusted to the ESCB under the Treaties and the Statute of the ESCB and of the ECB,
    — make recommendations and deliver opinions.

2. The European Central Bank may decide to publish its decisions, recommendations and opinions.

3. Within the limits and under the conditions adopted by the Council under the procedure laid down in Article 129(4), the European Central Bank shall be entitled to impose fines

or periodic penalty payments on undertakings for failure to comply with obligations under its regulations and decisions.

Article 133

Without prejudice to the powers of the European Central Bank, the European Parliament and the Council, acting in accordance with the ordinary legislative procedure, shall lay down the measures necessary for the use of the euro as the single currency. Such measures shall be adopted after consultation of the European Central Bank.

Chapter 3 INSTITUTIONAL PROVISIONS

Article 134 (ex Article 114 TEC)

1. In order to promote coordination of the policies of Member States to the full extent needed for the functioning of the internal market, an Economic and Financial Committee is hereby set up.

2. The Economic and Financial Committee shall have the following tasks:
    — to deliver opinions at the request of the Council or of the Commission, or on its own initiative for submission to those institutions,
    — to keep under review the economic and financial situation of the Member States and of the Union and to report regularly thereon to the Council and to the Commission, in particular on financial relations with third countries and international institutions,
    — without prejudice to Article 240, to contribute to the preparation of the work of the Council referred to in Articles 66, 75, 121(2), (3), (4) and (6), 122, 124, 125, 126, 127(6), 128(2), 129(3) and (4), 138, 140(2) and (3), 143, 144(2) and (3), and in Article 219, and to carry out other advisory and preparatory tasks assigned to it by the Council,
    — to examine, at least once a year, the situation regarding the movement of capital and the freedom of payments, as they result from the application of the Treaties and of measures adopted by the Council; the examination shall cover all measures relating to capital movements and payments; the Committee shall report to the Commission and to the Council on the outcome of this examination.

    The Member States, the Commission and the European Central Bank shall each appoint no more than two members of the Committee.

3. The Council shall, on a proposal from the Commission and after consulting the European Central Bank and the Committee referred to in this Article, lay down detailed provisions concerning the composition of the Economic and Financial Committee. The President of the Council shall inform the European Parliament of such a decision.

4. In addition to the tasks set out in paragraph 2, if and as long as there are Member States with a derogation as referred to in Article 139, the Committee shall keep under review the monetary and financial situation and the general payments system of those Member States and report regularly thereon to the Council and to the Commission.

Article 135 (ex Article 115 TEC)

For matters within the scope of Articles 121(4), 126 with the exception of paragraph 14, 138, 140(1), 140(2), first subparagraph, 140(3) and 219, the Council or a Member State may request the Commission to make a recommendation or a proposal, as appropriate. The Commission shall examine this request and submit its conclusions to the Council without delay.

Chapter 4 PROVISIONS SPECIFIC TO MEMBER STATES WHOSE CURRENCY IS THE EURO

Article 136

1. In order to ensure the proper functioning of economic and monetary union, and in accordance with the relevant provisions of the Treaties, the Council shall, in accordance with the relevant procedure from among those referred to in Articles 121 and 126, with the exception of the procedure set out in Article 126(14), adopt measures specific to those Member States whose currency is the euro:
    (a) to strengthen the coordination and surveillance of their budgetary discipline;
    (b) to set out economic policy guidelines for them, while ensuring that they are compatible with those adopted for the whole of the Union and are kept under surveillance.

2. For those measures set out in paragraph 1, only members of the Council representing Member States whose currency is the euro shall take part in the vote.

    A qualified majority of the said members shall be defined in accordance with Article 238(3)(a).

Article 137

Arrangements for meetings between ministers of those Member States whose currency is the euro are laid down by the Protocol on the Euro Group.

Article 138 (ex Article 111(4), TEC)

1. In order to secure the euro's place in the international monetary system, the Council, on a proposal from the Commission, shall adopt a decision establishing common positions on matters of particular interest for economic and monetary union within the competent international financial institutions and conferences. The Council shall act after consulting the European Central Bank.

2. The Council, on a proposal from the Commission, may adopt appropriate measures to ensure unified representation within the international financial institutions and conferences. The Council shall act after consulting the European Central Bank.

3. For the measures referred to in paragraphs 1 and 2, only members of the Council representing Member States whose currency is the euro shall take part in the vote.

    A qualified majority of the said members shall be defined in accordance with Article 238(3)(a).

Chapter 5 TRANSITIONAL PROVISIONS

Article 139

1. Member States in respect of which the Council has not decided that they fulfil the necessary conditions for the adoption of the euro shall hereinafter be referred to as 'Member States with a derogation'.

2. The following provisions of the Treaties shall not apply to Member States with a derogation:
    (a) adoption of the parts of the broad economic policy guidelines which concern the euro area generally (Article 121(2));
    (b) coercive means of remedying excessive deficits (Article 126(9) and (11));
    (c) the objectives and tasks of the ESCB (Article 127(1) to (3) and (5));
    (d) issue of the euro (Article 128);
    (e) acts of the European Central Bank (Article 132);

(f)   measures governing the use of the euro (Article 133);

(g)   monetary agreements and other measures relating to exchange-rate policy (Article 219);

(h)   appointment of members of the Executive Board of the European Central Bank (Article 283(2));

(i)   decisions establishing common positions on issues of particular relevance for economic and monetary union within the competent international financial institutions and conferences (Article 138(1));

(j)   measures to ensure unified representation within the international financial institutions and conferences (Article 138(2)).

In the Articles referred to in points (a) to (j), 'Member States' shall therefore mean Member States whose currency is the euro.

3.   Under Chapter IX of the Statute of the ESCB and of the ECB, Member States with a derogation and their national central banks are excluded from rights and obligations within the ESCB.

4.   The voting rights of members of the Council representing Member States with a derogation shall be suspended for the adoption by the Council of the measures referred to in the Articles listed in paragraph 2, and in the following instances:

(a)   recommendations made to those Member States whose currency is the euro in the framework of multilateral surveillance, including on stability programmes and warnings (Article 121(4));

(b)   measures relating to excessive deficits concerning those Member States whose currency is the euro (Article 126(6), (7), (8), (12) and (13)).

A qualified majority of the other members of the Council shall be defined in accordance with Article 238(3)(a).

Article 140 (ex Articles 121(1), 122(2), second sentence, and 123(5) TEC)

1.   At least once every two years, or at the request of a Member State with a derogation, the Commission and the European Central Bank shall report to the Council on the progress made by the Member States with a derogation in fulfilling their obligations regarding the achievement of economic and monetary union. These reports shall include an examination of the compatibility between the national legislation of each of these Member States, including the statutes of its national central bank, and Articles 130 and 131 and the Statute of the ESCB and of the ECB. The reports shall also examine the achievement of a high degree of sustainable convergence by reference to the fulfilment by each Member State of the following criteria:

— the achievement of a high degree of price stability; this will be apparent from a rate of inflation which is close to that of, at most, the three best performing Member States in terms of price stability,

— the sustainability of the government financial position; this will be apparent from having achieved a government budgetary position without a deficit that is excessive as determined in accordance with Article 126(6),

— the observance of the normal fluctuation margins provided for by the exchange-rate mechanism of the European Monetary System, for at least two years, without devaluing against the euro,

— the durability of convergence achieved by the Member State with a derogation and of its participation in the exchange-rate mechanism being reflected in the long-term interest-rate levels.

The four criteria mentioned in this paragraph and the relevant periods over which they are to be respected are developed further in a Protocol annexed to the Treaties. The reports of the Commission and the European Central Bank shall also take account of the results of the integration of markets, the situation and development of the balances of payments on current account and an examination of the development of unit labour costs and other price indices.

2. After consulting the European Parliament and after discussion in the European Council, the Council shall, on a proposal from the Commission, decide which Member States with a derogation fulfil the necessary conditions on the basis of the criteria set out in paragraph 1, and abrogate the derogations of the Member States concerned.

    The Council shall act having received a recommendation of a qualified majority of those among its members representing Member States whose currency is the euro. These members shall act within six months of the Council receiving the Commission's proposal.

    The qualified majority of the said members, as referred to in the second subparagraph, shall be defined in accordance with Article 238(3)(a).

3. If it is decided, in accordance with the procedure set out in paragraph 2, to abrogate a derogation, the Council shall, acting with the unanimity of the Member States whose currency is the euro and the Member State concerned, on a proposal from the Commission and after consulting the European Central Bank, irrevocably fix the rate at which the euro shall be substituted for the currency of the Member State concerned, and take the other measures necessary for the introduction of the euro as the single currency in the Member State concerned.

Article 141 (ex Articles 123(3) and 117(2) first five indents, TEC)

1. If and as long as there are Member States with a derogation, and without prejudice to Article 129(1), the General Council of the European Central Bank referred to in Article 44 of the Statute of the ESCB and of the ECB shall be constituted as a third decision-making body of the European Central Bank.

2. If and as long as there are Member States with a derogation, the European Central Bank shall, as regards those Member States:
    — strengthen cooperation between the national central banks,
    — strengthen the coordination of the monetary policies of the Member States, with the aim of ensuring price stability,
    — monitor the functioning of the exchange-rate mechanism,
    — hold consultations concerning issues falling within the competence of the national central banks and affecting the stability of financial institutions and markets,
    — carry out the former tasks of the European Monetary Cooperation Fund which had subsequently been taken over by the European Monetary Institute.

Article 142 (ex Article 124(1) TEC)

Each Member State with a derogation shall treat its exchange-rate policy as a matter of common interest. In so doing, Member States shall take account of the experience acquired in cooperation within the framework of the exchange-rate mechanism.

Article 143 (ex Article 119 TEC)

1. Where a Member State with a derogation is in difficulties or is seriously threatened with difficulties as regards its balance of payments either as a result of an overall disequilibrium in its balance of payments, or as a result of the type of currency at its disposal, and where such difficulties are liable in particular to jeopardise the functioning of the internal market or the implementation of the common commercial policy, the Commission shall immediately investigate the position of the State in question and the action which, making use of all the means at its disposal, that State has taken or may take in accordance with

the provisions of the Treaties. The Commission shall state what measures it recommends the State concerned to take.

If the action taken by a Member State with a derogation and the measures suggested by the Commission do not prove sufficient to overcome the difficulties which have arisen or which threaten, the Commission shall, after consulting the Economic and Financial Committee, recommend to the Council the granting of mutual assistance and appropriate methods therefor.

The Commission shall keep the Council regularly informed of the situation and of how it is developing.

2.   The Council shall grant such mutual assistance; it shall adopt directives or decisions laying down the conditions and details of such assistance, which may take such forms as:
(a)   a concerted approach to or within any other international organisations to which Member States with a derogation may have recourse;
(b)   measures needed to avoid deflection of trade where the Member State with a derogation which is in difficulties maintains or reintroduces quantitative restrictions against third countries;
(c)   the granting of limited credits by other Member States, subject to their agreement.

3.   If the mutual assistance recommended by the Commission is not granted by the Council or if the mutual assistance granted and the measures taken are insufficient, the Commission shall authorise the Member State with a derogation which is in difficulties to take protective measures, the conditions and details of which the Commission shall determine.

Such authorisation may be revoked and such conditions and details may be changed by the Council.

Article 144 (ex Article 120 TEC)
1.   Where a sudden crisis in the balance of payments occurs and a decision within the meaning of Article 143(2) is not immediately taken, a Member State with a derogation may, as a precaution, take the necessary protective measures. Such measures must cause the least possible disturbance in the functioning of the internal market and must not be wider in scope than is strictly necessary to remedy the sudden difficulties which have arisen.

2.   The Commission and the other Member States shall be informed of such protective measures not later than when they enter into force. The Commission may recommend to the Council the granting of mutual assistance under Article 143.

3.   After the Commission has delivered a recommendation and the Economic and Financial Committee has been consulted, the Council may decide that the Member State concerned shall amend, suspend or abolish the protective measures referred to above.

TITLE IX
EMPLOYMENT

Article 145 (ex Article 125 TEC)
Member States and the Union shall, in accordance with this Title, work towards developing a coordinated strategy for employment and particularly for promoting a skilled, trained and adaptable workforce and labour markets responsive to economic change with a view to achieving the objectives defined in Article 3 of the Treaty on European Union.

Article 146 (ex Article 126 TEC)

1.   Member States, through their employment policies, shall contribute to the achievement of the objectives referred to in Article 145 in a way consistent with the broad guidelines of the economic policies of the Member States and of the Union adopted pursuant to Article 121(2).

2.   Member States, having regard to national practices related to the responsibilities of management and labour, shall regard promoting employment as a matter of common concern and shall coordinate their action in this respect within the Council, in accordance with the provisions of Article 148.

Article 147 (ex Article 127 TEC)

1.   The Union shall contribute to a high level of employment by encouraging cooperation between Member States and by supporting and, if necessary, complementing their action. In doing so, the competences of the Member States shall be respected.

2.   The objective of a high level of employment shall be taken into consideration in the formulation and implementation of Union policies and activities.

Article 148 (ex Article 128 TEC)

1.   The European Council shall each year consider the employment situation in the Union and adopt conclusions thereon, on the basis of a joint annual report by the Council and the Commission.

2.   On the basis of the conclusions of the European Council, the Council, on a proposal from the Commission and after consulting the European Parliament, the Economic and Social Committee, the Committee of the Regions and the Employment Committee referred to in Article 150, shall each year draw up guidelines which the Member States shall take into account in their employment policies. These guidelines shall be consistent with the broad guidelines adopted pursuant to Article 121(2).

3.   Each Member State shall provide the Council and the Commission with an annual report on the principal measures taken to implement its employment policy in the light of the guidelines for employment as referred to in paragraph 2.

4.   The Council, on the basis of the reports referred to in paragraph 3 and having received the views of the Employment Committee, shall each year carry out an examination of the implementation of the employment policies of the Member States in the light of the guidelines for employment. The Council, on a recommendation from the Commission, may, if it considers it appropriate in the light of that examination, make recommendations to Member States.

5.   On the basis of the results of that examination, the Council and the Commission shall make a joint annual report to the European Council on the employment situation in the Union and on the implementation of the guidelines for employment.

Article 149 (ex Article 129 TEC)

The European Parliament and the Council, acting in accordance with the ordinary legislative procedure and after consulting the Economic and Social Committee and the Committee of the Regions, may adopt incentive measures designed to encourage cooperation between Member States and to support their action in the field of employment through initiatives aimed at developing exchanges of information and best practices, providing comparative analysis and advice as well as promoting innovative approaches and evaluating experiences, in particular by recourse to pilot projects.

Those measures shall not include harmonisation of the laws and regulations of the Member States.

Article 150 (ex Article 130 TEC)

The Council, acting by a simple majority after consulting the European Parliament, shall establish an Employment Committee with advisory status to promote coordination between Member States on employment and labour market policies. The tasks of the Committee shall be:

— to monitor the employment situation and employment policies in the Member States and the Union,

— without prejudice to Article 240, to formulate opinions at the request of either the Council or the Commission or on its own initiative, and to contribute to the preparation of the Council proceedings referred to in Article 148.

In fulfilling its mandate, the Committee shall consult management and labour.

Each Member State and the Commission shall appoint two members of the Committee.

TITLE X
SOCIAL POLICY

Article 151 (ex Article 136 TEC)

The Union and the Member States, having in mind fundamental social rights such as those set out in the European Social Charter signed at Turin on 18 October 1961 and in the 1989 Community Charter of the Fundamental Social Rights of Workers, shall have as their objectives the promotion of employment, improved living and working conditions, so as to make possible their harmonisation while the improvement is being maintained, proper social protection, dialogue between management and labour, the development of human resources with a view to lasting high employment and the combating of exclusion.

To this end the Union and the Member States shall implement measures which take account of the diverse forms of national practices, in particular in the field of contractual relations, and the need to maintain the competitiveness of the Union's economy.

They believe that such a development will ensue not only from the functioning of the internal market, which will favour the harmonisation of social systems, but also from the procedures provided for in the Treaties and from the approximation of provisions laid down by law, regulation or administrative action.

Article 152

The Union recognises and promotes the role of the social partners at its level, taking into account the diversity of national systems. It shall facilitate dialogue between the social partners, respecting their autonomy.

The Tripartite Social Summit for Growth and Employment shall contribute to social dialogue.

Article 153 (ex Article 137 TEC)

1. With a view to achieving the objectives of Article 151, the Union shall support and complement the activities of the Member States in the following fields:

   (a) improvement in particular of the working environment to protect workers' health and safety;
   (b) working conditions;
   (c) social security and social protection of workers;
   (d) protection of workers where their employment contract is terminated;
   (e) the information and consultation of workers;
   (f) representation and collective defence of the interests of workers and employers, including co-determination, subject to paragraph 5;

(g)   conditions of employment for third-country nationals legally residing in Union territory;
(h)   the integration of persons excluded from the labour market, without prejudice to Article 166;
(i)   equality between men and women with regard to labour market opportunities and treatment at work;
(j)   the combating of social exclusion;
(k)   the modernisation of social protection systems without prejudice to point (c).

2.   To this end, the European Parliament and the Council:
(a)   may adopt measures designed to encourage cooperation between Member States through initiatives aimed at improving knowledge, developing exchanges of information and best practices, promoting innovative approaches and evaluating experiences, excluding any harmonisation of the laws and regulations of the Member States;
(b)   may adopt, in the fields referred to in paragraph 1(a) to (i), by means of directives, minimum requirements for gradual implementation, having regard to the conditions and technical rules obtaining in each of the Member States. Such directives shall avoid imposing administrative, financial and legal constraints in a way which would hold back the creation and development of small and medium-sized undertakings.

The European Parliament and the Council shall act in accordance with the ordinary legislative procedure after consulting the Economic and Social Committee and the Committee of the Regions.

In the fields referred to in paragraph 1(c), (d), (f) and (g), the Council shall act unanimously, in accordance with a special legislative procedure, after consulting the European Parliament and the said Committees.

The Council, acting unanimously on a proposal from the Commission, after consulting the European Parliament, may decide to render the ordinary legislative procedure applicable to paragraph 1(d), (f) and (g).

3.   A Member State may entrust management and labour, at their joint request, with the implementation of directives adopted pursuant to paragraph 2, or, where appropriate, with the implementation of a Council decision adopted in accordance with Article 155.

In this case, it shall ensure that, no later than the date on which a directive or a decision must be transposed or implemented, management and labour have introduced the necessary measures by agreement, the Member State concerned being required to take any necessary measure enabling it at any time to be in a position to guarantee the results imposed by that directive or that decision.

4.   The provisions adopted pursuant to this Article:
—   shall not affect the right of Member States to define the fundamental principles of their social security systems and must not significantly affect the financial equilibrium thereof,
—   shall not prevent any Member State from maintaining or introducing more stringent protective measures compatible with the Treaties.

5.   The provisions of this Article shall not apply to pay, the right of association, the right to strike or the right to impose lock-outs.

Article 154 (ex Article 138 TEC)
1.   The Commission shall have the task of promoting the consultation of management and labour at Union level and shall take any relevant measure to facilitate their dialogue by ensuring balanced support for the parties.

2. To this end, before submitting proposals in the social policy field, the Commission shall consult management and labour on the possible direction of Union action.

3. If, after such consultation, the Commission considers Union action advisable, it shall consult management and labour on the content of the envisaged proposal. Management and labour shall forward to the Commission an opinion or, where appropriate, a recommendation.

4. On the occasion of the consultation referred to in paragraphs 2 and 3, management and labour may inform the Commission of their wish to initiate the process provided for in Article 155. The duration of this process shall not exceed nine months, unless the management and labour concerned and the Commission decide jointly to extend it.

Article 155 (ex Article 139 TEC)
1. Should management and labour so desire, the dialogue between them at Union level may lead to contractual relations, including agreements.

2. Agreements concluded at Union level shall be implemented either in accordance with the procedures and practices specific to management and labour and the Member States or, in matters covered by Article 153, at the joint request of the signatory parties, by a Council decision on a proposal from the Commission. The European Parliament shall be informed.

    The Council shall act unanimously where the agreement in question contains one or more provisions relating to one of the areas for which unanimity is required pursuant to Article 153(2).

Article 156 (ex Article 140 TEC)
With a view to achieving the objectives of Article 151 and without prejudice to the other provisions of the Treaties, the Commission shall encourage cooperation between the Member States and facilitate the coordination of their action in all social policy fields under this Chapter, particularly in matters relating to:
— employment,

— labour law and working conditions,

— basic and advanced vocational training,

— social security,

— prevention of occupational accidents and diseases,

— occupational hygiene,

— the right of association and collective bargaining between employers and workers.

To this end, the Commission shall act in close contact with Member States by making studies, delivering opinions and arranging consultations both on problems arising at national level and on those of concern to international organisations, in particular initiatives aiming at the establishment of guidelines and indicators, the organisation of exchange of best practice, and the preparation of the necessary elements for periodic monitoring and evaluation. The European Parliament shall be kept fully informed.

Before delivering the opinions provided for in this Article, the Commission shall consult the Economic and Social Committee.

Article 157 (ex Article 141 TEC)
1. Each Member State shall ensure that the principle of equal pay for male and female workers for equal work or work of equal value is applied.

2.   For the purpose of this Article, 'pay' means the ordinary basic or minimum wage or salary and any other consideration, whether in cash or in kind, which the worker receives directly or indirectly, in respect of his employment, from his employer.

Equal pay without discrimination based on sex means:
(a) that pay for the same work at piece rates shall be calculated on the basis of the same unit of measurement;
(b) that pay for work at time rates shall be the same for the same job.

3.   The European Parliament and the Council, acting in accordance with the ordinary legislative procedure, and after consulting the Economic and Social Committee, shall adopt measures to ensure the application of the principle of equal opportunities and equal treatment of men and women in matters of employment and occupation, including the principle of equal pay for equal work or work of equal value.

4.   With a view to ensuring full equality in practice between men and women in working life, the principle of equal treatment shall not prevent any Member State from maintaining or adopting measures providing for specific advantages in order to make it easier for the underrepresented sex to pursue a vocational activity or to prevent or compensate for disadvantages in professional careers.

Article 158 (ex Article 142 TEC)
Member States shall endeavour to maintain the existing equivalence between paid holiday schemes.

Article 159 (ex Article 143 TEC)
The Commission shall draw up a report each year on progress in achieving the objectives of Article 151, including the demographic situation in the Union. It shall forward the report to the European Parliament, the Council and the Economic and Social Committee.

Article 160 (ex Article 144 TEC)
The Council, acting by a simple majority after consulting the European Parliament, shall establish a Social Protection Committee with advisory status to promote cooperation on social protection policies between Member States and with the Commission. The tasks of the Committee shall be:
—   to monitor the social situation and the development of social protection policies in the Member States and the Union,

—   to promote exchanges of information, experience and good practice between Member States and with the Commission,

—   without prejudice to Article 240, to prepare reports, formulate opinions or undertake other work within its fields of competence, at the request of either the Council or the Commission or on its own initiative.

In fulfilling its mandate, the Committee shall establish appropriate contacts with management and labour.

Each Member State and the Commission shall appoint two members of the Committee.

Article 161 (ex Article 145 TEC)
The Commission shall include a separate chapter on social developments within the Union in its annual report to the European Parliament.

The European Parliament may invite the Commission to draw up reports on any particular problems concerning social conditions.

TITLE XI
THE EUROPEAN SOCIAL FUND

Article 162 (ex Article 146 TEC)
In order to improve employment opportunities for workers in the internal market and to contribute thereby to raising the standard of living, a European Social Fund is hereby established in accordance with the provisions set out below; it shall aim to render the employment of workers easier and to increase their geographical and occupational mobility within the Union, and to facilitate their adaptation to industrial changes and to changes in production systems, in particular through vocational training and retraining.

Article 163 (ex Article 147 TEC)
The Fund shall be administered by the Commission.

The Commission shall be assisted in this task by a Committee presided over by a Member of the Commission and composed of representatives of governments, trade unions and employers' organisations.

Article 164 (ex Article 148 TEC)
The European Parliament and the Council, acting in accordance with the ordinary legislative procedure and after consulting the Economic and Social Committee and the Committee of the Regions, shall adopt implementing regulations relating to the European Social Fund.

TITLE XII
EDUCATION, VOCATIONAL TRAINING, YOUTH AND SPORT

Article 165 (ex Article 149 TEC)
1. The Union shall contribute to the development of quality education by encouraging cooperation between Member States and, if necessary, by supporting and supplementing their action, while fully respecting the responsibility of the Member States for the content of teaching and the organisation of education systems and their cultural and linguistic diversity.

    The Union shall contribute to the promotion of European sporting issues, while taking account of the specific nature of sport, its structures based on voluntary activity and its social and educational function.

2. Union action shall be aimed at:
    — developing the European dimension in education, particularly through the teaching and dissemination of the languages of the Member States,
    — encouraging mobility of students and teachers, by encouraging inter alia, the academic recognition of diplomas and periods of study,
    — promoting cooperation between educational establishments,
    — developing exchanges of information and experience on issues common to the education systems of the Member States,
    — encouraging the development of youth exchanges and of exchanges of socio-educational instructors, and encouraging the participation of young people in democratic life in Europe,
    — encouraging the development of distance education,
    — developing the European dimension in sport, by promoting fairness and openness in sporting competitions and cooperation between bodies responsible for sports, and by protecting the physical and moral integrity of sportsmen and sportswomen, especially the youngest sportsmen and sportswomen.

3.   The Union and the Member States shall foster cooperation with third countries and the competent international organisations in the field of education and sport, in particular the Council of Europe.

4.   In order to contribute to the achievement of the objectives referred to in this Article:
     — the European Parliament and the Council, acting in accordance with the ordinary legislative procedure, after consulting the Economic and Social Committee and the Committee of the Regions, shall adopt incentive measures, excluding any harmonisation of the laws and regulations of the Member States,
     — the Council, on a proposal from the Commission, shall adopt recommendations.

Article 166 (ex Article 150 TEC)

1.   The Union shall implement a vocational training policy which shall support and supplement the action of the Member States, while fully respecting the responsibility of the Member States for the content and organisation of vocational training.

2.   Union action shall aim to:
     — facilitate adaptation to industrial changes, in particular through vocational training and retraining,
     — improve initial and continuing vocational training in order to facilitate vocational integration and reintegration into the labour market,
     — facilitate access to vocational training and encourage mobility of instructors and trainees and particularly young people,
     — stimulate cooperation on training between educational or training establishments and firms,
     — develop exchanges of information and experience on issues common to the training systems of the Member States.

3.   The Union and the Member States shall foster cooperation with third countries and the competent international organisations in the sphere of vocational training.

4.   The European Parliament and the Council, acting in accordance with the ordinary legislative procedure and after consulting the Economic and Social Committee and the Committee of the Regions, shall adopt measures to contribute to the achievement of the objectives referred to in this Article, excluding any harmonisation of the laws and regulations of the Member States, and the Council, on a proposal from the Commission, shall adopt recommendations.

TITLE XIII
CULTURE

Article 167 (ex Article 151 TEC)

1.   The Union shall contribute to the flowering of the cultures of the Member States, while respecting their national and regional diversity and at the same time bringing the common cultural heritage to the fore.

2.   Action by the Union shall be aimed at encouraging cooperation between Member States and, if necessary, supporting and supplementing their action in the following areas:
     — improvement of the knowledge and dissemination of the culture and history of the European peoples,
     — conservation and safeguarding of cultural heritage of European significance,
     — non-commercial cultural exchanges,
     — artistic and literary creation, including in the audiovisual sector.

3. The Union and the Member States shall foster cooperation with third countries and the competent international organisations in the sphere of culture, in particular the Council of Europe.

4. The Union shall take cultural aspects into account in its action under other provisions of the Treaties, in particular in order to respect and to promote the diversity of its cultures.

5. In order to contribute to the achievement of the objectives referred to in this Article:
    — the European Parliament and the Council acting in accordance with the ordinary legislative procedure and after consulting the Committee of the Regions, shall adopt incentive measures, excluding any harmonisation of the laws and regulations of the Member States,
    — the Council, on a proposal from the Commission, shall adopt recommendations.

TITLE XIV
PUBLIC HEALTH

Article 168 (ex Article 152 TEC)

1. A high level of human health protection shall be ensured in the definition and implementation of all Union policies and activities.

    Union action, which shall complement national policies, shall be directed towards improving public health, preventing physical and mental illness and diseases, and obviating sources of danger to physical and mental health. Such action shall cover the fight against the major health scourges, by promoting research into their causes, their transmission and their prevention, as well as health information and education, and monitoring, early warning of and combating serious cross-border threats to health.

    The Union shall complement the Member States' action in reducing drugs-related health damage, including information and prevention.

2. The Union shall encourage cooperation between the Member States in the areas referred to in this Article and, if necessary, lend support to their action. It shall in particular encourage cooperation between the Member States to improve the complementarity of their health services in cross-border areas.

    Member States shall, in liaison with the Commission, coordinate among themselves their policies and programmes in the areas referred to in paragraph 1. The Commission may, in close contact with the Member States, take any useful initiative to promote such coordination, in particular initiatives aiming at the establishment of guidelines and indicators, the organisation of exchange of best practice, and the preparation of the necessary elements for periodic monitoring and evaluation. The European Parliament shall be kept fully informed.

3. The Union and the Member States shall foster cooperation with third countries and the competent international organisations in the sphere of public health.

4. By way of derogation from Article 2(5) and Article 6(a) and in accordance with Article 4(2)(k) the European Parliament and the Council, acting in accordance with the ordinary legislative procedure and after consulting the Economic and Social Committee and the Committee of the Regions, shall contribute to the achievement of the objectives referred to in this Article through adopting in order to meet common safety concerns:
    (a) measures setting high standards of quality and safety of organs and substances of human origin, blood and blood derivatives; these measures shall not prevent any Member State from maintaining or introducing more stringent protective measures;
    (b) measures in the veterinary and phytosanitary fields which have as their direct objective the protection of public health;

(c) measures setting high standards of quality and safety for medicinal products and devices for medical use.

5. The European Parliament and the Council, acting in accordance with the ordinary legislative procedure and after consulting the Economic and Social Committee and the Committee of the Regions, may also adopt incentive measures designed to protect and improve human health and in particular to combat the major cross-border health scourges, measures concerning monitoring, early warning of and combating serious cross-border threats to health, and measures which have as their direct objective the protection of public health regarding tobacco and the abuse of alcohol, excluding any harmonisation of the laws and regulations of the Member States.

6. The Council, on a proposal from the Commission, may also adopt recommendations for the purposes set out in this Article.

7. Union action shall respect the responsibilities of the Member States for the definition of their health policy and for the organisation and delivery of health services and medical care. The responsibilities of the Member States shall include the management of health services and medical care and the allocation of the resources assigned to them. The measures referred to in paragraph 4(a) shall not affect national provisions on the donation or medical use of organs and blood.

TITLE XV
CONSUMER PROTECTION

Article 169 (ex Article 153 TEC)
1. In order to promote the interests of consumers and to ensure a high level of consumer protection, the Union shall contribute to protecting the health, safety and economic interests of consumers, as well as to promoting their right to information, education and to organise themselves in order to safeguard their interests.

2. The Union shall contribute to the attainment of the objectives referred to in paragraph 1 through:
   (a) measures adopted pursuant to Article 114 in the context of the completion of the internal market;
   (b) measures which support, supplement and monitor the policy pursued by the Member States.

3. The European Parliament and the Council, acting in accordance with the ordinary legislative procedure and after consulting the Economic and Social Committee, shall adopt the measures referred to in paragraph 2(b).

4. Measures adopted pursuant to paragraph 3 shall not prevent any Member State from maintaining or introducing more stringent protective measures. Such measures must be compatible with the Treaties. The Commission shall be notified of them.

TITLE XVI
TRANS-EUROPEAN NETWORKS

Article 170 (ex Article 154 TEC)
1. To help achieve the objectives referred to in Articles 26 and 174 and to enable citizens of the Union, economic operators and regional and local communities to derive full benefit from the setting-up of an area without internal frontiers, the Union shall contribute to the establishment and development of trans-European networks in the areas of transport, telecommunications and energy infrastructures.

2.   Within the framework of a system of open and competitive markets, action by the
      Union shall aim at promoting the interconnection and interoperability of national
      networks as well as access to such networks. It shall take account in particular of
      the need to link island, landlocked and peripheral regions with the central regions of
      the Union.

Article 171 (ex Article 155 TEC)

1.   In order to achieve the objectives referred to in Article 170, the Union:
      — shall establish a series of guidelines covering the objectives, priorities and broad lines
        of measures envisaged in the sphere of trans-European networks; these guidelines
        shall identify projects of common interest,
      — shall implement any measures that may prove necessary to ensure the interoperability
        of the networks, in particular in the field of technical standardisation,
      — may support projects of common interest supported by Member States, which are
        identified in the framework of the guidelines referred to in the first indent, particularly
        through feasibility studies, loan guarantees or interest-rate subsidies; the Union may
        also contribute, through the Cohesion Fund set up pursuant to Article 177, to the
        financing of specific projects in Member States in the area of transport infrastructure.
      The Union's activities shall take into account the potential economic viability of the
      projects.

2.   Member States shall, in liaison with the Commission, coordinate among themselves the
      policies pursued at national level which may have a significant impact on the achievement
      of the objectives referred to in Article 170. The Commission may, in close cooperation
      with the Member State, take any useful initiative to promote such coordination.

3.   The Union may decide to cooperate with third countries to promote projects of mutual
      interest and to ensure the interoperability of networks.

Article 172 (ex Article 156 TEC)

The guidelines and other measures referred to in Article 171(1) shall be adopted by the European
Parliament and the Council, acting in accordance with the ordinary legislative procedure and
after consulting the Economic and Social Committee and the Committee of the Regions.

Guidelines and projects of common interest which relate to the territory of a Member State shall
require the approval of the Member State concerned.

TITLE XVII
INDUSTRY

Article 173 (ex Article 157 TEC)

1.   The Union and the Member States shall ensure that the conditions necessary for the
      competitiveness of the Union's industry exist.

      For that purpose, in accordance with a system of open and competitive markets, their
      action shall be aimed at:
      — speeding up the adjustment of industry to structural changes,
      — encouraging an environment favourable to initiative and to the development of
        undertakings throughout the Union, particularly small and medium-sized undertakings,
      — encouraging an environment favourable to cooperation between undertakings,
      — fostering better exploitation of the industrial potential of policies of innovation,
        research and technological development.

2.   The Member States shall consult each other in liaison with the Commission and, where
      necessary, shall coordinate their action. The Commission may take any useful initiative to

promote such coordination, in particular initiatives aiming at the establishment of guidelines and indicators, the organisation of exchange of best practice, and the preparation of the necessary elements for periodic monitoring and evaluation. The European Parliament shall be kept fully informed.

3. The Union shall contribute to the achievement of the objectives set out in paragraph 1 through the policies and activities it pursues under other provisions of the Treaties. The European Parliament and the Council, acting in accordance with the ordinary legislative procedure and after consulting the Economic and Social Committee, may decide on specific measures in support of action taken in the Member States to achieve the objectives set out in paragraph 1, excluding any harmonisation of the laws and regulations of the Member States.

This Title shall not provide a basis for the introduction by the Union of any measure which could lead to a distortion of competition or contains tax provisions or provisions relating to the rights and interests of employed persons.

TITLE XVIII
ECONOMIC, SOCIAL AND TERRITORIAL COHESION

Article 174 (ex Article 158 TEC)
In order to promote its overall harmonious development, the Union shall develop and pursue its actions leading to the strengthening of its economic, social and territorial cohesion.

In particular, the Union shall aim at reducing disparities between the levels of development of the various regions and the backwardness of the least favoured regions.

Among the regions concerned, particular attention shall be paid to rural areas, areas affected by industrial transition, and regions which suffer from severe and permanent natural or demographic handicaps such as the northernmost regions with very low population density and island, cross- border and mountain regions.

Article 175 (ex Article 159 TEC)
Member States shall conduct their economic policies and shall coordinate them in such a way as, in addition, to attain the objectives set out in Article 174. The formulation and implementation of the Union's policies and actions and the implementation of the internal market shall take into account the objectives set out in Article 174 and shall contribute to their achievement. The Union shall also support the achievement of these objectives by the action it takes through the Structural Funds (European Agricultural Guidance and Guarantee Fund, Guidance Section; European Social Fund; European Regional Development Fund), the European Investment Bank and the other existing Financial Instruments.

The Commission shall submit a report to the European Parliament, the Council, the Economic and Social Committee and the Committee of the Regions every three years on the progress made towards achieving economic, social and territorial cohesion and on the manner in which the various means provided for in this Article have contributed to it. This report shall, if necessary, be accompanied by appropriate proposals.

If specific actions prove necessary outside the Funds and without prejudice to the measures decided upon within the framework of the other Union policies, such actions may be adopted by the Council acting in accordance with the ordinary legislative procedure and after consulting the Economic and Social Committee and the Committee of the Regions.

Article 176 (ex Article 160 TEC)
The European Regional Development Fund is intended to help to redress the main regional imbalances in the Union through participation in the development and structural adjustment of

regions whose development is lagging behind and in the conversion of declining industrial regions.

Article 177 (ex Article 161 TEC)
Without prejudice to Article 178, the European Parliament and the Council, acting by means of regulations in accordance with the ordinary legislative procedure and consulting the Economic and Social Committee and the Committee of the Regions, shall define the tasks, priority objectives and the organisation of the Structural Funds, which may involve grouping the Funds. The general rules applicable to them and the provisions necessary to ensure their effectiveness and the coordination of the Funds with one another and with the other existing Financial Instruments shall also be defined by the same procedure.

A Cohesion Fund set up in accordance with the same procedure shall provide a financial contribution to projects in the fields of environment and trans-European networks in the area of transport infrastructure.

Article 178 (ex Article 162 TEC)
Implementing regulations relating to the European Regional Development Fund shall be taken by the European Parliament and the Council, acting in accordance with the ordinary legislative procedure and after consulting the Economic and Social Committee and the Committee of the Regions.

With regard to the European Agricultural Guidance and Guarantee Fund, Guidance Section, and the European Social Fund, Articles 43 and 164 respectively shall continue to apply.

TITLE XIX
RESEARCH AND TECHNOLOGICAL DEVELOPMENT AND SPACE

Article 179 (ex Article 163 TEC)
1.   The Union shall have the objective of strengthening its scientific and technological bases by achieving a European research area in which researchers, scientific knowledge and technology circulate freely, and encouraging it to become more competitive, including in its industry, while promoting all the research activities deemed necessary by virtue of other Chapters of the Treaties.

2.   For this purpose the Union shall, throughout the Union, encourage undertakings, including small and medium-sized undertakings, research centres and universities in their research and technological development activities of high quality; it shall support their efforts to cooperate with one another, aiming, notably, at permitting researchers to cooperate freely across borders and at enabling undertakings to exploit the internal market potential to the full, in particular through the opening-up of national public contracts, the definition of common standards and the removal of legal and fiscal obstacles to that cooperation.

3.   All Union activities under the Treaties in the area of research and technological development, including demonstration projects, shall be decided on and implemented in accordance with the provisions of this Title.

Article 180 (ex Article 164 TEC)
In pursuing these objectives, the Union shall carry out the following activities, complementing the activities carried out in the Member States:
(a)   implementation of research, technological development and demonstration programmes, by promoting cooperation with and between undertakings, research centres and universities;

(b)   promotion of cooperation in the field of Union research, technological development and demonstration with third countries and international organisations;

(c)   dissemination and optimisation of the results of activities in Union research, technological development and demonstration;

(d)   stimulation of the training and mobility of researchers in the Union.

Article 181 (ex Article 165 TEC)

1.   The Union and the Member States shall coordinate their research and technological development activities so as to ensure that national policies and Union policy are mutually consistent.

2.   In close cooperation with the Member State, the Commission may take any useful initiative to promote the coordination referred to in paragraph 1, in particular initiatives aiming at the establishment of guidelines and indicators, the organisation of exchange of best practice, and the preparation of the necessary elements for periodic monitoring and evaluation. The European Parliament shall be kept fully informed.

Article 182 (ex Article 166 TEC)

1.   A multiannual framework programme, setting out all the activities of the Union, shall be adopted by the European Parliament and the Council, acting in accordance with the ordinary legislative procedure after consulting the Economic and Social Committee.

The framework programme shall:
— establish the scientific and technological objectives to be achieved by the activities provided for in Article 180 and fix the relevant priorities,
— indicate the broad lines of such activities,
— fix the maximum overall amount and the detailed rules for Union financial participation in the framework programme and the respective shares in each of the activities provided for.

2.   The framework programme shall be adapted or supplemented as the situation changes.

3.   The framework programme shall be implemented through specific programmes developed within each activity. Each specific programme shall define the detailed rules for implementing it, fix its duration and provide for the means deemed necessary. The sum of the amounts deemed necessary, fixed in the specific programmes, may not exceed the overall maximum amount fixed for the framework programme and each activity.

4.   The Council, acting in accordance with a special legislative procedure and after consulting the European Parliament and the Economic and Social Committee, shall adopt the specific programmes.

5.   As a complement to the activities planned in the multiannual framework programme, the European Parliament and the Council, acting in accordance with the ordinary legislative procedure and after consulting the Economic and Social Committee, shall establish the measures necessary for the implementation of the European research area.

Article 183 (ex Article 167 TEC)

For the implementation of the multiannual framework programme the Union shall:
— determine the rules for the participation of undertakings, research centres and universities,

— lay down the rules governing the dissemination of research results.

Article 184 (ex Article 168 TEC)

In implementing the multiannual framework programme, supplementary programmes may be decided on involving the participation of certain Member States only, which shall finance them subject to possible Union participation.

The Union shall adopt the rules applicable to supplementary programmes, particularly as regards the dissemination of knowledge and access by other Member States.

Article 185 (ex Article 169 TEC)

In implementing the multiannual framework programme, the Union may make provision, in agreement with the Member States concerned, for participation in research and development programmes undertaken by several Member States, including participation in the structures created for the execution of those programmes.

Article 186 (ex Article 170 TEC)

In implementing the multiannual framework programme the Union may make provision for cooperation in Union research, technological development and demonstration with third countries or international organisations.

The detailed arrangements for such cooperation may be the subject of agreements between the Union and the third parties concerned.

Article 187 (ex Article 171 TEC)

The Union may set up joint undertakings or any other structure necessary for the efficient execution of Union research, technological development and demonstration programmes.

Article 188 (ex Article 172 TEC)

The Council, on a proposal from the Commission and after consulting the European Parliament and the Economic and Social Committee, shall adopt the provisions referred to in Article 187.

The European Parliament and the Council, acting in accordance with the ordinary legislative procedure and after consulting the Economic and Social Committee, shall adopt the provisions referred to in Articles 183, 184 and 185. Adoption of the supplementary programmes shall require the agreement of the Member States concerned.

Article 189

1. To promote scientific and technical progress, industrial competitiveness and the implementation of its policies, the Union shall draw up a European space policy. To this end, it may promote joint initiatives, support research and technological development and coordinate the efforts needed for the exploration and exploitation of space.

2. To contribute to attaining the objectives referred to in paragraph 1, the European Parliament and the Council, acting in accordance with the ordinary legislative procedure, shall establish the necessary measures, which may take the form of a European space programme, excluding any harmonisation of the laws and regulations of the Member States.

3. The Union shall establish any appropriate relations with the European Space Agency.

4. This Article shall be without prejudice to the other provisions of this Title.

Article 190 (ex Article 173 TEC)

At the beginning of each year the Commission shall send a report to the European Parliament and to the Council. The report shall include information on research and technological development activities and the dissemination of results during the previous year, and the work programme for the current year.

TITLE XX
ENVIRONMENT

Article 191 (ex Article 174 TEC)

1. Union policy on the environment shall contribute to pursuit of the following objectives:
    — preserving, protecting and improving the quality of the environment,
    — protecting human health,
    — prudent and rational utilisation of natural resources,
    — promoting measures at international level to deal with regional or worldwide environmental problems, and in particular combating climate change.

2. Union policy on the environment shall aim at a high level of protection taking into account the diversity of situations in the various regions of the Union. It shall be based on the precautionary principle and on the principles that preventive action should be taken, that environmental damage should as a priority be rectified at source and that the polluter should pay.

    In this context, harmonisation measures answering environmental protection requirements shall include, where appropriate, a safeguard clause allowing Member States to take provisional measures, for non-economic environmental reasons, subject to a procedure of inspection by the Union.

3. In preparing its policy on the environment, the Union shall take account of:
    — available scientific and technical data,
    — environmental conditions in the various regions of the Union,
    — the potential benefits and costs of action or lack of action,
    — the economic and social development of the Union as a whole and the balanced development of its regions.

4. Within their respective spheres of competence, the Union and the Member States shall cooperate with third countries and with the competent international organisations. The arrangements for Union cooperation may be the subject of agreements between the Union and the third parties concerned.

    The previous subparagraph shall be without prejudice to Member States' competence to negotiate in international bodies and to conclude international agreements.

Article 192 (ex Article 175 TEC)

1. The European Parliament and the Council, acting in accordance with the ordinary legislative procedure and after consulting the Economic and Social Committee and the Committee of the Regions, shall decide what action is to be taken by the Union in order to achieve the objectives referred to in Article 191.

2. By way of derogation from the decision-making procedure provided for in paragraph 1 and without prejudice to Article 114, the Council acting unanimously in accordance with a special legislative procedure and after consulting the European Parliament, the Economic and Social Committee and the Committee of the Regions, shall adopt:
    (a) provisions primarily of a fiscal nature;
    (b) measures affecting:
        — town and country planning,
        — quantitative management of water resources or affecting, directly or indirectly, the availability of those resources,
        — land use, with the exception of waste management;
    (c) measures significantly affecting a Member State's choice between different energy sources and the general structure of its energy supply.

The Council, acting unanimously on a proposal from the Commission and after consulting the European Parliament, the Economic and Social Committee and the Committee of the Regions, may make the ordinary legislative procedure applicable to the matters referred to in the first subparagraph.

3. General action programmes setting out priority objectives to be attained shall be adopted by the European Parliament and the Council, acting in accordance with the ordinary legislative procedure and after consulting the Economic and Social Committee and the Committee of the Regions.

    The measures necessary for the implementation of these programmes shall be adopted under the terms of paragraph 1 or 2, as the case may be.

4. Without prejudice to certain measures adopted by the Union, the Member States shall finance and implement the environment policy.

5. Without prejudice to the principle that the polluter should pay, if a measure based on the provisions of paragraph 1 involves costs deemed disproportionate for the public authorities of a Member State, such measure shall lay down appropriate provisions in the form of:
    — temporary derogations, and/or
    — financial support from the Cohesion Fund set up pursuant to Article 177.

Article 193 (ex Article 176 TEC)

The protective measures adopted pursuant to Article 192 shall not prevent any Member State from maintaining or introducing more stringent protective measures. Such measures must be compatible with the Treaties. They shall be notified to the Commission.

TITLE XXI
ENERGY

Article 194

1. In the context of the establishment and functioning of the internal market and with regard for the need to preserve and improve the environment, Union policy on energy shall aim, in a spirit of solidarity between Member States, to:
    (a) ensure the functioning of the energy market;
    (b) ensure security of energy supply in the Union;
    (c) promote energy efficiency and energy saving and the development of new and renewable forms of energy; and
    (d) promote the interconnection of energy networks.

2. Without prejudice to the application of other provisions of the Treaties, the European Parliament and the Council, acting in accordance with the ordinary legislative procedure, shall establish the measures necessary to achieve the objectives in paragraph 1. Such measures shall be adopted after consultation of the Economic and Social Committee and the Committee of the Regions.

    Such measures shall not affect a Member State's right to determine the conditions for exploiting its energy resources, its choice between different energy sources and the general structure of its energy supply, without prejudice to Article 192(2)(c).

3. By way of derogation from paragraph 2, the Council, acting in accordance with a special legislative procedure, shall unanimously and after consulting the European Parliament, establish the measures referred to therein when they are primarily of a fiscal nature.

TITLE XXII
TOURISM

Article 195

1.   The Union shall complement the action of the Member States in the tourism sector, in particular by promoting the competitiveness of Union undertakings in that sector.

To that end, Union action shall be aimed at:
(a) encouraging the creation of a favourable environment for the development of undertakings in this sector;
(b) promoting cooperation between the Member States, particularly by the exchange of good practice.

2.   The European Parliament and the Council, acting in accordance with the ordinary legislative procedure, shall establish specific measures to complement actions within the Member States to achieve the objectives referred to in this Article, excluding any harmonisation of the laws and regulations of the Member States.

TITLE XXIII
CIVIL PROTECTION

Article 196

1.   The Union shall encourage cooperation between Member States in order to improve the effectiveness of systems for preventing and protecting against natural or man-made disasters.

Union action shall aim to:
(a) support and complement Member States' action at national, regional and local level in risk prevention, in preparing their civil-protection personnel and in responding to natural or man- made disasters within the Union;
(b) promote swift, effective operational cooperation within the Union between national civil- protection services;
(c) promote consistency in international civil-protection work.

2.   The European Parliament and the Council, acting in accordance with the ordinary legislative procedure shall establish the measures necessary to help achieve the objectives referred to in paragraph 1, excluding any harmonisation of the laws and regulations of the Member States.

TITLE XXIV
ADMINISTRATIVE COOPERATION

Article 197

1.   Effective implementation of Union law by the Member States, which is essential for the proper functioning of the Union, shall be regarded as a matter of common interest.

2.   The Union may support the efforts of Member States to improve their administrative capacity to implement Union law. Such action may include facilitating the exchange of information and of civil servants as well as supporting training schemes. No Member State shall be obliged to avail itself of such support. The European Parliament and the Council, acting by means of regulations in accordance with the ordinary legislative procedure, shall establish the necessary measures to this end, excluding any harmonisation of the laws and regulations of the Member States.

3.   This Article shall be without prejudice to the obligations of the Member States to implement Union law or to the prerogatives and duties of the Commission. It shall also be

without prejudice to other provisions of the Treaties providing for administrative cooperation among the Member States and between them and the Union.

Part Four ASSOCIATION OF THE OVERSEAS COUNTRIES AND TERRITORIES*
Article 198 (ex Article 182 TEC)

The Member States agree to associate with the Union the non-European countries and territories which have special relations with Denmark, France, the Netherlands and the United Kingdom. These countries and territories (hereinafter called the 'countries and territories') are listed in Annex II.

The purpose of association shall be to promote the economic and social development of the countries and territories and to establish close economic relations between them and the Union as a whole.

In accordance with the principles set out in the preamble to this Treaty, association shall serve primarily to further the interests and prosperity of the inhabitants of these countries and territories in order to lead them to the economic, social and cultural development to which they aspire.

Article 199 (ex Article 183 TEC)

Association shall have the following objectives.

1. Member States shall apply to their trade with the countries and territories the same treatment as they accord each other pursuant to the Treaties.

2. Each country or territory shall apply to its trade with Member States and with the other countries and territories the same treatment as that which it applies to the European State with which is has special relations.

3. The Member States shall contribute to the investments required for the progressive development of these countries and territories.

4. For investments financed by the Union, participation in tenders and supplies shall be open on equal terms to all natural and legal persons who are nationals of a Member State or of one of the countries and territories.

5. In relations between Member States and the countries and territories the right of establishment of nationals and companies or firms shall be regulated in accordance with the provisions and procedures laid down in the Chapter relating to the right of establishment and on a non- discriminatory basis, subject to any special provisions laid down pursuant to Article 203.

Article 200 (ex Article 184 TEC)

1. Customs duties on imports into the Member States of goods originating in the countries and territories shall be prohibited in conformity with the prohibition of customs duties between Member States in accordance with the provisions of the Treaties.

2. Customs duties on imports into each country or territory from Member States or from the other countries or territories shall be prohibited in accordance with the provisions of Article 30.

....

*   EDITOR'S NOTE; Annex II of the Treaties lists the overseas countries and territories to which the provisions of Part Four apply. These are: Greenland, New Caledonia and Dependencies, French Polynesia, French Southern and Antarctic Territories, Wallis and Futuna Islands, Mayotte, Saint Pierre and Miquelon, Aruba, Netherlands Antilles: Bonaire, Curaçao, Saba, Sint Eustatius, Sint Maarten, Anguilla, Cayman Islands, Falkland Islands, South Georgia and the South Sandwich Islands, Montserrat, Pitcairn, Saint Helena and Dependencies, British Antarctic Territory, British Indian Ocean Territory, Turks and Caicos Islands, British Virgin Islands, and Bermuda.

3.   The countries and territories may, however, levy customs duties which meet the needs of their development and industrialisation or produce revenue for their budgets.

The duties referred to in the preceding subparagraph may not exceed the level of those imposed on imports of products from the Member State with which each country or territory has special relations.

4.   Paragraph 2 shall not apply to countries and territories which, by reason of the particular international obligations by which they are bound, already apply a non-discriminatory customs tariff.

5.   The introduction of or any change in customs duties imposed on goods imported into the countries and territories shall not, either in law or in fact, give rise to any direct or indirect discrimination between imports from the various Member States.

Article 201 (ex Article 185 TEC)
If the level of the duties applicable to goods from a third country on entry into a country or territory is liable, when the provisions of Article 200(1) have been applied, to cause deflections of trade to the detriment of any Member State, the latter may request the Commission to propose to the other Member States the measures needed to remedy the situation.

Article 202 (ex Article 186 TEC)
Subject to the provisions relating to public health, public security or public policy, freedom of movement within Member States for workers from the countries and territories, and within the countries and territories for workers from Member States, shall be regulated by acts adopted in accordance with Article 203.

Article 203 (ex Article 187 TEC)
The Council, acting unanimously on a proposal from the Commission, shall, on the basis of the experience acquired under the association of the countries and territories with the Union and of the principles set out in the Treaties, lay down provisions as regards the detailed rules and the procedure for the association of the countries and territories with the Union. Where the provisions in question are adopted by the Council in accordance with a special legislative procedure, it shall act unanimously on a proposal from the Commission and after consulting the European Parliament.

Article 204 (ex Article 188 TEC)
The provisions of Articles 198 to 203 shall apply to Greenland, subject to the specific provisions for Greenland set out in the Protocol on special arrangements for Greenland, annexed to the Treaties.

Part Five THE UNION'S EXTERNAL ACTION

TITLE I
GENERAL PROVISIONS ON THE UNION'S EXTERNAL ACTION

Article 205
The Union's action on the international scene, pursuant to this Part, shall be guided by the principles, pursue the objectives and be conducted in accordance with the general provisions laid down in Chapter 1 of Title V of the Treaty on European Union.

TITLE II
COMMON COMMERCIAL POLICY

Article 206 (ex Article 131 TEC)
By establishing a customs union in accordance with Articles 28 to 32, the Union shall contribute, in the common interest, to the harmonious development of world trade, the

progressive abolition of restrictions on international trade and on foreign direct investment, and the lowering of customs and other barriers.

Article 207 (ex Article 133 TEC)

1. The common commercial policy shall be based on uniform principles, particularly with regard to changes in tariff rates, the conclusion of tariff and trade agreements relating to trade in goods and services, and the commercial aspects of intellectual property, foreign direct investment, the achievement of uniformity in measures of liberalisation, export policy and measures to protect trade such as those to be taken in the event of dumping or subsidies. The common commercial policy shall be conducted in the context of the principles and objectives of the Union's external action.

2. The European Parliament and the Council, acting by means of regulations in accordance with the ordinary legislative procedure, shall adopt the measures defining the framework for implementing the common commercial policy.

3. Where agreements with one or more third countries or international organisations need to be negotiated and concluded, Article 218 shall apply, subject to the special provisions of this Article.

    The Commission shall make recommendations to the Council, which shall authorise it to open the necessary negotiations. The Council and the Commission shall be responsible for ensuring that the agreements negotiated are compatible with internal Union policies and rules.

    The Commission shall conduct these negotiations in consultation with a special committee appointed by the Council to assist the Commission in this task and within the framework of such directives as the Council may issue to it. The Commission shall report regularly to the special committee and to the European Parliament on the progress of negotiations.

4. For the negotiation and conclusion of the agreements referred to in paragraph 3, the Council shall act by a qualified majority.

    For the negotiation and conclusion of agreements in the fields of trade in services and the commercial aspects of intellectual property, as well as foreign direct investment, the Council shall act unanimously where such agreements include provisions for which unanimity is required for the adoption of internal rules.

    The Council shall also act unanimously for the negotiation and conclusion of agreements:

    (a) in the field of trade in cultural and audiovisual services, where these agreements risk prejudicing the Union's cultural and linguistic diversity;
    (b) in the field of trade in social, education and health services, where these agreements risk seriously disturbing the national organisation of such services and prejudicing the responsibility of Member States to deliver them.

5. The negotiation and conclusion of international agreements in the field of transport shall be subject to Title VI of Part Three and to Article 218.

6. The exercise of the competences conferred by this Article in the field of the common commercial policy shall not affect the delimitation of competences between the Union and the Member States, and shall not lead to harmonisation of legislative or regulatory provisions of the Member States in so far as the Treaties exclude such harmonisation.

TITLE III
COOPERATION WITH THIRD COUNTRIES AND HUMANITARIAN AID

Chapter 1 DEVELOPMENT COOPERATION

Article 208 (ex Article 177 TEC)

1.   Union policy in the field of development cooperation shall be conducted within the framework of the principles and objectives of the Union's external action. The Union's development cooperation policy and that of the Member States complement and reinforce each other.

Union development cooperation policy shall have as its primary objective the reduction and, in the long term, the eradication of poverty. The Union shall take account of the objectives of development cooperation in the policies that it implements which are likely to affect developing countries.

2.   The Union and the Member States shall comply with the commitments and take account of the objectives they have approved in the context of the United Nations and other competent international organisations.

Article 209 (ex Article 179 TEC)

1.   The European Parliament and the Council, acting in accordance with the ordinary legislative procedure, shall adopt the measures necessary for the implementation of development cooperation policy, which may relate to multiannual cooperation programmes with developing countries or programmes with a thematic approach.

2.   The Union may conclude with third countries and competent international organisations any agreement helping to achieve the objectives referred to in Article 21 of the Treaty on European Union and in Article 208 of this Treaty.

The first subparagraph shall be without prejudice to Member States' competence to negotiate in international bodies and to conclude agreements.

3.   The European Investment Bank shall contribute, under the terms laid down in its Statute, to the implementation of the measures referred to in paragraph 1.

Article 210 (ex Article 180 TEC)

1.   In order to promote the complementarity and efficiency of their action, the Union and the Member States shall coordinate their policies on development cooperation and shall consult each other on their aid programmes, including in international organisations and during international conferences. They may undertake joint action. Member States shall contribute if necessary to the implementation of Union aid programmes.

2.   The Commission may take any useful initiative to promote the coordination referred to in paragraph 1.

Article 211 (ex Article 181 TEC)

Within their respective spheres of competence, the Union and the Member States shall cooperate with third countries and with the competent international organisations.

Chapter 2 ECONOMIC, FINANCIAL AND TECHNICAL COOPERATION WITH THIRD COUNTRIES

Article 212 (ex Article 181a TEC)

1.   Without prejudice to the other provisions of the Treaties, and in particular Articles 208 to 211, the Union shall carry out economic, financial and technical cooperation measures,

including assistance, in particular financial assistance, with third countries other than developing countries. Such measures shall be consistent with the development policy of the Union and shall be carried out within the framework of the principles and objectives of its external action. The Union's operations and those of the Member States shall complement and reinforce each other.

2.   The European Parliament and the Council, acting in accordance with the ordinary legislative procedure, shall adopt the measures necessary for the implementation of paragraph 1.

3.   Within their respective spheres of competence, the Union and the Member States shall cooperate with third countries and the competent international organisations. The arrangements for Union cooperation may be the subject of agreements between the Union and the third parties concerned.

The first subparagraph shall be without prejudice to the Member States' competence to negotiate in international bodies and to conclude international agreements.

Article 213
When the situation in a third country requires urgent financial assistance from the Union, the Council shall adopt the necessary decisions on a proposal from the Commission.

Chapter 3 HUMANITARIAN AID

Article 214
1.   The Union's operations in the field of humanitarian aid shall be conducted within the framework of the principles and objectives of the external action of the Union. Such operations shall be intended to provide ad hoc assistance and relief and protection for people in third countries who are victims of natural or man-made disasters, in order to meet the humanitarian needs resulting from these different situations. The Union's measures and those of the Member States shall complement and reinforce each other.

2.   Humanitarian aid operations shall be conducted in compliance with the principles of international law and with the principles of impartiality, neutrality and non-discrimination.

3.   The European Parliament and the Council, acting in accordance with the ordinary legislative procedure, shall establish the measures defining the framework within which the Union's humanitarian aid operations shall be implemented.

4.   The Union may conclude with third countries and competent international organisations any agreement helping to achieve the objectives referred to in paragraph 1 and in Article 21 of the Treaty on European Union.

The first subparagraph shall be without prejudice to Member States' competence to negotiate in international bodies and to conclude agreements.

5.   In order to establish a framework for joint contributions from young Europeans to the humanitarian aid operations of the Union, a European Voluntary Humanitarian Aid Corps shall be set up. The European Parliament and the Council, acting by means of regulations in accordance with the ordinary legislative procedure, shall determine the rules and procedures for the operation of the Corps.

6.   The Commission may take any useful initiative to promote coordination between actions of the Union and those of the Member States, in order to enhance the efficiency and complementarity of Union and national humanitarian aid measures.

7.   The Union shall ensure that its humanitarian aid operations are coordinated and consistent with those of international organisations and bodies, in particular those forming part of the United Nations system.

TITLE IV
RESTRICTIVE MEASURES

Article 215 (ex Article 301 TEC)

1.   Where a decision, adopted in accordance with Chapter 2 of Title V of the Treaty on European Union, provides for the interruption or reduction, in part or completely, of economic and financial relations with one or more third countries, the Council, acting by a qualified majority on a joint proposal from the High Representative of the Union for Foreign Affairs and Security Policy and the Commission, shall adopt the necessary measures. It shall inform the European Parliament thereof.

2.   Where a decision adopted in accordance with Chapter 2 of Title V of the Treaty on European Union so provides, the Council may adopt restrictive measures under the procedure referred to in paragraph 1 against natural or legal persons and groups or non-State entities.

3.   The acts referred to in this Article shall include necessary provisions on legal safeguards.

TITLE V
INTERNATIONAL AGREEMENTS

Article 216

1.   The Union may conclude an agreement with one or more third countries or international organisations where the Treaties so provide or where the conclusion of an agreement is necessary in order to achieve, within the framework of the Union's policies, one of the objectives referred to in the Treaties, or is provided for in a legally binding Union act or is likely to affect common rules or alter their scope.

2.   Agreements concluded by the Union are binding upon the institutions of the Union and on its Member States.

Article 217 (ex Article 310 TEC)

The Union may conclude with one or more third countries or international organisations agreements establishing an association involving reciprocal rights and obligations, common action and special procedure.

Article 218 (ex Article 300 TEC)

1.   Without prejudice to the specific provisions laid down in Article 207, agreements between the Union and third countries or international organisations shall be negotiated and concluded in accordance with the following procedure.

2.   The Council shall authorise the opening of negotiations, adopt negotiating directives, authorise the signing of agreements and conclude them.

3.   The Commission, or the High Representative of the Union for Foreign Affairs and Security Policy where the agreement envisaged relates exclusively or principally to the common foreign and security policy, shall submit recommendations to the Council, which shall adopt a decision authorising the opening of negotiations and, depending on the

subject of the agreement envisaged, nominating the Union negotiator or the head of the Union's negotiating team.

4.   The Council may address directives to the negotiator and designate a special committee in consultation with which the negotiations must be conducted.

5.   The Council, on a proposal by the negotiator, shall adopt a decision authorising the signing of the agreement and, if necessary, its provisional application before entry into force.

6.   The Council, on a proposal by the negotiator, shall adopt a decision concluding the agreement.

Except where agreements relate exclusively to the common foreign and security policy, the Council shall adopt the decision concluding the agreement:
(a)   after obtaining the consent of the European Parliament in the following cases:
     (i)   association agreements;
     (ii)   agreement on Union accession to the European Convention for the Protection of Human Rights and Fundamental Freedoms;
     (iii) agreements establishing a specific institutional framework by organising cooperation procedures;
     (iv)   agreements with important budgetary implications for the Union;
     (v)   agreements covering fields to which either the ordinary legislative procedure applies, or the special legislative procedure where consent by the European Parliament is required.
The European Parliament and the Council may, in an urgent situation, agree upon a time-limit for consent.

(b)   after consulting the European Parliament in other cases. The European Parliament shall deliver its opinion within a time-limit which the Council may set depending on the urgency of the matter. In the absence of an opinion within that time-limit, the Council may act.

7.   When concluding an agreement, the Council may, by way of derogation from paragraphs 5, 6 and 9, authorise the negotiator to approve on the Union's behalf modifications to the agreement where it provides for them to be adopted by a simplified procedure or by a body set up by the agreement. The Council may attach specific conditions to such authorisation.

8.   The Council shall act by a qualified majority throughout the procedure.

However, it shall act unanimously when the agreement covers a field for which unanimity is required for the adoption of a Union act as well as for association agreements and the agreements referred to in Article 212 with the States which are candidates for accession. The Council shall also act unanimously for the agreement on accession of the Union to the European Convention for the Protection of Human Rights and Fundamental Freedoms; the decision concluding this agreement shall enter into force after it has been approved by the Member States in accordance with their respective constitutional requirements.

9.   The Council, on a proposal from the Commission or the High Representative of the Union for Foreign Affairs and Security Policy, shall adopt a decision suspending application of an agreement and establishing the positions to be adopted on the Union's behalf in a body set up by an agreement, when that body is called upon to adopt acts having legal effects, with the exception of acts supplementing or amending the institutional framework of the agreement.

10.   The European Parliament shall be immediately and fully informed at all stages of the procedure.

11.   A Member State, the European Parliament, the Council or the Commission may obtain the opinion of the Court of Justice as to whether an agreement envisaged is compatible with the Treaties. Where the opinion of the Court is adverse, the agreement envisaged may not enter into force unless it is amended or the Treaties are revised.

Article 219 (ex Article 111(1) to (3) and (5) TEC)

1.   By way of derogation from Article 218, the Council, either on a recommendation from the European Central Bank or on a recommendation from the Commission and after consulting the European Central Bank, in an endeavour to reach a consensus consistent with the objective of price stability, may conclude formal agreements on an exchange-rate system for the euro in relation to the currencies of third States. The Council shall act unanimously after consulting the European Parliament and in accordance with the procedure provided for in paragraph 3.

      The Council may, either on a recommendation from the European Central Bank or on a recommendation from the Commission, and after consulting the European Central Bank, in an endeavour to reach a consensus consistent with the objective of price stability, adopt, adjust or abandon the central rates of the euro within the exchange-rate system. The President of the Council shall inform the European Parliament of the adoption, adjustment or abandonment of the euro central rates.

2.   In the absence of an exchange-rate system in relation to one or more currencies of third States as referred to in paragraph 1, the Council, either on a recommendation from the Commission and after consulting the European Central Bank or on a recommendation from the European Central Bank, may formulate general orientations for exchange-rate policy in relation to these currencies. These general orientations shall be without prejudice to the primary objective of the ESCB to maintain price stability.

3.   By way of derogation from Article 218, where agreements concerning monetary or foreign exchange regime matters need to be negotiated by the Union with one or more third States or international organisations, the Council, on a recommendation from the Commission and after consulting the European Central Bank, shall decide the arrangements for the negotiation and for the conclusion of such agreements. These arrangements shall ensure that the Union expresses a single position. The Commission shall be fully associated with the negotiations.

4.   Without prejudice to Union competence and Union agreements as regards economic and monetary union, Member States may negotiate in international bodies and conclude international agreements.

TITLE VI
THE UNION'S RELATIONS WITH INTERNATIONAL ORGANISATIONS AND THIRD COUNTRIES AND UNION DELEGATIONS

Article 220 (ex Articles 302 to 304 TEC)

1.   The Union shall establish all appropriate forms of cooperation with the organs of the United Nations and its specialised agencies, the Council of Europe, the Organisation for Security and Cooperation in Europe and the Organisation for Economic Cooperation and Development.

The Union shall also maintain such relations as are appropriate with other international organisations.

2.   The High Representative of the Union for Foreign Affairs and Security Policy and the Commission shall implement this Article.

Article 221

1.   Union delegations in third countries and at international organisations shall represent the Union.

2.   Union delegations shall be placed under the authority of the High Representative of the Union for Foreign Affairs and Security Policy. They shall act in close cooperation with Member States' diplomatic and consular missions.

TITLE VII
SOLIDARITY CLAUSE

Article 222

1.   The Union and its Member States shall act jointly in a spirit of solidarity if a Member State is the object of a terrorist attack or the victim of a natural or man-made disaster. The Union shall mobilise all the instruments at its disposal, including the military resources made available by the Member States, to:
   (a)   — prevent the terrorist threat in the territory of the Member States;
         — protect democratic institutions and the civilian population from any terrorist attack;
         — assist a Member State in its territory, at the request of its political authorities, in the event of a terrorist attack;
   (b) assist a Member State in its territory, at the request of its political authorities, in the event of a natural or man-made disaster.

2.   Should a Member State be the object of a terrorist attack or the victim of a natural or man- made disaster, the other Member States shall assist it at the request of its political authorities. To that end, the Member States shall coordinate between themselves in the Council.

3.   The arrangements for the implementation by the Union of the solidarity clause shall be defined by a decision adopted by the Council acting on a joint proposal by the Commission and the High Representative of the Union for Foreign Affairs and Security Policy. The Council shall act in accordance with Article 31(1) of the Treaty on European Union where this decision has defence implications. The European Parliament shall be informed.

For the purposes of this paragraph and without prejudice to Article 240, the Council shall be assisted by the Political and Security Committee with the support of the structures developed in the context of the common security and defence policy and by the Committee referred to in Article 71; the two committees shall, if necessary, submit joint opinions.

4.   The European Council shall regularly assess the threats facing the Union in order to enable the Union and its Member States to take effective action.

Part Six INSTITUTIONAL AND FINANCIAL PROVISIONS

TITLE I
INSTITUTIONAL PROVISIONS

Chapter 1 THE INSTITUTIONS

SECTION 1 THE EUROPEAN PARLIAMENT

Article 223 (ex Article 190(4) and (5) TEC)
1.   The European Parliament shall draw up a proposal to lay down the provisions necessary for the election of its Members by direct universal suffrage in accordance with a uniform procedure in all Member States or in accordance with principles common to all Member States.

The Council, acting unanimously in accordance with a special legislative procedure and after obtaining the consent of the European Parliament, which shall act by a majority of its component Members, shall lay down the necessary provisions. These provisions shall enter into force following their approval by the Member States in accordance with their respective constitutional requirements.

2.   The European Parliament, acting by means of regulations on its own initiative in accordance with a special legislative procedure after seeking an opinion from the Commission and with the consent of the Council, shall lay down the regulations and general conditions governing the performance of the duties of its Members. All rules or conditions relating to the taxation of Members or former Members shall require unanimity within the Council.

Article 224 (ex Article 191, second subparagraph, TEC)
The European Parliament and the Council, acting in accordance with the ordinary legislative procedure, by means of regulations, shall lay down the regulations governing political parties at European level referred to in Article 10(4) of the Treaty on European Union and in particular the rules regarding their funding.

Article 225 (ex Article 192, second subparagraph, TEC)
The European Parliament may, acting by a majority of its component Members, request the Commission to submit any appropriate proposal on matters on which it considers that a Union act is required for the purpose of implementing the Treaties. If the Commission does not submit a proposal, it shall inform the European Parliament of the reasons.

Article 226 (ex Article 193 TEC)
In the course of its duties, the European Parliament may, at the request of a quarter of its component Members, set up a temporary Committee of Inquiry to investigate, without prejudice to the powers conferred by the Treaties on other institutions or bodies, alleged contraventions or maladministration in the implementation of Union law, except where the alleged facts are being examined before a court and while the case is still subject to legal proceedings.

The temporary Committee of Inquiry shall cease to exist on the submission of its report.

The detailed provisions governing the exercise of the right of inquiry shall be determined by the European Parliament, acting by means of regulations on its own initiative in accordance with a special legislative procedure, after obtaining the consent of the Council and the Commission.

Article 227 (ex Article 194 TEC)
Any citizen of the Union, and any natural or legal person residing or having its registered office in a Member State, shall have the right to address, individually or in association with other citizens or persons, a petition to the European Parliament on a matter which comes within the Union's fields of activity and which affects him, her or it directly.

Article 228 (ex Article 195 TEC)
1.   A European Ombudsman, elected by the European Parliament, shall be empowered to receive complaints from any citizen of the Union or any natural or legal person residing or having its registered office in a Member State concerning instances of maladministration in the activities of the Union institutions, bodies, offices or agencies, with the exception of the Court of Justice of the European Union acting in its judicial role. He or she shall examine such complaints and report on them.

In accordance with his duties, the Ombudsman shall conduct inquiries for which he finds grounds, either on his own initiative or on the basis of complaints submitted to him direct or through a Member of the European Parliament, except where the alleged facts are or have been the subject of legal proceedings. Where the Ombudsman establishes an instance of maladministration, he shall refer the matter to the institution, body, office or agency concerned, which shall have a period of three months in which to inform him of its views. The Ombudsman shall then forward a report to the European Parliament and the institution, body, office or agency concerned. The person lodging the complaint shall be informed of the outcome of such inquiries.

The Ombudsman shall submit an annual report to the European Parliament on the outcome of his inquiries.

2.   The Ombudsman shall be elected after each election of the European Parliament for the duration of its term of office. The Ombudsman shall be eligible for reappointment.

The Ombudsman may be dismissed by the Court of Justice at the request of the European Parliament if he no longer fulfils the conditions required for the performance of his duties or if he is guilty of serious misconduct.

3.   The Ombudsman shall be completely independent in the performance of his duties. In the performance of those duties he shall neither seek nor take instructions from any Government, institution, body, office or entity. The Ombudsman may not, during his term of office, engage in any other occupation, whether gainful or not.

4.   The European Parliament acting by means of regulations on its own initiative in accordance with a special legislative procedure shall, after seeking an opinion from the Commission and with the consent of the Council, lay down the regulations and general conditions governing the performance of the Ombudsman's duties.

Article 229 (ex Article 196 TEC)
The European Parliament shall hold an annual session. It shall meet, without requiring to be convened, on the second Tuesday in March.

The European Parliament may meet in extraordinary part-session at the request of a majority of its component Members or at the request of the Council or of the Commission.

Article 230 (ex Article 197, second, third and fourth paragraph, TEC)
The Commission may attend all the meetings and shall, at its request, be heard.

The Commission shall reply orally or in writing to questions put to it by the European Parliament or by its Members.

The European Council and the Council shall be heard by the European Parliament in accordance with the conditions laid down in the Rules of Procedure of the European Council and those of the Council.

Article 231 (ex Article 198 TEC)
Save as otherwise provided in the Treaties, the European Parliament shall act by a majority of the votes cast.

The Rules of Procedure shall determine the quorum.

Article 232 (ex Article 199 TEC)
The European Parliament shall adopt its Rules of Procedure, acting by a majority of its Members.

The proceedings of the European Parliament shall be published in the manner laid down in the Treaties and in its Rules of Procedure.

Article 233 (ex Article 200 TEC)
The European Parliament shall discuss in open session the annual general report submitted to it by the Commission.

Article 234 (ex Article 201 TEC)
If a motion of censure on the activities of the Commission is tabled before it, the European Parliament shall not vote thereon until at least three days after the motion has been tabled and only by open vote.

If the motion of censure is carried by a two-thirds majority of the votes cast, representing a majority of the component Members of the European Parliament, the members of the Commission shall resign as a body and the High Representative of the Union for Foreign Affairs and Security Policy shall resign from duties that he or she carries out in the Commission. They shall remain in office and continue to deal with current business until they are replaced in accordance with Article 17 of the Treaty on European Union. In this case, the term of office of the members of the Commission appointed to replace them shall expire on the date on which the term of office of the members of the Commission obliged to resign as a body would have expired.

SECTION 2 THE EUROPEAN COUNCIL

Article 235
1.   Where a vote is taken, any member of the European Council may also act on behalf of not more than one other member.

Article 16(4) of the Treaty on European Union and Article 238(2) of this Treaty shall apply to the European Council when it is acting by a qualified majority. Where the European Council decides by vote, its President and the President of the Commission shall not take part in the vote.

Abstentions by members present in person or represented shall not prevent the adoption by the European Council of acts which require unanimity.

2.   The President of the European Parliament may be invited to be heard by the European Council.

3.   The European Council shall act by a simple majority for procedural questions and for the adoption of its Rules of Procedure.

4.   The European Council shall be assisted by the General Secretariat of the Council.

Article 236

The European Council shall adopt by a qualified majority:

(a)   a decision establishing the list of Council configurations, other than those of the General Affairs Council and of the Foreign Affairs Council, in accordance with Article 16(6) of the Treaty on European Union;

(b)   a decision on the Presidency of Council configurations, other than that of Foreign Affairs, in accordance with Article 16(9) of the Treaty on European Union.

SECTION 3 THE COUNCIL

Article 237 (ex Article 204 TEC)

The Council shall meet when convened by its President on his own initiative or at the request of one of its Members or of the Commission.

Article 238 (ex Article 205(1) and (2), TEC)

1.   Where it is required to act by a simple majority, the Council shall act by a majority of its component members.

2.   By way of derogation from Article 16(4) of the Treaty on European Union, as from 1 November 2014 and subject to the provisions laid down in the Protocol on transitional provisions, where the Council does not act on a proposal from the Commission or from the High Representative of the Union for Foreign Affairs and Security Policy, the qualified majority shall be defined as at least 72% of the members of the Council, representing Member States comprising at least 65% of the population of the Union.

3.   As from 1 November 2014 and subject to the provisions laid down in the Protocol on transitional provisions, in cases where, under the Treaties, not all the members of the Council participate in voting, a qualified majority shall be defined as follows:

(a)   A qualified majority shall be defined as at least 55% of the members of the Council representing the participating Member States, comprising at least 65% of the population of these States.
A blocking minority must include at least the minimum number of Council members representing more than 35% of the population of the participating Member States, plus one member, failing which the qualified majority shall be deemed attained;

(b)   By way of derogation from point (a), where the Council does not act on a proposal from the Commission or from the High Representative of the Union for Foreign Affairs and Security Policy, the qualified majority shall be defined as at least 72% of the members of the Council representing the participating Member States, comprising at least 65% of the population of these States.

4.   Abstentions by Members present in person or represented shall not prevent the adoption by the Council of acts which require unanimity.

Article 239 (ex Article 206 TEC)

Where a vote is taken, any Member of the Council may also act on behalf of not more than one other member.

Article 240 (ex Article 207 TEC)

1. A committee consisting of the Permanent Representatives of the Governments of the Member States shall be responsible for preparing the work of the Council and for carrying out the tasks assigned to it by the latter. The Committee may adopt procedural decisions in cases provided for in the Council's Rules of Procedure.

2. The Council shall be assisted by a General Secretariat, under the responsibility of a Secretary- General appointed by the Council.

   The Council shall decide on the organisation of the General Secretariat by a simple majority.

3. The Council shall act by a simple majority regarding procedural matters and for the adoption of its Rules of Procedure.

Article 241 (ex Article 208 TEC)

The Council, acting by a simple majority, may request the Commission to undertake any studies the Council considers desirable for the attainment of the common objectives, and to submit to it any appropriate proposals. If the Commission does not submit a proposal, it shall inform the Council of the reasons.

Article 242 (ex Article 209 TEC)

The Council, acting by a simple majority shall, after consulting the Commission, determine the rules governing the committees provided for in the Treaties.

Article 243 (ex Article 210 TEC)

The Council shall determine the salaries, allowances and pensions of the President of the European Council, the President of the Commission, the High Representative of the Union for Foreign Affairs and Security Policy, the Members of the Commission, the Presidents, Members and Registrars of the Court of Justice of the European Union, and the Secretary-General of the Council. It shall also determine any payment to be made instead of remuneration.

SECTION 4 THE COMMISSION

Article 244

In accordance with Article 17(5) of the Treaty on European Union, the Members of the Commission shall be chosen on the basis of a system of rotation established unanimously by the European Council and on the basis of the following principles:

(a) Member States shall be treated on a strictly equal footing as regards determination of the sequence of, and the time spent by, their nationals as members of the Commission; consequently, the difference between the total number of terms of office held by nationals of any given pair of Member States may never be more than one;

(b) subject to point (a), each successive Commission shall be so composed as to reflect satisfactorily the demographic and geographical range of all the Member States.

Article 245 (ex Article 213 TEC)

The Members of the Commission shall refrain from any action incompatible with their duties. Member States shall respect their independence and shall not seek to influence them in the performance of their tasks.

The Members of the Commission may not, during their term of office, engage in any other occupation, whether gainful or not. When entering upon their duties they shall give a solemn undertaking that, both during and after their term of office, they will respect the obligations arising therefrom and in particular their duty to behave with integrity and discretion as regards the acceptance, after they have ceased to hold office, of certain appointments or benefits. In the event of any breach of these obligations, the Court of Justice may, on application by the Council acting by a simple majority or the Commission, rule that the Member concerned be, according to the circumstances, either compulsorily retired in accordance with Article 247 or deprived of his right to a pension or other benefits in its stead.

Article 246 (ex Article 215 TEC)

Apart from normal replacement, or death, the duties of a Member of the Commission shall end when he resigns or is compulsorily retired.

A vacancy caused by resignation, compulsory retirement or death shall be filled for the remainder of the Member's term of office by a new Member of the same nationality appointed by the Council, by common accord with the President of the Commission, after consulting the European Parliament and in accordance with the criteria set out in the second subparagraph of Article 17(3) of the Treaty on European Union.

The Council may, acting unanimously on a proposal from the President of the Commission, decide that such a vacancy need not be filled, in particular when the remainder of the Member's term of office is short.

In the event of resignation, compulsory retirement or death, the President shall be replaced for the remainder of his term of office. The procedure laid down in the first subparagraph of Article 17(7) of the Treaty on European Union shall be applicable for the replacement of the President.

In the event of resignation, compulsory retirement or death, the High Representative of the Union for Foreign Affairs and Security Policy shall be replaced, for the remainder of his or her term of office, in accordance with Article 18(1) of the Treaty on European Union.

In the case of the resignation of all the Members of the Commission, they shall remain in office and continue to deal with current business until they have been replaced, for the remainder of their term of office, in accordance with Article 17 of the Treaty on European Union.

Article 247 (ex Article 216 TEC)

If any Member of the Commission no longer fulfils the conditions required for the performance of his duties or if he has been guilty of serious misconduct, the Court of Justice may, on application by the Council acting by a simple majority or the Commission, compulsorily retire him.

Article 248 (ex Article 217(2) TEC)

Without prejudice to Article 18(4) of the Treaty on European Union, the responsibilities incumbent upon the Commission shall be structured and allocated among its members by its President, in accordance with Article 17(6) of that Treaty. The President may reshuffle the allocation of those responsibilities during the Commission's term of office. The Members of the Commission shall carry out the duties devolved upon them by the President under his authority.

Article 249 (ex Articles 218(2) and 212 TEC)

1.   The Commission shall adopt its Rules of Procedure so as to ensure that both it and its departments operate. It shall ensure that these Rules are published.

2.   The Commission shall publish annually, not later than one month before the opening of the session of the European Parliament, a general report on the activities of the Union.

Article 250 (ex Article 219 TEC)

The Commission shall act by a majority of its Members.

Its Rules of Procedure shall determine the quorum.

SECTION 5   THE COURT OF JUSTICE OF THE EUROPEAN UNION

Article 251 (ex Article 221 TEC)

The Court of Justice shall sit in chambers or in a Grand Chamber, in accordance with the rules laid down for that purpose in the Statute of the Court of Justice of the European Union.

When provided for in the Statute, the Court of Justice may also sit as a full Court.

Article 252 (ex Article 222 TEC)

The Court of Justice shall be assisted by eight Advocates-General. Should the Court of Justice so request, the Council, acting unanimously, may increase the number of Advocates-General.

It shall be the duty of the Advocate-General, acting with complete impartiality and independence, to make, in open court, reasoned submissions on cases which, in accordance with the Statute of the Court of Justice of the European Union, require his involvement.

Article 253 (ex Article 223 TEC)

The Judges and Advocates-General of the Court of Justice shall be chosen from persons whose independence is beyond doubt and who possess the qualifications required for appointment to the highest judicial offices in their respective countries or who are jurisconsults of recognised competence; they shall be appointed by common accord of the governments of the Member States for a term of six years, after consultation of the panel provided for in Article 255.

Every three years there shall be a partial replacement of the Judges and Advocates-General, in accordance with the conditions laid down in the Statute of the Court of Justice of the European Union.

The Judges shall elect the President of the Court of Justice from among their number for a term of three years. He may be re-elected.

Retiring Judges and Advocates-General may be reappointed.

The Court of Justice shall appoint its Registrar and lay down the rules governing his service.

The Court of Justice shall establish its Rules of Procedure. Those Rules shall require the approval of the Council.

Article 254 (ex Article 224 TEC)

The number of Judges of the General Court shall be determined by the Statute of the Court of Justice of the European Union. The Statute may provide for the General Court to be assisted by Advocates- General.

The members of the General Court shall be chosen from persons whose independence is beyond doubt and who possess the ability required for appointment to high judicial office. They shall be appointed by common accord of the governments of the Member States for a term of six years, after consultation of the panel provided for in Article 255. The membership shall be partially renewed every three years. Retiring members shall be eligible for reappointment.

The Judges shall elect the President of the General Court from among their number for a term of three years. He may be re-elected.

The General Court shall appoint its Registrar and lay down the rules governing his service.

The General Court shall establish its Rules of Procedure in agreement with the Court of Justice.

Those Rules shall require the approval of the Council.

Unless the Statute of the Court of Justice of the European Union provides otherwise, the provisions of the Treaties relating to the Court of Justice shall apply to the General Court.

Article 255

A panel shall be set up in order to give an opinion on candidates' suitability to perform the duties of Judge and Advocate-General of the Court of Justice and the General Court before the governments of the Member States make the appointments referred to in Articles 253 and 254.

The panel shall comprise seven persons chosen from among former members of the Court of Justice and the General Court, members of national supreme courts and lawyers of recognised competence, one of whom shall be proposed by the European Parliament. The Council shall adopt a decision establishing the panel's operating rules and a decision appointing its members. It shall act on the initiative of the President of the Court of Justice.

Article 256 (ex Article 225 TEC)

1. The General Court shall have jurisdiction to hear and determine at first instance actions or proceedings referred to in Articles 263, 265, 268, 270 and 272, with the exception of those assigned to a specialised court set up under Article 257 and those reserved in the Statute for the Court of Justice. The Statute may provide for the General Court to have jurisdiction for other classes of action or proceeding.

   Decisions given by the General Court under this paragraph may be subject to a right of appeal to the Court of Justice on points of law only, under the conditions and within the limits laid down by the Statute.

2. The General Court shall have jurisdiction to hear and determine actions or proceedings brought against decisions of the specialised courts.

   Decisions given by the General Court under this paragraph may exceptionally be subject to review by the Court of Justice, under the conditions and within the limits laid down by the Statute, where there is a serious risk of the unity or consistency of Union law being affected.

3. The General Court shall have jurisdiction to hear and determine questions referred for a preliminary ruling under Article 267, in specific areas laid down by the Statute.

   Where the General Court considers that the case requires a decision of principle likely to affect the unity or consistency of Union law, it may refer the case to the Court of Justice for a ruling.

   Decisions given by the General Court on questions referred for a preliminary ruling may exceptionally be subject to review by the Court of Justice, under the conditions and within the limits laid down by the Statute, where there is a serious risk of the unity or consistency of Union law being affected.

Article 257 (ex Article 225a TEC)

The European Parliament and the Council, acting in accordance with the ordinary legislative procedure, may establish specialised courts attached to the General Court to hear and determine at first instance certain classes of action or proceeding brought in specific areas. The European Parliament and the Council shall act by means of regulations either on a proposal from the Commission after consultation of the Court of Justice or at the request of the Court of Justice after consultation of the Commission.

The regulation establishing a specialised court shall lay down the rules on the organisation of the court and the extent of the jurisdiction conferred upon it.

Decisions given by specialised courts may be subject to a right of appeal on points of law only or, when provided for in the regulation establishing the specialised court, a right of appeal also on matters of fact, before the General Court.

The members of the specialised courts shall be chosen from persons whose independence is beyond doubt and who possess the ability required for appointment to judicial office. They shall be appointed by the Council, acting unanimously.

The specialised courts shall establish their Rules of Procedure in agreement with the Court of Justice. Those Rules shall require the approval of the Council.

Unless the regulation establishing the specialised court provides otherwise, the provisions of the Treaties relating to the Court of Justice of the European Union and the provisions of the Statute of the Court of Justice of the European Union shall apply to the specialised courts. Title I of the Statute and Article 64 thereof shall in any case apply to the specialised courts.

Article 258 (ex Article 226 TEC)

If the Commission considers that a Member State has failed to fulfil an obligation under the Treaties, it shall deliver a reasoned opinion on the matter after giving the State concerned the opportunity to submit its observations.

If the State concerned does not comply with the opinion within the period laid down by the Commission, the latter may bring the matter before the Court of Justice of the European Union.

Article 259 (ex Article 227 TEC)

A Member State which considers that another Member State has failed to fulfil an obligation under the Treaties may bring the matter before the Court of Justice of the European Union.

Before a Member State brings an action against another Member State for an alleged infringement of an obligation under the Treaties, it shall bring the matter before the Commission.

The Commission shall deliver a reasoned opinion after each of the States concerned has been given the opportunity to submit its own case and its observations on the other party's case both orally and in writing.

If the Commission has not delivered an opinion within three months of the date on which the matter was brought before it, the absence of such opinion shall not prevent the matter from being brought before the Court.

Article 260 (ex Article 228 TEC)

1. If the Court of Justice of the European Union finds that a Member State has failed to fulfil an obligation under the Treaties, the State shall be required to take the necessary measures to comply with the judgment of the Court.

2. If the Commission considers that the Member State concerned has not taken the necessary measures to comply with the judgment of the Court, it may bring the case before the Court after giving that State the opportunity to submit its observations. It shall specify the amount of the lump sum or penalty payment to be paid by the Member State concerned which it considers appropriate in the circumstances.

    If the Court finds that the Member State concerned has not complied with its judgment it may impose a lump sum or penalty payment on it.

    This procedure shall be without prejudice to Article 259.

3. When the Commission brings a case before the Court pursuant to Article 258 on the grounds that the Member State concerned has failed to fulfil its obligation to notify measures transposing a directive adopted under a legislative procedure, it may, when it deems appropriate, specify the amount of the lump sum or penalty payment to be paid by the Member State concerned which it considers appropriate in the circumstances.

If the Court finds that there is an infringement it may impose a lump sum or penalty payment on the Member State concerned not exceeding the amount specified by the Commission. The payment obligation shall take effect on the date set by the Court in its judgment.

Article 261 (ex Article 229 TEC)
Regulations adopted jointly by the European Parliament and the Council, and by the Council, pursuant to the provisions of the Treaties, may give the Court of Justice of the European Union unlimited jurisdiction with regard to the penalties provided for in such regulations.

Article 262 (ex Article 229a TEC)
Without prejudice to the other provisions of the Treaties, the Council, acting unanimously in accordance with a special legislative procedure and after consulting the European Parliament, may adopt provisions to confer jurisdiction, to the extent that it shall determine, on the Court of Justice of the European Union in disputes relating to the application of acts adopted on the basis of the Treaties which create European intellectual property rights. These provisions shall enter into force after their approval by the Member States in accordance with their respective constitutional requirements.

Article 263 (ex Article 230 TEC)
The Court of Justice of the European Union shall review the legality of legislative acts, of acts of the Council, of the Commission and of the European Central Bank, other than recommendations and opinions, and of acts of the European Parliament and of the European Council intended to produce legal effects vis-à-vis third parties. It shall also review the legality of acts of bodies, offices or agencies of the Union intended to produce legal effects vis-à-vis third parties.

It shall for this purpose have jurisdiction in actions brought by a Member State, the European Parliament, the Council or the Commission on grounds of lack of competence, infringement of an essential procedural requirement, infringement of the Treaties or of any rule of law relating to their application, or misuse of powers.

The Court shall have jurisdiction under the same conditions in actions brought by the Court of Auditors, by the European Central Bank and by the Committee of the Regions for the purpose of protecting their prerogatives.

Any natural or legal person may, under the conditions laid down in the first and second paragraphs, institute proceedings against an act addressed to that person or which is of direct and individual concern to them, and against a regulatory act which is of direct concern to them and does not entail implementing measures.

Acts setting up bodies, offices and agencies of the Union may lay down specific conditions and arrangements concerning actions brought by natural or legal persons against acts of these bodies, offices or agencies intended to produce legal effects in relation to them.

The proceedings provided for in this Article shall be instituted within two months of the publication of the measure, or of its notification to the plaintiff, or, in the absence thereof, of the day on which it came to the knowledge of the latter, as the case may be.

Article 264 (ex Article 231 TEC)
If the action is well founded, the Court of Justice of the European Union shall declare the act concerned to be void.

However, the Court shall, if it considers this necessary, state which of the effects of the act which it has declared void shall be considered as definitive.

Article 265 (ex Article 232 TEC)
Should the European Parliament, the European Council, the Council, the Commission or the European Central Bank, in infringement of the Treaties, fail to act, the Member States and the other institutions of the Union may bring an action before the Court of Justice of the European Union to have the infringement established. This Article shall apply, under the same conditions, to bodies, offices and agencies of the Union which fail to act.

The action shall be admissible only if the institution, body, office or agency concerned has first been called upon to act. If, within two months of being so called upon, the institution, body, office or agency concerned has not defined its position, the action may be brought within a further period of two months.

Any natural or legal person may, under the conditions laid down in the preceding paragraphs, complain to the Court that an institution, body, office or agency of the Union has failed to address to that person any act other than a recommendation or an opinion.

Article 266 (ex Article 233 TEC)
The institution whose act has been declared void or whose failure to act has been declared contrary to the Treaties shall be required to take the necessary measures to comply with the judgment of the Court of Justice of the European Union.

This obligation shall not affect any obligation which may result from the application of the second paragraph of Article 340.

Article 267 (ex Article 234 TEC)
The Court of Justice of the European Union shall have jurisdiction to give preliminary rulings concerning:
(a)   the interpretation of the Treaties;
(b)   the validity and interpretation of acts of the institutions, bodies, offices or agencies of the Union;

Where such a question is raised before any court or tribunal of a Member State, that court or tribunal may, if it considers that a decision on the question is necessary to enable it to give judgment, request the Court to give a ruling thereon.

Where any such question is raised in a case pending before a court or tribunal of a Member State against whose decisions there is no judicial remedy under national law, that court or tribunal shall bring the matter before the Court.

If such a question is raised in a case pending before a court or tribunal of a Member State with regard to a person in custody, the Court of Justice of the European Union shall act with the minimum of delay.

Article 268 (ex Article 235 TEC)
The Court of Justice of the European Union shall have jurisdiction in disputes relating to compensation for damage provided for in the second and third paragraphs of Article 340.

Article 269
The Court of Justice shall have jurisdiction to decide on the legality of an act adopted by the European Council or by the Council pursuant to Article 7 of the Treaty on European Union solely at the request of the Member State concerned by a determination of the European Council or of the Council and in respect solely of the procedural stipulations contained in that Article.

Such a request must be made within one month from the date of such determination. The Court shall rule within one month from the date of the request.

Article 270 (ex Article 236 TEC)
The Court of Justice of the European Union shall have jurisdiction in any dispute between the Union and its servants within the limits and under the conditions laid down in the Staff Regulations of Officials and the Conditions of Employment of other servants of the Union.

Article 271 (ex Article 237 TEC)
The Court of Justice of the European Union shall, within the limits hereinafter laid down, have jurisdiction in disputes concerning:

(a)   the fulfilment by Member States of obligations under the Statute of the European Investment Bank. In this connection, the Board of Directors of the Bank shall enjoy the powers conferred upon the Commission by Article 258;

(b)   measures adopted by the Board of Governors of the European Investment Bank. In this connection, any Member State, the Commission or the Board of Directors of the Bank may institute proceedings under the conditions laid down in Article 263;

(c)   measures adopted by the Board of Directors of the European Investment Bank. Proceedings against such measures may be instituted only by Member States or by the Commission, under the conditions laid down in Article 263, and solely on the grounds of non-compliance with the procedure provided for in Article 19(2), (5), (6) and (7) of the Statute of the Bank;

(d)   the fulfilment by national central banks of obligations under the Treaties and the Statute of the ESCB and of the ECB. In this connection the powers of the Governing Council of the European Central Bank in respect of national central banks shall be the same as those conferred upon the Commission in respect of Member States by Article 258. If the Court finds that a national central bank has failed to fulfil an obligation under the Treaties, that bank shall be required to take the necessary measures to comply with the judgment of the Court.

Article 272 (ex Article 238 TEC)
The Court of Justice of the European Union shall have jurisdiction to give judgment pursuant to any arbitration clause contained in a contract concluded by or on behalf of the Union, whether that contract be governed by public or private law.

Article 273 (ex Article 239 TEC)
The Court of Justice shall have jurisdiction in any dispute between Member States which relates to the subject matter of the Treaties if the dispute is submitted to it under a special agreement between the parties.

Article 274 (ex Article 240 TEC)
Save where jurisdiction is conferred on the Court of Justice of the European Union by the Treaties, disputes to which the Union is a party shall not on that ground be excluded from the jurisdiction of the courts or tribunals of the Member States.

Article 275
The Court of Justice of the European Union shall not have jurisdiction with respect to the provisions relating to the common foreign and security policy nor with respect to acts adopted on the basis of those provisions.

However, the Court shall have jurisdiction to monitor compliance with Article 40 of the Treaty on European Union and to rule on proceedings, brought in accordance with the conditions laid down in the fourth paragraph of Article 263 of this Treaty, reviewing the legality of decisions providing for restrictive measures against natural or legal persons adopted by the Council on the basis of Chapter 2 of Title V of the Treaty on European Union.

Article 276
In exercising its powers regarding the provisions of Chapters 4 and 5 of Title V of Part Three relating to the area of freedom, security and justice, the Court of Justice of the European Union shall have no jurisdiction to review the validity or proportionality of operations carried out by the police or other law-enforcement services of a Member State or the exercise of the responsibilities incumbent upon Member States with regard to the maintenance of law and order and the safeguarding of internal security.

Article 277 (ex Article 241 TEC)
Notwithstanding the expiry of the period laid down in Article 263, sixth paragraph, any party may, in proceedings in which an act of general application adopted by an institution, body, office or agency of the Union is at issue, plead the grounds specified in Article 263, second paragraph, in order to invoke before the Court of Justice of the European Union the inapplicability of that act.

Article 278 (ex Article 242 TEC)
Actions brought before the Court of Justice of the European Union shall not have suspensory effect. The Court may, however, if it considers that circumstances so require, order that application of the contested act be suspended.

Article 279 (ex Article 243 TEC)
The Court of Justice of the European Union may in any cases before it prescribe any necessary interim measures.

Article 280 (ex Article 244 TEC)
The judgments of the Court of Justice of the European Union shall be enforceable under the conditions laid down in Article 299.

Article 281 (ex Article 245 TEC)
The Statute of the Court of Justice of the European Union shall be laid down in a separate Protocol.

The European Parliament and the Council, acting in accordance with the ordinary legislative procedure, may amend the provisions of the Statute, with the exception of Title I and Article 64. The European Parliament and the Council shall act either at the request of the Court of Justice and after consultation of the Commission, or on a proposal from the Commission and after consultation of the Court of Justice.

SECTION 6 THE EUROPEAN CENTRAL BANK

Article 282
1.   The European Central Bank, together with the national central banks, shall constitute the European System of Central Banks (ESCB). The European Central Bank, together with the national central banks of the Member States whose currency is the euro, which constitute the Eurosystem, shall conduct the monetary policy of the Union.

2.   The ESCB shall be governed by the decision-making bodies of the European Central Bank. The primary objective of the ESCB shall be to maintain price stability. Without prejudice to that objective, it shall support the general economic policies in the Union in order to contribute to the achievement of the latter's objectives.

3.   The European Central Bank shall have legal personality. It alone may authorise the issue of the euro. It shall be independent in the exercise of its powers and in the management of its finances. Union institutions, bodies, offices and agencies and the governments of the Member States shall respect that independence.

4.   The European Central Bank shall adopt such measures as are necessary to carry out its tasks in accordance with Articles 127 to 133, with Article 138, and with the conditions laid down in the Statute of the ESCB and of the ECB. In accordance with these same Articles, those Member States whose currency is not the euro, and their central banks, shall retain their powers in monetary matters.

5.   Within the areas falling within its responsibilities, the European Central Bank shall be consulted on all proposed Union acts, and all proposals for regulation at national level, and may give an opinion.

Article 283 (ex Article 112 TEC)

1.   The Governing Council of the European Central Bank shall comprise the members of the Executive Board of the European Central Bank and the Governors of the national central banks of the Member States whose currency is the euro.

2.   The Executive Board shall comprise the President, the Vice-President and four other members.

The President, the Vice-President and the other members of the Executive Board shall be appointed by the European Council, acting by a qualified majority, from among persons of recognised standing and professional experience in monetary or banking matters, on a recommendation from the Council, after it has consulted the European Parliament and the Governing Council of the European Central Bank.

Their term of office shall be eight years and shall not be renewable.

Only nationals of Member States may be members of the Executive Board.

Article 284 (ex Article 113 TEC)

1.   The President of the Council and a Member of the Commission may participate, without having the right to vote, in meetings of the Governing Council of the European Central Bank.

The President of the Council may submit a motion for deliberation to the Governing Council of the European Central Bank.

2.   The President of the European Central Bank shall be invited to participate in Council meetings when the Council is discussing matters relating to the objectives and tasks of the ESCB.

3.   The European Central Bank shall address an annual report on the activities of the ESCB and on the monetary policy of both the previous and current year to the European Parliament, the Council and the Commission, and also to the European Council. The President of the European Central Bank shall present this report to the Council and to the European Parliament, which may hold a general debate on that basis.

The President of the European Central Bank and the other members of the Executive Board may, at the request of the European Parliament or on their own initiative, be heard by the competent committees of the European Parliament.

SECTION 7   THE COURT OF AUDITORS

Article 285 (ex Article 246 TEC)

The Court of Auditors shall carry out the Union's audit.

It shall consist of one national of each Member State. Its Members shall be completely independent in the performance of their duties, in the Union's general interest.

Article 286 (ex Article 247 TEC)

1. The Members of the Court of Auditors shall be chosen from among persons who belong or have belonged in their respective States to external audit bodies or who are especially qualified for this office. Their independence must be beyond doubt.

2. The Members of the Court of Auditors shall be appointed for a term of six years. The Council, after consulting the European Parliament, shall adopt the list of Members drawn up in accordance with the proposals made by each Member State. The term of office of the Members of the Court of Auditors shall be renewable.

   They shall elect the President of the Court of Auditors from among their number for a term of three years. The President may be re-elected.

3. In the performance of these duties, the Members of the Court of Auditors shall neither seek nor take instructions from any government or from any other body. The Members of the Court of Auditors shall refrain from any action incompatible with their duties.

4. The Members of the Court of Auditors may not, during their term of office, engage in any other occupation, whether gainful or not. When entering upon their duties they shall give a solemn undertaking that, both during and after their term of office, they will respect the obligations arising therefrom and in particular their duty to behave with integrity and discretion as regards the acceptance, after they have ceased to hold office, of certain appointments or benefits.

5. Apart from normal replacement, or death, the duties of a Member of the Court of Auditors shall end when he resigns, or is compulsorily retired by a ruling of the Court of Justice pursuant to paragraph 6.

   The vacancy thus caused shall be filled for the remainder of the Member's term of office.

   Save in the case of compulsory retirement, Members of the Court of Auditors shall remain in office until they have been replaced.

6. A Member of the Court of Auditors may be deprived of his office or of his right to a pension or other benefits in its stead only if the Court of Justice, at the request of the Court of Auditors, finds that he no longer fulfils the requisite conditions or meets the obligations arising from his office.

7. The Council shall determine the conditions of employment of the President and the Members of the Court of Auditors and in particular their salaries, allowances and pensions. It shall also determine any payment to be made instead of remuneration.

8. The provisions of the Protocol on the privileges and immunities of the European Union applicable to the Judges of the Court of Justice of the European Union shall also apply to the Members of the Court of Auditors.

Article 287 (ex Article 248 TEC)

1. The Court of Auditors shall examine the accounts of all revenue and expenditure of the Union. It shall also examine the accounts of all revenue and expenditure of all bodies,

offices or agencies set up by the Union in so far as the relevant constituent instrument does not preclude such examination.

The Court of Auditors shall provide the European Parliament and the Council with a statement of assurance as to the reliability of the accounts and the legality and regularity of the underlying transactions which shall be published in the *Official Journal of the European Union*. This statement may be supplemented by specific assessments for each major area of Union activity.

2.   The Court of Auditors shall examine whether all revenue has been received and all expenditure incurred in a lawful and regular manner and whether the financial management has been sound. In doing so, it shall report in particular on any cases of irregularity.

The audit of revenue shall be carried out on the basis both of the amounts established as due and the amounts actually paid to the Union.

The audit of expenditure shall be carried out on the basis both of commitments undertaken and payments made.

These audits may be carried out before the closure of accounts for the financial year in question.

3.   The audit shall be based on records and, if necessary, performed on the spot in the other institutions of the Union, on the premises of any body, office or agency which manages revenue or expenditure on behalf of the Union and in the Member States, including on the premises of any natural or legal person in receipt of payments from the budget. In the Member States the audit shall be carried out in liaison with national audit bodies or, if these do not have the necessary powers, with the competent national departments. The Court of Auditors and the national audit bodies of the Member States shall cooperate in a spirit of trust while maintaining their independence. These bodies or departments shall inform the Court of Auditors whether they intend to take part in the audit.

The other institutions of the Union, any bodies, offices or agencies managing revenue or expenditure on behalf of the Union, any natural or legal person in receipt of payments from the budget, and the national audit bodies or, if these do not have the necessary powers, the competent national departments, shall forward to the Court of Auditors, at its request, any document or information necessary to carry out its task.

In respect of the European Investment Bank's activity in managing Union expenditure and revenue, the Court's rights of access to information held by the Bank shall be governed by an agreement between the Court, the Bank and the Commission. In the absence of an agreement, the Court shall nevertheless have access to information necessary for the audit of Union expenditure and revenue managed by the Bank.

4.   The Court of Auditors shall draw up an annual report after the close of each financial year. It shall be forwarded to the other institutions of the Union and shall be published, together with the replies of these institutions to the observations of the Court of Auditors, in the *Official Journal of the European Union*.

The Court of Auditors may also, at any time, submit observations, particularly in the form of special reports, on specific questions and deliver opinions at the request of one of the other institutions of the Union.

It shall adopt its annual reports, special reports or opinions by a majority of its Members. However, it may establish internal chambers in order to adopt certain categories of reports or opinions under the conditions laid down by its Rules of Procedure.

It shall assist the European Parliament and the Council in exercising their powers of control over the implementation of the budget.

The Court of Auditors shall draw up its Rules of Procedure. Those rules shall require the approval of the Council.

Chapter 2 LEGAL ACTS OF THE UNION, ADOPTION PROCEDURES AND OTHER PROVISIONS

SECTION 1 THE LEGAL ACTS OF THE UNION

Article 288 (ex Article 249 TEC)

To exercise the Union's competences, the institutions shall adopt regulations, directives, decisions, recommendations and opinions.

A regulation shall have general application. It shall be binding in its entirety and directly applicable in all Member States.

A directive shall be binding, as to the result to be achieved, upon each Member State to which it is addressed, but shall leave to the national authorities the choice of form and methods.

A decision shall be binding in its entirety. A decision which specifies those to whom it is addressed shall be binding only on them.

Recommendations and opinions shall have no binding force.

Article 289

1. The ordinary legislative procedure shall consist in the joint adoption by the European Parliament and the Council of a regulation, directive or decision on a proposal from the Commission. This procedure is defined in Article 294.

2. In the specific cases provided for by the Treaties, the adoption of a regulation, directive or decision by the European Parliament with the participation of the Council, or by the latter with the participation of the European Parliament, shall constitute a special legislative procedure.

3. Legal acts adopted by legislative procedure shall constitute legislative acts.

4. In the specific cases provided for by the Treaties, legislative acts may be adopted on the initiative of a group of Member States or of the European Parliament, on a recommendation from the European Central Bank or at the request of the Court of Justice or the European Investment Bank.

Article 290

1. A legislative act may delegate to the Commission the power to adopt non-legislative acts of general application to supplement or amend certain non-essential elements of the legislative act.

    The objectives, content, scope and duration of the delegation of power shall be explicitly defined in the legislative acts. The essential elements of an area shall be reserved for the legislative act and accordingly shall not be the subject of a delegation of power.

2. Legislative acts shall explicitly lay down the conditions to which the delegation is subject; these conditions may be as follows:
    (a) the European Parliament or the Council may decide to revoke the delegation;
    (b) the delegated act may enter into force only if no objection has been expressed by the European Parliament or the Council within a period set by the legislative act.

For the purposes of (a) and (b), the European Parliament shall act by a majority of its component members, and the Council by a qualified majority.

3.   The adjective 'delegated' shall be inserted in the title of delegated acts.

Article 291

1.   Member States shall adopt all measures of national law necessary to implement legally binding Union acts.

2.   Where uniform conditions for implementing legally binding Union acts are needed, those acts shall confer implementing powers on the Commission, or, in duly justified specific cases and in the cases provided for in Articles 24 and 26 of the Treaty on European Union, on the Council.

3.   For the purposes of paragraph 2, the European Parliament and the Council, acting by means of regulations in accordance with the ordinary legislative procedure, shall lay down in advance the rules and general principles concerning mechanisms for control by Member States of the Commission's exercise of implementing powers.

4.   The word 'implementing' shall be inserted in the title of implementing acts.

Article 292

The Council shall adopt recommendations. It shall act on a proposal from the Commission in all cases where the Treaties provide that it shall adopt acts on a proposal from the Commission. It shall act unanimously in those areas in which unanimity is required for the adoption of a Union act. The Commission, and the European Central Bank in the specific cases provided for in the Treaties, shall adopt recommendations.

SECTION 2 PROCEDURES FOR THE ADOPTION OF ACTS AND OTHER PROVISIONS

Article 293 (ex Article 250 TEC)

1.   Where, pursuant to the Treaties, the Council acts on a proposal from the Commission, it may amend that proposal only by acting unanimously, except in the cases referred to in paragraphs 10 and 13 of Article 294, in Articles 310, 312 and 314 and in the second paragraph of Article 315.

2.   As long as the Council has not acted, the Commission may alter its proposal at any time during the procedures leading to the adoption of a Union act.

Article 294 (ex Article 251 TEC)

1.   Where reference is made in the Treaties to the ordinary legislative procedure for the adoption of an act, the following procedure shall apply.

2.   The Commission shall submit a proposal to the European Parliament and the Council.

First reading

3.   The European Parliament shall adopt its position at first reading and communicate it to the Council.

4.   If the Council approves the European Parliament's position, the act concerned shall be adopted in the wording which corresponds to the position of the European Parliament.

5.   If the Council does not approve the European Parliament's position, it shall adopt its position at first reading and communicate it to the European Parliament.

6.   The Council shall inform the European Parliament fully of the reasons which led it to adopt its position at first reading. The Commission shall inform the European Parliament fully of its position.

Second reading

7.   If, within three months of such communication, the European Parliament:
   (a) approves the Council's position at first reading or has not taken a decision, the act concerned shall be deemed to have been adopted in the wording which corresponds to the position of the Council;
   (b) rejects, by a majority of its component members, the Council's position at first reading, the proposed act shall be deemed not to have been adopted;
   (c) proposes, by a majority of its component members, amendments to the Council's position at first reading, the text thus amended shall be forwarded to the Council and to the Commission, which shall deliver an opinion on those amendments.

8.   If, within three months of receiving the European Parliament's amendments, the Council, acting by a qualified majority:
   (a) approves all those amendments, the act in question shall be deemed to have been adopted;
   (b) does not approve all the amendments, the President of the Council, in agreement with the President of the European Parliament, shall within six weeks convene a meeting of the Conciliation Committee.

9.   The Council shall act unanimously on the amendments on which the Commission has delivered a negative opinion.

Conciliation

10.   The Conciliation Committee, which shall be composed of the members of the Council or their representatives and an equal number of members representing the European Parliament, shall have the task of reaching agreement on a joint text, by a qualified majority of the members of the Council or their representatives and by a majority of the members representing the European Parliament within six weeks of its being convened, on the basis of the positions of the European Parliament and the Council at second reading.

11.   The Commission shall take part in the Conciliation Committee's proceedings and shall take all necessary initiatives with a view to reconciling the positions of the European Parliament and the Council.

12.   If, within six weeks of its being convened, the Conciliation Committee does not approve the joint text, the proposed act shall be deemed not to have been adopted.

Third reading

13.   If, within that period, the Conciliation Committee approves a joint text, the European Parliament, acting by a majority of the votes cast, and the Council, acting by a qualified majority, shall each have a period of six weeks from that approval in which to adopt the act in question in accordance with the joint text. If they fail to do so, the proposed act shall be deemed not to have been adopted.

14.   The periods of three months and six weeks referred to in this Article shall be extended by a maximum of one month and two weeks respectively at the initiative of the European Parliament or the Council.

Special provisions

15.   Where, in the cases provided for in the Treaties, a legislative act is submitted to the ordinary legislative procedure on the initiative of a group of Member States, on a

recommendation by the European Central Bank, or at the request of the Court of Justice, paragraph 2, the second sentence of paragraph 6, and paragraph 9 shall not apply.

In such cases, the European Parliament and the Council shall communicate the proposed act to the Commission with their positions at first and second readings. The European Parliament or the Council may request the opinion of the Commission throughout the procedure, which the Commission may also deliver on its own initiative. It may also, if it deems it necessary, take part in the Conciliation Committee in accordance with paragraph 11.

Article 295

The European Parliament, the Council and the Commission shall consult each other and by common agreement make arrangements for their cooperation. To that end, they may, in compliance with the Treaties, conclude interinstitutional agreements which may be of a binding nature.

Article 296 (ex Article 253 TEC)

Where the Treaties do not specify the type of act to be adopted, the institutions shall select it on a case-by-case basis, in compliance with the applicable procedures and with the principle of proportionality.

Legal acts shall state the reasons on which they are based and shall refer to any proposals, initiatives, recommendations, requests or opinions required by the Treaties.
When considering draft legislative acts, the European Parliament and the Council shall refrain from adopting acts not provided for by the relevant legislative procedure in the area in question.

Article 297 (ex Article 254 TEC)

1. Legislative acts adopted under the ordinary legislative procedure shall be signed by the President of the European Parliament and by the President of the Council.

   Legislative acts adopted under a special legislative procedure shall be signed by the President of the institution which adopted them.

   Legislative acts shall be published in the *Official Journal of the European Union*. They shall enter into force on the date specified in them or, in the absence thereof, on the twentieth day following that of their publication.

2. Non-legislative acts adopted in the form of regulations, directives or decisions, when the latter do not specify to whom they are addressed, shall be signed by the President of the institution which adopted them.

   Regulations and directives which are addressed to all Member States, as well as decisions which do not specify to whom they are addressed, shall be published in the *Official Journal of the European Union*. They shall enter into force on the date specified in them or, in the absence thereof, on the twentieth day following that of their publication.

   Other directives, and decisions which specify to whom they are addressed, shall be notified to those to whom they are addressed and shall take effect upon such notification.

Article 298

1. In carrying out their missions, the institutions, bodies, offices and agencies of the Union shall have the support of an open, efficient and independent European administration.

2. In compliance with the Staff Regulations and the Conditions of Employment adopted on the basis of Article 336, the European Parliament and the Council, acting by means of

regulations in accordance with the ordinary legislative procedure, shall establish provisions to that end.

Article 299 (ex Article 256 TEC)

Acts of the Council, the Commission or the European Central Bank which impose a pecuniary obligation on persons other than States, shall be enforceable.

Enforcement shall be governed by the rules of civil procedure in force in the State in the territory of which it is carried out. The order for its enforcement shall be appended to the decision, without other formality than verification of the authenticity of the decision, by the national authority which the government of each Member State shall designate for this purpose and shall make known to the Commission and to the Court of Justice of the European Union.

When these formalities have been completed on application by the party concerned, the latter may proceed to enforcement in accordance with the national law, by bringing the matter directly before the competent authority.

Enforcement may be suspended only by a decision of the Court. However, the courts of the country concerned shall have jurisdiction over complaints that enforcement is being carried out in an irregular manner.

Chapter 3 THE UNION'S ADVISORY BODIES

Article 300

1. The European Parliament, the Council and the Commission shall be assisted by an Economic and Social Committee and a Committee of the Regions, exercising advisory functions.

2. The Economic and Social Committee shall consist of representatives of organisations of employers, of the employed, and of other parties representative of civil society, notably in socio-economic, civic, professional and cultural areas.

3. The Committee of the Regions shall consist of representatives of regional and local bodies who either hold a regional or local authority electoral mandate or are politically accountable to an elected assembly.

4. The members of the Economic and Social Committee and of the Committee of the Regions shall not be bound by any mandatory instructions. They shall be completely independent in the performance of their duties, in the Union's general interest.

5. The rules referred to in paragraphs 2 and 3 governing the nature of the composition of the Committees shall be reviewed at regular intervals by the Council to take account of economic, social and demographic developments within the Union. The Council, on a proposal from the Commission, shall adopt decisions to that end.

SECTION 1 THE ECONOMIC AND SOCIAL COMMITTEE

Article 301 (ex Article 258 TEC)

The number of members of the Economic and Social Committee shall not exceed 350.

The Council, acting unanimously on a proposal from the Commission, shall adopt a decision determining the Committee's composition.

The Council shall determine the allowances of members of the Committee.

Article 302 (ex Article 259 TEC)

1. The members of the Committee shall be appointed for five years The Council shall adopt the list of members drawn up in accordance with the proposals made by each Member State. The term of office of the members of the Committee shall be renewable.

2. The Council shall act after consulting the Commission. It may obtain the opinion of European bodies which are representative of the various economic and social sectors and of civil society to which the Union's activities are of concern.

Article 303 (ex Article 260 TEC)

The Committee shall elect its chairman and officers from among its members for a term of two and a half years.

It shall adopt its Rules of Procedure.

The Committee shall be convened by its chairman at the request of the European Parliament, the Council or of the Commission. It may also meet on its own initiative.

Article 304 (ex Article 262 TEC)

The Committee shall be consulted by the European Parliament, by the Council or by the Commission where the Treaties so provide. The Committee may be consulted by these institutions in all cases in which they consider it appropriate. It may issue an opinion on its own initiative in cases in which it considers such action appropriate.

The European Parliament, the Council or the Commission shall, if it considers it necessary, set the Committee, for the submission of its opinion, a time limit which may not be less than one month from the date on which the chairman receives notification to this effect. Upon expiry of the time limit, the absence of an opinion shall not prevent further action.

The opinion of the Committee, together with a record of the proceedings, shall be forwarded to the European Parliament, to the Council and to the Commission.

SECTION 2 THE COMMITTEE OF THE REGIONS

Article 305 (ex Article 263, second, third and fourth paragraphs, TEC)

The number of members of the Committee of the Regions shall not exceed 350.

The Council, acting unanimously on a proposal from the Commission, shall adopt a decision determining the Committee's composition.

The members of the Committee and an equal number of alternate members shall be appointed for five years. Their term of office shall be renewable. The Council shall adopt the list of members and alternate members drawn up in accordance with the proposals made by each Member State. When the mandate referred to in Article 300(3) on the basis of which they were proposed comes to an end, the term of office of members of the Committee shall terminate automatically and they shall then be replaced for the remainder of the said term of office in accordance with the same procedure. No member of the Committee shall at the same time be a Member of the European Parliament.

Article 306 (ex Article 264 TEC)

The Committee of the Regions shall elect its chairman and officers from among its members for a term of two and a half years.

It shall adopt its Rules of Procedure.

The Committee shall be convened by its chairman at the request of the European Parliament, the Council or of the Commission. It may also meet on its own initiative.

Article 307 (ex Article 265 TEC)
The Committee of the Regions shall be consulted by the European Parliament, by the Council or by the Commission where the Treaties so provide and in all other cases, in particular those which concern cross-border cooperation, in which one of these institutions considers it appropriate.

The European Parliament, the Council or the Commission shall, if it considers it necessary, set the Committee, for the submission of its opinion, a time limit which may not be less than one month from the date on which the chairman receives notification to this effect. Upon expiry of the time limit, the absence of an opinion shall not prevent further action.

Where the Economic and Social Committee is consulted pursuant to Article 304, the Committee of the Regions shall be informed by the European Parliament, the Council or the Commission of the request for an opinion. Where it considers that specific regional interests are involved, the Committee of the Regions may issue an opinion on the matter.

It may issue an opinion on its own initiative in cases in which it considers such action appropriate.

The opinion of the Committee, together with a record of the proceedings, shall be forwarded to the European Parliament, to the Council and to the Commission.

Chapter 4 THE EUROPEAN INVESTMENT BANK

Article 308 (ex Article 266 TEC)
The European Investment Bank shall have legal personality.

The members of the European Investment Bank shall be the Member States.

The Statute of the European Investment Bank is laid down in a Protocol annexed to the Treaties. The Council acting unanimously in accordance with a special legislative procedure, at the request of the European Investment Bank and after consulting the European Parliament and the Commission, or on a proposal from the Commission and after consulting the European Parliament and the European Investment Bank, may amend the Statute of the Bank.

Article 309 (ex Article 267 TEC)
The task of the European Investment Bank shall be to contribute, by having recourse to the capital market and utilising its own resources, to the balanced and steady development of the internal market in the interest of the Union. For this purpose the Bank shall, operating on a non-profit-making basis, grant loans and give guarantees which facilitate the financing of the following projects in all sectors of the economy:
(a)   projects for developing less-developed regions;

(b)   projects for modernising or converting undertakings or for developing fresh activities called for by the establishment or functioning of the internal market, where these projects are of such a size or nature that they cannot be entirely financed by the various means available in the individual Member States;

(c)   projects of common interest to several Member States which are of such a size or nature that they cannot be entirely financed by the various means available in the individual Member States.

In carrying out its task, the Bank shall facilitate the financing of investment programmes in conjunction with assistance from the Structural Funds and other Union Financial Instruments.

TITLE II
FINANCIAL PROVISIONS

Article 310 (ex Article 268 TEC)

1.   All items of revenue and expenditure of the Union shall be included in estimates to be drawn up for each financial year and shall be shown in the budget.

The Union's annual budget shall be established by the European Parliament and the Council in accordance with Article 314.

The revenue and expenditure shown in the budget shall be in balance.

2.   The expenditure shown in the budget shall be authorised for the annual budgetary period in accordance with the regulation referred to in Article 322.

3.   The implementation of expenditure shown in the budget shall require the prior adoption of a legally binding Union act providing a legal basis for its action and for the implementation of the corresponding expenditure in accordance with the regulation referred to in Article 322, except in cases for which that law provides.

4.   With a view to maintaining budgetary discipline, the Union shall not adopt any act which is likely to have appreciable implications for the budget without providing an assurance that the expenditure arising from such an act is capable of being financed within the limit of the Union's own resources and in compliance with the multiannual financial framework referred to in Article 312.

5.   The budget shall be implemented in accordance with the principle of sound financial management. Member States shall cooperate with the Union to ensure that the appropriations entered in the budget are used in accordance with this principle.

6.   The Union and the Member States, in accordance with Article 325, shall counter fraud and any other illegal activities affecting the financial interests of the Union.

Chapter 1 THE UNION'S OWN RESOURCES

Article 311 (ex Article 269 TEC)

The Union shall provide itself with the means necessary to attain its objectives and carry through its policies.

Without prejudice to other revenue, the budget shall be financed wholly from own resources.

The Council, acting in accordance with a special legislative procedure, shall unanimously and after consulting the European Parliament adopt a decision laying down the provisions relating to the system of own resources of the Union. In this context it may establish new categories of own resources or abolish an existing category. That decision shall not enter into force until it is approved by the Member States in accordance with their respective constitutional requirements.

The Council, acting by means of regulations in accordance with a special legislative procedure, shall lay down implementing measures for the Union's own resources system in so far as this is provided for in the decision adopted on the basis of the third paragraph. The Council shall act after obtaining the consent of the European Parliament.

Chapter 2 THE MULTIANNUAL FINANCIAL FRAMEWORK

Article 312

1.   The multiannual financial framework shall ensure that Union expenditure develops in an orderly manner and within the limits of its own resources.

It shall be established for a period of at least five years.

The annual budget of the Union shall comply with the multiannual financial framework.

2.   The Council, acting in accordance with a special legislative procedure, shall adopt a regulation laying down the multiannual financial framework. The Council shall act unanimously after obtaining the consent of the European Parliament, which shall be given by a majority of its component members.

The European Council may, unanimously, adopt a decision authorising the Council to act by a qualified majority when adopting the regulation referred to in the first subparagraph.

3.   The financial framework shall determine the amounts of the annual ceilings on commitment appropriations by category of expenditure and of the annual ceiling on payment appropriations. The categories of expenditure, limited in number, shall correspond to the Union's major sectors of activity.

The financial framework shall lay down any other provisions required for the annual budgetary procedure to run smoothly.

4.   Where no Council regulation determining a new financial framework has been adopted by the end of the previous financial framework, the ceilings and other provisions corresponding to the last year of that framework shall be extended until such time as that act is adopted.

5.   Throughout the procedure leading to the adoption of the financial framework, the European Parliament, the Council and the Commission shall take any measure necessary to facilitate its adoption.

Chapter 3 THE UNION'S ANNUAL BUDGET

Article 313 (ex Article 272(1), TEC)
The financial year shall run from 1 January to 31 December.

Article 314 (ex Article 272(2) to (10), TEC)
The European Parliament and the Council, acting in accordance with a special legislative procedure, shall establish the Union's annual budget in accordance with the following provisions.

1.   With the exception of the European Central Bank, each institution shall, before 1 July, draw up estimates of its expenditure for the following financial year. The Commission shall consolidate these estimates in a draft budget, which may contain different estimates.

The draft budget shall contain an estimate of revenue and an estimate of expenditure.

2.   The Commission shall submit a proposal containing the draft budget to the European Parliament and to the Council not later than 1 September of the year preceding that in which the budget is to be implemented.

The Commission may amend the draft budget during the procedure until such time as the Conciliation Committee, referred to in paragraph 5, is convened.

3.   The Council shall adopt its position on the draft budget and forward it to the European Parliament not later than 1 October of the year preceding that in which the budget is to be implemented. The Council shall inform the European Parliament in full of the reasons which led it to adopt its position.

4.   If, within forty-two days of such communication, the European Parliament:
      (a) approves the position of the Council, the budget shall be adopted;
      (b) has not taken a decision, the budget shall be deemed to have been adopted;

(c) adopts amendments by a majority of its component members, the amended draft shall be forwarded to the Council and to the Commission. The President of the European Parliament, in agreement with the President of the Council, shall immediately convene a meeting of the Conciliation Committee. However, if within ten days of the draft being forwarded the Council informs the European Parliament that it has approved all its amendments, the Conciliation Committee shall not meet.

5.   The Conciliation Committee, which shall be composed of the members of the Council or their representatives and an equal number of members representing the European Parliament, shall have the task of reaching agreement on a joint text, by a qualified majority of the members of the Council or their representatives and by a majority of the representatives of the European Parliament within twenty-one days of its being convened, on the basis of the positions of the European Parliament and the Council.

The Commission shall take part in the Conciliation Committee's proceedings and shall take all the necessary initiatives with a view to reconciling the positions of the European Parliament and the Council.

6.   If, within the twenty-one days referred to in paragraph 5, the Conciliation Committee agrees on a joint text, the European Parliament and the Council shall each have a period of fourteen days from the date of that agreement in which to approve the joint text.

7.   If, within the period of fourteen days referred to in paragraph 6:
(a) the European Parliament and the Council both approve the joint text or fail to take a decision, or if one of these institutions approves the joint text while the other one fails to take a decision, the budget shall be deemed to be definitively adopted in accordance with the joint text; or
(b) the European Parliament, acting by a majority of its component members, and the Council both reject the joint text, or if one of these institutions rejects the joint text while the other one fails to take a decision, a new draft budget shall be submitted by the Commission; or
(c) the European Parliament, acting by a majority of its component members, rejects the joint text while the Council approves it, a new draft budget shall be submitted by the Commission; or
(d) the European Parliament approves the joint text whilst the Council rejects it, the European Parliament may, within fourteen days from the date of the rejection by the Council and acting by a majority of its component members and three-fifths of the votes cast, decide to confirm all or some of the amendments referred to in paragraph 4(c). Where a European Parliament amendment is not confirmed, the position agreed in the Conciliation Committee on the budget heading which is the subject of the amendment shall be retained. The budget shall be deemed to be definitively adopted on this basis.

8.   If, within the twenty-one days referred to in paragraph 5, the Conciliation Committee does not agree on a joint text, a new draft budget shall be submitted by the Commission.

9.   When the procedure provided for in this Article has been completed, the President of the European Parliament shall declare that the budget has been definitively adopted.

10.   Each institution shall exercise the powers conferred upon it under this Article in compliance with the Treaties and the acts adopted thereunder, with particular regard to the Union's own resources and the balance between revenue and expenditure.

Article 315 (ex Article 273 TEC)

If, at the beginning of a financial year, the budget has not yet been definitively adopted, a sum equivalent to not more than one twelfth of the budget appropriations for the preceding financial year may be spent each month in respect of any chapter of the budget in accordance with the provisions of the Regulations made pursuant to Article 322; that sum shall not, however, exceed one twelfth of the appropriations provided for in the same chapter of the draft budget.

The Council on a proposal by the Commission, may, provided that the other conditions laid down in the first paragraph are observed, authorise expenditure in excess of one twelfth in accordance with the regulations made pursuant to Article 322. The Council shall forward the decision immediately to the European Parliament.

The decision referred to in the second paragraph shall lay down the necessary measures relating to resources to ensure application of this Article, in accordance with the acts referred to in Article 311.

It shall enter into force thirty days following its adoption if the European Parliament, acting by a majority of its component Members, has not decided to reduce this expenditure within that time- limit.

Article 316 (ex Article 271 TEC)

In accordance with conditions to be laid down pursuant to Article 322, any appropriations, other than those relating to staff expenditure, that are unexpended at the end of the financial year may be carried forward to the next financial year only.

Appropriations shall be classified under different chapters grouping items of expenditure according to their nature or purpose and subdivided in accordance with the regulations made pursuant to Article 322.

The expenditure of the European Parliament, the European Council and the Council, the Commission and the Court of Justice of the European Union shall be set out in separate parts of the budget, without prejudice to special arrangements for certain common items of expenditure.

Chapter 4 IMPLEMENTATION OF THE BUDGET AND DISCHARGE

Article 317 (ex Article 274 TEC)

The Commission shall implement the budget in cooperation with the Member States, in accordance with the provisions of the regulations made pursuant to Article 322, on its own responsibility and within the limits of the appropriations, having regard to the principles of sound financial management. Member States shall cooperate with the Commission to ensure that the appropriations are used in accordance with the principles of sound financial management.

The regulations shall lay down the control and audit obligations of the Member States in the implementation of the budget and the resulting responsibilities. They shall also lay down the responsibilities and detailed rules for each institution concerning its part in effecting its own expenditure.

Within the budget, the Commission may, subject to the limits and conditions laid down in the regulations made pursuant to Article 322, transfer appropriations from one chapter to another or from one subdivision to another.

Article 318 (ex Article 275 TEC)

The Commission shall submit annually to the European Parliament and to the Council the accounts of the preceding financial year relating to the implementation of the budget. The

Commission shall also forward to them a financial statement of the assets and liabilities of the Union.

The Commission shall also submit to the European Parliament and to the Council an evaluation report on the Union's finances based on the results achieved, in particular in relation to the indications given by the European Parliament and the Council pursuant to Article 319.

Article 319 (ex Article 276 TEC)

1. The European Parliament, acting on a recommendation from the Council, shall give a discharge to the Commission in respect of the implementation of the budget. To this end, the Council and the European Parliament in turn shall examine the accounts, the financial statement and the evaluation report referred to in Article 318, the annual report by the Court of Auditors together with the replies of the institutions under audit to the observations of the Court of Auditors, the statement of assurance referred to in Article 287(1), second subparagraph and any relevant special reports by the Court of Auditors.

2. Before giving a discharge to the Commission, or for any other purpose in connection with the exercise of its powers over the implementation of the budget, the European Parliament may ask to hear the Commission give evidence with regard to the execution of expenditure or the operation of financial control systems. The Commission shall submit any necessary information to the European Parliament at the latter's request.

3. The Commission shall take all appropriate steps to act on the observations in the decisions giving discharge and on other observations by the European Parliament relating to the execution of expenditure, as well as on comments accompanying the recommendations on discharge adopted by the Council.

    At the request of the European Parliament or the Council, the Commission shall report on the measures taken in the light of these observations and comments and in particular on the instructions given to the departments which are responsible for the implementation of the budget. These reports shall also be forwarded to the Court of Auditors.

Chapter 5 COMMON PROVISIONS

Article 320 (ex Article 277 TEC)
The multiannual financial framework and the annual budget shall be drawn up in euro.

Article 321 (ex Article 278 TEC)
The Commission may, provided it notifies the competent authorities of the Member States concerned, transfer into the currency of one of the Member States its holdings in the currency of another Member State, to the extent necessary to enable them to be used for purposes which come within the scope of the Treaties. The Commission shall as far as possible avoid making such transfers if it possesses cash or liquid assets in the currencies which it needs.

The Commission shall deal with each Member State through the authority designated by the State concerned. In carrying out financial operations the Commission shall employ the services of the bank of issue of the Member State concerned or of any other financial institution approved by that State.

Article 322 (ex Article 279 TEC)

1. The European Parliament and the Council, acting in accordance with the ordinary legislative procedure, and after consulting the Court of Auditors, shall adopt by means of regulations:
    (a) the financial rules which determine in particular the procedure to be adopted for establishing and implementing the budget and for presenting and auditing accounts;

(b) rules providing for checks on the responsibility of financial actors, in particular authorising officers and accounting officers.

2.   The Council, acting on a proposal from the Commission and after consulting the European Parliament and the Court of Auditors, shall determine the methods and procedure whereby the budget revenue provided under the arrangements relating to the Union's own resources shall be made available to the Commission, and determine the measures to be applied, if need be, to meet cash requirements.

Article 323
The European Parliament, the Council and the Commission shall ensure that the financial means are made available to allow the Union to fulfil its legal obligations in respect of third parties.

Article 324
Regular meetings between the Presidents of the European Parliament, the Council and the Commission shall be convened, on the initiative of the Commission, under the budgetary procedures referred to in this Title. The Presidents shall take all the necessary steps to promote consultation and the reconciliation of the positions of the institutions over which they preside in order to facilitate the implementation of this Title.

Chapter 6 COMBATTING FRAUD

Article 325 (ex Article 280 TEC)
1.   The Union and the Member States shall counter fraud and any other illegal activities affecting the financial interests of the Union through measures to be taken in accordance with this Article, which shall act as a deterrent and be such as to afford effective protection in the Member States, and in all the Union's institutions, bodies, offices and agencies.

2.   Member States shall take the same measures to counter fraud affecting the financial interests of the Union as they take to counter fraud affecting their own financial interests.

3.   Without prejudice to other provisions of the Treaties, the Member States shall coordinate their action aimed at protecting the financial interests of the Union against fraud. To this end they shall organise, together with the Commission, close and regular cooperation between the competent authorities.

4.   The European Parliament and the Council, acting in accordance with the ordinary legislative procedure, after consulting the Court of Auditors, shall adopt the necessary measures in the fields of the prevention of and fight against fraud affecting the financial interests of the Union with a view to affording effective and equivalent protection in the Member States and in all the Union's institutions, bodies, offices and agencies.

5.   The Commission, in cooperation with Member States, shall each year submit to the European Parliament and to the Council a report on the measures taken for the implementation of this Article.

TITLE III
ENHANCED COOPERATION

Article 326 (ex Articles 27a to 27e, 40 to 40b and 43 to 45 TEU and ex Articles 11 and 11a TEC)
Any enhanced cooperation shall comply with the Treaties and Union law.

Such cooperation shall not undermine the internal market or economic, social and territorial cohesion. It shall not constitute a barrier to or discrimination in trade between Member States, nor shall it distort competition between them.

Article 327 (ex Articles 27a to 27e, 40 to 40b and 43 to 45 TEU and ex Articles 11 and 11a TEC)

Any enhanced cooperation shall respect the competences, rights and obligations of those Member States which do not participate in it. Those Member States shall not impede its implementation by the participating Member States.

Article 328 (ex Articles 27a to 27e, 40 to 40b and 43 to 45 TEU and ex Articles 11 and 11a TEC)

1. When enhanced cooperation is being established, it shall be open to all Member States, subject to compliance with any conditions of participation laid down by the authorising decision. It shall also be open to them at any other time, subject to compliance with the acts already adopted within that framework, in addition to those conditions.

    The Commission and the Member States participating in enhanced cooperation shall ensure that they promote participation by as many Member States as possible.

2. The Commission and, where appropriate, the High Representative of the Union for Foreign Affairs and Security Policy shall keep the European Parliament and the Council regularly informed regarding developments in enhanced cooperation.

Article 329 (ex Articles 27a to 27e, 40 to 40b and 43 to 45 TEU and ex Articles 11 and 11a TEC)

1. Member States which wish to establish enhanced cooperation between themselves in one of the areas covered by the Treaties, with the exception of fields of exclusive competence and the common foreign and security policy, shall address a request to the Commission, specifying the scope and objectives of the enhanced cooperation proposed. The Commission may submit a proposal to the Council to that effect. In the event of the Commission not submitting a proposal, it shall inform the Member States concerned of the reasons for not doing so.

    Authorisation to proceed with the enhanced cooperation referred to in the first subparagraph shall be granted by the Council, on a proposal from the Commission and after obtaining the consent of the European Parliament.

2. The request of the Member States which wish to establish enhanced cooperation between themselves within the framework of the common foreign and security policy shall be addressed to the Council. It shall be forwarded to the High Representative of the Union for Foreign Affairs and Security Policy, who shall give an opinion on whether the enhanced cooperation proposed is consistent with the Union's common foreign and security policy, and to the Commission, which shall give its opinion in particular on whether the enhanced cooperation proposed is consistent with other Union policies. It shall also be forwarded to the European Parliament for information.

    Authorisation to proceed with enhanced cooperation shall be granted by a decision of the Council acting unanimously.

Article 330 (ex Articles 27a to 27e, 40 to 40b and 43 to 45 TEU and ex Articles 11 and 11a TEC)

All members of the Council may participate in its deliberations, but only members of the Council representing the Member States participating in enhanced cooperation shall take part in the vote.

Unanimity shall be constituted by the votes of the representatives of the participating Member States only.

A qualified majority shall be defined in accordance with Article 238(3).

Article 331 (ex Articles 27a to 27e, 40 to 40b and 43 to 45 TEU and ex Articles 11 and 11a TEC)

1. Any Member State which wishes to participate in enhanced cooperation in progress in one of the areas referred to in Article 329(1) shall notify its intention to the Council and the Commission.

   The Commission shall, within four months of the date of receipt of the notification, confirm the participation of the Member State concerned. It shall note where necessary that the conditions of participation have been fulfilled and shall adopt any transitional measures necessary with regard to the application of the acts already adopted within the framework of enhanced cooperation.

   However, if the Commission considers that the conditions of participation have not been fulfilled, it shall indicate the arrangements to be adopted to fulfil those conditions and shall set a deadline for re- examining the request. On the expiry of that deadline, it shall re-examine the request, in accordance with the procedure set out in the second subparagraph. If the Commission considers that the conditions of participation have still not been met, the Member State concerned may refer the matter to the Council, which shall decide on the request. The Council shall act in accordance with Article 330. It may also adopt the transitional measures referred to in the second subparagraph on a proposal from the Commission.

2. Any Member State which wishes to participate in enhanced cooperation in progress in the framework of the common foreign and security policy shall notify its intention to the Council, the High Representative of the Union for Foreign Affairs and Security Policy and the Commission.

   The Council shall confirm the participation of the Member State concerned, after consulting the High Representative of the Union for Foreign Affairs and Security Policy and after noting, where necessary, that the conditions of participation have been fulfilled. The Council, on a proposal from the High Representative, may also adopt any transitional measures necessary with regard to the application of the acts already adopted within the framework of enhanced cooperation. However, if the Council considers that the conditions of participation have not been fulfilled, it shall indicate the arrangements to be adopted to fulfil those conditions and shall set a deadline for re-examining the request for participation.

   For the purposes of this paragraph, the Council shall act unanimously and in accordance with Article 330.

Article 332 (ex Articles 27a to 27e, 40 to 40b and 43 to 45 TEU and ex Articles 11 and 11a TEC)

Expenditure resulting from implementation of enhanced cooperation, other than administrative costs entailed for the institutions, shall be borne by the participating Member States, unless all members of the Council, acting unanimously after consulting the European Parliament, decide otherwise.

Article 333 (ex Articles 27a to 27e, 40 to 40b and 43 to 45 TEU and ex Articles 11 and 11a TEC)

1. Where a provision of the Treaties which may be applied in the context of enhanced cooperation stipulates that the Council shall act unanimously, the Council, acting

unanimously in accordance with the arrangements laid down in Article 330, may adopt a decision stipulating that it will act by a qualified majority.

2.   Where a provision of the Treaties which may be applied in the context of enhanced cooperation stipulates that the Council shall adopt acts under a special legislative procedure, the Council, acting unanimously in accordance with the arrangements laid down in Article 330, may adopt a decision stipulating that it will act under the ordinary legislative procedure. The Council shall act after consulting the European Parliament.

3.   Paragraphs 1 and 2 shall not apply to decisions having military or defence implications.

Article 334 (ex Articles 27a to 27e, 40 to 40b and 43 to 45 TEU and ex Articles 11 and 11a TEC)
The Council and the Commission shall ensure the consistency of activities undertaken in the context of enhanced cooperation and the consistency of such activities with the policies of the Union, and shall cooperate to that end.

Part Seven GENERAL AND FINAL PROVISIONS

Article 335 (ex Article 282 TEC)
In each of the Member States, the Union shall enjoy the most extensive legal capacity accorded to legal persons under their laws; it may, in particular, acquire or dispose of movable and immovable property and may be a party to legal proceedings. To this end, the Union shall be represented by the Commission. However, the Union shall be represented by each of the institutions, by virtue of their administrative autonomy, in matters relating to their respective operation.

Article 336 (ex Article 283 TEC)
The European Parliament and the Council shall, acting by means of regulations in accordance with the ordinary legislative procedure and after consulting the other institutions concerned, lay down the Staff Regulations of Officials of the European Union and the Conditions of Employment of other servants of the Union.

Article 337 (ex Article 284 TEC)
The Commission may, within the limits and under conditions laid down by the Council acting by a simple majority in accordance with the provisions of the Treaties, collect any information and carry out any checks required for the performance of the tasks entrusted to it.

Article 338 (ex Article 285 TEC)
1.   Without prejudice to Article 5 of the Protocol on the Statute of the European System of Central Banks and of the European Central Bank, the European Parliament and the Council, acting in accordance with the ordinary legislative procedure, shall adopt measures for the production of statistics where necessary for the performance of the activities of the Union.

2.   The production of Union statistics shall conform to impartiality, reliability, objectivity, scientific independence, cost-effectiveness and statistical confidentiality; it shall not entail excessive burdens on economic operators.

Article 339 (ex Article 287 TEC)
The members of the institutions of the Union, the members of committees, and the officials and other servants of the Union shall be required, even after their duties have ceased, not to disclose information of the kind covered by the obligation of professional secrecy, in particular information about undertakings, their business relations or their cost components.

Article 340 (ex Article 288 TEC)
The contractual liability of the Union shall be governed by the law applicable to the contract in question.

In the case of non-contractual liability, the Union shall, in accordance with the general principles common to the laws of the Member States, make good any damage caused by its institutions or by its servants in the performance of their duties.

Notwithstanding the second paragraph, the European Central Bank shall, in accordance with the general principles common to the laws of the Member States, make good any damage caused by it or by its servants in the performance of their duties.

The personal liability of its servants towards the Union shall be governed by the provisions laid down in their Staff Regulations or in the Conditions of Employment applicable to them.

Article 341 (ex Article 289 TEC)
The seat of the institutions of the Union shall be determined by common accord of the governments of the Member States.

Article 342 (ex Article 290 TEC)
The rules governing the languages of the institutions of the Union shall, without prejudice to the provisions contained in the Statute of the Court of Justice of the European Union, be determined by the Council, acting unanimously by means of regulations.

Article 343 (ex Article 291 TEC)
The Union shall enjoy in the territories of the Member States such privileges and immunities as are necessary for the performance of its tasks, under the conditions laid down in the Protocol of 8 April 1965 on the privileges and immunities of the European Union. The same shall apply to the European Central Bank and the European Investment Bank.

Article 344 (ex Article 292 TEC)
Member States undertake not to submit a dispute concerning the interpretation or application of the Treaties to any method of settlement other than those provided for therein.

Article 345 (ex Article 295 TEC)
The Treaties shall in no way prejudice the rules in Member States governing the system of property ownership.

Article 346 (ex Article 296 TEC)
1.   The provisions of the Treaties shall not preclude the application of the following rules:
      (a) no Member State shall be obliged to supply information the disclosure of which it considers contrary to the essential interests of its security;
      (b) any Member State may take such measures as it considers necessary for the protection of the essential interests of its security which are connected with the production of or trade in arms, munitions and war material; such measures shall not adversely affect the conditions of competition in the internal market regarding products which are not intended for specifically military purposes.

2.   The Council may, acting unanimously on a proposal from the Commission, make changes to the list, which it drew up on 15 April 1958, of the products to which the provisions of paragraph 1(b) apply.

Article 347 (ex Article 297 TEC)
Member States shall consult each other with a view to taking together the steps needed to prevent the functioning of the internal market being affected by measures which a Member

State may be called upon to take in the event of serious internal disturbances affecting the maintenance of law and order, in the event of war, serious international tension constituting a threat of war, or in order to carry out obligations it has accepted for the purpose of maintaining peace and international security.

Article 348 (ex Article 298 TEC)
If measures taken in the circumstances referred to in Articles 346 and 347 have the effect of distorting the conditions of competition in the internal market, the Commission shall, together with the State concerned, examine how these measures can be adjusted to the rules laid down in the Treaties.

By way of derogation from the procedure laid down in Articles 258 and 259, the Commission or any Member State may bring the matter directly before the Court of Justice if it considers that another Member State is making improper use of the powers provided for in Articles 346 and 347. The Court of Justice shall give its ruling in camera.

Article 349 (ex Article 299(2), second, third and fourth subparagraphs, TEC)
Taking account of the structural social and economic situation of Guadeloupe, French Guiana, Martinique, Réunion, Saint-Barthélemy, Saint-Martin, the Azores, Madeira and the Canary Islands, which is compounded by their remoteness, insularity, small size, difficult topography and climate, economic dependence on a few products, the permanence and combination of which severely restrain their development, the Council, on a proposal from the Commission and after consulting the European Parliament, shall adopt specific measures aimed, in particular, at laying down the conditions of application of the Treaties to those regions, including common policies. Where the specific measures in question are adopted by the Council in accordance with a special legislative procedure, it shall also act on a proposal from the Commission and after consulting the European Parliament.

The measures referred to in the first paragraph concern in particular areas such as customs and trade policies, fiscal policy, free zones, agriculture and fisheries policies, conditions for supply of raw materials and essential consumer goods, State aids and conditions of access to structural funds and to horizontal Union programmes.

The Council shall adopt the measures referred to in the first paragraph taking into account the special characteristics and constraints of the outermost regions without undermining the integrity and the coherence of the Union legal order, including the internal market and common policies.

Article 350 (ex Article 306 TEC)
The provisions of the Treaties shall not preclude the existence or completion of regional unions between Belgium and Luxembourg, or between Belgium, Luxembourg and the Netherlands, to the extent that the objectives of these regional unions are not attained by application of the Treaties.

Article 351 (ex Article 307 TEC)
The rights and obligations arising from agreements concluded before 1 January 1958 or, for acceding States, before the date of their accession, between one or more Member States on the one hand, and one or more third countries on the other, shall not be affected by the provisions of the Treaties.

To the extent that such agreements are not compatible with the Treaties, the Member State or States concerned shall take all appropriate steps to eliminate the incompatibilities established. Member States shall, where necessary, assist each other to this end and shall, where appropriate, adopt a common attitude.

In applying the agreements referred to in the first paragraph, Member States shall take into account the fact that the advantages accorded under the Treaties by each Member State form an integral part of the establishment of the Union and are thereby inseparably linked with the creation of common institutions, the conferring of powers upon them and the granting of the same advantages by all the other Member States.

Article 352 (ex Article 308 TEC)

1. If action by the Union should prove necessary, within the framework of the policies defined in the Treaties, to attain one of the objectives set out in the Treaties, and the Treaties have not provided the necessary powers, the Council, acting unanimously on a proposal from the Commission and after obtaining the consent of the European Parliament, shall adopt the appropriate measures. Where the measures in question are adopted by the Council in accordance with a special legislative procedure, it shall also act unanimously on a proposal from the Commission and after obtaining the consent of the European Parliament.

2. Using the procedure for monitoring the subsidiarity principle referred to in Article 5(3) of the Treaty on European Union, the Commission shall draw national Parliaments' attention to proposals based on this Article.

3. Measures based on this Article shall not entail harmonisation of Member States' laws or regulations in cases where the Treaties exclude such harmonisation.

4. This Article cannot serve as a basis for attaining objectives pertaining to the common foreign and security policy and any acts adopted pursuant to this Article shall respect the limits set out in Article 40, second paragraph, of the Treaty on European Union.

Article 353

Article 48(7) of the Treaty on European Union shall not apply to the following Articles:

— Article 311, third and fourth paragraphs,

— Article 312(2), first subparagraph,

— Article 352, and

— Article 354.

Article 354 (ex Article 309 TEC)

For the purposes of Article 7 of the Treaty on European Union on the suspension of certain rights resulting from Union membership, the member of the European Council or of the Council representing the Member State in question shall not take part in the vote and the Member State in question shall not be counted in the calculation of the one third or four fifths of Member States referred to in paragraphs 1 and 2 of that Article. Abstentions by members present in person or represented shall not prevent the adoption of decisions referred to in paragraph 2 of that Article.

For the adoption of the decisions referred to in paragraphs 3 and 4 of Article 7 of the Treaty on European Union, a qualified majority shall be defined in accordance with Article 238(3)(b) of this Treaty.

Where, following a decision to suspend voting rights adopted pursuant to paragraph 3 of Article 7 of the Treaty on European Union, the Council acts by a qualified majority on the basis of a provision of the Treaties, that qualified majority shall be defined in accordance with Article 238(3)(b) of this Treaty, or, where the Council acts on a proposal from the Commission or from the High Representative of the Union for Foreign Affairs and Security Policy, in accordance with Article 238(3)(a).

For the purposes of Article 7 of the Treaty on European Union, the European Parliament shall act by a two-thirds majority of the votes cast, representing the majority of its component Members.

Article 355 (ex Article 299(2), first subparagraph, and Article 299(3) to (6) TEC)

In addition to the provisions of Article 52 of the Treaty on European Union relating to the territorial scope of the Treaties, the following provisions shall apply:

1. The provisions of the Treaties shall apply to Guadeloupe, French Guiana, Martinique, Réunion, Saint-Barthélemy, Saint-Martin, the Azores, Madeira and the Canary Islands in accordance with Article 349.

2. The special arrangements for association set out in Part Four shall apply to the overseas countries and territories listed in Annex II.

    The Treaties shall not apply to those overseas countries and territories having special relations with the United Kingdom of Great Britain and Northern Ireland which are not included in the aforementioned list.

3. The provisions of the Treaties shall apply to the European territories for whose external relations a Member State is responsible.

4. The provisions of the Treaties shall apply to the Åland Islands in accordance with the provisions set out in Protocol 2 to the Act concerning the conditions of accession of the Republic of Austria, the Republic of Finland and the Kingdom of Sweden.

5. Notwithstanding Article 52 of the Treaty on European Union and paragraphs 1 to 4 of this Article:
    (a) the Treaties shall not apply to the Faeroe Islands;
    (b) the Treaties shall not apply to the United Kingdom Sovereign Base Areas of Akrotiri and Dhekelia in Cyprus except to the extent necessary to ensure the implementation of the arrangements set out in the Protocol on the Sovereign Base Areas of the United Kingdom of Great Britain and Northern Ireland in Cyprus annexed to the Act concerning the conditions of accession of the Czech Republic, the Republic of Estonia, the Republic of Cyprus, the Republic of Latvia, the Republic of Lithuania, the Republic of Hungary, the Republic of Malta, the Republic of Poland, the Republic of Slovenia and the Slovak Republic to the European Union and in accordance with the terms of that Protocol;
    (c) the Treaties shall apply to the Channel Islands and the Isle of Man only to the extent necessary to ensure the implementation of the arrangements for those islands set out in the Treaty concerning the accession of new Member States to the European Economic Community and to the European Atomic Energy Community signed on 22 January 1972.

6. The European Council may, on the initiative of the Member State concerned, adopt a decision amending the status, with regard to the Union, of a Danish, French or Netherlands country or territory referred to in paragraphs 1 and 2. The European Council shall act unanimously after consulting the Commission.

Article 356 (ex Article 312 TEC)

This Treaty is concluded for an unlimited period.

Article 357 (ex Article 313 TEC)

This Treaty shall be ratified by the High Contracting Parties in accordance with their respective constitutional requirements. The Instruments of ratification shall be deposited with the Government of the Italian Republic.

This Treaty shall enter into force on the first day of the month following the deposit of the Instrument of ratification by the last signatory State to take this step. If, however, such deposit is made less than 15 days before the beginning of the following month, this Treaty shall not enter into force until the first day of the second month after the date of such deposit.

Article 358

The provisions of Article 55 of the Treaty on European Union shall apply to this Treaty.

IN WITNESS WHEREOF, the undersigned Plenipotentiaries have signed this Treaty.

Done at Rome this twenty-fifth day of March in the year one thousand nine hundred and fifty-seven.

(List of signatories not reproduced)

PROTOCOLS
OJ C 83, 30.3.2010, p. 201*

---

*   EDITOR'S NOTE: The following Protocols have been omitted: Nos 4–7, 10–11, 16–18, 22–23, 28–29, 31–35 and 37.

PROTOCOL (NO 1) ON THE ROLE OF NATIONAL PARLIAMENTS IN THE EUROPEAN UNION

THE HIGH CONTRACTING PARTIES,

RECALLING that the way in which national Parliaments scrutinise their governments in relation to the activities of the Union is a matter for the particular constitutional organisation and practice of each Member State,

DESIRING to encourage greater involvement of national Parliaments in the activities of the European Union and to enhance their ability to express their views on draft legislative acts of the Union as well as on other matters which may be of particular interest to them,

HAVE AGREED UPON the following provisions, which shall be annexed to the Treaty on European Union, to the Treaty on the Functioning of the European Union and to the Treaty establishing the European Atomic Energy Community:

TITLE I
INFORMATION FOR NATIONAL PARLIAMENTS

Article 1
Commission consultation documents (green and white papers and communications) shall be forwarded directly by the Commission to national Parliaments upon publication. The Commission shall also forward the annual legislative programme as well as any other instrument of legislative planning or policy to national Parliaments, at the same time as to the European Parliament and the Council.

Article 2
Draft legislative acts sent to the European Parliament and to the Council shall be forwarded to national Parliaments.

For the purposes of this Protocol, "draft legislative acts" shall mean proposals from the Commission, initiatives from a group of Member States, initiatives from the European Parliament, requests from the Court of Justice, recommendations from the European Central Bank and requests from the European Investment Bank, for the adoption of a legislative act.

Draft legislative acts originating from the Commission shall be forwarded to national Parliaments directly by the Commission, at the same time as to the European Parliament and the Council.

Draft legislative acts originating from the European Parliament shall be forwarded to national Parliaments directly by the European Parliament.

Draft legislative acts originating from a group of Member States, the Court of Justice, the European Central Bank or the European Investment Bank shall be forwarded to national Parliaments by the Council.

Article 3

National Parliaments may send to the Presidents of the European Parliament, the Council and the Commission a reasoned opinion on whether a draft legislative act complies with the principle of subsidiarity, in accordance with the procedure laid down in the Protocol on the application of the principles of subsidiarity and proportionality.

If the draft legislative act originates from a group of Member States, the President of the Council shall forward the reasoned opinion or opinions to the governments of those Member States.
If the draft legislative act originates from the Court of Justice, the European Central Bank or the European Investment Bank, the President of the Council shall forward the reasoned opinion or opinions to the institution or body concerned.

Article 4

An eight-week period shall elapse between a draft legislative act being made available to national Parliaments in the official languages of the Union and the date when it is placed on a provisional agenda for the Council for its adoption or for adoption of a position under a legislative procedure. Exceptions shall be possible in cases of urgency, the reasons for which shall be stated in the act or position of the Council. Save in urgent cases for which due reasons have been given, no agreement may be reached on a draft legislative act during those eight weeks. Save in urgent cases for which due reasons have been given, a ten-day period shall elapse between the placing of a draft legislative act on the provisional agenda for the Council and the adoption of a position.

Article 5

The agendas for and the outcome of meetings of the Council, including the minutes of meetings where the Council is deliberating on draft legislative acts, shall be forwarded directly to national Parliaments, at the same time as to Member States' governments.

Article 6

When the European Council intends to make use of the first or second subparagraphs of Article 48(7) of the Treaty on European Union, national Parliaments shall be informed of the initiative of the European Council at least six months before any decision is adopted.

Article 7

The Court of Auditors shall forward its annual report to national Parliaments, for information, at the same time as to the European Parliament and to the Council.

Article 8

Where the national Parliamentary system is not unicameral, Articles 1 to 7 shall apply to the component chambers.

TITLE II
INTERPARLIAMENTARY COOPERATION

Article 9

The European Parliament and national Parliaments shall together determine the organisation and promotion of effective and regular interparliamentary cooperation within the Union.

Article 10

A conference of Parliamentary Committees for Union Affairs may submit any contribution it deems appropriate for the attention of the European Parliament, the Council and the

Commission. That conference shall in addition promote the exchange of information and best practice between national Parliaments and the European Parliament, including their special committees. It may also organise interparliamentary conferences on specific topics, in particular to debate matters of common foreign and security policy, including common security and defence policy. Contributions from the conference shall not bind national Parliaments and shall not prejudge their positions.

PROTOCOL (NO 2) ON THE APPLICATION OF THE PRINCIPLES OF SUBSIDIARITY AND PROPORTIONALITY

THE HIGH CONTRACTING PARTIES,

WISHING to ensure that decisions are taken as closely as possible to the citizens of the Union,

RESOLVED to establish the conditions for the application of the principles of subsidiarity and proportionality, as laid down in Article 5 of the Treaty on European Union, and to establish a system for monitoring the application of those principles,

HAVE AGREED UPON the following provisions, which shall be annexed to the Treaty on European Union and to the Treaty on the Functioning of the European Union:

Article 1
Each institution shall ensure constant respect for the principles of subsidiarity and proportionality, as laid down in Article 5 of the Treaty on European Union.

Article 2
Before proposing legislative acts, the Commission shall consult widely. Such consultations shall, where appropriate, take into account the regional and local dimension of the action envisaged. In cases of exceptional urgency, the Commission shall not conduct such consultations. It shall give reasons for its decision in its proposal.

Article 3
For the purposes of this Protocol, 'draft legislative acts' shall mean proposals from the Commission, initiatives from a group of Member States, initiatives from the European Parliament, requests from the Court of Justice, recommendations from the European Central Bank and requests from the European Investment Bank, for the adoption of a legislative act.

Article 4
The Commission shall forward its draft legislative acts and its amended drafts to national Parliaments at the same time as to the Union legislator.

The European Parliament shall forward its draft legislative acts and its amended drafts to national Parliaments.

The Council shall forward draft legislative acts originating from a group of Member States, the Court of Justice, the European Central Bank or the European Investment Bank and amended drafts to national Parliaments.

Upon adoption, legislative resolutions of the European Parliament and positions of the Council shall be forwarded by them to national Parliaments.

Article 5
Draft legislative acts shall be justified with regard to the principles of subsidiarity and proportionality. Any draft legislative act should contain a detailed statement making it possible to appraise compliance with the principles of subsidiarity and proportionality. This statement

should contain some assessment of the proposal's financial impact and, in the case of a directive, of its implications for the rules to be put in place by Member States, including, where necessary, the regional legislation. The reasons for concluding that a Union objective can be better achieved at Union level shall be substantiated by qualitative and, wherever possible, quantitative indicators. Draft legislative acts shall take account of the need for any burden, whether financial or administrative, falling upon the Union, national governments, regional or local authorities, economic operators and citizens, to be minimised and commensurate with the objective to be achieved.

Article 6
Any national Parliament or any chamber of a national Parliament may, within eight weeks from the date of transmission of a draft legislative act, in the official languages of the Union, send to the Presidents of the European Parliament, the Council and the Commission a reasoned opinion stating why it considers that the draft in question does not comply with the principle of subsidiarity. It will be for each national Parliament or each chamber of a national Parliament to consult, where appropriate, regional parliaments with legislative powers.

If the draft legislative act originates from a group of Member States, the President of the Council shall forward the opinion to the governments of those Member States.
If the draft legislative act originates from the Court of Justice, the European Central Bank or the European Investment Bank, the President of the Council shall forward the opinion to the institution or body concerned.

Article 7
1. The European Parliament, the Council and the Commission, and, where appropriate, the group of Member States, the Court of Justice, the European Central Bank or the European Investment Bank, if the draft legislative act originates from them, shall take account of the reasoned opinions issued by national Parliaments or by a chamber of a national Parliament.

    Each national Parliament shall have two votes, shared out on the basis of the national Parliamentary system. In the case of a bicameral Parliamentary system, each of the two chambers shall have one vote.

2. Where reasoned opinions on a draft legislative act's non-compliance with the principle of subsidiarity represent at least one third of all the votes allocated to the national Parliaments in accordance with the second subparagraph of paragraph 1, the draft must be reviewed. This threshold shall be a quarter in the case of a draft legislative act submitted on the basis of Article 76 of the Treaty on the Functioning of the European Union on the area of freedom, security and justice.

    After such review, the Commission or, where appropriate, the group of Member States, the European Parliament, the Court of Justice, the European Central Bank or the European Investment Bank, if the draft legislative act originates from them, may decide to maintain, amend or withdraw the draft. Reasons must be given for this decision.

3. Furthermore, under the ordinary legislative procedure, where reasoned opinions on the non-compliance of a proposal for a legislative act with the principle of subsidiarity represent at least a simple majority of the votes allocated to the national Parliaments in accordance with the second subparagraph of paragraph 1, the proposal must be reviewed. After such review, the Commission may decide to maintain, amend or withdraw the proposal.

    If it chooses to maintain the proposal, the Commission will have, in a reasoned opinion, to justify why it considers that the proposal complies with the principle of subsidiarity.

This reasoned opinion, as well as the reasoned opinions of the national Parliaments, will have to be submitted to the Union legislator, for consideration in the procedure:

(a) before concluding the first reading, the legislator (the European Parliament and the Council) shall consider whether the legislative proposal is compatible with the principle of subsidiarity, taking particular account of the reasons expressed and shared by the majority of national Parliaments as well as the reasoned opinion of the Commission;

(b) if, by a majority of 55% of the members of the Council or a majority of the votes cast in the European Parliament, the legislator is of the opinion that the proposal is not compatible with the principle of subsidiarity, the legislative proposal shall not be given further consideration.

Article 8

The Court of Justice of the European Union shall have jurisdiction in actions on grounds of infringement of the principle of subsidiarity by a legislative act, brought in accordance with the rules laid down in Article 263 of the Treaty on the Functioning of the European Union by Member States, or notified by them in accordance with their legal order on behalf of their national Parliament or a chamber thereof.

In accordance with the rules laid down in the said Article, the Committee of the Regions may also bring such actions against legislative acts for the adoption of which the Treaty on the Functioning of the European Union provides that it be consulted.

Article 9

The Commission shall submit each year to the European Council, the European Parliament, the Council and national Parliaments a report on the application of Article 5 of the Treaty on European Union. This annual report shall also be forwarded to the Economic and Social Committee and the Committee of the Regions.

PROTOCOL (NO 3) ON THE STATUTE OF THE COURT OF JUSTICE OF THE EUROPEAN UNION

THE HIGH CONTRACTING PARTIES,

DESIRING to lay down the Statute of the Court of Justice of the European Union provided for in Article 281 of the Treaty on the Functioning of the European Union,

HAVE AGREED UPON the following provisions, which shall be annexed to the Treaty on European Union, the Treaty on the Functioning of the European Union and the Treaty establishing the European Atomic Energy Community:

Article 1

The Court of Justice of the European Union shall be constituted and shall function in accordance with the provisions of the Treaties, of the Treaty establishing the European Atomic Energy Community (EAEC Treaty) and of this Statute.

TITLE I
JUDGES AND ADVOCATES-GENERAL

Article 2

Before taking up his duties each Judge shall, before the Court of Justice sitting in open court, take an oath to perform his duties impartially and conscientiously and to preserve the secrecy of the deliberations of the Court.

Article 3

The Judges shall be immune from legal proceedings. After they have ceased to hold office, they shall continue to enjoy immunity in respect of acts performed by them in their official capacity, including words spoken or written.

The Court of Justice, sitting as a full Court, may waive the immunity. If the decision concerns a member of the General Court or of a specialised court, the Court shall decide after consulting the court concerned.

Where immunity has been waived and criminal proceedings are instituted against a Judge, he shall be tried, in any of the Member States, only by the court competent to judge the members of the highest national judiciary.

Articles 11 to 14 and Article 17 of the Protocol on the privileges and immunities of the European Union shall apply to the Judges, Advocates-General, Registrar and Assistant Rapporteurs of the Court of Justice of the European Union, without prejudice to the provisions relating to immunity from legal proceedings of Judges which are set out in the preceding paragraphs.

Article 4

The Judges may not hold any political or administrative office.

They may not engage in any occupation, whether gainful or not, unless exemption is exceptionally granted by the Council, acting by a simple majority.

When taking up their duties, they shall give a solemn undertaking that, both during and after their term of office, they will respect the obligations arising therefrom, in particular the duty to behave with integrity and discretion as regards the acceptance, after they have ceased to hold office, of certain appointments or benefits.

Any doubt on this point shall be settled by decision of the Court of Justice. If the decision concerns a member of the General Court or of a specialised court, the Court shall decide after consulting the court concerned.

Article 5

Apart from normal replacement, or death, the duties of a Judge shall end when he resigns.

Where a Judge resigns, his letter of resignation shall be addressed to the President of the Court of Justice for transmission to the President of the Council. Upon this notification a vacancy shall arise on the bench.

Save where Article 6 applies, a Judge shall continue to hold office until his successor takes up his duties.

Article 6

A Judge may be deprived of his office or of his right to a pension or other benefits in its stead only if, in the unanimous opinion of the Judges and Advocates-General of the Court of Justice, he no longer fulfils the requisite conditions or meets the obligations arising from his office. The Judge concerned shall not take part in any such deliberations. If the person concerned is a member of the General Court or of a specialised court, the Court shall decide after consulting the court concerned.

The Registrar of the Court shall communicate the decision of the Court to the President of the European Parliament and to the President of the Commission and shall notify it to the President of the Council.

In the case of a decision depriving a Judge of his office, a vacancy shall arise on the bench upon this latter notification.

Article 7
A Judge who is to replace a member of the Court whose term of office has not expired shall be appointed for the remainder of his predecessor's term.

Article 8
The provisions of Articles 2 to 7 shall apply to the Advocates-General.

TITLE II
ORGANISATION OF THE COURT OF JUSTICE

Article 9
When, every three years, the Judges are partially replaced, 14 and 13 Judges shall be replaced alternately.

When, every three years, the Advocates-General are partially replaced, four Advocates-General shall be replaced on each occasion.

Article 10
The Registrar shall take an oath before the Court of Justice to perform his duties impartially and conscientiously and to preserve the secrecy of the deliberations of the Court of Justice.

Article 11
The Court of Justice shall arrange for replacement of the Registrar on occasions when he is prevented from attending the Court of Justice.

Article 12
Officials and other servants shall be attached to the Court of Justice to enable it to function. They shall be responsible to the Registrar under the authority of the President.

Article 13
At the request of the Court of Justice, the European Parliament and the Council may, acting in accordance with the ordinary legislative procedure, provide for the appointment of Assistant Rapporteurs and lay down the rules governing their service. The Assistant Rapporteurs may be required, under conditions laid down in the Rules of Procedure, to participate in preparatory inquiries in cases pending before the Court and to cooperate with the Judge who acts as Rapporteur.

The Assistant Rapporteurs shall be chosen from persons whose independence is beyond doubt and who possess the necessary legal qualifications; they shall be appointed by the Council, acting by a simple majority. They shall take an oath before the Court to perform their duties impartially and conscientiously and to preserve the secrecy of the deliberations of the Court.

Article 14
The Judges, the Advocates-General and the Registrar shall be required to reside at the place where the Court of Justice has its seat.

Article 15

The Court of Justice shall remain permanently in session. The duration of the judicial vacations shall be determined by the Court with due regard to the needs of its business.

Article 16

The Court of Justice shall form chambers consisting of three and five Judges. The Judges shall elect the Presidents of the chambers from among their number. The Presidents of the chambers of five Judges shall be elected for three years. They may be re-elected once.

The Grand Chamber shall consist of 13 Judges. It shall be presided over by the President of the Court. The Presidents of the chambers of five Judges and other Judges appointed in accordance with the conditions laid down in the Rules of Procedure shall also form part of the Grand Chamber.

The Court shall sit in a Grand Chamber when a Member State or an institution of the Union that is party to the proceedings so requests.

The Court shall sit as a full Court where cases are brought before it pursuant to Article 228(2), Article 245(2), Article 247 or Article 286(6) of the Treaty on the Functioning of the European Union.

Moreover, where it considers that a case before it is of exceptional importance, the Court may decide, after hearing the Advocate-General, to refer the case to the full Court.

Article 17

Decisions of the Court of Justice shall be valid only when an uneven number of its members is sitting in the deliberations.

Decisions of the chambers consisting of either three or five Judges shall be valid only if they are taken by three Judges.

Decisions of the Grand Chamber shall be valid only if nine Judges are sitting.

Decisions of the full Court shall be valid only if 15 Judges are sitting.

In the event of one of the Judges of a chamber being prevented from attending, a Judge of another chamber may be called upon to sit in accordance with conditions laid down in the Rules of Procedure.

Article 18

No Judge or Advocate-General may take part in the disposal of any case in which he has previously taken part as agent or adviser or has acted for one of the parties, or in which he has been called upon to pronounce as a member of a court or tribunal, of a commission of inquiry or in any other capacity.

If, for some special reason, any Judge or Advocate-General considers that he should not take part in the judgment or examination of a particular case, he shall so inform the President. If, for some special reason, the President considers that any Judge or Advocate-General should not sit or make submissions in a particular case, he shall notify him accordingly.

Any difficulty arising as to the application of this Article shall be settled by decision of the Court of Justice.

A party may not apply for a change in the composition of the Court or of one of its chambers on the grounds of either the nationality of a Judge or the absence from the Court or from the chamber of a Judge of the nationality of that party.

TITLE III
PROCEDURE BEFORE THE COURT OF JUSTICE

Article 19

The Member States and the institutions of the Union shall be represented before the Court of Justice by an agent appointed for each case; the agent may be assisted by an adviser or by a lawyer.

The States, other than the Member States, which are parties to the Agreement on the European Economic Area and also the EFTA Surveillance Authority referred to in that Agreement shall be represented in same manner.

Other parties must be represented by a lawyer.

Only a lawyer authorised to practise before a court of a Member State or of another State which is a party to the Agreement on the European Economic Area may represent or assist a party before the Court.

Such agents, advisers and lawyers shall, when they appear before the Court, enjoy the rights and immunities necessary to the independent exercise of their duties, under conditions laid down in the Rules of Procedure.

As regards such advisers and lawyers who appear before it, the Court shall have the powers normally accorded to courts of law, under conditions laid down in the Rules of Procedure.

University teachers being nationals of a Member State whose law accords them a right of audience shall have the same rights before the Court as are accorded by this Article to lawyers.

Article 20

The procedure before the Court of Justice shall consist of two parts: written and oral.

The written procedure shall consist of the communication to the parties and to the institutions of the Union whose decisions are in dispute, of applications, statements of case, defences and observations, and of replies, if any, as well as of all papers and documents in support or of certified copies of them.

Communications shall be made by the Registrar in the order and within the time laid down in the Rules of Procedure.

The oral procedure shall consist of the reading of the report presented by a Judge acting as Rapporteur, the hearing by the Court of agents, advisers and lawyers and of the submissions of the Advocate-General, as well as the hearing, if any, of witnesses and experts.

Where it considers that the case raises no new point of law, the Court may decide, after hearing the Advocate-General, that the case shall be determined without a submission from the Advocate- General.

Article 21

A case shall be brought before the Court of Justice by a written application addressed to the Registrar. The application shall contain the applicant's name and permanent address and the description of the signatory, the name of the party or names of the parties against whom the application is made, the subject-matter of the dispute, the form of order sought and a brief statement of the pleas in law on which the application is based.

The application shall be accompanied, where appropriate, by the measure the annulment of which is sought or, in the circumstances referred to in Article 265 of the Treaty on the Functioning of the European Union, by documentary evidence of the date on which an institution was, in accordance with those Articles, requested to act. If the documents are not submitted with the application, the Registrar shall ask the party concerned to produce them within a reasonable period, but in that event the rights of the party shall not lapse even if such documents are produced after the time limit for bringing proceedings.

Article 22
A case governed by Article 18 of the EAEC Treaty shall be brought before the Court of Justice by an appeal addressed to the Registrar. The appeal shall contain the name and permanent address of the applicant and the description of the signatory, a reference to the decision against which the appeal is brought, the names of the respondents, the subject-matter of the dispute, the submissions and a brief statement of the grounds on which the appeal is based.

The appeal shall be accompanied by a certified copy of the decision of the Arbitration Committee which is contested.

If the Court rejects the appeal, the decision of the Arbitration Committee shall become final.

If the Court annuls the decision of the Arbitration Committee, the matter may be re-opened, where appropriate, on the initiative of one of the parties in the case, before the Arbitration Committee. The latter shall conform to any decisions on points of law given by the Court.

Article 23
In the cases governed by Article 267 of the Treaty on the Functioning of the European Union, the decision of the court or tribunal of a Member State which suspends its proceedings and refers a case to the Court of Justice shall be notified to the Court by the court or tribunal concerned. The decision shall then be notified by the Registrar of the Court to the parties, to the Member States and to the Commission, and to the institution, body, office or agency of the Union which adopted the act the validity or interpretation of which is in dispute.

Within two months of this notification, the parties, the Member States, the Commission and, where appropriate, the institution, body, office or agency which adopted the act the validity or interpretation of which is in dispute, shall be entitled to submit statements of case or written observations to the Court.

In the cases governed by Article 267 of the Treaty on the Functioning of the European Union, the decision of the national court or tribunal shall, moreover, be notified by the Registrar of the Court to the States, other than the Member States, which are parties to the Agreement on the European Economic Area and also to the EFTA Surveillance Authority referred to in that Agreement which may, within two months of notification, where one of the fields of application of that Agreement is concerned, submit statements of case or written observations to the Court.

Where an agreement relating to a specific subject matter, concluded by the Council and one or more non-member States, provides that those States are to be entitled to submit statements of case or written observations where a court or tribunal of a Member State refers to the Court of Justice for a preliminary ruling a question falling within the scope of the agreement, the decision of the national court or tribunal containing that question shall also be notified to the non-member States concerned. Within two months from such notification, those States may lodge at the Court statements of case or written observations.

Article 23a (1)
The Rules of Procedure may provide for an expedited or accelerated procedure and, for references for a preliminary ruling relating to the area of freedom, security and justice, an urgent procedure.

Those procedures may provide, in respect of the submission of statements of case or written observations, for a shorter period than that provided for by Article 23, and, in derogation from the fourth paragraph of Article 20, for the case to be determined without a submission from the Advocate General.

In addition, the urgent procedure may provide for restriction of the parties and other interested persons mentioned in Article 23, authorised to submit statements of case or written observations and, in cases of extreme urgency, for the written stage of the procedure to be omitted.

Article 24
The Court of Justice may require the parties to produce all documents and to supply all information which the Court considers desirable. Formal note shall be taken of any refusal.

The Court may also require the Member States and institutions, bodies, offices and agencies not being parties to the case to supply all information which the Court considers necessary for the proceedings.

Article 25
The Court of Justice may at any time entrust any individual, body, authority, committee or other organisation it chooses with the task of giving an expert opinion.

Article 26
Witnesses may be heard under conditions laid down in the Rules of Procedure.

Article 27
With respect to defaulting witnesses the Court of Justice shall have the powers generally granted to courts and tribunals and may impose pecuniary penalties under conditions laid down in the Rules of Procedure.

Article 28
Witnesses and experts may be heard on oath taken in the form laid down in the Rules of Procedure or in the manner laid down by the law of the country of the witness or expert.

Article 29
The Court of Justice may order that a witness or expert be heard by the judicial authority of his place of permanent residence.

The order shall be sent for implementation to the competent judicial authority under conditions laid down in the Rules of Procedure. The documents drawn up in compliance with the letters rogatory shall be returned to the Court under the same conditions.

The Court shall defray the expenses, without prejudice to the right to charge them, where appropriate, to the parties.

Article 30
A Member State shall treat any violation of an oath by a witness or expert in the same manner as if the offence had been committed before one of its courts with jurisdiction in civil proceedings. At the instance of the Court of Justice, the Member State concerned shall prosecute the offender before its competent court.

Article 31
The hearing in court shall be public, unless the Court of Justice, of its own motion or on application by the parties, decides otherwise for serious reasons.

Article 32
During the hearings the Court of Justice may examine the experts, the witnesses and the parties themselves. The latter, however, may address the Court of Justice only through their representatives.

Article 33
Minutes shall be made of each hearing and signed by the President and the Registrar.

Article 34
The case list shall be established by the President.

Article 35
The deliberations of the Court of Justice shall be and shall remain secret.

Article 36
Judgments shall state the reasons on which they are based. They shall contain the names of the Judges who took part in the deliberations.

Article 37
Judgments shall be signed by the President and the Registrar. They shall be read in open court.

Article 38
The Court of Justice shall adjudicate upon costs.

Article 39
The President of the Court of Justice may, by way of summary procedure, which may, in so far as necessary, differ from some of the rules contained in this Statute and which shall be laid down in the Rules of Procedure, adjudicate upon applications to suspend execution, as provided for in Article 278 of the Treaty on the Functioning of the European Union and Article 157 of the EAEC Treaty, or to prescribe interim measures pursuant to Article 279 of the Treaty on the Functioning of the European Union, or to suspend enforcement in accordance with the fourth paragraph of Article 299 of the Treaty on the Functioning of the European Union or the third paragraph of Article 164 of the EAEC Treaty.

Should the President be prevented from attending, his place shall be taken by another Judge under conditions laid down in the Rules of Procedure.

The ruling of the President or of the Judge replacing him shall be provisional and shall in no way prejudice the decision of the Court on the substance of the case.

Article 40
Member States and institutions of the Union may intervene in cases before the Court of Justice.

The same right shall be open to the bodies, offices and agencies of the Union and to any other person which can establish an interest in the result of a case submitted to the Court. Natural or legal persons shall not intervene in cases between Member States, between institutions of the Union or between Member States and institutions of the Union.

Without prejudice to the second paragraph, the States, other than the Member States, which are parties to the Agreement on the European Economic Area, and also the EFTA Surveillance Authority referred to in that Agreement, may intervene in cases before the Court where one of the fields of application of that Agreement is concerned.

An application to intervene shall be limited to supporting the form of order sought by one of the parties.

Article 41

Where the defending party, after having been duly summoned, fails to file written submissions in defence, judgment shall be given against that party by default. An objection may be lodged against the judgment within one month of it being notified. The objection shall not have the effect of staying enforcement of the judgment by default unless the Court of Justice decides otherwise.

Article 42

Member States, institutions, bodies, offices and agencies of the Union and any other natural or legal persons may, in cases and under conditions to be determined by the Rules of Procedure, institute third-party proceedings to contest a judgment rendered without their being heard, where the judgment is prejudicial to their rights.

Article 43

If the meaning or scope of a judgment is in doubt, the Court of Justice shall construe it on application by any party or any institution of the Union establishing an interest therein.

Article 44

An application for revision of a judgment may be made to the Court of Justice only on discovery of a fact which is of such a nature as to be a decisive factor, and which, when the judgment was given, was unknown to the Court and to the party claiming the revision.

The revision shall be opened by a judgment of the Court expressly recording the existence of a new fact, recognising that it is of such a character as to lay the case open to revision and declaring the application admissible on this ground.

No application for revision may be made after the lapse of 10 years from the date of the judgment.

Article 45

Periods of grace based on considerations of distance shall be determined by the Rules of Procedure.

No right shall be prejudiced in consequence of the expiry of a time limit if the party concerned proves the existence of unforeseeable circumstances or of force majeure.

Article 46

Proceedings against the Union in matters arising from non-contractual liability shall be barred after a period of five years from the occurrence of the event giving rise thereto. The period of limitation shall be interrupted if proceedings are instituted before the Court of Justice or if prior to such proceedings an application is made by the aggrieved party to the relevant institution of the Union. In the latter event the proceedings must be instituted within the period of two months provided for in Article 263 of the Treaty on the Functioning of the European Union; the provisions of the second paragraph of Article 265 of the Treaty on the Functioning of the European Union shall apply where appropriate.

This Article shall also apply to proceedings against the European Central Bank regarding non-contractual liability.

TITLE IV
GENERAL COURT

Article 47

The first paragraph of Article 9, Articles 14 and 15, the first, second, fourth and fifth paragraphs of Article 17 and Article 18 shall apply to the General Court and its members.

The fourth paragraph of Article 3 and Articles 10, 11 and 14 shall apply to the Registrar of the General Court mutatis mutandis.

Article 48
The General Court shall consist of 27 Judges.

Article 49
The Members of the General Court may be called upon to perform the task of an Advocate-General.

It shall be the duty of the Advocate-General, acting with complete impartiality and independence, to make, in open court, reasoned submissions on certain cases brought before the General Court in order to assist the General Court in the performance of its task.

The criteria for selecting such cases, as well as the procedures for designating the Advocates-General, shall be laid down in the Rules of Procedure of the General Court.

A Member called upon to perform the task of Advocate-General in a case may not take part in the judgment of the case.

Article 50

The General Court shall sit in chambers of three or five Judges. The Judges shall elect the Presidents of the chambers from among their number. The Presidents of the chambers of five Judges shall be elected for three years. They may be re-elected once.

The composition of the chambers and the assignment of cases to them shall be governed by the Rules of Procedure. In certain cases governed by the Rules of Procedure, the General Court may sit as a full court or be constituted by a single Judge.

The Rules of Procedure may also provide that the General Court may sit in a Grand Chamber in cases and under the conditions specified therein.

Article 51
By way of derogation from the rule laid down in Article 256(1) of the Treaty on the Functioning of the European Union, jurisdiction shall be reserved to the Court of Justice in the actions referred to in Articles 263 and 265 of the Treaty on the Functioning of the European Union when they are brought by a Member State against:
(a) an act of or failure to act by the European Parliament or the Council, or by those institutions acting jointly, except for:
— decisions taken by the Council under the third subparagraph of Article 108(2) of the Treaty on the Functioning of the European Union;
— acts of the Council adopted pursuant to a Council regulation concerning measures to protect trade within the meaning of Article 207 of the Treaty on the Functioning of the European Union;
— acts of the Council by which the Council exercises implementing powers in accordance with the second paragraph of Article 291 of the Treaty on the Functioning of the European Union;
(b) against an act of or failure to act by the Commission under the first paragraph of Article 331 of the Treaty on the Functioning of the European Union.

Jurisdiction shall also be reserved to the Court of Justice in the actions referred to in the same Articles when they are brought by an institution of the Union against an act of or failure to act by the European Parliament, the Council, both those institutions acting jointly, or the

Commission, or brought by an institution of the Union against an act of or failure to act by the European Central Bank.

Article 52

The President of the Court of Justice and the President of the General Court shall determine, by common accord, the conditions under which officials and other servants attached to the Court of Justice shall render their services to the General Court to enable it to function. Certain officials or other servants shall be responsible to the Registrar of the General Court under the authority of the President of the General Court.

Article 53

The procedure before the General Court shall be governed by Title III.

Such further and more detailed provisions as may be necessary shall be laid down in its Rules of Procedure. The Rules of Procedure may derogate from the fourth paragraph of Article 40 and from Article 41 in order to take account of the specific features of litigation in the field of intellectual property.

Notwithstanding the fourth paragraph of Article 20, the Advocate-General may make his reasoned submissions in writing.

Article 54

Where an application or other procedural document addressed to the General Court is lodged by mistake with the Registrar of the Court of Justice, it shall be transmitted immediately by that Registrar to the Registrar of the General Court; likewise, where an application or other procedural document addressed to the Court of Justice is lodged by mistake with the Registrar of the General Court, it shall be transmitted immediately by that Registrar to the Registrar of the Court of Justice.

Where the General Court finds that it does not have jurisdiction to hear and determine an action in respect of which the Court of Justice has jurisdiction, it shall refer that action to the Court of Justice; likewise, where the Court of Justice finds that an action falls within the jurisdiction of the General Court, it shall refer that action to the General Court, whereupon that Court may not decline jurisdiction.

Where the Court of Justice and the General Court are seised of cases in which the same relief is sought, the same issue of interpretation is raised or the validity of the same act is called in question, the General Court may, after hearing the parties, stay the proceedings before it until such time as the Court of Justice has delivered judgment or, where the action is one brought pursuant to Article 263 of the Treaty on the Functioning of the European Union, may decline jurisdiction so as to allow the Court of Justice to rule on such actions. In the same circumstances, the Court of Justice may also decide to stay the proceedings before it; in that event, the proceedings before the General Court shall continue.

Where a Member State and an institution of the Union are challenging the same act, the General Court shall decline jurisdiction so that the Court of Justice may rule on those applications.

Article 55

Final decisions of the General Court, decisions disposing of the substantive issues in part only or disposing of a procedural issue concerning a plea of lack of competence or inadmissibility, shall be notified by the Registrar of the General Court to all parties as well as all Member States and the institutions of the Union even if they did not intervene in the case before the General Court.

Article 56

An appeal may be brought before the Court of Justice, within two months of the notification of the decision appealed against, against final decisions of the General Court and decisions of that Court disposing of the substantive issues in part only or disposing of a procedural issue concerning a plea of lack of competence or inadmissibility.

Such an appeal may be brought by any party which has been unsuccessful, in whole or in part, in its submissions. However, interveners other than the Member States and the institutions of the Union may bring such an appeal only where the decision of the General Court directly affects them.

With the exception of cases relating to disputes between the Union and its servants, an appeal may also be brought by Member States and institutions of the Union which did not intervene in the proceedings before the General Court. Such Member States and institutions shall be in the same position as Member States or institutions which intervened at first instance.

Article 57

Any person whose application to intervene has been dismissed by the General Court may appeal to the Court of Justice within two weeks from the notification of the decision dismissing the application.

The parties to the proceedings may appeal to the Court of Justice against any decision of the General Court made pursuant to Article 278 or Article 279 or the fourth paragraph of Article 299 of the Treaty on the Functioning of the European Union or Article 157 or the third paragraph of Article 164 of the EAEC Treaty within two months from their notification.

The appeal referred to in the first two paragraphs of this Article shall be heard and determined under the procedure referred to in Article 39.

Article 58

An appeal to the Court of Justice shall be limited to points of law. It shall lie on the grounds of lack of competence of the General Court, a breach of procedure before it which adversely affects the interests of the appellant as well as the infringement of Union law by the General Court.

No appeal shall lie regarding only the amount of the costs or the party ordered to pay them.

Article 59

Where an appeal is brought against a decision of the General Court, the procedure before the Court of Justice shall consist of a written part and an oral part. In accordance with conditions laid down in the Rules of Procedure, the Court of Justice, having heard the Advocate-General and the parties, may dispense with the oral procedure.

Article 60

Without prejudice to Articles 278 and 279 of the Treaty on the Functioning of the European Union or Article 157 of the EAEC Treaty, an appeal shall not have suspensory effect.

By way of derogation from Article 280 of the Treaty on the Functioning of the European Union, decisions of the General Court declaring a regulation to be void shall take effect only as from the date of expiry of the period referred to in the first paragraph of Article 56 of this Statute or, if an appeal shall have been brought within that period, as from the date of dismissal of the appeal, without prejudice, however, to the right of a party to apply to the Court of Justice, pursuant to Articles 278 and 279 of the Treaty on the Functioning of the European Union or Article 157 of the EAEC Treaty, for the suspension of the effects of the regulation which has been declared void or for the prescription of any other interim measure.

Article 61

If the appeal is well founded, the Court of Justice shall quash the decision of the General Court. It may itself give final judgment in the matter, where the state of the proceedings so permits, or refer the case back to the General Court for judgment.

Where a case is referred back to the General Court, that Court shall be bound by the decision of the Court of Justice on points of law.

When an appeal brought by a Member State or an institution of the Union, which did not intervene in the proceedings before the General Court, is well founded, the Court of Justice may, if it considers this necessary, state which of the effects of the decision of the General Court which has been quashed shall be considered as definitive in respect of the parties to the litigation.

Article 62

In the cases provided for in Article 256(2) and (3) of the Treaty on the Functioning of the European Union, where the First Advocate-General considers that there is a serious risk of the unity or consistency of Union law being affected, he may propose that the Court of Justice review the decision of the General Court.

The proposal must be made within one month of delivery of the decision by the General Court. Within one month of receiving the proposal made by the First Advocate-General, the Court of Justice shall decide whether or not the decision should be reviewed.

Article 62a

The Court of Justice shall give a ruling on the questions which are subject to review by means of an urgent procedure on the basis of the file forwarded to it by the General Court.

Those referred to in Article 23 of this Statute and, in the cases provided for in Article 256(2) of the EC Treaty, the parties to the proceedings before the General Court shall be entitled to lodge statements or written observations with the Court of Justice relating to questions which are subject to review within a period prescribed for that purpose.

The Court of Justice may decide to open the oral procedure before giving a ruling.

Article 62b

In the cases provided for in Article 256(2) of the Treaty on the Functioning of the European Union, without prejudice to Articles 278 and 279 of the Treaty on the Functioning of the European Union, proposals for review and decisions to open the review procedure shall not have suspensory effect. If the Court of Justice finds that the decision of the General Court affects the unity or consistency of Union law, it shall refer the case back to the General Court which shall be bound by the points of law decided by the Court of Justice; the Court of Justice may state which of the effects of the decision of the General Court are to be considered as definitive in respect of the parties to the litigation. If, however, having regard to the result of the review, the outcome of the proceedings flows from the findings of fact on which the decision of the General Court was based, the Court of Justice shall give final judgment.

In the cases provided for in Article 256(3) of the Treaty on the Functioning of the European Union, in the absence of proposals for review or decisions to open the review procedure, the answer(s) given by the General Court to the questions submitted to it shall take effect upon expiry of the periods prescribed for that purpose in the second paragraph of Article 62. Should a review procedure be opened, the answer(s) subject to review shall take effect following that procedure, unless the Court of Justice decides otherwise. If the Court of Justice finds that the decision of the General Court affects the unity or consistency of Union law, the answer given by the Court of Justice to the questions subject to review shall be substituted for that given by the General Court.

TITLE IVA
SPECIALISED COURTS

Article 62c
The provisions relating to the jurisdiction, composition, organisation and procedure of the specialised courts established under Article 257 of the Treaty on the Functioning of the European Union are set out in an Annex to this Statute.

TITLE V
FINAL PROVISIONS

Article 63
The Rules of Procedure of the Court of Justice and of the General Court shall contain any provisions necessary for applying and, where required, supplementing this Statute.

Article 64
The rules governing the language arrangements applicable at the Court of Justice of the European Union shall be laid down by a regulation of the Council acting unanimously. This regulation shall be adopted either at the request of the Court of Justice and after consultation of the Commission and the European Parliament, or on a proposal from the Commission and after consultation of the Court of Justice and of the European Parliament.

Until those rules have been adopted, the provisions of the Rules of Procedure of the Court of Justice and of the Rules of Procedure of the General Court governing language arrangements shall continue to apply. By way of derogation from Articles 253 and 254 of the Treaty on the Functioning of the European Union, those provisions may only be amended or repealed with the unanimous consent of the Council.

ANNEX I (omitted).
(1)   Article inserted by Decision 2008/79/EC, Euratom (OJ L 24, 29.1.2008, p. 42).

PROTOCOL (NO 8) RELATING TO ARTICLE 6(2) OF THE TREATY ON EUROPEAN UNION ON THE ACCESSION OF THE UNION TO THE EUROPEAN CONVENTION ON THE PROTECTION OF HUMAN RIGHTS AND FUNDAMENTAL FREEDOMS

THE HIGH CONTRACTING PARTIES,

HAVE AGREED UPON the following provisions, which shall be annexed to the Treaty on European Union and to the Treaty on the Functioning of the European Union:

Article 1
The agreement relating to the accession of the Union to the European Convention on the Protection of Human Rights and Fundamental Freedoms (hereinafter referred to as the 'European Convention') provided for in Article 6(2) of the Treaty on European Union shall make provision for preserving the specific characteristics of the Union and Union law, in particular with regard to:
(a)   the specific arrangements for the Union's possible participation in the control bodies of the European Convention;

(b) the mechanisms necessary to ensure that proceedings by non-Member States and individual applications are correctly addressed to Member States and/or the Union as appropriate.

Article 2
The agreement referred to in Article 1 shall ensure that accession of the Union shall not affect the competences of the Union or the powers of its institutions. It shall ensure that nothing therein affects the situation of Member States in relation to the European Convention, in particular in relation to the Protocols thereto, measures taken by Member States derogating from the European Convention in accordance with Article 15 thereof and reservations to the European Convention made by Member States in accordance with Article 57 thereof.

Article 3
Nothing in the agreement referred to in Article 1 shall affect Article 344 of the Treaty on the Functioning of the European Union.

PROTOCOL (NO 9) ON THE DECISION OF THE COUNCIL RELATING TO THE IMPLEMENTATION OF ARTICLE 16(4) OF THE TREATY ON EUROPEAN UNION AND ARTICLE 238(2) OF THE TREATY ON THE FUNCTIONING OF THE EUROPEAN UNION BETWEEN 1 NOVEMBER 2014 AND 31 MARCH 2017 ON THE ONE HAND, AND AS FROM 1 APRIL 2017 ON THE OTHER

THE HIGH CONTRACTING PARTIES,

TAKING INTO ACCOUNT the fundamental importance that agreeing on the Decision of the Council relating to the implementation of Article 16(4) of the Treaty on European Union and Article 238(2) of the Treaty on the Functioning of the European Union between 1 November 2014 and 31 March 2017 on the one hand, and as from 1 April 2017 on the other (hereinafter 'the Decision'), had when approving the Treaty of Lisbon,

HAVE AGREED UPON the following provisions, which shall be annexed to the Treaty on European Union and to the Treaty on the Functioning of the European Union:

Sole Article
Before the examination by the Council of any draft which would aim either at amending or abrogating the Decision or any of its provisions, or at modifying indirectly its scope or its meaning through the modification of another legal act of the Union, the European Council shall hold a preliminary deliberation on the said draft, acting by consensus in accordance with Article 15(4) of the Treaty on European Union.

PROTOCOL (NO 12) ON THE EXCESSIVE DEFICIT PROCEDURE

THE HIGH CONTRACTING PARTIES,

DESIRING TO lay down the details of the excessive deficit procedure referred to in Article 126 of the Treaty on the Functioning of the European Union,

HAVE AGREED upon the following provisions, which shall be annexed to the Treaty on European Union and to the Treaty on the Functioning of the European Union:

Article 1
The reference values referred to in Article 126(2) of the Treaty on the Functioning of the European Union are:
— 3% for the ratio of the planned or actual government deficit to gross domestic product at market prices;
— 60% for the ratio of government debt to gross domestic product at market prices.

Article 2

In Article 126 of the said Treaty and in this Protocol:

— "government" means general government, that is central government, regional or local government and social security funds, to the exclusion of commercial operations, as defined in the European System of Integrated Economic Accounts;

— "deficit" means net borrowing as defined in the European System of Integrated Economic Accounts;

— "investment" means gross fixed capital formation as defined in the European System of Integrated Economic Accounts;

— "debt" means total gross debt at nominal value outstanding at the end of the year and consolidated between and within the sectors of general government as defined in the first indent.

Article 3

In order to ensure the effectiveness of the excessive deficit procedure, the governments of the Member States shall be responsible under this procedure for the deficits of general government as defined in the first indent of Article 2. The Member States shall ensure that national procedures in the budgetary area enable them to meet their obligations in this area deriving from these Treaties. The Member States shall report their planned and actual deficits and the levels of their debt promptly and regularly to the Commission.

Article 4

The statistical data to be used for the application of this Protocol shall be provided by the Commission.

PROTOCOL (NO 13) ON THE CONVERGENCE CRITERIA

THE HIGH CONTRACTING PARTIES,

DESIRING to lay down the details of the convergence criteria which shall guide the Union in taking decisions to end the derogations of those Member States with a derogation, referred to in Article 140 of the Treaty on the Functioning of the European Union,

HAVE AGREED upon the following provisions, which shall be annexed to the Treaty on European Union and to the Treaty on the Functioning of the European Union:

Article 1

The criterion on price stability referred to in the first indent of Article 140(1) of the Treaty on the Functioning of the European Union shall mean that a Member State has a price performance that is sustainable and an average rate of inflation, observed over a period of one year before the examination, that does not exceed by more than 1 ½ percentage points that of, at most, the three best performing Member States in terms of price stability. Inflation shall be measured by means of the consumer price index on a comparable basis taking into account differences in national definitions.

Article 2

The criterion on the government budgetary position referred to in the second indent of Article 140(1) of the said Treaty shall mean that at the time of the examination the Member State is not the subject of a Council decision under Article 126(6) of the said Treaty that an excessive deficit exists.

Article 3

The criterion on participation in the Exchange Rate mechanism of the European Monetary System referred to in the third indent of Article 140(1) of the said Treaty shall mean that a Member State has respected the normal fluctuation margins provided for by the exchange-rate mechanism on the European Monetary System without severe tensions for at least the last two years before the examination. In particular, the Member State shall not have devalued its currency's bilateral central rate against the euro on its own initiative for the same period.

Article 4

The criterion on the convergence of interest rates referred to in the fourth indent of Article 140(1) of the said Treaty shall mean that, observed over a period of one year before the examination, a Member State has had an average nominal long-term interest rate that does not exceed by more than two percentage points that of, at most, the three best performing Member States in terms of price stability. Interest rates shall be measured on the basis of long-term government bonds or comparable securities, taking into account differences in national definitions.

Article 5

The statistical data to be used for the application of this Protocol shall be provided by the Commission.

Article 6

The Council shall, acting unanimously on a proposal from the Commission and after consulting the European Parliament, the ECB and the Economic and Financial Committee, adopt appropriate provisions to lay down the details of the convergence criteria referred to in Article 140(1) of the said Treaty, which shall then replace this Protocol.

PROTOCOL (NO 14) ON THE EURO GROUP

THE HIGH CONTRACTING PARTIES,

DESIRING to promote conditions for stronger economic growth in the European Union and, to that end, to develop ever-closer coordination of economic policies within the euro area,

CONSCIOUS of the need to lay down special provisions for enhanced dialogue between the Member States whose currency is the euro, pending the euro becoming the currency of all Member States of the Union,

HAVE AGREED UPON the following provisions, which shall be annexed to the Treaty on European Union and to the Treaty on the Functioning of the European Union:

Article 1

The Ministers of the Member States whose currency is the euro shall meet informally. Such meetings shall take place, when necessary, to discuss questions related to the specific responsibilities they share with regard to the single currency. The Commission shall take part in the meetings. The European Central Bank shall be invited to take part in such meetings, which shall be prepared by the representatives of the Ministers with responsibility for finance of the Member States whose currency is the euro and of the Commission.

Article 2

The Ministers of the Member States whose currency is the euro shall elect a president for two and a half years, by a majority of those Member States.

PROTOCOL (NO 15) ON CERTAIN PROVISIONS RELATING TO THE UNITED KINGDOM OF GREAT BRITAIN AND NORTHERN IRELAND

THE HIGH CONTRACTING PARTIES,

RECOGNISING that the United Kingdom shall not be obliged or committed to adopt the euro without a separate decision to do so by its government and parliament,

GIVEN that on 16 October 1996 and 30 October 1997 the United Kingdom government notified the Council of its intention not to participate in the third stage of economic and monetary union,

NOTING the practice of the government of the United Kingdom to fund its borrowing requirement by the sale of debt to the private sector,

HAVE AGREED upon the following provisions, which shall be annexed to the Treaty on European Union and to the Treaty on the Functioning of the European Union:

1.   Unless the United Kingdom notifies the Council that it intends to adopt the euro, it shall be under no obligation to do so.

2.   In view of the notice given to the Council by the United Kingdom government on 16 October 1996 and 30 October 1997, paragraphs 3 to 8 and 10 shall apply to the United Kingdom.

3.   The United Kingdom shall retain its powers in the field of monetary policy according to national law.

4.   Articles 119, second paragraph, 126(1), (9) and (11), 127(1) to (5), 128, 130, 131, 132, 133, 138, 140(3), 219, 282(2), with the exception of the first and last sentences thereof, 282(5), and 283 of the Treaty on the Functioning of the European Union shall not apply to the United Kingdom. The same applies to Article 121(2) of this Treaty as regards the adoption of the parts of the broad economic policy guidelines which concern the euro area generally. In these provisions references to the Union or the Member States shall not include the United Kingdom and references to national central banks shall not include the Bank of England.

5.   The United Kingdom shall endeavour to avoid an excessive government deficit.

Articles 143 and 144 of the Treaty on the Functioning of the European Union shall continue to apply to the United Kingdom. Articles 134(4) and 142 shall apply to the United Kingdom as if it had a derogation.

6.   The voting rights of the United Kingdom shall be suspended in respect of acts of the Council referred to in the Articles listed in paragraph 4 and in the instances referred to in the first subparagraph of Article 139(4) of the Treaty on the Functioning of the European Union. For this purpose the second subparagraph of Article 139(4) of the Treaty shall apply.

The United Kingdom shall also have no right to participate in the appointment of the President, the Vice-President and the other members of the Executive Board of the ECB under the second subparagraph of Article 283(2) of the said Treaty.

7.   Articles 3, 4, 6, 7, 9.2, 10.1, 10.3, 11.2, 12.1, 14, 16, 18 to 20, 22, 23, 26, 27, 30 to 34 and 49 of the Protocol on the Statute of the European System of Central Banks and of the European Central Bank ('the Statute') shall not apply to the United Kingdom.

In those Articles, references to the Union or the Member States shall not include the United Kingdom and references to national central banks or shareholders shall not include the Bank of England.

References in Articles 10.3 and 30.2 of the Statute to 'subscribed capital of the ECB' shall not include capital subscribed by the Bank of England.

8.   Article 141(1) of the Treaty on the Functioning of the European Union and Articles 43 to 47 of the Statute shall have effect, whether or not there is any Member State with a derogation, subject to the following amendments:

(a)   References in Article 43 to the tasks of the ECB and the EMI shall include those tasks that still need to be performed in the third stage owing to any decision of the United Kingdom not to adopt the euro.

(b)   In addition to the tasks referred to in Article 46, the ECB shall also give advice in relation to and contribute to the preparation of any decision of the Council with regard to the United Kingdom taken in accordance with paragraphs 9(a) and 9(c).

(c)   The Bank of England shall pay up its subscription to the capital of the ECB as a contribution to its operational costs on the same basis as national central banks of Member States with a derogation.

9.   The United Kingdom may notify the Council at any time of its intention to adopt the euro. In that event:

(a)   The United Kingdom shall have the right to adopt the euro provided only that it satisfies the necessary conditions. The Council, acting at the request of the United Kingdom and under the conditions and in accordance with the procedure laid down in Article 140(1) and (2) of the Treaty on the Functioning of the European Union, shall decide whether it fulfils the necessary conditions.

(b)   The Bank of England shall pay up its subscribed capital, transfer to the ECB foreign reserve assets and contribute to its reserves on the same basis as the national central bank of a Member State whose derogation has been abrogated.

(c)   The Council, acting under the conditions and in accordance with the procedure laid down in Article 140(3) of the said Treaty, shall take all other necessary decisions to enable the United Kingdom to adopt the euro.

If the United Kingdom adopts the euro pursuant to the provisions of this Protocol, paragraphs 3 to 8 shall cease to have effect.

10.   Notwithstanding Article 123 of the Treaty on the Functioning of the European Union and Article 21.1 of the Statute, the Government of the United Kingdom may maintain its 'ways and means' facility with the Bank of England if and so long as the United Kingdom does not adopt the euro.

PROTOCOL (NO 19) ON THE SCHENGEN *ACQUIS* INTEGRATED INTO THE FRAMEWORK OF THE EUROPEAN UNION

THE HIGH CONTRACTING PARTIES,

NOTING that the Agreements on the gradual abolition of checks at common borders signed by some Member States of the European Union in Schengen on 14 June 1985 and on 19 June 1990, as well as related agreements and the rules adopted on the basis of these agreements, have been integrated into the framework of the European Union by the Treaty of Amsterdam of 2 October 1997,

DESIRING to preserve the Schengen *acquis*, as developed since the entry into force of the Treaty of Amsterdam, and to develop this *acquis* in order to contribute towards achieving the objective of offering citizens of the Union an area of freedom, security and justice without internal borders,

TAKING INTO ACCOUNT the special position of Denmark,

TAKING INTO ACCOUNT the fact that Ireland and the United Kingdom of Great Britain and Northern Ireland do not participate in all the provisions of the Schengen *acquis*; that provision should, however, be made to allow those Member States to accept other provisions of this *acquis* in full or in part,

RECOGNISING that, as a consequence, it is necessary to make use of the provisions of the Treaties concerning closer cooperation between some Member States,

TAKING INTO ACCOUNT the need to maintain a special relationship with the Republic of Iceland and the Kingdom of Norway, both States being bound by the provisions of the Nordic passport union, together with the Nordic States which are members of the European Union,

HAVE AGREED UPON the following provisions, which shall be annexed to the Treaty on European Union and to the Treaty on the Functioning of the European Union:

Article 1
The Kingdom of Belgium, the Republic of Bulgaria, the Czech Republic, the Kingdom of Denmark, the Federal Republic of Germany, the Republic of Estonia, the Hellenic Republic, the Kingdom of Spain, the French Republic, the Italian Republic, the Republic of Cyprus, the Republic of Latvia, the Republic of Lithuania, the Grand Duchy of Luxembourg, the Republic of Hungary, Malta, the Kingdom of the Netherlands, the Republic of Austria, the Republic of Poland, the Portuguese Republic, Romania, the Republic of Slovenia, the Slovak Republic, the Republic of Finland and the Kingdom of Sweden shall be authorised to establish closer cooperation among themselves in areas covered by provisions defined by the Council which constitute the Schengen *acquis*. This cooperation shall be conducted within the institutional and legal framework of the European Union and with respect for the relevant provisions of the Treaties.

Article 2
The Schengen *acquis* shall apply to the Member States referred to in Article 1, without prejudice to Article 3 of the Act of Accession of 16 April 2003 or to Article 4 of the Act of Accession of 25 April 2005. The Council will substitute itself for the Executive Committee established by the Schengen agreements.

Article 3
The participation of Denmark in the adoption of measures constituting a development of the Schengen *acquis*, as well as the implementation of these measures and their application to Denmark, shall be governed by the relevant provisions of the Protocol on the position of Denmark.

Article 4
Ireland and the United Kingdom of Great Britain and Northern Ireland may at any time request to take part in some or all of the provisions of the Schengen *acquis*.
The Council shall decide on the request with the unanimity of its members referred to in Article 1 and of the representative of the Government of the State concerned.

Article 5
1. Proposals and initiatives to build upon the Schengen *acquis* shall be subject to the relevant provisions of the Treaties.

    In this context, where either Ireland or the United Kingdom has not notified the Council in writing within a reasonable period that it wishes to take part, the authorisation referred to in Article 329 of the Treaty on the Functioning of the European Union shall be deemed to have been granted to the Member States referred to in Article 1 and to Ireland or the United Kingdom where either of them wishes to take part in the areas of cooperation in question.

2.   Where either Ireland or the United Kingdom is deemed to have given notification pursuant to a decision under Article 4, it may nevertheless notify the Council in writing, within three months, that it does not wish to take part in such a proposal or initiative. In that case, Ireland or the United Kingdom shall not take part in its adoption. As from the latter notification, the procedure for adopting the measure building upon the Schengen *acquis* shall be suspended until the end of the procedure set out in paragraphs 3 or 4 or until the notification is withdrawn at any moment during that procedure.

3.   For the Member State having made the notification referred to in paragraph 2, any decision taken by the Council pursuant to Article 4 shall, as from the date of entry into force of the proposed measure, cease to apply to the extent considered necessary by the Council and under the conditions to be determined in a decision of the Council acting by a qualified majority on a proposal from the Commission. That decision shall be taken in accordance with the following criteria: the Council shall seek to retain the widest possible measure of participation of the Member State concerned without seriously affecting the practical operability of the various parts of the Schengen *acquis*, while respecting their coherence. The Commission shall submit its proposal as soon as possible after the notification referred to in paragraph 2. The Council shall, if needed after convening two successive meetings, act within four months of the Commission proposal.

4.   If, by the end of the period of four months, the Council has not adopted a decision, a Member State may, without delay, request that the matter be referred to the European Council. In that case, the European Council shall, at its next meeting, acting by a qualified majority on a proposal from the Commission, take a decision in accordance with the criteria referred to in paragraph 3.

5.   If, by the end of the procedure set out in paragraphs 3 or 4, the Council or, as the case may be, the European Council has not adopted its decision, the suspension of the procedure for adopting the measure building upon the Schengen *acquis* shall be terminated. If the said measure is subsequently adopted any decision taken by the Council pursuant to Article 4 shall, as from the date of entry into force of that measure, cease to apply for the Member State concerned to the extent and under the conditions decided by the Commission, unless the said Member State has withdrawn its notification referred to in paragraph 2 before the adoption of the measure. The Commission shall act by the date of this adoption. When taking its decision, the Commission shall respect the criteria referred to in paragraph 3.

Article 6
The Republic of Iceland and the Kingdom of Norway shall be associated with the implementation of the Schengen *acquis* and its further development. Appropriate procedures shall be agreed to that effect in an Agreement to be concluded with those States by the Council, acting by the unanimity of its Members mentioned in Article 1. Such Agreement shall include provisions on the contribution of Iceland and Norway to any financial consequences resulting from the implementation of this Protocol.

A separate Agreement shall be concluded with Iceland and Norway by the Council, acting unanimously, for the establishment of rights and obligations between Ireland and the United Kingdom of Great Britain and Northern Ireland on the one hand, and Iceland and Norway on the other, in domains of the Schengen *acquis* which apply to these States.

Article 7
For the purposes of the negotiations for the admission of new Member States into the European Union, the Schengen *acquis* and further measures taken by the institutions within its scope shall be regarded as an *acquis* which must be accepted in full by all States candidates for admission.

PROTOCOL (NO 20) ON THE APPLICATION OF CERTAIN ASPECTS OF ARTICLE 26 OF THE TREATY ON THE FUNCTIONING OF THE EUROPEAN UNION TO THE UNITED KINGDOM AND TO IRELAND

THE HIGH CONTRACTING PARTIES,

DESIRING to settle certain questions relating to the United Kingdom and Ireland,

HAVING REGARD to the existence for many years of special travel arrangements between the United Kingdom and Ireland,

HAVE AGREED UPON the following provisions, which shall be annexed to the Treaty on European Union and the Treaty on the Functioning of the European Union:

Article 1
The United Kingdom shall be entitled, notwithstanding Articles 26 and 77 of the Treaty on the Functioning of the European Union, any other provision of that Treaty or of the Treaty on European Union, any measure adopted under those Treaties, or any international agreement concluded by the Union or by the Union and its Member States with one or more third States, to exercise at its frontiers with other Member States such controls on persons seeking to enter the United Kingdom as it may consider necessary for the purpose:

(a)   of verifying the right to enter the United Kingdom of citizens of Member States and of their dependants exercising rights conferred by Union law, as well as citizens of other States on whom such rights have been conferred by an agreement by which the United Kingdom is bound; and

(b)   of determining whether or not to grant other persons permission to enter the United Kingdom.

Nothing in Articles 26 and 77 of the Treaty on the Functioning of the European Union or in any other provision of that Treaty or of the Treaty on European Union or in any measure adopted under them shall prejudice the right of the United Kingdom to adopt or exercise any such controls. References to the United Kingdom in this Article shall include territories for whose external relations the United Kingdom is responsible.

Article 2
The United Kingdom and Ireland may continue to make arrangements between themselves relating to the movement of persons between their territories ('the Common Travel Area'), while fully respecting the rights of persons referred to in Article 1, first paragraph, point (a) of this Protocol.

Accordingly, as long as they maintain such arrangements, the provisions of Article 1 of this Protocol shall apply to Ireland under the same terms and conditions as for the United Kingdom. Nothing in Articles 26 and 77 of the Treaty on the Functioning of the European Union, in any other provision of that Treaty or of the Treaty on European Union or in any measure adopted under them, shall affect any such arrangements.

Article 3
The other Member States shall be entitled to exercise at their frontiers or at any point of entry into their territory such controls on persons seeking to enter their territory from the United

Kingdom or any territories whose external relations are under its responsibility for the same purposes stated in Article 1 of this Protocol, or from Ireland as long as the provisions of Article 1 of this Protocol apply to Ireland.

Nothing in Articles 26 and 77 of the Treaty on the Functioning of the European Union or in any other provision of that Treaty or of the Treaty on European Union or in any measure adopted under them shall prejudice the right of the other Member States to adopt or exercise any such controls.

PROTOCOL (NO 21) ON THE POSITION OF THE UNITED KINGDOM AND IRELAND IN RESPECT OF THE AREA OF FREEDOM, SECURITY AND JUSTICE

THE HIGH CONTRACTING PARTIES,

DESIRING to settle certain questions relating to the United Kingdom and Ireland,

HAVING REGARD to the Protocol on the application of certain aspects of Article 26 of the Treaty on the Functioning of the European Union to the United Kingdom and to Ireland,

HAVE AGREED UPON the following provisions, which shall be annexed to the Treaty on European Union and the Treaty on the Functioning of the European Union:

Article 1
Subject to Article 3, the United Kingdom and Ireland shall not take part in the adoption by the Council of proposed measures pursuant to Title V of Part Three of the Treaty on the Functioning of the European Union. The unanimity of the members of the Council, with the exception of the representatives of the governments of the United Kingdom and Ireland, shall be necessary for decisions of the Council which must be adopted unanimously.

For the purposes of this Article, a qualified majority shall be defined in accordance with Article 238(3) of the Treaty on the Functioning of the European Union.

Article 2
In consequence of Article 1 and subject to Articles 3, 4 and 6, none of the provisions of Title V of Part Three of the Treaty on the Functioning of the European Union, no measure adopted pursuant to that Title, no provision of any international agreement concluded by the Union pursuant to that Title, and no decision of the Court of Justice interpreting any such provision or measure shall be binding upon or applicable in the United Kingdom or Ireland; and no such provision, measure or decision shall in any way affect the competences, rights and obligations of those States; and no such provision, measure or decision shall in any way affect the Community or Union *acquis* nor form part of Union law as they apply to the United Kingdom or Ireland.

Article 3
1.   The United Kingdom or Ireland may notify the President of the Council in writing, within three months after a proposal or initiative has been presented to the Council pursuant to Title V of Part Three of the Treaty on the Functioning of the European Union, that it wishes to take part in the adoption and application of any such proposed measure, whereupon that State shall be entitled to do so.

The unanimity of the members of the Council, with the exception of a member which has not made such a notification, shall be necessary for decisions of the Council which must be adopted unanimously. A measure adopted under this paragraph shall be binding upon all Member States which took part in its adoption.

Measures adopted pursuant to Article 70 of the Treaty on the Functioning of the European Union shall lay down the conditions for the participation of the United

Kingdom and Ireland in the evaluations concerning the areas covered by Title V of Part Three of that Treaty.

For the purposes of this Article, a qualified majority shall be defined in accordance with Article 238(3) of the Treaty on the Functioning of the European Union.

2.   If after a reasonable period of time a measure referred to in paragraph 1 cannot be adopted with the United Kingdom or Ireland taking part, the Council may adopt such measure in accordance with Article 1 without the participation of the United Kingdom or Ireland. In that case Article 2 applies.

Article 4
The United Kingdom or Ireland may at any time after the adoption of a measure by the Council pursuant to Title V of Part Three of the Treaty on the Functioning of the European Union notify its intention to the Council and to the Commission that it wishes to accept that measure. In that case, the procedure provided for in Article 331(1) of the Treaty on the Functioning of the European Union shall apply mutatis mutandis.

Article 4a
1.   The provisions of this Protocol apply for the United Kingdom and Ireland also to measures proposed or adopted pursuant to Title V of Part Three of the Treaty on the Functioning of the European Union amending an existing measure by which they are bound.

2.   However, in cases where the Council, acting on a proposal from the Commission, determines that the non-participation of the United Kingdom or Ireland in the amended version of an existing measure makes the application of that measure inoperable for other Member States or the Union, it may urge them to make a notification under Article 3 or 4. For the purposes of Article 3, a further period of two months starts to run as from the date of such determination by the Council.

If at the expiry of that period of two months from the Council's determination the United Kingdom or Ireland has not made a notification under Article 3 or Article 4, the existing measure shall no longer be binding upon or applicable to it, unless the Member State concerned has made a notification under Article 4 before the entry into force of the amending measure. This shall take effect from the date of entry into force of the amending measure or of expiry of the period of two months, whichever is the later.

For the purpose of this paragraph, the Council shall, after a full discussion of the matter, act by a qualified majority of its members representing the Member States participating or having participated in the adoption of the amending measure. A qualified majority of the Council shall be defined in accordance with Article 238(3)(a) of the Treaty on the Functioning of the European Union.

3.   The Council, acting by a qualified majority on a proposal from the Commission, may determine that the United Kingdom or Ireland shall bear the direct financial consequences, if any, necessarily and unavoidably incurred as a result of the cessation of its participation in the existing measure.

4.   This Article shall be without prejudice to Article 4.

Article 5
A Member State which is not bound by a measure adopted pursuant to Title V of Part Three of the Treaty on the Functioning of the European Union shall bear no financial consequences of that measure other than administrative costs entailed for the institutions, unless all

members of the Council, acting unanimously after consulting the European Parliament, decide otherwise.

Article 6
Where, in cases referred to in this Protocol, the United Kingdom or Ireland is bound by a measure adopted by the Council pursuant to Title V of Part Three of the Treaty on the Functioning of the European Union, the relevant provisions of the Treaties shall apply to that State in relation to that measure.

Article 6a
The United Kingdom and Ireland shall not be bound by the rules laid down on the basis of Article 16 of the Treaty on the Functioning of the European Union which relate to the processing of personal data by the Member States when carrying out activities which fall within the scope of Chapter 4 or Chapter 5 of Title V of Part Three of that Treaty where the United Kingdom and Ireland are not bound by the rules governing the forms of judicial cooperation in criminal matters or police cooperation which require compliance with the provisions laid down on the basis of Article 16.

Article 7
Articles 3, 4 and 4a shall be without prejudice to the Protocol on the Schengen *acquis* integrated into the framework of the European Union.

Article 8
Ireland may notify the Council in writing that it no longer wishes to be covered by the terms of this Protocol. In that case, the normal treaty provisions will apply to Ireland.

Article 9
With regard to Ireland, this Protocol shall not apply to Article 75 of the Treaty on the Functioning of the European Union.

PROTOCOL (NO 23) ON EXTERNAL RELATIONS OF THE MEMBER STATES WITH REGARD TO THE CROSSING OF EXTERNAL BORDERS

THE HIGH CONTRACTING PARTIES,

TAKING INTO ACCOUNT the need of the Member States to ensure effective controls at their external borders, in cooperation with third countries where appropriate,

HAVE AGREED UPON the following provisions, which shall be annexed to the Treaty on European Union and to the Treaty on the Functioning of the European Union:

The provisions on the measures on the crossing of external borders included in Article 77(2)(b) of the Treaty on the Functioning of the European Union shall be without prejudice to the competence of Member States to negotiate or conclude agreements with third countries as long as they respect Union law and other relevant international agreements.

PROTOCOL (NO 24) ON ASYLUM FOR NATIONALS OF MEMBER STATES OF THE EUROPEAN UNION

THE HIGH CONTRACTING PARTIES,

WHEREAS, in accordance with Article 6(1) of the Treaty on European Union, the Union recognises the rights, freedoms and principles set out in the Charter of Fundamental Rights,

WHEREAS pursuant to Article 6(3) of the Treaty on European Union, fundamental rights, as guaranteed by the European Convention for the Protection of Human Rights and Fundamental Freedoms, constitute part of the Union's law as general principles,

WHEREAS the Court of Justice of the European Union has jurisdiction to ensure that in the interpretation and application of Article 6, paragraphs (1) and (3) of the Treaty on European Union the law is observed by the European Union,

WHEREAS pursuant to Article 49 of the Treaty on European Union any European State, when applying to become a Member of the Union, must respect the values set out in Article 2 of the Treaty on European Union,

BEARING IN MIND that Article 7 of the Treaty on European Union establishes a mechanism for the suspension of certain rights in the event of a serious and persistent breach by a Member State of those values,

RECALLING that each national of a Member State, as a citizen of the Union, enjoys a special status and protection which shall be guaranteed by the Member States in accordance with the provisions of Part Two of the Treaty on the Functioning of the European Union,

BEARING IN MIND that the Treaties establish an area without internal frontiers and grant every citizen of the Union the right to move and reside freely within the territory of the Member States,

WISHING to prevent the institution of asylum being resorted to for purposes alien to those for which it is intended,

WHEREAS this Protocol respects the finality and the objectives of the Geneva Convention of 28 July 1951 relating to the status of refugees,

HAVE AGREED UPON the following provisions, which shall be annexed to the Treaty on European Union and to the Treaty on the Functioning of the European Union:

Sole Article
Given the level of protection of fundamental rights and freedoms by the Member States of the European Union, Member States shall be regarded as constituting safe countries of origin in respect of each other for all legal and practical purposes in relation to asylum matters. Accordingly, any application for asylum made by a national of a Member State may be taken into consideration or declared admissible for processing by another Member State only in the following cases:

(a)   if the Member State of which the applicant is a national proceeds after the entry into force of the Treaty of Amsterdam, availing itself of the provisions of Article 15 of the European Convention for the Protection of Human Rights and Fundamental Freedoms, to take measures derogating in its territory from its obligations under that Convention;

(b)   if the procedure referred to Article 7(1) of the Treaty on European Union has been initiated and until the Council, or, where appropriate, the European Council, takes a decision in respect thereof with regard to the Member State of which the applicant is a national;

(c)   if the Council has adopted a decision in accordance with Article 7(1) of the Treaty on European Union in respect of the Member State of which the applicant is a national or if the European Council has adopted a decision in accordance with Article 7(2) of that Treaty in respect of the Member State of which the applicant is a national;

(d)   if a Member State should so decide unilaterally in respect of the application of a national of another Member State; in that case the Council shall be immediately informed; the application shall be dealt with on the basis of the presumption that it is manifestly unfounded without affecting in any way, whatever the cases may be, the decision-making power of the Member State.

PROTOCOL (NO 25) ON THE EXERCISE OF SHARED COMPETENCE

THE HIGH CONTRACTING PARTIES,

HAVE AGREED UPON the following provisions, which shall be annexed to the Treaty on European Union and to the Treaty on the Functioning of the European Union:

Sole Article
With reference to Article 2(2) of the Treaty on the Functioning of the European Union on shared competence, when the Union has taken action in a certain area, the scope of this exercise of competence only covers those elements governed by the Union act in question and therefore does not cover the whole area.

PROTOCOL (NO 26) ON SERVICES OF GENERAL INTEREST

THE HIGH CONTRACTING PARTIES,

WISHING to emphasise the importance of services of general interest,

HAVE AGREED UPON the following interpretative provisions, which shall be annexed to the Treaty on European Union and to the Treaty on the Functioning of the European Union:

Article 1
The shared values of the Union in respect of services of general economic interest within the meaning of Article 14 of the Treaty on the Functioning of the European Union include in particular:
—   the essential role and the wide discretion of national, regional and local authorities in providing, commissioning and organising services of general economic interest as closely as possible to the needs of the users;
—   the diversity between various services of general economic interest and the differences in the needs and preferences of users that may result from different geographical, social or cultural situations;
—   a high level of quality, safety and affordability, equal treatment and the promotion of universal access and of user rights.

Article 2
The provisions of the Treaties do not affect in any way the competence of Member States to provide, commission and organise non-economic services of general interest.

PROTOCOL (NO 27) ON THE INTERNAL MARKET AND COMPETITION

THE HIGH CONTRACTING PARTIES,

CONSIDERING that the internal market as set out in Article 3 of the Treaty on European Union includes a system ensuring that competition is not distorted,

HAVE AGREED that:

To this end, the Union shall, if necessary, take action under the provisions of the Treaties, including under Article 352 of the Treaty on the Functioning of the European Union.

This protocol shall be annexed to the Treaty on European Union and to the Treaty on the Functioning of the European Union.

PROTOCOL (No 30) ON THE APPLICATION OF THE CHARTER OF FUNDAMENTAL RIGHTS OF THE EUROPEAN UNION TO POLAND AND TO THE UNITED KINGDOM

THE HIGH CONTRACTING PARTIES,

WHEREAS in Article 6 of the Treaty on European Union, the Union recognises the rights, freedoms and principles set out in the Charter of Fundamental Rights of the European Union,

WHEREAS the Charter is to be applied in strict accordance with the provisions of the aforementioned Article 6 and Title VII of the Charter itself,

WHEREAS the aforementioned Article 6 requires the Charter to be applied and interpreted by the courts of Poland and of the United Kingdom strictly in accordance with the explanations referred to in that Article,

WHEREAS the Charter contains both rights and principles,

WHEREAS the Charter contains both provisions which are civil and political in character and those which are economic and social in character,

WHEREAS the Charter reaffirms the rights, freedoms and principles recognised in the Union and makes those rights more visible, but does not create new rights or principles,

RECALLING the obligations devolving upon Poland and the United Kingdom under the Treaty on European Union, the Treaty on the Functioning of the European Union, and Union law generally,

NOTING the wish of Poland and the United Kingdom to clarify certain aspects of the application of the Charter,

DESIROUS therefore of clarifying the application of the Charter in relation to the laws and administrative action of Poland and of the United Kingdom and of its justiciability within Poland and within the United Kingdom,

REAFFIRMING that references in this Protocol to the operation of specific provisions of the Charter are strictly without prejudice to the operation of other provisions of the Charter,

REAFFIRMING that this Protocol is without prejudice to the application of the Charter to other Member States,

REAFFIRMING that this Protocol is without prejudice to other obligations devolving upon Poland and the United Kingdom under the Treaty on European Union, the Treaty on the Functioning of the European Union, and Union law generally,

HAVE AGREED UPON the following provisions, which shall be annexed to the Treaty on European Union and to the Treaty on the Functioning of the European Union:

Article 1
1. The Charter does not extend the ability of the Court of Justice of the European Union, or any court or tribunal of Poland or of the United Kingdom, to find that the laws, regulations or administrative provisions, practices or action of Poland or of the United

Kingdom are inconsistent with the fundamental rights, freedoms and principles that it reaffirms.

2. In particular, and for the avoidance of doubt, nothing in Title IV of the Charter creates justiciable rights applicable to Poland or the United Kingdom except in so far as Poland or the United Kingdom has provided for such rights in its national law.

Article 2
To the extent that a provision of the Charter refers to national laws and practices, it shall only apply to Poland or the United Kingdom to the extent that the rights or principles that it contains are recognised in the law or practices of Poland or of the United Kingdom.

PROTOCOL (No 36) ON TRANSITIONAL PROVISIONS

THE HIGH CONTRACTING PARTIES,

WHEREAS, in order to organise the transition from the institutional provisions of the Treaties applicable prior to the entry into force of the Treaty of Lisbon to the provisions contained in that Treaty, it is necessary to lay down transitional provisions,

HAVE AGREED UPON the following provisions, which shall be annexed to the Treaty on European Union, to the Treaty on the Functioning of the European Union and to the Treaty establishing the European Atomic Energy Community:

Article 1
In this Protocol, the words 'the Treaties' shall mean the Treaty on European Union, the Treaty on the Functioning of the European Union and the Treaty establishing the European Atomic Energy Community.

TITLE I
PROVISIONS CONCERNING THE EUROPEAN PARLIAMENT

Article 2
In accordance with the second subparagraph of Article 14(2) of the Treaty on European Union, the European Council shall adopt a decision determining the composition of the European Parliament in good time before the 2009 European Parliament elections.
Until the end of the 2004–2009 parliamentary term, the composition and the number of representatives elected to the European Parliament shall remain the same as on the date of the entry into force of the Treaty of Lisbon.

TITLE II
PROVISIONS CONCERNING THE QUALIFIED MAJORITY

Article 3
1. In accordance with Article 16(4) of the Treaty on European Union, the provisions of that paragraph and of Article 238(2) of the Treaty on the Functioning of the European Union relating to the definition of the qualified majority in the European Council and the Council shall take effect on 1 November 2014.

2. Between 1 November 2014 and 31 March 2017, when an act is to be adopted by qualified majority, a member of the Council may request that it be adopted in accordance with the qualified majority as defined in paragraph 3. In that case, paragraphs 3 and 4 shall apply.

3.   Until 31 October 2014, the following provisions shall remain in force, without prejudice to the second subparagraph of Article 235(1) of the Treaty on the Functioning of the European Union.

For acts of the European Council and of the Council requiring a qualified majority, members' votes shall be weighted as follows:

Belgium 12	Luxembourg 4
Bulgaria 10	Hungary 12
Czech Republic 12	Malta 3
Denmark 7	Netherlands 13
Germany 29	Austria 10
Estonia 4	Poland 27
Ireland 7	Portugal 12
Greece 12	Romania 14
Spain 27	Slovenia 4
France 29	Slovakia 7
Italy 29	Finland 7
Cyprus 4	Sweden 10
Latvia 4	United Kingdom 29
Lithuania 7	

Acts shall be adopted if there are at least 255 votes in favour representing a majority of the members where, under the Treaties, they must be adopted on a proposal from the Commission. In other cases decisions shall be adopted if there are at least 255 votes in favour representing at least two thirds of the members.

A member of the European Council or the Council may request that, where an act is adopted by the European Council or the Council by a qualified majority, a check is made to ensure that the Member States comprising the qualified majority represent at least 62% of the total population of the Union. If that proves not to be the case, the act shall not be adopted.

4.   Until 31 October 2014, the qualified majority shall, in cases where, under the Treaties, not all the members of the Council participate in voting, namely in the cases where reference is made to the qualified majority as defined in Article 238(3) of the Treaty on the Functioning of the European Union, be defined as the same proportion of the weighted votes and the same proportion of the number of the Council members and, if appropriate, the same percentage of the population of the Member States concerned as laid down in paragraph 3 of this Article.

TITLE III
PROVISIONS CONCERNING THE CONFIGURATIONS OF THE COUNCIL

Article 4
Until the entry into force of the decision referred to in the first subparagraph of Article 16(6) of the Treaty on European Union, the Council may meet in the configurations laid down in the second and third subparagraphs of that paragraph and in the other configurations on the list established by a decision of the General Affairs Council, acting by a simple majority.

TITLE IV
PROVISIONS CONCERNING THE COMMISSION, INCLUDING THE HIGH REPRESENTATIVE OF THE UNION FOR FOREIGN AFFAIRS AND SECURITY POLICY

Article 5

The members of the Commission in office on the date of entry into force of the Treaty of Lisbon shall remain in office until the end of their term of office. However, on the day of the appointment of the High Representative of the Union for Foreign Affairs and Security Policy, the term of office of the member having the same nationality as the High Representative shall end.

TITLE V
PROVISIONS CONCERNING THE SECRETARY-GENERAL OF THE COUNCIL, HIGH REPRESENTATIVE FOR THE COMMON FOREIGN AND SECURITY POLICY, AND THE DEPUTY SECRETARY-GENERAL OF THE COUNCIL

Article 6

The terms of office of the Secretary-General of the Council, High Representative for the common foreign and security policy, and the Deputy Secretary-General of the Council shall end on the date of entry into force of the Treaty of Lisbon. The Council shall appoint a Secretary-General in conformity with Article 240(2) of the Treaty on the Functioning of the European Union.

TITLE VI
PROVISIONS CONCERNING ADVISORY BODIES

Article 7

Until the entry into force of the decision referred to in Article 301 of the Treaty on the Functioning of the European Union, the allocation of members of the Economic and Social Committee shall be as follows:

Belgium 12	Spain 21
Bulgaria 12	France 24
Czech Republic 12	Italy 24
Denmark 9	Cyprus 6
Germany 24	Latvia 7
Estonia 7	Lithuania 9
Ireland 9	Luxembourg 6
Greece 12	Hungary 12
Malta 5	Slovenia 7
Netherlands 12	Slovakia 9
Austria 12	Finland 9
Poland 21	Sweden 12
Portugal 12	United Kingdom 24
Romania 15	

Article 8

Until the entry into force of the decision referred to in Article 305 of the Treaty on the Functioning of the European Union, the allocation of members of the Committee of the Regions shall be as follows:

Belgium 12
Bulgaria 12
Czech Republic 12
Denmark 9
Germany 24
Estonia 7
Ireland 9
Greece 12
Spain 21
France 24
Italy 24
Cyprus 6
Latvia 7
Lithuania 9

Luxembourg 6
Hungary 12
Malta 5
Netherlands 12
Austria 12
Poland 21
Portugal 12
Romania 15
Slovenia 7
Slovakia 9
Finland 9
Sweden 12
United Kingdom 24

TITLE VII
TRANSITIONAL PROVISIONS CONCERNING ACTS ADOPTED ON THE BASIS OF TITLES V AND VI OF THE TREATY ON EUROPEAN UNION PRIOR TO THE ENTRY INTO FORCE OF THE TREATY OF LISBON

Article 9
The legal effects of the acts of the institutions, bodies, offices and agencies of the Union adopted on the basis of the Treaty on European Union prior to the entry into force of the Treaty of Lisbon shall be preserved until those acts are repealed, annulled or amended in implementation of the Treaties. The same shall apply to agreements concluded between Member States on the basis of the Treaty on European Union.

Article 10
1. As a transitional measure, and with respect to acts of the Union in the field of police cooperation and judicial cooperation in criminal matters which have been adopted before the entry into force of the Treaty of Lisbon, the powers of the institutions shall be the following at the date of entry into force of that Treaty: the powers of the Commission under Article 258 of the Treaty on the Functioning of the European Union shall not be applicable and the powers of the Court of Justice of the European Union under Title VI of the Treaty on European Union, in the version in force before the entry into force of the Treaty of Lisbon, shall remain the same, including where they have been accepted under Article 35(2) of the said Treaty on European Union.

2. The amendment of an act referred to in paragraph 1 shall entail the applicability of the powers of the institutions referred to in that paragraph as set out in the Treaties with respect to the amended act for those Member States to which that amended act shall apply.

3. In any case, the transitional measure mentioned in paragraph 1 shall cease to have effect five years after the date of entry into force of the Treaty of Lisbon.

4. At the latest six months before the expiry of the transitional period referred to in paragraph 3, the United Kingdom may notify to the Council that it does not accept, with respect to the acts referred to in paragraph 1, the powers of the institutions referred to in paragraph 1 as set out in the Treaties. In case the United Kingdom has made that notification, all acts referred to in paragraph 1 shall cease to apply to it as from the date of expiry of the transitional period referred to in paragraph 3. This subparagraph shall not apply with respect to the amended acts which are applicable to the United Kingdom as referred to in paragraph 2.

The Council, acting by a qualified majority on a proposal from the Commission, shall determine the necessary consequential and transitional arrangements. The United Kingdom shall not participate in the adoption of this decision. A qualified majority of the Council shall be defined in accordance with Article 238(3)(a) of the Treaty on the Functioning of the European Union.

The Council, acting by a qualified majority on a proposal from the Commission, may also adopt a decision determining that the United Kingdom shall bear the direct financial consequences, if any, necessarily and unavoidably incurred as a result of the cessation of its participation in those acts.

5. The United Kingdom may, at any time afterwards, notify the Council of its wish to participate in acts which have ceased to apply to it pursuant to paragraph 4, first subparagraph. In that case, the relevant provisions of the Protocol on the Schengen *acquis* integrated into the framework of the European Union or of the Protocol on the position of the United Kingdom and Ireland in respect of the area of freedom, security and justice, as the case may be, shall apply. The powers of the institutions with regard to those acts shall be those set out in the Treaties. When acting under the relevant Protocols, the Union institutions and the United Kingdom shall seek to re-establish the widest possible measure of participation of the United Kingdom in the *acquis* of the Union in the area of freedom, security and justice without seriously affecting the practical operability of the various parts thereof, while respecting their coherence.

II Tables of Equivalences

CONSOLIDATED VERSION OF THE TREATY ON EUROPEAN UNION – TABLES OF EQUIVALENCES*

OJ C 83, 30.3.2010, p. 361

TREATY ON EUROPEAN UNION[1]

Old numbering of the TEU	New numbering of the TEU
TITLE I — COMMON PROVISIONS	TITLE I — COMMON PROVISIONS
Article 1	Article 1
	Article 2
Article 2	Article 3
Article 3 (repealed) (1)	
	Article 4
	Article 5 (2)
Article 4 (repealed) (3)	
Article 5 (repealed) (4)	
Article 6	Article 6
Article 7	Article 7
	Article 8
TITLE II — PROVISIONS AMENDING THE TEC WITH A VIEW TO ESTABLISHING THE EC	TITLE II — PROVISIONS ON DEMOCRATIC PRINCIPLES
Article 8 (repealed) (5)	Article 9
	Article 10 (6)
	Article 11
	Article 12
TITLE III — PROVISIONS AMENDING THE TREATY ESTABLISHING THE EUROPEAN COAL AND STEEL COMMUNITY	TITLE III — PROVISIONS ON THE INSTITUTIONS
Article 9 (repealed) (7)	Article 13
	Article 14 (8)

---

*   Tables of equivalences as referred to in Article 5 of the Treaty of Lisbon. The original centre column, which set out the intermediate numbering as used in that Treaty, has been omitted.

Old numbering of the TEU	New numbering of the TEU
	Article 15 (9)
	Article 16 (10)
	Article 17 (11)
	Article 18
	Article 19 (12)
TITLE IV — PROVISIONS AMENDING THE TREATY ESTABLISHING THE EUROPEAN ATOMIC ENERGY COMMUNITY	TITLE IV — PROVISIONS ON ENHANCED COOPERATION
Article 10 (repealed) (13)	
Articles 27a to 27e (replaced)	
Articles 40 to 40b (replaced)	
Articles 43 to 45 (replaced)	
	Article 20 (14)
TITLE V — PROVISIONS ON A COMMON FOREIGN AND SECURITY POLICY	TITLE V — GENERAL PROVISIONS ON THE UNION'S EXTERNAL ACTION AND SPECIFIC PROVISIONS ON THE COMMON FOREIGN AND SECURITY POLICY
	Chapter 1 — General provisions on the Union's external action
	Article 21
	Article 22
	Chapter 2 — Specific provisions on the common foreign and security policy
	Section 1 — Common provisions
	Article 23
Article 11	Article 24
Article 12	Article 25
Article 13	Article 26
	Article 27
Article 14	Article 28
Article 15	Article 29
Article 22 (moved)	Article 30
Article 23 (moved)	Article 31
Article 16	Article 32
Article 17 (moved)	*Article 42*
Article 18	Article 33
Article 19	Article 34
Article 20	Article 35
Article 21	Article 36
Article 22 (moved)	*Article 30*
Article 23 (moved)	*Article 31*
Article 24	Article 37
Article 25	Article 38
	Article 39
Article 47 (moved)	Article 40

Old numbering of the TEU	New numbering of the TEU
Article 26 (repealed)	
Article 27 (repealed)	
Article 27a (replaced) (15)	*Article 20*
Article 27b (replaced) (15)	*Article 20*
Article 27c (replaced) (15)	*Article 20*
Article 27d (replaced) (15)	*Article 20*
Article 27e (replaced) (15)	*Article 20*
Article 28	Article 41
	Section 2 — Provisions on the common security and defence policy
Article 17 (moved)	Article 42
	Article 43
	Article 44
	Article 45
	Article 46
TITLE VI — PROVISIONS ON POLICE AND JUDICIAL COOPERATION IN CRIMINAL MATTERS (repealed) (16)	
Article 29 (replaced) (17)	
Article 30 (replaced) (18)	
Article 31 (replaced) (19)	
Article 32 (replaced) (20)	
Article 33 (replaced) (21)	
Article 34 (repealed)	
Article 35 (repealed)	
Article 36 (replaced) (22)	
Article 37 (repealed)	
Article 38 (repealed)	
Article 39 (repealed)	
Article 40 (replaced) (23)	*Article 20*
Article 40 A (replaced) (23)	*Article 20*
Article 40 B (replaced) (23)	*Article 20*
Article 41 (repealed)	
Article 42 (repealed)	
TITLE VII — PROVISIONS ON ENHANCED COOPERATION (replaced) (24)	
TITLE IV — PROVISIONS ON ENHANCED COOPERATION	
Article 43 (replaced) (24)	*Article 20*
Article 43 A (replaced) (24)	*Article 20*
Article 43 B (replaced) (24)	*Article 20*
Article 44 (replaced) (24)	*Article 20*
Article 44 A (replaced) (24)	*Article 20*
Article 45 (replaced) (24)	*Article 20*

Old numbering of the TEU	New numbering of the TEU
TITLE VIII—FINAL PROVISIONS	TITLE VI—FINAL PROVISIONS
Article 46 (repealed)	
	Article 47
Article 47 (replaced)	*Article 40*
Article 48	Article 48
Article 49	Article 49
	Article 50
	Article 51
	Article 52
Article 50 (repealed)	
Article 51	Article 53
Article 52	Article 54
Article 53	Article 55

(1) Replaced, in substance, by Article 7 of the Treaty on the Functioning of the European Union ('TFEU') and by Articles 13(1) and 21, paragraph 3, second subparagraph of the Treaty on European Union ('TEU').

(2) Replaces Article 5 of the Treaty establishing the European Community ('TEC').

(3) Replaced, in substance, by Article 15.

(4) Replaced, in substance, by Article 13, paragraph 2.

(5) Article 8 TEU, which was in force until the entry into force of the Treaty of Lisbon (hereinafter 'current'), amended the TEC. Those amendments are incorporated into the latter Treaty and Article 8 is repealed. Its number is used to insert a new provision.

(6) Paragraph 4 replaces, in substance, the first subparagraph of Article 191 TEC.

(7) The current Article 9 TEU amended the Treaty establishing the European Coal and Steel Community. This latter expired on 23 July 2002. Article 9 is repealed and the number thereof is used to insert another provision.

(8) — Paragraphs 1 and 2 replace, in substance, Article 189 TEC;
— paragraphs 1 to 3 replace, in substance, paragraphs 1 to 3 of Article 190 TEC;
— paragraph 1 replaces, in substance, the first subparagraph of Article 192 TEC;
— paragraph 4 replaces, in substance, the first subparagraph of Article 197 TEC.

(9) Replaces, in substance, Article 4.

(10) — Paragraph 1 replaces, in substance, the first and second indents of Article 202 TEC;
— paragraphs 2 and 9 replace, in substance, Article 203 TEC;
— paragraphs 4 and 5 replace, in substance, paragraphs 2 and 4 of Article 205 TEC.

(11) Paragraph 1 replaces, in substance, Article 211 TEC;
— paragraphs 3 and 7 replace, in substance, Article 214 TEC.
— paragraph 6 replaces, in substance, paragraphs 1, 3 and 4 of Article 217 TEC.

(12) — Replaces, in substance, Article 220 TEC.
— the second subparagraph of paragraph 2 replaces, in substance, the first subparagraph of Article 221 TEC.

(13) The current Article 10 TEU amended the Treaty establishing the European Atomic Energy Community. Those amendments are incorporated into the Treaty of Lisbon. Article 10 is repealed and the number thereof is used to insert another provision.

(14) Also replaces Articles 11 and 11a TEC.

(15) The current Articles 27a to 27e, on enhanced cooperation, are also replaced by Articles 326 to 334 TFEU.

(16) The current provisions of Title VI of the TEU, on police and judicial cooperation in criminal matters, are replaced by the provisions of Chapters 1, 5 and 5 of Title IV of Part Three of the TFEU.

(17) Replaced by Article 67 TFEU.

(18) Replaced by Articles 87 and 88 TFEU.

(19) Replaced by Articles 82, 83 and 85 TFEU.

(20) Replaced by Article 89 TFEU.

(21) Replaced by Article 72 TFEU.

(22) Replaced by Article 71 TFEU.

(23) The current Articles 40 to 40 B TEU, on enhanced cooperation, are also replaced by Articles 326 to 334 TFEU.

(24) The current Articles 43 to 45 and Title VII of the TEU, on enhanced cooperation, are also replaced by Articles 326 to 334 TFEU.

TREATY ON THE FUNCTIONING OF THE EUROPEAN UNION

Old numbering of the TEU	New numbering of the TEU
PART ONE — PRINCIPLES	PART ONE — PRINCIPLES
Article 1 (repealed)	
	Article 1
Article 2 (repealed) (25)	
	Title I — Categories and areas of Union competence
	Article 2
	Article 3
	Article 4
	Article 5
	Article 6
	Title II — Provisions having general Application
	Article 7
Article 3, paragraph 1 (repealed) (26)	
Article 3, paragraph 2	Article 8
Article 4 (moved)	*Article 119*
Article 5 (replaced) (27)	
	Article 9
	Article 10
Article 6	Article 11
Article 153, paragraph 2 (moved)	Article 12
	Article 13 (28)
Article 7 (repealed) (29)	
Article 8 (repealed) (30)	
Article 9 (repealed)	
Article 10 (repealed) (31)	
Article 11 (replaced) (32)	*Articles 326 to 334*
Article 11a (replaced) (32)	*Articles 326 to 334*
Article 12 (repealed)	*Article 18*
Article 13 (moved)	*Article 19*
Article 14 (moved)	*Article 26*
Article 15 (moved)	*Article 27*
Article 16	Article 14
Article 255 (moved)	Article 15
Article 286 (moved)	Article 16
	Article 17
PART TWO — CITIZENSHIP OF THE UNION	PART TWO — NON-DISCRIMINATION AND CITIZENSHIP OF THE UNION
Article 12 (moved)	Article 18
Article 13 (moved)	Article 19
Article 17	Article 20
Article 18	Article 21
Article 19	Article 22
Article 20	Article 23
Article 21	Article 24
Article 22	Article 25

Old numbering of the TEU	New numbering of the TEU
PART THREE — COMMUNITY POLICIES	PART THREE — POLICIES AND INTERNAL ACTIONS OF THE UNION
	Title I — The internal market
Article 14 (moved)	Article 26
Article 15 (moved)	Article 27
Title I — Free movement of goods	Title II — Free movement of goods
Article 23	Article 28
Article 24	Article 29
Chapter 1 — The customs union	Chapter 1 — The customs union
Article 25	Article 30
Article 26	Article 31
Article 27	Article 32
Part Three, Title X, Customs cooperation (moved)	Chapter 2 — Customs cooperation
Article 135 (moved)	Article 33
Chapter 2 — Prohibition of quantitative restrictions between Member States	Chapter 3 — Prohibition of quantitative restrictions between Member States
Article 28	Article 34
Article 29	Article 35
Article 30	Article 36
Article 31	Article 37
Title II — Agriculture	Title III — Agriculture and fisheries
Article 32	Article 38
Article 33	Article 39
Article 34	Article 40
Article 35	Article 41
Article 36	Article 42
Article 37	Article 43
Article 38	Article 44
Title III — Free movement of persons, services and capital	Title IV — Free movement of persons, services and capital
Chapter 1 — Workers	Chapter 1 — Workers
Article 39	Article 45
Article 40	Article 46
Article 41	Article 47
Article 42	Article 48
Chapter 2 — Right of establishment	Chapter 2 — Right of establishment
Article 43	Article 49
Article 44	Article 50
Article 45	Article 51
Article 46	Article 52
Article 47	Article 53
Article 48	Article 54
Article 294 (moved)	Article 55
Chapter 3 — Services	Chapter 3 — Services

Old numbering of the TEU	New numbering of the TEU
Article 49	Article 56
Article 50	Article 57
Article 51	Article 58
Article 52	Article 59
Article 53	Article 60
Article 54	Article 61
Article 55	Article 62
Chapter 4 — Capital and payments	Chapter 4 — Capital and payments
Article 56	Article 63
Article 57	Article 64
Article 58	Article 65
Article 59	Article 66
Article 60 (moved)	*Article 75*
Title IV — Visas, asylum, immigration and other policies related to free movement of persons	Title V — Area of freedom, security and justice
	Chapter 1 — General provisions
Article 61	Article 67 (33)
	Article 68
	Article 69
	Article 70
	Article 71 (34)
Article 64, paragraph 1 (replaced)	Article 72 (35)
	Article 73
Article 66 (replaced)	Article 74
Article 60 (moved)	Article 75
	Article 76
	Chapter 2 — Policies on border checks, asylum and immigration
Article 62	Article 77
Article 63, points 1 et 2, and Article 64, paragraph 2 (36)	Article 78
Article 63, points 3 and 4	Article 79
	Article 80
Article 64, paragraph 1 (replaced)	*Article 72*
	Chapter 3 — Judicial cooperation in civil matters
Article 65	Article 81
Article 66 (replaced)	*Article 74*
Article 67 (repealed)	
Article 68 (repealed)	
Article 69 (repealed)	
	Chapter 4 — Judicial cooperation in criminal matters
	Article 82 (37)
	Article 83 (37)
	Article 84
	Article 85 (37)

Old numbering of the TEU	New numbering of the TEU
	Article 86
	Chapter 5 — Police cooperation
	Article 87 (38)
	Article 88 (38)
	Article 89 (39)
Title V — Transport	Title VI — Transport
Article 70	Article 90
Article 71	Article 91
Article 72	Article 92
Article 73	Article 93
Article 74	Article 94
Article 75	Article 95
Article 76	Article 96
Article 77	Article 97
Article 78	Article 98
Article 79	Article 99
Article 80	Article 100
Title VI — Common rules on competition, competition, taxation and approximation	Title VII — Common rules on competition, taxation and approximation of laws
Chapter 1 — Rules on competition	Chapter 1 — Rules on competition
Section 1 — Rules applying to undertakings	Section 1 — Rules applying to undertakings
Article 81	Article 101
Article 82	Article 102
Article 83	Article 103
Article 84	Article 104
Article 85	Article 105
Article 86	Article 106
Section 2 — Aids granted by States	Section 2 — Aids granted by States
Article 87	Article 107
Article 88	Article 108
Article 89	Article 109
Chapter 2 — Tax provisions	Chapter 2 — Tax provisions
Article 90	Article 110
Article 91	Article 111
Article 92	Article 112
Article 93	Article 113
Chapter 3 — Approximation of laws	Chapter 3 — Approximation of laws
Article 95 (moved)	Article 114
Article 94 (moved)	Article 115
Article 96	Article 116
Article 97	Article 117
	Article 118
Title VII — Economic and monetary policy	Title VIII — Economic and monetary policy
Article 4 (moved)	Article 119
Chapter 1 — Economic policy	Chapter 1 — Economic policy
Article 98	Article 120
Article 99	Article 121
Article 100	Article 122

Old numbering of the TEU	New numbering of the TEU
Article 101	Article 123
Article 102	Article 124
Article 103	Article 125
Article 104	Article 126
Chapter 2 — monetary policy	Chapter 2 — monetary policy
Article 105	Article 127
Article 106	Article 128
Article 107	Article 129
Article 108	Article 130
Article 109	Article 131
Article 110	Article 132
Article 111, paras. 1 to 3 & 5 (moved)	*Article 219*
Article 111, para. 4 (moved)	*Article 138*
	Article 133
Chapter 3 — Institutional provisions	Chapter 3 — Institutional provisions
Article 112 (moved)	*Article 283*
Article 113 (moved)	*Article 284*
Article 114	Article 134
Article 115	Article 135
	Chapter 4 — Provisions specific to Member States whose currency is the euro
	Article 136
	Article 137
Article 111, paragraph 4 (moved)	Article 138
Chapter 4 — Transitional provisions	Chapter 5 — Transitional provisions
Article 116 (repealed)	
	Article 139
Article 117, paras. 1, 2, sixth indent, and 3 to 9 (repealed)	
Article 117, para. 2, first five indents (moved)	*Article 141, para. 2*
Article 121, para. 1 (moved)	Article 140 (40)
Article 122, para. 2, second sentence (moved)	
Article 123, para. 5 (moved)	
Article 118 (repealed)	
Article 123, para. 3 (moved)	Article 141 (41)
Article 117, para. 2, first five indents (moved)	
Article 124, para. 1 (moved)	Article 142
Article 119	Article 143
Article 120	Article 144
Article 121, para. 1 (moved)	*Article 140, para. 1*
Article 121, paras. 2 to 4 (repealed)	
Article 122, paras. 1, 2, first sentence, 3, 4, 5 and 6 (repealed)	
Article 122, para. 2, second sentence (moved)	*Article 140, para. 2, first subpara.*
Article 123, paragraphs 1, 2 and 4 (repealed)	
Article 123, para. 3 (moved)	*Article 141, para. 1*
Article 123, para. 5 (moved)	*Article 140, para. 3*

Old numbering of the TEU	New numbering of the TEU
Article 124, para. 1 (moved)	*Article 142*
Article 124, para. 2 (repealed)	
Title VIII — Employment	Title IX — Employment
Article 125	Article 145
Article 126	Article 146
Article 127	Article 147
Article 128	Article 148
Article 129	Article 149
Article 130	Article 150
Title IX — Common commercial policy (moved)	*Part Five, Title II, common commercial policy*
Article 131 (moved)	*Article 206*
Article 132 (repealed)	
Article 133 (moved)	*Article 207*
Article 134 (repealed)	
Title X — Customs cooperation (moved)	*Part Three, Title II, Chapter 2, Customs cooperation*
Article 135 (moved)	*Article 33*
Title XI — Social policy, education, vocational training and youth	Title X — Social policy
Chapter 1 — social provisions (repealed)	
Article 136	Article 151
	Article 152
Article 137	Article 153
Article 138	Article 154
Article 139	Article 155
Article 140	Article 156
Article 141	Article 157
Article 142	Article 158
Article 143	Article 159
Article 144	Article 160
Article 145	Article 161
Chapter 2 — The European Social Fund	Title XI — The European Social Fund
Article 146	Article 162
Article 147	Article 163
Article 148	Article 164
Chapter 3 — Education, vocational training and youth	Title XII — Education, vocational training, youth and sport
Article 149	Article 165
Article 150	Article 166
Title XII — Culture	Title XIII — Culture
Article 151	Article 167
Title XIII — Public health	Title XIV — Public health
Article 152	Article 168
Title XIV — Consumer protection	Title XV — Consumer protection
Article 153, paras. 1, 3, 4 and 5	Article 169
Article 153, para. 2 (moved)	*Article 12*
Title XV — Trans–European networks	Title XVI — Trans–European networks

Old numbering of the TEU	New numbering of the TEU
Article 154	Article 170
Article 155	Article 171
Article 156	Article 172
Title XVI — Industry	Title XVII — Industry
Article 157	Article 173
Title XVII — Economic and social cohesion	Title XVIII — Economic, social and territorial cohesion
Article 158	Article 174
Article 159	Article 175
Article 160	Article 176
Article 161	Article 177
Article 162	Article 178
Title XVIII — Research and technological development	Title XIX — Research and technological development and space
Article 163	Article 179
Article 164	Article 180
Article 165	Article 181
Article 166	Article 182
Article 167	Article 183
Article 168	Article 184
Article 169	Article 185
Article 170	Article 186
Article 171	Article 187
Article 172	Article 188
	Article 189
Article 173	Article 190
Title XIX — Environment	Title XX — Environment
Article 174	Article 191
Article 175	Article 192
Article 176	Article 193
	Title XXI — Energy
	Article 194
	Title XXII — Tourism
	Article 195
	Title XXIII — Civil protection
	Article 196
	Title XXIV — Administrative cooperation
	Article 197
Title XX — Development cooperation (moved)	*Part Five, Title III, Chapter 1, Development cooperation*
Article 177 (moved)	*Article 208*
Article 178 (repealed) (42)	
Article 179 (moved)	*Article 209*
Article 180 (moved)	*Article 210*
Article 181 (moved)	*Article 211*
Title XXI — Economic, financial and technical cooperation with third countries (moved)	*Part Five, Title III, Chapter 2, Economic, financial and technical cooperation with third countries*
Article 181a (moved)	*Article 212*

Old numbering of the TEU	New numbering of the TEU
PART FOUR — ASSOCIATION OF THE OVERSEAS COUNTRIES AND TERRITORIES	PART FOUR — ASSOCIATION OF THE OVERSEAS COUNTRIES AND TERRITORIES
Article 182	Article 198
Article 183	Article 199
Article 184	Article 200
Article 185	Article 201
Article 186	Article 202
Article 187	Article 203
Article 188	Article 204
	PART FIVE — EXTERNAL ACTION BY THE UNION
	Title I — General provisions on the Union's external action
	Article 205
Part Three, Title IX, Common commercial policy (moved)	Title II — Common commercial policy
Article 131 (moved)	Article 206
Article 133 (moved)	Article 207
	Title III — Cooperation with third countries and humanitarian aid
Part Three, Title XX, Development cooperation (moved)	Chapter 1 — Development cooperation
Article 177 (moved)	Article 208 (43)
Article 179 (moved)	Article 209
Article 180 (moved)	Article 210
Article 181 (moved)	Article 211
Part Three, Title XXI, Economic, financial and technical cooperation with third countries (moved)	Chapter 2 — Economic, financial and technical cooperation with third countries
Article 181a (moved)	Article 212
	Article 213
	Chapter 3 — Humanitarian aid
	Article 214
	Title IV — Restrictive measures
Article 301 (replaced)	Article 215
	Title V — International agreements
	Article 216
Article 310 (moved)	Article 217
Article 300 (replaced)	Article 218
Article 111, paras. 1 to 3 and 5 (moved)	Article 219
	Title VI — The Union's relations with international organisations and third countries and the Union delegations
Articles 302 to 304 (replaced)	Article 220
	Article 221
	Title VII — Solidarity clause
	Article 222

Old numbering of the TEU	New numbering of the TEU
PART FIVE — INSTITUTIONS OF THE COMMUNITY	PART SIX — INSTITUTIONAL AND FINANCIAL PROVISIONS
Title I — Institutional provisions	Title I — Institutional provisions
Chapter 1 — The institutions	Chapter 1 — The institutions
Section 1 — The European Parliament	Section 1 — The European Parliament
Article 189 (repealed) (44)	
Article 190, paras. 1 to 3 (repealed) (45)	
Article 190, paras. 4 and 5	Article 223
Article 191, first para. (repealed) (46)	
Article 191, second para.	Article 224
Article 192, first para. (repealed) (47)	
Article 192, second para.	Article 225
Article 193	Article 226
Article 194	Article 227
Article 195	Article 228
Article 196	Article 229
Article 197, first para. (repealed) (48)	
Article 197, second, third & fourth paras.	
	Article 230
Article 198	Article 231
Article 199	Article 232
Article 200	Article 233
Article 201	Article 234
	Section 2 — The European Council
	Article 235
	Article 236
Section 2 — The Council	Section 3 — The Council
Article 202 (repealed) (49)	
Article 203 (repealed) (50)	
Article 204	Article 237
Article 205, paras. 2 and 4 (repealed) (51)	
Article 205, paras. 1 and 3	Article 238
Article 206	Article 239
Article 207	Article 240
Article 208	Article 241
Article 209	Article 242
Article 210	Article 243
Section 3 — The Commission	Section 4 — The Commission
Article 211 (repealed) (52)	
	Article 244
Article 212 (moved)	*Article 249, para. 2*
Article 213	Article 245
Article 214 (repealed) (53)	
Article 215	Article 246
Article 216	Article 247
Article 217, paras. 1, 3 and 4 (repealed) (54)	

Old numbering of the TEU	New numbering of the TEU
Article 217, para. 2	Article 248
Article 218, para. 1 (repealed) (55)	
Article 218, para. 2	Article 249
Article 219	Article 250
Section 4 — The Court of Justice	Section 5 — The Court of Justice of the European Union
Article 220 (repealed) (56)	
Article 221, first para. (repealed) (57)	
Article 221, second and third paras.	Article 251
Article 222	Article 252
Article 223	Article 253
Article 224 (58)	Article 254
	Article 255
Article 225	Article 256
Article 225a	Article 257
Article 226	Article 258
Article 227	Article 259
Article 228	Article 260
Article 229	Article 261
Article 229a	Article 262
Article 230	Article 263
Article 231	Article 264
Article 232	Article 265
Article 233	Article 266
Article 234	Article 267
Article 235	Article 268
	Article 269
Article 236	Article 270
Article 237	Article 271
Article 238	Article 272
Article 239	Article 273
Article 240	Article 274
	Article 275
	Article 276
Article 241	Article 277
Article 242	Article 278
Article 243	Article 279
Article 244	Article 280
Article 245	Article 281
	Section 6 — The European Central Bank
	Article 282
Article 112 (moved)	Article 283
Article 113 (moved)	Article 284
Section 5 — The Court of Auditors	Section 7 — The Court of Auditors
Article 246	Article 285
Article 247	Article 286
Article 248	Article 287

Old numbering of the TEU	New numbering of the TEU
Chapter 2 — Provisions common to several institutions	Chapter 2 — Legal acts of the Union, adoption procedures and other provisions
	Section 1 — The legal acts of the Union
Article 249	Article 288
	Article 289
	Article 290 (59)
	Article 291 (59)
	Article 292
	Section 2 — Procedures for the adoption of acts and other provisions
Article 250	Article 293
Article 251	Article 294
Article 252 (repealed)	
	Article 295
Article 253	Article 296
Article 254	Article 297
	Article 298
Article 255 (moved)	*Article 15*
Article 256	Article 299
	Chapter 3 — The Union's advisory bodies
	Article 300
Chapter 3 — The Economic and Social Committee	Section 1 — The Economic and Social Committee
Article 257 (repealed) (60)	
Article 258, first, second and fourth paras.	Article 301
Article 258, third para. (repealed) (61)	
Article 259	Article 302
Article 260	Article 303
Article 261 (repealed)	
Article 262	Article 304
Chapter 4 — The Committee of the Regions	Section 2 — The Committee of the Regions
Article 263, first and fifth paras. (repealed) (62)	
Article 263, second to fourth paras.	Article 305
Article 264	Article 306
Article 265	Article 307
Chapter 5 — The European Investment Bank	Chapter 4 — The European Investment
Article 266	Article 308
Article 267	Article 309
Title II — Financial provisions	Title II — Financial provisions
Article 268	Article 310
	Chapter 1 — The Union's own resources
Article 269	Article 311
Article 270 (repealed) (63)	
	Chapter 2 — The multiannual financial framework
	Article 312
	Chapter 3 — The Union's annual budget

Old numbering of the TEU	New numbering of the TEU
Article 272, para. 1 (moved)	Article 313
Article 271 (moved)	*Article 316*
Article 272, para. 1 (moved)	*Article 313*
Article 272, paras. 2 to 10	Article 314
Article 273	Article 315
Article 271 (moved)	Article 316
	Chapter 4 — Implementation of the budget and discharge
Article 274	Article 317
Article 275	Article 318
Article 276	Article 319
	Chapter 5 — Common provisions
Article 277	Article 320
Article 278	Article 321
Article 279	Article 322
	Article 323
	Article 324
	Chapter 6 — Combating fraud
Article 280	Article 325
	Title III — Enhanced cooperation
Articles 11 and 11a (replaced)	Article 326 (64)
Articles 11 and 11a (replaced)	Article 327 (64)
Articles 11 and 11a (replaced)	Article 328 (64)
Articles 11 and 11a (replaced)	Article 329 (64)
Articles 11 and 11a (replaced)	Article 330 (64)
Articles 11 and 11a (replaced)	Article 331 (64)
Articles 11 and 11a (replaced)	Article 332 (64)
Articles 11 and 11a (replaced)	Article 333 (64)
Articles 11 and 11a (replaced)	Article 334 (64)
PART SIX — GENERAL AND FINAL PROVISIONS	PART SEVEN — GENERAL AND FINAL PROVISIONS
Article 281 (repealed) (65)	
Article 282	Article 335
Article 283	Article 336
Article 284	Article 337
Article 285	Article 338
Article 286 (replaced)	*Article 16*
Article 287	Article 339
Article 288	Article 340
Article 289	Article 341
Article 290	Article 342
Article 291	Article 343
Article 292	Article 344
Article 293 (repealed)	
Article 294 (moved)	*Article 55*
Article 295	Article 345
Article 296	Article 346

Old numbering of the TEU	New numbering of the TEU
Article 297	Article 347
Article 298	Article 348
Article 299, para. 1 (repealed) (66)	
Article 299, para. 2, second, third & fourth subparas.	Article 349
Article 299, para. 2, first subpara. and paras. 3 to 6 (moved)	*Article 355*
Article 300 (replaced)	*Article 218*
Article 301 (replaced)	*Article 215*
Article 302 (replaced)	*Article 220*
Article 303 (replaced)	*Article 220*
Article 304 (replaced)	*Article 220*
Article 305 (repealed)	
Article 306	Article 350
Article 307	Article 351
Article 308	Article 352
	Article 353
Article 309	Article 354
Article 310 (moved)	*Article 217*
Article 311 (repealed) (67)	
Article 299, para. 2, first subpara., and paras. 3 to 6 (moved)	Article 355
Article 312	Article 356
	Final Provisions
Article 313	Article 357
	Article 358
Article 314 (repealed) (68)	

(25) Replaced, in substance, by Article 3 TEU.
(26) Replaced, in substance, by Articles 3 to 6 TFEU.
(27) Replaced, in substance, by Article 5 TEU.
(28) Insertion of the operative part of the protocol on protection and welfare of animals.
(29) Replaced, in substance, by Article 13 TEU.
(30) Replaced, in substance, by Article 13 TEU and Article 282, para. 1, TFEU.
(31) Replaced, in substance, by Article 4, para. 3, TEU.
(32) Also replaced by Article 20 TEU.
(33) Also replaces the current Article 29 TEU.
(34) Also replaces the current Article 36 TEU.
(35) Also replaces the current Article 33 TEU.
(36) Points 1 and 2 of Article 63 EC are replaced by paragraphs 1 and 2 of Article 78 TFEU, and paragraph 2 of Article 64 is replaced by paragraph 3 of Article 78 TFEU.
(37) Replaces the current Article 31 TEU.
(38) Replaces the current Article 30 TEU.
(39) Replaces the current Article 32 TEU.
(40) — Article 140, para. 1 takes over the wording of para. 1 of Article 121.
        — Article 140, para. 2 takes over the second sentence of para. 2 of Article 122.
        — Article 140, para. 3 takes over para. 5 of Article 123.
(41) — Article 141, para. 1 takes over para. 3 of Article 123.
        — Article 141, para. 2 takes over the first five indents of para. 2 of Article 117.
(42) Replaced, in substance, by the second sentence of the second subpara. of para. 1 of Article 208 TFUE.
(43) The second sentence of the second subpara. of para. 1 replaces, in substance, Article 178 TEC.
(44) Replaced, in substance, by Article 14, paras. 1 and 2, TEU.
(45) Replaced, in substance, by Article 14, paras. 1 to 3, TEU.
(46) Replaced, in substance, by Article 11, para. 4, TEU.

(47) Replaced, in substance, by Article 14, para. 1, TEU.
(48) Replaced, in substance, by Article 14, para. 4, TEU.
(49) Replaced, in substance, by Article 16, para. 1, TEU and by Articles 290 and 291 TFEU.
(50) Replaced, in substance, by Article 16, paras. 2 and 9 TEU.
(51) Replaced, in substance, by Article 16, paras. 4 and 5 TEU.
(52) Replaced, in substance, by Article 17, para. 1 TEU.
(53) Replaced, in substance, by Article 17, paras. 3 and 7 TEU.
(54) Replaced, in substance, by Article 17, para. 6, TEU.
(55) Replaced, in substance, by Article 295 TFEU.
(56) Replaced, in substance, by Article 19 TEU.
(57) Replaced, in substance, by Article 19, para. 2, first subpara., of the TEU.
(58) The first sentence of the first subpara. is replaced, in substance, by Article 19, para. 2, second subpara. of the TEU.
(59) Replaces, in substance, the third indent of Article 202 TEC.
(60) Replaced, in substance, by Article 300, para. 2 of the TFEU.
(61) Replaced, in substance, by Article 300, para. 4 of the TFEU.
(62) Replaced, in substance, by Article 300, paras. 3 and 4, TFEU.
(63) Replaced, in substance, by Article 310, para. 4, TFEU.
(64) Also replaces the current Articles 27a to 27e, 40 to 40b, and 43 to 45 TEU.
(64) Also replaces the current Articles 27a to 27e, 40 to 40b, and 43 to 45 TEU.
(65) Replaced, in substance, by Article 47 TEU.
(66) Replaced, in substance by Article 52 TEU.
(67) Replaced, in substance by Article 51 TEU.
(68) Replaced, in substance by Article 55 TEU.

III Charter of Fundamental Rights of the European Union

CHARTER OF FUNDAMENTAL RIGHTS OF THE EUROPEAN UNION

OJ C83, 30.3.2010, p. 389*

SOLEMN PROCLAMATION

The European Parliament, the Council and the Commission solemnly proclaim the following text as the Charter of Fundamental Rights of the European Union.

CHARTER OF FUNDAMENTAL RIGHTS OF THE EUROPEAN UNION

PREAMBLE

The peoples of Europe, in creating an ever closer union among them, are resolved to share a peaceful future based on common values.

Conscious of its spiritual and moral heritage, the Union is founded on the indivisible, universal values of human dignity, freedom, equality and solidarity; it is based on the principles of democracy and the rule of law. It places the individual at the heart of its activities, by

---

* EDITOR'S NOTE: The text reproduced below adapts the wording of the Charter proclaimed on 7 December 2000 (OJ C 364, 18.12.2000, p. 1), and has replaced it from the date of entry into force of the Treaty of Lisbon, 1 December 2009. The adapted text was first published in 2007. For the text of the 'explanations' relating to the Charter, as adapted, see OJ C 303, 14.12.2007, p. 17. The 'rights, freedoms and principles' set out in the Charter have the 'same legal value' as the Treaties according to Article 6(1) of the Treaty on European Union. The Charter is also subject to the provisions of Protocol (No 30), annexed to the Treaties, which concerns its application to Poland and the United Kingdom (see Part I of this edition).

establishing the citizenship of the Union and by creating an area of freedom, security and justice.

The Union contributes to the preservation and to the development of these common values while respecting the diversity of the cultures and traditions of the peoples of Europe as well as the national identities of the Member States and the organisation of their public authorities at national, regional and local levels; it seeks to promote balanced and sustainable development and ensures free movement of persons, services, goods and capital, and the freedom of establishment.

To this end, it is necessary to strengthen the protection of fundamental rights in the light of changes in society, social progress and scientific and technological developments by making those rights more visible in a Charter.

This Charter reaffirms, with due regard for the powers and tasks of the Union and for the principle of subsidiarity, the rights as they result, in particular, from the constitutional traditions and international obligations common to the Member States, the European Convention for the Protection of Human Rights and Fundamental Freedoms, the Social Charters adopted by the Union and by the Council of Europe and the case-law of the Court of Justice of the European Union and of the European Court of Human Rights. In this context the Charter will be interpreted by the courts of the Union and the Member States with due regard to the explanations prepared under the authority of the Praesidium of the Convention which drafted the Charter and updated under the responsibility of the Praesidium of the European Convention.

Enjoyment of these rights entails responsibilities and duties with regard to other persons, to the human community and to future generations.

The Union therefore recognises the rights, freedoms and principles set out hereafter.

TITLE I
DIGNITY

Article 1 Human dignity
Human dignity is inviolable. It must be respected and protected.

Article 2 Right to life
1.   Everyone has the right to life.

2.   No one shall be condemned to the death penalty, or executed.

Article 3 Right to the integrity of the person
1.   Everyone has the right to respect for his or her physical and mental integrity.

2.   In the fields of medicine and biology, the following must be respected in particular:
     (a) the free and informed consent of the person concerned, according to the procedures laid down by law;
     (b) the prohibition of eugenic practices, in particular those aiming at the selection of persons;
     (c) the prohibition on making the human body and its parts as such a source of financial gain;
     (d) the prohibition of the reproductive cloning of human beings.

Article 4 *Prohibition* of torture and inhuman or degrading treatment or punishment
No one shall be subjected to torture or to inhuman or degrading treatment or punishment.

Article 5 *Prohibition* of slavery and forced labour
1.   No one shall be held in slavery or servitude.

2.   No one shall be required to perform forced or compulsory labour.

3.   Trafficking in human beings is prohibited.

TITLE II
FREEDOMS

Article 6 Right to liberty and security
Everyone has the right to liberty and security of person.

Article 7 Respect for private and family life
Everyone has the right to respect for his or her private and family life, home and
communications.

Article 8 Protection of personal data
1.   Everyone has the right to the protection of personal data concerning him or her.

2.   Such data must be processed fairly for specified purposes and on the basis of the consent
      of the person concerned or some other legitimate basis laid down by law. Everyone has
      the right of access to data which has been collected concerning him or her, and the right to
      have it rectified.

3.   Compliance with these rules shall be subject to control by an independent authority.

Article 9 Right to marry and right to found a family
The right to marry and the right to found a family shall be guaranteed in accordance with the
national laws governing the exercise of these rights.

Article 10 Freedom of thought, conscience and religion
1.   Everyone has the right to freedom of thought, conscience and religion. This right includes
      freedom to change religion or belief and freedom, either alone or in community with
      others and in public or in private, to manifest religion or belief, in worship, teaching,
      practice and observance.

2.   The right to conscientious objection is recognised, in accordance with the national laws
      governing the exercise of this right.

Article 11 Freedom of expression and information
1.   Everyone has the right to freedom of expression. This right shall include freedom to hold
      opinions and to receive and impart information and ideas without interference by public
      authority and regardless of frontiers.

2.   The freedom and pluralism of the media shall be respected.

Article 12 Freedom of assembly and of association
1.   Everyone has the right to freedom of peaceful assembly and to freedom of association
      at all levels, in particular in political, trade union and civic matters, which implies the

right of everyone to form and to join trade unions for the protection of his or her interests.

2. Political parties at Union level contribute to expressing the political will of the citizens of the Union.

Article 13 Freedom of the arts and sciences
The arts and scientific research shall be free of constraint. Academic freedom shall be respected.

Article 14 Right to education
1. Everyone has the right to education and to have access to vocational and continuing training.

2. This right includes the possibility to receive free compulsory education.

3. The freedom to found educational establishments with due respect for democratic principles and the right of parents to ensure the education and teaching of their children in conformity with their religious, philosophical and pedagogical convictions shall be respected, in accordance with the national laws governing the exercise of such freedom and right.

Article 15 Freedom to choose an occupation and right to engage in work
1. Everyone has the right to engage in work and to pursue a freely chosen or accepted occupation.

2. Every citizen of the Union has the freedom to seek employment, to work, to exercise the right of establishment and to provide services in any Member State.

3. Nationals of third countries who are authorised to work in the territories of the Member States are entitled to working conditions equivalent to those of citizens of the Union.

Article 16 Freedom to conduct a business
The freedom to conduct a business in accordance with Union law and national laws and practices is recognised.

Article 17 Right to property
1. Everyone has the right to own, use, dispose of and bequeath his or her lawfully acquired possessions. No one may be deprived of his or her possessions, except in the public interest and in the cases and under the conditions provided for by law, subject to fair compensation being paid in good time for their loss. The use of property may be regulated by law in so far as is necessary for the general interest.

2. Intellectual property shall be protected.

Article 18 Right to asylum
The right to asylum shall be guaranteed with due respect for the rules of the Geneva Convention of 28 July 1951 and the Protocol of 31 January 1967 relating to the status of refugees and in accordance with the Treaty on European Union and the Treaty on the Functioning of the European Union (hereinafter referred to as 'the Treaties').

Article 19 Protection in the event of removal, expulsion or extradition
1. Collective expulsions are prohibited.

2.   No one may be removed, expelled or extradited to a State where there is a serious risk that he or she would be subjected to the death penalty, torture or other inhuman or degrading treatment or punishment.

TITLE III
EQUALITY

Article 20 Equality before the law
Everyone is equal before the law.

Article 21 Non-discrimination
1.   Any discrimination based on any ground such as sex, race, colour, ethnic or social origin, genetic features, language, religion or belief, political or any other opinion, membership of a national minority, property, birth, disability, age or sexual orientation shall be prohibited.

2.   Within the scope of application of the Treaties and without prejudice to any of their specific provisions, any discrimination on grounds of nationality shall be prohibited.

Article 22 Cultural, religious and linguistic diversity
The Union shall respect cultural, religious and linguistic diversity.

Article 23 Equality between women and men
Equality between women and men must be ensured in all areas, including employment, work and pay.

The principle of equality shall not prevent the maintenance or adoption of measures providing for specific advantages in favour of the under-represented sex.

Article 24 The rights of the child
1.   Children shall have the right to such protection and care as is necessary for their well-being. They may express their views freely. Such views shall be taken into consideration on matters which concern them in accordance with their age and maturity.

2.   In all actions relating to children, whether taken by public authorities or private institutions, the child's best interests must be a primary consideration.

3.   Every child shall have the right to maintain on a regular basis a personal relationship and direct contact with both his or her parents, unless that is contrary to his or her interests.

Article 25 The rights of the elderly
The Union recognises and respects the rights of the elderly to lead a life of dignity and independence and to participate in social and cultural life.

Article 26 Integration of persons with disabilities
The Union recognises and respects the right of persons with disabilities to benefit from measures designed to ensure their independence, social and occupational integration and participation in the life of the community.

TITLE IV
SOLIDARITY

Article 27 Workers' right to information and consultation within the undertaking
Workers or their representatives must, at the appropriate levels, be guaranteed information and consultation in good time in the cases and under the conditions provided for by Union law and national laws and practices.

Article 28 Right of collective bargaining and action
Workers and employers, or their respective organisations, have, in accordance with Union law and national laws and practices, the right to negotiate and conclude collective agreements at the appropriate levels and, in cases of conflicts of interest, to take collective action to defend their interests, including strike action.

Article 29 Right of access to placement services
Everyone has the right of access to a free placement service.

Article 30 Protection in the event of unjustified dismissal
Every worker has the right to protection against unjustified dismissal, in accordance with Union law and national laws and practices.

Article 31 Fair and just working conditions
1.   Every worker has the right to working conditions which respect his or her health, safety and dignity.

2.   Every worker has the right to limitation of maximum working hours, to daily and weekly rest periods and to an annual period of paid leave.

Article 32 Prohibition of child labour and protection of young people at work
The employment of children is prohibited. The minimum age of admission to employment may not be lower than the minimum school-leaving age, without prejudice to such rules as may be more favourable to young people and except for limited derogations.

Young people admitted to work must have working conditions appropriate to their age and be protected against economic exploitation and any work likely to harm their safety, health or physical, mental, moral or social development or to interfere with their education.

Article 33 Family and professional life
1.   The family shall enjoy legal, economic and social protection.

2.   To reconcile family and professional life, everyone shall have the right to protection from dismissal for a reason connected with maternity and the right to paid maternity leave and to parental leave following the birth or adoption of a child.

Article 34 Social security and social assistance
1.   The Union recognises and respects the entitlement to social security benefits and social services providing protection in cases such as maternity, illness, industrial accidents, dependency or old age, and in the case of loss of employment, in accordance with the rules laid down by Union law and national laws and practices.

2.   Everyone residing and moving legally within the European Union is entitled to social security benefits and social advantages in accordance with Union law and national laws and practices.

3. In order to combat social exclusion and poverty, the Union recognises and respects the right to social and housing assistance so as to ensure a decent existence for all those who lack sufficient resources, in accordance with the rules laid down by Union law and national laws and practices.

Article 35 Health care
Everyone has the right of access to preventive health care and the right to benefit from medical treatment under the conditions established by national laws and practices. A high level of human health protection shall be ensured in the definition and implementation of all the Union's policies and activities.

Article 36 Access to services of general economic interest
The Union recognises and respects access to services of general economic interest as provided for in national laws and practices, in accordance with the Treaties, in order to promote the social and territorial cohesion of the Union.

Article 37 Environmental protection
A high level of environmental protection and the improvement of the quality of the environment must be integrated into the policies of the Union and ensured in accordance with the principle of sustainable development.

Article 38 Consumer protection
Union policies shall ensure a high level of consumer protection.

TITLE V
CITIZENS' RIGHTS

Article 39 Right to vote and to stand as a candidate at elections to the European Parliament
1. Every citizen of the Union has the right to vote and to stand as a candidate at elections to the European Parliament in the Member State in which he or she resides, under the same conditions as nationals of that State.

2. Members of the European Parliament shall be elected by direct universal suffrage in a free and secret ballot.

Article 40 Right to vote and to stand as a candidate at municipal elections
Every citizen of the Union has the right to vote and to stand as a candidate at municipal elections in the Member State in which he or she resides under the same conditions as nationals of that State.

Article 41 Right to good administration
1. Every person has the right to have his or her affairs handled impartially, fairly and within a reasonable time by the institutions, bodies, offices and agencies of the Union.

2. This right includes:
    (a) the right of every person to be heard, before any individual measure which would affect him or her adversely is taken;
    (b) the right of every person to have access to his or her file, while respecting the legitimate interests of confidentiality and of professional and business secrecy;
    (c) the obligation of the administration to give reasons for its decisions.

3.   Every person has the right to have the Union make good any damage caused by its institutions or by its servants in the performance of their duties, in accordance with the general principles common to the laws of the Member States.

4.   Every person may write to the institutions of the Union in one of the languages of the Treaties and must have an answer in the same language.

Article 42 Right of access to documents
Any citizen of the Union, and any natural or legal person residing or having its registered office in a Member State, has a right of access to documents of the institutions, bodies, offices and agencies of the Union, whatever their medium.

Article 43 European Ombudsman
Any citizen of the Union and any natural or legal person residing or having its registered office in a Member State has the right to refer to the European Ombudsman cases of maladministration in the activities of the institutions, bodies, offices or agencies of the Union, with the exception of the Court of Justice of the European Union acting in its judicial role.

Article 44 Right to petition
Any citizen of the Union and any natural or legal person residing or having its registered office in a Member State has the right to petition the European Parliament.

Article 45 Freedom of movement and of residence
1.   Every citizen of the Union has the right to move and reside freely within the territory of the Member States.

2.   Freedom of movement and residence may be granted, in accordance with the Treaties, to nationals of third countries legally resident in the territory of a Member State.

Article 46 Diplomatic and consular protection
Every citizen of the Union shall, in the territory of a third country in which the Member State of which he or she is a national is not represented, be entitled to protection by the diplomatic or consular authorities of any Member State, on the same conditions as the nationals of that Member State.

TITLE VI
JUSTICE

Article 47 Right to an effective remedy and to a fair trial
Everyone whose rights and freedoms guaranteed by the law of the Union are violated has the right to an effective remedy before a tribunal in compliance with the conditions laid down in this Article.

Everyone is entitled to a fair and public hearing within a reasonable time by an independent and impartial tribunal previously established by law. Everyone shall have the possibility of being advised, defended and represented.

Legal aid shall be made available to those who lack sufficient resources in so far as such aid is necessary to ensure effective access to justice.

Article 48 Presumption of innocence and right of defence
1.   Everyone who has been charged shall be presumed innocent until proved guilty according to law.

2.   Respect for the rights of the defence of anyone who has been charged shall be guaranteed.

Article 49 Principles of legality and proportionality of criminal offences and penalties
1.   No one shall be held guilty of any criminal offence on account of any act or omission which did not constitute a criminal offence under national law or international law at the time when it was committed. Nor shall a heavier penalty be imposed than the one that was applicable at the time the criminal offence was committed. If, subsequent to the commission of a criminal offence, the law provides for a lighter penalty, that penalty shall be applicable.

2.   This Article shall not prejudice the trial and punishment of any person for any act or omission which, at the time when it was committed, was criminal according to the general principles recognised by the community of nations.

3.   The severity of penalties must not be disproportionate to the criminal offence.

Article 50 Right not to be tried or punished twice in criminal proceedings for the same criminal offence
No one shall be liable to be tried or punished again in criminal proceedings for an offence for which he or she has already been finally acquitted or convicted within the Union in accordance with the law.

TITLE VII
GENERAL PROVISIONS GOVERNING THE INTERPRETATION AND APPLICATION OF THE CHARTER

Article 51 Field of application
1.   The provisions of this Charter are addressed to the institutions, bodies, offices and agencies of the Union with due regard for the principle of subsidiarity and to the Member States only when they are implementing Union law. They shall therefore respect the rights, observe the principles and promote the application thereof in accordance with their respective powers and respecting the limits of the powers of the Union as conferred on it in the Treaties.

2.   The Charter does not extend the field of application of Union law beyond the powers of the Union or establish any new power or task for the Union, or modify powers and tasks as defined in the Treaties.

Article 52 Scope and interpretation of rights and principles
1.   Any limitation on the exercise of the rights and freedoms recognised by this Charter must be provided for by law and respect the essence of those rights and freedoms. Subject to the principle of proportionality, limitations may be made only if they are necessary and genuinely meet objectives of general interest recognised by the Union or the need to protect the rights and freedoms of others.

2.   Rights recognised by this Charter for which provision is made in the Treaties shall be exercised under the conditions and within the limits defined by those Treaties.

3.   In so far as this Charter contains rights which correspond to rights guaranteed by the Convention for the Protection of Human Rights and Fundamental Freedoms, the meaning and scope of those rights shall be the same as those laid down by the said Convention. This provision shall not prevent Union law providing more extensive protection.

4.   In so far as this Charter recognises fundamental rights as they result from the constitutional traditions common to the Member States, those rights shall be interpreted in harmony with those traditions.

5. The provisions of this Charter which contain principles may be implemented by legislative and executive acts taken by institutions, bodies, offices and agencies of the Union, and by acts of Member States when they are implementing Union law, in the exercise of their respective powers. They shall be judicially cognisable only in the interpretation of such acts and in the ruling on their legality.

6. Full account shall be taken of national laws and practices as specified in this Charter.

7. The explanations drawn up as a way of providing guidance in the interpretation of this Charter shall be given due regard by the courts of the Union and of the Member States.

Article 53 Level of protection
Nothing in this Charter shall be interpreted as restricting or adversely affecting human rights and fundamental freedoms as recognised, in their respective fields of application, by Union law and international law and by international agreements to which the Union or all the Member States are party, including the European Convention for the Protection of Human Rights and Fundamental Freedoms, and by the Member States' constitutions.

Article 54 Prohibition of abuse of rights
Nothing in this Charter shall be interpreted as implying any right to engage in any activity or to perform any act aimed at the destruction of any of the rights and freedoms recognised in this Charter or at their limitation to a greater extent than is provided for herein.

IV Provisions Governing the Institutions

A) The Court of Justice – procedural texts

Extracts from the Rules of Procedure of the Court of Justice

OJ L 176, 4.7.1991, p. 7 as amended and consolidated. Text effective from the date of publication in the Official Journal,

OJ L 92, 13.4.2010, p. 12[1]

[1]   EDITOR'S NOTE: These Rules of Procedure were issued by the Court of Justice in accordance with its powers under Article 253 TFEU (ex 223 TEC). The Rules of Procedure are also subject to the institutional provisions contained in Articles 251-281 TFEU and Protocol (No.3) on the Statute of the Court of Justice of the European Union. For the text of the Statute of the Court of Justice see the Protocols in Part I of this edition. Complete versions of the consolidated texts of the Rules of Procedure of the Court of Justice and the General Court (previously the Court of First Instance) can be found on the Court of Justice's web pages at: http://curia.europa.eu/jcms/jcms/ Jo2_7031 (Court of Justice) and http://curia.europa.eu/jcms/jcms/Jo2_7040 (General Court).

TITLE 1
ORGANISATION OF THE COURT

Chapter 1 JUDGES AND ADVOCATES GENERAL

Article 2
The term of office of a Judge shall begin on the date laid down in his instrument of appointment. In the absence of any provisions regarding the date, the term shall begin on the date of the instrument.

Article 3
1. Before taking up his duties, a Judge shall at the first public sitting of the Court which he attends after his appointment take the following oath:

    'I swear that I will perform my duties impartially and conscientiously; I swear that I will preserve the secrecy of the deliberations of the Court'.

2. Immediately after taking the oath, a Judge shall sign a declaration by which he solemnly undertakes that, both during and after his term of office, he will respect the obligations arising therefrom, and in particular the duty to behave with integrity and discretion as regards the acceptance, after he has ceased to hold office, of certain appointments and benefits.

Article 4
When the Court is called upon to decide whether a Judge no longer fulfils the requisite conditions or no longer meets the obligations arising from his office, the President shall invite the Judge concerned to make representations to the Court, in closed session and in the absence of the Registrar.

Article 5
Articles 2, 3 and 4 of these Rules shall apply to Advocates General.

Article 6
Judges and Advocates General shall rank equally in precedence according to their seniority in office. Where there is equal seniority in office, precedence shall be determined by age.

Retiring Judges and Advocates General who are reappointed shall retain their former precedence.

Chapter 2 PRESIDENCY OF THE COURT AND CONSTITUTION OF THE CHAMBERS

Article 7
1. The Judges shall, immediately after the partial replacement provided for in Article 253 TFEU, elect one of their number as President of the Court for a term of three years.

2. If the office of the President of the Court falls vacant before the normal date of expiry thereof, the Court shall elect a successor for the remainder of the term.

3. The elections provided for in this Article shall be by secret ballot. The Judge obtaining the votes of more than half the Judges composing the Court shall be elected. If no Judge obtains that majority, further ballots shall be held until that majority is attained.

Article 8
The President shall direct the judicial business and the administration of the Court; he shall preside at hearings and deliberations.

Article 9
1. The Court shall set up Chambers of five and three Judges in accordance with Article 16 of the Statute and shall decide which Judges shall be attached to them.

    The Court shall designate the Chamber or Chambers of five Judges which, for a period of one year, shall be responsible for cases of the kind referred to in Article 104b.

    The composition of the Chambers and the designation of the Chamber or Chambers responsible for cases of the kind referred to in Article 104b shall be published in the *Official Journal of the European Union.*

2. As soon as an application initiating proceedings has been lodged, the President shall designate a Judge to act as Rapporteur.

    For cases of the kind referred to in Article 104b, the Judge-Rapporteur shall be selected from among the Judges of the Chamber designated in accordance with paragraph 1 of this Article, on a proposal from the President of that Chamber. If the Chamber decides that the case is not to be dealt with under the urgent procedure, the President of the Court may reassign the case to a Judge-Rapporteur attached to another Chamber.

    The President of the Court shall take the necessary steps if a Judge-Rapporteur is absent or prevented from acting.

3. For cases assigned to a formation of the Court in accordance with Article 44(3), the word 'Court' in these Rules shall mean that formation.

4. In cases assigned to a Chamber of five or three Judges, the powers of the President of the Court shall be exercised by the President of the Chamber.

Article 10
1. The Judges shall, immediately after the election of the President of the Court, elect the Presidents of the Chambers of five Judges for a term of three years.

    The Judges shall elect the Presidents of the Chambers of three Judges for a term of one year.

    The Court shall appoint for a period of one year the First Advocate General.

    The provisions of Article 7(2) and (3) shall apply.

The elections and appointment made in pursuance of this paragraph shall be published in the *Official Journal of the European Union.*

2.   The First Advocate General shall assign each case to an Advocate General as soon as the Judge-Rapporteur has been designated by the President. He shall take the necessary steps if an Advocate General is absent or prevented from acting.

Article 11

When the President of the Court is absent or is prevented from attending or when the office of President is vacant, the functions of President shall be exercised by a President of a Chamber of five Judges according to the order of precedence laid down in Article 6 of these Rules.

When the President of the Court and the Presidents of the Chambers of five Judges are all absent or prevented from attending at the same time, or their posts are vacant at the same time, the functions of President shall be exercised by one of the Presidents of the Chambers of three Judges according to the order of precedence laid down in Article 6 of these Rules.

If the President of the Court and all the Presidents of Chambers are all absent or prevented from attending at the same time, or their posts are vacant at the same time, the functions of President shall be exercised by one of the other Judges according to the order of precedence laid down in Article 6 of these Rules.

Chapter 2A FORMATIONS OF THE COURT

Article 11a

The Court shall sit in the following formations:

–   the full Court, composed of all the Judges;

–   the Grand Chamber, composed of 13 Judges in accordance with Article 11b,

–   Chambers composed of five or three Judges in accordance with Article 11c.

Article 11b

1.   For each case the Grand Chamber shall be composed of the President of the Court, the Presidents of the Chambers of five Judges, the Judge-Rapporteur and the number of Judges necessary to reach 13. The last-mentioned Judges shall be designated from the list referred to in paragraph 2, following the order laid down therein. The starting-point on that list, in every case assigned to the Grand Chamber, shall be the name of the Judge immediately following the last Judge designated from the list for the preceding case assigned to that formation of the Court.

2.   After the election of the President of the Court and of the Presidents of the Chambers of five Judges, a list of the other Judges shall be drawn up for the purposes of determining the composition of the Grand Chamber. That list shall follow the order laid down in Article 6 of these Rules, alternating with the reverse order: the first Judge on that list shall be the first according to the order laid down in that Article, the second Judge shall be the last according to that order, the third Judge shall be the second according to that order, the fourth Judge the penultimate according to that order, and so on.

The list shall be published in the *Official Journal of the European Union.*

3.   In cases which are assigned to the Grand Chamber between the beginning of a year in which there is a partial replacement of Judges and the moment when that replacement has

taken place, two substitute Judges shall also sit. Those substitute Judges shall be the two Judges appearing in the list referred to in the previous paragraph immediately after the last Judge designated for the composition of the Grand Chamber in the case.

The substitute Judges shall replace, in the order of the list referred to in the previous paragraph, such Judges as are unable to take part in the decision on the case.

Article 11c

1. The Chambers of five Judges and three Judges shall, for each case, be composed of the President of the Chamber, the Judge-Rapporteur and the number of Judges required to attain the number of five and three Judges respectively. Those last-mentioned Judges shall be designated from the lists referred to in paragraph 2 and following the order laid down in them.

   The startingpoint in those lists, for every case assigned to a Chamber, shall be the name of the Judge immediately following the last Judge designated from the list for the preceding case assigned to the Chamber concerned.

2. For the composition of the Chambers of five Judges, after the election of the Presidents of those Chambers lists shall be drawn up including all the Judges attached to the Chamber concerned, with the exception of its President. The lists shall be drawn up in the same way as the list referred to in Article 11b(2).

   For the composition of the Chambers of three Judges, after the election of the Presidents of those Chambers lists shall be drawn up including all the Judges attached to the Chamber concerned, with the exception of its President. The lists shall be drawn up according to the order laid down in Article 6 of these Rules.

   The lists referred to in this paragraph shall be published in the *Official Journal of the European Union*.

Article 11d

1. Where the Court considers that several cases must be heard and determined together by one and the same formation of the Court, the composition of that formation shall be that fixed for the case in respect of which the preliminary report was first examined.

2. Where a Chamber to which a case has been assigned refers the case back to the Court under Article 44(4), in order that it may be reassigned to a formation composed of a greater number of Judges, that formation shall include the members of the Chamber which has referred the case back.

Article 11e

When a member of the formation determining a case is prevented from attending, he shall be replaced by a Judge according to the order of the lists referred to in Article 11b(2) or 11c(2).

When the President of the Court is prevented from attending, the functions of the President of the Grand Chamber shall be exercised in accordance with the provisions of Article 11.

When the President of a Chamber of five Judges is prevented from attending, the functions of President of the Chamber shall be exercised by a President of a Chamber of three Judges, where necessary according to the order laid down in Article 6 of these Rules or, if that Chamber does not include a President of a Chamber of three Judges, by one of the other Judges according to the order laid down in Article 6.

When the President of a Chamber of three Judges is prevented from attending, the functions of President of the Chamber shall be exercised by a Judge of that Chamber according to the order laid down in Article 6 of these Rules.

(The remaining Chapters in Title I have been omitted).

TITLE II
PROCEDURE

Chapter 1 WRITTEN PROCEDURE

Article 37

1. The original of every pleading must be signed by the party's agent or lawyer.

    The original, accompanied by all annexes referred to therein, shall be lodged together with five copies for the Court and a copy for every other party to the proceedings. Copies shall be certified by the party lodging them.

2. Institutions shall in addition produce, within time-limits laid down by the Court, translations of all pleadings into the other languages provided for by Article 1 of Council Regulation No 1. The second subparagraph of paragraph 1 of this Article shall apply.

3. All pleadings shall bear a date. In the reckoning of time-limits for taking steps in proceedings, only the date of lodgment at the Registry shall be taken into account.

4. To every pleading there shall be annexed a file containing the documents relied on in support of it, together with a schedule listing them.

5. Where in view of the length of a document only extracts from it are annexed to the pleading, the whole document or a full copy of it shall be lodged at the Registry.

6. Without prejudice to the provisions of paragraphs 1 to 5, the date on which a copy of the signed original of a pleading, including the schedule of documents referred to in paragraph 4, is received at the Registry by telefax or other technical means of communication available to the Court shall be deemed to be the date of lodgment for the purposes of compliance with the time-limits for taking steps in proceedings, provided that the signed original of the pleading, accompanied by the annexes and copies referred to in the second subparagraph of paragraph 1 above, is lodged at the Registry no later than days thereafter. Article 81(2) shall not be applicable to this period of 10 days.

7. Without prejudice to the first subparagraph of paragraph 1 or to paragraphs 2 to 5, the Court may by decision determine the criteria for a procedural document sent to the Registry by electronic means to be deemed to be the original of that document. That decision shall be published in the *Official Journal of the European Union.*

Article 38

1. An application of the kind referred to in Article 21 of the Statute shall state:
    (a) the name and address of the applicant;
    (b) the designation of the party against whom the application is made;
    (c) the subject-matter of the proceedings and a summary of the pleas in law on which the application is based;
    (d) the form of order sought by the applicant;
    (e) where appropriate, the nature of any evidence offered in support.

2. For the purpose of the proceedings, the application shall state an address for service in the place where the Court has its seat and the name of the person who is authorised and has expressed willingness to accept service.

    In addition to, or instead of, specifying an address for service as referred to in the first subparagraph, the application may state that the lawyer or agent agrees that service is to be effected on him by telefax or other technical means of communication.

    If the application does not comply with the requirements referred to in the first and second subparagraphs, all service on the party concerned for the purpose of the proceedings shall be effected, for so long as the defect has not been cured, by registered letter addressed to the agent or lawyer of that party. By way of derogation from Article 79(1), service shall then be deemed to be duly effected by the lodging of the registered letter at the post office of the place where the Court has its seat.

3. The lawyer acting for a party must lodge at the Registry a certificate that he is authorised to practise before a court of a Member State or of another State which is a party to the EEA Agreement.

4. The application shall be accompanied, where appropriate, by the documents specified in the second paragraph of Article 21 of the Statute.

5. An application made by a legal person governed by private law shall be accompanied by:
    (a) the instrument or instruments constituting or regulating that legal person or a recent extract from the register of companies, firms or associations or any other proof of its existence in law;
    (b) proof that the authority granted to the applicant's lawyer has been properly conferred on him by someone authorised for the purpose.

6. An application submitted under Article 273 TFEU shall be accompanied by a copy of the special agreement concluded between the Member States concerned.

7. If an application does not comply with the requirements set out in paragraphs 3 to 6 of this Article, the Registrar shall prescribe a reasonable period within which the applicant is to comply with them whether by putting the application itself in order or by producing any of the abovementioned documents. If the applicant fails to put the application in order or to produce the required documents within the time prescribed, the Court shall, after hearing the Advocate General, decide whether the non-compliance with these conditions renders the application formally inadmissible.

Article 39
The application shall be served on the defendant. In a case where Article 38(7) applies, service shall be effected as soon as the application has been put in order or the Court has declared it admissible notwithstanding the failure to observe the formal requirements set out in that Article.

Article 40
1. Within one month after service on him of the application, the defendant shall lodge a defence, stating:
    (a) the name and address of the defendant;
    (b) the arguments of fact and law relied on;
    (c) the form of order sought by the defendant;
    (d) the nature of any evidence offered by him.
    The provisions of Article 38(2) to (5) of these Rules shall apply to the defence.

2.   The time-limit laid down in paragraph 1 of this Article may be extended by the President on a reasoned application by the defendant.

Article 41

1.   The application initiating the proceedings and the defence may be supplemented by a reply from the applicant and by a rejoinder from the defendant.

2.   The President shall fix the time-limits within which these pleadings are to be lodged.

Article 42

1.   In reply or rejoinder a party may offer further evidence. The party must, however, give reasons for the delay in offering it.

2.   No new plea in law may be introduced in the course of proceedings unless it is based on matters of law or of fact which come to light in the course of the procedure.

    If in the course of the procedure one of the parties puts forward a new plea in law which is so based, the President may, even after the expiry of the normal procedural time-limits, acting on a report of the Judge-Rapporteur and after hearing the Advocate General, allow the other party time to answer on that plea.

    The decision on the admissibility of the plea shall be reserved for the final judgment.

Article 43

The Court may, at any time, after hearing the parties and the Advocate General, if the assignment referred to in Article 10(2) has taken place, order that two or more cases concerning the same subject-matter shall, on account of the connection between them, be joined for the purposes of the written or oral procedure or of the final judgment. The cases may subsequently be disjoined. The President may refer these matters to the Court.

Chapter 1A THE PRELIMINARY REPORT AND ASSIGNMENT OF CASES TO FORMATIONS

Article 44

1.   The President shall fix a date on which the Judge-Rapporteur is to present his preliminary report to the general meeting of the Court, either:
    (a) after the rejoinder has been lodged; or
    (b) where no reply or no rejoinder has been lodged within the time-limit fixed in accordance with Article 41(2); or
    (c) where the party concerned has waived his right to lodge a reply or rejoinder; or
    (d) where the expedited procedure referred to in Article 62a is to be applied, when the President fixes a date for the hearing.

2.   The preliminary report shall contain recommendations as to whether a preparatory inquiry or any other preparatory step should be undertaken and as to the formation to which the case should be assigned. It shall also contain the Judge-Rapporteur's recommendation, if any, as to whether to dispense with a hearing as provided for in Article 44a and as to whether to dispense with an Opinion of the Advocate General pursuant to the fifth subparagraph of Article 20 of the Statute.

    The Court shall decide, after hearing the Advocate General, what action to take upon the recommendations of the Judge-Rapporteur.

3.   The Court shall assign to the Chambers of five and three Judges any case brought before it in so far as the difficulty or importance of the case or particular circumstances are not such as to require that it should be assigned to the Grand Chamber.

However, a case may not be assigned to a Chamber of five or three Judges if a Member State or an institution of the Union, being a party to the proceedings, has requested that the case be decided by the Grand Chamber. For the purposes of this provision, 'party to the proceedings' means any Member State or any institution which is a party to or an intervener in the proceedings or which has submitted written observations in any reference of a kind mentioned in Article 103. A request such as that referred to in this subparagraph may not be made in proceedings between the Union and its servants.

The Court shall sit as a full Court where cases are brought before it pursuant to the provisions referred to in the fourth paragraph of Article 16 of the Statute. It may assign a case to the full Court where, in accordance with the fifth paragraph of Article 16 of the Statute, it considers that the case is of exceptional importance.

4. The formation to which a case has been assigned may, at any stage of the proceedings, refer the case back to the Court in order that it may be reassigned to a formation composed of a greater number of Judges.

5. Where a preparatory inquiry has been opened, the formation determining the case may, if it does not undertake it itself, assign the inquiry to the Judge-Rapporteur. Where the oral procedure is opened without an inquiry, the President of the formation determining the case shall fix the opening date.

Article 44a

Without prejudice to any special provisions laid down in these Rules, the procedure before the Court shall also include an oral part. However, after the pleadings referred to in Article 40(1) and, as the case may be, in Article 41(1) have been lodged, the Court, acting on a report from the Judge-Rapporteur and after hearing the Advocate General, and if none of the parties has submitted an application setting out the reasons for which he wishes to be heard, may decide otherwise. The application shall be submitted within a period of three weeks from notification to the party of the close of the written procedure. That period may be extended by the President.

Chapter 2 PREPARATORY INQUIRIES AND OTHER PREPARATORY MEASURES

SECTION 1 – MEASURES OF INQUIRY

Article 45

1. The Court, after hearing the Advocate General, shall prescribe the measures of inquiry that it considers appropriate by means of an order setting out the facts to be proved. Before the Court decides on the measures of inquiry referred to in paragraph 2(c), (d) and (e) the parties shall be heard.

The order shall be served on the parties.

2. Without prejudice to Articles 24 and 25 of the Statute, the following measures of inquiry may be adopted:
   (a) the personal appearance of the parties;
   (b) a request for information and production of documents;
   (c) oral testimony;
   (d) the commissioning of an expert's report;
   (e) an inspection of the place or thing in question.

3. The Advocate General shall take part in the measures of inquiry.

4. Evidence may be submitted in rebuttal and previous evidence may be amplified.

Article 46

The parties shall be entitled to attend the measures of inquiry.

SECTION 2 – THE SUMMONING AND EXAMINATION OF WITNESSES AND EXPERTS

Article 47

1.   The Court may, either of its own motion or on application by a party, and after hearing the Advocate General, order that certain facts be proved by witnesses. The order of the Court shall set out the facts to be established.

The Court may summon a witness of its own motion or on application by a party or at the instance of the Advocate General.

An application by a party for the examination of a witness shall state precisely about what facts and for what reasons the witness should be examined.

2.   The witness shall be summoned by an order of the Court containing the following information:
(a) the surname, forenames, description and address of the witness;
(b) an indication of the facts about which the witness is to be examined;
(c) where appropriate, particulars of the arrangements made by the Court for reimbursement of expenses incurred by the witness, and of the penalties which may be imposed on defaulting witnesses.
The order shall be served on the parties and the witnesses.

3.   The Court may make the summoning of a witness for whose examination a party has applied conditional upon the deposit with the cashier of the Court of a sum sufficient to cover the taxed costs thereof; the Court shall fix the amount of the payment.

The cashier shall advance the funds necessary in connection with the examination of any witness summoned by the Court of its own motion.

4.   After the identity of the witness has been established, the President shall inform him that he will be required to vouch the truth of his evidence in the manner laid down in these Rules.

The witness shall give his evidence to the Court, the parties having been given notice to attend. After the witness has given his main evidence the President may, at the request of a party or of his own motion, put questions to him.

The other Judges and the Advocate General may do likewise.

Subject to the control of the President, questions may be put to witnesses by the representatives of the parties.

5.   After giving his evidence, the witness shall take the following oath:

'I swear that I have spoken the truth, the whole truth and nothing but the truth.'

The Court may, after hearing the parties, exempt a witness from taking the oath.

6.   The Registrar shall draw up minutes in which the evidence of each witness is reproduced.

The minutes shall be signed by the President or by the Judge-Rapporteur responsible for conducting the examination of the witness, and by the Registrar. Before the minutes are thus signed, witnesses must be given an opportunity to check the content of the minutes and to sign them.

The minutes shall constitute an official record.

Article 48

1. Witnesses who have been duly summoned shall obey the summons and attend for examination.

2. If a witness who has been duly summoned fails to appear before the Court, the Court may impose upon him a pecuniary penalty not exceeding EUR 5 000* and may order that a further summons be served on the witness at his own expense. [*See Article 2 of Council Regulation (EC) No 1103/97 of 17 June 1997 on certain provisions relating to the introduction of the euro (OJ L 162 of 19.6.1997, p. 1]*.

    The same penalty may be imposed upon a witness who, without good reason, refuses to give evidence or to take the oath or where appropriate to make a solemn affirmation equivalent thereto.

3. If the witness proffers a valid excuse to the Court, the pecuniary penalty imposed on him may be cancelled. The pecuniary penalty imposed may be reduced at the request of the witness where he establishes that it is disproportionate to his income.

4. Penalties imposed and other measures ordered under this Article shall be enforced in accordance with Articles 280 TFEU and 299 TFEU and Article 164 TEAEC.

Article 49

1. The Court may order that an expert's report be obtained. The order appointing the expert shall define his task and set a time-limit within which he is to make his report.

2. The expert shall receive a copy of the order, together with all the documents necessary for carrying out his task. He shall be under the supervision of the Judge-Rapporteur, who may be present during his investigation and who shall be kept informed of his progress in carrying out his task.

    The Court may request the parties or one of them to lodge security for the costs of the expert's report.

3. At the request of the expert, the Court may order the examination of witnesses. Their examination shall be carried out in accordance with Article 47 of these Rules.

4. The expert may give his opinion only on points which have been expressly referred to him.

5. After the expert has made his report, the Court may order that he be examined, the parties having been given notice to attend.

    Subject to the control of the President, questions may be put to the expert by the representatives of the parties.

6. After making his report, the expert shall take the following oath before the Court:

    'I swear that I have conscientiously and impartially carried out my task.'

    The Court may, after hearing the parties, exempt the expert from taking the oath.

Article 50

1. If one of the parties objects to a witness or to an expert on the ground that he is not a competent or proper person to act as witness or expert or for any other reason, or if a witness or expert refuses to give evidence, to take the oath or to make a solemn affirmation equivalent thereto, the matter shall be resolved by the Court.

2.   An objection to a witness or to an expert shall be raised within two weeks after service of the order summoning the witness or appointing the expert; the statement of objection must set out the grounds of objection and indicate the nature of any evidence offered.

Article 51

1.   Witnesses and experts shall be entitled to reimbursement of their travel and subsistence expenses. The cashier of the Court may make a payment to them towards these expenses in advance.

2.   Witnesses shall be entitled to compensation for loss of earnings, and experts to fees for their services. The cashier of the Court shall pay witnesses and experts their compensation or fees after they have carried out their respective duties or tasks.

Article 52

The Court may, on application by a party or of its own motion, issue letters rogatory for the examination of witnesses or experts, as provided for in the supplementary rules mentioned in Article 125 of these Rules.

Article 53

1.   The Registrar shall draw up minutes of every hearing. The minutes shall be signed by the President and by the Registrar and shall constitute an official record.

2.   The parties may inspect the minutes and any expert's report at the Registry and obtain copies at their own expense.

SECTION 3 – CLOSURE OF THE PREPARATORY INQUIRY

Article 54

Unless the Court prescribes a period within which the parties may lodge written observations, the President shall fix the date for the opening of the oral procedure after the preparatory inquiry has been completed.

Where a period had been prescribed for the lodging of written observations, the President shall fix the date for the opening of the oral procedure after that period has expired.

SECTION 4 – PREPARATORY MEASURES

Article 54a

The Judge-Rapporteur and the Advocate General may request the parties to submit within a specified period all such information relating to the facts, and all such documents or other particulars, as they may consider relevant. The information and/or documents provided shall be communicated to the other parties.

Chapter Three ORAL PROCEDURE

Article 55

1.   Subject to the priority of decisions provided for in Article 85 of these Rules, the Court shall deal with the cases before it in the order in which the preparatory inquiries in them have been completed. Where the preparatory inquiries in several cases are completed simultaneously, the order in which they are to be dealt with shall be determined by the dates of entry in the register of the applications initiating them respectively.

2.   The President may in special circumstances order that a case be given priority over others.

The President may in special circumstances, after hearing the parties and the Advocate General, either on his own initiative or at the request of one of the parties, defer a case to be dealt with at a later date. On a joint application by the parties the President may order that a case be deferred.

Article 56

1. The proceedings shall be opened and directed by the President, who shall be responsible for the proper conduct of the hearing.

2. The oral proceedings in cases heard *in camera* shall not be published.

Article 57

The President may in the course of the hearing put questions to the agents, advisers or lawyers of the parties.

The other Judges and the Advocate General may do likewise.

Article 58

A party may address the Court only through his agent, adviser or lawyer.

Article 59

1. The Advocate General shall deliver his opinion orally at the end of the oral procedure.

2. After the Advocate General has delivered his opinion, the President shall declare the oral procedure closed.

Article 60

The Court may at any time, in accordance with Article 45(1), after hearing the Advocate General, order any measure of inquiry to be taken or that a previous inquiry be repeated or expanded. The Court may direct the Judge-Rapporteur to carry out the measures so ordered.

Article 61

The Court may after hearing the Advocate General order the reopening of the oral procedure.

Article 62

1. The Registrar shall draw up minutes of every hearing. The minutes shall be signed by the President and by the Registrar and shall constitute an official record.

2. The parties may inspect the minutes at the Registry and obtain copies at their own expense.

Chapter 3A EXPEDITED PROCEDURES

Article 62a

1. On application by the applicant or the defendant, the President may exceptionally decide, on the basis of a recommendation by the Judge-Rapporteur and after hearing the other party and the Advocate General, that a case is to be determined pursuant to an expedited procedure derogating from the provisions of these Rules, where the particular urgency of the case requires the Court to give its ruling with the minimum of delay.

   An application for a case to be decided under an expedited procedure shall be made by a separate document lodged at the same time as the application initiating the proceedings or the defence, as the case may be.

2.   Under the expedited procedure, the originating application and the defence may be supplemented by a reply and a rejoinder only if the President considers this to be necessary.

An intervener may lodge a statement in intervention only if the President considers this to be necessary.

3.   Once the defence has been lodged or, if the decision to adjudicate under an expedited procedure is not made until after that pleading has been lodged, once that decision has been taken, the President shall fix a date for the hearing, which shall be communicated forthwith to the parties. He may postpone the date of the hearing where the organisation of measures of inquiry or of other preparatory measures so requires.

Without prejudice to Article 42, the parties may supplement their arguments and offer further evidence in the course of the oral procedure. They must, however, give reasons for the delay in offering such further evidence.

4.   The Court shall give its ruling after hearing the Advocate General.

Chapter 4 JUDGMENTS

Article 63
The judgment shall contain:
–   a statement that it is the judgment of the Court,
–   the date of its delivery,
–   the names of the President and of the Judges taking part in it,
–   the name of the Advocate General,
–   the name of the Registrar,
–   the description of the parties,
–   the names of the agents, advisers and lawyers of the parties,
–   a statement of the forms of order sought by the parties,
–   a statement that the Advocate General has been heard,
–   a summary of the facts,
–   the grounds for the decision,
–   the operative part of the judgment, including the decision as to costs.

Article 64
1.   The judgment shall be delivered in open court; the parties shall be given notice to attend to hear it.

2.   The original of the judgment, signed by the President, by the Judges who took part in the deliberations and by the Registrar, shall be sealed and deposited at the

Registry; the parties shall be served with certified copies of the judgment.

3.   The Registrar shall record on the original of the judgment the date on which it was delivered.

Article 65
The judgment shall be binding from the date of its delivery.

Article 66

1. Without prejudice to the provisions relating to the interpretation of judgments the Court may, of its own motion or on application by a party made within two weeks after the delivery of a judgment, rectify clerical mistakes, errors in calculation and obvious slips in it.

2. The parties, whom the Registrar shall duly notify, may lodge written observations within a period prescribed by the President.

3. The Court shall take its decision in closed session after hearing the Advocate General.

4. The original of the rectification order shall be annexed to the original of the rectified judgment. A note of this order shall be made in the margin of the original of the rectified judgment.

Article 67

If the Court should omit to give a decision on a specific head of claim or on costs, any party may within a month after service of the judgment apply to the Court to supplement its judgment.

The application shall be served on the opposite party and the President shall prescribe a period within which that party may lodge written observations.

After these observations have been lodged, the Court shall, after hearing the Advocate General, decide both on the admissibility and on the substance of the application.

Article 68

The Registrar shall arrange for the publication of reports of cases before the Court.

(The remaining chapters in Title II have been omitted)

TITLE III
SPECIAL FORMS OF PROCEDURE

(Chapters 1–8 omitted)

Chapter 9 PRELIMINARY RULINGS AND OTHER REFERENCES FOR INTERPRETATION

Article 103

1. In cases governed by Article 23 of the Statute, the procedure shall be governed by the provisions of these Rules, subject to adaptations necessitated by the nature of the reference for a preliminary ruling.

2. The provisions of paragraph 1 shall apply to the references for a preliminary ruling provided for in the Protocol concerning the interpretation by the Court of Justice of the Convention of 29 February 1968 on the mutual recognition of companies and legal persons and the Protocol concerning the interpretation by the Court of Justice of the Convention of 27 September 1968 on jurisdiction and the enforcement of judgments in civil and commercial matters, signed at Luxembourg on 3 June 1971, and to the references provided for by Article 4 of the latter Protocol.

    The provisions of paragraph 1 shall apply also to references for interpretation provided for by other existing or future agreements.

Article 104

1. The decisions of national courts or tribunals referred to in Article 103 shall be communicated to the Member States in the original version, accompanied by a translation

into the official language of the State to which they are addressed. Where appropriate on account of the length of the national court's decision, such translation shall be replaced by the translation into the official language of the State to which it is addressed of a summary of the decision, which will serve as a basis for the position to be adopted by that State. The summary shall include the full text of the question or questions referred for a preliminary ruling. That summary shall contain, in particular, in so far as that information appears in the national court's decision, the subject-matter of the main proceedings, the essential arguments of the parties in the main proceedings, a succinct presentation of the reasoning in the reference for a preliminary ruling and the case-law and the provisions of European Union and domestic law relied on.

In the cases governed by the third paragraph of Article 23 of the Statute, the decisions of national courts or tribunals shall be notified to the States, other than the Member States, which are parties to the EEA Agreement and also to the EFTA Surveillance Authority in the original version, accompanied by a translation of the decision, or where appropriate of a summary, into one of the languages mentioned in Article 29(1), to be chosen by the addressee of the notification.

Where a non-Member State has the right to take part in proceedings for a preliminary ruling pursuant to the fourth paragraph of Article 23 of the Statute, the original version of the decision of the national court or tribunal shall be communicated to it together with a translation of the decision, or where appropriate of a summary, into one of the languages mentioned in Article 29(1), to be chosen by the non-Member State concerned.

2.   As regards the representation and attendance of the parties to the main proceedings in the preliminary ruling procedure the Court shall take account of the rules of procedure of the national court or tribunal which made the reference.

3.   Where a question referred to the Court for a preliminary ruling is identical to a question on which the Court has already ruled, or where the answer to such a question may be clearly deduced from existing case-law, the Court may, after hearing the Advocate General, at any time give its decision by reasoned order in which reference is made to its previous judgment or to the relevant case-law.

The Court may also give its decision by reasoned order, after informing the court or tribunal which referred the question to it, hearing any observations submitted by the persons referred to in Article 23 of the Statute and after hearing the Advocate General, where the answer to the question referred to the Court for a preliminary ruling admits of no reasonable doubt.

4.   Without prejudice to paragraph (3) of this Article, the procedure before the Court in the case of a reference for a preliminary ruling shall also include an oral part.

However, after the statements of case or written observations referred to Article 23 of the Statute have been submitted, the Court, acting on a report from the Judge Rapporteur, after informing the persons who under the aforementioned provisions are entitled to submit such statements or observations, may, after hearing the Advocate General, decide otherwise, provided that none of those persons has submitted an application setting out the reasons for which he wishes to be heard. The application shall be submitted within a period of three weeks from service on the party or person of the written statements of case or written observations which have been lodged. That period may be extended by the President.

5.   The Court may, after hearing the Advocate General, request clarification from the national court.

6.   It shall be for the national court or tribunal to decide as to the costs of the reference.

In special circumstances the Court may grant, by way of legal aid, assistance for the purpose of facilitating the representation or attendance of a party.

Article 104a

At the request of the national court, the President may exceptionally decide, on a proposal from the Judge-Rapporteur and after hearing the Advocate General, to apply an accelerated procedure derogating from the provisions of these Rules to a reference for a preliminary ruling, where the circumstances referred to establish that a ruling on the question put to the Court is a matter of exceptional urgency.

In that event, the President may immediately fix the date for the hearing, which shall be notified to the parties in the main proceedings and to the other persons referred to in Article 23 of the Statute when the decision making the reference is served.

The parties and other interested persons referred to in the preceding paragraph may lodge statements of case or written observations within a period prescribed by the President, which shall not be less than 15 days. The President may request the parties and other interested persons to restrict the matters addressed in their statement of case or written observations to the essential points of law raised by the question referred.

The statements of case or written observations, if any, shall be notified to the parties and to the other persons referred to above prior to the hearing.

The Court shall rule after hearing the Advocate General.

Article 104b

1.   A reference for a preliminary ruling which raises one or more questions in the areas covered by Title V of Part Three of the Treaty on the Functioning of the European Union may, at the request of the national court or tribunal or, exceptionally, of the Court's own motion, be dealt with under an urgent procedure which derogates from the provisions of these Rules.

The national court or tribunal shall set out, in its request, the matters of fact and law which establish the urgency and justify the application of that exceptional procedure and shall, in so far as possible, indicate the answer it proposes to the questions referred.

If the national court or tribunal has not submitted a request for the urgent procedure to be applied, the President of the Court may, if the application of that procedure appears, prima facie, to be required, ask the Chamber referred to below to consider whether it is necessary to deal with the reference under that procedure.

The decision to deal with a reference for a preliminary ruling under the urgent procedure shall be taken by the designated Chamber, acting on a report of the Judge-Rapporteur and after hearing the Advocate General. The composition of that Chamber shall be determined in accordance with Article 11c on the day on which the case is assigned to the Judge-Rapporteur if the application of the urgent procedure is requested by the national court or tribunal, or, if the application of that procedure is considered at the request of the President of the Court, on the day on which that request is made.

2.   A reference for a preliminary ruling of the kind referred to in the preceding paragraph shall, where the national court or tribunal has requested the application of the urgent procedure or where the President has requested the designated Chamber to consider whether it is necessary to deal with the reference under that procedure, be notified forthwith by the Registrar to the parties to the action before the national court or

tribunal, to the Member State from which the reference is made and to the institutions referred to in the first paragraph of Article 23 of the Statute, in accordance with that provision.

The decision as to whether or not to deal with the reference for a preliminary ruling under the urgent procedure shall be notified forthwith to the national court or tribunal and to the parties, Member State and institutions referred to in the preceding subparagraph. The decision to deal with the reference under the urgent procedure shall prescribe the period within which those parties or entities may lodge statements of case or written observations. The decision may specify the matters of law to which such statements of case or written observations must relate and may specify the maximum length of those documents.

As soon as the notification referred to in the first subparagraph above has been made, the reference for a preliminary ruling shall also be communicated to the interested persons referred to in Article 23 of the Statute, other than the persons notified, and the decision whether or not to deal with the reference for a preliminary ruling under the urgent procedure shall be communicated to those interested persons as soon as the notification referred to in the second subparagraph has been made.

The parties and other interested persons referred to in Article 23 of the Statute shall be informed as soon as may be possible of the foreseeable date of the hearing.

Where the reference is not to be dealt with under the urgent procedure, the proceedings shall continue in accordance with the provisions of Article 23 of the Statute and the applicable provisions of these Rules.

3.   A reference for a preliminary ruling which is to be dealt with under an urgent procedure, together with the statements of case or written observations which have been lodged, shall be served on the persons referred to in Article 23 of the Statute other than the parties and the entities referred to in the first subparagraph of the preceding paragraph of this Article. The reference for a preliminary ruling shall be accompanied by a translation, where appropriate in summary form, in accordance with Article 104(1).

The statements of case or written observations which have been lodged shall also be served on the parties and the other persons referred to in the first subparagraph of Article 104b(2).

The date of the hearing shall be notified to the parties and those other persons at the same time as the documents referred to in the preceding paragraphs are served.

4.   The Chamber may, in cases of extreme urgency, decide to omit the written part of the procedure referred to in the second subparagraph of paragraph 2 of this Article.

5.   The designated Chamber shall rule after hearing the Advocate General.

It may decide to sit in a formation of three Judges. In that event, it shall be composed of the President of the designated Chamber, the Judge-Rapporteur and the first Judge or, as the case may be, the first two Judges designated from the list referred to in Article 11c(2) on the date on which the composition of the designated Chamber is determined in accordance with the fourth subparagraph of paragraph 1 of this Article.

It may also decide to refer the case back to the Court in order for it to be assigned to a formation composed of a greater number of Judges. The urgent procedure shall continue before the new formation, where necessary after the reopening of the oral procedure.

6.   The procedural documents referred to in this Article shall be deemed to have been lodged on the transmission to the Registry, by telefax or other technical means of communication

available to the Court, of a copy of the signed original and the documents relied on in support of it, together with the schedule referred to in Article 37(4). The original of the document and the annexes referred to above shall be sent to the Registry.

Where this Article requires that a document be notified to or served on a person, such notification or service may be effected by the transmission of a copy of the document by telefax or other technical means of communication available to the Court and the addressee.

(Chapter 10 omitted).

Chapter 11 OPINIONS

Article 107
1.   A request by the European Parliament for an opinion pursuant to Article 218 TFEU shall be served on the Council, on the European Commission and on the Member States. Such a request by the Council shall be served on the European Commission and on the European Parliament. Such a request by the European Commission shall be served on the Council, on the European Parliament and on the Member States. Such a request by a Member State shall be served on the Council, on the European Commission, on the European Parliament and on the other Member States.

The President shall prescribe a period within which the institutions and Member States which have been served with a request may submit their written observations.

2.   The Opinion may deal not only with the question whether the envisaged agreement is compatible which the provisions of the Treaties but also with the question whether the Union or any Union institution has the power to enter into that agreement.

Article 108
1.   As soon as the request for an Opinion has been lodged, the President shall designate a Judge to act as Rapporteur.

2.   The Court sitting in closed session shall, after hearing the Advocates General, deliver a reasoned Opinion.

3.   The Opinion, signed by the President, by the Judges who took part in the deliberations and by the Registrar, shall be served on the Council, the European Commission, the European Parliament and the Member States.

Article 109
(repealed)

(The remaining chapters in Title III are omitted)

TITLE IV
APPEALS AGAINST DECISIONS OF THE GENERAL COURT

Article 110
Without prejudice to the arrangements laid down in Article 29(2)(b) and (c) and the fourth subparagraph of Article 29(3) of these Rules, in appeals against decisions of the General Court as referred to in Articles 56 and 57 of the Statute, the language of the case shall be the language of the decision of the General Court against which the appeal is brought.

Article 111
1.   An appeal shall be brought by lodging an application at the Registry of the Court of
      Justice or of the General Court.

2.   The Registry of the General Court shall immediately transmit to the Registry of
      the Court of Justice the papers in the case at first instance and, where necessary,
      the appeal.

Article 112
1.   An appeal shall contain:
      (a) the name and address of the appellant;
      (b) the names of the other parties to the proceedings before the General Court;
      (c) the pleas in law and legal arguments relied on;
      (d) the form or order sought by the appellant.
      Article 37 and Article 38(2) and (3) of these Rules shall apply to appeals.

2.   The decision of the General Court appealed against shall be attached to the appeal. The
      appeal shall state the date on which the decision appealed against was notified to the
      appellant.

3.   If an appeal does not comply with Article 38(3) or with paragraph 2 of this Article,
      Article 38(7) of these Rules shall apply.

Article 113
1.   An appeal may seek:
      –   to set aside, in whole or in part, the decision of the General Court;
      –   the same form of order, in whole or in part, as that sought at first instance and shall
          not seek a different form of order.

2.   The subject-matter of the proceedings before the General Court may not be changed in the
      appeal.

Article 114
Notice of the appeal shall be served on all the parties to the proceedings before the General
Court. Article 39 of these Rules shall apply.

Article 115
1.   Any party to the proceedings before the General Court may lodge a response within two
      months after service on him of notice of the appeal. The time-limit for lodging a response
      shall not be extended.

2.   A response shall contain:
      (a) the name and address of the party lodging it;
      (b) the date on which notice of the appeal was served on him;
      (c) the pleas in law and legal arguments relied on;
      (d) the form of order sought by the respondent.
      Article 37 and Article 38(2) and (3) of these Rules shall apply.

Article 116
1.   A response may seek:
      –   to dismiss, in whole or in part, the appeal or to set aside, in whole or in part, the
          decision of the General Court;
      –   the same form of order, in whole or in part, as that sought at first instance and shall
          not seek a different form of order.

2.   The subject-matter of the proceedings before the General Court may not be changed in the response.

Article 117
1.   The appeal and the response may be supplemented by a reply and a rejoinder where the President, on application made by the appellant within seven days of service of the response, considers such further pleading necessary and expressly allows the submission of a reply in order to enable the appellant to put forward his point of view or in order to provide a basis for the decision on the appeal. The President shall prescribe the date by which the reply is to be submitted and, upon service of that pleading, the date by which the rejoinder is to be submitted.

2.   Where the response seeks to set aside, in whole or in part, the decision of the General Court on a plea in law which was not raised in the appeal, the appellant or any other party may submit a reply on that plea alone within two months of the service of the response in question. Paragraph 1 shall apply to any further pleading following such a reply.

Article 118
Subject to the following provisions, Articles 42(2), 43, 44, 55 to 90, 93, 95 to 100 and 102 of these Rules shall apply to the procedure before the Court of Justice on appeal from a decision of the General Court.

Article 119
Where the appeal is, in whole or in part, clearly inadmissible or clearly unfounded, the Court may at any time, acting on a report from the Judge-Rapporteur and after hearing the Advocate General, by reasoned order dismiss the appeal in whole or in part.

Article 120
After the submission of pleadings as provided for in Article 115(1) and, if any, Article 117(1) and (2) of these Rules, the Court, acting on a report from the Judge-Rapporteur and after hearing the Advocate General and the parties, may decide to dispense with the oral part of the procedure unless one of the parties submits an application setting out the reasons for which he wishes to be heard. The application shall be submitted within a period of three weeks from notification to the party of the close of the written procedure.

That period may be extended by the President.

Article 121
The report referred to in Article 44(2) shall be presented to the Court after the pleadings provided for in Article 115(1) and where appropriate Article 117(1) and (2) of these Rules have been lodged. Where no such pleadings are lodged, the same procedure shall apply after the expiry of the period prescribed for lodging them.

Article 122
Where the appeal is unfounded or where the appeal is well founded and the Court itself gives final judgment in the case, the Court shall make a decision as to costs.
In proceedings between the Union and its servants:
–   Article 70 of these Rules shall apply only to appeals brought by institutions;

–   by way of derogation from Article 69(2) of these Rules, the Court may, in appeals brought by officials or other servants of an institution, order the parties to share the costs where equity so requires.

If the appeal is withdrawn Article 69(5) shall apply.

When an appeal brought by a Member State or an institution which did not intervene in the proceedings before the General Court is well founded, the Court of Justice may order that the parties share the costs or that the successful appellant pay the costs which the appeal has caused an unsuccessful party to incur.

Article 123
An application to intervene made to the Court in appeal proceedings shall be lodged before the expiry of a period of one month running from the publication referred to in Article 16(6).

TITLE IVA
REVIEW OF DECISIONS OF THE GENERAL COURT

Article 123a
Without prejudice to the arrangements laid down in Article 29(2)(b) and (c) and the fourth and fifth subparagraphs of Article 29(3) of these Rules, where, in accordance with the second paragraph of Article 62 of the Statute, the Court decides to review a decision of the General Court, the language of the case shall be the language of the decision of the General Court which is subject to review.

Article 123b
A special Chamber shall be set up for the purpose of deciding, in accordance with Article 123d, whether a decision of the General Court is to be reviewed in accordance with Article 62 of the Statute.

That Chamber shall be composed of the President of the Court and of four of the Presidents of the Chambers of five Judges designated according to the order of precedence laid down in Article 6 of these Rules.

Article 123c
As soon as the date for the delivery of a decision to be given under Article 256(2) or (3) TFEU is fixed, the Registry of the General Court shall inform the Registry of the Court of Justice. The decision shall be communicated immediately upon its delivery.

Article 123d
The proposal of the First Advocate General to review a decision of the General Court shall be forwarded to the President of the Court of Justice and notice of that transmission shall be given to the Registrar at the same time. Where the decision of the General Court has been given under Article 256(3) TFEU, the Registrar shall forthwith inform the General Court, the national court and the parties to the proceedings before the national court of the proposal to review.

As soon as the proposal to review has been received, the President shall designate the Judge-Rapporteur from among the Judges of the Chamber referred to in Article 123b.

That Chamber, acting on a report from the Judge-Rapporteur, shall decide whether the decision of the General Court is to be reviewed. The decision to review the decision of the General Court shall indicate the questions which are to be reviewed.

Where the decision of the General Court has been given under Article 256(2) TFEU, the General Court, the parties to the proceedings before it and the other interested parties referred to in the second paragraph of Article 62a of the Statute shall forthwith be informed by the Registrar of the decision of the Court of Justice to review the decision of the General Court.

Where the decision of the General Court has been given under Article 256(3) TFEU, the General Court, the national court, the parties to the proceedings before the national court and the other interested parties referred to in the second paragraph of Article 62a of the Statute shall forthwith be informed by the Registrar of the decision of the Court of Justice as to whether or not the decision of the General Court is to be reviewed. Notice of a decision to review the decision of the General Court shall be given in the *Official Journal of the European Union*.

Article 123e
The decision to review a decision of the General Court shall be notified to the parties and other interested parties referred to in the second paragraph of Article 62a of the Statute.

The notification to the Member States, and the States, other than the Member States, which are parties to the EEA Agreement, as well as the EFTA Surveillance Authority, shall be accompanied by a translation of the decision of the Court of Justice in accordance with the provisions of the first and second subparagraphs of Article 104(1) of these Rules. The decision of the Court of Justice shall also be communicated to the General Court and, in cases involving a decision given by that Court under Article 256(3) TFEU, to the national court concerned.

Within one month of the notification referred to in the preceding paragraph, the parties and other persons to whom the decision of the Court of Justice has been notified may lodge statements or written observations on the questions which are subject to review.

As soon as a decision to review a decision of the General Court has been taken, the First Advocate General shall assign the review to an Advocate General.

After designating the Judge-Rapporteur, the President shall fix the date on which the latter is to present a preliminary report to the general meeting of the Court. That report shall contain the recommendations of the Judge-Rapporteur as to whether any preparatory steps should be taken, as to the formation of the Court to which the review should be assigned and as to whether a hearing should take place, and also as to the manner in which the Advocate General should present his views. The Court shall decide, after hearing the Advocate General, what action to take upon the recommendations of the Judge-Rapporteur.

Where the decision of the General Court which is subject to review was given under Article 256(2) TFEU, the Court of Justice shall make a decision as to costs.

(Remaining provisions omitted).

COURT OF JUSTICE INFORMATION NOTE
on references from national courts for a preliminary ruling
OJ C 297, 5.12.2009, p. 1*

. . . .

I. GENERAL

1.   The preliminary ruling system is a fundamental mechanism of European Union law aimed at enabling national courts to ensure uniform interpretation and application of that law in all the Member States.

2.   The Court of Justice of the European Union has jurisdiction to give preliminary rulings on

. . . .

(*This note replaces the information note published in OJ 2005 C 143, p. 1 and the supplement to that note published in OJ 2008 C 64.)

the interpretation of European Union law and on the validity of acts of the institutions, bodies, offices or agencies of the Union. That general jurisdiction is conferred on it by Article 19(3)(b) of the Treaty on European Union (OJEU 2008 C 115, p. 13) ('the TEU') and Article 267 of the Treaty on the Functioning of the European Union (OJEU 2008 C 115, p. 47) ('the TFEU').

3.   Article 256(3) TFEU provides that the General Court is to have jurisdiction to hear and determine questions referred for a preliminary ruling under Article 267, in specific areas laid down by the Statute. Since no provisions have been introduced into the Statute in that regard, the Court of Justice alone has jurisdiction to give preliminary rulings.

4.   While Article 267 TFEU confers on the Court of Justice a general jurisdiction, a number of provisions exist which lay down exceptions to or restrictions on that jurisdiction. This is true in particular of Articles 275 and 276 TFEU and Article 10 of Protocol (No 36) on Transitional Provisions of the Treaty of Lisbon (OJEU 2008 C 115, p. 322).

5.   The preliminary ruling procedure being based on cooperation between the Court of Justice and national courts, it may be helpful, in order to ensure that that cooperation is effective, to provide the national courts with the following information.

6.   This practical information, which is in no way binding, is intended to provide guidance to national courts as to whether it is appropriate to make a reference for a preliminary ruling and, should they proceed, to help them formulate and submit questions to the Court.

THE ROLE OF THE COURT OF JUSTICE IN THE PRELIMINARY RULING PROCEDURE

7.   Under the preliminary ruling procedure, the Court's role is to give an interpretation of European Union law or to rule on its validity, not to apply that law to the factual situation underlying the main proceedings, which is the task of the national court. It is not for the Court either to decide issues of fact raised in the main proceedings or to resolve differences of opinion on the interpretation or application of rules of national law.

8.   In ruling on the interpretation or validity of European Union law, the Court makes every effort to give a reply which will be of assistance in resolving the dispute, but it is for the referring court to draw the appropriate conclusions from that reply, if necessary by disapplying the rule of national law in question.

THE DECISION TO SUBMIT A QUESTION TO THE COURT

The originator of the question

9.   Under Article 267 TFEU, any court or tribunal of a Member State, in so far as it is called upon to give a ruling in proceedings intended to arrive at a decision of a judicial nature, may as a rule refer a question to the Court of Justice for a preliminary ruling (1). Status as a court or tribunal is interpreted by the Court of Justice as a self-standing concept of European Union law.

10. It is for the national court alone to decide whether to refer a question to the Court of Justice for a preliminary ruling, whether or not the parties to the main proceedings have requested it to do so.

References on interpretation

11. Any court or tribunal may refer a question to the Court of Justice on the interpretation of a rule of European Union law if it considers it necessary to do so in order to resolve a dispute brought before it.

12. However, courts or tribunals against whose decisions there is no judicial remedy under national law must, as a rule, refer such a question to the Court, unless the Court has already ruled on the point (and there is no new context that raises any serious doubt as to whether that case-law may be applied), or unless the correct interpretation of the rule of law in question is obvious.

13. Thus, a court or tribunal against whose decisions there is a judicial remedy may, in particular when it considers that sufficient guidance is given by the case-law of the Court of Justice, itself decide on the correct interpretation of European Union law and its application to the factual situation before it. However, a reference for a preliminary ruling may prove particularly useful, at an appropriate stage of the proceedings, when there is a new question of interpretation of general interest for the uniform application of European Union law in all the Member States, or where the existing case-law does not appear to be applicable to a new set of facts.

14. It is for the national court to explain why the interpretation sought is necessary to enable it to give judgment.

References on determination of validity

15. Although national courts may reject pleas raised before them challenging the validity of acts of an institution, body, office or agency of the Union, the Court of Justice has exclusive jurisdiction to declare such an act invalid.

16. All national courts must therefore refer a question to the Court when they have doubts about the validity of such an act, stating the reasons for which they consider that that act may be invalid.

17. However, if a national court has serious doubts about the validity of an act of an institution, body, office or agency of the Union on which a national measure is based, it may exceptionally suspend application of that measure temporarily or grant other interim relief with respect to it. It must then refer the question of validity to the Court of Justice, stating the reasons for which it considers the act to be invalid.

THE STAGE AT WHICH TO SUBMIT A QUESTION FOR A PRELIMINARY RULING

18. A national court or tribunal may refer a question to the Court for a preliminary ruling as soon as it finds that a ruling on the point or points of interpretation or validity is necessary to enable it to give judgment; it is the national court which is in the best position to decide at what stage of the proceedings such a question should be referred.

19. It is, however, desirable that a decision to seek a preliminary ruling should be taken when the national proceedings have reached a stage at which the national court is able to define the factual and legal context of the question, so that the Court of Justice has available to it all the information necessary to check, where appropriate, that European Union law applies to the main proceedings. It may also be in the interests of justice to refer a question for a preliminary ruling only after both sides have been heard.

20. The decision by which a national court or tribunal refers a question to the Court of Justice for a preliminary ruling may be in any form allowed by national law as regards procedural steps. It must however be borne in mind that it is that document which serves as the basis of the proceedings before the Court and that it must therefore contain such information as will enable the latter to give a reply which is of assistance to the national court. Moreover, it is only the actual reference for a preliminary ruling which is notified to the interested persons entitled to submit observations to the Court, in particular the Member States and the institutions, and which is translated.

21. Owing to the need to translate the reference, it should be drafted simply, clearly and precisely, avoiding superfluous detail.

22. A maximum of about 10 pages is often sufficient to set out in a proper manner the context of a reference for a preliminary ruling. The order for reference must be succinct but sufficiently complete and must contain all the relevant information to give the Court and the interested persons entitled to submit observations a clear understanding of the factual and legal context of the main proceedings. In particular, the order for reference must:
   — include a brief account of the subject-matter of the dispute and the relevant findings of fact, or, at least, set out the factual situation on which the question referred is based;
   — set out the tenor of any applicable national provisions and identify, where necessary, the relevant national case-law, giving in each case precise references (for example, a page of an official journal or specific law report, with any internet reference);
   — identify the European Union law provisions relevant to the case as accurately as possible;
   — explain the reasons which prompted the national court to raise the question of the interpretation or validity of the European Union law provisions, and the relationship between those provisions and the national provisions applicable to the main proceedings;
   — include, if need be, a summary of the main relevant arguments of the parties to the main proceedings.
   In order to make it easier to read and refer to the document, it is helpful if the different points or paragraphs of the order for reference are numbered.

23. Finally, the referring court may, if it considers itself able, briefly state its view on the answer to be given to the questions referred for a preliminary ruling.

24. The question or questions themselves should appear in a separate and clearly identified section of the order for reference, generally at the beginning or the end. It must be possible to understand them without referring to the statement of the grounds for the reference, which will however provide the necessary background for a proper assessment.

THE EFFECTS OF THE REFERENCE FOR A PRELIMINARY RULING ON THE NATIONAL PROCEEDINGS

25. A reference for a preliminary ruling calls for the national proceedings to be stayed until the Court of Justice has given its ruling.

26. However, the national court may still order protective measures, particularly in connection with a reference on determination of validity (see point 17 above).

COSTS AND LEGAL AID

27. Preliminary ruling proceedings before the Court of Justice are free of charge and the Court does not rule on the costs of the parties to the main proceedings; it is for the national court to rule on those costs.

28. If a party has insufficient means and where it is possible under national rules, the national court may grant that party legal aid to cover the costs, including those of lawyers' fees, which it incurs before the Court. The Court itself may also grant legal aid where the party in question is not already in receipt of legal aid under national rules or to the extent to which that aid does not cover, or covers only partly, costs incurred before the Court.

COMMUNICATION BETWEEN THE NATIONAL COURT AND THE COURT OF JUSTICE

29. The order for reference and the relevant documents (including, where applicable, the case file or a copy of the case file) are to be sent by the national court directly to the Court of Justice, by registered post (addressed to the Registry of the Court of Justice, L-2925 Luxembourg, telephone +352 4303-1).

30. The Court Registry will stay in contact with the national court until a ruling is given, and will send it copies of the procedural documents.

31. The Court of Justice will send its ruling to the national court. It would welcome information from the national court on the action taken upon its ruling in the national proceedings and, where appropriate, a copy of the national court's final decision.

II. THE URGENT PRELIMINARY RULING PROCEDURE (PPU)

32. This part of the note provides practical information on the urgent preliminary ruling procedure applicable to references relating to the area of freedom, security and justice. The procedure is governed by Article 23a of Protocol (No 3) on the Statute of the Court of Justice of the European Union (OJEU 2008 C 115, p. 210) and Article 104b of the Rules of Procedure of the Court of Justice. National courts may request that this procedure be applied or request the application of the accelerated procedure under the conditions laid down in Article 23a of the Protocol and Article 104a of the Rules of Procedure.

CONDITIONS FOR THE APPLICATION OF THE URGENT PRELIMINARY RULING PROCEDURE

33. The urgent preliminary ruling procedure is applicable only in the areas covered by Title V of Part Three of the TFEU, which relates to the area of freedom, security and justice.

34. The Court of Justice decides whether this procedure is to be applied. Such a decision is generally taken only on a reasoned request from the referring court. Exceptionally, the Court may decide of its own motion to deal with a reference under the urgent preliminary ruling procedure, where that appears to be required.

35. The urgent preliminary ruling procedure simplifies the various stages of the proceedings before the Court, but its application entails significant constraints for the Court and for the parties and other interested persons participating in the procedure, particularly the Member States.

36. It should therefore be requested only where it is absolutely necessary for the Court to give its ruling on the reference as quickly as possible. Although it is not possible to provide an exhaustive list of such situations, particularly because of the varied and evolving nature of the rules of European Union law governing the area of freedom, security and justice, a national court or tribunal might, for example, consider submitting a request for the urgent preliminary ruling procedure to be applied in the following situations: in the case, referred

to in the fourth paragraph of Article 267 TFEU, of a person in custody or deprived of his liberty, where the answer to the question raised is decisive as to the assessment of that person's legal situation or, in proceedings concerning parental authority or custody of children, where the identity of the court having jurisdiction under European Union law depends on the answer to the question referred for a preliminary ruling.

THE REQUEST FOR APPLICATION OF THE URGENT PRELIMINARY RULING PROCEDURE

37.   To enable the Court to decide quickly whether the urgent preliminary ruling procedure should be applied, the request must set out the matters of fact and law which establish the urgency and, in particular, the risks involved in following the normal preliminary ruling procedure.

38.   In so far as it is able to do so, the referring court should briefly state its view on the answer to be given to the question(s) referred. Such a statement makes it easier for the parties and other interested persons participating in the procedure to define their positions and facilitates the Court's decision, thereby contributing to the rapidity of the procedure.

39.   The request for the urgent preliminary ruling procedure must be submitted in a form that enables the Court Registry to establish immediately that the file must be dealt with in a particular way. Accordingly, the request should be submitted in a document separate from the order for reference itself, or in a covering letter expressly setting out the request.

40.   As regards the order for reference itself, it is particularly important that it should be succinct where the matter is urgent, as this will help to ensure the rapidity of the procedure.

COMMUNICATION BETWEEN THE COURT OF JUSTICE, THE NATIONAL COURT AND THE PARTIES

41.   As regards communication with the national court or tribunal and the parties before it, national courts or tribunals which submit a request for an urgent preliminary ruling procedure are requested to state the e-mail address or any fax number which may be used by the Court of Justice, together with the e-mail addresses or any fax numbers of the representatives of the parties to the proceedings.

42.   A copy of the signed order for reference together with a request for the urgent preliminary ruling procedure can initially be sent to the Court by e-mail (ECJ-Registry@curia.europa.eu) or by fax (+352 43 37 66). Processing of the reference and of the request can then begin upon receipt of the e-mailed or faxed copy. The originals of those documents must, however, be sent to the Court Registry as soon as possible.

(1)   Article 10(1) to (3) of Protocol No 36 provides that the powers of the Court of Justice in relation to acts adopted before the entry into force of the Treaty of Lisbon (OJ 2007 C 306, p. 1) under Title VI of the TEU, in the field of police cooperation and judicial cooperation in criminal matters, and which have not since been amended, are, however, to remain the same for a maximum period of five years from the date of entry into force of the Treaty of Lisbon (1 December 2009). During that period, such acts may, therefore, form the subject-matter of a reference for a preliminary ruling only where the order for reference is made by a court of a Member State which has accepted the jurisdiction of the Court of Justice, it being a matter for each State to determine whether the right to refer a question to the Court is to be available to all of its national courts or is to be reserved to the courts of last instance.

B) Presidency of the Council

European Council Decision of 1 December 2009
on the exercise of the Presidency of the Council OJ L 315, 2.12.2009, p. 50

THE EUROPEAN COUNCIL,

Having regard to the Treaty on the European Union, and in particular Article 16(9) thereof,

Having regard to the Treaty on the Functioning of the European Union, and in particular Article 236(b) thereof,

Whereas:
(1) Declaration (no 9) annexed to the Final Act of the Intergovernmental Conference which has adopted the Treaty of Lisbon foresees that the European Council adopts, on the date of entry into force of the Treaty, the Decision the text of which is contained in the said Declaration.

(2) It is therefore appropriate to adopt that Decision,

HAS ADOPTED THIS DECISION:

Article 1
1. The Presidency of the Council, with the exception of the Foreign Affairs configuration, shall be held by pre-established groups of three Member States for a period of 18 months. The groups shall be made up on a basis of equal rotation among the Member States, taking into account their diversity and geographical balance within the Union.

2. Each member of the group shall in turn chair for a six-month period all configurations of the Council, with the exception of the Foreign Affairs configuration. The other members of the group shall assist the Chair in all its responsibilities on the basis of a common programme. Members of the team may decide alternative arrangements among themselves.

Article 2
The Committee of Permanent Representatives of the Governments of the Member States shall be chaired by a representative of the Member State chairing the General Affairs Council. The Chair of the Political and Security Committee shall be held by a representative of the High Representative of the Union for Foreign Affairs and Security Policy. The chair of the preparatory bodies of the various Council configurations, with the exception of the Foreign Affairs configuration, shall fall to the member of the group chairing the relevant configuration, unless decided otherwise in accordance with Article 4.

Article 3
The General Affairs Council shall ensure consistency and continuity in the work of the different Council configurations in the framework of multiannual programmes in cooperation with the Commission. The Member States holding the Presidency shall take all necessary measures for the organisation and smooth operation of the Council's work, with the assistance of the General Secretariat of the Council.

Article 4
The Council shall adopt a decision establishing the measures for the implementation of this decision.

Article 5
This Decision shall enter into force on the day of its adoption. It shall be published in the *Official Journal of the European Union.*

C) Implementing Powers and Law Making

Council Decision of 28 June 1999

laying down the procedures for the exercise of implementing powers conferred on the Commission
OJ L 184, 17.7.1999, L184/23[1]

THE COUNCIL OF THE EUROPEAN UNION,

Having regard to the Treaty establishing the European Community, and in particular the third indent of Article 202 thereof,

Having regard to the proposal from the Commission,

Having regard to the opinion of the European Parliament,

Whereas:
(1)   in the instruments which it adopts, the Council has to confer on the Commission powers for the implementation of the rules which the Council lays down; the Council may impose certain requirements in respect of the exercise of these powers; it may also reserve to itself the right, in specific and substantiated cases, to exercise directly implementing powers;

(2)   the Council adopted Decision 87/373/EEC of 13 July 1987 laying down the procedures for the exercise of implementing powers conferred on the Commission (3); that Decision has provided for a limited number of procedures for the exercise of such powers;

(3)   declaration No 31 annexed to the Final Act of the Intergovernmental Conference which adopted the Amsterdam Treaty calls on the Commission to submit to the Council a proposal amending Decision 87/373/EEC;

(4)   for reasons of clarity, rather than amending Decision 87/373/EEC, it has been considered more appropriate to replace that Decision by a new Decision and, therefore, to repeal Decision 87/373/EEC;

(5)   the first purpose of this Decision is, with a view to achieving greater consistency and predictability in the choice of type of committee, to provide for criteria relating to the choice of committee procedures, it being understood that such criteria are of a non-binding nature with the exception of those governing the regulatory procedure with scrutiny;

---

[1]   EDITOR'S NOTE: As amended by Council Decision 2006/512/EC, OJ L 200, 22.7.2006, p. 11. All other footnotes contained in the Decision have been omitted. As of 1 June 2010, this Council Decision has not been amended following the adoption of the Treaty of Lisbon. It may include references to the old version of the Treaty on European Union (TEU) and/or the now replaced Treaty establishing the European Community (TEC). Reference should be made to the Tables of Equivalences accompanying the consolidated Treaties in Part II of this edition for the conversion of old Treaty article numbers to new ones.

(6) in this regard, the management procedure should be followed as regards management measures such as those relating to the application of the common agricultural and common fisheries policies or to the implementation of programmes with substantial budgetary implications; such management measures should be taken by the Commission by a procedure ensuring decision-making within suitable periods; however, where non-urgent measures are referred to the Council, the Commission should exercise its discretion to defer application of the measures;

(7) the regulatory procedure should be followed as regards measures of general scope designed to apply essential provisions of basic instruments, including measures concerning the protection of the health or safety of humans, animals or plants, as well as measures designed to adapt or update certain non-essential provisions of a basic instrument; such implementing measures should be adopted by an effective procedure which complies in full with the Commission's right of initiative in legislative matters;

(7a) it is necessary to follow the regulatory procedure with scrutiny as regards measures of general scope which seek to amend nonessential elements of a basic instrument adopted in accordance with the procedure referred to in Article 251 of the Treaty, *inter alia* by deleting some of those elements or by supplementing the instrument by the addition of new nonessential elements. This procedure should enable the two arms of the legislative authority to scrutinise such measures before they are adopted. The essential elements of a legislative act may only be amended by the legislator on the basis of the Treaty;

(8) the advisory procedure should be followed in any case in which it is considered to be the most appropriate; the advisory procedure will continue to be used in those cases where it currently applies;

(9) the second purpose of this Decision is to simplify the requirements for the exercise of implementing powers conferred on the Commission as well as to improve the involvement of the European Parliament in those cases where the basic instrument conferring implementation powers on the Commission was adopted in accordance with the procedure laid down in Article 251 of the Treaty; it has been accordingly considered appropriate to reduce the number of procedures as well as to adjust them in line with the respective powers of the institutions involved and notably to give the European Parliament an opportunity to have its views taken into consideration by, respectively, the Commission or the Council in cases where it considers that, respectively, a draft measure submitted to a committee or a proposal submitted to the Council under the regulatory procedure exceeds the implementing powers provided for in the basic instrument;

(10) the third purpose of this Decision is to improve information to the European Parliament by providing that the Commission should inform it on a regular basis of committee proceedings, that the Commission should transmit to it documents related to activities of committees and inform it whenever the Commission transmits to the Council measures or proposals for measures to be taken; particular attention will be paid to the provision of information to the European Parliament on the proceedings of committees in the framework of the regulatory procedure with scrutiny, so as to ensure that the European Parliament takes a decision within the stipulated deadline;

(11) the fourth purpose of this Decision is to improve information to the public concerning committee procedures and therefore to make applicable to committees the principles and conditions on public access to documents applicable to the Commission, to provide for a list of all committees which assist the Commission in the exercise of implementing powers and for an annual report on the working of committees to be published as well as to provide for all references to documents related to committees which have been transmitted to the European Parliament to be made public in a register;

(12)   the specific committee procedures created for the implementation of the common commercial policy and the competition rules laid down by the Treaties that are not currently based upon Decision 87/373/EEC are not in any way affected by this Decision,

HAS DECIDED AS FOLLOWS:

Article 1

Other than in specific and substantiated cases where the basic instrument reserves to the Council the right to exercise directly certain implementing powers itself, such powers shall be conferred on the Commission in accordance with the relevant provisions in the basic instrument. These provisions shall stipulate the essential elements of the powers thus conferred. Where the basic instrument imposes specific procedural requirements for the adoption of implementing measures, such requirements shall be in conformity with the procedures provided for by Articles 3, 4, 5, 5a and 6.

Article 2

1.   Without prejudice to paragraph 2, the choice of procedural methods for the adoption of implementing measures shall be guided by the following criteria:

(a)   management measures, such as those relating to the application of the common agricultural and common fisheries policies, or to the implementation of programmes with substantial budgetary implications, should be adopted by use of the management procedure;

(b)   measures of general scope designed to apply essential provisions of basic instruments, including measures concerning the protection of the health or safety of humans, animals or plants, should be adopted by use of the regulatory procedure; where a basic instrument stipulates that certain non-essential provisions of the instrument may be adapted or updated by way of implementing procedures, such measures should be adopted by use of the regulatory procedure;

(c)   without prejudice to points (a) and (b), the advisory procedure shall be used in any case in which it is considered to be the most appropriate.

2.   Where a basic instrument, adopted in accordance with the procedure referred to in Article 251 of the Treaty, provides for the adoption of measures of general scope designed to amend non-essential elements of that instrument, *inter alia* by deleting some of those elements or by supplementing the instrument by the addition of new non-essential elements, those measures shall be adopted in accordance with the regulatory procedure with scrutiny.

Article 3 Advisory procedure

1.   The Commission shall be assisted by an advisory committee composed of the representatives of the Member States and chaired by the representative of the Commission.

2.   The representative of the Commission shall submit to the Committee a draft of the measures to be taken. The committee shall deliver its opinion on the draft, within a time-limit which the chairman may lay down according to the urgency of the matter, if necessary by taking a vote.

3.   The opinion shall be recorded in the minutes; in addition, each Member State shall have the right to ask to have its position recorded in the minutes.

4.   The Commission shall take the utmost account of the opinion delivered by the committee. It shall inform the committee of the manner in which the opinion has been taken into account.

Article 4 Management procedure

1.   The Commission shall be assisted by a management committee composed of the representatives of the Member States and chaired by the representative of the Commission.

2. The representative of the Commission shall submit to the committee a draft of the measures to be taken. The committee shall deliver its opinion on the draft within a time-limit which the chairman may lay down according to the urgency of the matter. The opinion shall be delivered by the majority laid down in Article 205(2) and (4) of the Treaty, in the case of decisions which the Council is required to adopt on a proposal from the Commission. The votes of the representatives of the Member States within the committee shall be weighted in the manner set out in that Article. The chairman shall not vote.

3. The Commission shall, without prejudice to Article 8, adopt measures which shall apply immediately. However, if these measures are not in accordance with the opinion of the committee, they shall be communicated by the Commission to the Council forthwith. In that event, the Commission may defer application of the measures which it has decided on for a period to be laid down in each basic instrument but which shall in no case exceed three months from the date of such communication.

4. The Council, acting by qualified majority, may take a different decision within the period provided for by paragraph 3.

Article 5 Regulatory procedure

1. The Commission shall be assisted by a regulatory committee composed of the representatives of the Member States and chaired by the representative of the Commission.

2. The representative of the Commission shall submit to the committee a draft of the measures to be taken. The committee shall deliver its opinion on the draft within a time-limit which the chairman may lay down according to the urgency of the matter. The opinion shall be delivered by the majority laid down in Article 205(2) and (4) of the Treaty in the case of decisions which the Council is required to adopt on a proposal from the Commission. The votes of the representatives of the Member States within the Committee shall be weighted in the manner set out in that Article. The chairman shall not vote.

3. The Commission shall, without prejudice to Article 8, adopt the measures envisaged if they are in accordance with the opinion of the committee.

4. If the measures envisaged are not in accordance with the opinion of the committee, or if no opinion is delivered, the Commission shall, without delay, submit to the Council a proposal relating to the measures to be taken and shall inform the European Parliament.

5. If the European Parliament considers that a proposal submitted by the Commission pursuant to a basic instrument adopted in accordance with the procedure laid down in Article 251 of the Treaty exceeds the implementing powers provided for in that basic instrument, it shall inform the Council of its position.

6. The Council may, where appropriate in view of any such position, act by qualified majority on the proposal, within a period to be laid down in each basic instrument but which shall in no case exceed three months from the date of referral to the Council.

If within that period the Council has indicated by qualified majority that it opposes the proposal, the Commission shall re-examine it. It may submit an amended proposal to the Council, re-submit its proposal or present a legislative proposal on the basis of the Treaty.

If on the expiry of that period the Council has neither adopted the proposed implementing act nor indicated its opposition to the proposal for implementing measures, the proposed implementing act shall be adopted by the Commission.

Article 5a Regulatory procedure with scrutiny

1.   The Commission shall be assisted by a Regulatory Procedure with Scrutiny Committee composed of the representatives of the Member States and chaired by the representative of the Commission.

2.   The representative of the Commission shall submit to the Committee a draft of the measures to be taken. The Committee shall deliver its opinion on the draft within a time-limit which the chairman may lay down according to the urgency of the matter. The opinion shall be delivered by the majority laid down in Article 205(2) and (4) of the Treaty in the case of decisions which the Council is required to adopt on a proposal from the Commission. The votes of the representatives of the Member States within the Committee shall be weighted in the manner set out in that Article. The chairman shall not vote.

3.   If the measures envisaged by the Commission are in accordance with the opinion of the Committee, the following procedure shall apply:
   (a)   the Commission shall without delay submit the draft measures for scrutiny by the European Parliament and the Council;
   (b)   the European Parliament, acting by a majority of its component members, or the Council, acting by a qualified majority, may oppose the adoption of the said draft by the Commission, justifying their opposition by indicating that the draft measures proposed by the Commission exceed the implementing powers provided for in the basic instrument or that the draft is not compatible with the aim or the content of the basic instrument or does not respect the principles of subsidiarity or proportionality;
   (c)   if, within three months from the date of referral to them, the European Parliament or the Council opposes the draft measures, the latter shall not be adopted by the Commission. In that event, the Commission may submit to the Committee an amended draft of the measures or present a legislative proposal on the basis of the Treaty;
   (d)   if, on expiry of that period, neither the European Parliament nor the Council has opposed the draft measures, the latter shall be adopted by the Commission.

4.   If the measures envisaged by the Commission are not in accordance with the opinion of the Committee, or if no opinion is delivered, the following procedure shall apply:
   (a)   the Commission shall without delay submit a proposal relating to the measures to be taken to the Council and shall forward it to the European Parliament at the same time;
   (b)   the Council shall act on the proposal by a qualified majority within two months from the date of referral to it;
   (c)   if, within that period, the Council opposes the proposed measures by a qualified majority, the measures shall not be adopted. In that event, the Commission may submit to the Council an amended proposal or present a legislative proposal on the basis of the Treaty;
   (d)   if the Council envisages adopting the proposed measures, it shall without delay submit them to the European Parliament. If the Council does not act within the two-month period, the Commission shall without delay submit the measures for scrutiny by the European Parliament;
   (e)   the European Parliament, acting by a majority of its component members within four months from the forwarding of the proposal in accordance with point (a), may oppose the adoption of the measures in question, justifying their opposition by indicating that the proposed measures exceed the implementing powers provided for in the basic instrument or are not compatible with the aim or the content of the basic instrument or do not respect the principles of subsidiarity or proportionality;
   (f)   if, within that period, the European Parliament opposes the proposed measures, the latter shall not be adopted. In that event, the Commission may submit to the ommittee an amended draft of the measures or present a legislative proposal on the basis of the Treaty;

(g) if, on expiry of that period, the European Parliament has not opposed the proposed measures, the latter shall be adopted by the Council or by the Commission, as the case may be.

5. By way of derogation from paragraphs 3 and 4, a basic instrument may in duly substantiated exceptional cases provide:
(a) that the time-limits laid down in paragraphs 3(c), 4(b) and 4(e) shall be extended by an additional month, when justified by the complexity of the measures; or
(b) that the time-limits laid down in paragraphs 3(c), 4(b) and 4(e) shall be curtailed where justified on the grounds of efficiency.

6. A basic instrument may provide that if, on imperative grounds of urgency, the time-limits for the regulatory procedure with scrutiny referred to in paragraphs 3, 4 and 5 cannot be complied with, the following procedure shall apply:
(a) if the measures envisaged by the Commission are in accordance with the opinion of the Committee, the Commission shall adopt the measures, which shall immediately be implemented. The Commission shall without delay communicate them to the European Parliament and to the Council;
(b) within a time-limit of one month following that communication, the European Parliament, acting by a majority of its component members, or the Council, acting by a qualified majority, may oppose the measures adopted by the Commission, on the grounds that the measures exceed the implementing powers provided for in the basic instrument or are not compatible with the aim or the content of the basic instrument or do not respect the principles of subsidiarity or proportionality;
(c) in the event of opposition by the European Parliament or the Council, the Commission shall repeal the measures. It may however provisionally maintain the measures in force if warranted on health protection, safety or environmental grounds. In that event, it shall without delay submit to the Committee an amended draft of the measures or a legislative proposal on the basis of the Treaty. The provisional measures shall remain in force until they are replaced by a definitive instrument.

Article 6 Safeguard procedure
The following procedure may be applied where the basic instrument confers on the Commission the power to decide on safeguard measures:
(a) the Commission shall notify the Council and the Member States of any decision regarding safeguard measures. It may be stipulated that before adopting its decision, the Commission shall consult the Member States in accordance with procedures to be determined in each case;

(b) Any Member State may refer the Commission's decision to the Council within a time-limit to be determined within the basic instrument in question;

(c) the Council, acting by a qualified majority, may take a different decision within a time-limit to be determined in the basic instrument in question. Alternatively, it may be stipulated in the basic instrument that the Council, acting by qualified majority, may confirm, amend or revoke the decision adopted by the Commission and that, if the Council has not taken a decision within the abovementioned time-limit, the decision of the Commission is deemed to be revoked.

Article 7
1. Each committee shall adopt its own rules of procedure on the proposal of its chairman, on the basis of standard rules of procedure which shall be published in the *Official Journal of the European Communities*.

Insofar as necessary existing committees shall adapt their rules of procedure to the standard rules of procedure.

2. The principles and conditions on public access to documents applicable to the Commission shall apply to the committees.

3. The European Parliament shall be informed by the Commission of committee proceedings on a regular basis following arrangements which ensure that the transmission system is transparent and that the information forwarded and the various stages of the procedure are identified. To that end, it shall receive agendas for committee meetings, draft measures submitted to the committees for the implementation of instruments adopted by the procedure provided for by Article 251 of the Treaty, and the results of voting and summary records of the meetings and lists of the authorities and organisations to which the persons designated by the Member States to represent them belong. The European Parliament shall also be kept informed whenever the Commission transmits to the Council measures or proposals for measures to be taken.

4. The Commission shall, within six months of the date on which this Decision takes effect, publish in the *Official Journal of the European Communities*, a list of all committees which assist the Commission in the exercise of implementing powers. This list shall specify, in relation to each committee, the basic instrument(s) under which the committee is established. From 2000 onwards, the Commission shall also publish an annual report on the working of committees.

5. The references of all documents sent to the European Parliament pursuant to paragraph 3 shall be made public in a register to be set up by the Commission in 2001.

Article 8
If the European Parliament indicates, in a Resolution setting out the grounds on which it is based, that draft implementing measures, the adoption of which is contemplated and which have been submitted to a committee pursuant to a basic instrument adopted under Article 251 of the Treaty, would exceed the implementing powers provided for in the basic instrument, the Commission shall re-examine the draft measures. Taking the Resolution into account and within the time-limits of the procedure under way, the Commission may submit new draft measures to the committee, continue with the procedure or submit a proposal to the European Parliament and the Council on the basis of the Treaty.

The Commission shall inform the European Parliament and the committee of the action which it intends to take on the Resolution of the European Parliament and of its reasons for doing so.

Article 9
Decision 87/373/EEC shall be repealed.

Article 10
This Decision shall take effect on the day following that of its publication in the *Official Journal of the European Communities*.

DECLARATIONS ON COUNCIL DECISION 1999/468/EC OF 28 JUNE 1999

laying down the procedures for the exercise of implementing powers conferred on the Commission
OJ C 203, 17.7.1999, p. 1

1. COMMISSION STATEMENT (AD ARTICLE 4)

Under the management procedure, the Commission would recall that its constant practice is to try to secure a satisfactory decision which will also muster the widest possible support within the Committee.

The commission will take account of the position of the members of the Committee and act in such a way as to avoid going against any predominant position which might emerge against the appropriateness of an implementing measure.

2. COUNCIL AND COMMISSION STATEMENT

The Commission and the Council agree that provisions relating to committees assisting the Commission in the exercise of implementing powers provided for in application of Decision 87/373/EEC should be adjusted without delay in order to align them with Articles 3, 4, 5 and 6 of Decision 1999/468/EC in accordance with the appropriate legislative procedures.

Such adjustment should be made as follows:

—   current procedure I would be turned into the new advisory procedure;

—   current procedures II(a) and II(b) would be turned into the new management procedure;

—   current procedures III(a) and III(b) would be turned into the new regulatory procedure.

a modification of the type of committee provided for in a basic instrument should be made, on a case by case basis, in the course of normal revision of legislation, guided inter alia by the criteria provided for in Article 2.

Such adjustment or modification should be made in compliance with the obligations incumbent on the Community institutions. It should not have the effect of jeopardising attainment of the objectives of the basic instrument or the effectiveness of Community action.

3. COMMISSION STATEMENT (AD ARTICLE 5)

In the review of proposals for implementing measures concerning particularly sensitive sectors, the Commission, in order to find a balanced solution, will act in such a way as to avoid going against any predominant position which might emerge within the Council against the appropriateness of an implementing measure.

AGREEMENT BETWEEN THE EUROPEAN PARLIAMENT AND THE COMMISSION

of 3 June 2008
on procedures for implementing Council Decision 1999/468/EC laying down the procedures for the exercise of implementing powers conferred on the Commission, as amended by Decision 2006/512/EC
OJ C 143, 10.6.2008, p. 1[1]

INFORMATION TO THE EUROPEAN PARLIAMENT

1.   Pursuant to Article 7(3) of Decision 1999/468/EC [1], the European Parliament is to be informed by the Commission on a regular basis of proceedings of committees [2] in accordance with arrangements which ensure that the transmission system is transparent

---

[1]   EDITOR'S NOTE: As of 1 June 2010 this Agreement has not been amended following the adoption of the Treaty of Lisbon. It may include references to the old version of the Treaty on European Union (TEU) and/or the now replaced Treaty establishing the European Community (TEC). Reference should be made to the Tables of Equivalences accompanying the consolidated Treaties in Part II of this edition for the conversion of old Treaty article numbers to new ones.

and efficient and that the information forwarded and the various stages of the procedure are identified. To that end, it is to receive, at the same time as the members of the committees and on the same terms, the draft agendas for committee meetings, the draft implementing measures submitted to those committees pursuant to basic instruments adopted in accordance with the procedure provided for by Article 251 of the Treaty, the results of voting, summary records of the meetings and lists of the authorities to which the persons designated by the Member States to represent them belong.

REGISTER

2.   The Commission will establish a register containing all documents forwarded to the European Parliament [3]. The European Parliament will have direct access to this register. In accordance with Article 7(5) of Decision 1999/468/EC, references of all documents transmitted to the European Parliament will be made public.

3.   In accordance with the undertakings given by the Commission in its statement on Article 7(3) of Decision 1999/468/EC [4], and once the appropriate technical arrangements have been made, the register provided for in paragraph 2 will enable, in particular:
    — a clear identification of the documents covered by the same procedure and of any changes to the implementing measure at each stage of the procedure,
    — an indication of the stage of the procedure and the timetable,
    — a clear distinction between the draft measures received by the European Parliament at the same time as the committee members in accordance with the right to information and the final draft following the committee's opinion that is forwarded to the European Parliament,
    — a clear identification of any modification in comparison to documents already forwarded to the European Parliament.

4.   When, after a transitional period starting from the entry into force of this Agreement, the European Parliament and the Commission conclude that the system is operational and satisfactory, the transmission of documents to the European Parliament shall be made by electronic notification with a link to the register provided for in paragraph 2. This decision shall be taken through an exchange of letters between the presidents of both institutions. During the transitional period, the documents will be forwarded to the European Parliament as an attachment to an electronic mail.

5.   Furthermore, the Commission agrees to forward to the European Parliament, for information and at the request of the parliamentary committee responsible, specific draft measures implementing basic instruments which, although not adopted in accordance with the procedure provided for by Article 251 of the Treaty, are of particular importance to the European Parliament. These measures shall be entered in the register provided for in paragraph 2 with a notification thereof to the European Parliament.

6.   In addition to the summary records referred to in paragraph 1, the European Parliament may request access to minutes of committee meetings [5]. The Commission will examine each request, on a case by case basis, under the confidentiality rules set out in Annex 1 to the Framework Agreement on relations between the European Parliament and the Commission [6].

CONFIDENTIAL DOCUMENTS

7.   Confidential documents will be processed in accordance with internal administrative procedures drawn up by each institution with a view to providing all the requisite guarantees.

European Parliament resolutions under Article 8 of Decision 1999/468/EC

8. Pursuant to Article 8 of Decision 1999/468/EC, the European Parliament may indicate, in a resolution setting out the grounds on which it is based, that draft measures implementing a basic instrument adopted in accordance with the procedure provided for by Article 251 of the Treaty would exceed the implementing powers provided for in that basic instrument.

9. The European Parliament is to adopt such resolutions in accordance with its Rules of Procedure; it is to have a period of one month in which to do so, beginning on the date of receipt of the final draft of the implementing measures in the language versions submitted to the members of the committee concerned.

10. The European Parliament and the Commission agree that it is appropriate to establish a shorter time limit on a permanent basis for some types of urgent implementing measures on which a decision must be taken within a shorter period of time in the interests of sound management. This applies in particular to some types of measure relating to external action, including humanitarian and emergency aid, to health and safety protection, to transport security and safety and to exemptions from public procurement rules. An agreement between the Member of the Commission and the Chair of the parliamentary committee responsible will lay down the types of measure concerned and the applicable time limits. Such an agreement may be revoked at any time by either side.

11. Without prejudice to the cases referred to in paragraph 10, the time limit will be shorter in urgent cases and in the case of measures relating to day-to-day administrative matters and/or having a limited period of validity. That time limit may be very short in extremely urgent cases, in particular on public health grounds. The Member of the Commission responsible is to set the appropriate time limit and to state the reason for that time limit. The European Parliament may in such cases use a procedure whereby application of Article 8 of Decision 1999/468/EC is delegated to the parliamentary committee responsible, which may send a response to the Commission within the relevant time limit.

12. As soon as the Commission's services foresee that draft measures covered by paragraphs 10 and 11 might have to be submitted to a committee, they will informally warn the secretariat of the parliamentary committee or committees responsible thereof. As soon as initial draft measures have been submitted to the members of the committee, the Commission's services will notify the secretariat of the parliamentary committee or committees of their urgency and of the time limits that will apply once the final draft has been submitted.

13. Following the adoption by the European Parliament of a resolution as referred to in paragraph 8 or a response as referred to in paragraph 11, the Member of the Commission responsible is to inform the European Parliament or, where appropriate, the parliamentary committee responsible of the action the Commission intends to take thereon.

14. Data pursuant to paragraphs 10 to 13 will be entered in the register.

REGULATORY PROCEDURE WITH SCRUTINY

15. Where the regulatory procedure with scrutiny applies, and following the vote in the committee, the Commission will inform the European Parliament of the applicable time limits. Subject to paragraph 16, these time limits will start to run only once the European Parliament has received all language versions.

16. Where shorter time limits apply (Article 5a(5)(b) of Decision 1999/468/EC) and in cases of urgency (Article 5a(6) of Decision 1999/468/EC), the time limits shall start to run from

the date of receipt by the European Parliament of the final draft implementing measures in the language versions submitted to the members of the committee, unless the Chair of the parliamentary committee objects. In any event, the Commission will endeavour to forward all language versions to the European Parliament as soon as possible. As soon as the Commission's services foresee that draft measures covered by Article 5a(5)(b) or (6) might have to be submitted to a committee, they will informally warn the secretariat of the parliamentary committee or committees responsible thereof.

FINANCIAL SERVICES

17. In accordance with its statement on Article 7(3) of Decision 1999/468/EC, in respect of financial services the Commission undertakes to:

— ensure that the Commission official chairing a committee meeting informs the European Parliament, at its request, after each meeting, of any discussions concerning draft implementing measures that have been submitted to that committee,
— give an oral or written reply to any questions regarding discussions concerning draft implementing measures submitted to a committee.

Finally, the Commission will ensure that the undertakings made at Parliament's plenary sitting of 5 February 2002 [7] and restated at its plenary sitting of 31 March 2004 [8] and those referred to in points 1 to 7 of the letter of 2 October 2001 [9] from Commissioner Bolkestein to the Chair of the European Parliament's Committee on Economic and Monetary Affairs are honoured in respect of the entire financial services sector (including securities, banks, insurance, pensions and accounting).[10]

CALENDAR OF PARLIAMENTARY WORK

18. Except where shorter time limits apply or in cases of urgency, the Commission will take into account, when transmitting draft implementing measures under this Agreement, the European Parliament's periods of recess (winter, summer and European elections) in order to ensure that Parliament is able to exercise its prerogatives within the time limits laid down in Decision 1999/468/EC and this Agreement.[11]

(Remaining provisions and signatories omitted)

[1]   OJ 1999, L184/23. Decision as amended by Decision 2006/512/EC (OJ 2006, L 200/11).

[2]   Throughout this Agreement, the word "committee" shall be taken to refer to committees established in accordance with Decision 1999/468/EC, except where it is specified that another committee is referred to.

[3]   The target date for the establishment of the register is 31 March 2008.

[4]   OJ 2006, C171/21.

[5]   See the judgment of the Court of First Instance of the European Communities of 19 July 1999 in Case T-188/97, Rothmans v Commission [1999] ECR II-2463.

[6]   OJ 2006, C117E/123 (footnote corrected by OJ 2006, C 154/24).

[7]   OJ 2002, C284E/19.

[8]   OJ 2004, C103E/446 and Verbatim Report of Proceedings (CRE) for Parliament's plenary sitting of 31 March 2004, under "Vote".

[9]   OJ 2002, C284E/83.

[10] OJ 2000, L256/19.

[11] OJ 1996, C102/1.

INTERINSTITUTIONAL AGREEMENT OF 16 DECEMBER 2003

on better law-making

OJ C 321, 31.12.2003, p. 1[1]

. . . .

THE EUROPEAN PARLIAMENT, THE COUNCIL OF THE EUROPEAN UNION AND THE COMMISSION OF THE EUROPEAN COMMUNITIES,

Having regard to the Treaty establishing the European Community and, in particular, to Article 5 thereof and the Protocol on the application of the principles of subsidiarity and proportionality annexed thereto,

Having regard to the Treaty on European Union,

Drawing attention to Declaration No 18 on the estimated costs under Commission proposals and to Declaration No 19 on the implementation of Community law, both of which are annexed to the Maastricht Final Act,

Drawing attention to the Interinstitutional Agreements of 25 October 1993 on the procedures for implementing the principle of subsidiarity(1), of 20 December 1994 on accelerated working method for the official codification of legislative texts(2), of 22 December 1998 on common guidelines for the quality of drafting of Community legislation(3), and of 28 November 2001 on a more structured use of the recasting technique for legal acts(4),

Noting the Presidency Conclusions of the meetings of the European Council held on 21 and 22 June 2002 in Seville and on 20 and 21 March 2003 in Brussels,

Emphasising that this Agreement is concluded without prejudice to the outcome of the Intergovernmental Conference which will be held following the Convention on the Future of Europe,

HAVE AGREED AS FOLLOWS:

COMMON COMMITMENTS AND OBJECTIVES

1. The European Parliament, the Council of the European Union and the Commission of the European Communities hereby agree to improve the quality of law-making by means of a series of initiatives and procedures set out in this interinstitutional agreement.

2. In exercising the powers and in compliance with the procedures laid down in the Treaty, and recalling the importance which they attach to the Community method, the three Institutions agree to observe general principles such as democratic legitimacy, subsidiarity and proportionality, and legal certainty. They further agree to promote simplicity, clarity and consistency in the drafting of laws and the utmost transparency of the legislative process.

    They call on the Member States to ensure a proper and prompt transposition of Community law into national law within the prescribed time limits, pursuant to the Presidency Conclusions of the European Council at its Stockholm, Barcelona and Seville meetings.

. . . .

[1]   EDITOR'S NOTE: As of 1 June 2010 this Agreement has not been amended following the adoption of the Treaty of Lisbon. It may include references to the old version of the Treaty on European Union (TEU) and/or the now replaced Treaty establishing the European Community (TEC). Reference should be made to the Tables of Equivalences accompanying the consolidated Treaties in Part II of this edition for the conversion of old Treaty article numbers to new ones.

BETTER COORDINATION OF THE LEGISLATIVE PROCESS

3.   The three Institutions agree to ensure that general coordination of their legislative activity is improved, thereby providing an essential foundation for better law-making within the European Union.

4.   The three Institutions agree to improve the coordination of their preparatory and legislative work in the context of the codecision procedure and to publicise it in appropriate fashion.

The Council will inform the European Parliament in good time of the draft multiannual strategic programme which it recommends for adoption by the European Council. The three Institutions will forward to each other their respective annual legislative timetables with a view to reaching agreement on joint annual programming.

In particular, the European Parliament and the Council will seek to establish, for each legislative proposal, an indicative timetable for the various stages leading to the final adoption of that proposal.

Wherever multiannual programming has an interinstitutional impact, the three Institutions will initiate cooperation through the appropriate channels.

As far as possible, the Commission's annual law-making and work programme will include indications as to the choice of legislative instrument and the legal basis envisaged for each measure to be put forward.

5.   The three Institutions will, in the interests of efficiency, ensure as far as possible a better synchronisation of the treatment of common dossiers by the preparatory bodies(5) of each branch of the legislative authority(6).

6.   The three Institutions will keep each other permanently informed about their work throughout the legislative process. This information will be based on appropriate procedures, including dialogue between the European Parliament, in committee and plenary, and the Council Presidency and the Commission.

7.   The Commission will submit an annual progress report on its legislative proposals.

8.   The Commission will ensure that, as a general rule, Commissioners are present for discussions at European Parliament committee meetings and plenary sittings on draft legislation for which they are responsible.

The Council will continue the practice of maintaining intensive contact with the European Parliament by means of regular participation in plenary debates, as far as possible by the Ministers concerned. The Council will also endeavour to participate regularly in the work of the parliamentary committees and in other meetings, preferably at ministerial level or at some other appropriate level.

9.   The Commission will take account of requests made by the European Parliament or the Council, on the basis respectively of Article 192 or Article 208 of the EC Treaty, for the submission of legislative proposals. It will reply rapidly and appropriately to the parliamentary committees concerned and to the Council's preparatory bodies.

GREATER TRANSPARENCY AND ACCESSIBILITY

10.   The three Institutions confirm the importance which they attach to greater transparency and to the increased provision of information to the public at every stage of their legislative work, whilst taking into account their respective rules of procedure. They will ensure in

particular that public debates at political level are broadcast as widely as possible through the systematic use of new communication technologies such as, inter alia, satellite broadcasting and Internet video-streaming. They will also ensure that the public has greater access to EUR-Lex.

11. The three Institutions will hold a joint press conference to announce the successful outcome of the legislative process in the codecision procedure, once they have reached agreement, whether after first reading, second reading or conciliation.

CHOICE OF LEGISLATIVE INSTRUMENT AND LEGAL BASIS

12. The Commission will explain and justify to the European Parliament and to the Council its choice of legislative instrument, where possible as part of its annual work programme or of the normal dialogue procedures and, at all events, in the explanatory memoranda attached to its initiatives. It will consider any request in this connection from the legislative authority, and it will take account of the results of any consultations which it has undertaken before tabling its proposals.

It will ensure that the action it proposes is as simple as is compatible with the proper attainment of the objective of the measure and the need for effective implementation.

13. The three Institutions recall the definition of the term "directive" (Article 249 of the EC Treaty) and the relevant provisions of the Protocol on the application of the principles of subsidiarity and proportionality. In its proposals for directives, the Commission will ensure that a proper balance is struck between general principles and detailed provisions, in a manner that avoids excessive use of Community implementing measures.

14. The Commission will provide a clear and comprehensive justification for the legal basis used for each proposal. In the event of a change being made to the legal basis after any Commission proposal has been presented, the European Parliament will be duly re-consulted by the Institution concerned, in full compliance with the case-law of the Court of Justice of the European Communities.

15. In the explanatory memoranda to its proposals, the Commission will, in every instance, set out the legal arrangements which currently exist at Community level in the area affected by the proposal. The Commission will also explain in its explanatory memoranda how the measures proposed are justified in the light of the principles of subsidiarity and proportionality. The Commission will also give an account of the scope and the results of the prior consultation and the impact analyses that it has undertaken.

USE OF ALTERNATIVE METHODS OF REGULATION

16. The three Institutions recall the Community's obligation to legislate only where it is necessary, in accordance with the Protocol on the application of the principles of subsidiarity and proportionality. They recognise the need to use, in suitable cases or where the Treaty does not specifically require the use of a legal instrument, alternative regulation mechanisms.

17. The Commission will ensure that any use of co-regulation or self-regulation is always consistent with Community law and that it meets the criteria of transparency (in particular the publicising of agreements) and representativeness of the parties involved. It must also represent added value for the general interest. These mechanisms will not be applicable where fundamental rights or important political options are at stake or in situations where the rules must be applied in a uniform fashion in all Member States. They must ensure swift and flexible regulation which does not affect the principles of competition or the unity of the internal market.

CO-REGULATION

18. Co-regulation means the mechanism whereby a Community legislative act entrusts the attainment of the objectives defined by the legislative authority to parties which are recognised in the field (such as economic operators, the social partners, non-governmental organisations, or associations).

   This mechanism may be used on the basis of criteria defined in the legislative act so as to enable the legislation to be adapted to the problems and sectors concerned, to reduce the legislative burden by concentrating on essential aspects and to draw on the experience of the parties concerned.

19. The legislative act must abide by the principle of proportionality defined in the EC Treaty. Agreements between social partners must comply with the provisions laid down in Articles 138 and 139 of the EC Treaty. In the explanatory memoranda to its proposals, the Commission will explain to the competent legislative authority its reasons for proposing the use of this mechanism.

20. In the context defined by the basic legislative act, the parties affected by that act may conclude voluntary agreements for the purpose of determining practical arrangements.

   The draft agreements will be forwarded by the Commission to the legislative authority. In accordance with its responsibilities, the Commission will verify whether or not those draft agreements comply with Community law (and, in particular, with the basic legislative act).

   At the request of inter alia the European Parliament or of the Council, on a case-by-case basis and depending on the subject, the basic legislative act may include a provision for a two-month period of grace following notification of a draft agreement to the European Parliament and the Council. During that period, each Institution may either suggest amendments, if it is considered that the draft agreement does not meet the objectives laid down by the legislative authority, or object to the entry into force of that agreement and, possibly, ask the Commission to submit a proposal for a legislative act.

21. A legislative act which serves as the basis for a co-regulation mechanism will indicate the possible extent of co-regulation in the area concerned. The competent legislative authority will define in the act the relevant measures to be taken in order to follow up its application, in the event of non-compliance by one or more parties or if the agreement fails. These measures may provide, for example, for the regular supply of information by the Commission to the legislative authority on follow-up to application or for a revision clause under which the Commission will report at the end of a specific period and, where necessary, propose an amendment to the legislative act or any other appropriate legislative measure.

SELF-REGULATION

22. Self-regulation is defined as the possibility for economic operators, the social partners, non-governmental organisations or associations to adopt amongst themselves and for themselves common guidelines at European level (particularly codes of practice or sectoral agreements).

   As a general rule, this type of voluntary initiative does not imply that the Institutions have adopted any particular stance, in particular where such initiatives are undertaken in areas which are not covered by the Treaties or in which the Union has not hitherto legislated. As one of its responsibilities, the Commission will scrutinise self-regulation practices in order to verify that they comply with the provisions of the EC Treaty.

23. The Commission will notify the European Parliament and the Council of the self-regulation practices which it regards, on the one hand, as contributing to the attainment of the EC Treaty objectives and as being compatible with its provisions and, on the other, as being satisfactory in terms of the representativeness of the parties concerned, sectoral and geographical cover and the added value of the commitments given. It will, nonetheless, consider the possibility of putting forward a proposal for a legislative act, in particular at the request of the competent legislative authority or in the event of a failure to observe the above practices.

IMPLEMENTING MEASURES (COMMITTEE PROCEDURE)

24. The three Institutions emphasise the important role played by implementing measures in legislation. They note the outcome of the Convention on the Future of Europe relating to the establishment of rules governing the exercise by the Commission of the implementing powers conferred on it.

The European Parliament and the Council emphasise that, in accordance with their respective powers, they have begun consideration of the proposal which the Commission adopted on 11 December 2002 with a view to amending Council Decision 1999/468/EC(7).

IMPROVING THE QUALITY OF LEGISLATION

25. The three Institutions, exercising their respective powers, will ensure that legislation is of good quality, namely that it is clear, simple and effective. The Institutions consider that improvement of the pre-legislative consultation process and more frequent use of impact assessments (both ex ante and ex post) will help towards this objective. They are committed to the full application of the Interinstitutional Agreement of 22 December 1998 on common guidelines for the quality of drafting of Community legislation.

(a) Pre-legislative consultation
26. During the period preceding the submission of legislative proposals, the Commission will, having informed the European Parliament and the Council, conduct the widest possible consultations, the results of which will be made public. In certain cases, where the Commission deems it appropriate, the Commission may submit a pre-legislative consultation document on which the European Parliament and the Council may choose to deliver an opinion.

(b) Impact analyses
27. Pursuant to the Protocol on the application of the principles of subsidiarity and proportionality, the Commission will take due account in its legislative proposals of their financial or administrative implications, for the Union and the Member States in particular. Furthermore, each of the three Institutions will take into account the objective of ensuring that application in the Member States is appropriate and effective.

28. The three Institutions agree on the positive contribution of impact assessments in improving the quality of Community legislation, with particular regard to the scope and substance thereof.

29. The Commission will continue to implement the integrated advance impact-assessment process for major items of draft legislation, combining in one single evaluation the impact assessments relating inter alia to social, economic and environmental aspects. The results of the assessments will be made fully and freely available to the European Parliament, the Council and the general public. In the explanatory memorandum to its proposals, the

Commission will indicate the manner in which the impact assessments have influenced them.

30.   Where the codecision procedure applies, the European Parliament and Council may, on the basis of jointly defined criteria and procedures, have impact assessments carried out prior to the adoption of any substantive amendment, either at first reading or at the conciliation stage. As soon as possible after this Agreement is adopted, the three Institutions will carry out an assessment of their respective experiences and will consider the possibility of establishing a common methodology.

(c) Consistency of texts

31.   The European Parliament and the Council will make all appropriate arrangements for improving the scrutiny carried out by their respective departments of the wording of texts adopted under the codecision procedure, with a view to avoiding any inaccuracies or inconsistencies. To this end, the Institutions may agree on a short period of grace in order to allow such legal verification to be performed before the act is finally adopted.

BETTER TRANSPOSITION AND APPLICATION

32.   The three Institutions emphasise the need for Member States to comply with Article 10 of the EC Treaty, they call upon the Member States to ensure that Community law is properly and promptly transposed into national law within the prescribed deadlines; and they deem such transposition to be essential to the consistent and effective application of that legislation by the courts, the administrations, members of the public and economic and social operators.

33.   The three Institutions will ensure that all directives include a binding time limit for the transposition of their provisions into national law. They will insert into directives a time limit for transposition that is as short as possible and that generally does not exceed two years. The three Institutions hope that the Member States will make a renewed effort as regards the transposition of directives within the time limits which they specify. In this connection, the European Parliament and the Council note that the Commission is proposing to step up cooperation with the Member States.

The three Institutions point out that, under the EC Treaty, the Commission has the power to initiate an infringement procedure in instances where a Member State fails to transpose legislation within the stipulated time limit; and the European Parliament and Council note the commitments given by the Commission on this subject(8).

34.   The Commission will draw up annual reports on the transposition of directives in the various Member States, with tables showing transposition rates. Those reports will be communicated to the European Parliament and to the Council, and will be made public.

The Council will encourage the Member States to draw up, for themselves and in the interests of the Community, their own tables which will, as far as possible, illustrate the correlation between the directives and the transposition measures and to make them public. It calls on those Member States which have not yet done so to appoint a transposition coordinator as soon as possible.

SIMPLIFYING AND REDUCING THE VOLUME OF LEGISLATION

35. In order to make Community law easier to read and to apply, the three Institutions agree, firstly, to update and condense existing legislation and, secondly, significantly to simplify it. They will take the Commission's multiannual programme as a basis for this task.

Legislation will be updated and condensed inter alia through the repeal of acts which are no longer applied and through the codification or recasting of other acts.

The purpose of legislative simplification is to improve and adapt legislation by amending or replacing acts and provisions which are too unwieldy and too complex to be applied. Such simplification will be carried out through the recasting of existing acts or by means of new legislative proposals, whilst maintaining the substance of Community policies. In this connection, the Commission will select the areas of current law which are suitable for simplification, on the basis of criteria laid down once the legislative authority has been consulted.

36. Within six months of the date upon which this Agreement comes into force, the European Parliament and the Council, whose task it would be as legislative authority to adopt at the final stage the proposals for simplified acts, need to modify their working methods by introducing, for example, ad hoc structures with the specific task of simplifying legislation.

IMPLEMENTATION AND MONITORING OF THE AGREEMENT

37. The implementation of this Agreement will be monitored by the High-Level Technical Group for Interinstitutional Cooperation.

38. The three Institutions will take the necessary steps to ensure that their staff have the means and resources required for the proper implementation of the provisions of this Agreement.

(Signatories omitted)

(1) OJ 1993, C329/135.

(2) OJ 1996, C102/2.

(3) OJ 1999, C73/1.

(4) OJ 2002, C77/1.

(5) Committee at the European Parliament; the working party and Permanent Representatives' Committee at the Council.

(6) For the purposes of this Agreement, "legislative authority" means only the European Parliament and the Council.

(7) OJ 1999, L184/23.

(8) Commission communication of 12 December 2002 on better monitoring of the application of Community law, COM(2002) 725 final, p. 20 and 21.

D) Access to Documents

Regulation (EC) No 1049/2001 of the European Parliament and of the Council of 30 May 2001

regarding public access to European Parliament, Council and Commission documents
OJ L 145, 31.5.2001, p. 43[1]

(footnotes omitted)

THE EUROPEAN PARLIAMENT AND THE COUNCIL OF THE EUROPEAN UNION,

Having regard to the Treaty establishing the European Community, and in particular Article 255(2) thereof,

Having regard to the proposal from the Commission,

Acting in accordance with the procedure referred to in Article 251 of the Treaty,

Whereas:

(1)   The second subparagraph of Article 1 of the Treaty on European Union enshrines the concept of openness, stating that the Treaty marks a new stage in the process of creating an ever closer union among the peoples of Europe, in which decisions are taken as openly as possible and as closely as possible to the citizen.

(2)   Openness enables citizens to participate more closely in the decision-making process and guarantees that the administration enjoys greater legitimacy and is more effective and more accountable to the citizen in a democratic system. Openness contributes to strengthening the principles of democracy and respect for fundamental rights as laid down in Article 6 of the EU Treaty and in the Charter of Fundamental Rights of the European Union.

(3)   The conclusions of the European Council meetings held at Birmingham, Edinburgh and Copenhagen stressed the need to introduce greater transparency into the work of the Union institutions. This Regulation consolidates the initiatives that the institutions have already taken with a view to improving the transparency of the decision-making process.

(4)   The purpose of this Regulation is to give the fullest possible effect to the right of public access to documents and to lay down the general principles and limits on such access in accordance with Article 255(2) of the EC Treaty.

(5)   Since the question of access to documents is not covered by provisions of the Treaty establishing the European Coal and Steel Community and the Treaty establishing the European Atomic Energy Community, the European Parliament, the Council and the Commission should, in accordance with Declaration No 41 attached to the Final Act of the Treaty of Amsterdam, draw guidance from this Regulation as regards documents concerning the activities covered by those two Treaties.

[1]   EDITOR'S NOTE: As of 1 June 2010 this Regulation has not been amended following the adoption of the Treaty of Lisbon. It may include references to the old version of the Treaty on European Union (TEU) and/or the now replaced Treaty establishing the European Community (TEC). Reference should be made to the Tables of Equivalences accompanying the consolidated Treaties in Part II of this edition for the conversion of old Treaty article numbers to new ones.

(6)   Wider access should be granted to documents in cases where the institutions are acting in their legislative capacity, including under delegated powers, while at the same time preserving the effectiveness of the institutions' decision-making process. Such documents should be made directly accessible to the greatest possible extent.

(7)   In accordance with Articles 28(1) and 41(1) of the EU Treaty, the right of access also applies to documents relating to the common foreign and security policy and to police and judicial cooperation in criminal matters. Each institution should respect its security rules.

(8)   In order to ensure the full application of this Regulation to all activities of the Union, all agencies established by the institutions should apply the principles laid down in this Regulation.

(9)   On account of their highly sensitive content, certain documents should be given special treatment. Arrangements for informing the European Parliament of the content of such documents should be made through interinstitutional agreement.

(10)   In order to bring about greater openness in the work of the institutions, access to documents should be granted by the European Parliament, the Council and the Commission not only to documents drawn up by the institutions, but also to documents received by them. In this context, it is recalled that Declaration No 35 attached to the Final Act of the Treaty of Amsterdam provides that a Member State may request the Commission or the Council not to communicate to third parties a document originating from that State without its prior agreement.

(11)   In principle, all documents of the institutions should be accessible to the public. However, certain public and private interests should be protected by way of exceptions. The institutions should be entitled to protect their internal consultations and deliberations where necessary to safeguard their ability to carry out their tasks. In assessing the exceptions, the institutions should take account of the principles in Community legislation concerning the protection of personal data, in all areas of Union activities.

(12)   All rules concerning access to documents of the institutions should be in conformity with this Regulation.

(13)   In order to ensure that the right of access is fully respected, a two-stage administrative procedure should apply, with the additional possibility of court proceedings or complaints to the Ombudsman.

(14)   Each institution should take the measures necessary to inform the public of the new provisions in force and to train its staff to assist citizens exercising their rights under this Regulation. In order to make it easier for citizens to exercise their rights, each institution should provide access to a register of documents.

(15)   Even though it is neither the object nor the effect of this Regulation to amend national legislation on access to documents, it is nevertheless clear that, by virtue of the principle of loyal cooperation which governs relations between the institutions and the Member States, Member States should take care not to hamper the proper application of this Regulation and should respect the security rules of the institutions.

(16)   This Regulation is without prejudice to existing rights of access to documents for Member States, judicial authorities or investigative bodies.

(17)   In accordance with Article 255(3) of the EC Treaty, each institution lays down specific provisions regarding access to its documents in its rules of procedure. Council Decision 93/731/EC of 20 December 1993 on public access to Council documents, Commission Decision 94/90/ECSC, EC, Euratom of 8 February 1994 on public access to Commission

documents, European Parliament Decision 97/632/EC, ECSC, Euratom of 10 July 1997 on public access to European Parliament documents, and the rules on confidentiality of Schengen documents should therefore, if necessary, be modified or be repealed,

HAVE ADOPTED THIS REGULATION:

Article 1 Purpose
The purpose of this Regulation is:
(a)   to define the principles, conditions and limits on grounds of public or private interest governing the right of access to European Parliament, Council and Commission (hereinafter referred to as "the institutions") documents provided for in Article 255 of the EC Treaty in such a way as to ensure the widest possible access to documents,

(b)   to establish rules ensuring the easiest possible exercise of this right, and

(c)   to promote good administrative practice on access to documents.

Article 2 Beneficiaries and scope
1.   Any citizen of the Union, and any natural or legal person residing or having its registered office in a Member State, has a right of access to documents of the institutions, subject to the principles, conditions and limits defined in this Regulation.

2.   The institutions may, subject to the same principles, conditions and limits, grant access to documents to any natural or legal person not residing or not having its registered office in a Member State.

3.   This Regulation shall apply to all documents held by an institution, that is to say, documents drawn up or received by it and in its possession, in all areas of activity of the European Union.

4.   Without prejudice to Articles 4 and 9, documents shall be made accessible to the public either following a written application or directly in electronic form or through a register. In particular, documents drawn up or received in the course of a legislative procedure shall be made directly accessible in accordance with Article 12.

5.   Sensitive documents as defined in Article 9(1) shall be subject to special treatment in accordance with that Article.

6.   This Regulation shall be without prejudice to rights of public access to documents held by the institutions which might follow from instruments of international law or acts of the institutions implementing them.

Article 3 Definitions
For the purpose of this Regulation:
(a)   "document" shall mean any content whatever its medium (written on paper or stored in electronic form or as a sound, visual or audiovisual recording) concerning a matter relating to the policies, activities and decisions falling within the institution's sphere of responsibility;

(b)   "third party" shall mean any natural or legal person, or any entity outside the institution concerned, including the Member States, other Community or non-Community institutions and bodies and third countries.

Article 4 Exceptions
1.   The institutions shall refuse access to a document where disclosure would undermine the protection of:

   (a) the public interest as regards:
- public security,
- defence and military matters,
- international relations,
- the financial, monetary or economic policy of the Community or a Member State;

   (b) privacy and the integrity of the individual, in particular in accordance with Community legislation regarding the protection of personal data.

2.   The institutions shall refuse access to a document where disclosure would undermine the protection of:
- commercial interests of a natural or legal person, including intellectual property,
- court proceedings and legal advice,
- the purpose of inspections, investigations and audits,

unless there is an overriding public interest in disclosure.

3.   Access to a document, drawn up by an institution for internal use or received by an institution, which relates to a matter where the decision has not been taken by the institution, shall be refused if disclosure of the document would seriously undermine the institution's decision-making process, unless there is an overriding public interest in disclosure.

Access to a document containing opinions for internal use as part of deliberations and preliminary consultations within the institution concerned shall be refused even after the decision has been taken if disclosure of the document would seriously undermine the institution's decision-making process, unless there is an overriding public interest in disclosure.

4.   As regards third-party documents, the institution shall consult the third party with a view to assessing whether an exception in paragraph 1 or 2 is applicable, unless it is clear that the document shall or shall not be disclosed.

5.   A Member State may request the institution not to disclose a document originating from that Member State without its prior agreement.

6.   If only parts of the requested document are covered by any of the exceptions, the remaining parts of the document shall be released.

7.   The exceptions as laid down in paragraphs 1 to 3 shall only apply for the period during which protection is justified on the basis of the content of the document. The exceptions may apply for a maximum period of 30 years. In the case of documents covered by the exceptions relating to privacy or commercial interests and in the case of sensitive documents, the exceptions may, if necessary, continue to apply after this period.

Article 5 Documents in the Member States

Where a Member State receives a request for a document in its possession, originating from an institution, unless it is clear that the document shall or shall not be disclosed, the Member State shall consult with the institution concerned in order to take a decision that does not jeopardise the attainment of the objectives of this Regulation.

The Member State may instead refer the request to the institution.

Article 6 Applications

1.   Applications for access to a document shall be made in any written form, including electronic form, in one of the languages referred to in Article 314 of the EC Treaty and in a sufficiently precise manner to enable the institution to identify the document. The applicant is not obliged to state reasons for the application.

2.   If an application is not sufficiently precise, the institution shall ask the applicant to clarify the application and shall assist the applicant in doing so, for example, by providing information on the use of the public registers of documents.

3.   In the event of an application relating to a very long document or to a very large number of documents, the institution concerned may confer with the applicant informally, with a view to finding a fair solution.

4.   The institutions shall provide information and assistance to citizens on how and where applications for access to documents can be made.

Article 7 Processing of initial applications

1.   An application for access to a document shall be handled promptly. An acknowledgement of receipt shall be sent to the applicant. Within 15 working days from registration of the application, the institution shall either grant access to the document requested and provide access in accordance with Article 10 within that period or, in a written reply, state the reasons for the total or partial refusal and inform the applicant of his or her right to make a confirmatory application in accordance with paragraph 2 of this Article.

2.   In the event of a total or partial refusal, the applicant may, within 15 working days of receiving the institution's reply, make a confirmatory application asking the institution to reconsider its position.

3.   In exceptional cases, for example in the event of an application relating to a very long document or to a very large number of documents, the time-limit provided for in paragraph 1 may be extended by 15 working days, provided that the applicant is notified in advance and that detailed reasons are given.

4.   Failure by the institution to reply within the prescribed time-limit shall entitle the applicant to make a confirmatory application.

Article 8 Processing of confirmatory applications

1.   A confirmatory application shall be handled promptly. Within 15 working days from registration of such an application, the institution shall either grant access to the document requested and provide access in accordance with Article 10 within that period or, in a written reply, state the reasons for the total or partial refusal. In the event of a total or partial refusal, the institution shall inform the applicant of the remedies open to him or her, namely instituting court proceedings against the institution and/or making a complaint to the Ombudsman, under the conditions laid down in Articles 230 and 195 of the EC Treaty, respectively.

2.   In exceptional cases, for example in the event of an application relating to a very long document or to a very large number of documents, the time limit provided for in paragraph 1 may be extended by 15 working days, provided that the applicant is notified in advance and that detailed reasons are given.

3.   Failure by the institution to reply within the prescribed time limit shall be considered as a negative reply and entitle the applicant to institute court proceedings against the institution and/or make a complaint to the Ombudsman, under the relevant provisions of the EC Treaty.

Article 9 Treatment of sensitive documents

1.   Sensitive documents are documents originating from the institutions or the agencies established by them, from Member States, third countries or International Organisations, classified as "TRÈS SECRET/TOP SECRET", "SECRET" or "CONFIDENTIEL" in accordance with the rules of the institution concerned, which protect essential interests of

the European Union or of one or more of its Member States in the areas covered by Article 4(1)(a), notably public security, defence and military matters.

2.   Applications for access to sensitive documents under the procedures laid down in Articles 7 and 8 shall be handled only by those persons who have a right to acquaint themselves with those documents. These persons shall also, without prejudice to Article 11(2), assess which references to sensitive documents could be made in the public register.

3.   Sensitive documents shall be recorded in the register or released only with the consent of the originator.

4.   An institution which decides to refuse access to a sensitive document shall give the reasons for its decision in a manner which does not harm the interests protected in Article 4.

5.   Member States shall take appropriate measures to ensure that when handling applications for sensitive documents the principles in this Article and Article 4 are respected.

6.   The rules of the institutions concerning sensitive documents shall be made public.

7.   The Commission and the Council shall inform the European Parliament regarding sensitive documents in accordance with arrangements agreed between the institutions.

Article 10 Access following an application
1.   The applicant shall have access to documents either by consulting them on the spot or by receiving a copy, including, where available, an electronic copy, according to the applicant's preference. The cost of producing and sending copies may be charged to the applicant. This charge shall not exceed the real cost of producing and sending the copies. Consultation on the spot, copies of less than 20 A4 pages and direct access in electronic form or through the register shall be free of charge.

2.   If a document has already been released by the institution concerned and is easily accessible to the applicant, the institution may fulfil its obligation of granting access to documents by informing the applicant how to obtain the requested document.

3.   Documents shall be supplied in an existing version and format (including electronically or in an alternative format such as Braille, large print or tape) with full regard to the applicant's preference.

Article 11 Registers
1.   To make citizens' rights under this Regulation effective, each institution shall provide public access to a register of documents. Access to the register should be provided in electronic form. References to documents shall be recorded in the register without delay.

2.   For each document the register shall contain a reference number (including, where applicable, the interinstitutional reference), the subject matter and/or a short description of the content of the document and the date on which it was received or drawn up and recorded in the register. References shall be made in a manner which does not undermine protection of the interests in Article 4.

3.   The institutions shall immediately take the measures necessary to establish a register which shall be operational by 3 June 2002.

Article 12 Direct access in electronic form or through a register
1.   The institutions shall as far as possible make documents directly accessible to the public in electronic form or through a register in accordance with the rules of the institution concerned.

2.   In particular, legislative documents, that is to say, documents drawn up or received in the course of procedures for the adoption of acts which are legally binding in or for the Member States, should, subject to Articles 4 and 9, be made directly accessible.

3.   Where possible, other documents, notably documents relating to the development of policy or strategy, should be made directly accessible.

4.   Where direct access is not given through the register, the register shall as far as possible indicate where the document is located.

Article 13 Publication in the *Official Journal*

1.   In addition to the acts referred to in Article 254(1) and (2) of the EC Treaty and the first paragraph of Article 163 of the Euratom Treaty, the following documents shall, subject to Articles 4 and 9 of this Regulation, be published in the *Official Journal*:
    (a) Commission proposals;
    (b) common positions adopted by the Council in accordance with the procedures referred to in Articles 251 and 252 of the EC Treaty and the reasons underlying those common positions, as well as the European Parliament's positions in these procedures;
    (c) framework decisions and decisions referred to in Article 34(2) of the EU Treaty;
    (d) conventions established by the Council in accordance with Article 34(2) of the EU Treaty;
    (e) conventions signed between Member States on the basis of Article 293 of the EC Treaty;
    (f) international agreements concluded by the Community or in accordance with Article 24 of the EU Treaty.

2.   As far as possible, the following documents shall be published in the *Official Journal*:
    (a) initiatives presented to the Council by a Member State pursuant to Article 67(1) of the EC Treaty or pursuant to Article 34(2) of the EU Treaty;
    (b) common positions referred to in Article 34(2) of the EU Treaty;
    (c) directives other than those referred to in Article 254(1) and (2) of the EC Treaty, decisions other than those referred to in Article 254(1) of the EC Treaty, recommendations and opinions.

3.   Each institution may in its rules of procedure establish which further documents shall be published in the *Official Journal*.

Article 14 Information

1.   Each institution shall take the requisite measures to inform the public of the rights they enjoy under this Regulation.

2.   The Member States shall cooperate with the institutions in providing information to the citizens.

Article 15 Administrative practice in the institutions

1.   The institutions shall develop good administrative practices in order to facilitate the exercise of the right of access guaranteed by this Regulation.

2.   The institutions shall establish an interinstitutional committee to examine best practice, address possible conflicts and discuss future developments on public access to documents.

Article 16 Reproduction of documents

This Regulation shall be without prejudice to any existing rules on copyright which may limit a third party's right to reproduce or exploit released documents.

Article 17 Reports

1.   Each institution shall publish annually a report for the preceding year including the number of cases in which the institution refused to grant access to documents, the reasons for such refusals and the number of sensitive documents not recorded in the register.

2.   At the latest by 31 January 2004, the Commission shall publish a report on the implementation of the principles of this Regulation and shall make recommendations, including, if appropriate, proposals for the revision of this Regulation and an action programme of measures to be taken by the institutions.

Article 18 Application measures

1.   Each institution shall adapt its rules of procedure to the provisions of this Regulation. The adaptations shall take effect from 3 December 2001.

2.   Within six months of the entry into force of this Regulation, the Commission shall examine the conformity of Council Regulation (EEC, Euratom) No 354/83 of 1 February 1983 concerning the opening to the public of the historical archives of the European Economic Community and the European Atomic Energy Community with this Regulation in order to ensure the preservation and archiving of documents to the fullest extent possible.

3.   Within six months of the entry into force of this Regulation, the Commission shall examine the conformity of the existing rules on access to documents with this Regulation.

Article 19 Entry into force

This Regulation shall enter into force on the third day following that of its publication in the *Official Journal* of the European Communities.

It shall be applicable from 3 December 2001.

This Regulation shall be binding in its entirety and directly applicable in all Member States.

(Date of signing and signatories omitted)

INTERINSTITUTIONAL AGREEMENT OF 20 NOVEMBER 2002

between the European Parliament and the Council concerning access by the European Parliament to sensitive information of the Council in the field of security and defence policy OJ C298, 30.11.2002, p. 1[1]

....

(footnotes omitted)

THE EUROPEAN PARLIAMENT AND THE COUNCIL,

Whereas:

(1)   Article 21 of the Treaty on European Union states that the Council Presidency shall consult the European Parliament on the main aspects and the basic choices of the common foreign and security policy and shall ensure that the views of the European Parliament are duly taken into consideration. That Article also stipulates that the

....

[1]   EDITOR'S NOTE: As of 1 June 2010 this Agreement has not been amended following the adoption of the Treaty of Lisbon. It may include references to the old version of the Treaty on European Union (TEU) and/or the now replaced Treaty establishing the European Community (TEC). Reference should be made to the Tables of Equivalences accompanying the consolidated Treaties in Part II of this edition for the conversion of old Treaty article numbers to new ones.

European Parliament shall be kept regularly informed by the Council Presidency and the Commission of the development of the common foreign and security policy. A mechanism should be introduced to ensure that these principles are implemented in this field.

(2)   In view of the specific nature and the especially sensitive content of certain highly classified information in the field of security and defence policy, special arrangements should be introduced for the handling of documents containing such information.

(3)   In conformity with Article 9(7) of Regulation (EC) No 1049/2001 of the European Parliament and of the Council of 30 May 2001 regarding public access to European Parliament, Council and Commission documents(1), the Council is to inform the European Parliament regarding sensitive documents as defined in Article 9(1) of that Regulation in accordance with arrangements agreed between the institutions.

(4)   In most Member States there are specific mechanisms for the transmission and handling of classified information between governments and national parliaments. This Interinstitutional Agreement should provide the European Parliament with treatment inspired by best practices in Member States,

HAVE CONCLUDED THIS INTERINSTITUTIONAL AGREEMENT:

1 SCOPE

1.1   This Interinstitutional Agreement deals with access by the European Parliament to sensitive information, i.e. information classified as TRÈS SECRET/TOP SECRET, SECRET or CONFIDENTIEL, whatever its origin, medium or state of completion, held by the Council in the field of security and defence policy and the handling of documents so classified.

1.2   Information originating from a third State or international organisation shall be transmitted with the agreement of that State or organisation.

Where information originating from a Member State is transmitted to the Council without explicit restriction on its dissemination to other institutions other than its classification, the rules in sections 2 and 3 of this Interinstitutional Agreement shall apply. Otherwise, such information shall be transmitted with the agreement of the Member State in question.

In the case of a refusal of the transmission of information originating from a third State, an international organisation or a Member State, the Council shall give the reasons.

1.3   The provisions of this Interinstitutional Agreement shall apply in accordance with applicable law and without prejudice to Decision 95/167/EC, Euratom, ECSC of the European Parliament, the Council and the Commission of 19 April 1995 on the detailed provisions governing the exercise of the European Parliament's right of inquiry(2) and without prejudice to existing arrangements, especially the Interinstitutional Agreement of 6 May 1999 between the European Parliament, the Council and the Commission on budgetary discipline and improvement of the budgetary procedure(3).

2 GENERAL RULES

2.1   The two institutions shall act in accordance with their mutual duties of sincere cooperation and in a spirit of mutual trust as well as in conformity with the relevant Treaty provisions. Communication and handling of the information covered by this Interinstitutional Agreement must have due regard for the interests which classification is designed to protect, and in particular the public interest as regards the security and defence of the European Union or of one or more of its Member States or military and non-military crisis management.

2.2   At the request of one of the persons referred to in point 3.1 below, the Presidency of the Council or the Secretary-General/High Representative shall inform them with all due despatch of the content of any sensitive information required for the exercise of the powers conferred on the European Parliament by the Treaty on European Union in the field covered by the present Interinstitutional Agreement, taking into account the public interest in matters relating to the security and defence of the European Union or of one or more of its Member States or military and non-military crisis management, in accordance with the arrangements laid down in section 3 below.

3   ARRANGEMENTS FOR ACCESS TO AND HANDLING OF SENSITIVE INFORMATION

3.1   In the context of this Interinstitutional Agreement, the President of the European Parliament or the Chairman of the European Parliament's Committee on Foreign Affairs, Human Rights, Common Security and Defence Policy may request that the Presidency of the Council or the Secretary-General/High Representative convey information to this committee on developments in European security and defence policy, including sensitive information to which point 3.3 applies.

3.2   In the event of a crisis or at the request of the President of the European Parliament or of the Chairman of the Committee on Foreign Affairs, Human Rights, Common Security and Defence Policy, such information shall be provided at the earliest opportunity.

3.3   In this framework, the President of the European Parliament and a special committee chaired by the Chairman of the Committee on Foreign Affairs, Human Rights, Common Security and Defence Policy and composed of four members designated by the Conference of Presidents shall be informed by the Presidency of the Council or the Secretary-General/High Representative of the content of the sensitive information where it is required for the exercise of the powers conferred on the European Parliament by the Treaty on European Union in the field covered by the present Interinstitutional Agreement. The President of the European Parliament and the special committee may ask to consult the documents in question on the premises of the Council.

Where this is appropriate and possible in the light of the nature and content of the information or documents concerned, these shall be made available to the President of the European Parliament, who shall select one of the following options:

(a)   information intended for the chairman of the Committee on Foreign Affairs, Human Rights, Common Security and Defence Policy;
(b)   access to information restricted to the members of the Committee on Foreign Affairs, Human Rights, Common Security and Defence Policy only;
(c)   discussion in the Committee on Foreign Affairs, Human Rights, Common Security and Defence Policy, meeting in camera, in accordance with arrangements which may vary by virtue of the degree of confidentiality involved;
(d)   communication of documents from which information has been expunged in the light of the degree of secrecy required.

These options are not applicable if sensitive information is classified as TRÈS SECRET//TOP SECRET.

As to information or documents classified as SECRET or CONFIDENTIEL, the selection by the President of the European Parliament of one of these options shall be previously agreed with the Council.

The information or documents in question shall not be published or forwarded to any other addressee.

4 FINAL PROVISIONS

4.1   The European Parliament and the Council, each for its own part, shall take all necessary measures to ensure the implementation of this Interinstitutional Agreement, including the steps required for the security clearance of the persons involved.

4.2   The two institutions are willing to discuss comparable Interinstitutional Agreements covering classified information in other areas of the Council's activities, on the understanding that the provisions of this Interinstitutional Agreement do not constitute a precedent for the Union's or the Community's other areas of activity and shall not affect the substance of any other Interinstitutional Agreements.

4.3   This Interinstitutional Agreement shall be reviewed after two years at the request of either of the two institutions in the light of experience gained in implementing it.

(*Date of signing and signatories omitted*)

ANNEX

This Interinstitutional Agreement shall be implemented in conformity with the relevant applicable regulations and in particular with the principle according to which the consent of the originator is a necessary condition for the transmission of classified information as laid down in point 1.2.

Consultation of sensitive documents by the members of the Special Committee of the European Parliament shall take place in a secured room at the Council premises.

This Interinstitutional Agreement shall enter into force after the European Parliament has adopted internal security measures which are in accordance with the principles laid down in point 2.1 and comparable to those of the other institutions in order to guarantee an equivalent level of protection of the sensitive information concerned.

V Internal Market

A) Free Movement of Goods

Commission Directive of 22 December 1969
on the abolition of measures which have an effect equivalent to quantitative restrictions on imports
OJ English special edition: Series I Chapter 1970(I), p. 17[1]

(Preamble omitted)

Article 1
The purpose of this Directive is to abolish the measures referred to in Articles 2 and 3, which were operative at the date of entry into force of the EEC Treaty.

Article 2
1. This Directive covers measures, other than those applicable equally to domestic or imported products, which hinder imports which could otherwise take place, including measures which make importation more difficult or costly than the disposal of domestic production.

2. In particular, it covers measures which make imports or the disposal, at any marketing stage, of imported products subject to a condition-other than a formality-which is required in respect of imported products only, or a condition differing from that required for domestic products and more difficult to satisfy. Equally, it covers, in particular, measures which favour domestic products or grant them a preference, other than an aid, to which conditions may or may not be attached.

3. The measures referred to must be taken to include those measures which:
    (a) lay down, for imported products only, minimum or maximum prices below or above which imports are prohibited, reduced or made subject to conditions liable to hinder importation;
    (b) lay down less favourable prices for imported products than for domestic products;
    (c) fix profit margins or any other price components for imported products only or fix these differently for domestic products and for imported products, to the detriment of the latter;

---

[1]   EDITOR'S NOTE: This Directive refers to the original European Economic Community (EEC) Treaty article numbers in force at the time of its adoption. The replacement article numbers contained in the Treaty on the Functioning of the European Union (TFEU) have been inserted in closed brackets after each Treaty reference for ease of conversion.

(d) preclude any increase in the price of the imported product corresponding to the supplementary costs and charges inherent in importation;

(e) fix the prices of products solely on the basis of the cost price or the quality of domestic products at such a level as to create a hindrance to importation;

(f) lower the value of an imported product, in particular by causing a reduction in its intrinsic value, or increase its costs;

(g) make access of imported products to the domestic market conditional upon having an agent or representative in the territory of the importing Member State;

(h) lay down conditions of payment in respect of imported products only, or subject imported products to conditions which are different from those laid down for domestic products and more difficult to satisfy;

(i) require, for imports only, the giving of guarantees or making of payments on account;

(j) subject imported products only to conditions, in respect, in particular of shape, size, weight, composition, presentation, identification or putting up, or subject imported products to conditions which are different from those for domestic products and more difficult to satisfy;

(k) hinder the purchase by private individuals of imported products only, or encourage, require or give preference to the purchase of domestic products only;

(l) totally or partially preclude the use of national facilities or equipment in respect of imported products only, or totally or partially confine the use of such facilities or equipment to domestic products only;

(m) prohibit or limit publicity in respect of imported products only, or totally or partially confine publicity to domestic products only;

(n) prohibit, limit or require stocking in respect of imported products only; totally or partially confine the use of stocking facilities to domestic products only, or make the stocking of imported products subject to conditions which are different from those required for domestic products and more difficult to satisfy;

(o) make importation subject to the granting of reciprocity by one or more Member States;

(p) prescribe that imported products are to conform, totally or partially, to rules other than those of the importing country;

(q) specify time limits for imported products which are insufficient or excessive in relation to the normal course of the various transactions to which these time limits apply;

(r) subject imported products to controls or, other than those inherent in the customs clearance procedure, to which domestic products are not subject or which are stricter in respect of imported products than they are in respect of domestic products, without this being necessary in order to ensure equivalent protection;

(s) confine names which are not indicative of origin or source to domestic products only.

Article 3

This Directive also covers measures governing the marketing of products which deal, in particular, with shape, size, weight, composition, presentation, identification or putting up and which are equally applicable to domestic and imported products, where the restrictive effect of such measures on the free movement of goods exceeds the effects intrinsic to trade rules.
This is the case, in particular, where:

— the restrictive effects on the free movement of goods are out of proportion to their purpose;

— the same objective can be attained by other means which are less of a hindrance to trade.

Article 4

1. Member States shall take all necessary steps in respect of products which must be allowed to enjoy free movement pursuant to Articles 9 and 10 of the Treaty [Articles 28 and 29

TFEU] to abolish measures having an effect equivalent to quantitative restrictions on imports and covered by this Directive.

2.   Member States shall inform the Commission of measures taken pursuant to this Directive.

Article 5
1.   This Directive does not apply to measures:
   (a) which fall under Article 37 (1) of the EEC Treaty [Article 37(1) TFEU];
   (b) which are referred to in Article 44 of the EEC Treaty [now repealed] or form an integral part of a national organisation of an agricultural market not yet replaced by a common organisation.

2.   This Directive shall apply without prejudice to the application, in particular, of Articles 36 and 223 of the EEC Treaty [Articles 36 and 346 TFEU].

Article 6
This Directive is addressed to the Member States.

(Date of signing and signatory omitted)

COMMUNICATION FROM THE COMMISSION
concerning the consequences of the judgment given by the Court of Justice on 20 February 1979 in Case 120/78 ('Cassis de Dijon')
OJ C 256, 3.10.1980, p. 2[1]

The following is the text of a letter which has been sent to the Member States; the European Parliament and the Council have also been notified of it.

In the Commission's Communication of 6 November 1978 on "Safeguarding free trade within the Community", it was emphasized that the free movement of goods is being affected by a growing number of restrictive measures.

The judgment delivered by the Court of Justice on 20 February 1979 in Case 120/78 (the "Cassis de Dijon" case), and recently reaffirmed in the judgment of 26 June 1980 in Case 788/79, has given the Commission some interpretative guidance enabling it to monitor more strictly the application of the Treaty rules on the free movement of goods, particularly Articles 30 to 36 of the EEC Treaty [Articles 34–36 TFEU].

The Court gives a very general definition of the barriers to free trade which are prohibited by the provisions of Article 30 et seq. of the EEC Treaty [Article 34 et.seq TFEU]. These are taken to include "any national measure capable of hindering, directly or indirectly, actually or potentially, intra-Community trade".

In its judgment of 20 February 1979 the Court indicates the scope of this definition as it applies to technical and commercial rules.

---

[1]   EDITOR'S NOTE: This Communication refers to the original European Economic Community (EEC) Treaty article numbers in force at the time of its publication. The replacement article numbers contained in the Treaty on the Functioning of the European Union (TFEU) have been inserted in closed brackets after each Treaty reference for ease of conversion.

Any product lawfully produced and marketed in one Member State must, in principle, be admitted to the market of any other Member State.

Technical and commercial rules, even those equally applicable to national and imported products, may create barriers to trade only where those rules are necessary to satisfy mandatory requirements and to serve a purpose which is in the general interest and for which they are an essential guarantee. This purpose must be such as to take precedence over the requirements of the free movement of goods, which constitutes one of the fundamental rules of the Community.

The conclusions in terms of policy which the Commission draws from this new guidance are set out below.

— Whereas Member States may, with respect to domestic products and in the absence of relevant Community provisions, regulate the terms on which such products are marketed, the case is different for products imported from other Member States.

Any product imported from another Member State must in principle be admitted to the territory of the importing Member State if it has been lawfully produced, that is, conforms to rules and processes of manufacture that are customarily and traditionally accepted in the exporting country, and is marketed in the territory of the latter.

This principle implies that Member States, when drawing up commercial or technical rules liable to affect the free movement of goods, may not take an exclusively national viewpoint and take account only of requirements confined to domestic products. The proper functioning of the common market demands that each Member State also give consideration to the legitimate requirements of the other Member States.

— Only under very strict conditions does the Court accept exceptions to this principle; barriers to trade resulting from differences between commercial and technical rules are only admissible: – if the rules are necessary, that is appropriate and not excessive, in order to satisfy mandatory requirements (public health, protection of consumers or the environment, the fairness of commercial transactions, etc.);
— if the rules serve a purpose in the general interest which is compelling enough to justify an exception to a fundamental rule of the Treaty such as the free movement of goods;
— if the rules are essential for such a purpose to be attained, i.e. are the means which are the most appropriate and at the same time least hinder trade.

The Court's interpretation has induced the Commission to set out a number of guidelines.

— The principles deduced by the Court imply that a Member State may not in principle prohibit the sale in its territory of a product lawfully produced and marketed in another Member State even if the product is produced according to technical or quality requirements which differ from those imposed on its domestic products. Where a product "suitably and satisfactorily" fulfils the legitimate objective of a Member State's own rules (public safety, protection of the consumer or the environment, etc.), the importing country cannot justify prohibiting its sale in its territory by claiming that the way it fulfils the objective is different from that imposed on domestic products.

In such a case, an absolute prohibition of sale could not be considered "necessary" to satisfy a "mandatory requirement" because it would not be an "essential guarantee" in the sense defined in the Court's judgment.

The Commission will therefore have to tackle a whole body of commercial rules which lay down that products manufactured and marketed in one Member State must fulfil technical or qualitative conditions in order to be admitted to the market of another and specifically in all cases where the trade barriers occasioned by such rules are inadmissible according to the very strict criteria set out by the Court.

The Commission is referring in particular to rules covering the composition, designation, presentation and packaging of products as well as rules requiring compliance with certain technical standards.

— The Commission's work of harmonization will henceforth have to be directed mainly at national laws having an impact on the functioning of the common market where barriers to trade to be removed arise from national provisions which are admissible under the criteria set by the Court.

The Commission will be concentrating on sectors deserving priority because of their economic relevance to the creation of a single internal market.

To forestall later difficulties, the Commission will be informing Member States of potential objections, under the terms of Community law, to provisions they may be considering introducing which come to the attention of the Commission.

It will be producing suggestions soon on the procedures to be followed in such cases.

The Commission is confident that this approach will secure greater freedom of trade for the Community's manufacturers, so strengthening the industrial base of the Community, while meeting the expectations of consumers.

COUNCIL REGULATION (EC) No 2679/98 OF 7 DECEMBER 1998

on the functioning of the internal market in relation to the free movement of goods among the Member States,[1]
OJ L 337, 12.12.1998, p. 8

(footnotes omitted)

THE COUNCIL OF THE EUROPEAN UNION,

Having regard to the Treaty establishing the European Community, and in particular Article 235 [Article 352 TFEU] thereof,

Having regard to the proposal from the Commission,

Having regard to the opinion of the European Parliament,

Having regard to the opinion of the Economic and Social Committee,

(1)   Whereas, as provided for in Article 7a of the Treaty [Article 26 TFEU], the internal market comprises an area without internal frontiers in which, in particular, the free movement of goods is ensured in accordance with Articles 30 to 36 of the Treaty [Articles 34–36 TFEU];

(2)   Whereas breaches of this principle, such as occur when in a given Member State the free movement of goods is obstructed by actions of private individuals, may cause grave disruption to the proper functioning of the internal market and inflict serious losses on the individuals affected;

---

[1]   EDITOR'S NOTE: This Regulation refers to the old EC Treaty article numbers effective prior to the Treaty of Amsterdam, 1999. The replacement article numbers contained in the Treaty on the Functioning of the European Union (TFEU) have been inserted in closed brackets after each Treaty reference for ease of conversion.

(3)   Whereas, in order to ensure fulfilment of the obligations arising from the Treaty, and, in particular, to ensure the proper functioning of the internal market, Member States should, on the one hand, abstain from adopting measures or engaging in conduct liable to constitute an obstacle to trade and, on the other hand, take all necessary and proportionate measures with a view to facilitating the free movement of goods in their territory;

(4)   Whereas such measures must not affect the exercise of fundamental rights, including the right or freedom to strike;

(5)   Whereas this Regulation does not prevent any actions which may be necessary in certain cases at Community level to respond to problems in the functioning of the internal market, taking into account, where appropriate, the application of this Regulation;

(6)   Whereas Member States have exclusive competence as regards the maintenance of public order and the safeguarding of internal security as well as in determining whether, when and which measures are necessary and proportionate in order to facilitate the free movement of goods in their territory in a given situation;

(7)   Whereas there should be adequate and rapid exchange of information between the Member States and the Commission on obstacles to the free movement of goods;

(8)   Whereas a Member State on the territory of which obstacles to the free movement of goods occur should take all necessary and proportionate measures to restore as soon as possible the free movement of goods in their territory in order to avoid the risk that the disruption or loss in question will continue, increase or intensify and that there may be a breakdown in trade and in the contractual relations which underlie it; whereas such Member State should inform the Commission and, if requested, other Member States of the measures it has taken or intends to take in order to fulfil this objective;

(9)   Whereas the Commission, in fulfilment of its duty under the Treaty, should notify the Member State concerned of its view that a breach has occurred and the Member State should respond to that notification;

(10)   Whereas the Treaty provides for no powers, other than those in Article 235 [Article 352 TFEU] thereof, for the adoption of this Regulation,

HAS ADOPTED THIS REGULATION:

Article 1
For the purpose of this Regulation:
1.   the term "obstacle" shall mean an obstacle to the free movement of goods among Member States which is attributable to a Member State, whether it involves action or inaction on its part, which may constitute a breach of Articles 30 to 36 of the Treaty [Articles 34–36 TFEU] and which:
   (a) leads to serious disruption of the free movement of goods by physically or otherwise preventing, delaying or diverting their import into, export from or transport across a Member State,
   (b) causes serious loss to the individuals affected, and
   (c) requires immediate action in order to prevent any continuation, increase or intensification of the disruption or loss in question;

2.   the term "inaction" shall cover the case when the competent authorities of a Member State, in the presence of an obstacle caused by actions taken by private individuals, fail to

take all necessary and proportionate measures within their powers with a view to removing the obstacle and ensuring the free movement of goods in their territory.

Article 2
This Regulation may not be interpreted as affecting in any way the exercise of fundamental rights as recognised in Member States, including the right or freedom to strike. These rights may also include the right or freedom to take other actions covered by the specific industrial relations systems in Member States.

Article 3
1. When an obstacle occurs or when there is a threat thereof
   (a) any Member State (whether or not it is the Member State concerned) which has relevant information shall immediately transmit it to the Commission, and
   (b) the Commission shall immediately transmit to the Member States that information and any information from any other source which it may consider relevant.

2. The Member State concerned shall respond as soon as possible to requests for information from the Commission and from other Member States concerning the nature of the obstacle or threat and the action which it has taken or proposes to take. Information exchange between Member States shall also be transmitted to the Commission.

Article 4
1. When an obstacle occurs, and subject to Article 2, the Member State concerned shall
   (a) take all necessary and proportionate measures so that the free movement of goods is assured in the territory of the Member State in accordance with the Treaty, and
   (b) inform the Commission of the actions which its authorities have taken or intend to take.

2. The Commission shall immediately transmit the information received under paragraph 1(b) to the other Member States.

Article 5
1. Where the Commission considers that an obstacle is occurring in a Member State, it shall notify the Member State concerned of the reasons that have led the Commission to such a conclusion and shall request the Member State to take all necessary and proportionate measures to remove the said obstacle within a period which it shall determine with reference to the urgency of the case.

2. In reaching its conclusion, the Commission shall have regard to Article 2.

3. The Commission may publish in the *Official Journal of the European Communities* the text of the notification which it has sent to the Member State concerned and shall immediately transmit the text to any party which requests it.

4. The Member State shall, within five working days of receipt of the text, either:
   — inform the Commission of the steps which it has taken or intends to take to implement paragraph 1, or
   — communicate a reasoned submission as to why there is no obstacle constituting a breach of Articles 30 to 36 of the Treaty [Articles 34–36 TFEU].

5. In exceptional cases, the Commission may allow an extension of the deadline mentioned in paragraph 4 if the Member State submits a duly substantiated request and the grounds cited are deemed acceptable.

This Regulation shall be binding in its entirety and directly applicable in all Member States.

(Date of signing and signatory omitted)

RESOLUTION OF THE COUNCIL AND OF THE REPRESENTATIVES OF THE GOVERNMENTS OF THE MEMBER STATES, MEETING WITHIN THE COUNCIL

of 7 December 1998 on the free movement of goods,
OJ L 337, 12.12.98, p. 10[1]

....

(preamble and footnote omitted)

1. MEMBER STATES undertake to do all within their powers, taking into account the protection of fundamental rights, including the right or freedom to strike, to maintain the free movement of goods and to deal rapidly with actions which seriously disrupt the free movement of goods, as defined in Regulation (EC) No 2679/98.

2. MEMBER STATES undertake to inform their economic operators of such disruptions and of efforts to overcome them.

3. MEMBER STATES agree to ensure that rapid and effective review procedures are available for any person who has been harmed as a result of a breach of the Treaty caused by an obstacle within the meaning of Article 1 of Regulation (EC) No 2679/98. They undertake to take all reasonable and proportionate steps to inform persons affected by a breach of the Treaty of this kind, of the existence of such remedies and of the procedure to be followed in pursuing them.

4. MEMBER STATES also agree to take the necessary steps, in accordance with the provisions of the Treaty, to make sure that requests for debate on the free movement of goods can be dealt with swiftly at the appropriate level within the Council, should a given situation warrant such attention.

5. THE COUNCIL notes the Commission's intention to impose tight deadlines for procedures under Article 169 of the Treaty [Article 258 TFEU] regarding cases falling within the scope of Regulation (EC) No 2679/98 and requests the Commission to inform the Council of specific initiatives to be taken in this respect.

6. MEMBER STATES take note that in cases referred to in paragraph 5 the time set by the Commission for submission of observations may be as short as five working days, as may also the time for response to a reasoned opinion.

7. THE COUNCIL invites the Court of Justice of the European Communities to consider whether cases within the scope of Regulation (EC) No 2679/98 can be expedited and promises to examine any proposals to amend the Rules of Procedure of the Court of Justice urgently and with an open mind.

....

[1]   EDITOR'S NOTE: This Resolution refers to the old EC Treaty article numbers effective prior to the Treaty of Amsterdam, 1999. The replacement article numbers contained in the Treaty on the Functioning of the European Union (TFEU) have been inserted in closed brackets after each Treaty reference for ease of conversion.

8.   THE COUNCIL invites the Commission to submit a report on the application of
Regulation (EC) No 2679/98 two years after the entry into force thereof.

B) FREE MOVEMENT OF PERSONS

REGULATION (EEC) No 1612/68 OF THE COUNCIL OF 15 OCTOBER 1968

on freedom of movement for workers within the Community, Part I,
OJ English special edition: Series I Chapter 1968(II) p. 475*

....

(Preamble and footnotes omitted)

Part I EMPLOYMENT AND WORKERS' FAMILIES

Title I ELIGIBILITY FOR EMPLOYMENT

Article 1
1.   Any national of a Member State, shall, irrespective of his place of residence, have the
right to take up an activity as an employed person, and to pursue such activity, within
the territory of another Member State in accordance with the provisions laid down by
law, regulation or administrative action governing the employment of nationals of that
State.

2.   He shall, in particular, have the right to take up available employment in the territory of
another Member State with the same priority as nationals of that State.

Article 2
Any national of a Member State and any employer pursuing an activity in the territory
of a Member State may exchange their applications for and offers of employment, and may
conclude and perform contracts of employment in accordance with the provisions in force laid
down by law, regulation or administrative action, without any discrimination resulting
therefrom.

Article 3
1.   Under this Regulation, provisions laid down by law, regulation or administrative action
or administrative practices of a Member State shall not apply:
— where they limit application for and offers of employment, or the right of foreign
nationals to take up and pursue employment or subject these to conditions not
applicable in respect of their own nationals; or
— where, though applicable irrespective of nationality, their exclusive or principal aim
or effect is to keep nationals of other Member States away from the employment
offered.
This provision shall not apply to conditions relating to linguistic knowledge required by
reason of the nature of the post to be filled.

....

*   As amended by Council Regulation (EEC) No 312/76 of 9 February 1976, OJ L 39, 14.2.1976, p. 2, Council
Regulation (EEC) No 2434/92 of 27 July 1992, OJ L 245, 26.8.1992, p. 1, Directive 2004/38/EC of the European
Parliament and of the Council of 29 April 2004, OJ L 229, 29.6.2004, p. 35; and corrected by Corrigendum, OJ L
999, 1.1.1973, p. 28 (16/12/68)

2.   There shall be included in particular among the provisions or practices of a Member State referred to in the first subparagraph of paragraph 1 those which:
(a) prescribe a special recruitment procedure for foreign nationals;
(b) limit or restrict the advertising of vacancies in the press or through any other medium or subject it to conditions other than those applicable in respect of employers pursuing their activities in the territory of that Member State;
(c) subject eligibility for employment to conditions of registration with employment offices or impede recruitment of individual workers, where persons who do not reside in the territory of that State are concerned.

Article 4
1.   Provisions laid down by law, regulation or administrative action of the Member States which restrict by number or percentage the employment of foreign nationals in any undertaking, branch of activity or region, or at a national level, shall not apply to nationals of the other Member States.

2.   When in a Member State the granting of any benefit to undertakings is subject to a minimum percentage of national workers being employed, nationals of the other Member States shall be counted as national workers, subject to the provisions of the Council Directive of 15 October 1963.

Article 5
A national of a Member State who seeks employment in the territory of another Member State shall receive the same assistance there as that afforded by the employment offices in that State to their own nationals seeking employment.

Article 6
1.   The engagement and recruitment of a national of one Member State for a post in another Member State shall not depend on medical, vocational or other criteria which are discriminatory on grounds of nationality by comparison with those applied to nationals of the other Member State who wish to pursue the same activity.

2.   Nevertheless, a national who holds an offer in his name from an employer in a Member State other than that of which he is a national may have to undergo a vocational test, if the employer expressly requests this when making his offer of employment.

Title II EMPLOYMENT AND EQUALITY OF TREATMENT

Article 7
1.   A worker who is a national of a Member State may not, in the territory of another Member State, be treated differently from national workers by reason of his nationality in respect of any conditions of employment and work, in particular as regards remuneration, dismissal, and should he become unemployed, reinstatement or re-employment;

2.   He shall enjoy the same social and tax advantages as national workers.

3.   He shall also, by virtue of the same right and under the same conditions as national workers, have access to training in vocational schools and retraining centres.

4.   Any clause of a collective or individual agreement or of any other collective regulation concerning eligibility for employment, employment, remuneration and other conditions of work or dismissal shall be null and void in so far as it lays down or authorises discriminatory conditions in respect of workers who are nationals of the other Member States.

Article 8

1.   A worker who is a national of a Member State and who is employed in the territory of another Member State shall enjoy equality of treatment as regards membership of trade unions and the exercise of rights attaching thereto, including the right to vote and to be eligible for the administration or management posts of a trade union; he may be excluded from taking part in the management of bodies governed by public law and from holding an office governed by public law. Furthermore, he shall have the right of eligibility for workers' representative bodies in the undertaking. The provisions of this Article shall not affect laws or regulations in certain Member States which grant more extensive rights to workers coming from the other Member States.

Article 9

1.   A worker who is a national of a Member State and who is employed in the territory of another Member State shall enjoy all the rights and benefits accorded to national workers in matters of housing, including ownership of the housing he needs.

2.   Such a worker may, with the same right as nationals, put his name down on the housing lists in the region in which he is employed, where such lists exist; he shall enjoy the resultant benefits and priorities.

      If his family has remained in the country whence he came, they shall be considered for this purpose as residing in the said region, where national workers benefit from a similar presumption.

(Article 10 and 11 have been repealed by Directive 2004/38/EC)

TITLE III WORKERS' FAMILIES

Article 12

The children of a national of a Member State who is or has been employed in the territory of another Member State shall be admitted to that State's general educational, apprenticeship and vocational training courses under the same conditions as the nationals of that State, if such children are residing in its territory.

Member States shall encourage all efforts to enable such children to attend these courses under the best possible conditions.

(Parts II–IV omitted)

Council Directive 77/486/EEC of 25 July 1977
on the education of the children of migrant workers,
OJ L 199, 6.8.1977, p. 32[1]

....

(footnotes omitted)

THE COUNCIL OF THE EUROPEAN COMMUNITIES,

Having regard to the Treaty establishing the European Economic Community, and in particular Article 49 thereof [Article 46 TFEU],

....

[1]   EDITOR'S NOTE: This Directive refers to the original European Economic Community (EEC) Treaty article numbers in force at the time of its publication. The replacement article numbers contained in the Treaty on the Functioning of the European Union (TFEU) have been inserted in closed brackets after each Treaty reference for ease of conversion.

Having regard to the proposal from the Commission,

Having regard to the opinion of the European Parliament,

Having regard to the opinion of the Economic and Social Committee,

Whereas in its resolution of 21 January 1974 concerning a social action programme, the Council included in its priority actions those designed to improve the conditions of freedom of movement for workers relating in particular to reception and to the education of their children;

Whereas in order to permit the integration of such children into the educational environment and the school system of the host State, they should be able to receive suitable tuition including teaching of the language of the host State;

Whereas host Member States should also take, in conjunction with the Member States of origin, appropriate measures to promote the teaching of the mother tongue and of the culture of the country of origin of the abovementioned children, with a view principally to facilitating their possible reintegration into the Member State of origin,

HAS ADOPTED THIS DIRECTIVE:

Article 1
This Directive shall apply to children for whom school attendance is compulsory under the laws of the host State, who are dependants of any worker who is a national of another Member State, where such children are resident in the territory of the Member State in which that national carries on or has carried on an activity as an employed person.

Article 2
Member States shall, in accordance with their national circumstances and legal systems, take appropriate measures to ensure that free tuition to facilitate initial reception is offered in their territory to the children referred to in Article 1, including, in particular, the teaching – adapted to the specific needs of such children – of the official language or one of the official languages of the host State.

Member States shall take the measures necessary for the training and further training of the teachers who are to provide this tuition.

Article 3
Member States shall, in accordance with their national circumstances and legal systems, and in cooperation with States of origin, take appropriate measures to promote, in coordination with normal education, teaching of the mother tongue and culture of the country of origin for the children referred to in Article 1.

Article 4
The Member States shall take the necessary measures to comply with this Directive within four years of its notification and shall forthwith inform the Commission thereof.

The Member States shall also inform the Commission of all laws, regulations and administrative or other provisions which they adopt in the field governed by this Directive.

Article 5
The Member States shall forward to the Commission within five years of the notification of this Directive, and subsequently at regular intervals at the request of the Commission, all relevant information to enable the Commission to report to the Council on the application of this Directive.

Article 6
This Directive is addressed to the Member States.

DIRECTIVE 2004/38/EC OF THE EUROPEAN PARLIAMENT AND OF THE COUNCIL OF 29 APRIL 2004

on the right of citizens of the Union and their family members to move and reside freely within the territory of the Member States amending Regulation (EEC) No 1612/68 and repealing Directives 64/221/EEC, 68/360/EEC, 72/194/EEC, 73/148/EEC, 75/34/EEC, 75/35/EEC, 90/364/EEC, 90/365/EEC and 93//96/EEC
OJ L 229, 29.6.2004, p. 35*[1]

....

(footnotes omitted)

THE EUROPEAN PARLIAMENT AND THE COUNCIL OF THE EUROPEAN UNION,

Having regard to the Treaty establishing the European Community, and in particular Articles 12, 18, 40, 44 and 52 thereof,

Having regard to the proposal from the Commission,

Having regard to the opinion of the European Economic and Social Committee,

Having regard to the opinion of the Committee of the Regions,

Acting in accordance with the procedure laid down in Article 251 of the Treaty,

Whereas:

(1)   Citizenship of the Union confers on every citizen of the Union a primary and individual right to move and reside freely within the territory of the Member States, subject to the limitations and conditions laid down in the Treaty and to the measures adopted to give it effect.

(2)   The free movement of persons constitutes one of the fundamental freedoms of the internal market, which comprises an area without internal frontiers, in which freedom is ensured in accordance with the provisions of the Treaty.

(3)   Union citizenship should be the fundamental status of nationals of the Member States when they exercise their right of free movement and residence. It is therefore necessary to codify and review the existing Community instruments dealing separately with workers, self-employed persons, as well as students and other inactive persons in order to simplify and strengthen the right of free movement and residence of all Union citizens.

....

(*as corrected at: OJ L 30, 3.2.2005, p. 27, and OJ L 197, 28.7.2005)

[1]   EDITOR'S NOTE: As of 1 June 2010 this Directive has not been amended following the adoption of the Treaty of Lisbon. It includes references to the old Treaty article numbers. Reference should be made to the Tables of Equivalences accompanying the consolidated Treaties in Part II of this edition for the conversion of old Treaty article numbers to new ones.

(4)   With a view to remedying this sector-by-sector, piecemeal approach to the right of free movement and residence and facilitating the exercise of this right, there needs to be a single legislative act to amend Council Regulation (EEC) No 1612/68 of 15 October 1968 on freedom of movement for workers within the Community, and to repeal the following acts: Council Directive 68/360/EEC of 15 October 1968 on the abolition of restrictions on movement and residence within the Community for workers of Member States and their families, Council Directive 73/148/EEC of 21 May 1973 on the abolition of restrictions on movement and residence within the Community for nationals of Member States with regard to establishment and the provision of services, Council Directive 90/364/EEC of 28 June 1990 on the right of residence, Council Directive 90/365/EEC of 28 June 1990 on the right of residence for employees and self-employed persons who have ceased their occupational activity and Council Directive 93/96/EEC of 29 October 1993 on the right of residence for students.

(5)   The right of all Union citizens to move and reside freely within the territory of the Member States should, if it is to be exercised under objective conditions of freedom and dignity, be also granted to their family members, irrespective of nationality. For the purposes of this Directive, the definition of «family member» should also include the registered partner if the legislation of the host Member State treats registered partnership as equivalent to marriage.

(6)   In order to maintain the unity of the family in a broader sense and without prejudice to the prohibition of discrimination on grounds of nationality, the situation of those persons who are not included in the definition of family members under this Directive, and who therefore do not enjoy an automatic right of entry and residence in the host Member State, should be examined by the host Member State on the basis of its own national legislation, in order to decide whether entry and residence could be granted to such persons, taking into consideration their relationship with the Union citizen or any other circumstances, such as their financial or physical dependence on the Union citizen.

(7)   The formalities connected with the free movement of Union citizens within the territory of Member States should be clearly defined, without prejudice to the provisions applicable to national border controls.

(8)   With a view to facilitating the free movement of family members who are not nationals of a Member State, those who have already obtained a residence card should be exempted from the requirement to obtain an entry visa within the meaning of Council Regulation (EC) No 539/2001 of 15 March 2001 listing the third countries whose nationals must be in possession of visas when crossing the external borders and those whose nationals are exempt from that requirement or, where appropriate, of the applicable national legislation.

(9)   Union citizens should have the right of residence in the host Member State for a period not exceeding three months without being subject to any conditions or any formalities other than the requirement to hold a valid identity card or passport, without prejudice to a more favourable treatment applicable to job-seekers as recognised by the case-law of the Court of Justice.

(10)   Persons exercising their right of residence should not, however, become an unreasonable burden on the social assistance system of the host Member State during an initial period of residence. Therefore, the right of residence for Union citizens and their family members for periods in excess of three months should be subject to conditions.

(11) The fundamental and personal right of residence in another Member State is conferred directly on Union citizens by the Treaty and is not dependent upon their having fulfilled administrative procedures.

(12) For periods of residence of longer than three months, Member States should have the possibility to require Union citizens to register with the competent authorities in the place of residence, attested by a registration certificate issued to that effect.

(13) The residence card requirement should be restricted to family members of Union citizens who are not nationals of a Member State for periods of residence of longer than three months.

(14) The supporting documents required by the competent authorities for the issuing of a registration certificate or of a residence card should be comprehensively specified in order to avoid divergent administrative practices or interpretations constituting an undue obstacle to the exercise of the right of residence by Union citizens and their family members.

(15) Family members should be legally safeguarded in the event of the death of the Union citizen, divorce, annulment of marriage or termination of a registered partnership. With due regard for family life and human dignity, and in certain conditions to guard against abuse, measures should therefore be taken to ensure that in such circumstances family members already residing within the territory of the host Member State retain their right of residence exclusively on a personal basis.

(16) As long as the beneficiaries of the right of residence do not become an unreasonable burden on the social assistance system of the host Member State they should not be expelled. Therefore, an expulsion measure should not be the automatic consequence of recourse to the social assistance system. The host Member State should examine whether it is a case of temporary difficulties and take into account the duration of residence, the personal circumstances and the amount of aid granted in order to consider whether the beneficiary has become an unreasonable burden on its social assistance system and to proceed to his expulsion. In no case should an expulsion measure be adopted against workers, self-employed persons or job-seekers as defined by the Court of Justice save on grounds of public policy or public security.

(17) Enjoyment of permanent residence by Union citizens who have chosen to settle long term in the host Member State would strengthen the feeling of Union citizenship and is a key element in promoting social cohesion, which is one of the fundamental objectives of the Union. A right of permanent residence should therefore be laid down for all Union citizens and their family members who have resided in the host Member State in compliance with the conditions laid down in this Directive during a continuous period of five years without becoming subject to an expulsion measure.

(18) In order to be a genuine vehicle for integration into the society of the host Member State in which the Union citizen resides, the right of permanent residence, once obtained, should not be subject to any conditions.

(19) Certain advantages specific to Union citizens who are workers or self-employed persons and to their family members, which may allow these persons to acquire a right of permanent residence before they have resided five years in the host Member State, should be maintained, as these constitute acquired rights, conferred by Commission Regulation (EEC) No 1251/70 of 29 June 1970 on the right of workers to remain in the territory of a Member State after having been employed in that State and Council Directive 75/34/EEC of 17 December 1974 concerning the right of nationals of a Member State to remain

in the territory of another Member State after having pursued therein an activity in a self-employed capacity.

(20) In accordance with the prohibition of discrimination on grounds of nationality, all Union citizens and their family members residing in a Member State on the basis of this Directive should enjoy, in that Member State, equal treatment with nationals in areas covered by the Treaty, subject to such specific provisions as are expressly provided for in the Treaty and secondary law.

(21) However, it should be left to the host Member State to decide whether it will grant social assistance during the first three months of residence, or for a longer period in the case of job-seekers, to Union citizens other than those who are workers or self-employed persons or who retain that status or their family members, or maintenance assistance for studies, including vocational training, prior to acquisition of the right of permanent residence, to these same persons.

(22) The Treaty allows restrictions to be placed on the right of free movement and residence on grounds of public policy, public security or public health. In order to ensure a tighter definition of the circumstances and procedural safeguards subject to which Union citizens and their family members may be denied leave to enter or may be expelled, this Directive should replace Council Directive 64/221/EEC of 25 February 1964 on the coordination of special measures concerning the movement and residence of foreign nationals, which are justified on grounds of public policy, public security or public health.

(23) Expulsion of Union citizens and their family members on grounds of public policy or public security is a measure that can seriously harm persons who, having availed themselves of the rights and freedoms conferred on them by the Treaty, have become genuinely integrated into the host Member State. The scope for such measures should therefore be limited in accordance with the principle of proportionality to take account of the degree of integration of the persons concerned, the length of their residence in the host Member State, their age, state of health, family and economic situation and the links with their country of origin.

(24) Accordingly, the greater the degree of integration of Union citizens and their family members in the host Member State, the greater the degree of protection against expulsion should be. Only in exceptional circumstances, where there are imperative grounds of public security, should an expulsion measure be taken against Union citizens who have resided for many years in the territory of the host Member State, in particular when they were born and have resided there throughout their life. In addition, such exceptional circumstances should also apply to an expulsion measure taken against minors, in order to protect their links with their family, in accordance with the United Nations Convention on the Rights of the Child, of 20 November 1989.

(25) Procedural safeguards should also be specified in detail in order to ensure a high level of protection of the rights of Union citizens and their family members in the event of their being denied leave to enter or reside in another Member State, as well as to uphold the principle that any action taken by the authorities must be properly justified.

(26) In all events, judicial redress procedures should be available to Union citizens and their family members who have been refused leave to enter or reside in another Member State.

(27) In line with the case-law of the Court of Justice prohibiting Member States from issuing orders excluding for life persons covered by this Directive from their territory, the right of Union citizens and their family members who have been excluded from the territory of a Member State to submit a fresh application after a reasonable period, and in any event

after a three year period from enforcement of the final exclusion order, should be confirmed.

(28) To guard against abuse of rights or fraud, notably marriages of convenience or any other form of relationships contracted for the sole purpose of enjoying the right of free movement and residence, Member States should have the possibility to adopt the necessary measures.

(29) This Directive should not affect more favourable national provisions.

(30) With a view to examining how further to facilitate the exercise of the right of free movement and residence, a report should be prepared by the Commission in order to evaluate the opportunity to present any necessary proposals to this effect, notably on the extension of the period of residence with no conditions.

(31) This Directive respects the fundamental rights and freedoms and observes the principles recognised in particular by the Charter of Fundamental Rights of the European Union. In accordance with the prohibition of discrimination contained in the Charter, Member States should implement this Directive without discrimination between the beneficiaries of this Directive on grounds such as sex, race, colour, ethnic or social origin, genetic characteristics, language, religion or beliefs, political or other opinion, membership of an ethnic minority, property, birth, disability, age or sexual orientation,

HAVE ADOPTED THIS DIRECTIVE:

Chapter I GENERAL PROVISIONS

Article 1 Subject
This Directive lays down:
(a) the conditions governing the exercise of the right of free movement and residence within the territory of the Member States by Union citizens and their family members;

(b) the right of permanent residence in the territory of the Member States for Union citizens and their family members;

(c) the limits placed on the rights set out in (a) and (b) on grounds of public policy, public security or public health.

Article 2 Definitions
For the purposes of this Directive:
1. 'Union citizen' means any person having the nationality of a Member State;

2. 'family member' means:
    (a) the spouse;
    (b) the partner with whom the Union citizen has contracted a registered partnership, on the basis of the legislation of a Member State, if the legislation of the host Member State treats registered partnerships as equivalent to marriage and in accordance with the conditions laid down in the relevant legislation of the host Member State;
    (c) the direct descendants who are under the age of 21 or are dependants and those of the spouse or partner as defined in point (b);
    (d) the dependent direct relatives in the ascending line and those of the spouse or partner as defined in point (b);

3. 'host Member State' means the Member State to which a Union citizen moves in order to exercise his/her right of free movement and residence.

Article 3 Beneficiaries

1.   This Directive shall apply to all Union citizens who move to or reside in a Member State other than that of which they are a national, and to their family members as defined in point 2 of Article 2 who accompany or join them.

2.   Without prejudice to any right to free movement and residence the persons concerned may have in their own right, the host Member State shall, in accordance with its national legislation, facilitate entry and residence for the following persons:

(a)   any other family members, irrespective of their nationality, not falling under the definition in point 2 of Article 2 who, in the country from which they have come, are dependants or members of the household of the Union citizen having the primary right of residence, or where serious health grounds strictly require the personal care of the family member by the Union citizen;

(b)   the partner with whom the Union citizen has a durable relationship, duly attested.

The host Member State shall undertake an extensive examination of the personal circumstances and shall justify any denial of entry or residence to these people.

Chapter II RIGHT OF EXIT AND ENTRY

Article 4 Right of exit

1.   Without prejudice to the provisions on travel documents applicable to national border controls, all Union citizens with a valid identity card or passport and their family members who are not nationals of a Member State and who hold a valid passport shall have the right to leave the territory of a Member State to travel to another Member State.

2.   No exit visa or equivalent formality may be imposed on the persons to whom paragraph 1 applies.

3.   Member States shall, acting in accordance with their laws, issue to their own nationals, and renew, an identity card or passport stating their nationality.

4.   The passport shall be valid at least for all Member States and for countries through which the holder must pass when travelling between Member States. Where the law of a Member State does not provide for identity cards to be issued, the period of validity of any passport on being issued or renewed shall be not less than five years.

Article 5 Right of entry

1.   Without prejudice to the provisions on travel documents applicable to national border controls, Member States shall grant Union citizens leave to enter their territory with a valid identity card or passport and shall grant family members who are not nationals of a Member State leave to enter their territory with a valid passport.

No entry visa or equivalent formality may be imposed on Union citizens.

2.   Family members who are not nationals of a Member State shall only be required to have an entry visa in accordance with Regulation (EC) No 539/2001 or, where appropriate, with national law. For the purposes of this Directive, possession of the valid residence card referred to in Article 10 shall exempt such family members from the visa requirement.

Member States shall grant such persons every facility to obtain the necessary visas. Such visas shall be issued free of charge as soon as possible and on the basis of an accelerated procedure.

3.   The host Member State shall not place an entry or exit stamp in the passport of family members who are not nationals of a Member State provided that they present the residence card provided for in Article 10.

4.   Where a Union citizen, or a family member who is not a national of a Member State, does not have the necessary travel documents or, if required, the necessary visas, the Member State concerned shall, before turning them back, give such persons every reasonable opportunity to obtain the necessary documents or have them brought to them within a reasonable period of time or to corroborate or prove by other means that they are covered by the right of free movement and residence.

5.   The Member State may require the person concerned to report his/her presence within its territory within a reasonable and non-discriminatory period of time. Failure to comply with this requirement may make the person concerned liable to proportionate and non-discriminatory sanctions.

Chapter III RIGHT OF RESIDENCE

Article 6 Right of residence for up to three months
1.   Union citizens shall have the right of residence on the territory of another Member State for a period of up to three months without any conditions or any formalities other than the requirement to hold a valid identity card or passport.

2.   The provisions of paragraph 1 shall also apply to family members in possession of a valid passport who are not nationals of a Member State, accompanying or joining the Union citizen.

Article 7 Right of residence for more than three months
1.   All Union citizens shall have the right of residence on the territory of another Member State for a period of longer than three months if they:
   (a) are workers or self-employed persons in the host Member State; or
   (b) have sufficient resources for themselves and their family members not to become a burden on the social assistance system of the host Member State during their period of residence and have comprehensive sickness insurance cover in the host Member State; or
   (c) are enrolled at a private or public establishment, accredited or financed by the host Member State on the basis of its legislation or administrative practice, for the principal purpose of following a course of study, including vocational training; and have comprehensive sickness insurance cover in the host Member State and assure the relevant national authority, by means of a declaration or by such equivalent means as they may choose, that they have sufficient resources for themselves and their family members not to become a burden on the social assistance system of the host Member State during their period of residence; or
   (d) are family members accompanying or joining a Union citizen who satisfies the conditions referred to in points (a), (b) or (c).

2.   The right of residence provided for in paragraph 1 shall extend to family members who are not nationals of a Member State, accompanying or joining the Union citizen in the host Member State, provided that such Union citizen satisfies the conditions referred to in paragraph 1(a), (b) or (c).

3.   For the purposes of paragraph 1(a), a Union citizen who is no longer a worker or self-employed person shall retain the status of worker or self-employed person in the following circumstances:
   (a) he/she is temporarily unable to work as the result of an illness or accident;
   (b) he/she is in duly recorded involuntary unemployment after having been employed for more than one year and has registered as a job-seeker with the relevant employment office;

(c) he/she is in duly recorded involuntary unemployment after completing a fixed-term employment contract of less than a year or after having become involuntarily unemployed during the first twelve months and has registered as a job-seeker with the relevant employment office. In this case, the status of worker shall be retained for no less than six months;

(d) he/she embarks on vocational training. Unless he/she is involuntarily unemployed, the retention of the status of worker shall require the training to be related to the previous employment.

4. By way of derogation from paragraphs 1(d) and 2 above, only the spouse, the registered partner provided for in Article 2(2)(b) and dependent children shall have the right of residence as family members of a Union citizen meeting the conditions under 1(c) above. Article 3(2) shall apply to his/her dependent direct relatives in the ascending lines and those of his/her spouse or registered partner.

Article 8 Administrative formalities for Union citizens

1. Without prejudice to Article 5(5), for periods of residence longer than three months, the host Member State may require Union citizens to register with the relevant authorities.

2. The deadline for registration may not be less than three months from the date of arrival. A registration certificate shall be issued immediately, stating the name and address of the person registering and the date of the registration. Failure to comply with the registration requirement may render the person concerned liable to proportionate and non-discriminatory sanctions.

3. For the registration certificate to be issued, Member States may only require that,

    Union citizens to whom point (a) of Article 7(1) applies present a valid identity card or passport, a confirmation of engagement from the employer or a certificate of employment, or proof that they are self-employed persons,

    Union citizens to whom point (b) of Article 7(1) applies present a valid identity card or passport and provide proof that they satisfy the conditions laid down therein,

    Union citizens to whom point (c) of Article 7(1) applies present a valid identity card or passport, provide proof of enrolment at an accredited establishment and of comprehensive sickness insurance cover and the declaration or equivalent means referred to in point (c) of Article 7(1). Member States may not require this declaration to refer to any specific amount of resources.

4. Member States may not lay down a fixed amount which they regard as 'sufficient resources', but they must take into account the personal situation of the person concerned. In all cases this amount shall not be higher than the threshold below which nationals of the host Member State become eligible for social assistance, or, where this criterion is not applicable, higher than the minimum social security pension paid by the host Member State.

5. For the registration certificate to be issued to family members of Union citizens, who are themselves Union citizens, Member States may require the following documents to be presented:
    (a) a valid identity card or passport;
    (b) a document attesting to the existence of a family relationship or of a registered partnership;
    (c) where appropriate, the registration certificate of the Union citizen whom they are accompanying or joining;
    (d) in cases falling under points (c) and (d) of Article 2(2), documentary evidence that the conditions laid down therein are met;

(e) in cases falling under Article 3(2)(a), a document issued by the relevant authority in the country of origin or country from which they are arriving certifying that they are dependants or members of the household of the Union citizen, or proof of the existence of serious health grounds which strictly require the personal care of the family member by the Union citizen;

(f) in cases falling under Article 3(2)(b), proof of the existence of a durable relationship with the Union citizen.

Article 9 Administrative formalities for family members who are not nationals of a Member State

1. Member States shall issue a residence card to family members of a Union citizen who are not nationals of a Member State, where the planned period of residence is for more than three months.

2. The deadline for submitting the residence card application may not be less than three months from the date of arrival.

3. Failure to comply with the requirement to apply for a residence card may make the person concerned liable to proportionate and non-discriminatory sanctions.

Article 10 Issue of residence cards

1. The right of residence of family members of a Union citizen who are not nationals of a Member State shall be evidenced by the issuing of a document called 'Residence card of a family member of a Union citizen' no later than six months from the date on which they submit the application. A certificate of application for the residence card shall be issued immediately.

2. For the residence card to be issued, Member States shall require presentation of the following documents:

(a) a valid passport;

(b) a document attesting to the existence of a family relationship or of a registered partnership;

(c) the registration certificate or, in the absence of a registration system, any other proof of residence in the host Member State of the Union citizen whom they are accompanying or joining;

(d) in cases falling under points (c) and (d) of Article 2(2), documentary evidence that the conditions laid down therein are met;

(e) in cases falling under Article 3(2)(a), a document issued by the relevant authority in the country of origin or country from which they are arriving certifying that they are dependants or members of the household of the Union citizen, or proof of the existence of serious health grounds which strictly require the personal care of the family member by the Union citizen;

(f) in cases falling under Article 3(2)(b), proof of the existence of a durable relationship with the Union citizen.

Article 11 Validity of the residence card

1. The residence card provided for by Article 10(1) shall be valid for five years from the date of issue or for the envisaged period of residence of the Union citizen, if this period is less than five years.

2. The validity of the residence card shall not be affected by temporary absences not exceeding six months a year, or by absences of a longer duration for compulsory military service or by one absence of a maximum of 12 consecutive months for important reasons such as pregnancy and childbirth, serious illness, study or vocational training, or a posting in another Member State or a third country.

Article 12 Retention of the right of residence by family members in the event of death or departure of the Union citizen

1. Without prejudice to the second subparagraph, the Union citizen's death or departure from the host Member State shall not affect the right of residence of his/her family members who are nationals of a Member State.

   Before acquiring the right of permanent residence, the persons concerned must meet the conditions laid down in points (a), (b), (c) or (d) of Article 7(1).

2. Without prejudice to the second subparagraph, the Union citizen's death shall not entail loss of the right of residence of his/her family members who are not nationals of a Member State and who have been residing in the host Member State as family members for at least one year before the Union citizen's death.

   Before acquiring the right of permanent residence, the right of residence of the persons concerned shall remain subject to the requirement that they are able to show that they are workers or self-employed persons or that they have sufficient resources for themselves and their family members not to become a burden on the social assistance system of the host Member State during their period of residence and have comprehensive sickness insurance cover in the host Member State, or that they are members of the family, already constituted in the host Member State, of a person satisfying these requirements.

   'Sufficient resources' shall be as defined in Article 8(4).

   Such family members shall retain their right of residence exclusively on a personal basis.

3. The Union citizen's departure from the host Member State or his/her death shall not entail loss of the right of residence of his/her children or of the parent who has actual custody of the children, irrespective of nationality, if the children reside in the host Member State and are enrolled at an educational establishment, for the purpose of studying there, until the completion of their studies.

Article 13 Retention of the right of residence by family members in the event of divorce, annulment of marriage or termination of registered partnership

1. Without prejudice to the second subparagraph, divorce, annulment of the Union citizen's marriage or termination of his/her registered partnership, as referred to in point 2(b) of Article 2 shall not affect the right of residence of his/her family members who are nationals of a Member State.

   Before acquiring the right of permanent residence, the persons concerned must meet the conditions laid down in points (a), (b), (c) or (d) of Article 7(1).

2. Without prejudice to the second subparagraph, divorce, annulment of marriage or termination of the registered partnership referred to in point 2(b) of Article 2 shall not entail loss of the right of residence of a Union citizen's family members who are not nationals of a Member State where:

   (a) prior to initiation of the divorce or annulment proceedings or termination of the registered partnership referred to in point 2(b) of Article 2, the marriage or registered partnership has lasted at least three years, including one year in the host Member State; or

   (b) by agreement between the spouses or the partners referred to in point 2(b) of Article 2 or by court order, the spouse or partner who is not a national of a Member State has custody of the Union citizen's children; or

   (c) this is warranted by particularly difficult circumstances, such as having been a victim of domestic violence while the marriage or registered partnership was subsisting; or

(d) by agreement between the spouses or partners referred to in point 2(b) of Article 2 or by court order, the spouse or partner who is not a national of a Member State has the right of access to a minor child, provided that the court has ruled that such access must be in the host Member State, and for as long as is required.

Before acquiring the right of permanent residence, the right of residence of the persons concerned shall remain subject to the requirement that they are able to show that they are workers or self-employed persons or that they have sufficient resources for themselves and their family members not to become a burden on the social assistance system of the host Member State during their period of residence and have comprehensive sickness insurance cover in the host Member State, or that they are members of the family, already constituted in the host Member State, of a person satisfying these requirements. 'Sufficient resources' shall be as defined in Article 8(4).

Such family members shall retain their right of residence exclusively on personal basis.

Article 14 Retention of the right of residence

1. Union citizens and their family members shall have the right of residence provided for in Article 6, as long as they do not become an unreasonable burden on the social assistance system of the host Member State.

2. Union citizens and their family members shall have the right of residence provided for in Articles 7, 12 and 13 as long as they meet the conditions set out therein.

    In specific cases where there is a reasonable doubt as to whether a Union citizen or his/her family members satisfies the conditions set out in Articles 7, 12 and 13, Member States may verify if these conditions are fulfilled. This verification shall not be carried out systematically.

3. An expulsion measure shall not be the automatic consequence of a Union citizen's or his or her family member's recourse to the social assistance system of the host Member State.

4. By way of derogation from paragraphs 1 and 2 and without prejudice to the provisions of Chapter VI, an expulsion measure may in no case be adopted against Union citizens or their family members if:
    (a) the Union citizens are workers or self-employed persons, or
    (b) the Union citizens entered the territory of the host Member State in order to seek employment. In this case, the Union citizens and their family members may not be expelled for as long as the Union citizens can provide evidence that they are continuing to seek employment and that they have a genuine chance of being engaged.

Article 15 Procedural safeguards

1. The procedures provided for by Articles 30 and 31 shall apply by analogy to all decisions restricting free movement of Union citizens and their family members on grounds other than public policy, public security or public health.

2. Expiry of the identity card or passport on the basis of which the person concerned entered the host Member State and was issued with a registration certificate or residence card shall not constitute a ground for expulsion from the host Member State.

3. The host Member State may not impose a ban on entry in the context of an expulsion decision to which paragraph 1 applies.

Chapter IV RIGHT OF PERMANENT RESIDENCE

SECTION I ELIGIBILITY

Article 16 General rule for Union citizens and their family members

1.   Union citizens who have resided legally for a continuous period of five years in the host Member State shall have the right of permanent residence there. This right shall not be subject to the conditions provided for in Chapter III.

2.   Paragraph 1 shall apply also to family members who are not nationals of a Member State and have legally resided with the Union citizen in the host Member State for a continuous period of five years.

3.   Continuity of residence shall not be affected by temporary absences not exceeding a total of six months a year, or by absences of a longer duration for compulsory military service, or by one absence of a maximum of 12 consecutive months for important reasons such as pregnancy and childbirth, serious illness, study or vocational training, or a posting in another Member State or a third country.

4.   Once acquired, the right of permanent residence shall be lost only through absence from the host Member State for a period exceeding two consecutive years.

Article 17 Exemptions for persons no longer working in the host Member State and their family members

1.   By way of derogation from Article 16, the right of permanent residence in the host Member State shall be enjoyed before completion of a continuous period of five years of residence by:

(a) workers or self-employed persons who, at the time they stop working, have reached the age laid down by the law of that Member State for entitlement to an old age pension or workers who cease paid employment to take early retirement, provided that they have been working in that Member State for at least the preceding twelve months and have resided there continuously for more than three years.

If the law of the host Member State does not grant the right to an old age pension to certain categories of self-employed persons, the age condition shall be deemed to have been met once the person concerned has reached the age of 60;

(b) workers or self-employed persons who have resided continuously in the host Member State for more than two years and stop working there as a result of permanent incapacity to work.

If such incapacity is the result of an accident at work or an occupational disease entitling the person concerned to a benefit payable in full or in part by an institution in the host Member State, no condition shall be imposed as to length of residence;

(c) workers or self-employed persons who, after three years of continuous employment and residence in the host Member State, work in an employed or self-employed capacity in another Member State, while retaining their place of residence in the host Member State, to which they return, as a rule, each day or at least once a week.

For the purposes of entitlement to the rights referred to in points (a) and (b), periods of employment spent in the Member State in which the person concerned is working shall be regarded as having been spent in the host Member State.

Periods of involuntary unemployment duly recorded by the relevant employment office, periods not worked for reasons not of the person's own making and absences from work or cessation of work due to illness or accident shall be regarded as periods of employment.

2. The conditions as to length of residence and employment laid down in point (a) of paragraph 1 and the condition as to length of residence laid down in point (b) of paragraph 1 shall not apply if the worker's or the self-employed person's spouse or partner as referred to in point 2(b) of Article 2 is a national of the host Member State or has lost the nationality of that Member State by marriage to that worker or self-employed person.

3. Irrespective of nationality, the family members of a worker or a self-employed person who are residing with him in the territory of the host Member State shall have the right of permanent residence in that Member State, if the worker or self-employed person has acquired himself the right of permanent residence in that Member State on the basis of paragraph 1.

4. If, however, the worker or self-employed person dies while still working but before acquiring permanent residence status in the host Member State on the basis of paragraph 1, his family members who are residing with him in the host Member State shall acquire the right of permanent residence there, on condition that:
    (a) the worker or self-employed person had, at the time of death, resided continuously on the territory of that Member State for two years; or
    (b) the death resulted from an accident at work or an occupational disease; or
    (c) the surviving spouse lost the nationality of that Member State following marriage to the worker or self-employed person.

Article 18 Acquisition of the right of permanent residence by certain family members who are not nationals of a Member State
Without prejudice to Article 17, the family members of a Union citizen to whom Articles 12(2) and 13(2) apply, who satisfy the conditions laid down therein, shall acquire the right of permanent residence after residing legally for a period of five consecutive years in the host Member State.

SECTION II ADMINISTRATIVE FORMALITIES

Article 19 Document certifying permanent residence for Union citizens
1. Upon application Member States shall issue Union citizens entitled to permanent residence, after having verified duration of residence, with a document certifying permanent residence.

2. The document certifying permanent residence shall be issued as soon as possible.

Article 20 Permanent residence card for family members who are not nationals of a Member State
1. Member States shall issue family members who are not nationals of a Member State entitled to permanent residence with a permanent residence card within six months of the submission of the application. The permanent residence card shall be renewable automatically every 10 years.

2. The application for a permanent residence card shall be submitted before the residence card expires. Failure to comply with the requirement to apply for a permanent residence card may render the person concerned liable to proportionate and non-discriminatory sanctions.

3. Interruption in residence not exceeding two consecutive years shall not affect the validity of the permanent residence card.

Article 21 Continuity of residence
For the purposes of this Directive, continuity of residence may be attested by any means of proof in use in the host Member State. Continuity of residence is broken by any expulsion decision duly enforced against the person concerned.

Chapter V PROVISIONS COMMON TO THE RIGHT OF RESIDENCE AND THE RIGHT OF PERMANENT RESIDENCE

Article 22 Territorial scope

The right of residence and the right of permanent residence shall cover the whole territory of the host Member State. Member States may impose territorial restrictions on the right of residence and the right of permanent residence only where the same restrictions apply to their own nationals.

Article 23 Related rights

Irrespective of nationality, the family members of a Union citizen who have the right of residence or the right of permanent residence in a Member State shall be entitled to take up employment or self-employment there.

Article 24 Equal treatment

1.   Subject to such specific provisions as are expressly provided for in the Treaty and secondary law, all Union citizens residing on the basis of this Directive in the territory of the host Member State shall enjoy equal treatment with the nationals of that Member State within the scope of the Treaty. The benefit of this right shall be extended to family members who are not nationals of a Member State and who have the right of residence or permanent residence.

2.   By way of derogation from paragraph 1, the host Member State shall not be obliged to confer entitlement to social assistance during the first three months of residence or, where appropriate, the longer period provided for in Article 14(4)(b), nor shall it be obliged, prior to acquisition of the right of permanent residence, to grant maintenance aid for studies, including vocational training, consisting in student grants or student loans to persons other than workers, self-employed persons, persons who retain such status and members of their families.

Article 25 General provisions concerning residence documents

1.   Possession of a registration certificate as referred to in Article 8, of a document certifying permanent residence, of a certificate attesting submission of an application for a family member residence card, of a residence card or of a permanent residence card, may under no circumstances be made a precondition for the exercise of a right or the completion of an administrative formality, as entitlement to rights may be attested by any other means of proof.

2.   All documents mentioned in paragraph 1 shall be issued free of charge or for a charge not exceeding that imposed on nationals for the issuing of similar documents.

Article 26 Checks

Member States may carry out checks on compliance with any requirement deriving from their national legislation for non-nationals always to carry their registration certificate or residence card, provided that the same requirement applies to their own nationals as regards their identity card. In the event of failure to comply with this requirement, Member States may impose the same sanctions as those imposed on their own nationals for failure to carry their identity card.

Chapter VI RESTRICTIONS ON THE RIGHT OF ENTRY AND THE RIGHT OF RESIDENCE ON GROUNDS OF PUBLIC POLICY, PUBLIC SECURITY OR PUBLIC HEALTH

Article 27 General principles

1.   Subject to the provisions of this Chapter, Member States may restrict the freedom of movement and residence of Union citizens and their family members, irrespective of

nationality, on grounds of public policy, public security or public health. These grounds shall not be invoked to serve economic ends.

2.   Measures taken on grounds of public policy or public security shall comply with the principle of proportionality and shall be based exclusively on the personal conduct of the individual concerned. Previous criminal convictions shall not in themselves constitute grounds for taking such measures.

The personal conduct of the individual concerned must represent a genuine, present and sufficiently serious threat affecting one of the fundamental interests of society. Justifications that are isolated from the particulars of the case or that rely on considerations of general prevention shall not be accepted.

3.   In order to ascertain whether the person concerned represents a danger for public policy or public security, when issuing the registration certificate or, in the absence of a registration system, not later than three months from the date of arrival of the person concerned on its territory or from the date of reporting his/her presence within the territory, as provided for in Article 5(5), or when issuing the residence card, the host Member State may, should it consider this essential, request the Member State of origin and, if need be, other Member States to provide information concerning any previous police record the person concerned may have. Such enquiries shall not be made as a matter of routine. The Member State consulted shall give its reply within two months.

4.   The Member State which issued the passport or identity card shall allow the holder of the document who has been expelled on grounds of public policy, public security, or public health from another Member State to re-enter its territory without any formality even if the document is no longer valid or the nationality of the holder is in dispute.

Article 28 Protection against expulsion

1.   Before taking an expulsion decision on grounds of public policy or public security, the host Member State shall take account of considerations such as how long the individual concerned has resided on its territory, his/her age, state of health, family and economic situation, social and cultural integration into the host Member State and the extent of his/her links with the country of origin.

2.   The host Member State may not take an expulsion decision against Union citizens or their family members, irrespective of nationality, who have the right of permanent residence on its territory, except on serious grounds of public policy or public security.

3.   An expulsion decision may not be taken against Union citizens, except if the decision is based on imperative grounds of public security, as defined by Member States, if they:
(a) have resided in the host Member State for the previous 10 years; or
(b) are a minor, except if the expulsion is necessary for the best interests of the child, as provided for in the United Nations Convention on the Rights of the Child of 20 November 1989.

Article 29 Public health

1.   The only diseases justifying measures restricting freedom of movement shall be the diseases with epidemic potential as defined by the relevant instruments of the World Health Organisation and other infectious diseases or contagious parasitic diseases if they are the subject of protection provisions applying to nationals of the host Member State.

2.   Diseases occurring after a three-month period from the date of arrival shall not constitute grounds for expulsion from the territory.

3.   Where there are serious indications that it is necessary, Member States may, within three months of the date of arrival, require persons entitled to the right of residence to undergo, free of charge, a medical examination to certify that they are not suffering from any of the conditions referred to in paragraph 1. Such medical examinations may not be required as a matter of routine.

Article 30 Notification of decisions

1.   The persons concerned shall be notified in writing of any decision taken under Article 27(1), in such a way that they are able to comprehend its content and the implications for them.

2.   The persons concerned shall be informed, precisely and in full, of the public policy, public security or public health grounds on which the decision taken in their case is based, unless this is contrary to the interests of State security.

3.   The notification shall specify the court or administrative authority with which the person concerned may lodge an appeal, the time limit for the appeal and, where applicable, the time allowed for the person to leave the territory of the Member State. Save in duly substantiated cases of urgency, the time allowed to leave the territory shall be not less than one month from the date of notification.

Article 31 Procedural safeguards

1.   The persons concerned shall have access to judicial and, where appropriate, administrative redress procedures in the host Member State to appeal against or seek review of any decision taken against them on the grounds of public policy, public security or public health.

2.   Where the application for appeal against or judicial review of the expulsion decision is accompanied by an application for an interim order to suspend enforcement of that decision, actual removal from the territory may not take place until such time as the decision on the interim order has been taken, except:

where the expulsion decision is based on a previous judicial decision; or

where the persons concerned have had previous access to judicial review; or

where the expulsion decision is based on imperative grounds of public security under Article 28(3).

3.   The redress procedures shall allow for an examination of the legality of the decision, as well as of the facts and circumstances on which the proposed measure is based. They shall ensure that the decision is not disproportionate, particularly in view of the requirements laid down in Article 28.

4.   Member States may exclude the individual concerned from their territory pending the redress procedure, but they may not prevent the individual from submitting his/her defence in person, except when his/her appearance may cause serious troubles to public policy or public security or when the appeal or judicial review concerns a denial of entry to the territory.

Article 32 Duration of exclusion orders

1.   Persons excluded on grounds of public policy or public security may submit an application for lifting of the exclusion order after a reasonable period, depending on the circumstances, and in any event after three years from enforcement of the final exclusion order which has been validly adopted in accordance with Community law, by putting forward arguments to establish that there has been a material change in the circumstances which justified the decision ordering their exclusion.

The Member State concerned shall reach a decision on this application within six months of its submission.

2.   The persons referred to in paragraph 1 shall have no right of entry to the territory of the Member State concerned while their application is being considered.

Article 33 Expulsion as a penalty or legal consequence

1.   Expulsion orders may not be issued by the host Member State as a penalty or legal consequence of a custodial penalty, unless they conform to the requirements of Articles 27, 28 and 29.

2.   If an expulsion order, as provided for in paragraph 1, is enforced more than two years after it was issued, the Member State shall check that the individual concerned is currently and genuinely a threat to public policy or public security and shall assess whether there has been any material change in the circumstances since the expulsion order was issued.

Chapter VII FINAL PROVISIONS

Article 34 Publicity

Member States shall disseminate information concerning the rights and obligations of Union citizens and their family members on the subjects covered by this Directive, particularly by means of awareness-raising campaigns conducted through national and local media and other means of communication.

Article 35 Abuse of rights

Member States may adopt the necessary measures to refuse, terminate or withdraw any right conferred by this Directive in the case of abuse of rights or fraud, such as marriages of convenience. Any such measure shall be proportionate and subject to the procedural safeguards provided for in Articles 30 and 31.

Article 36 Sanctions

Member States shall lay down provisions on the sanctions applicable to breaches of national rules adopted for the implementation of this Directive and shall take the measures required for their application. The sanctions laid down shall be effective and proportionate. Member States shall notify the Commission of these provisions not later than 30 April 2006 and as promptly as possible in the case of any subsequent changes.

Article 37 More favourable national provisions

The provisions of this Directive shall not affect any laws, regulations or administrative provisions laid down by a Member State which would be more favourable to the persons covered by this Directive.

Article 38 Repeals

1.   Articles 10 and 11 of Regulation (EEC) No 1612/68 shall be repealed with effect from 30 April 2006.

2.   Directives 64/221/EEC, 68/360/EEC, 72/194/EEC, 73/148/EEC, 75/34/EEC, 75/35/ EEC, 90/364/EEC, 90/365/EEC and 93/96/EEC shall be repealed with effect from 30 April 2006.

3.   References made to the repealed provisions and Directives shall be construed as being made to this Directive.

Article 39 Report

No later than 30 April 2008 the Commission shall submit a report on the application of this Directive to the European Parliament and the Council, together with any necessary proposals, notably on the opportunity to extend the period of time during which Union citizens and their family members may reside in the territory of the host Member State without any conditions. The Member States shall provide the Commission with the information needed to produce the report.

Article 40 Transposition

1.   Member States shall bring into force the laws, regulations and administrative provisions necessary to comply with this Directive by 30 April 2006.

When Member States adopt those measures, they shall contain a reference to this Directive or shall be accompanied by such a reference on the occasion of their official publication. The methods of making such reference shall be laid down by the Member States.

2.   Member States shall communicate to the Commission the text of the provisions of national law which they adopt in the field covered by this Directive together with a table showing how the provisions of this Directive correspond to the national provisions adopted.

Article 41 Entry into force

This Directive shall enter into force on the day of its publication in the *Official Journal of the European Union.*

Article 42 Addressees

This Directive is addressed to the Member States.

(*Date of signing and signatories omitted*)

DIRECTIVE 2005/36/EC OF THE EUROPEAN PARLIAMENT AND OF THE COUNCIL OF 7 SEPTEMBER 2005

on the recognition of professional qualifications
OJ L 255, 30.9.2005, p. 22, as amended and corrected*

....

(*As amended by: Council Directive 2006/100/EC of 20 November 2006 L 363/141, 20.12.2006; Commission Regulation (EC) No 1430/2007 of 5 December 2007 L 320/3, 6.12.2007; Commission Regulation (EC) No 755/2008 of 31 July 2008 L205/10, 1.8.2008; and Regulation (EC) No 1137/2008 of the European Parliament and of the Council of 22 October 2008 L 311/1, 21.11.2008). Corrected at: OJ L 271/18, 16.10.2007, (2005/36/EC); and OJ L 93/28, 4.4.2008, (2005/36/EC).[1]

(*Annexes II–VII are omitted due to their length*)

THE EUROPEAN PARLIAMENT AND THE COUNCIL OF THE EUROPEAN UNION,

Having regard to the Treaty establishing the European Community, and in particular Article 40, Article 47(1), the first and third sentences of Article 47(2), and Article 55 thereof,

---

[1]   EDITOR'S NOTE: As of 1 June 2010 this Directive has not been amended following the adoption of the Treaty of Lisbon. It includes references to the old Treaty article numbers. Reference should be made to the Tables of Equivalences accompanying the consolidated Treaties in Part II of this edition for the conversion of old Treaty article numbers to new ones.

Having regard to the proposal from the Commission,

Having regard to the opinion of the European Economic and Social Committee,

Acting in accordance with the procedure laid down in Article 251 of the Treaty,

Whereas:

(1)   Pursuant to Article 3(1)(c) of the Treaty, the abolition, as between Member States, of obstacles to the free movement of persons and services is one of the objectives of the Community. For nationals of the Member States, this includes, in particular, the right to pursue a profession, in a self-employed or employed capacity, in a Member State other than the one in which they have obtained their professional qualifications. In addition, Article 47(1) of the Treaty lays down that directives shall be issued for the mutual recognition of diplomas, certificates and other evidence of formal qualifications.

(Recital 2 omitted)

(3)   The guarantee conferred by this Directive on persons having acquired their professional qualifications in a Member State to have access to the same profession and pursue it in another Member State with the same rights as nationals is without prejudice to compliance by the migrant professional with any non-discriminatory conditions of pursuit which might be laid down by the latter Member State, provided that these are objectively justified and proportionate.

(Remainder of the preamble and all footnotes omitted)

TITLE I GENERAL PROVISIONS

Article 1 Purpose

This Directive establishes rules according to which a Member State which makes access to or pursuit of a regulated profession in its territory contingent upon possession of specific professional qualifications (referred to hereinafter as the host Member State) shall recognise professional qualifications obtained in one or more other Member States (referred to hereinafter as the home Member State) and which allow the holder of the said qualifications to pursue the same profession there, for access to and pursuit of that profession.

Article 2 Scope

1.   This Directive shall apply to all nationals of a Member State wishing to pursue a regulated profession in a Member State, including those belonging to the liberal professions, other than that in which they obtained their professional qualifications, on either a self-employed or employed basis.

2.   Each Member State may permit Member State nationals in possession of evidence of professional qualifications not obtained in a Member State to pursue a regulated profession within the meaning of Article 3(1)(a) on its territory in accordance with its rules. In the case of professions covered by Title III, Chapter III, this initial recognition shall respect the minimum training conditions laid down in that Chapter.

3.   Where, for a given regulated profession, other specific arrangements directly related to the recognition of professional qualifications are established in a separate instrument of Community law, the corresponding provisions of this Directive shall not apply.

Article 3 Definitions

1.   For the purposes of this Directive, the following definitions apply:

(a) "regulated profession": a professional activity or group of professional activities, access to which, the pursuit of which, or one of the modes of pursuit of which is subject, directly or indirectly, by virtue of legislative, regulatory or administrative provisions to the possession of specific professional qualifications; in particular, the use of a professional title limited by legislative, regulatory or administrative provisions to holders of a given professional qualification shall constitute a mode of pursuit. Where the first sentence of this definition does not apply, a profession referred to in paragraph 2 shall be treated as a regulated profession;

(b) "professional qualifications": qualifications attested by evidence of formal qualifications, an attestation of competence referred to in Article 11, point (a) (i) and/or professional experience;

(c) "evidence of formal qualifications": diplomas, certificates and other evidence issued by an authority in a Member State designated pursuant to legislative, regulatory or administrative provisions of that Member State and certifying successful completion of professional training obtained mainly in the Community. Where the first sentence of this definition does not apply, evidence of formal qualifications referred to in paragraph 3 shall be treated as evidence of formal qualifications;

(d) "competent authority": any authority or body empowered by a Member State specifically to issue or receive training diplomas and other documents or information and to receive the applications, and take the decisions, referred to in this Directive;

(e) "regulated education and training": any training which is specifically geared to the pursuit of a given profession and which comprises a course or courses complemented, where appropriate, by professional training, or probationary or professional practice. The structure and level of the professional training, probationary or professional practice shall be determined by the laws, regulations or administrative provisions of the Member State concerned or monitored or approved by the authority designated for that purpose;

(f) "professional experience": the actual and lawful pursuit of the profession concerned in a Member State;

(g) "adaptation period": the pursuit of a regulated profession in the host Member State under the responsibility of a qualified member of that profession, such period of supervised practice possibly being accompanied by further training. This period of supervised practice shall be the subject of an assessment. The detailed rules governing the adaptation period and its assessment as well as the status of a migrant under supervision shall be laid down by the competent authority in the host Member State.

The status enjoyed in the host Member State by the person undergoing the period of supervised practice, in particular in the matter of right of residence as well as obligations, social rights and benefits, allowances and remuneration, shall be established by the competent authorities in that Member State in accordance with applicable Community law;

(h) "aptitude test": a test limited to the professional knowledge of the applicant, made by the competent authorities of the host Member State with the aim of assessing the ability of the applicant to pursue a regulated profession in that Member State. In order to permit this test to be carried out, the competent authorities shall draw up a list of subjects which, on the basis of a comparison of the education and training required in the Member State and that received by the applicant, are not covered by the diploma or other evidence of formal qualifications possessed by the applicant. The aptitude test must take account of the fact that the applicant is a qualified professional in the home Member State or the Member State from which he comes. It shall cover subjects to be selected from those on the list, knowledge of which is essential in order to be able to pursue the profession in the host Member State. The test may also include knowledge of the professional rules applicable to the activities in question in the host Member State.

The detailed application of the aptitude test and the status, in the host Member State, of the applicant who wishes to prepare himself for the aptitude test in that State shall be determined by the competent authorities in that Member State;

(i) "manager of an undertaking": any person who in an undertaking in the occupational field in question has pursued an activity:

(i) as a manager of an undertaking or a manager of a branch of an undertaking; or

(ii) as a deputy to the proprietor or the manager of an undertaking where that post involves responsibility equivalent to that of the proprietor or manager represented; or

(iii) in a managerial post with duties of a commercial and/or technical nature and with responsibility for one or more departments of the undertaking.

2. A profession practised by the members of an association or organisation listed in Annex I shall be treated as a regulated profession.

The purpose of the associations or organisations referred to in the first subparagraph is, in particular, to promote and maintain a high standard in the professional field concerned. To that end they are recognised in a special form by a Member State and award evidence of formal qualifications to their members, ensure that their members respect the rules of professional conduct which they prescribe, and confer on them the right to use a title or designatory letters or to benefit from a status corresponding to those formal qualifications.

On each occasion that a Member State grants recognition to an association or organisation referred to in the first subparagraph, it shall inform the Commission, which shall publish an appropriate notification in the *Official Journal of the European Union*.

3. Evidence of formal qualifications issued by a third country shall be regarded as evidence of formal qualifications if the holder has three years' professional experience in the profession concerned on the territory of the Member State which recognised that evidence of formal qualifications in accordance with Article 2(2), certified by that Member State.

Article 4 Effects of recognition

1. The recognition of professional qualifications by the host Member State allows the beneficiary to gain access in that Member State to the same profession as that for which he is qualified in the home Member State and to pursue it in the host Member State under the same conditions as its nationals.

2. For the purposes of this Directive, the profession which the applicant wishes to pursue in the host Member State is the same as that for which he is qualified in his home Member State if the activities covered are comparable.

TITLE II FREE PROVISION OF SERVICES

Article 5 Principle of the free provision of services

1. Without prejudice to specific provisions of Community law, as well as to Articles 6 and 7 of this Directive, Member States shall not restrict, for any reason relating to professional qualifications, the free provision of services in another Member State:

(a) if the service provider is legally established in a Member State for the purpose of pursuing the same profession there (hereinafter referred to as the Member State of establishment), and

(b) where the service provider moves, if he has pursued that profession in the Member State of establishment for at least two years during the 10 years preceding the provision of services when the profession is not regulated in that Member State. The condition requiring two years' pursuit shall not apply when either the profession or the education and training leading to the profession is regulated.

2.   The provisions of this title shall only apply where the service provider moves to the territory of the host Member State to pursue, on a temporary and occasional basis, the profession referred to in paragraph 1.

The temporary and occasional nature of the provision of services shall be assessed case by case, in particular in relation to its duration, its frequency, its regularity and its continuity.

3.   Where a service provider moves, he shall be subject to professional rules of a professional, statutory or administrative nature which are directly linked to professional qualifications, such as the definition of the profession, the use of titles and serious professional malpractice which is directly and specifically linked to consumer protection and safety, as well as disciplinary provisions which are applicable in the host Member State to professionals who pursue the same profession in that Member State.

Article 6   Exemptions

Pursuant to Article 5(1), the host Member State shall exempt service providers established in another Member State from the requirements which it places on professionals established in its territory relating to:

(a)   authorisation by, registration with or membership of a professional organisation or body. In order to facilitate the application of disciplinary provisions in force on their territory according to Article 5(3), Member States may provide either for automatic temporary registration with or for pro forma membership of such a professional organisation or body, provided that such registration or membership does not delay or complicate in any way the provision of services and does not entail any additional costs for the service provider. A copy of the declaration and, where applicable, of the renewal referred to in Article 7(1), accompanied, for professions which have implications for public health and safety referred to in Article 7(4) or which benefit from automatic recognition under Title III Chapter III, by a copy of the documents referred to in Article 7(2) shall be sent by the competent authority to the relevant professional organisation or body, and this shall constitute automatic temporary registration or pro forma membership for this purpose;

(b)   registration with a public social security body for the purpose of settling accounts with an insurer relating to activities pursued for the benefit of insured persons.

The service provider shall, however, inform in advance or, in an urgent case, afterwards, the body referred to in point (b) of the services which he has provided.

Article 7   Declaration to be made in advance, if the service provider moves

1.   Member States may require that, where the service provider first moves from one Member State to another in order to provide services, he shall inform the competent authority in the host Member State in a written declaration to be made in advance including the details of any insurance cover or other means of personal or collective protection with regard to professional liability. Such declaration shall be renewed once a year if the service provider intends to provide temporary or occasional services in that Member State during that year. The service provider may supply the declaration by any means.

2.   Moreover, for the first provision of services or if there is a material change in the situation substantiated by the documents, Member States may require that the declaration be accompanied by the following documents:
(a)   proof of the nationality of the service provider;
(b)   an attestation certifying that the holder is legally established in a Member State for

the purpose of pursuing the activities concerned and that he is not prohibited from practising, even temporarily, at the moment of delivering the attestation;

(c) evidence of professional qualifications;

(d) for cases referred to in Article 5(1)(b), any means of proof that the service provider has pursued the activity concerned for at least two years during the previous ten years;

(e) for professions in the security sector, where the Member State so requires for its own nationals, evidence of no criminal convictions.

3.   The service shall be provided under the professional title of the Member State of establishment, in so far as such a title exists in that Member State for the professional activity in question. That title shall be indicated in the official language or one of the official languages of the Member State of establishment in such a way as to avoid any confusion with the professional title of the host Member State. Where no such professional title exists in the Member State of establishment, the service provider shall indicate his formal qualification in the official language or one of the official languages of that Member State. By way of exception, the service shall be provided under the professional title of the host Member State for cases referred to in Title III Chapter III.

4.   For the first provision of services, in the case of regulated professions having public health or safety implications, which do not benefit from automatic recognition under Title III Chapter III, the competent authority of the host Member State may check the professional qualifications of the service provider prior to the first provision of services. Such a prior check shall be possible only where the purpose of the check is to avoid serious damage to the health or safety of the service recipient due to a lack of professional qualification of the service provider and where this does not go beyond what is necessary for that purpose.

Within a maximum of one month of receipt of the declaration and accompanying documents, the competent authority shall endeavour to inform the service provider either of its decision not to check his qualifications or of the outcome of such check. Where there is a difficulty which would result in delay, the competent authority shall notify the service provider within the first month of the reason for the delay and the timescale for a decision, which must be finalised within the second month of receipt of completed documentation.

Where there is a substantial difference between the professional qualifications of the service provider and the training required in the host Member State, to the extent that that difference is such as to be harmful to public health or safety, the host Member State shall give the service provider the opportunity to show, in particular by means of an aptitude test, that he has acquired the knowledge or competence lacking. In any case, it must be possible to provide the service within one month of a decision being taken in accordance with the previous subparagraph.

In the absence of a reaction of the competent authority within the deadlines set in the previous subparagraphs, the service may be provided.

In cases where qualifications have been verified under this paragraph, the service shall be provided under the professional title of the host Member State.

Article 8 Administrative cooperation

1.   The competent authorities of the host Member State may ask the competent authorities of the Member State of establishment, for each provision of services, to provide any information relevant to the legality of the service provider's establishment and his good conduct, as well as the absence of any disciplinary or criminal sanctions of a professional nature. The competent authorities of the Member State of establishment shall provide this information in accordance with the provisions of Article 56.

2.   The competent authorities shall ensure the exchange of all information necessary for complaints by a recipient of a service against a service provider to be correctly pursued. Recipients shall be informed of the outcome of the complaint.

Article 9 Information to be given to the recipients of the service
In cases where the service is provided under the professional title of the Member State of establishment or under the formal qualification of the service provider, in addition to the other requirements relating to information contained in Community law, the competent authorities of the host Member State may require the service provider to furnish the recipient of the service with any or all of the following information:

(a)   if the service provider is registered in a commercial register or similar public register, the register in which he is registered, his registration number, or equivalent means of identification contained in that register;

(b)   if the activity is subject to authorisation in the Member State of establishment, the name and address of the competent supervisory authority;

(c)   any professional association or similar body with which the service provider is registered;

(d)   the professional title or, where no such title exists, the formal qualification of the service provider and the Member State in which it was awarded;

(e)   if the service provider performs an activity which is subject to VAT, the VAT identification number referred to in Article 22(1) of the sixth Council Directive 77/388/EEC of 17 May 1977 on the harmonisation of the laws of the Member States relating to turnover taxes – Common system of value added tax: uniform basis of assessment [23];

(f)   details of any insurance cover or other means of personal or collective protection with regard to professional liability.

TITLE III FREEDOM OF ESTABLISHMENT

Chapter I GENERAL SYSTEM FOR THE RECOGNITION OF EVIDENCE OF TRAINING

Article 10 Scope
This Chapter applies to all professions which are not covered by Chapters II and III of this Title and in the following cases in which the applicant, for specific and exceptional reasons, does not satisfy the conditions laid down in those Chapters:

(a)   for activities listed in Annex IV, when the migrant does not meet the requirements set out in Articles 17, 18 and 19;

(b)   for doctors with basic training, specialised doctors, nurses responsible for general care, dental practitioners, specialised dental practitioners, veterinary surgeons, midwives, pharmacists and architects, when the migrant does not meet the requirements of effective and lawful professional practice referred to in Articles 23, 27, 33, 37, 39, 43 and 49;

(c)   for architects, when the migrant holds evidence of formal qualification not listed in Annex V, point 5.7;

(d)   without prejudice to Article 21(1), 23 and 27, for doctors, nurses, dental practitioners, veterinary surgeons, midwives, pharmacists and architects holding evidence of formal qualifications as a specialist who must have taken part in the training leading to the possession of a title listed in Annex V, points 5.1.1, 5.2.2, 5.3.2, 5.4.2, 5.5.2, 5.6.2 and 5.7.1, and solely for the purpose of the recognition of the relevant specialty;

(e)   for nurses responsible for general care and specialized nurses holding evidence of formal qualifications as a specialist who have taken part in the training leading to the possession of a title listed in Annex V, point 5.2.2, when the migrant seeks recognition in another Member State where the relevant professional activities are pursued by specialised nurses without training as general care nurse;

(f)   for specialised nurses without training as general care nurse, when the migrant seeks recognition in another Member State where the relevant professional activities are pursued by nurses responsible for general care, specialised nurses without training as general care nurse or specialised nurses holding evidence of formal qualifications as a specialist who have taken part in the training leading to the possession of the titles listed in Annex V, point 5.22;

(g)   for migrants meeting the requirements set out in Article 3(3).

Article 11 Levels of qualification

For the purpose of applying Article 13, the professional qualifications are grouped under the following levels as described below:

(a)   an attestation of competence issued by a competent authority in the home Member State designated pursuant to legislative, regulatory or administrative provisions of that Member State, on the basis of:
- (i)   either a training course not forming part of a certificate or diploma within the meaning of points (b), (c), (d) or (e), or a specific examination without prior training, or full-time pursuit of the profession in a Member State for three consecutive years or for an equivalent duration on a part-time basis during the previous 10 years,
- (ii)   or general primary or secondary education, attesting that the holder has acquired general knowledge;

(b)   a certificate attesting to a successful completion of a secondary course,
- (i)   either general in character, supplemented by a course of study or professional training other than those referred to in point (c) and/or by the probationary or professional practice required in addition to that course,
- (ii)   or technical or professional in character, supplemented where appropriate by a course of study or professional training as referred to in point (i), and/or by the probationary or professional practice required in addition to that course;

(c)   a diploma certifying successful completion of
- (i)   either training at post-secondary level other than that referred to in points (d) and (e) of a duration of at least one year or of an equivalent duration on a part-time basis, one of the conditions of entry of which is, as a general rule, the successful completion of the secondary course required to obtain entry to university or higher education or the completion of equivalent school education of the second secondary level, as well as the professional training which may be required in addition to that post-secondary course; or
- (ii)   in the case of a regulated profession, training with a special structure, included in Annex II, equivalent to the level of training provided for under (i), which provides a comparable professional standard and which prepares the trainee for a comparable level of responsibilities and functions;

(d)   a diploma certifying successful completion of training at post-secondary level of at least three and not more than four years' duration, or of an equivalent duration on a part-time basis, at a university or establishment of higher education or another establishment providing the same level of training, as well as the professional training which may be required in addition to that post-secondary course;

(e)   a diploma certifying that the holder has successfully completed a post-secondary course of at least four years' duration, or of an equivalent duration on a part-time basis, at a university or establishment of higher education or another establishment of equivalent level and, where appropriate, that he has successfully completed the professional training required in addition to the post-secondary course.

The Commission may adapt the list in Annex II to take account of training which meets the requirements provided for in point (c)(ii) of the first paragraph. Those measures, designed to amend non-essential elements of this Directive, shall be adopted in accordance with the regulatory procedure with scrutiny referred to in Article 58(3).

Article 12 Equal treatment of qualifications

Any evidence of formal qualifications or set of evidence of formal qualifications issued by a competent authority in a Member State, certifying successful completion of training in the Community which is recognised by that Member State as being of an equivalent level and which confers on the holder the same rights of access to or pursuit of a profession or prepares for the pursuit of that profession, shall be treated as evidence of formal qualifications of the type covered by Article 11, including the level in question.

Any professional qualification which, although not satisfying the requirements contained in the legislative, regulatory or administrative provisions in force in the home Member State for access to or the pursuit of a profession, confers on the holder acquired rights by virtue of these provisions, shall also be treated as such evidence of formal qualifications under the same conditions as set out in the first subparagraph. This applies in particular if the home Member State raises the level of training required for admission to a profession and for its exercise, and if an individual who has undergone former training, which does not meet the requirements of the new qualification, benefits from acquired rights by virtue of national legislative, regulatory or administrative provisions; in such case this former training is considered by the host Member State, for the purposes of the application of Article 13, as corresponding to the level of the new training.

Article 13 Conditions for recognition

1. If access to or pursuit of a regulated profession in a host Member State is contingent upon possession of specific professional qualifications, the competent authority of that Member State shall permit access to and pursuit of that profession, under the same conditions as apply to its nationals, to applicants possessing the attestation of competence or evidence of formal qualifications required by another Member State in order to gain access to and pursue that profession on its territory.

    Attestations of competence or evidence of formal qualifications shall satisfy the following conditions:
    (a) they shall have been issued by a competent authority in a Member State, designated in accordance with the legislative, regulatory or administrative provisions of that Member State;
    (b) they shall attest a level of professional qualification at least equivalent to the level immediately prior to that which is required in the host Member State, as described in Article 11.

2. Access to and pursuit of the profession, as described in paragraph 1, shall also be granted to applicants who have pursued the profession referred to in that paragraph on a full-time basis for two years during the previous 10 years in another Member State which does not regulate that profession, providing they possess one or more attestations of competence or documents providing evidence of formal qualifications.

    Attestations of competence and evidence of formal qualifications shall satisfy the following conditions:

(a) they shall have been issued by a competent authority in a Member State, designated in accordance with the legislative, regulatory or administrative provisions of that Member State;

(b) they shall attest a level of professional qualification at least equivalent to the level immediately prior to that required in the host Member State, as described in Article 11;

(c) they shall attest that the holder has been prepared for the pursuit of the profession in question.

The two years' professional experience referred to in the first subparagraph may not, however, be required if the evidence of formal qualifications which the applicant possesses certifies regulated education and training within the meaning of Article 3(1)(e) at the levels of qualifications described in Article 11, points (b), (c), (d) or (e). The regulated education and training listed in Annex III shall be considered as such regulated education and training at the level described in Article 11, point (c).

The Commission may adapt the list in Annex III to take account of regulated education and training which provides a comparable professional standard and which prepares the trainee for a comparable level of responsibilities and functions. Those measures, designed to amend non-essential elements of this Directive, shall be adopted in accordance with the regulatory procedure with scrutiny referred to in Article 58(3).

3. By way of derogation from paragraph 1, point (b) and to paragraph 2, point (b), the host Member State shall permit access and pursuit of a regulated profession where access to this profession is contingent in its territory upon possession of a qualification certifying successful completion of higher or university education of four years' duration, and where the applicant possesses a qualification referred to in Article 11, point (c).

Article 14 Compensation measures

1. Article 13 does not preclude the host Member State from requiring the applicant to complete an adaptation period of up to three years or to take an aptitude test if:

(a) the duration of the training of which he provides evidence under the terms of Article 13, paragraph 1 or 2, is at least one year shorter than that required by the host Member State;

(b) the training he has received covers substantially different matters than those covered by the evidence of formal qualifications required in the host Member State;

(c) the regulated profession in the host Member State comprises one or more regulated professional activities which do not exist in the corresponding profession in the applicant's home Member State within the meaning of Article 4(2), and that difference consists in specific training which is required in the host Member State and which covers substantially different matters from those covered by the applicant's attestation of competence or evidence of formal qualifications.

2. If the host Member State makes use of the option provided for in paragraph 1, it must offer the applicant the choice between an adaptation period and an aptitude test.

Where a Member State considers, with respect to a given profession, that it is necessary to derogate from the requirement, set out in the previous subparagraph, that it give the applicant a choice between an adaptation period and an aptitude test, it shall inform the other Member States and the Commission in advance and provide sufficient justification for the derogation.

If, after receiving all necessary information, the Commission considers that the derogation referred to in the second subparagraph is inappropriate or that it is not in accordance with Community law, it shall, within three months, ask the Member State in question to refrain from taking the envisaged measure. In the absence of a response from the Commission within the abovementioned deadline, the derogation may be applied.

3. By way of derogation from the principle of the right of the applicant to choose, as laid down in paragraph 2, for professions whose pursuit requires precise knowledge of national law and in respect of which the provision of advice and/or assistance concerning national law is an essential and constant aspect of the professional activity, the host Member State may stipulate either an adaptation period or an aptitude test.

    This applies also to the cases provided for in Article 10 points (b) and (c), in Article 10 point (d) concerning doctors and dental practitioners in Article 10 point (f) when the migrant seeks recognition in another Member State where the relevant professional activities are pursued by nurses responsible for general care or specialised nurses holding evidence of formal qualifications as a specialist who have taken part in the training leading to the possession of the titles listed in Annex V, point 5.2.2 and in Article 10 point (g).

    In the cases covered by Article 10 point (a), the host Member State may require an adaptation period or an aptitude test if the migrant envisages pursuing professional activities in a self-employed capacity or as a manager of an undertaking which require the knowledge and the application of the specific national rules in force, provided that knowledge and application of those rules are required by the competent authorities of the host Member State for access to such activities by its own nationals.

4. For the purpose of applying paragraph 1 points (b) and (c), "substantially different matters" means matters of which knowledge is essential for pursuing the profession and with regard to which the training received by the migrant shows important differences in terms of duration or content from the training required by the host Member State.

5. Paragraph 1 shall be applied with due regard to the principle of proportionality. In particular, if the host Member State intends to require the applicant to complete an adaptation period or take an aptitude test, it must first ascertain whether the knowledge acquired by the applicant in the course of his professional experience in a Member State or in a third country, is of a nature to cover, in full or in part, the substantial difference referred to in paragraph 4.

Article 15 Waiving of compensation measures on the basis of common platforms
1. For the purpose of this Article, "common platforms" is defined as a set of criteria of professional qualifications which are suitable for compensating for substantial differences which have been identified between the training requirements existing in the various Member States for a given profession. These substantial differences shall be identified by comparison between the duration and contents of the training in at least two thirds of the Member States, including all Member States which regulate this profession. The differences in the contents of the training may result from substantial differences in the scope of the professional activities.

2. Common platforms as defined in paragraph 1 may be submitted to the Commission by Member States or by professional associations or organisations which are representative at national and European level. If the Commission, after consulting the Member States, is of the opinion that a draft common platform facilitates the mutual recognition of professional qualifications, it may present draft measures with a view to their adoption. Those measures, designed to amend non-essential elements of this Directive by supplementing it, shall be adopted in accordance with the regulatory procedure with scrutiny referred to in Article 58(3).

3. Where the applicant's professional qualifications satisfy the criteria established in the measure adopted in accordance with paragraph 2, the host Member State shall waive the application of compensation measures under Article 14.

4.   Paragraphs 1 to 3 shall not affect the competence of Member States to decide the professional qualifications required for the pursuit of professions in their territory as well as the contents and the organisation of their systems of education and professional training.

5.   If a Member State considers that the criteria established in a measure adopted in accordance with paragraph 2 no longer offer adequate guarantees with regard to professional qualifications, it shall inform the Commission accordingly. The Commission shall, if appropriate, present a draft measure for adoption. That measure, designed to amend non-essential elements of this Directive by supplementing it, shall be adopted in accordance with the regulatory procedure with scrutiny referred to in Article 58(3).

6.   The Commission shall, by 20 October 2010, submit to the European Parliament and the Council a report on the operation of this Article and, if necessary, appropriate proposals for amending this Article.

Chapter II RECOGNITION OF PROFESSIONAL EXPERIENCE

Article 16 Requirements regarding professional experience
If, in a Member State, access to or pursuit of one of the activities listed in Annex IV is contingent upon possession of general, commercial or professional knowledge and aptitudes, that Member State shall recognise previous pursuit of the activity in another Member State as sufficient proof of such knowledge and aptitudes. The activity must have been pursued in accordance with Articles 17, 18 and 19.

Article 17 Activities referred to in list I of Annex IV
1.   For the activities in list I of Annex IV, the activity in question must have been previously pursued:
 (a) for six consecutive years on a self-employed basis or as a manager of an undertaking; or
 (b) for three consecutive years on a self-employed basis or as a manager of an undertaking, where the beneficiary proves that he has received previous training of at least three years for the activity in question, evidenced by a certificate recognised by the Member State or judged by a competent professional body to be fully valid; or
 (c) for four consecutive years on a self-employed basis or as a manager of an undertaking, where the beneficiary can prove that he has received, for the activity in question, previous training of at least two years' duration, attested by a certificate recognised by the Member State or judged by a competent professional body to be fully valid; or
 (d) for three consecutive years on a self-employed basis, if the beneficiary can prove that he has pursued the activity in question on an employed basis for at least five years; or
 (e) for five consecutive years in an executive position, of which at least three years involved technical duties and responsibility for at least one department of the company, if the beneficiary can prove that he has received, for the activity in question, previous training of at least three years' duration, as attested by a certificate recognised by the Member State or judged by a competent professional body to be fully valid.

2.   In cases (a) and (d), the activity must not have finished more than 10 years before the date on which the complete application was submitted by the person concerned to the competent authority referred to in Article 56.

3.   Paragraph 1(e) shall not apply to activities in Group ex 855, hairdressing establishments, of the ISIC Nomenclature.

Article 18 Activities referred to in list II of Annex IV
1.   For the activities in list II of Annex IV, the activity in question must have been previously pursued:
(a) for five consecutive years on a self-employed basis or as a manager of an undertaking, or
(b) for three consecutive years on a self-employed basis or as a manager of an undertaking, where the beneficiary proves that he has received previous training of at least three years for the activity in question, evidenced by a certificate recognised by the Member State or judged by a competent professional body to be fully valid, or
(c) for four consecutive years on a self-employed basis or as a manager of an undertaking, where the beneficiary can prove that he has received, for the activity in question, previous training of at least two years' duration, attested by a certificate recognised by the Member State or judged by a competent professional body to be fully valid, or
(d) for three consecutive years on a self-employed basis or as a manager of an undertaking, if the beneficiary can prove that he has pursued the activity in question on an employed basis for at least five years, or
(e) for five consecutive years on an employed basis, if the beneficiary can prove that he has received, for the activity in question, previous training of at least three years' duration, as attested by a certificate recognised by the Member State or judged by a competent professional body to be fully valid, or
(f) for six consecutive years on an employed basis, if the beneficiary can prove that he has received previous training in the activity in question of at least two years' duration, as attested by a certificate recognised by the Member State or judged by a competent professional body to be fully valid.
2.   In cases (a) and (d), the activity must not have finished more than 10 years before the date on which the complete application was submitted by the person concerned to the competent authority referred to in Article 56.

Article 19 Activities referred to in list III of Annex IV
1.   For the activities in list III of Annex IV, the activity in question must have been previously pursued:
(a) for three consecutive years, either on a self-employed basis or as a manager of an undertaking, or
(b) for two consecutive years, either on a self-employed basis or as a manager of an undertaking, if the beneficiary can prove that he has received previous training for the activity in question, as attested by a certificate recognised by the Member State or judged by a competent professional body to be fully valid, or
(c) for two consecutive years, either on a self-employed basis or as a manager of an undertaking, if the beneficiary can prove that he has pursued the activity in question on an employed basis for at least three years, or
(d) for three consecutive years, on an employed basis, if the beneficiary can prove that he has received previous training for the activity in question, as attested by a certificate recognised by the Member State or judged by a competent professional body to be fully valid.
2.   In cases (a) and (c), the activity must not have finished more than 10 years before the date on which the complete application was submitted by the person concerned to the competent authority referred to in Article 56.

Article 20 Adaptation of the lists of activities in Annex IV
The Commission may adapt the lists of activities in Annex IV which are the subject of recognition of professional experience pursuant to Article 16 with a view to updating or

clarifying the nomenclature, provided that this does not involve any change in the activities related to the individual categories. Those measures, designed to amend non-essential elements of this Directive, shall be adopted in accordance with the regulatory procedure with scrutiny referred to in Article 58(3).

Chapter III RECOGNITION ON THE BASIS OF COORDINATION OF MINIMUM TRAINING CONDITIONS

SECTION 1 GENERAL PROVISIONS

Article 21 Principle of automatic recognition

1. Each Member State shall recognise evidence of formal qualifications as doctor giving access to the professional activities of doctor with basic training and specialised doctor, as nurse responsible for general care, as dental practitioner, as specialised dental practitioner, as veterinary surgeon, as pharmacist and as architect, listed in Annex V, points 5.1.1, 5.1.2, 5.2.2, 5.3.2, 5.3.3, 5.4.2, 5.6.2 and 5.7.1 respectively, which satisfy the minimum training conditions referred to in Articles 24, 25, 31, 34, 35, 38, 44 and 46 respectively, and shall, for the purposes of access to and pursuit of the professional activities, give such evidence the same effect on its territory as the evidence of formal qualifications which it itself issues.

    Such evidence of formal qualifications must be issued by the competent bodies in the Member States and accompanied, where appropriate, by the certificates listed in Annex V, points 5.1.1, 5.1.2, 5.2.2, 5.3.2, 5.3.3, 5.4.2, 5.6.2 and 5.7.1 respectively.

    The provisions of the first and second subparagraphs do not affect the acquired rights referred to in Articles 23, 27, 33, 37, 39 and 49.

2. Each Member State shall recognise, for the purpose of pursuing general medical practice in the framework of its national social security system, evidence of formal qualifications listed in Annex V, point 5.1.4 and issued to nationals of the Member States by the other Member States in accordance with the minimum training conditions laid down in Article 28.

    The provisions of the previous subparagraph do not affect the acquired rights referred to in Article 30.

3. Each Member State shall recognise evidence of formal qualifications as a midwife, awarded to nationals of Member States by the other Member States, listed in Annex V, point 5.5.2, which complies with the minimum training conditions referred to in Article 40 and satisfies the criteria set out in Article 41, and shall, for the purposes of access to and pursuit of the professional activities, give such evidence the same effect on its territory as the evidence of formal qualifications which it itself issues. This provision does not affect the acquired rights referred to in Articles 23 and 43.

4. Member States shall not be obliged to give effect to evidence of formal qualifications referred to in Annex V, point 5.6.2, for the setting up of new pharmacies open to the public. For the purposes of this paragraph, pharmacies which have been open for less than three years shall also be considered as new pharmacies.

5. Evidence of formal qualifications as an architect referred to in Annex V, point 5.7.1, which is subject to automatic recognition pursuant to paragraph 1, proves completion of a course of training which began not earlier than during the academic reference year referred to in that Annex.

6. Each Member State shall make access to and pursuit of the professional activities of doctors, nurses responsible for general care, dental practitioners, veterinary surgeons,

midwives and pharmacists subject to possession of evidence of formal qualifications referred to in Annex V, points 5.1.1, 5.1.2, 5.1.4, 5.2.2, 5.3.2, 5.3.3, 5.4.2, 5.5.2 and 5.6.2 respectively, attesting that the person concerned has acquired, over the duration of his training, and where appropriate, the knowledge and skills referred to in Articles 24(3), 31(6), 34(3), 38(3), 40(3) and 44(3).

The Commission may adapt the knowledge and skills referred to in Articles 24(3), 31(6), 34(3), 38(3), 40(3) and 44(3) to scientific and technical progress. Those measures, designed to amend non-essential elements of this Directive, shall be adopted in accordance with the regulatory procedure with scrutiny referred to in Article 58(3).

Such updates shall not entail, for any Member State, an amendment of its existing legislative principles regarding the structure of professions as regards training and conditions of access by natural persons.

7.   Each Member State shall notify the Commission of the legislative, regulatory and administrative provisions which it adopts with regard to the issuing of evidence of formal qualifications in the area covered by this Chapter. In addition, for evidence of formal qualifications in the area referred to in Section 8, this notification shall be addressed to the other Member States.

The Commission shall publish an appropriate communication in the *Official Journal of the European Union*, indicating the titles adopted by the Member States for evidence of formal qualifications and, where appropriate, the body which issues the evidence of formal qualifications, the certificate which accompanies it and the corresponding professional title referred to in Annex V, points 5.1.1, 5.1.2, 5.1.3, 5.1.4, 5.2.2, 5.3.2, 5.3.3, 5.4.2, 5.5.2, 5.6.2 and 5.7.1 respectively.

Article 22 Common provisions on training

With regard to the training referred to in Articles 24, 25, 28, 31, 34, 35, 38, 40, 44 and 46:

(a)   Member States may authorise part-time training under conditions laid down by the competent authorities; those authorities shall ensure that the overall duration, level and quality of such training is not lower than that of continuous full-time training;

(b)   in accordance with the procedures specific to each Member State, continuing education and training shall ensure that persons who have completed their studies are able to keep abreast of professional developments to the extent necessary to maintain safe and effective practice.

Article 23 Acquired rights

1.   Without prejudice to the acquired rights specific to the professions concerned, in cases where the evidence of formal qualifications as doctor giving access to the professional activities of doctor with basic training and specialised doctor, as nurse responsible for general care, as dental practitioner, as specialised dental practitioner, as veterinary surgeon, as midwife and as pharmacist held by Member States nationals does not satisfy all the training requirements referred to in Articles 24, 25, 31, 34, 35, 38, 40 and 44, each Member State shall recognise as sufficient proof evidence of formal qualifications issued by those Member States insofar as such evidence attests successful completion of training which began before the reference dates laid down in Annex V, points 5.1.1, 5.1.2, 5.2.2, 5.3.2, 5.3.3, 5.4.2, 5.5.2 and 5.6.2 and is accompanied by a certificate stating that the holders have been effectively and lawfully engaged in the activities in question for at least three consecutive years during the five years preceding the award of the certificate.

2.   The same provisions shall apply to evidence of formal qualifications as doctor giving access to the professional activities of doctor with basic training and specialised doctor, as

nurse responsible for general care, as dental practitioner, as specialised dental practitioner, as veterinary surgeon, as midwife and as pharmacist, obtained in the territory of the former German Democratic Republic, which does not satisfy all the minimum training requirements laid down in Articles 24, 25, 31, 34, 35, 38, 40 and 44 if such evidence certifies successful completion of training which began before:

(a) 3 October 1990 for doctors with basic training, nurses responsible for general care, dental practitioners with basic training, specialised dental practitioners, veterinary surgeons, midwives and pharmacists, and

(b) 3 April 1992 for specialised doctors.

The evidence of formal qualifications referred to in the first subparagraph confers on the holder the right to pursue professional activities throughout German territory under the same conditions as evidence of formal qualifications issued by the competent German authorities referred to in Annex V, points 5.1.1, 5.1.2, 5.2.2, 5.3.2, 5.3.3, 5.4.2, 5.5.2 and 5.6.2.

3.   Without prejudice to the provisions of Article 37(1), each Member State shall recognise evidence of formal qualifications as doctor giving access to the professional activities of doctor with basic training and specialised doctor, as nurse responsible for general care, as veterinary surgeon, as midwife, as pharmacist and as architect held by Member States nationals and issued by the former Czechoslovakia, or whose training commenced, for the Czech Republic and Slovakia, before 1 January 1993, where the authorities of either of the two aforementioned Member States attest that such evidence of formal qualifications has the same legal validity within their territory as the evidence of formal qualifications which they issue and, with respect to architects, as the evidence of formal qualifications specified for those Member States in Annex VI, point 6, as regards access to the professional activities of doctor with basic training, specialised doctor, nurse responsible for general care, veterinary surgeon, midwife, pharmacist with respect to the activities referred to in Article 45(2), and architect with respect to the activities referred to in Article 48, and the pursuit of such activities.

Such an attestation must be accompanied by a certificate issued by those same authorities stating that such persons have effectively and lawfully been engaged in the activities in question within their territory for at least three consecutive years during the five years prior to the date of issue of the certificate.

4.   Each Member State shall recognise evidence of formal qualifications as doctor giving access to the professional activities of doctor with basic training and specialised doctor, as nurse responsible for general care, as dental practitioner, as specialised dental practitioner, as veterinary surgeon, as midwife, as pharmacist and as architect held by nationals of the Member States and issued by the former Soviet Union, or whose training commenced

(a)   for Estonia, before 20 August 1991,

(b)   for Latvia, before 21 August 1991,

(c)   for Lithuania, before 11 March 1990,

where the authorities of any of the three aforementioned Member States attest that such evidence has the same legal validity within their territory as the evidence which they issue and, with respect to architects, as the evidence of formal qualifications specified for those Member States in Annex VI, point 6, as regards access to the professional activities of doctor with basic training, specialised doctor, nurse responsible for general care, dental practitioner, specialised dental practitioner, veterinary surgeon, midwife, pharmacist with respect to the activities referred to in Article 45(2), and architect with respect to the activities referred to in Article 48, and the pursuit of such activities.

Such an attestation must be accompanied by a certificate issued by those same authorities stating that such persons have effectively and lawfully been engaged in the activities in question within their territory for at least three consecutive years during the five years prior to the date of issue of the certificate.

With regard to evidence of formal qualifications as veterinary surgeons issued by the former Soviet Union or in respect of which training commenced, for Estonia, before 20 August 1991, the attestation referred to in the preceding subparagraph must be accompanied by a certificate issued by the Estonian authorities stating that such persons have effectively and lawfully been engaged in the activities in question within their territory for at least five consecutive years during the seven years prior to the date of issue of the certificate.

5. Each Member State shall recognise evidence of formal qualifications as doctor giving access to the professional activities of doctor with basic training and specialised doctor, as nurse responsible for general care, as dental practitioner, as specialised dental practitioner, as veterinary surgeon, as midwife, as pharmacist and as architect held by nationals of the Member States and issued by the former Yugoslavia, or whose training commenced, for Slovenia, before 25 June 1991, where the authorities of the aforementioned Member State attest that such evidence has the same legal validity within their territory as the evidence which they issue and, with respect to architects, as the evidence of formal qualifications specified for those Member States in Annex VI, point 6, as regards access to the professional activities of doctor with basic training, specialised doctor, nurse responsible for general care, dental practitioner, specialised dental practitioner, veterinary surgeon, midwife, pharmacist with respect to the activities referred to in Article 45(2), and architect with respect to the activities referred to in Article 48, and the pursuit of such activities.

Such an attestation must be accompanied by a certificate issued by those same authorities stating that such persons have effectively and lawfully been engaged in the activities in question within their territory for at least three consecutive years during the five years prior to the date of issue of the certificate.

6. Each Member State shall recognise as sufficient proof for Member State nationals whose evidence of formal qualifications as a doctor, nurse responsible for general care, dental practitioner, veterinary surgeon, midwife and pharmacist does not correspond to the titles given for that Member State in Annex V, points 5.1.1, 5.1.2, 5.1.3, 5.1.4, 5.2.2, 5.3.2, 5.3.3, 5.4.2, 5.5.2 and 5.6.2, evidence of formal qualifications issued by those Member States accompanied by a certificate issued by the competent authorities or bodies.

The certificate referred to in the first subparagraph shall state that the evidence of formal qualifications certifies successful completion of training in accordance with Articles 24, 25, 28, 31, 34, 35, 38, 40 and 44 respectively and is treated by the Member State which issued it in the same way as the qualifications whose titles are listed in Annex V, points 5.1.1, 5.1.2, 5.1.3, 5.1.4, 5.2.2, 5.3.2, 5.3.3, 5.4.2, 5.5.2 and 5.6.2.

Article 23a Specific circumstances

1. By way of derogation from the present Directive, Bulgaria may authorise the holders of the qualification of 'фелдшер' (feldsher) awarded in Bulgaria before 31 December 1999 and exercising this profession under the Bulgarian national social security scheme on 1 January 2000 to continue to exercise the said profession, even if parts of their activity fall under the provisions of the present Directive concerning doctors of medicine and nurses responsible for general care respectively.

2. The holders of the Bulgarian qualification of 'фелдшер' (feldsher) referred to in paragraph 1 are not entitled to obtain professional recognition in other Member States as doctors of medicine nor as nurses responsible for general care under this Directive.

SECTION 2 DOCTORS OF MEDICINE

Article 24 Basic medical training

1.   Admission to basic medical training shall be contingent upon possession of a diploma or certificate providing access, for the studies in question, to universities.

2.   Basic medical training shall comprise a total of at least six years of study or 5500 hours of theoretical and practical training provided by, or under the supervision of, a university.

For persons who began their studies before 1 January 1972, the course of training referred to in the first subparagraph may comprise six months of full-time practical training at university level under the supervision of the competent authorities.

3.   Basic medical training shall provide an assurance that the person in question has acquired the following knowledge and skills:
   (a)   adequate knowledge of the sciences on which medicine is based and a good understanding of the scientific methods including the principles of measuring biological functions, the evaluation of scientifically established facts and the analysis of data;
   (b)   sufficient understanding of the structure, functions and behaviour of healthy and sick persons, as well as relations between the state of health and physical and social surroundings of the human being;
   (c)   adequate knowledge of clinical disciplines and practices, providing him with a coherent picture of mental and physical diseases, of medicine from the points of view of prophylaxis, diagnosis and therapy and of human reproduction;
   (d)   suitable clinical experience in hospitals under appropriate supervision.

Article 25 Specialist medical training

1.   Admission to specialist medical training shall be contingent upon completion and validation of six years of study as part of a training programme referred to in Article 24 in the course of which the trainee has acquired the relevant knowledge of basic medicine.

2.   Specialist medical training shall comprise theoretical and practical training at a university or medical teaching hospital or, where appropriate, a medical care establishment approved for that purpose by the competent authorities or bodies.

The Member States shall ensure that the minimum duration of specialist medical training courses referred to in Annex V, point 5.1.3 is not less than the duration provided for in that point. Training shall be given under the supervision of the competent authorities or bodies. It shall include personal participation of the trainee specialised doctor in the activity and responsibilities entailed by the services in question.

3.   Training shall be given on a full-time basis at specific establishments which are recognised by the competent authorities. It shall entail participation in the full range of medical activities of the department where the training is given, including duty on call, in such a way that the trainee specialist devotes all his professional activity to his practical and theoretical training throughout the entire working week and throughout the year, in accordance with the procedures laid down by the competent authorities. Accordingly, these posts shall be the subject of appropriate remuneration.

4.   The Member States shall make the issuance of evidence of specialist medical training contingent upon possession of evidence of basic medical training referred to in Annex V, point 5.1.1.

5.   The Commission may adapt the minimum periods of training referred to in Annex V, point 5.1.3, to scientific and technical progress. Those measures, designed to amend

non-essential elements of this Directive, shall be adopted in accordance with the regulatory procedure with scrutiny referred to in Article 58(3).

Article 26 Types of specialist medical training

Evidence of formal qualifications as a specialised doctor referred to in Article 21 is such evidence awarded by the competent authorities or bodies referred to in Annex V, point 5.1.2 as corresponds, for the specialised training in question, to the titles in use in the various Member States and referred to in Annex V, point 5.1.3.

The Commission may include in Annex V, point 5.1.3, new medical specialties common to at least two-fifths of the Member States with a view to updating this Directive in the light of changes in national legislation. That measure, designed to amend non-essential elements of this Directive, shall be adopted in accordance with the regulatory procedure with scrutiny referred to in Article 58(3).

Article 27 Acquired rights specific to specialised doctors

1.   A host Member State may require of specialised doctors whose part-time specialist medical training was governed by legislative, regulatory and administrative provisions in force as of 20 June 1975 and who began their specialist training no later than 31 December 1983 that their evidence of formal qualifications be accompanied by a certificate stating that they have been effectively and lawfully engaged in the relevant activities for at least three consecutive years during the five years preceding the award of that certificate.

2.   Every Member State shall recognise the qualification of specialised doctors awarded in Spain to doctors who completed their specialist training before 1 January 1995, even if that training does not satisfy the minimum training requirements provided for in Article 25, in so far as that qualification is accompanied by a certificate issued by the competent Spanish authorities and attesting that the person concerned has passed the examination in specific professional competence held in the context of exceptional measures concerning recognition laid down in Royal Decree 1497/99, with a view to ascertaining that the person concerned possesses a level of knowledge and skill comparable to that of doctors who possess a qualification as a specialised doctor defined for Spain in Annex V, points 5.1.2 and 5.1.3.

3.   Every Member State which has repealed its legislative, regulatory or administrative provisions relating to the award of evidence of formal qualifications as a specialised doctor referred to in Annex V, points 5.1.2 and 5.1.3 and which has adopted measures relating to acquired rights benefiting its nationals, shall grant nationals of other Member States the right to benefit from those measures, in so far as such evidence of formal qualifications was issued before the date on which the host Member State ceased to issue such evidence for the specialty in question.

The dates on which these provisions were repealed are set out in Annex V, point 5.1.3.

Article 28 Specific training in general medical practice

1.   Admission to specific training in general medical practice shall be contingent on the completion and validation of six years of study as part of a training programme referred to in Article 24.

2.   The specific training in general medical practice leading to the award of evidence of formal qualifications issued before 1 January 2006 shall be of a duration of at least two years on a full-time basis. In the case of evidence of formal qualifications issued after that date, the training shall be of a duration of at least three years on a full-time basis.

Where the training programme referred to in Article 24 comprises practical training given by an approved hospital possessing appropriate general medical equipment and services or as part of an approved general medical practice or an approved centre in which doctors provide primary medical care, the duration of that practical training may, up to a maximum of one year, be included in the duration provided for in the first subparagraph for certificates of training issued on or after 1 January 2006.

The option provided for in the second subparagraph shall be available only for Member States in which the specific training in general medical practice lasted two years as of 1 January 2001.

3.   The specific training in general medical practice shall be carried out on a full-time basis, under the supervision of the competent authorities or bodies. It shall be more practical than theoretical.

The practical training shall be given, on the one hand, for at least six months in an approved hospital possessing appropriate equipment and services and, on the other hand, for at least six months as part of an approved general medical practice or an approved centre at which doctors provide primary health care.

The practical training shall take place in conjunction with other health establishments or structures concerned with general medicine. Without prejudice to the minimum periods laid down in the second subparagraph, however, the practical training may be given during a period of not more than six months in other approved establishments or health structures concerned with general medicine.

The training shall require the personal participation of the trainee in the professional activity and responsibilities of the persons with whom he is working.

4.   Member States shall make the issuance of evidence of formal qualifications in general medical practice subject to possession of evidence of formal qualifications in basic medical training referred to in Annex V, point 5.1.1.

5.   Member States may issue evidence of formal qualifications referred to in Annex V, point 5.1.4 to a doctor who has not completed the training provided for in this Article but who has completed a different, supplementary training, as attested by evidence of formal qualifications issued by the competent authorities in a Member State. They may not, however, award evidence of formal qualifications unless it attests knowledge of a level qualitatively equivalent to the knowledge acquired from the training provided for in this Article.

Member States shall determine, inter alia, the extent to which the complementary training and professional experience already acquired by the applicant may replace the training provided for in this Article.

The Member States may only issue the evidence of formal qualifications referred to in Annex V, point 5.1.4 if the applicant has acquired at least six months' experience of general medicine in a general medical practice or a centre in which doctors provide primary health care of the types referred to in paragraph 3.

Article 29 Pursuit of the professional activities of general practitioners

Each Member State shall, subject to the provisions relating to acquired rights, make the pursuit of the activities of a general practitioner in the framework of its national social security system contingent upon possession of evidence of formal qualifications referred to in Annex V, point 5.1.4.

Member States may exempt persons who are currently undergoing specific training in general medicine from this condition.

Article 30 Acquired rights specific to general practitioners

1. Each Member State shall determine the acquired rights. It shall, however, confer as an acquired right the right to pursue the activities of a general practitioner in the framework of its national social security system, without the evidence of formal qualifications referred to in Annex V, point 5.1.4, on all doctors who enjoy this right as of the reference date stated in that point by virtue of provisions applicable to the medical profession giving access to the professional activities of doctor with basic training and who are established as of that date on its territory, having benefited from the provisions of Articles 21 or 23.

   The competent authorities of each Member State shall, on demand, issue a certificate stating the holder's right to pursue the activities of general practitioner in the framework of their national social security systems, without the evidence of formal qualifications referred to in Annex V, point 5.1.4, to doctors who enjoy acquired rights pursuant to the first subparagraph.

2. Every Member State shall recognise the certificates referred to in paragraph 1, second subparagraph, awarded to nationals of Member States by the other Member States, and shall give such certificates the same effect on its territory as evidence of formal qualifications which it awards and which permit the pursuit of the activities of a general practitioner in the framework of its national social security system.

SECTION 3 NURSES RESPONSIBLE FOR GENERAL CARE

Article 31 Training of nurses responsible for general care

1. Admission to training for nurses responsible for general care shall be contingent upon completion of general education of 10 years, as attested by a diploma, certificate or other evidence issued by the competent authorities or bodies in a Member State or by a certificate attesting success in an examination, of an equivalent level, for admission to a school of nursing.

2. Training of nurses responsible for general care shall be given on a full-time basis and shall include at least the programme described in Annex V, point 5.2.1.

   The Commission may adapt the content listed in Annex V, point 5.2.1, to scientific and technical progress. That measure, designed to amend non-essential elements of this Directive, shall be adopted in accordance with the regulatory procedure with scrutiny referred to in Article 58(3).

   Such updates may not entail, for any Member State, any amendment of its existing legislative principles relating to the structure of professions as regards training and the conditions of access by natural persons.

3. The training of nurses responsible for general care shall comprise at least three years of study or 4600 hours of theoretical and clinical training, the duration of the theoretical training representing at least one-third and the duration of the clinical training at least one half of the minimum duration of the training. Member States may grant partial exemptions to persons who have received part of their training on courses which are of at least an equivalent level.

   The Member States shall ensure that institutions providing nursing training are responsible for the coordination of theoretical and clinical training throughout the entire study programme.

4. Theoretical training is that part of nurse training from which trainee nurses acquire the professional knowledge, insights and skills necessary for organising, dispensing and

evaluating overall health care. The training shall be given by teachers of nursing care and by other competent persons, in nursing schools and other training establishments selected by the training institution.

5.　Clinical training is that part of nurse training in which trainee nurses learn, as part of a team and in direct contact with a healthy or sick individual and/or community, to organise, dispense and evaluate the required comprehensive nursing care, on the basis of the knowledge and skills which they have acquired. The trainee nurse shall learn not only how to work in a team, but also how to lead a team and organise overall nursing care, including health education for individuals and small groups, within the health institute or in the community.

This training shall take place in hospitals and other health institutions and in the community, under the responsibility of nursing teachers, in cooperation with and assisted by other qualified nurses. Other qualified personnel may also take part in the teaching process.

Trainee nurses shall participate in the activities of the department in question insofar as those activities are appropriate to their training, enabling them to learn to assume the responsibilities involved in nursing care.

6.　Training for nurses responsible for general care shall provide an assurance that the person in question has acquired the following knowledge and skills:
(a)　adequate knowledge of the sciences on which general nursing is based, including sufficient understanding of the structure, physiological functions and behaviour of healthy and sick persons, and of the relationship between the state of health and the physical and social environment of the human being;
(b)　sufficient knowledge of the nature and ethics of the profession and of the general principles of health and nursing;
(c)　adequate clinical experience; such experience, which should be selected for its training value, should be gained under the supervision of qualified nursing staff and in places where the number of qualified staff and equipment are appropriate for the nursing care of the patient;
(d)　the ability to participate in the practical training of health personnel and experience of working with such personnel;
(e)　experience of working with members of other professions in the health sector.

Article 32 Pursuit of the professional activities of nurses responsible for general care
For the purposes of this Directive, the professional activities of nurses responsible for general care are the activities pursued on a professional basis and referred to in Annex V, point 5.2.2.

Article 33 Acquired rights specific to nurses responsible for general care
1.　Where the general rules of acquired rights apply to nurses responsible for general care, the activities referred to in Article 23 must have included full responsibility for the planning, organisation and administration of nursing care delivered to the patient.

2.　As regards the Polish qualification of nurse responsible for general care, only the following acquired rights provisions shall apply. In the case of nationals of the Member States whose evidence of formal qualifications as nurse responsible for general care was awarded by, or whose training started in, Poland before 1 May 2004 and who do not satisfy the minimum training requirements laid down in Article 31, Member States shall recognise the following evidence of formal qualifications as nurse responsible for general care as being sufficient proof if accompanied by a certificate stating that those Member State nationals have effectively and lawfully been engaged in the activities of a nurse responsible for general care in Poland for the period specified below:

(a) evidence of formal qualifications as a nurse at degree level (dyplom licencjata pielęgniarstwa) — at least three consecutive years during the five years prior to the date of issue of the certificate,

(b) evidence of formal qualifications as a nurse certifying completion of post-secondary education obtained from a medical vocational school (dyplom pielęgniarki albo pielęgniarki dyplomowanej) — at least five consecutive years during the seven years prior to the date of issue of the certificate.

The said activities must have included taking full responsibility for the planning, organisation and administration of nursing care delivered to the patient.

3. Member States shall recognise evidence of formal qualifications in nursing awarded in Poland, to nurses who completed training before 1 May 2004, which did not comply with the minimum training requirements laid down in Article 31, attested by the diploma "bachelor" which has been obtained on the basis of a special upgrading programme contained in Article 11 of the Act of 20 April 2004 on the amendment of the Act on professions of nurse and midwife and on some other legal acts (Official Journal of the Republic of Poland of 30 April 2004 No 92, pos. 885), and the Regulation of the Minister of Health of 11 May 2004 on the detailed conditions of delivering studies for nurses and midwives, who hold a certificate of secondary school (final examination — matura) and are graduates of medical lyceum and medical vocational schools teaching in a profession of a nurse and a midwife (Official Journal of the Republic of Poland of 13 May 2004 No 110, pos. 1170), with the aim of verifying that the person concerned has a level of knowledge and competence comparable to that of nurses holding the qualifications which, in the case of Poland, are defined in Annex V, point 5.2.2.

Article 33(a)

As regards the Romanian qualification of nurse responsible for general care, only the following acquired rights provisions will apply:

In the case of nationals of the Member States whose evidence of formal qualifications as nurse responsible for general care were awarded by, or whose training started in, Romania before the date of accession and which does not satisfy the minimum training requirements laid down in Article 31, Member States shall recognise the evidence of formal qualification as nurse responsible for general care (*Certificat de competence profesionale de asistent medical generalist*) with postsecondary education obtained from a *scoală postliceală*, as being sufficient proof if accompanied by a certificate stating that those Member State nationals have effectively and lawfully been engaged in the activities of a nurse responsible for general care in Romania for a period of at least five consecutive years during the seven years prior to the date of issue of the certificate.

The said activities must have included taking full responsibility for the planning, organisation and carrying out of the nursing care of the patient.

SECTION 4 DENTAL PRACTITIONERS

Article 34 Basic dental training

1. Admission to basic dental training presupposes possession of a diploma or certificate giving access, for the studies in question, to universities or higher institutes of a level recognised as equivalent, in a Member State.

2. Basic dental training shall comprise a total of at least five years of full-time theoretical and practical study, comprising at least the programme described in Annex V, point 5.3.1 and

given in a university, in a higher institute providing training recognised as being of an equivalent level or under the supervision of a university.

The Commission may adapt the content listed in Annex V, point 5.3.1, to scientific and technical progress. That measure, designed to amend non-essential elements of this Directive, shall be adopted in accordance with the regulatory procedure with scrutiny referred to in Article 58(3).

Such updates may not entail, for any Member State, any amendment of its existing legislative principles relating to the system of professions as regards training and the conditions of access by natural persons.

3. Basic dental training shall provide an assurance that the person in question has acquired the following knowledge and skills:
    (a) adequate knowledge of the sciences on which dentistry is based and a good understanding of scientific methods, including the principles of measuring biological functions, the evaluation of scientifically established facts and the analysis of data;
    (b) adequate knowledge of the constitution, physiology and behaviour of healthy and sick persons as well as the influence of the natural and social environment on the state of health of the human being, in so far as these factors affect dentistry;
    (c) adequate knowledge of the structure and function of the teeth, mouth, jaws and associated tissues, both healthy and diseased, and their relationship to the general state of health and to the physical and social well-being of the patient;
    (d) adequate knowledge of clinical disciplines and methods, providing the dentist with a coherent picture of anomalies, lesions and diseases of the teeth, mouth, jaws and associated tissues and of preventive, diagnostic and therapeutic dentistry;
    (e) suitable clinical experience under appropriate supervision.
    This training shall provide him with the skills necessary for carrying out all activities involving the prevention, diagnosis and treatment of anomalies and diseases of the teeth, mouth, jaws and associated tissues.

Article 35 Specialist dental training
1. Admission to specialist dental training shall entail the completion and validation of five years of theoretical and practical instruction within the framework of the training referred to in Article 34, or possession of the documents referred to in Articles 23 and 37.

2. Specialist dental training shall comprise theoretical and practical instruction in a university centre, in a treatment teaching and research centre or, where appropriate, in a health establishment approved for that purpose by the competent authorities or bodies.

    Full-time specialist dental courses shall be of a minimum of three years' duration supervised by the competent authorities or bodies. It shall involve the personal participation of the dental practitioner training to be a specialist in the activity and in the responsibilities of the establishment concerned.

    The Commission may adapt the minimum period of training referred to in the second subparagraph to scientific and technical progress. That measure, designed to amend non-essential elements of this Directive, shall be adopted in accordance with the regulatory procedure with scrutiny referred to in Article 58(3).

3. The Member States shall make the issuance of evidence of specialist dental training contingent upon possession of evidence of basic dental training referred to in Annex V, point 5.3.2.

Article 36 Pursuit of the professional activities of dental practitioners

1.   For the purposes of this Directive, the professional activities of dental practitioners are the activities defined in paragraph 3 and pursued under the professional qualifications listed in Annex V, point 5.3.2.

2.   The profession of dental practitioner shall be based on dental training referred to in Article 34 and shall constitute a specific profession which is distinct from other general or specialised medical professions. Pursuit of the activities of a dental practitioner requires the possession of evidence of formal qualifications referred to in Annex V, point 5.3.2. Holders of such evidence of formal qualifications shall be treated in the same way as those to whom Articles 23 or 37 apply.

3.   The Member States shall ensure that dental practitioners are generally able to gain access to and pursue the activities of prevention, diagnosis and treatment of anomalies and diseases affecting the teeth, mouth, jaws and adjoining tissue, having due regard to the regulatory provisions and rules of professional ethics on the reference dates referred to in Annex V, point 5.3.2.

Article 37 Acquired rights specific to dental practitioners

1.   Every Member State shall, for the purposes of the pursuit of the professional activities of dental practitioners under the qualifications listed in Annex V, point 5.3.2, recognise evidence of formal qualifications as a doctor issued in Italy, Spain, Austria, the Czech Republic, Slovakia and Romania to persons who began their medical training on or before the reference date stated in that Annex for the Member State concerned, accompanied by a certificate issued by the competent authorities of that Member State.

The certificate must show that the two following conditions are met:
(a) that the persons in question have been effectively, lawfully and principally engaged in that Member State in the activities referred to in Article 36 for at least three consecutive years during the five years preceding the award of the certificate;
(b) that those persons are authorised to pursue the said activities under the same conditions as holders of evidence of formal qualifications listed for that Member State in Annex V, point 5.3.2.
Persons who have successfully completed at least three years of study, certified by the competent authorities in the Member State concerned as being equivalent to the training referred to in Article 34, shall be exempt from the three-year practical work experience referred to in the second subparagraph, point (a).

With regard to the Czech Republic and Slovakia, evidence of formal qualifications obtained in the former Czechoslovakia shall be accorded the same level of recognition as Czech and Slovak evidence of formal qualifications and under the same conditions as set out in the preceding subparagraphs.

2.   Each Member State shall recognise evidence of formal qualifications as a doctor issued in Italy to persons who began their university medical training after 28 January 1980 and no later than 31 December 1984, accompanied by a certificate issued by the competent Italian authorities.

The certificate must show that the three following conditions are met:
(a) that the persons in question passed the relevant aptitude test held by the competent Italian authorities with a view to establishing that those persons possess a level of knowledge and skills comparable to that of persons possessing evidence of formal qualifications listed for Italy in Annex V, point 5.3.2;

(b) that they have been effectively, lawfully and principally engaged in the activities referred to in Article 36 in Italy for at least three consecutive years during the five years preceding the award of the certificate;

(c) that they are authorised to engage in or are effectively, lawfully and principally engaged in the activities referred to in Article 36, under the same conditions as the holders of evidence of formal qualifications listed for Italy in Annex V, point 5.3.2.

Persons who have successfully completed at least three years of study certified by the competent authorities as being equivalent to the training referred to in Article 34 shall be exempt from the aptitude test referred to in the second subparagraph, point (a).

Persons who began their university medical training after 31 December 1984 shall be treated in the same way as those referred to above, provided that the abovementioned three years of study began before 31 December 1994.

SECTION 5 VETERINARY SURGEONS

Article 38 The training of veterinary surgeons

1.   The training of veterinary surgeons shall comprise a total of at least five years of full-time theoretical and practical study at a university or at a higher institute providing training recognised as being of an equivalent level, or under the supervision of a university, covering at least the study programme referred to in Annex V, point 5.4.1.

The Commission may adapt the content listed in Annex V, point 5.4.1, to scientific and technical progress. That measure, designed to amend non-essential elements of this Directive, shall be adopted in accordance with the regulatory procedure with scrutiny referred to in Article 58(3).

Such updates may not entail, for any Member State, any amendment of its existing legislative principles relating to the structure of professions as regards training and conditions of access by natural persons.

2.   Admission to veterinary training shall be contingent upon possession of a diploma or certificate entitling the holder to enter, for the studies in question, university establishments or institutes of higher education recognised by a Member State to be of an equivalent level for the purpose of the relevant study.

3.   Training as a veterinary surgeon shall provide an assurance that the person in question has acquired the following knowledge and skills:

(a) adequate knowledge of the sciences on which the activities of the veterinary surgeon are based;

(b) adequate knowledge of the structure and functions of healthy animals, of their husbandry, reproduction and hygiene in general, as well as their feeding, including the technology involved in the manufacture and preservation of foods corresponding to their needs;

(c) adequate knowledge of the behaviour and protection of animals;

(d) adequate knowledge of the causes, nature, course, effects, diagnosis and treatment of the diseases of animals, whether considered individually or in groups, including a special knowledge of the diseases which may be transmitted to humans;

(e) adequate knowledge of preventive medicine;

(f) adequate knowledge of the hygiene and technology involved in the production, manufacture and putting into circulation of animal foodstuffs or foodstuffs of animal origin intended for human consumption;

(g) adequate knowledge of the laws, regulations and administrative provisions relating to the subjects listed above;

(h) adequate clinical and other practical experience under appropriate supervision.

Article 39 Acquired rights specific to veterinary surgeons

Without prejudice to Article 23(4), with regard to nationals of Member States whose evidence of formal qualifications as a veterinary surgeon was issued by, or whose training commenced in, Estonia before 1 May 2004, Member States shall recognise such evidence of formal qualifications as a veterinary surgeon if it is accompanied by a certificate stating that such persons have effectively and lawfully been engaged in the activities in question in Estonia for at least five consecutive years during the seven years prior to the date of issue of the certificate.

SECTION 6 MIDWIVES

Article 40 The training of midwives

1.   The training of midwives shall comprise a total of at least:
  (a) specific full-time training as a midwife comprising at least three years of theoretical and practical study (route I) comprising at least the programme described in Annex V, point 5.5.1, or
  (b) specific full-time training as a midwife of 18 months' duration (route II), comprising at least the study programme described in Annex V, point 5.5.1, which was not the subject of equivalent training of nurses responsible for general care.

The Member States shall ensure that institutions providing midwife training are responsible for coordinating theory and practice throughout the programme of study.

The Commission may adapt the content listed in Annex V, point 5.5.1, to scientific and technical progress. That measure, designed to amend non-essential elements of this Directive, shall be adopted in accordance with the regulatory procedure with scrutiny referred to in Article 58(3).

Such updates must not entail, for any Member State, any amendment of existing legislative principles relating to the structure of professions as regards training and the conditions of access by natural persons.

2.   Access to training as a midwife shall be contingent upon one of the following conditions:
  (a) completion of at least the first 10 years of general school education for route I, or
  (b) possession of evidence of formal qualifications as a nurse responsible for general care referred to in Annex V, point 5.2.2 for route II.

3.   Training as a midwife shall provide an assurance that the person in question has acquired the following knowledge and skills:
  (a) adequate knowledge of the sciences on which the activities of midwives are based, particularly obstetrics and gynaecology;
  (b) adequate knowledge of the ethics of the profession and the professional legislation;
  (c) detailed knowledge of biological functions, anatomy and physiology in the field of obstetrics and of the newly born, and also a knowledge of the relationship between the state of health and the physical and social environment of the human being, and of his behaviour;
  (d) adequate clinical experience gained in approved institutions under the supervision of staff qualified in midwifery and obstetrics;
  (e) adequate understanding of the training of health personnel and experience of working with such.

Article 41 Procedures for the recognition of evidence of formal qualifications as a midwife

1.   The evidence of formal qualifications as a midwife referred to in Annex V, point 5.5.2 shall be subject to automatic recognition pursuant to Article 21 in so far as they satisfy one of the following criteria:
  (a) full-time training of at least three years as a midwife:

(i)   either made contingent upon possession of a diploma, certificate or other evidence of qualification giving access to universities or higher education institutes, or otherwise guaranteeing an equivalent level of knowledge; or

(ii) followed by two years of professional practice for which a certificate has been issued in accordance with paragraph 2;

(b) full-time training as a midwife of at least two years or 3600 hours, contingent upon possession of evidence of formal qualifications as a nurse responsible for general care referred to in Annex V, point 5.2.2;

(c) full-time training as a midwife of at least 18 months or 3000 hours, contingent upon possession of evidence of formal qualifications as a nurse responsible for general care referred to in Annex V, point 5.2.2 and followed by one year's professional practice for which a certificate has been issued in accordance with paragraph 2.

2.   The certificate referred to in paragraph 1 shall be issued by the competent authorities in the home Member State. It shall certify that the holder, after obtaining evidence of formal qualifications as a midwife, has satisfactorily pursued all the activities of a midwife for a corresponding period in a hospital or a health care establishment approved for that purpose.

Article 42 Pursuit of the professional activities of a midwife

1.   The provisions of this section shall apply to the activities of midwives as defined by each Member State, without prejudice to paragraph 2, and pursued under the professional titles set out in Annex V, point 5.5.2.

2.   The Member States shall ensure that midwives are able to gain access to and pursue at least the following activities:

(a) provision of sound family planning information and advice;

(b) diagnosis of pregnancies and monitoring normal pregnancies; carrying out the examinations necessary for the monitoring of the development of normal pregnancies;

(c) prescribing or advising on the examinations necessary for the earliest possible diagnosis of pregnancies at risk;

(d) provision of programmes of parenthood preparation and complete preparation for childbirth including advice on hygiene and nutrition;

(e) caring for and assisting the mother during labour and monitoring the condition of the foetus in utero by the appropriate clinical and technical means;

(f) conducting spontaneous deliveries including where required episiotomies and in urgent cases breech deliveries;

(g) recognising the warning signs of abnormality in the mother or infant which necessitate referral to a doctor and assisting the latter where appropriate; taking the necessary emergency measures in the doctor's absence, in particular the manual removal of the placenta, possibly followed by manual examination of the uterus;

(h) examining and caring for the new-born infant; taking all initiatives which are necessary in case of need and carrying out where necessary immediate resuscitation;

(i) caring for and monitoring the progress of the mother in the post-natal period and giving all necessary advice to the mother on infant care to enable her to ensure the optimum progress of the new-born infant;

(j) carrying out treatment prescribed by doctors;

(k) drawing up the necessary written reports.

Article 43 Acquired rights specific to midwives

1.   Every Member State shall, in the case of Member State nationals whose evidence of formal qualifications as a midwife satisfies all the minimum training requirements laid down in Article 40 but, by virtue of Article 41, is not recognised unless it is accompanied

by a certificate of professional practice referred to in Article 41(2), recognise as sufficient proof evidence of formal qualifications issued by those Member States before the reference date referred to in Annex V, point 5.5.2, accompanied by a certificate stating that those nationals have been effectively and lawfully engaged in the activities in question for at least two consecutive years during the five years preceding the award of the certificate.

2. The conditions laid down in paragraph 1 shall apply to the nationals of Member States whose evidence of formal qualifications as a midwife certifies completion of training received in the territory of the former German Democratic Republic and satisfying all the minimum training requirements laid down in Article 40 but where the evidence of formal qualifications, by virtue of Article 41, is not recognised unless it is accompanied by the certificate of professional experience referred to in Article 41(2), where it attests a course of training which began before 3 October 1990.

3. As regards the Polish evidence of formal qualifications as a midwife, only the following acquired rights provisions shall apply.

In the case of Member States nationals whose evidence of formal qualifications as a midwife was awarded by, or whose training commenced in, Poland before 1 May 2004, and who do not satisfy the minimum training requirements as set out in Article 40, Member States shall recognise the following evidence of formal qualifications as a midwife if accompanied by a certificate stating that such persons have effectively and lawfully been engaged in the activities of a midwife for the period specified below:

(a) evidence of formal qualifications as a midwife at degree level (dyplom licencjata położnictwa): at least three consecutive years during the five years prior to the date of issue of the certificate,

(b) evidence of formal qualifications as a midwife certifying completion of post-secondary education obtained from a medical vocational school (dyplom położnej): at least five consecutive years during the seven years prior to the date of issue of the certificate.

4. Member States shall recognise evidence of formal qualifications in midwifery awarded in Poland, to midwives who completed training before 1 May 2004, which did not comply with the minimum training requirements laid down in Article 40, attested by the diploma "bachelor" which has been obtained on the basis of a special upgrading programme contained in Article 11 of the Act of 20 April 2004 on the amendment of the Act on professions of nurse and midwife and on some other legal acts (Official Journal of the Republic of Poland of 30 April 2004 No 92, pos. 885), and the Regulation of the Minister of Health of 11 May 2004 on the detailed conditions of delivering studies for nurses and midwives, who hold a certificate of secondary school (final examination — matura) and are graduates of medical lyceum and medical vocational schools teaching in a profession of a nurse and a midwife (Official Journal of the Republic of Poland of 13 May 2004 No 110, pos 1170), with the aim of verifying that the person concerned has a level of knowledge and competence comparable to that of midwives holding the qualifications which, in the case of Poland, are defined in Annex V, point 5.5.2.

Article 43(a)

As regards the Romanian qualifications in midwifery, only the following acquired rights provisions will apply:

In the case of nationals of the Member States whose evidence of formal qualifications as a midwife (asistent medical obstetrică-ginecologie/obstetrics-gynecology nurse) were awarded by Romania before the date of accession and which do not satisfy the minimum training requirements laid down in Article 40, Member States shall recognise the said evidence of formal qualifications as being sufficient proof for the purposes of carrying out the activities of midwife, if they are accompanied by a certificate stating that those Member State nationals have effectively and lawfully been engaged in the activities of midwife in Romania, for at least five consecutive years during the seven years prior to the issue of the certificate.

SECTION 7 PHARMACIST

Article 44 Training as a pharmacist

1. Admission to a course of training as a pharmacist shall be contingent upon possession of a diploma or certificate giving access, in a Member State, to the studies in question, at universities or higher institutes of a level recognised as equivalent.

2. Evidence of formal qualifications as a pharmacist shall attest to training of at least five years' duration, including at least:
    (a) four years of full-time theoretical and practical training at a university or at a higher institute of a level recognised as equivalent, or under the supervision of a university;
    (b) six-month traineeship in a pharmacy which is open to the public or in a hospital, under the supervision of that hospital's pharmaceutical department.

    That training cycle shall include at least the programme described in Annex V, point 5.6.1. The Commission may adapt the content listed in Annex V, point 5.6.1, to scientific and technical progress. That measure, designed to amend non-essential elements of this Directive, shall be adopted in accordance with the regulatory procedure with scrutiny referred to in Article 58(3).

    Such updates must not entail, for any Member State, any amendment of existing legislative principles relating to the structure of professions as regards training and the conditions of access by natural persons.

3. Training for pharmacists shall provide an assurance that the person concerned has acquired the following knowledge and skills:
    (a) adequate knowledge of medicines and the substances used in the manufacture of medicines;
    (b) adequate knowledge of pharmaceutical technology and the physical, chemical, biological and microbiological testing of medicinal products;
    (c) adequate knowledge of the metabolism and the effects of medicinal products and of the action of toxic substances, and of the use of medicinal products;
    (d) adequate knowledge to evaluate scientific data concerning medicines in order to be able to supply appropriate information on the basis of this knowledge;
    (e) adequate knowledge of the legal and other requirements associated with the pursuit of pharmacy.

Article 45 Pursuit of the professional activities of a pharmacist

1. For the purposes of this Directive, the activities of a pharmacist are those, access to which and pursuit of which are contingent, in one or more Member States, upon professional qualifications and which are open to holders of evidence of formal qualifications of the types listed in Annex V, point 5.6.2.

2. The Member States shall ensure that the holders of evidence of formal qualifications in pharmacy at university level or a level deemed to be equivalent, which satisfies the provisions of Article 44, are able to gain access to and pursue at least the following activities, subject to the requirement, where appropriate, of supplementary professional experience:
    (a) preparation of the pharmaceutical form of medicinal products;
    (b) manufacture and testing of medicinal products;
    (c) testing of medicinal products in a laboratory for the testing of medicinal products;

(d) storage, preservation and distribution of medicinal products at the wholesale stage;

(e) preparation, testing, storage and supply of medicinal products in pharmacies open to the public;

(f) preparation, testing, storage and dispensing of medicinal products in hospitals;

(g) provision of information and advice on medicinal products.

3. If a Member State makes access to or pursuit of one of the activities of a pharmacist contingent upon supplementary professional experience, in addition to possession of evidence of formal qualifications referred to in Annex V, point 5.6.2, that Member State shall recognise as sufficient proof in this regard a certificate issued by the competent authorities in the home Member State stating that the person concerned has been engaged in those activities in the home Member State for a similar period.

4. The recognition referred to in paragraph 3 shall not apply with regard to the two-year period of professional experience required by the Grand Duchy of Luxembourg for the grant of a State public pharmacy concession.

5. If, on 16 September 1985, a Member State had a competitive examination in place designed to select from among the holders referred to in paragraph 2, those who are to be authorised to become owners of new pharmacies whose creation has been decided on as part of a national system of geographical division, that Member State may, by way of derogation from paragraph 1, proceed with that examination and require nationals of Member States who possess evidence of formal qualifications as a pharmacist referred to in Annex V, point 5.6.2 or who benefit from the provisions of Article 23 to take part in it.

SECTION 8 ARCHITECT

Article 46 Training of architects

1. Training as an architect shall comprise a total of at least four years of full-time study or six years of study, at least three years of which on a full-time basis, at a university or comparable teaching institution. The training must lead to successful completion of a university-level examination.

That training, which must be of university level, and of which architecture is the principal component, must maintain a balance between theoretical and practical aspects of architectural training and guarantee the acquisition of the following knowledge and skills:

(a) ability to create architectural designs that satisfy both aesthetic and technical requirements;

(b) adequate knowledge of the history and theories of architecture and the related arts, technologies and human sciences;

(c) knowledge of the fine arts as an influence on the quality of architectural design;

(d) adequate knowledge of urban design, planning and the skills involved in the planning process;

(e) understanding of the relationship between people and buildings, and between buildings and their environment, and of the need to relate buildings and the spaces between them to human needs and scale;

(f) understanding of the profession of architecture and the role of the architect in society, in particular in preparing briefs that take account of social factors;

(g) understanding of the methods of investigation and preparation of the brief for a design project;

(h) understanding of the structural design, constructional and engineering problems associated with building design;

(i) adequate knowledge of physical problems and technologies and of the function of buildings so as to provide them with internal conditions of comfort and protection against the climate;

(j) the necessary design skills to meet building users' requirements within the constraints imposed by cost factors and building regulations;

(k) adequate knowledge of the industries, organisations, regulations and procedures involved in translating design concepts into buildings and integrating plans into overall planning.

2. The Commission may adapt the knowledge and skills listed in paragraph 1 to scientific and technical progress. That measure, designed to amend non-essential elements of this Directive, shall be adopted in accordance with the regulatory procedure with scrutiny referred to in Article 58(3).

Such updates must not entail, for any Member State, any amendment of existing legislative principles relating to the structure of professions as regards training and the conditions of access by natural persons.

Article 47 Derogations from the conditions for the training of architects

1. By way of derogation from Article 46, the following shall also be recognised as satisfying Article 21: training existing as of 5 August 1985, provided by "Fachhochschulen" in the Federal Republic of Germany over a period of three years, satisfying the requirements referred to in Article 46 and giving access to the activities referred to in Article 48 in that Member State under the professional title of "architect", in so far as the training was followed by a four-year period of professional experience in the Federal Republic of Germany, as attested by a certificate issued by the professional association in whose roll the name of the architect wishing to benefit from the provisions of this Directive appears.

The professional association must first ascertain that the work performed by the architect concerned in the field of architecture represents convincing application of the full range of knowledge and skills listed in Article 46(1). That certificate shall be awarded in line with the same procedure as that applying to registration in the professional association's roll.

2. By way of derogation from Article 46, the following shall also be recognised as satisfying Article 21: training as part of social betterment schemes or part-time university studies which satisfies the requirements referred to in Article 46, as attested by an examination in architecture passed by a person who has been working for seven years or more in the field of architecture under the supervision of an architect or architectural bureau. The examination must be of university level and be equivalent to the final examination referred to in Article 46(1), first subparagraph.

Article 48 Pursuit of the professional activities of architects

1. For the purposes of this Directive, the professional activities of an architect are the activities regularly carried out under the professional title of "architect".

2. Nationals of a Member State who are authorised to use that title pursuant to a law which gives the competent authority of a Member State the power to award that title to Member States nationals who are especially distinguished by the quality of their work in the field of architecture shall be deemed to satisfy the conditions required for the pursuit of the activities of an architect, under the professional title of "architect". The architectural nature of the activities of the persons concerned shall be attested by a certificate awarded by their home Member State.

Article 49 Acquired rights specific to architects

1. Each Member State shall accept evidence of formal qualifications as an architect listed in Annex VI, awarded by the other Member States, and attesting a course of training which began no later than the reference academic year referred to in that Annex, even if they do not satisfy the minimum requirements laid down in Article 46, and shall, for the purposes

of access to and pursuit of the professional activities of an architect, give such evidence the same effect on its territory as evidence of formal qualifications as an architect which it itself issues.

Under these circumstances, certificates issued by the competent authorities of the Federal Republic of Germany attesting that evidence of formal qualifications issued on or after 8 May 1945 by the competent authorities of the German Democratic Republic is equivalent to such evidence listed in that Annex, shall be recognised.

2. Without prejudice to paragraph 1, every Member State shall recognise the following evidence of formal qualifications and shall, for the purposes of access to and pursuit of the professional activities of an architect performed, give them the same effect on its territory as evidence of formal qualifications which it itself issues: certificates issued to nationals of Member States by the Member States which have enacted rules governing the access to and pursuit of the activities of an architect as of the following dates:
(a) 1 January 1995 for Austria, Finland and Sweden;
(b) 1 May 2004 for the Czech Republic, Estonia, Cyprus, Latvia, Lithuania, Hungary, Malta, Poland, Slovenia and Slovakia;
(c) 5 August 1987 for the other Member States.
The certificates referred to in the first subparagraph shall certify that the holder was authorized, no later than the respective date, to use the professional title of architect, and that he has been effectively engaged, in the context of those rules, in the activities in question for at least three consecutive years during the five years preceding the award of the certificate.

Chapter IV COMMON PROVISIONS ON ESTABLISHMENT

Article 50 Documentation and formalities

1. Where the competent authorities of the host Member State decide on an application for authorisation to pursue the regulated profession in question by virtue of this Title, those authorities may demand the documents and certificates listed in Annex VII.

The documents referred to in Annex VII, point 1(d), (e) and (f), shall not be more than three months old by the date on which they are submitted.

The Member States, bodies and other legal persons shall guarantee the confidentiality of the information which they receive.

2. In the event of justified doubts, the host Member State may require from the competent authorities of a Member State confirmation of the authenticity of the attestations and evidence of formal qualifications awarded in that other Member State, as well as, where applicable, confirmation of the fact that the beneficiary fulfils, for the professions referred to in Chapter III of this Title, the minimum training conditions set out respectively in Articles 24, 25, 28, 31, 34, 35, 38, 40, 44 and 46.

3. In cases of justified doubt, where evidence of formal qualifications, as defined in Article 3(1)(c), has been issued by a competent authority in a Member State and includes training received in whole or in part in an establishment legally established in the territory of another Member State, the host Member State shall be entitled to verify with the competent body in the Member State of origin of the award:
(a) whether the training course at the establishment which gave the training has been formally certified by the educational establishment based in the Member State of origin of the award;
(b) whether the evidence of formal qualifications issued is the same as that which would have been awarded if the course had been followed entirely in the Member State of origin of the award; and

(c)   whether the evidence of formal qualifications confers the same professional rights in the territory of the Member State of origin of the award.

4.   Where a host Member State requires its nationals to swear a solemn oath or make a sworn statement in order to gain access to a regulated profession, and where the wording of that oath or statement cannot be used by nationals of the other Member States, the host Member State shall ensure that the persons concerned can use an appropriate equivalent wording.

Article 51 Procedure for the mutual recognition of professional qualifications

1.   The competent authority of the host Member State shall acknowledge receipt of the application within one month of receipt and inform the applicant of any missing document.

2.   The procedure for examining an application for authorisation to practise a regulated profession must be completed as quickly as possible and lead to a duly substantiated decision by the competent authority in the host Member State in any case within three months after the date on which the applicant's complete file was submitted. However, this deadline may be extended by one month in cases falling under Chapters I and II of this Title.

3.   The decision, or failure to reach a decision within the deadline, shall be subject to appeal under national law.

Article 52 Use of professional titles

1.   If, in a host Member State, the use of a professional title relating to one of the activities of the profession in question is regulated, nationals of the other Member States who are authorised to practise a regulated profession on the basis of Title III shall use the professional title of the host Member State, which corresponds to that profession in that Member State, and make use of any associated initials.

2.   Where a profession is regulated in the host Member State by an association or organisation within the meaning of Article 3(2), nationals of Member States shall not be authorised to use the professional title issued by that organisation or association, or its abbreviated form, unless they furnish proof that they are members of that association or organisation.

If the association or organisation makes membership contingent upon certain qualifications, it may do so, only under the conditions laid down in this Directive, in respect of nationals of other Member States who possess professional qualifications.

TITLE IV DETAILED RULES FOR PURSUING THE PROFESSION

Article 53 Knowledge of languages

Persons benefiting from the recognition of professional qualifications shall have a knowledge of languages necessary for practising the profession in the host Member State.

Article 54 Use of academic titles

Without prejudice to Articles 7 and 52, the host Member State shall ensure that the right shall be conferred on the persons concerned to use academic titles conferred on them in the home Member State, and possibly an abbreviated form thereof, in the language of the home Member State. The host Member State may require that title to be followed by the name and address of the establishment or examining board which awarded it. Where an academic title of the home

Member State is liable to be confused in the host Member State with a title which, in the latter Member State, requires supplementary training not acquired by the beneficiary, the host Member State may require the beneficiary to use the academic title of the home Member State in an appropriate form, to be laid down by the host Member State.

Article 55 Approval by health insurance funds

Without prejudice to Article 5(1) and Article 6, first subparagraph, point (b), Member States which require persons who acquired their professional qualifications in their territory to complete a preparatory period of in-service training and/or a period of professional experience in order to be approved by a health insurance fund, shall waive this obligation for the holders of evidence of professional qualifications of doctor and dental practitioner acquired in other Member States.

TITLE V ADMINISTRATIVE COOPERATION AND RESPONSIBILITY FOR IMPLEMENTATION

Article 56 Competent authorities

1. The competent authorities of the host Member State and of the home Member State shall work in close collaboration and shall provide mutual assistance in order to facilitate application of this Directive. They shall ensure the confidentiality of the information which they exchange.

2. The competent authorities of the host and home Member States shall exchange information regarding disciplinary action or criminal sanctions taken or any other serious, specific circumstances which are likely to have consequences for the pursuit of activities under this Directive, respecting personal data protection legislation provided for in Directives 95/46/EC of the European Parliament and of the Council of 24 October 1995 on the protection of individuals with regard to the processing of personal data and on the free movement of such data [24] and 2002/58/EC of the European Parliament and of the Council of 12 July 2002 concerning the processing of personal data and the protection of privacy in the electronic communications sector (Directive on privacy and electronic communications) [25].

    The home Member State shall examine the veracity of the circumstances and its authorities shall decide on the nature and scope of the investigations which need to be carried out and shall inform the host Member State of the conclusions which it draws from the information available to it.

3. Each Member State shall, no later than 20 October 2007, designate the authorities and bodies competent to award or receive evidence of formal qualifications and other documents or information, and those competent to receive applications and take the decisions referred to in this Directive, and shall forthwith inform the other Member States and the Commission thereof.

4. Each Member State shall designate a coordinator for the activities of the authorities referred to in paragraph 1 and shall inform the other Member States and the Commission thereof.

    The coordinators' remit shall be:
    (a) to promote uniform application of this Directive;
    (b) to collect all the information which is relevant for application of this Directive, such as on the conditions for access to regulated professions in the Member States.
    For the purpose of fulfilling the remit described in point (b), the coordinators may solicit the help of the contact points referred to in Article 57.

Article 57 Contact points

Each Member State shall designate, no later than 20 October 2007, a contact point whose remit shall be:

(a)   to provide the citizens and contact points of the other Member States with such information as is necessary concerning the recognition of professional qualifications provided for in this Directive, such as information on the national legislation governing the professions and the pursuit of those professions, including social legislation, and, where appropriate, the rules of ethics;

(b)   to assist citizens in realising the rights conferred on them by this Directive, in cooperation, where appropriate, with the other contact points and the competent authorities in the host Member State.

At the Commission's request, the contact points shall inform the Commission of the result of enquiries with which they are dealing pursuant to the provisions of point (b) within two months of receiving them.

Article 58 Committee procedure

1.   The Commission shall be assisted by a Committee on the recognition of professional qualifications.

2.   Where reference is made to this paragraph, Articles 5 and 7 of Decision 1999/468/EC shall apply, having regard to the provisions of Article 8 thereof. The period provided for in Article 5(6) of Decision 1999/468/EC shall be set at two months.

3.   Where reference is made to this paragraph, Article 5a(1) to (4) and Article 7 of Decision 1999/468/EC shall apply, having regard to the provisions of Article 8 thereof.

Article 59 Consultation

The Commission shall ensure the consultation of experts from the professional groups concerned in an appropriate manner in particular in the context of the work of the committee referred to in Article 58 and shall provide a reasoned report on these consultations to that committee.

TITLE VI OTHER PROVISIONS

Article 60 Reports

1.   As from 20 October 2007, Member States shall, every two years, send a report to the Commission on the application of the system. In addition to general observations, the report shall contain a statistical summary of decisions taken and a description of the main problems arising from the application of this Directive.

2.   As from 20 October 2007, the Commission shall draw up every five years a report on the implementation of this Directive.

Article 61 Derogation clause

If, for the application of one of the provisions of this Directive, a Member State encounters major difficulties in a particular area, the Commission shall examine those difficulties in collaboration with the Member State concerned.

Where appropriate, the Commission shall decide, in accordance with the procedure referred to in Article 58(2), to permit the Member State in question to derogate from the provision in question for a limited period.

Article 62 Repeal

Directives 77/452/EEC, 77/453/EEC, 78/686/EEC, 78/687/EEC, 78/1026/EEC, 78/1027/EEC, 80/154/EEC, 80/155/EEC, 85/384/EEC, 85/432/EEC, 85/433/EEC, 89/48/EEC, 92/51/EEC, 93/16/EEC and 1999/42/EC are repealed with effect from 20 October 2007. References to the repealed Directives shall be understood as references to this Directive and the acts adopted on the basis of those Directives shall not be affected by the repeal.

Article 63 Transposition

Member States shall bring into force the laws, regulations and administrative provisions necessary to comply with this Directive by 20 October 2007 at the latest. They shall forthwith inform the Commission thereof.

When Member States adopt these measures, they shall contain a reference to this Directive or be accompanied by such a reference on the occasion of their official publication. Member States shall determine how such reference is to be made.

Article 64 Entry into force

This Directive shall enter into force on the 20th day following its publication in the *Official Journal of the European Union.*

Article 65 Addressees

This Directive is addressed to the Member States.

(Date of signing and signatories omitted)

ANNEX I

List of professional associations or organisations fulfilling the conditions of Article 3(2)

IRELAND [1]

1. The Institute of Chartered Accountants in Ireland [2]

2. The Institute of Certified Public Accountants in Ireland [2]

3. The Association of Certified Accountants [2]

4. Institution of Engineers of Ireland

5. Irish Planning Institute

UNITED KINGDOM

1. Institute of Chartered Accountants in England and Wales

2. Institute of Chartered Accountants of Scotland

3. Institute of Chartered Accountants in Ireland

4. Chartered Association of Certified Accountants

5. Chartered Institute of Loss Adjusters

6. Chartered Institute of Management Accountants

7. Institute of Chartered Secretaries and Administrators

8. Chartered Insurance Institute

9. Institute of Actuaries

10. Faculty of Actuaries

11. Chartered Institute of Bankers

12. Institute of Bankers in Scotland

13. Royal Institution of Chartered Surveyors

14. Royal Town Planning Institute

15. Chartered Society of Physiotherapy

16. Royal Society of Chemistry

17. British Psychological Society

18. Library Association

19. Institute of Chartered Foresters

20. Chartered Institute of Building

21. Engineering Council

22. Institute of Energy

23. Institution of Structural Engineers

24. Institution of Civil Engineers

25. Institution of Mining Engineers

26. Institution of Mining and Metallurgy

27. Institution of Electrical Engineers

28. Institution of Gas Engineers

29. Institution of Mechanical Engineers

30. Institution of Chemical Engineers

31. Institution of Production Engineers

32. Institution of Marine Engineers

33. Royal Institution of Naval Architects

34. Royal Aeronautical Society

35. Institute of Metals

36. Chartered Institution of Building Services Engineers

37. Institute of Measurement and Control

38. British Computer Society

   [1] Irish nationals are also members of the following associations or organisations in the United Kingdom:
   — Institute of Chartered Accountants in England and Wales
   — Institute of Chartered Accountants of Scotland
   — Institute of Actuaries
   — Faculty of Actuaries
   — The Chartered Institute of Management Accountants

— Institute of Chartered Secretaries and Administrators
— Royal Town Planning Institute
— Royal Institution of Chartered Surveyors
— Chartered Institute of Building.
[2] Only for the activity of auditing accounts.

(*Annexes II–VII omitted*).

C) Free Movement of Services

Directive 2006/123/EC of the European Parliament and of the Council of 12 December 2006
on services in the internal market
OJ L 376, 27.12.06, p. 36[1]

. . . .

Chapter I GENERAL PROVISIONS

Article 1 Subject matter
1. This Directive establishes general provisions facilitating the exercise of the freedom of establishment for service providers and the free movement of services, while maintaining a high quality of services.

2. This Directive does not deal with the liberalisation of services of general economic interest, reserved to public or private entities, nor with the privatisation of public entities providing services.

3. This Directive does not deal with the abolition of monopolies providing services nor with aids granted by Member States which are covered by Community rules on competition.

    This Directive does not affect the freedom of Member States to define, in conformity with Community law, what they consider to be services of general economic interest, how those services should be organised and financed, in compliance with the State aid rules, and what specific obligations they should be subject to.

4. This Directive does not affect measures taken at Community level or at national level, in conformity with Community law, to protect or promote cultural or linguistic diversity or media pluralism.

5. This Directive does not affect Member States' rules of criminal law. However, Member States may not restrict the freedom to provide services by applying criminal law provisions which specifically regulate or affect access to or exercise of a service activity in circumvention of the rules laid down in this Directive.

6. This Directive does not affect labour law, that is any legal or contractual provision concerning employment conditions, working conditions, including health

. . . .

[1] EDITOR'S NOTE: Article 1 summarises the balance of issues set out in the preamble of 118 paragraphs. Due to its length the preamble has been omitted. For the full text see EUR-Lex reference 32006L0123. As of 1 June 2010 this Directive has not been amended following the adoption of the Treaty of Lisbon. It includes references to the old Treaty article numbers. Reference should be made to the Tables of Equivalences accompanying the consolidated Treaties in Part II of this edition for the conversion of old Treaty article numbers to new ones.

and safety at work and the relationship between employers and workers, which Member States apply in accordance with national law which respects Community law. Equally, this Directive does not affect the social security legislation of the Member States.

7.   This Directive does not affect the exercise of fundamental rights as recognised in the Member States and by Community law. Nor does it affect the right to negotiate, conclude and enforce collective agreements and to take industrial action in accordance with national law and practices which respect Community law.

Article 2 Scope

1.   This Directive shall apply to services supplied by providers established in a Member State.

2.   This Directive shall not apply to the following activities:
   (a) non-economic services of general interest;
   (b) financial services, such as banking, credit, insurance and re-insurance, occupational or personal pensions, securities, investment funds, payment and investment advice, including the services listed in Annex I to Directive 2006/48/EC;
   (c) electronic communications services and networks, and associated facilities and services, with respect to matters covered by Directives 2002/19/EC, 2002/20/EC, 2002/21/EC, 2002/22/EC and 2002/58/EC;
   (d) services in the field of transport, including port services, falling within the scope of Title V of the Treaty;
   (e) services of temporary work agencies;
   (f) healthcare services whether or not they are provided via healthcare facilities, and regardless of the ways in which they are organised and financed at national level or whether they are public or private;
   (g) audiovisual services, including cinematographic services, whatever their mode of production, distribution and transmission, and radio broadcasting;
   (h) gambling activities which involve wagering a stake with pecuniary value in games of chance, including lotteries, gambling in casinos and betting transactions;
   (i) activities which are connected with the exercise of official authority as set out in Article 45 of the Treaty;
   (j) social services relating to social housing, childcare and support of families and persons permanently or temporarily in need which are provided by the State, by providers mandated by the State or by charities recognised as such by the State;
   (k) private security services;
   (l) services provided by notaries and bailiffs, who are appointed by an official act of government.

3.   This Directive shall not apply to the field of taxation.

Article 3 Relationship with other provisions of Community law

1.   If the provisions of this Directive conflict with a provision of another Community act governing specific aspects of access to or exercise of a service activity in specific sectors or for specific professions, the provision of the other Community act shall prevail and shall apply to those specific sectors or professions. These include:
   (a) Directive 96/71/EC;
   (b) Regulation (EEC) No 1408/71;
   (c) Council Directive 89/552/EEC of 3 October 1989 on the coordination of certain

provisions laid down by law, regulation or administrative action in Member States concerning the pursuit of television broadcasting activities;

(d)   Directive 2005/36/EC.

2.   This Directive does not concern rules of private international law, in particular rules governing the law applicable to contractual and non contractual obligations, including those which guarantee that consumers benefit from the protection granted to them by the consumer protection rules laid down in the consumer legislation in force in their Member State.

3.   Member States shall apply the provisions of this Directive in compliance with the rules of the Treaty on the right of establishment and the free movement of services.

Article 4 Definitions

For the purposes of this Directive, the following definitions shall apply:

1)   "service" means any self-employed economic activity, normally provided for remuneration, as referred to in Article 50 of the Treaty;

2)   "provider" means any natural person who is a national of a Member State, or any legal person as referred to in Article 48 of the Treaty and established in a Member State, who offers or provides a service;

3)   "recipient" means any natural person who is a national of a Member State or who benefits from rights conferred upon him by Community acts, or any legal person as referred to in Article 48 of the Treaty and established in a Member State, who, for professional or non-professional purposes, uses, or wishes to use, a service;

4)   "Member State of establishment" means the Member State in whose territory the provider of the service concerned is established;

5)   "establishment" means the actual pursuit of an economic activity, as referred to in Article 43 of the Treaty, by the provider for an indefinite period and through a stable infrastructure from where the business of providing services is actually carried out;

6)   "authorisation scheme" means any procedure under which a provider or recipient is in effect required to take steps in order to obtain from a competent authority a formal decision, or an implied decision, concerning access to a service activity or the exercise thereof;

7)   "requirement" means any obligation, prohibition, condition or limit provided for in the laws, regulations or administrative provisions of the Member States or in consequence of case-law, administrative practice, the rules of professional bodies, or the collective rules of professional associations or other professional organisations, adopted in the exercise of their legal autonomy; rules laid down in collective agreements negotiated by the social partners shall not as such be seen as requirements within the meaning of this Directive;

8)   "overriding reasons relating to the public interest" means reasons recognised as such in the case law of the Court of Justice, including the following grounds: public policy; public security; public safety; public health; preserving the financial equilibrium of the social security system; the protection of consumers, recipients of services and workers; fairness of trade transactions; combating fraud; the protection of the environment and the urban environment; the health of animals; intellectual property; the conservation of the national historic and artistic heritage; social policy objectives and cultural policy objectives;

9)   "competent authority" means any body or authority which has a supervisory or regulatory role in a Member State in relation to service activities, including, in particular,

administrative authorities, including courts acting as such, professional bodies, and those professional associations or other professional organisations which, in the exercise of their legal autonomy, regulate in a collective manner access to service activities or the exercise thereof;

10) "Member State where the service is provided" means the Member State where the service is supplied by a provider established in another Member State;

11) "regulated profession" means a professional activity or a group of professional activities as referred to in Article 3(1)(a) of Directive 2005/36/EC;

12) "commercial communication" means any form of communication designed to promote, directly or indirectly, the goods, services or image of an undertaking, organisation or person engaged in commercial, industrial or craft activity or practising a regulated profession. The following do not in themselves constitute commercial communications:
(a) information enabling direct access to the activity of the undertaking, organisation or person, including in particular a domain name or an electronic-mailing address;
(b) communications relating to the goods, services or image of the undertaking, organisation or person, compiled in an independent manner, particularly when provided for no financial consideration.

Chapter II ADMINISTRATIVE SIMPLIFICATION

Article 5 Simplification of procedures

1. Member States shall examine the procedures and formalities applicable to access to a service activity and to the exercise thereof. Where procedures and formalities examined under this paragraph are not sufficiently simple, Member States shall simplify them.

2. The Commission may introduce harmonised forms at Community level, in accordance with the procedure referred to in Article 40(2). These forms shall be equivalent to certificates, attestations and any other documents required of a provider.

3. Where Member States require a provider or recipient to supply a certificate, attestation or any other document proving that a requirement has been satisfied, they shall accept any document from another Member State which serves an equivalent purpose or from which it is clear that the requirement in question has been satisfied. They may not require a document from another Member State to be produced in its original form, or as a certified copy or as a certified translation, save in the cases provided for in other Community instruments or where such a requirement is justified by an overriding reason relating to the public interest, including public order and security.

   The first subparagraph shall not affect the right of Member States to require non-certified translations of documents in one of their official languages.

4. Paragraph 3 shall not apply to the documents referred to in Article 7(2) and 50 of Directive 2005/36/EC, in Articles 45(3), 46, 49 and 50 of Directive 2004/18/EC of the European Parliament and of the Council of 31 March 2004 on the coordination of procedures for the award of public works contracts, public supply contracts and public service contracts, in Article 3(2) of Directive 98/5/EC of the European Parliament and of the Council of 16 February 1998 to facilitate practice of the profession of lawyer on a permanent basis in a Member State other than that in which the qualification was obtained, in the First Council Directive 68/151/EEC of 9 March 1968 on coordination of safeguards which, for the protection of the interests of members and others, are required by Member States of companies within the meaning of the second paragraph of Article 58 of the Treaty, with a view to making such safeguards equivalent throughout the Community and in the Eleventh Council Directive 89/666/EECof 21 December 1989

concerning disclosure requirements in respect of branches opened in a Member State by certain types of company governed by the law of another State.

Article 6 Points of single contact

1.   Member States shall ensure that it is possible for providers to complete the following procedures and formalities through points of single contact:

    (a) all procedures and formalities needed for access to his service activities, in particular, all declarations, notifications or applications necessary for authorisation from the competent authorities, including applications for inclusion in a register, a roll or a database, or for registration with a professional body or association;

    (b) any applications for authorisation needed to exercise his service activities.

2.   The establishment of points of single contact shall be without prejudice to the allocation of functions and powers among the authorities within national systems.

Article 7 Right to information

1.   Member States shall ensure that the following information is easily accessible to providers and recipients through the points of single contact:

    (a) requirements applicable to providers established in their territory, in particular those requirements concerning the procedures and formalities to be completed in order to access and to exercise service activities;

    (b) the contact details of the competent authorities enabling the latter to be contacted directly, including the details of those authorities responsible for matters concerning the exercise of service activities;

    (c) the means of, and conditions for, accessing public registers and databases on providers and services;

    (d) the means of redress which are generally available in the event of dispute between the competent authorities and the provider or the recipient, or between a provider and a recipient or between providers;

    (e) the contact details of the associations or organisations, other than the competent authorities, from which providers or recipients may obtain practical assistance.

2.   Member States shall ensure that it is possible for providers and recipients to receive, at their request, assistance from the competent authorities, consisting in information on the way in which the requirements referred to in point (a) of paragraph 1 are generally interpreted and applied. Where appropriate, such advice shall include a simple step-by-step guide. The information shall be provided in plain and intelligible language.

3.   Member States shall ensure that the information and assistance referred to in paragraphs 1 and 2 are provided in a clear and unambiguous manner, that they are easily accessible at a distance and by electronic means and that they are kept up to date.

4.   Member States shall ensure that the points of single contact and the competent authorities respond as quickly as possible to any request for information or assistance as referred to in paragraphs 1 and 2 and, in cases where the request is faulty or unfounded, inform the applicant accordingly without delay.

5.   Member States and the Commission shall take accompanying measures in order to encourage points of single contact to make the information provided for in this Article available in other Community languages. This does not interfere with Member States' legislation on the use of languages.

6.   The obligation for competent authorities to assist providers and recipients does not require those authorities to provide legal advice in individual cases but concerns only general information on the way in which requirements are usually interpreted or applied.

Article 8 Procedures by electronic means

1. Member States shall ensure that all procedures and formalities relating to access to a service activity and to the exercise thereof may be easily completed, at a distance and by electronic means, through the relevant point of single contact and with the relevant competent authorities.

2. Paragraph 1 shall not apply to the inspection of premises on which the service is provided or of equipment used by the provider or to physical examination of the capability or of the personal integrity of the provider or of his responsible staff.

3. The Commission shall, in accordance with the procedure referred to in Article 40(2), adopt detailed rules for the implementation of paragraph 1 of this Article with a view to facilitating the interoperability of information systems and use of procedures by electronic means between Member States, taking into account common standards developed at Community level.

Chapter III FREEDOM OF ESTABLISHMENT FOR PROVIDERS

SECTION 1 AUTHORISATIONS

Article 9 Authorisation schemes

1. Member States shall not make access to a service activity or the exercise thereof subject to an authorisation scheme unless the following conditions are satisfied:
    (a) the authorisation scheme does not discriminate against the provider in question;
    (b) the need for an authorisation scheme is justified by an overriding reason relating to the public interest;
    (c) the objective pursued cannot be attained by means of a less restrictive measure, in particular because an a posteriori inspection would take place too late to be genuinely effective.

2. In the report referred to in Article 39(1), Member States shall identify their authorisation schemes and give reasons showing their compatibility with paragraph 1 of this Article.

3. This section shall not apply to those aspects of authorisation schemes which are governed directly or indirectly by other Community instruments.

Article 10 Conditions for the granting of authorisation

1. Authorisation schemes shall be based on criteria which preclude the competent authorities from exercising their power of assessment in an arbitrary manner.

2. The criteria referred to in paragraph 1 shall be:
    (a) non-discriminatory;
    (b) justified by an overriding reason relating to the public interest;
    (c) proportionate to that public interest objective;
    (d) clear and unambiguous;
    (e) objective;
    (f) made public in advance;
    (g) transparent and accessible.

3. The conditions for granting authorisation for a new establishment shall not duplicate requirements and controls which are equivalent or essentially comparable as regards their purpose to which the provider is already subject in another Member State or in the same Member State. The liaison points referred to in Article 28(2) and the provider shall assist the competent authority by providing any necessary information regarding those requirements.

4.   The authorisation shall enable the provider to have access to the service activity, or to exercise that activity, throughout the national territory, including by means of setting up agencies, subsidiaries, branches or offices, except where an authorisation for each individual establishment or a limitation of the authorisation to a certain part of the territory is justified by an overriding reason relating to the public interest.

5.   The authorisation shall be granted as soon as it is established, in the light of an appropriate examination, that the conditions for authorisation have been met.

6.   Except in the case of the granting of an authorisation, any decision from the competent authorities, including refusal or withdrawal of an authorisation, shall be fully reasoned and shall be open to challenge before the courts or other instances of appeal.

7.   This Article shall not call into question the allocation of the competences, at local or regional level, of the Member States' authorities granting authorisations.

Article 11 Duration of authorisation

1.   An authorisation granted to a provider shall not be for a limited period, except where:
      (a) the authorisation is being automatically renewed or is subject only to the continued fulfilment of requirements;
      (b) the number of available authorisations is limited by an overriding reason relating to the public interest; or
      (c) a limited authorisation period can be justified by an overriding reason relating to the public interest.

2.   Paragraph 1 shall not concern the maximum period before the end of which the provider must actually commence his activity after receiving authorisation.

3.   Member States shall require a provider to inform the relevant point of single contact provided for in Article 6 of the following changes:
      (a) the creation of subsidiaries whose activities fall within the scope of the authorisation scheme;
      (b) changes in his situation which result in the conditions for authorisation no longer being met.

4.   This Article shall be without prejudice to the Member States' ability to revoke authorisations, when the conditions for authorisation are no longer met.

Article 12 Selection from among several candidates

1.   Where the number of authorisations available for a given activity is limited because of the scarcity of available natural resources or technical capacity, Member States shall apply a selection procedure to potential candidates which provides full guarantees of impartiality and transparency, including, in particular, adequate publicity about the launch, conduct and completion of the procedure.

2.   In the cases referred to in paragraph 1, authorisation shall be granted for an appropriate limited period and may not be open to automatic renewal nor confer any other advantage on the provider whose authorisation has just expired or on any person having any particular links with that provider.

3.   Subject to paragraph 1 and to Articles 9 and 10, Member States may take into account, in establishing the rules for the selection procedure, considerations of public health, social policy objectives, the health and safety of employees or self-employed persons, the protection of the environment, the preservation of cultural heritage and other overriding reasons relating to the public interest, in conformity with Community law.

Article 13 Authorisation procedures

1. Authorisation procedures and formalities shall be clear, made public in advance and be such as to provide the applicants with a guarantee that their application will be dealt with objectively and impartially.

2. Authorisation procedures and formalities shall not be dissuasive and shall not unduly complicate or delay the provision of the service. They shall be easily accessible and any charges which the applicants may incur from their application shall be reasonable and proportionate to the cost of the authorisation procedures in question and shall not exceed the cost of the procedures.

3. Authorisation procedures and formalities shall provide applicants with a guarantee that their application will be processed as quickly as possible and, in any event, within a reasonable period which is fixed and made public in advance. The period shall run only from the time when all documentation has been submitted. When justified by the complexity of the issue, the time period may be extended once, by the competent authority, for a limited time. The extension and its duration shall be duly motivated and shall be notified to the applicant before the original period has expired.

4. Failing a response within the time period set or extended in accordance with paragraph 3, authorisation shall be deemed to have been granted. Different arrangements may nevertheless be put in place, where justified by overriding reasons relating to the public interest, including a legitimate interest of third parties.

5. All applications for authorisation shall be acknowledged as quickly as possible. The acknowledgement must specify the following:
    (a) the period referred to in paragraph 3;
    (b) the available means of redress;
    (c) where applicable, a statement that in the absence of a response within the period specified, the authorisation shall be deemed to have been granted.

6. In the case of an incomplete application, the applicant shall be informed as quickly as possible of the need to supply any additional documentation, as well as of any possible effects on the period referred to in paragraph 3.

7. When a request is rejected because it fails to comply with the required procedures or formalities, the applicant shall be informed of the rejection as quickly as possible.

SECTION 2 REQUIREMENTS PROHIBITED OR SUBJECT TO EVALUATION

Article 14 Prohibited requirements

Member States shall not make access to, or the exercise of, a service activity in their territory subject to compliance with any of the following:

1) discriminatory requirements based directly or indirectly on nationality or, in the case of companies, the location of the registered office, including in particular:
    (a) nationality requirements for the provider, his staff, persons holding the share capital or members of the provider's management or supervisory bodies;
    (b) a requirement that the provider, his staff, persons holding the share capital or members of the provider's management or supervisory bodies be resident within the territory;

2) a prohibition on having an establishment in more than one Member State or on being entered in the registers or enrolled with professional bodies or associations of more than one Member State;

3) restrictions on the freedom of a provider to choose between a principal or a secondary establishment, in particular an obligation on the provider to have its principal

establishment in their territory, or restrictions on the freedom to choose between establishment in the form of an agency, branch or subsidiary;

4)   conditions of reciprocity with the Member State in which the provider already has an establishment, save in the case of conditions of reciprocity provided for in Community instruments concerning energy;

5)   the case-by-case application of an economic test making the granting of authorisation subject to proof of the existence of an economic need or market demand, an assessment of the potential or current economic effects of the activity or an assessment of the appropriateness of the activity in relation to the economic planning objectives set by the competent authority; this prohibition shall not concern planning requirements which do not pursue economic aims but serve overriding reasons relating to the public interest;

6)   the direct or indirect involvement of competing operators, including within consultative bodies, in the granting of authorisations or in the adoption of other decisions of the competent authorities, with the exception of professional bodies and associations or other organisations acting as the competent authority; this prohibition shall not concern the consultation of organisations, such as chambers of commerce or social partners, on matters other than individual applications for authorisation, or a consultation of the public at large;

7)   an obligation to provide or participate in a financial guarantee or to take out insurance from a provider or body established in their territory. This shall not affect the possibility for Member States to require insurance or financial guarantees as such, nor shall it affect requirements relating to the participation in a collective compensation fund, for instance for members of professional bodies or organisations;

8)   an obligation to have been pre-registered, for a given period, in the registers held in their territory or to have previously exercised the activity for a given period in their territory.

Article 15 Requirements to be evaluated

1.   Member States shall examine whether, under their legal system, any of the requirements listed in paragraph 2 are imposed and shall ensure that any such requirements are compatible with the conditions laid down in paragraph 3. Member States shall adapt their laws, regulations or administrative provisions so as to make them compatible with those conditions.

2.   Member States shall examine whether their legal system makes access to a service activity or the exercise of it subject to compliance with any of the following non-discriminatory requirements:
(a) quantitative or territorial restrictions, in particular in the form of limits fixed according to population or of a minimum geographical distance between providers;
(b) an obligation on a provider to take a specific legal form;
(c) requirements which relate to the shareholding of a company;
(d) requirements, other than those concerning matters covered by Directive 2005/36/EC or provided for in other Community instruments, which reserve access to the service activity in question to particular providers by virtue of the specific nature of the activity;
(e) a ban on having more than one establishment in the territory of the same State;
(f) requirements fixing a minimum number of employees;
(g) fixed minimum and/or maximum tariffs with which the provider must comply;
(h) an obligation on the provider to supply other specific services jointly with his service.

3.   Member States shall verify that the requirements referred to in paragraph 2 satisfy the following conditions:

(a) non-discrimination: requirements must be neither directly nor indirectly discriminatory according to nationality nor, with regard to companies, according to the location of the registered office;

(b) necessity: requirements must be justified by an overriding reason relating to the public interest;

(c) proportionality: requirements must be suitable for securing the attainment of the objective pursued; they must not go beyond what is necessary to attain that objective and it must not be possible to replace those requirements with other, less restrictive measures which attain the same result.

4. Paragraphs 1, 2 and 3 shall apply to legislation in the field of services of general economic interest only insofar as the application of these paragraphs does not obstruct the performance, in law or in fact, of the particular task assigned to them.

5. In the mutual evaluation report provided for in Article 39(1), Member States shall specify the following:

(a) the requirements that they intend to maintain and the reasons why they consider that those requirements comply with the conditions set out in paragraph 3;

(b) the requirements which have been abolished or made less stringent.

6. From 28 December 2006 Member States shall not introduce any new requirement of a kind listed in paragraph 2, unless that requirement satisfies the conditions laid down in paragraph 3.

7. Member States shall notify the Commission of any new laws, regulations or administrative provisions which set requirements as referred to in paragraph 6, together with the reasons for those requirements. The Commission shall communicate the provisions concerned to the other Member States. Such notification shall not prevent Member States from adopting the provisions in question.

Within a period of 3 months from the date of receipt of the notification, the Commission shall examine the compatibility of any new requirements with Community law and, where appropriate, shall adopt a decision requesting the Member State in question to refrain from adopting them or to abolish them.

The notification of a draft national law in accordance with Directive 98/34/EC shall fulfil the obligation of notification provided for in this Directive.

Chapter IV FREE MOVEMENT OF SERVICES

SECTION 1 FREEDOM TO PROVIDE SERVICES AND RELATED DEROGATIONS

Article 16 Freedom to provide services

1. Member States shall respect the right of providers to provide services in a Member State other than that in which they are established.

The Member State in which the service is provided shall ensure free access to and free exercise of a service activity within its territory.

Member States shall not make access to or exercise of a service activity in their territory subject to compliance with any requirements which do not respect the following principles:

(a) non-discrimination: the requirement may be neither directly nor indirectly discriminatory with regard to nationality or, in the case of legal persons, with regard to the Member State in which they are established;

(b) necessity: the requirement must be justified for reasons of public policy, public security, public health or the protection of the environment;

(c) proportionality: the requirement must be suitable for attaining the objective pursued, and must not go beyond what is necessary to attain that objective.

2. Member States may not restrict the freedom to provide services in the case of a provider established in another Member State by imposing any of the following requirements:
   (a) an obligation on the provider to have an establishment in their territory;
   (b) an obligation on the provider to obtain an authorisation from their competent authorities including entry in a register or registration with a professional body or association in their territory, except where provided for in this Directive or other instruments of Community law;
   (c) a ban on the provider setting up a certain form or type of infrastructure in their territory, including an office or chambers, which the provider needs in order to supply the services in question;
   (d) the application of specific contractual arrangements between the provider and the recipient which prevent or restrict service provision by the self-employed;
   (e) an obligation on the provider to possess an identity document issued by its competent authorities specific to the exercise of a service activity;
   (f) requirements, except for those necessary for health and safety at work, which affect the use of equipment and material which are an integral part of the service provided;
   (g) restrictions on the freedom to provide the services referred to in Article 19.

3. The Member State to which the provider moves shall not be prevented from imposing requirements with regard to the provision of a service activity, where they are justified for reasons of public policy, public security, public health or the protection of the environment and in accordance with paragraph 1. Nor shall that Member State be prevented from applying, in accordance with Community law, its rules on employment conditions, including those laid down in collective agreements.

4. By 28 December 2011 the Commission shall, after consultation of the Member States and the social partners at Community level, submit to the European Parliament and the Council a report on the application of this Article, in which it shall consider the need to propose harmonisation measures regarding service activities covered by this Directive.

Article 17 Additional derogations from the freedom to provide services
Article 16 shall not apply to:
1) services of general economic interest which are provided in another Member State, inter alia:
   (a) in the postal sector, services covered by Directive 97/67/EC of the European Parliament and of the Council of 15 December 1997 on common rules for the development of the internal market of Community postal services and the improvement of quality of service;
   (b) in the electricity sector, services covered by Directive 2003/54/EC of the European Parliament and of the Council of 26 June 2003 concerning common rules for the internal market in electricity;
   (c) in the gas sector, services covered by Directive 2003/55/EC of the European Parliament and of the Council of 26 June 2003 concerning common rules for the internal market in natural gas;
   (d) water distribution and supply services and waste water services;
   (e) treatment of waste;

2) matters covered by Directive 96/71/EC;

3) matters covered by Directive 95/46/EC of the European Parliament and of the Council of 24 October 1995 on the protection of individuals with regard to the processing of personal data and on the free movement of such data;

4)   matters covered by Council Directive 77/249/EEC of 22 March 1977 to facilitate the effective exercise by lawyers of freedom to provide services;

5)   the activity of judicial recovery of debts;

6)   matters covered by Title II of Directive 2005/36/EC, as well as requirements in the Member State where the service is provided which reserve an activity to a particular profession;

7)   matters covered by Regulation (EEC) No 1408/71;

8)   as regards administrative formalities concerning the free movement of persons and their residence, matters covered by the provisions of Directive 2004/38/EC that lay down administrative formalities of the competent authorities of the Member State where the service is provided with which beneficiaries must comply;

9)   as regards third country nationals who move to another Member State in the context of the provision of a service, the possibility for Member States to require visa or residence permits for third country nationals who are not covered by the mutual recognition regime provided for in Article 21 of the Convention implementing the Schengen Agreement of 14 June 1985 on the gradual abolition of checks at the common borders or the possibility to oblige third country nationals to report to the competent authorities of the Member State in which the service is provided on or after their entry;

10)   as regards the shipment of waste, matters covered by Council Regulation (EEC) No 259/93 of 1 February 1993 on the supervision and control of shipments of waste within, into and out of the European Community;

11)   copyright, neighbouring rights and rights covered by Council Directive 87/54/EEC of 16 December 1986 on the legal protection of topographies of semiconductor products and by Directive 96/9/EC of the European Parliament and of the Council of 11 March 1996 on the legal protection of databases, as well as industrial property rights;

12)   acts requiring by law the involvement of a notary;

13)   matters covered by Directive 2006/43/EC of the European Parliament and of the Council of 17 May 2006 on statutory audit of annual accounts and consolidated accounts;

14)   the registration of vehicles leased in another Member State;

15)   provisions regarding contractual and non-contractual obligations, including the form of contracts, determined pursuant to the rules of private international law.

Article 18 Case-by-case derogations

1.   By way of derogation from Article 16, and in exceptional circumstances only, a Member State may, in respect of a provider established in another Member State, take measures relating to the safety of services.

2.   The measures provided for in paragraph 1 may be taken only if the mutual assistance procedure laid down in Article 35 is complied with and the following conditions are fulfilled:
     (a) the national provisions in accordance with which the measure is taken have not been subject to Community harmonisation in the field of the safety of services;
     (b) the measures provide for a higher level of protection of the recipient than would be the case in a measure taken by the Member State of establishment in accordance with its national provisions;
     (c) the Member State of establishment has not taken any measures or has taken measures which are insufficient as compared with those referred to in Article 35(2);
     (d) the measures are proportionate.

3.   Paragraphs 1 and 2 shall be without prejudice to provisions, laid down in Community instruments, which guarantee the freedom to provide services or which allow derogations therefrom.

SECTION 2 RIGHTS OF RECIPIENTS OF SERVICES

Article 19 Prohibited restrictions

Member States may not impose on a recipient requirements which restrict the use of a service supplied by a provider established in another Member State, in particular the following requirements:

(a)   an obligation to obtain authorisation from or to make a declaration to their competent authorities;

(b)   discriminatory limits on the grant of financial assistance by reason of the fact that the provider is established in another Member State or by reason of the location of the place at which the service is provided.

Article 20 Non-discrimination

1.   Member States shall ensure that the recipient is not made subject to discriminatory requirements based on his nationality or place of residence.

2.   Member States shall ensure that the general conditions of access to a service, which are made available to the public at large by the provider, do not contain discriminatory provisions relating to the nationality or place of residence of the recipient, but without precluding the possibility of providing for differences in the conditions of access where those differences are directly justified by objective criteria.

Article 21 Assistance for recipients

1.   Member States shall ensure that recipients can obtain, in their Member State of residence, the following information:

(a)   general information on the requirements applicable in other Member States relating to access to, and exercise of, service activities, in particular those relating to consumer protection;

(b)   general information on the means of redress available in the case of a dispute between a provider and a recipient;

(c)   the contact details of associations or organisations, including the centres of the European Consumer Centres Network, from which providers or recipients may obtain practical assistance.

Where appropriate, advice from the competent authorities shall include a simple step-by-step guide. Information and assistance shall be provided in a clear and unambiguous manner, shall be easily accessible at a distance, including by electronic means, and shall be kept up to date.

2.   Member States may confer responsibility for the task referred to in paragraph 1 on points of single contact or on any other body, such as the centres of the European Consumer Centres Network, consumer associations or Euro Info Centres.

Member States shall communicate to the Commission the names and contact details of the designated bodies. The Commission shall transmit them to all Member States.

3.   In fulfilment of the requirements set out in paragraphs 1 and 2, the body approached by the recipient shall, if necessary, contact the relevant body for the Member State concerned. The latter shall send the information requested as soon as possible to the requesting body which shall forward the information to the recipient. Member States shall ensure that those bodies give each other mutual assistance and shall put in place all possible measures

for effective cooperation. Together with the Commission, Member States shall put in place practical arrangements necessary for the implementation of paragraph 1.

4.   The Commission shall, in accordance with the procedure referred to in Article 40(2), adopt measures for the implementation of paragraphs 1, 2 and 3 of this Article, specifying the technical mechanisms for the exchange of information between the bodies of the various Member States and, in particular, the interoperability of information systems, taking into account common standards.

Chapter V QUALITY OF SERVICES

Article 22 Information on providers and their services

1.   Member States shall ensure that providers make the following information available to the recipient:

(a) the name of the provider, his legal status and form, the geographic address at which he is established and details enabling him to be contacted rapidly and communicated with directly and, as the case may be, by electronic means;

(b) where the provider is registered in a trade or other similar public register, the name of that register and the provider's registration number, or equivalent means of identification in that register;

(c) where the activity is subject to an authorisation scheme, the particulars of the relevant competent authority or the single point of contact;

(d) where the provider exercises an activity which is subject to VAT, the identification number referred to in Article 22(1) of Sixth Council Directive 77/388/EEC of 17 May 1977 on the harmonisation of the laws of the Member States relating to turnover taxes – Common system of value added tax: uniform basis of assessment;

(e) in the case of the regulated professions, any professional body or similar institution with which the provider is registered, the professional title and the Member State in which that title has been granted;

(f) the general conditions and clauses, if any, used by the provider;

(g) the existence of contractual clauses, if any, used by the provider concerning the law applicable to the contract and/or the competent courts;

(h) the existence of an after-sales guarantee, if any, not imposed by law;

(i) the price of the service, where a price is pre-determined by the provider for a given type of service;

(j) the main features of the service, if not already apparent from the context;

(k) the insurance or guarantees referred to in Article 23(1), and in particular the contact details of the insurer or guarantor and the territorial coverage.

2.   Member States shall ensure that the information referred to in paragraph 1, according to the provider's preference:

(a) is supplied by the provider on his own initiative;

(b) is easily accessible to the recipient at the place where the service is provided or the contract concluded;

(c) can be easily accessed by the recipient electronically by means of an address supplied by the provider;

(d) appears in any information documents supplied to the recipient by the provider which set out a detailed description of the service he provides.

3.   Member States shall ensure that, at the recipient's request, providers supply the following additional information:

(a) where the price is not pre-determined by the provider for a given type of service, the price of the service or, if an exact price cannot be given, the method for calculating the price so that it can be checked by the recipient, or a sufficiently detailed estimate;

(b) as regards the regulated professions, a reference to the professional rules applicable in the Member State of establishment and how to access them;

(c) information on their multidisciplinary activities and partnerships which are directly linked to the service in question and on the measures taken to avoid conflicts of interest. That information shall be included in any information document in which providers give a detailed description of their services;

(d) any codes of conduct to which the provider is subject and the address at which these codes may be consulted by electronic means, specifying the language version available;

(e) where a provider is subject to a code of conduct, or member of a trade association or professional body which provides for recourse to a non-judicial means of dispute settlement, information in this respect. The provider shall specify how to access detailed information on the characteristics of, and conditions for, the use of non-judicial means of dispute settlement.

4.   Member States shall ensure that the information which a provider must supply in accordance with this Chapter is made available or communicated in a clear and unambiguous manner, and in good time before conclusion of the contract or, where there is no written contract, before the service is provided.

5.   The information requirements laid down in this Chapter are in addition to requirements already provided for in Community law and do not prevent Member States from imposing additional information requirements applicable to providers established in their territory.

6.   The Commission may, in accordance with the procedure referred to in Article 40(2), specify the content of the information provided for in paragraphs 1 and 3 of this Article according to the specific nature of certain activities and may specify the practical means of implementing paragraph 2 of this Article.

Article 23 Professional liability insurance and guarantees

1.   Member States may ensure that providers whose services present a direct and particular risk to the health or safety of the recipient or a third person, or to the financial security of the recipient, subscribe to professional liability insurance appropriate to the nature and extent of the risk, or provide a guarantee or similar arrangement which is equivalent or essentially comparable as regards its purpose.

2.   When a provider establishes himself in their territory, Member States may not require professional liability insurance or a guarantee from the provider where he is already covered by a guarantee which is equivalent, or essentially comparable as regards its purpose and the cover it provides in terms of the insured risk, the insured sum or a ceiling for the guarantee and possible exclusions from the cover, in another Member State in which the provider is already established. Where equivalence is only partial, Member States may require a supplementary guarantee to cover those aspects not already covered.

When a Member State requires a provider established in its territory to subscribe to professional liability insurance or to provide another guarantee, that Member State shall accept as sufficient evidence attestations of such insurance cover issued by credit institutions and insurers established in other Member States.

3.   Paragraphs 1 and 2 shall not affect professional insurance or guarantee arrangements provided for in other Community instruments.

4.   For the implementation of paragraph 1, the Commission may, in accordance with the regulatory procedure referred to in Article 40(2), establish a list of services which exhibit the characteristics referred to in paragraph 1 of this Article. The Commission may also, in

accordance with the procedure referred to in Article 40(3), adopt measures designed to amend non-essential elements of this Directive by supplementing it by establishing common criteria for defining, for the purposes of the insurance or guarantees referred to in paragraph 1 of this Article, what is appropriate to the nature and extent of the risk.

5.   For the purpose of this Article
      — "direct and particular risk" means a risk arising directly from the provision of the service,
      — "health and safety" means, in relation to a recipient or a third person, the prevention of death or serious personal injury,
      — "financial security" means, in relation to a recipient, the prevention of substantial losses of money or of value of property,
      — "professional liability insurance" means insurance taken out by a provider in respect of potential liabilities to recipients and, where applicable, third parties arising out of the provision of the service.

Article 24 Commercial communications by the regulated professions

1.   Member States shall remove all total prohibitions on commercial communications by the regulated professions.

2.   Member States shall ensure that commercial communications by the regulated professions comply with professional rules, in conformity with Community law, which relate, in particular, to the independence, dignity and integrity of the profession, as well as to professional secrecy, in a manner consistent with the specific nature of each profession. Professional rules on commercial communications shall be non-discriminatory, justified by an overriding reason relating to the public interest and proportionate.

Article 25 Multidisciplinary activities

1.   Member States shall ensure that providers are not made subject to requirements which oblige them to exercise a given specific activity exclusively or which restrict the exercise jointly or in partnership of different activities.

      However, the following providers may be made subject to such requirements:
      (a) the regulated professions, in so far as is justified in order to guarantee compliance with the rules governing professional ethics and conduct, which vary according to the specific nature of each profession, and is necessary in order to ensure their independence and impartiality;
      (b) providers of certification, accreditation, technical monitoring, test or trial services, in so far as is justified in order to ensure their independence and impartiality.

2.   Where multidisciplinary activities between providers referred to in points (a) and (b) of paragraph 1 are authorised, Member States shall ensure the following:
      (a) that conflicts of interest and incompatibilities between certain activities are prevented;
      (b) that the independence and impartiality required for certain activities is secured;
      (c) that the rules governing professional ethics and conduct for different activities are compatible with one another, especially as regards matters of professional secrecy.

3.   In the report referred to in Article 39(1), Member States shall indicate which providers are subject to the requirements laid down in paragraph 1 of this Article, the content of those requirements and the reasons for which they consider them to be justified.

Article 26 Policy on quality of services

1. Member States shall, in cooperation with the Commission, take accompanying measures to encourage providers to take action on a voluntary basis in order to ensure the quality of service provision, in particular through use of one of the following methods:

   (a) certification or assessment of their activities by independent or accredited bodies;

   (b) drawing up their own quality charter or participation in quality charters or labels drawn up by professional bodies at Community level.

2. Member States shall ensure that information on the significance of certain labels and the criteria for applying labels and other quality marks relating to services can be easily accessed by providers and recipients.

3. Member States shall, in cooperation with the Commission, take accompanying measures to encourage professional bodies, as well as chambers of commerce and craft associations and consumer associations, in their territory to cooperate at Community level in order to promote the quality of service provision, especially by making it easier to assess the competence of a provider.

4. Member States shall, in cooperation with the Commission, take accompanying measures to encourage the development of independent assessments, notably by consumer associations, in relation to the quality and defects of service provision, and, in particular, the development at Community level of comparative trials or testing and the communication of the results.

5. Member States, in cooperation with the Commission, shall encourage the development of voluntary European standards with the aim of facilitating compatibility between services supplied by providers in different Member States, information to the recipient and the quality of service provision.

Article 27 Settlement of disputes

1. Member States shall take the general measures necessary to ensure that providers supply contact details, in particular a postal address, fax number or e-mail address and telephone number to which all recipients, including those resident in another Member State, can send a complaint or a request for information about the service provided. Providers shall supply their legal address if this is not their usual address for correspondence.

   Member States shall take the general measures necessary to ensure that providers respond to the complaints referred to in the first subparagraph in the shortest possible time and make their best efforts to find a satisfactory solution.

2. Member States shall take the general measures necessary to ensure that providers are obliged to demonstrate compliance with the obligations laid down in this Directive as to the provision of information and to demonstrate that the information is accurate.

3. Where a financial guarantee is required for compliance with a judicial decision, Member States shall recognise equivalent guarantees lodged with a credit institution or insurer established in another Member State. Such credit institutions must be authorised in a Member State in accordance with Directive 2006/48/EC and such insurers in accordance, as appropriate, with First Council Directive 73/239/EEC of 24 July 1973 on the coordination of laws, regulations and administrative provisions relating to the taking-up and pursuit of the business of direct insurance other than life assurance and Directive 2002/83/EC of the European Parliament and of the Council of 5 November 2002 concerning life assurance.

4. Member States shall take the general measures necessary to ensure that providers who are subject to a code of conduct, or are members of a trade association or professional body,

which provides for recourse to a non-judicial means of dispute settlement inform the recipient thereof and mention that fact in any document which presents their services in detail, specifying how to access detailed information on the characteristics of, and conditions for, the use of such a mechanism.

Chapter VI ADMINISTRATIVE COOPERATION

Article 28 Mutual assistance – general obligations

1.   Member States shall give each other mutual assistance, and shall put in place measures for effective cooperation with one another, in order to ensure the supervision of providers and the services they provide.

2.   For the purposes of this Chapter, Member States shall designate one or more liaison points, the contact details of which shall be communicated to the other Member States and the Commission. The Commission shall publish and regularly update the list of liaison points.

3.   Information requests and requests to carry out any checks, inspections and investigations under this Chapter shall be duly motivated, in particular by specifying the reason for the request. Information exchanged shall be used only in respect of the matter for which it was requested.

4.   In the event of receiving a request for assistance from competent authorities in another Member State, Member States shall ensure that providers established in their territory supply their competent authorities with all the information necessary for supervising their activities in compliance with their national laws.

5.   In the event of difficulty in meeting a request for information or in carrying out checks, inspections or investigations, the Member State in question shall rapidly inform the requesting Member State with a view to finding a solution.

6.   Member States shall supply the information requested by other Member States or the Commission by electronic means and within the shortest possible period of time.

7.   Member States shall ensure that registers in which providers have been entered, and which may be consulted by the competent authorities in their territory, may also be consulted, in accordance with the same conditions, by the equivalent competent authorities of the other Member States.

8.   Member States shall communicate to the Commission information on cases where other Member States do not fulfil their obligation of mutual assistance. Where necessary, the Commission shall take appropriate steps, including proceedings provided for in Article 226 of the Treaty, in order to ensure that the Member States concerned comply with their obligation of mutual assistance. The Commission shall periodically inform Member States about the functioning of the mutual assistance provisions.

Article 29 Mutual assistance – general obligations for the Member State of establishment

1.   With respect to providers providing services in another Member State, the Member State of establishment shall supply information on providers established in its territory when requested to do so by another Member State and, in particular, confirmation that a provider is established in its territory and, to its knowledge, is not exercising his activities in an unlawful manner.

2.   The Member State of establishment shall undertake the checks, inspections and investigations requested by another Member State and shall inform the latter of the results and, as the case may be, of the measures taken. In so doing, the competent authorities

shall act to the extent permitted by the powers vested in them in their Member State. The competent authorities can decide on the most appropriate measures to be taken in each individual case in order to meet the request by another Member State.

3.   Upon gaining actual knowledge of any conduct or specific acts by a provider established in its territory which provides services in other Member States, that, to its knowledge, could cause serious damage to the health or safety of persons or to the environment, the Member State of establishment shall inform all other Member States and the Commission within the shortest possible period of time.

Article 30 Supervision by the Member State of establishment in the event of the temporary movement of a provider to another Member State

1.   With respect to cases not covered by Article 31(1), the Member State of establishment shall ensure that compliance with its requirements is supervised in conformity with the powers of supervision provided for in its national law, in particular through supervisory measures at the place of establishment of the provider.

2.   The Member State of establishment shall not refrain from taking supervisory or enforcement measures in its territory on the grounds that the service has been provided or caused damage in another Member State.

3.   The obligation laid down in paragraph 1 shall not entail a duty on the part of the Member State of establishment to carry out factual checks and controls in the territory of the Member State where the service is provided. Such checks and controls shall be carried out by the authorities of the Member State where the provider is temporarily operating at the request of the authorities of the Member State of establishment, in accordance with Article 31.

Article 31 Supervision by the Member State where the service is provided in the event of the temporary movement of the provider

1.   With respect to national requirements which may be imposed pursuant to Articles 16 or 17, the Member State where the service is provided is responsible for the supervision of the activity of the provider in its territory. In conformity with Community law, the Member State where the service is provided:
       (a)   shall take all measures necessary to ensure the provider complies with those requirements as regards the access to and the exercise of the activity;
       (b)   shall carry out the checks, inspections and investigations necessary to supervise the service provided.

2.   With respect to requirements other than those referred to in paragraph 1, where a provider moves temporarily to another Member State in order to provide a service without being established there, the competent authorities of that Member State shall participate in the supervision of the provider in accordance with paragraphs 3 and 4.

3.   At the request of the Member State of establishment, the competent authorities of the Member State where the service is provided shall carry out any checks, inspections and investigations necessary for ensuring the effective supervision by the Member State of establishment. In so doing, the competent authorities shall act to the extent permitted by the powers vested in them in their Member State. The competent authorities may decide on the most appropriate measures to be taken in each individual case in order to meet the request by the Member State of establishment.

4.   On their own initiative, the competent authorities of the Member State where the service is provided may conduct checks, inspections and investigations on the spot, provided that those checks, inspections or investigations are not discriminatory, are not

motivated by the fact that the provider is established in another Member State and are proportionate.

Article 32 Alert mechanism

1. Where a Member State becomes aware of serious specific acts or circumstances relating to a service activity that could cause serious damage to the health or safety of persons or to the environment in its territory or in the territory of other Member States, that Member State shall inform the Member State of establishment, the other Member States concerned and the Commission within the shortest possible period of time.

2. The Commission shall promote and take part in the operation of a European network of Member States' authorities in order to implement paragraph 1.

3. The Commission shall adopt and regularly update, in accordance with the procedure referred to in Article 40(2), detailed rules concerning the management of the network referred to in paragraph 2 of this Article.

Article 33 Information on the good repute of providers

1. Member States shall, at the request of a competent authority in another Member State, supply information, in conformity with their national law, on disciplinary or administrative actions or criminal sanctions and decisions concerning insolvency or bankruptcy involving fraud taken by their competent authorities in respect of the provider which are directly relevant to the provider's competence or professional reliability. The Member State which supplies the information shall inform the provider thereof.

   A request made pursuant to the first subparagraph must be duly substantiated, in particular as regards the reasons for the request for information.

2. Sanctions and actions referred to in paragraph 1 shall only be communicated if a final decision has been taken. With regard to other enforceable decisions referred to in paragraph 1, the Member State which supplies the information shall specify whether a particular decision is final or whether an appeal has been lodged in respect of it, in which case the Member State in question should provide an indication of the date when the decision on appeal is expected.

   Moreover, that Member State shall specify the provisions of national law pursuant to which the provider was found guilty or penalised.

3. Implementation of paragraphs 1and 2 must comply with rules on the provision of personal data and with rights guaranteed to persons found guilty or penalised in the Member States concerned, including by professional bodies. Any information in question which is public shall be accessible to consumers.

Article 34 Accompanying measures

1. The Commission, in cooperation with Member States, shall establish an electronic system for the exchange of information between Member States, taking into account existing information systems.

2. Member States shall, with the assistance of the Commission, take accompanying measures to facilitate the exchange of officials in charge of the implementation of mutual assistance and training of such officials, including language and computer training.

3. The Commission shall assess the need to establish a multi-annual programme in order to organise relevant exchanges of officials and training.

Article 35 Mutual assistance in the event of case-by-case derogations

1. Where a Member State intends to take a measure pursuant to Article 18, the procedure laid down in paragraphs 2 to 6 of this Article shall apply without prejudice to court proceedings, including preliminary proceedings and acts carried out in the framework of a criminal investigation.

2. The Member State referred to in paragraph 1 shall ask the Member State of establishment to take measures with regard to the provider, supplying all relevant information on the service in question and the circumstances of the case.

    The Member State of establishment shall check, within the shortest possible period of time, whether the provider is operating lawfully and verify the facts underlying the request. It shall inform the requesting Member State within the shortest possible period of time of the measures taken or envisaged or, as the case may be, the reasons why it has not taken any measures.

3. Following communication by the Member State of establishment as provided for in the second subparagraph of paragraph 2, the requesting Member State shall notify the Commission and the Member State of establishment of its intention to take measures, stating the following:
    (a) the reasons why it believes the measures taken or envisaged by the Member State of establishment are inadequate;
    (b) the reasons why it believes the measures it intends to take fulfil the conditions laid down in Article 18.

4. The measures may not be taken until fifteen working days after the date of notification provided for in paragraph 3.

5. Without prejudice to the possibility for the requesting Member State to take the measures in question upon expiry of the period specified in paragraph 4, the Commission shall, within the shortest possible period of time, examine the compatibility with Community law of the measures notified.

    Where the Commission concludes that the measure is incompatible with Community law, it shall adopt a decision asking the Member State concerned to refrain from taking the proposed measures or to put an end to the measures in question as a matter of urgency.

6. In the case of urgency, a Member State which intends to take a measure may derogate from paragraphs 2, 3 and 4. In such cases, the measures shall be notified within the shortest possible period of time to the Commission and the Member State of establishment, stating the reasons for which the Member State considers that there is urgency.

Article 36 Implementing measures

In accordance with the procedure referred to in Article 40(3), the Commission shall adopt the implementing measures designed to amend non-essential elements of this Chapter by supplementing it by specifying the time-limits provided for in Articles 28 and 35. The Commission shall also adopt, in accordance with the procedure referred to in Article 40(2), the practical arrangements for the exchange of information by electronic means between Member States, and in particular the interoperability provisions for information systems.

Chapter VII CONVERGENCE PROGRAMME

Article 37 Codes of conduct at Community level

1. Member States shall, in cooperation with the Commission, take accompanying measures to encourage the drawing up at Community level, particularly by professional bodies,

organisations and associations, of codes of conduct aimed at facilitating the provision of services or the establishment of a provider in another Member State, in conformity with Community law.

2.   Member States shall ensure that the codes of conduct referred to in paragraph 1 are accessible at a distance, by electronic means.

Article 38 Additional harmonisation

The Commission shall assess, by 28 December 2010 the possibility of presenting proposals for harmonisation instruments on the following subjects:

(a)   access to the activity of judicial recovery of debts;

(b)   private security services and transport of cash and valuables.

Article 39 Mutual evaluation

1.   By 28 December 2009 at the latest, Member States shall present a report to the Commission, containing the information specified in the following provisions:

(a) Article 9(2), on authorisation schemes;

(b) Article 15(5), on requirements to be evaluated;

(c) Article 25(3), on multidisciplinary activities.

2.   The Commission shall forward the reports provided for in paragraph 1 to the Member States, which shall submit their observations on each of the reports within six months of receipt. Within the same period, the Commission shall consult interested parties on those reports.

3.   The Commission shall present the reports and the Member States' observations to the Committee referred to in Article 40(1), which may make observations.

4.   In the light of the observations provided for in paragraphs 2 and 3, the Commission shall, by 28 December 2010 at the latest, present a summary report to the European Parliament and to the Council, accompanied where appropriate by proposals for additional initiatives.

5.   By 28 December 2009 at the latest, Member States shall present a report to the Commission on the national requirements whose application could fall under the third subparagraph of Article 16(1) and the first sentence of Article 16(3), providing reasons why they consider that the application of those requirements fulfil the criteria referred to in the third subparagraph of Article 16(1) and the first sentence of Article 16(3).

Thereafter, Member States shall transmit to the Commission any changes in their requirements, including new requirements, as referred to above, together with the reasons for them.

The Commission shall communicate the transmitted requirements to other Member States. Such transmission shall not prevent the adoption by Member States of the provisions in question. The Commission shall on an annual basis thereafter provide analyses and orientations on the application of these provisions in the context of this Directive.

Article 40 Committee procedure

1.   The Commission shall be assisted by a Committee.

2.   Where reference is made to this paragraph, Articles 5 and 7 of Decision 1999/468/EC shall apply, having regard to the provisions of Article 8 thereof. The period laid down in Article 5(6) of Decision 1999/468/EC shall be set at three months.

3.   Where reference is made to this paragraph, Article 5a(1) to (4), and Article 7 of Decision 1999/468/EC shall apply, having regard to the provisions of Article 8 thereof.

Article 41 Review clause

The Commission, by 28 December 2011 and every three years thereafter, shall present to the European Parliament and to the Council a comprehensive report on the application of this Directive. This report shall, in accordance with Article 16(4), address in particular the application of Article 16. It shall also consider the need for additional measures for matters excluded from the scope of application of this Directive. It shall be accompanied, where appropriate, by proposals for amendment of this Directive with a view to completing the Internal Market for services.

Article 42 Amendment of Directive 98/27/EC

In the Annex to Directive 98/27/EC of the European Parliament and of the Council of 19 May 1998 on injunctions for the protection of consumers' interests, the following point shall be added:

"13. Directive 2006/123/EC of the European Parliament and of the Council of 12 December 2006 on services in the internal market (OJ L 376, 27.12.2006, p. 36)"

Article 43 Protection of personal data

The implementation and application of this Directive and, in particular, the provisions on supervision shall respect the rules on the protection of personal data as provided for in Directives 95/46/EC and 2002/58/EC.

Chapter VIII FINAL PROVISIONS

Article 44 Transposition

1.   Member States shall bring into force the laws, regulations and administrative provisions necessary to comply with this Directive before 28 December 2009.

They shall forthwith communicate to the Commission the text of those measures.

When Member States adopt these measures, they shall contain a reference to this Directive or shall be accompanied by such a reference on the occasion of their official publication. The methods of making such reference shall be laid down by Member States.

2.   Member States shall communicate to the Commission the text of the main provisions of national law which they adopt in the field covered by this Directive.

Article 45 Entry into force

This Directive shall enter into force on the day following that of its publication in the *Official Journal of the European Union*.

Article 46 Addressees

This Directive is addressed to the Member States.

(*date of signing, signatories and footnotes omitted*)

VI Competition Law

COMMISSION NOTICE

on the definition of relevant market for the purposes of Community competition law

OJ C 372, 09.12.97, p. 5[1]

....

I. INTRODUCTION

1. The purpose of this notice is to provide guidance as to how the Commission applies the concept of relevant product and geographic market in its ongoing enforcement of Community competition law, in particular the application of Council Regulation No 17 and (EEC) No 4064/89, their equivalents in other sectoral applications such as transport, coal and steel, and agriculture, and the relevant provisions of the EEA Agreement (1). Throughout this notice, references to Articles 85 and 86 of the Treaty [Articles 101 and 102 TFEU] and to merger control are to be understood as referring to the equivalent provisions in the EEA Agreement and the ECSC Treaty.

2. Market definition is a tool to identify and define the boundaries of competition between firms. It serves to establish the framework within which competition policy is applied by the Commission. The main purpose of market definition is to identify in a systematic way the competitive constraints that the undertakings involved (2) face. The objective of defining a market in both its product and geographic dimension is to identify those actual competitors of the undertakings involved that are capable of constraining those undertakings' behaviour and of preventing them from behaving independently of effective competitive pressure. It is from this perspective that the market definition makes it possible inter alia to calculate market shares that would convey meaningful information regarding market power for the purposes of assessing dominance or for the purposes of applying Article 85 [Article 101].

3. It follows from point 2 that the concept of 'relevant market' is different from other definitions of market often used in other contexts. For instance, companies often use the term 'market' to refer to the area where it sells its products or to refer broadly to the industry or sector where it belongs.

....

[1]   EDITOR'S NOTE: This Commission Notice refers to the old EC Treaty article numbers effective prior to the Treaty of Amsterdam, 1999. In this edition the replacement article numbers contained in the Treaty on the Functioning of the European Union (TFEU) have been inserted in closed brackets after each Treaty reference for ease of conversion

4. The definition of the relevant market in both its product and its geographic dimensions often has a decisive influence on the assessment of a competition case. By rendering public the procedures which the Commission follows when considering market definition and by indicating the criteria and evidence on which it relies to reach a decision, the Commission expects to increase the transparency of its policy and decision-making in the area of competition policy.

5. Increased transparency will also result in companies and their advisers being able to better anticipate the possibility that the Commission may raise competition concerns in an individual case. Companies could, therefore, take such a possibility into account in their own internal decision-making when contemplating, for instance, acquisitions, the creation of joint ventures, or the establishment of certain agreements. It is also intended that companies should be in a better position to understand what sort of information the Commission considers relevant for the purposes of market definition.

6. The Commission's interpretation of 'relevant market' is without prejudice to the interpretation which may be given by the Court of Justice or the Court of First Instance of the European Communities.

II. DEFINITION OF RELEVANT MARKET

Definition of relevant product market and relevant geographic market

7. The Regulations based on Article 85 and 86 of the Treaty [Articles 101 and 102 TFEU], in particular in section 6 of Form A/B with respect to Regulation No 17, as well as in section 6 of Form CO with respect to Regulation (EEC) No 4064/89 on the control of concentrations having a Community dimension have laid down the following definitions, 'Relevant product markets' are defined as follows:

    'A relevant product market comprises all those products and/or services which are regarded as interchangeable or substitutable by the consumer, by reason of the products' characteristics, their prices and their intended use'.

8. 'Relevant geographic markets' are defined as follows:

    'The relevant geographic market comprises the area in which the undertakings concerned are involved in the supply and demand of products or services, in which the conditions of competition are sufficiently homogeneous and which can be distinguished from neighbouring areas because the conditions of competition are appreciably different in those area'.

9. The relevant market within which to assess a given competition issue is therefore established by the combination of the product and geographic markets. The Commission interprets the definitions in paragraphs 7 an 8 (which reflect the case-law of the Court of Justice and the Court of First Instance as well as its own decision-making practice) according to the orientations defined in this notice.

Concept of relevant market and objectives of Community competition policy

10. The concept of relevant market is closely related to the objectives pursued under Community competition policy. For example, under the Community's merger control, the objective in controlling structural changes in the supply of a product/service is to prevent the creation or reinforcement of a dominant position as a result of which effective competition would be significantly impeded in a substantial part of the common market. Under the Community's competition rules, a dominant position is such that a firm or group of firms would be in a position to behave to an appreciable extent independently of

its competitors, customers and ultimately of its consumers (3). Such a position would usually arise when a firm or group of firms accounted for a large share of the supply in any given market, provided that other factors analysed in the assessment (such as entry barriers, customers' capacity to react, etc.) point in the same direction.

11.   The same approach is followed by the Commission in its application of Article 86 of the Treaty [Article 102 TFEU] to firms that enjoy a single or collective dominant position. Within the meaning of Regulation No 17, the Commission has the power to investigate and bring to an end abuses of such a dominant position, which must also be defined by reference to the relevant market. Markets may also need to be defined in the application of Article 85 of the Treaty [Article 101 TFEU], in particular, in determining whether an appreciable restriction of competition exists or in establishing if the condition pursuant to Article 85 (3) (b) [Article 101(3)(b) TFEU] for an exemption from the application of Article 85 (1) [Article 101(1) TFEU] is met.

12.   The criteria for defining the relevant market are applied generally for the analysis of certain types of behaviour in the market and for the analysis of structural changes in the supply of products. This methodology, though, might lead to different results depending on the nature of the competition issue being examined. For instance, the scope of the geographic market might be different when analysing a concentration, where the analysis is essentially prospective, from an analysis of past behaviour. The different time horizon considered in each case might lead to the result that different geographic markets are defined for the same products depending on whether the Commission is examining a change in the structure of supply, such as a concentration or a cooperative joint venture, or examining issues relating to certain past behaviour.

Basic principles for market definition

Competitive constraints

13.   Firms are subject to three main sources or competitive constraints: demand substitutability, supply substitutability and potential competition. From an economic point of view, for the definition of the relevant market, demand substitution constitutes the most immediate and effective disciplinary force on the suppliers of a given product, in particular in relation to their pricing decisions. A firm or a group of firms cannot have a significant impact on the prevailing conditions of sale, such as prices, if its customers are in a position to switch easily to available substitute products or to suppliers located elsewhere. Basically, the exercise of market definition consists in identifying the effective alternative sources of supply for the customers of the undertakings involved, in terms both of products/services and of geographic location of suppliers.

14.   The competitive constraints arising from supply side substitutability other then those described in paragraphs 20 to 23 and from potential competition are in general less immediate and in any case require an analysis of additional factors. As a result such constraints are taken into account at the assessment stage of competition analysis.

Demand substitution

15.   The assessment of demand substitution entails a determination of the range of products which are viewed as substitutes by the consumer. One way of making this determination can be viewed as a speculative experiment, postulating a hypothetical small, lasting change in relative prices and evaluating the likely reactions of customers to that increase. The exercise of market definition focuses on prices for operational and practical purposes, and more precisely on demand substitution arising from small, permanent changes in relative prices. This concept can provide clear indications as to the evidence that is relevant in defining markets.

16.   Conceptually, this approach means that, starting from the type of products that the undertakings involved sell and the area in which they sell them, additional products and areas will be included in, or excluded from, the market definition depending on whether competition from these other products and areas affect or restrain sufficiently the pricing of the parties' products in the short term.

17.   The question to be answered is whether the parties' customers would switch to readily available substitutes or to suppliers located elsewhere in response to a hypothetical small (in the range 5% to 10 %) but permanent relative price increase in the products and areas being considered. If substitution were enough to make the price increase unprofitable because of the resulting loss of sales, additional substitutes and areas are included in the relevant market. This would be done until the set of products and geographical areas is such that small, permanent increases in relative prices would be profitable. The equivalent analysis is applicable in cases concerning the concentration of buying power, where the starting point would then be the supplier and the price test serves to identify the alternative distribution channels or outlets for the supplier's products. In the application of these principles, careful account should be taken of certain particular situations as described within paragraphs 56 and 58.

18.   A practical example of this test can be provided by its application to a merger of, for instance, soft-drink bottlers. An issue to examine in such a case would be to decide whether different flavours of soft drinks belong to the same market. In practice, the question to address would be whether consumers of flavour A would switch to other flavours when confronted with a permanent price increase of 5% to 10% for flavour A. If a sufficient number of consumers would switch to, say, flavour B, to such an extent that the price increase for flavour A would not be profitable owing to the resulting loss of sales, then the market would comprise at least flavours A and B. The process would have to be extended in addition to other available flavours until a set of products is identified for which a price rise would not induce a sufficient substitution in demand.

19.   Generally, and in particular for the analysis of merger cases, the price to take into account will be the prevailing market price. This may not be the case where the prevailing price has been determined in the absence of sufficient competition. In particular for the investigation of abuses of dominant positions, the fact that the prevailing price might already have been substantially increased will be taken into account.

Supply substitution

20.   Supply-side substitutability may also be taken into account when defining markets in those situations in which its effects are equivalent to those of demand substitution in terms of effectiveness and immediacy. This means that suppliers are able to switch production to the relevant products and market them in the short term (4) without incurring significant additional costs or risks in response to small and permanent changes in relative prices. When these conditions are met, the additional production that is put on the market will have a disciplinary effect on the competitive behaviour of the companies involved. Such an impact in terms of effectiveness and immediacy is equivalent to the demand substitution effect.

21.   These situations typically arise when companies market a wide range of qualities or grades of one product; even if, for a given final customer or group of consumers, the different qualities are not substitutable, the different qualities will be grouped into one product market, provided that most of the suppliers are able to offer and sell the various qualities immediately and without the significant increases in costs described above. In such cases, the relevant product market will encompass all products that are substitutable in demand and supply, and the current sales of those products will be aggregated so as to give the

total value or volume of the market. The same reasoning may lead to group different geographic areas.

22.   A practical example of the approach to supply-side substitutability when defining product markets is to be found in the case of paper. Paper is usually supplied in a range of different qualities, from standard writing paper to high quality papers to be used, for instance, to publish art books. From a demand point of view, different qualities of paper cannot be used for any given use, i.e. an art book or a high quality publication cannot be based on lower quality papers. However, paper plants are prepared to manufacture the different qualities, and production can be adjusted with negligible costs and in a short time-frame. In the absence of particular difficulties in distribution, paper manufacturers are able therefore, to compete for orders of the various qualities, in particular if orders are placed with sufficient lead time to allow for modification of production plans. Under such circumstances, the Commission would not define a separate market for each quality of paper and its respective use. The various qualities of paper are included in the relevant market, and their sales added up to estimate total market value and volume.

23.   When supply-side substitutability would entail the need to adjust significantly existing tangible and intangible assets, additional investments, strategic decisions or time delays, it will not be considered at the stage of market definition. Examples where supply-side substitution did not induce the Commission to enlarge the market are offered in the area of consumer products, in particular for branded beverages. Although bottling plants may in principle bottle different beverages, there are costs and lead times involved (in terms of advertising, product testing and distribution) before the products can actually be sold. In these cases, the effects of supply-side substitutability and other forms of potential competition would then be examined at a later stage.

Potential competition

24.   The third source of competitive constraint, potential competition, is not taken into account when defining markets, since the conditions under which potential competition will actually represent an effective competitive constraint depend on the analysis of specific factors and circumstances related to the conditions of entry. If required, this analysis is only carried out at a subsequent stage, in general once the position of the companies involved in the relevant market has already been ascertained, and when such position gives rise to concerns from a competition point of view.

III.   EVIDENCE RELIED ON TO DEFINE RELEVANT MARKETS
THE PROCESS OF DEFINING THE RELEVANT MARKET IN PRACTICE

Product dimension

25.   There is a range of evidence permitting an assessment of the extent to which substitution would take place. In individual cases, certain types of evidence will be determinant, depending very much on the characteristics and specificity of the industry and products or services that are being examined. The same type of evidence may be of no importance in other cases. In most cases, a decision will have to be based on the consideration of a number of criteria and different items of evidence. The Commission follows an open approach to empirical evidence, aimed at making an effective use of all available information which may be relevant in individual cases. The Commission does not follow a rigid hierarchy of different sources of information or types of evidence.

26. The process of defining relevant markets may be summarized as follows: on the basis of the preliminary information available or information submitted by the undertakings involved, the Commission will usually be in a position to broadly establish the possible relevant markets within which, for instance, a concentration or a restriction of competition has to be assessed. In general, and for all practical purposes when handling individual cases, the question will usually be to decide on a few alternative possible relevant markets. For instance, with respect to the product market, the issue will often be to establish whether product A and product B belong or do not belong to the same product market. it is often the case that the inclusion of product B would be enough to remove any competition concerns.

27. In such situations it is not necessary to consider whether the market includes additional products, or to reach a definitive conclusion on the precise product market. If under the conceivable alternative market definitions the operation in question does not raise competition concerns, the question of market definition will be left open, reducing thereby the burden on companies to supply information.

Geographic dimension

28. The Commission's approach to geographic market definition might be summarized as follows: it will take a preliminary view of the scope of the geographic market on the basis of broad indications as to the distribution of market shares between the parties and their competitors, as well as a preliminary analysis of pricing and price differences at national and Community or EEA level. This initial view is used basically as a working hypothesis to focus the Commission's enquiries for the purposes of arriving at a precise geographic market definition.

29. The reasons behind any particular configuration of prices and market shares need to be explored. Companies might enjoy high market shares in their domestic markets just because of the weight of the past, and conversely, a homogeneous presence of companies throughout the EEA might be consistent with national or regional geographic markets. The initial working hypothesis will therefore be checked against an analysis of demand characteristics (importance of national or local preferences, current patterns of purchases of customers, product differentiation/brands, other) in order to establish whether companies in different areas do indeed constitute a real alternative source of supply for consumers. The theoretical experiment is again based on substitution arising from changes in relative prices, and the question to answer is again whether the customers of the parties would switch their orders to companies located elsewhere in the short term and at a negligible cost.

30. If necessary, a further check on supply factors will be carried out to ensure that those companies located in differing areas do not face impediments in developing their sales on competitive terms throughout the whole geographic market. This analysis will include an examination of requirements for a local presence in order to sell in that area the conditions of access to distribution channels, costs associated with setting up a distribution network, and the presence or absence of regulatory barriers arising from public procurement, price regulations, quotas and tariffs limiting trade or production, technical standards, monopolies, freedom of establishment, requirements for administrative authorizations, packaging regulations, etc. In short, the Commission will identify possible obstacles and barriers isolating companies located in a given area from the competitive pressure of companies located outside that area, so as to determine the precise degree of market interpenetration at national, European or global level.

31. The actual pattern and evolution of trade flows offers useful supplementary indications as to the economic importance of each demand or supply factor mentioned above, and the

extent to which they may or may not constitute actual barriers creating different geographic markets. The analysis of trade flows will generally address the question of transport costs and the extent to which these may hinder trade between different areas, having regard to plant location, costs of production and relative price levels.

Market integration in the Community

32. Finally, the Commission also takes into account the continuing process of market integration, in particular in the Community, when defining geographic markets, especially in the area of concentrations and structural joint ventures. The measures adopted and implemented in the internal market programme to remove barriers to trade and further integrate the Community markets cannot be ignored when assessing the effects on competition of a concentration or a structural joint venture. A situation where national markets have been artificially isolated from each other because of the existence of legislative barriers that have now been removed will generally lead to a cautious assessment of past evidence regarding prices, market shares or trade patterns. A process of market integration that would, in the short term, lead to wider geographic markets may therefore be taken into consideration when defining the geographic market for the purposes of assessing concentrations and joint ventures.

The process of gathering evidence

33. When a precise market definition is deemed necessary, the Commission will often contact the main customers and the main companies in the industry to enquire into their views about the boundaries of product and geographic markets and to obtain the necessary factual evidence to reach a conclusion. The Commission might also contact the relevant professional associations, and companies active in upstream markets, so as to be able to define, in so far as necessary, separate product and geographic markets, for different levels of production or distribution of the products/services in question. It might also request additional information to the undertakings involved.

34. Where appropriate, the Commission will address written requests for information to the market players mentioned above. These requests will usually include questions relating to the perceptions of companies about reactions to hypothetical price increases and their views of the boundaries of the relevant market. They will also ask for provision of the factual information the Commission deems necessary to reach a conclusion on the extent of the relevant market. The Commission might also discuss with marketing directors or other officers of those companies to gain a better understanding on how negotiations between suppliers and customers take place and better understand issues relating to the definition of the relevant market. Where appropriate, they might also carry out visits or inspections to the premises of the parties, their customers and/or their competitors, in order to better understand how products are manufactured and sold.

35. The type of evidence relevant to reach a conclusion as to the product market can be categorized as follows:

Evidence to define markets – product dimension

36. An analysis of the product characteristics and its intended use allows the Commission, as a first step, to limit the field of investigation of possible substitutes. However, product characteristics and intended use are insufficient to show whether two products are demand substitutes. Functional interchangeability or similarity in characteristics may not, in themselves, provide sufficient criteria, because the responsiveness of customers to relative price changes may be determined by other considerations as well. For example, there may be different competitive constraints in the original equipment market for car components and in spare parts, thereby leading to a separate delineation of two relevant

markets. Conversely, differences in product characteristics are not in themselves sufficient to exclude demand substitutability, since this will depend to a large extent on how customers value different characteristics.

37. The type of evidence the Commission considers relevant to assess whether two products are demand substitutes can be categorized as follows:

38. Evidence of substitution in the recent past. In certain cases, it is possible to analyse evidence relating to recent past events or shocks in the market that offer actual examples of substitution between two products. When available, this sort of information will normally be fundamental for market definition. If there have been changes in relative prices in the past (all else being equal), the reactions in terms of quantities demanded will be determinant in establishing substitutability. Launches of new products in the past can also offer useful information, when it is possible to precisely analyse which products have lost sales to the new product.

39. There are a number of quantitative tests that have specifically been designed for the purpose of delineating markets. These tests consist of various econometric and statistical approaches estimates of elasticities and cross-price elasticities (5) for the demand of a product, tests based on similarity of price movements over time, the analysis of causality between price series and similarity of price levels and/or their convergence. The Commission takes into account the available quantitative evidence capable of withstanding rigorous scrutiny for the purposes of establishing patterns of substitution in the past.

40. Views of customers and competitors. The Commission often contacts the main customers and competitors of the companies involved in its enquiries, to gather their views on the boundaries of the product market as well as most of the factual information it requires to reach a conclusion on the scope of the market. Reasoned answers of customers and competitors as to what would happen if relative prices for the candidate products were to increase in the candidate geographic area by a small amount (for instance of 5% to 10 %) are taken into account when they are sufficiently backed by factual evidence.

41. Consumer preferences. In the case of consumer goods, it may be difficult for the Commission to gather the direct views of end consumers about substitute products. Marketing studies that companies have commissioned in the past and that are used by companies in their own decision-making as to pricing of their products and/or marketing actions may provide useful information for the Commission's delineation of the relevant market. Consumer surveys on usage patterns and attitudes, data from consumer's purchasing patterns, the views expressed by retailers and more generally, market research studies submitted by the parties and their competitors are taken into account to establish whether an economically significant proportion of consumers consider two products as substitutable, also taking into account the importance of brands for the products in question. The methodology followed in consumer surveys carried out ad hoc by the undertakings involved or their competitors for the purposes of a merger procedure or a procedure pursuant to Regulation No 17 will usually be scrutinized with utmost care. Unlike pre-existing studies, they have not been prepared in the normal course of business for the adoption of business decisions.

42. Barriers and costs associated with switching demand to potential substitutes. There are a number of barriers and costs that might prevent the Commission from considering two prima facie demand substitutes as belonging to one single product market. It is not possible to provide an exhaustive list of all the possible barriers to substitution and of switching costs. These barriers or obstacles might have a wide range of origins, and in its decisions, the Commission has been confronted with regulatory barriers or other forms of

State intervention, constraints arising in downstream markets, need to incur specific capital investment or loss in current output in order to switch to alternative inputs, the location of customers, specific investment in production process, learning and human capital investment, retooling costs or other investments, uncertainty about quality and reputation of unknown suppliers, and others.

43.   Different categories of customers and price discrimination. The extent of the product market might be narrowed in the presence of distinct groups of customers. A distinct group of customers for the relevant product may constitute a narrower, distinct market when such ha group could be subject to price discrimination. This will usually be the case when two conditions are met: (a) it is possible to identify clearly which group an individual customer belongs to at the moment of selling the relevant products to him, and (b) trade among customers or arbitrage by third parties should not be feasible.

Evidence for defining markets – geographic dimension

44.   The type of evidence the Commission considers relevant to reach a conclusion as to the geographic market can be categorized as follows:

45.   Past evidence of diversion of orders to other areas. In certain cases, evidence on changes in prices between different areas and consequent reactions by customers might be available. Generally, the same quantitative tests used for product market definition might as well be used in geographic market definition, bearing in mind that international comparisons of prices might be more complex due to a number of factors such as exchange rate movements, taxation and product differentiation.

46.   Basic demand characteristics. The nature of demand for the relevant product may in itself determine the scope of the geographical market. Factors such as national preferences or preferences for national brands, language, culture and life style, and the need for a local presence have a strong potential to limit the geographic scope of competition.

47.   Views of customers and competitors. Where appropriate, the Commission will contact the main customers and competitors of the parties in its enquiries, to gather their views on the boundaries of the geographic market as well as most of the factual information it requires to reach a conclusion on the scope of the market when they are sufficiently backed by factual evidence.

48.   Current geographic pattern of purchases. An examination of the customers' current geographic pattern of purchases provides useful evidence as to the possible scope of the geographic market. When customers purchase from companies located anywhere in the Community or the EEA on similar terms, or they procure their supplies through effective tendering procedures in which companies from anywhere in the Community or the EEA submit bids, usually the geographic market will be considered to be Community-wide.

49.   Trade flows/pattern of shipments. When the number of customers is so large that it is not possible to obtain through them a clear picture of geographic purchasing patterns, information on trade flows might be used alternatively, provided that the trade statistics are available with a sufficient degree of detail for the relevant products. Trade flows, and above all, the rationale behind trade flows provide useful insights and information for the purpose of establishing the scope of the geographic market but are not in themselves conclusive.

50.   Barriers and switching costs associated to divert orders to companies located in other areas. The absence of trans-border purchases or trade flows, for instance, does not necessarily mean that the market is at most national in scope. Still, barriers isolating the national market have to identified before it is concluded that the relevant geographic

market in such a case is national. Perhaps the clearest obstacle for a customer to divert its orders to other areas is the impact of transport costs and transport restrictions arising from legislation or from the nature of the relevant products. The impact of transport costs will usually limit the scope of the geographic market for bulky, low-value products, bearing in mind that a transport disadvantage might also be compensated by a comparative advantage in other costs (labour costs or raw materials). Access to distribution in a given area, regulatory barriers still existing in certain sectors, quotas and custom tariffs might also constitute barriers isolating a geographic area from the competitive pressure of companies located outside that area. Significant switching costs in procuring supplies from companies located in other countries constitute additional sources of such barriers.

51.   On the basis of the evidence gathered, the Commission will then define a geographic market that could range from a local dimension to a global one, and there are examples of both local and global markets in past decisions of the Commission.

52.   The paragraphs above describe the different factors which might be relevant to define markets. This does not imply that in each individual case it will be necessary to obtain evidence and assess each of these factors. Often in practice the evidence provided by a subset of these factors will be sufficient to reach a conclusion, as shown in the past decisional practice of the Commission.

IV. CALCULATION OF MARKET SHARE

53.   The definition of the relevant market in both its product and geographic dimensions allows the identification the suppliers and the customers/consumers active on that market. On that basis, a total market size and market shares for each supplier can be calculated on the basis of their sales of the relevant products in the relevant area. In practice, the total market size and market shares are often available from market sources, i.e. companies' estimates, studies commissioned from industry consultants and/or trade associations. When this is not the case, or when available estimates are not reliable, the Commission will usually ask each supplier in the relevant market to provide its own sales in order to calculate total market size and market shares.

54.   If sales are usually the reference to calculate market shares, there are nevertheless other indications that, depending on the specific products or industry in question, can offer useful information such as, in particular, capacity, the number of players in bidding markets, units of fleet as in aerospace, or the reserves held in the case of sectors such as mining.

55.   As a rule of thumb, both volume sales and value sales provide useful information. In cases of differentiated products, sales in value and their associated market share will usually be considered to better reflect the relative position and strength of each supplier.

V. ADDITIONAL CONSIDERATIONS

56.   There are certain areas where the application of the principles above has to be undertaken with care. This is the case when considering primary and secondary markets, in particular, when the behaviour of undertakings at a point in time has to be analysed pursuant to Article 86 [Article 102 TFEU]. The method of defining markets in these cases is the same, i.e. assessing the responses of customers based on their purchasing decisions to relative price changes, but taking into account as well, constraints on substitution imposed by conditions in the connected markets. A narrow definition of market for secondary products, for instance, spare parts, may result when compatibility with the primary

product is important. Problems of finding compatible secondary products together with the existence of high prices and a long lifetime of the primary products may render relative price increases of secondary products profitable. A different market definition may result if significant substitution between secondary products is possible or if the characteristics of the primary products make quick and direct consumer responses to relative price increases of the secondary products feasible.

57. In certain cases, the existence of chains of substitution might lead to the definition of a relevant market where products or areas at the extreme of the market are not directly substitutable. An example might be provided by the geographic dimension of a product with significant transport costs. In such cases, deliveries from a given plant are limited to a certain area around each plant by the impact of transport costs. In principle, such an area could constitute the relevant geographic market. However, if the distribution of plants is such that there are considerable overlaps between the areas around different plants, it is possible that the pricing of those products will be constrained by a chain substitution effect, and lead to the definition of a broader geographic market. The same reasoning may apply if product B is a demand substitute for products A and C. Even if products A and C are not direct demand substitutes, they might be found to be in the same relevant product market since their respective pricing might be constrained by substitution to B.

58. From a practical perspective, the concept of chains of substitution has to be corroborated by actual evidence, for instance related to price interdependence at the extremes of the chains of substitution, in order to lead to an extension of the relevant market in an individual case. Price levels at the extremes of the chains would have to be of the same magnitude as well.
   (1) The focus of assessment in State aid cases is the aid recipient and the industry/sector concerned rather than identification of competitive constraints faced by the aid recipient. When consideration of market power and therefore of the relevant market are raised in any particular case, elements of the approach outlined here might serve as a basis for the assessment of State aid cases.
   (2) For the purposes of this notice, the undertakings involved will be, in the case of a concentration, the parties to the concentration; in investigations within the meaning of Article 86 of the Treaty, [Article 102 TFEU] the undertaking being investigated or the complainants; for investigations within the meaning of Article 85 [Article 101 TFEU], the parties to the Agreement.
   (3) Definition given by the Court of Justice in its judgment of 13 February 1979 in Case 85/76, Hoffmann-La Roche [1979] ECR 461, and confirmed in subsequent judgments.
   (4) That is such a period that does not entail a significant adjustment of existing tangible and intangible assets (see paragraph 23).
   (5) Own-price elasticity of demand for product X is a measure of the responsiveness of demand for X to percentage change in its own price. Cross-price elasticity between products X and Y is the responsiveness of demand for product X to percentage change in the price of product Y.

COMMISSION REGULATION (EC) No 2658/2000
OF 29 NOVEMBER 2000

on the application of Article 81(3) of the Treaty to
categories of specialisation agreements

OJ 2000, L304/3*

....

(*As amended by the Act concerning the conditions of accession of the Czech Republic, the
Republic of Estonia, the Republic of Cyprus, the Republic of Latvia, the Republic of Lithuania,
the Republic of Hungary, the Republic of Malta, the Republic of Poland, the Republic of
Slovenia and the Slovak Republic and the adjustments to the Treaties on which the European
Union is founded, OJ L 236, 23.9.2003, p. 33)[1]

(footnotes omitted)

THE COMMISSION OF THE EUROPEAN COMMUNITIES,

Having regard to the Treaty establishing the European Community,

Having regard to Council Regulation (EEC) No 2821/71 of 20 December 1971 on the
application of Article 85(3) of the Treaty to categories of agreements, decisions and concerted
practices, as last amended by the Act of Accession of Austria, Finland and Sweden, and in
particular Article 1(1)(c) thereof,

Having published a draft of this Regulation,

Having consulted the Advisory Committee on Restrictive Practices and Dominant Positions,

Whereas:

(1) Regulation (EEC) No 2821/71 empowers the Commission to apply Article 81(3)
(formerly Article 85(3)) of the Treaty by regulation to certain categories of agreements,
decisions and concerted practices falling within the scope of Article 81(1) which have as
their object specialisation, including agreements necessary for achieving it.

(2) Pursuant to Regulation (EEC) No 2821/71, in particular, the Commission has
adopted Regulation (EEC) No 417/85 of 19 December 1984 on the application of
Article 85(3) of the Treaty to categories of specialisation agreements, as last amended by
Regulation (EC) No 2236/97. Regulation (EEC) No 417/85 expires on 31 December
2000.

(3) A new regulation should meet the two requirements of ensuring effective protection of
competition and providing adequate legal security for undertakings. The pursuit of these
objectives should take account of the need to simplify administrative supervision and the
legislative framework to as great an extent as possible. Below a certain level of market
power it can, for the application of Article 81(3), in general be presumed that
the positive effects of specialisation agreements will outweigh any negative effects on
competition.

(4) Regulation (EEC) No 2821/71 requires the exempting regulation of the Commission to
define the categories of agreements, decisions and concerted practices to which it applies,
to specify the restrictions or clauses which may, or may not, appear in the agreements,

....

[1]   EDITOR'S NOTE: As of 1 June 2010 this Regulation has not been amended following the adoption of the Treaty of
      Lisbon. It includes references to the old Treaty article numbers. Reference should be made to the Tables of
      Equivalences accompanying the consolidated Treaties in Part II of this edition for the conversion of old Treaty article
      numbers to new ones.

decisions and concerted practices, and to specify the clauses which must be contained in the agreements, decisions and concerted practices or the other conditions which must be satisfied.

(5)   It is appropriate to move away from the approach of listing exempted clauses and to place greater emphasis on defining the categories of agreements which are exempted up to a certain level of market power and on specifying the restrictions or clauses which are not to be contained in such agreements. This is consistent with an economics-based approach which assesses the impact of agreements on the relevant market.

(6)   For the application of Article 81(3) by regulation, it is not necessary to define those agreements which are capable of falling within Article 81(1). In the individual assessment of agreements under Article 81(1), account has to be taken of several factors, and in particular the market structure on the relevant market.

(7)   The benefit of the block exemption should be limited to those agreements for which it can be assumed with sufficient certainty that they satisfy the conditions of Article 81(3).

(8)   Agreements on specialisation in production generally contribute to improving the production or distribution of goods, because the undertakings concerned can concentrate on the manufacture of certain products and thus operate more efficiently and supply the products more cheaply. Agreements on specialisation in the provision of services can also be said to generally give rise to similar improvements. It is likely that, given effective competition, consumers will receive a fair share of the resulting benefit.

(9)   Such advantages can arise equally from agreements whereby one participant gives up the manufacture of certain products or provision of certain services in favour of another participant ("unilateral specialisation"), from agreements whereby each participant gives up the manufacture of certain products or provision of certain services in favour of another participant ("reciprocal specialisation") and from agreements whereby the participants undertake to jointly manufacture certain products or provide certain services ("joint production").

(10)   As unilateral specialisation agreements between non-competitors may benefit from the block exemption provided by Commission Regulation (EC) No 2790/1999 of 22 December 1999 on the application of Article 81(3) of the Treaty to categories of vertical agreements and concerted practices, the application of the present Regulation to unilateral specialisation agreements should be limited to agreements between competitors.

(11)   All other agreements entered into between undertakings relating to the conditions under which they specialise in the production of goods and/or services should fall within the scope of this Regulation. The block exemption should also apply to provisions contained in specialisation agreements which do not constitute the primary object of such agreements, but are directly related to and necessary for their implementation, and to certain related purchasing and marketing arrangements.

(12)   To ensure that the benefits of specialisation will materialise without one party leaving the market downstream of production, unilateral and reciprocal specialisation agreements should only be covered by this Regulation where they provide for supply and purchase obligations. These obligations may, but do not have to, be of an exclusive nature.

(13)   It can be presumed that, where the participating undertakings' share of the relevant market does not exceed 20%, specialisation agreements as defined in this Regulation will,

as a general rule, give rise to economic benefits in the form of economies of scale or scope or better production technologies, while allowing consumers a fair share of the resulting benefits.

(14) This Regulation should not exempt agreements containing restrictions which are not indispensable to attain the positive effects mentioned above. In principle certain severe anti-competitive restraints relating to the fixing of prices charged to third parties, limitation of output or sales, and allocation of markets or customers should be excluded from the benefit of the block exemption established by this Regulation irrespective of the market share of the undertakings concerned.

(15) The market share limitation, the non-exemption of certain agreements and the conditions provided for in this Regulation normally ensure that the agreements to which the block exemption applies do not enable the participating undertakings to eliminate competition in respect of a substantial part of the products or services in question.

(16) In particular cases in which the agreements falling under this Regulation nevertheless have effects incompatible with Article 81(3) of the Treaty, the Commission may withdraw the benefit of the block exemption.

(17) In order to facilitate the conclusion of specialisation agreements, which can have a bearing on the structure of the participating undertakings, the period of validity of this Regulation should be fixed at 10 years.

(18) This Regulation is without prejudice to the application of Article 82 of the Treaty.

(19) In accordance with the principle of the primacy of Community law, no measure taken pursuant to national laws on competition should prejudice the uniform application throughout the common market of the Community competition rules or the full effect of any measures adopted in implementation of those rules, including this Regulation,

HAS ADOPTED THIS REGULATION:

Article 1 Exemption

1. Pursuant to Article 81(3) of the Treaty and subject to the provisions of this Regulation, it is hereby declared that Article 81(1) shall not apply to the following agreements entered into between two or more undertakings (hereinafter referred to as "the parties") which relate to the conditions under which those undertakings specialise in the production of products (hereinafter referred to as "specialisation agreements"):

    (a) unilateral specialisation agreements, by virtue of which one party agrees to cease production of certain products or to refrain from producing those products and to purchase them from a competing undertaking, while the competing undertaking agrees to produce and supply those products; or

    (b) reciprocal specialisation agreements, by virtue of which two or more parties on a reciprocal basis agree to cease or refrain from producing certain but different products and to purchase these products from the other parties, who agree to supply them; or

    (c) joint production agreements, by virtue of which two or more parties agree to produce certain products jointly.

    This exemption shall apply to the extent that such specialisation agreements contain restrictions of competition falling within the scope of Article 81(1) of the Treaty.

2. The exemption provided for in paragraph 1 shall also apply to provisions contained in specialisation agreements, which do not constitute the primary object of such agreements,

but are directly related to and necessary for their implementation, such as those concerning the assignment or use of intellectual property rights.

The first subparagraph does, however, not apply to provisions which have the same object as the restrictions of competition enumerated in Article 5(1).

Article 2 Definitions

For the purposes of this Regulation:

1.   "Agreement" means an agreement, a decision of an association of undertakings or a concerted practice.

2.   "Participating undertakings" means undertakings party to the agreement and their respective connected undertakings.

3.   "Connected undertakings" means:
   (a) undertakings in which a party to the agreement, directly or indirectly:
      (i)   has the power to exercise more than half the voting rights, or
      (ii) has the power to appoint more than half the members of the supervisory board, board of management or bodies legally representing the undertaking, or
      (iii) has the right to manage the undertaking's affairs;
   (b) undertakings which directly or indirectly have, over a party to the agreement, the rights or powers listed in (a);
   (c) undertakings in which an undertaking referred to in (b) has, directly or indirectly, the rights or powers listed in (a);
   (d) undertakings in which a party to the agreement together with one or more of the undertakings referred to in (a), (b) or (c), or in which two or more of the latter undertakings, jointly have the rights or powers listed in (a);
   (e) undertakings in which the rights or the powers listed in (a) are jointly held by:
      (i)   parties to the agreement or their respective connected undertakings referred to in (a) to (d), or
      (ii) one or more of the parties to the agreement or one or more of their connected undertakings referred to in (a) to (d) and one or more third parties.

4.   "Product" means a good and/or a service, including both intermediary goods and/or services and final goods and/or services, with the exception of distribution and rental services.

5.   "Production" means the manufacture of goods or the provision of services and includes production by way of subcontracting.

6.   "Relevant market" means the relevant product and geographic market(s) to which the products, which are the subject matter of a specialisation agreement, belong.

7.   "Competing undertaking" means an undertaking that is active on the relevant market (an actual competitor) or an undertaking that would, on realistic grounds, undertake the necessary additional investments or other necessary switching costs so that it could enter the relevant market in response to a small and permanent increase in relative prices (a potential competitor).

8.   "Exclusive supply obligation" means an obligation not to supply a competing undertaking other than a party to the agreement with the product to which the specialisation agreement relates.

9.   "Exclusive purchase obligation" means an obligation to purchase the product to which the specialisation agreement relates only from the party which agrees to supply it.

Article 3 Purchasing and marketing arrangements

The exemption provided for in Article 1 shall also apply where:

(a) the parties accept an exclusive purchase and/or exclusive supply obligation in the context of a unilateral or reciprocal specialisation agreement or a joint production agreement, or

(b) the parties do not sell the products which are the object of the specialisation agreement independently but provide for joint distribution or agree to appoint a third party distributor on an exclusive or non-exclusive basis in the context of a joint production agreement provided that the third party is not a competing undertaking.

Article 4 Market share threshold

The exemption provided for in Article 1 shall apply on condition that the combined market share of the participating undertakings does not exceed 20% of the relevant market.

Article 5 Agreements not covered by the exemption

1. The exemption provided for in Article 1 shall not apply to agreements which, directly or indirectly, in isolation or in combination with other factors under the control of the parties, have as their object:

   (a) the fixing of prices when selling the products to third parties;

   (b) the limitation of output or sales; or

   (c) the allocation of markets or customers.

2. Paragraph 1 shall not apply to:

   (a) provisions on the agreed amount of products in the context of unilateral or reciprocal specialisation agreements or the setting of the capacity and production volume of a production joint venture in the context of a joint production agreement;

   (b) the setting of sales targets and the fixing of prices that a production joint venture charges to its immediate customers in the context of point (b) of Article 3.

Article 6 Application of the market share threshold

1. For the purposes of applying the market share threshold provided for in Article 4 the following rules shall apply:

   (a) the market share shall be calculated on the basis of the market sales value; if market sales value data are not available, estimates based on other reliable market information, including market sales volumes, may be used to establish the market share of the undertaking concerned;

   (b) the market share shall be calculated on the basis of data relating to the preceding calendar year;

   (c) the market share held by the undertakings referred to in point 3(e) of Article 2 shall be apportioned equally to each undertaking having the rights or the powers listed in point 3(a) of Article 2.

2. If the market share referred to in Article 4 is initially not more than 20% but subsequently rises above this level without exceeding 25%, the exemption provided for in Article 1 shall continue to apply for a period of two consecutive calendar years following the year in which the 20% threshold was first exceeded.

3. If the market share referred to in Article 4 is initially not more than 20% but subsequently rises above 25%, the exemption provided for in Article 1 shall continue to apply for one calendar year following the year in which the level of 25% was first exceeded.

4.   The benefit of paragraphs 2 and 3 may not be combined so as to exceed a period of two calendar years.

Article 7 Withdrawal

The Commission may withdraw the benefit of this Regulation, pursuant to Article 7 of Regulation (EEC) No 2821/71, where, either on its own initiative or at the request of a Member State or of a natural or legal person claiming a legitimate interest, it finds in a particular case that an agreement to which the exemption provided for in Article 1 applies nevertheless has effects which are incompatible with the conditions laid down in Article 81(3) of the Treaty, and in particular where:

(a) the agreement is not yielding significant results in terms of rationalisation or consumers are not receiving a fair share of the resulting benefit, or

(b) the products which are the subject of the specialisation are not subject in the common market or a substantial part thereof to effective competition from identical products or products considered by users to be equivalent in view of their characteristics, price and intended use.

Article 8 Transitional period

The prohibition laid down in Article 81(1) of the Treaty shall not apply during the period from 1 January 2001 to 30 June 2002 in respect of agreements already in force on 31 December 2000 which do not satisfy the conditions for exemption provided for in this Regulation but which satisfy the conditions for exemption provided for in Regulation (EEC) No 417/85.

Article 8a

The prohibition in Article 81(1) of the Treaty shall not apply to agreements which were in existence at the date of accession of the Czech Republic, Estonia, Cyprus, Latvia, Lithuania, Hungary, Malta, Poland, Slovenia and Slovakia and which, by reason of accession, fall within the scope of Article 81(1) if, within six months from the date of accession, they are so amended that they comply with the conditions laid down in this Regulation.

Article 9 Period of validity

This Regulation shall enter into force on 1 January 2001.

It shall expire on 31 December 2010.

This Regulation shall be binding in its entirety and directly applicable in all Member States.

(*date of signing and signatory omitted*)

COMMISSION REGULATION (EC) No 2659/2000 OF 29 NOVEMBER 2000

on the application of Article 81(3) of the Treaty to categories of research and development agreements, as amended*

OJ L 304, 5.12.2000, p. 7

(*As amended by the Act concerning the conditions of accession of the Czech Republic, the Republic of Estonia, the Republic of Cyprus, the Republic of Latvia, the Republic of Lithuania, the Republic of Hungary, the Republic of Malta, the Republic of Poland, the Republic of Slovenia and the Slovak Republic and the adjustments to the Treaties on which the European Union is founded, OJ L 236, 23.9.2003, p. 33)[1]

(footnotes omitted)

THE COMMISSION OF THE EUROPEAN COMMUNITIES,

Having regard to the Treaty establishing the European Community,

Having regard to Council Regulation (EEC) No 2821/71 of 20 December 1971 on application of Article 85(3) of the Treaty to categories of agreements, decisions and concerted practices, as last amended by the Act of Accession of Austria, Finland and Sweden, and in particular Article 1(1)(b) thereof,

Having published a draft of this Regulation,

Having consulted the Advisory Committee on Restrictive Practices and Dominant Positions,

Whereas:

(1)   Regulation (EEC) No 2821/71 empowers the Commission to apply Article 81(3) (formerly Article 85(3)) of the Treaty by regulation to certain categories of agreements, decisions and concerted practices falling within the scope of Article 81(1) which have as their object the research and development of products or processes up to the stage of industrial application, and exploitation of the results, including provisions regarding intellectual property rights.

(2)   Article 163(2) of the Treaty calls upon the Community to encourage undertakings, including small and medium-sized undertakings, in their research and technological development activities of high quality, and to support their efforts to cooperate with one another. Pursuant to Council Decision 1999/65/EC of 22 December 1998 concerning the rules for the participation of undertakings, research centres and universities and for the dissemination of research results for the implementation of the fifth framework programme of the European Community (1998–2002) and Commission Regulation (EC) No 996/1999 on the implementation of Decision 1999/65/EC, indirect research and technological development (RTD) actions supported under the fifth framework programme of the Community are required to be carried out cooperatively.

(3)   Agreements on the joint execution of research work or the joint development of the results of the research, up to but not including the stage of industrial application, generally do not fall within the scope of Article 81(1) of the Treaty. In certain circumstances, however, such as where the parties agree not to carry out other research and development in the same field, thereby forgoing the opportunity of gaining competitive advantages over the other parties, such agreements may fall within Article 81(1) and should therefore be included within the scope of this Regulation.

(4)   Pursuant to Regulation (EEC) No 2821/71, the Commission has, in particular, adopted Regulation (EEC) No 418/85 of 19 December 1984 on the application of Article 85(3) of the Treaty to categories of research and development agreements, as last amended by Regulation (EC) No 2236/97. Regulation (EEC) No 418/85 expires on 31 December 2000.

---

[1]   EDITOR'S NOTE: As of 1 June 2010 this Regulation has not been amended following the adoption of the Treaty of Lisbon. It includes references to the old Treaty article numbers. Reference should be made to the Tables of Equivalences accompanying the consolidated Treaties in Part II of this edition for the conversion of old Treaty article numbers to new ones.

(5)   A new regulation should meet the two requirements of ensuring effective protection of competition and providing adequate legal security for undertakings. The pursuit of these objectives should take account of the need to simplify administrative supervision and the legislative framework to as great an extent possible. Below a certain level of market power it can, for the application of Article 81(3), in general be presumed that the positive effects of research and development agreements will outweigh any negative effects on competition.

(6)   Regulation (EEC) No 2821/71 requires the exempting regulation of the Commission to define the categories of agreements, decisions and concerted practices to which it applies, to specify the restrictions or clauses which may, or may not, appear in the agreements, decisions and concerted practices, and to specify the clauses which must be contained in the agreements, decisions and concerted practices or the other conditions which must be satisfied.

(7)   It is appropriate to move away from the approach of listing exempted clauses and to place greater emphasis on defining the categories of agreements which are exempted up to a certain level of market power and on specifying the restrictions or clauses which are not to be contained in such agreements. This is consistent with an economics based approach which assesses the impact of agreements on the relevant market.

(8)   For the application of Article 81(3) by regulation, it is not necessary to define those agreements which are capable of falling within Article 81(1). In the individual assessment of agreements under Article 81(1), account has to be taken of several factors, and in particular the market structure on the relevant market.

(9)   The benefit of the block exemption should be limited to those agreements for which it can be assumed with sufficient certainty that they satisfy the conditions of Article 81(3).

(10)   Cooperation in research and development and in the exploitation of the results generally promotes technical and economic progress by increasing the dissemination of know-how between the parties and avoiding duplication of research and development work, by stimulating new advances through the exchange of complementary know-how, and by rationalising the manufacture of the products or application of the processes arising out of the research and development.

(11)   The joint exploitation of results can be considered as the natural consequence of joint research and development. It can take different forms such as manufacture, the exploitation of intellectual property rights that substantially contribute to technical or economic progress, or the marketing of new products.

(12)   Consumers can generally be expected to benefit from the increased volume and effectiveness of research and development through the introduction of new or improved products or services or the reduction of prices brought about by new or improved processes.

(13)   In order to attain the benefits and objectives of joint research and development the benefit of this Regulation should also apply to provisions contained in research and development agreements which do not constitute the primary object of such agreements, but are directly related to and necessary for their implementation.

(14)   In order to justify the exemption, the joint exploitation should relate to products or processes for which the use of the results of the research and development is decisive, and each of the parties is given the opportunity of exploiting any results that interest it. However, where academic bodies, research institutes or undertakings which supply research and development as a commercial service without normally being active in the

exploitation of results participate in research and development, they may agree to use the results of research and development solely for the purpose of further research. Similarly, non-competitors may agree to limit their right to exploitation to one or more technical fields of application to facilitate cooperation between parties with complementary skills.

(15) The exemption granted under this Regulation should be limited to research and development agreements which do not afford the undertakings the possibility of eliminating competition in respect of a substantial part of the products or services in question. It is necessary to exclude from the block exemption agreements between competitors whose combined share of the market for products or services capable of being improved or replaced by the results of the research and development exceeds a certain level at the time the agreement is entered into.

(16) In order to guarantee the maintenance of effective competition during joint exploitation of the results, provision should be made for the block exemption to cease to apply if the parties' combined share of the market for the products arising out of the joint research and development becomes too great. The exemption should continue to apply, irrespective of the parties' market shares, for a certain period after the commencement of joint exploitation, so as to await stabilisation of their market shares, particularly after the introduction of an entirely new product, and to guarantee a minimum period of return on the investments involved.

(17) This Regulation should not exempt agreements containing restrictions which are not indispensable to attain the positive effects mentioned above. In principle certain severe anti-competitive restraints such as limitations on the freedom of parties to carry out research and development in a field unconnected to the agreement, the fixing of prices charged to third parties, limitations on output or sales, allocation of markets or customers, and limitations on effecting passive sales for the contract products in territories reserved for other parties should be excluded from the benefit of the block exemption established by this Regulation irrespective of the market share of the undertakings concerned.

(18) The market share limitation, the non-exemption of certain agreements, and the conditions provided for in this Regulation normally ensure that the agreements to which the block exemption applies do not enable the participating undertakings to eliminate competition in respect of a substantial part of the products or services in question.

(19) In particular cases in which the agreements falling under this Regulation nevertheless have effects incompatible with Article 81(3) of the Treaty, the Commission may withdraw the benefit of the block exemption.

(20) Agreements between undertakings which are not competing manufacturers of products capable of being improved or replaced by the results of the research and development will only eliminate effective competition in research and development in exceptional circumstances. It is therefore appropriate to enable such agreements to benefit from the block exemption irrespective of market share and to address such exceptional cases by way of withdrawal of its benefit.

(21) As research and development agreements are often of a long-term nature, especially where the cooperation extends to the exploitation of the results, the period of validity of this Regulation should be fixed at 10 years.

(22) This Regulation is without prejudice to the application of Article 82 of the Treaty.

(23) In accordance with the principle of the primacy of Community law, no measure taken pursuant to national laws on competition should prejudice the uniform application

throughout the common market of the Community competition rules or the full effect of any measures adopted in implementation of those rules, including this Regulation,

HAS ADOPTED THIS REGULATION:

Article 1 Exemption

1. Pursuant to Article 81(3) of the Treaty and subject to the provisions of this Regulation, it is hereby declared that Article 81(1) shall not apply to agreements entered into between two or more undertakings (hereinafter referred to as "the parties") which relate to the conditions under which those undertakings pursue:
    (a) joint research and development of products or processes and joint exploitation of the results of that research and development;
    (b) joint exploitation of the results of research and development of products or processes jointly carried out pursuant to a prior agreement between the same parties; or
    (c) joint research and development of products or processes excluding joint exploitation of the results.
    This exemption shall apply to the extent that such agreements (hereinafter referred to as "research and development agreements") contain restrictions of competition falling within the scope of Article 81(1).

2. The exemption provided for in paragraph 1 shall also apply to provisions contained in research and development agreements which do not constitute the primary object of such agreements, but are directly related to and necessary for their implementation, such as an obligation not to carry out, independently or together with third parties, research and development in the field to which the agreement relates or in a closely connected field during the execution of the agreement.

    The first subparagraph does, however, not apply to provisions which have the same object as the restrictions of competition enumerated in Article 5(1).

Article 2 Definitions

For the purposes of this Regulation:

1. "agreement" means an agreement, a decision of an association of undertakings or a concerted practice;

2. "participating undertakings" means undertakings party to the research and development agreement and their respective connected undertakings;

3. "connected undertakings" means:
    (a) undertakings in which a party to the research and development agreement, directly or indirectly:
        (i) has the power to exercise more than half the voting rights,
        (ii) has the power to appoint more than half the members of the supervisory board, board of management or bodies legally representing the undertaking, or
        (iii) has the right to manage the undertaking's affairs;
    (b) undertakings which directly or indirectly have, over a party to the research and development agreement, the rights or powers listed in (a);
    (c) undertakings in which an undertaking referred to in (b) has, directly or indirectly, the rights or powers listed in (a);
    (d) undertakings in which a party to the research and development agreement together with one or more of the undertakings referred to in (a), (b) or (c), or in which two or more of the latter undertakings, jointly have the rights or powers listed in (a);
    (e) undertakings in which the rights or the powers listed in (a) are jointly held by:

> (i) parties to the research and development agreement or their respective connected undertakings referred to in (a) to (d), or
>
> (ii) one or more of the parties to the research and development agreement or one or more of their connected undertakings referred to in (a) to (d) and one or more third parties;

4. "research and development" means the acquisition of know-how relating to products or processes and the carrying out of theoretical analysis, systematic study or experimentation, including experimental production, technical testing of products or processes, the establishment of the necessary facilities and the obtaining of intellectual property rights for the results;

5. "product" means a good and/or a service, including both intermediary goods and/or services and final goods and/or services;

6. "contract process" means a technology or process arising out of the joint research and development;

7. "contract product" means a product arising out of the joint research and development or manufactured or provided applying the contract processes;

8. "exploitation of the results" means the production or distribution of the contract products or the application of the contract processes or the assignment or licensing of intellectual property rights or the communication of know-how required for such manufacture or application;

9. "intellectual property rights" includes industrial property rights, copyright and neighbouring rights;

10. "know-how" means a package of non-patented practical information, resulting from experience and testing, which is secret, substantial and identified: in this context, "secret" means that the know-how is not generally known or easily accessible; "substantial" means that the know-how includes information which is indispensable for the manufacture of the contract products or the application of the contract processes; "identified" means that the know-how is described in a sufficiently comprehensive manner so as to make it possible to verify that it fulfils the criteria of secrecy and substantiality;

11. research and development, or exploitation of the results, are carried out "jointly" where the work involved is:
    (a) carried out by a joint team, organisation or undertaking,
    (b) jointly entrusted to a third party, or
    (c) allocated between the parties by way of specialisation in research, development, production or distribution;

12. "competing undertaking" means an undertaking that is supplying a product capable of being improved or replaced by the contract product (an actual competitor) or an undertaking that would, on realistic grounds, undertake the necessary additional investments or other necessary switching costs so that it could supply such a product in response to a small and permanent increase in relative prices (a potential competitor);

13. "relevant market for the contract products" means the relevant product and geographic market(s) to which the contract products belong.

Article 3 Conditions for exemption

1. The exemption provided for in Article 1 shall apply subject to the conditions set out in paragraphs 2 to 5.

2.   All the parties must have access to the results of the joint research and development for the purposes of further research or exploitation. However, research institutes, academic bodies, or undertakings which supply research and development as a commercial service without normally being active in the exploitation of results may agree to confine their use of the results for the purposes of further research.

3.   Without prejudice to paragraph 2, where the research and development agreement provides only for joint research and development, each party must be free independently to exploit the results of the joint research and development and any pre-existing know-how necessary for the purposes of such exploitation. Such right to exploitation may be limited to one or more technical fields of application, where the parties are not competing undertakings at the time the research and development agreement is entered into.

4.   Any joint exploitation must relate to results which are protected by intellectual property rights or constitute know-how, which substantially contribute to technical or economic progress and the results must be decisive for the manufacture of the contract products or the application of the contract processes.

5.   Undertakings charged with manufacture by way of specialisation in production must be required to fulfil orders for supplies from all the parties, except where the research and development agreement also provides for joint distribution.

Article 4 Market share threshold and duration of exemption

1.   Where the participating undertakings are not competing undertakings, the exemption provided for in Article 1 shall apply for the duration of the research and development. Where the results are jointly exploited, the exemption shall continue to apply for seven years from the time the contract products are first put on the market within the common market.

2.   Where two or more of the participating undertakings are competing undertakings, the exemption provided for in Article 1 shall apply for the period referred to in paragraph 1 only if, at the time the research and development agreement is entered into, the combined market share of the participating undertakings does not exceed 25% of the relevant market for the products capable of being improved or replaced by the contract products.

3.   After the end of the period referred to in paragraph 1, the exemption shall continue to apply as long as the combined market share of the participating undertakings does not exceed 25% of the relevant market for the contract products.

Article 5 Agreements not covered by the exemption

1.   The exemption provided for in Article 1 shall not apply to research and development agreements which, directly or indirectly, in isolation or in combination with other factors under the control of the parties, have as their object:
   (a)   the restriction of the freedom of the participating undertakings to carry out research and development independently or in cooperation with third parties in a field unconnected with that to which the research and development relates or, after its completion, in the field to which it relates or in a connected field;
   (b)   the prohibition to challenge after completion of the research and development the validity of intellectual property rights which the parties hold in the common market and which are relevant to the research and development or, after the expiry of the research and development agreement, the validity of intellectual property rights which the parties hold in the common market and which protect the results of the research and development, without prejudice to the possibility to provide for termination of

the research and development agreement in the event of one of the parties challenging the validity of such intellectual property rights;
(c) the limitation of output or sales;
(d) the fixing of prices when selling the contract product to third parties;
(e) the restriction of the customers that the participating undertakings may serve, after the end of seven years from the time the contract products are first put on the market within the common market;
(f) the prohibition to make passive sales of the contract products in territories reserved for other parties;
(g) the prohibition to put the contract products on the market or to pursue an active sales policy for them in territories within the common market that are reserved for other parties after the end of seven years from the time the contract products are first put on the market within the common market;
(h) the requirement not to grant licences to third parties to manufacture the contract products or to apply the contract processes where the exploitation by at least one of the parties of the results of the joint research and development is not provided for or does not take place;
(i) the requirement to refuse to meet demand from users or resellers in their respective territories who would market the contract products in other territories within the common market; or
(j) the requirement to make it difficult for users or resellers to obtain the contract products from other resellers within the common market, and in particular to exercise intellectual property rights or take measures so as to prevent users or resellers from obtaining, or from putting on the market within the common market, products which have been lawfully put on the market within the Community by another party or with its consent.

2.   Paragraph 1 shall not apply to:
(a) the setting of production targets where the exploitation of the results includes the joint production of the contract products;
(b) the setting of sales targets and the fixing of prices charged to immediate customers where the exploitation of the results includes the joint distribution of the contract products.

Article 6 Application of the market share threshold
1.   For the purposes of applying the market share threshold provided for in Article 4 the following rules shall apply:
(a) the market share shall be calculated on the basis of the market sales value; if market sales value data are not available, estimates based on other reliable market information, including market sales volumes, may be used to establish the market share of the undertaking concerned;
(b) the market share shall be calculated on the basis of data relating to the preceding calendar year;
(c) the market share held by the undertakings referred to in point 3(e) of Article 2 shall be apportioned equally to each undertaking having the rights or the powers listed in point 3(a) of Article 2.

2.   If the market share referred to in Article 4(3) is initially not more than 25% but subsequently rises above this level without exceeding 30 %, the exemption provided for in Article 1 shall continue to apply for a period of two consecutive calendar years following the year in which the 25% threshold was first exceeded.

3.   If the market share referred to in Article 4(3) is initially not more than 25% but subsequently rises above 30 %, the exemption provided for in Article 1 shall continue to

apply for one calendar year following the year in which the level of 30% was first exceeded.

4.   The benefit of paragraphs 2 and 3 may not be combined so as to exceed a period of two calendar years.

Article 7 Withdrawal

The Commission may withdraw the benefit of this Regulation, pursuant to Article 7 of Regulation (EEC) No 2821/71, where, either on its own initiative or at the request of a Member State or of a natural or legal person claiming a legitimate interest, it finds in a particular case that a research and development agreement to which the exemption provided for in Article 1 applies nevertheless has effects which are incompatible with the conditions laid down in Article 81(3) of the Treaty, and in particular where:

   (a) the existence of the research and development agreement substantially restricts the scope for third parties to carry out research and development in the relevant field because of the limited research capacity available elsewhere;

   (b) because of the particular structure of supply, the existence of the research and development agreement substantially restricts the access of third parties to the market for the contract products;

   (c) without any objectively valid reason, the parties do not exploit the results of the joint research and development;

   (d) the contract products are not subject in the whole or a substantial part of the common market to effective competition from identical products or products considered by users as equivalent in view of their characteristics, price and intended use;

   (e) the existence of the research and development agreement would eliminate effective competition in research and development on a particular market.

Article 8 Transitional period

The prohibition laid down in Article 81(1) of the Treaty shall not apply during the period from 1 January 2001 to 30 June 2002 in respect of agreements already in force on 31 December 2000 which do not satisfy the conditions for exemption provided for in this Regulation but which satisfy the conditions for exemption provided for in Regulation (EEC) No 418/85.

Article 8a

The prohibition in Article 81(1) of the Treaty shall not apply to agreements which were in existence at the date of accession of the Czech Republic, Estonia, Cyprus, Latvia, Lithuania, Hungary, Malta, Poland, Slovenia and Slovakia and which, by reason of accession, fall within the scope of Article 81(1) if, within six months from the date of accession, they are so amended that they comply with the conditions laid down in this Regulation.

Article 9 Period of validity

This Regulation shall enter into force on 1 January 2001.

It shall expire on 31 December 2010.

This Regulation shall be binding in its entirety and directly applicable in all Member States.

(*date of signing and signatories deleted*)

COMMISSION NOTICE

on agreements of minor importance which do not appreciably restrict competition under Article 81(1) of the Treaty establishing the European Community (*de minimis*)(1)

OJ C 368, 22.12.2001, p. 13[1]

I

1.   Article 81(1) prohibits agreements between undertakings which may affect trade between Member States and which have as their object or effect the prevention, restriction or distortion of competition within the common market. The Court of Justice of the European Communities has clarified that this provision is not applicable where the impact of the agreement on intra-Community trade or on competition is not appreciable.

2.   In this notice the Commission quantifies, with the help of market share thresholds, what is not an appreciable restriction of competition under Article 81 of the EC Treaty. This negative definition of appreciability does not imply that agreements between undertakings which exceed the thresholds set out in this notice appreciably restrict competition. Such agreements may still have only a negligible effect on competition and may therefore not be prohibited by Article 81(1)(2).

3.   Agreements may in addition not fall under Article 81(1) because they are not capable of appreciably affecting trade between Member States. This notice does not deal with this issue. It does not quantify what does not constitute an appreciable effect on trade. It is however acknowledged that agreements between small and medium-sized undertakings, as defined in the Annex to Commission Recommendation 96/280/EC(3), are rarely capable of appreciably affecting trade between Member States. Small and medium-sized undertakings are currently defined in that recommendation as undertakings which have fewer than 250 employees and have either an annual turnover not exceeding EUR 40 million or an annual balance-sheet total not exceeding EUR 27 million.

4.   In cases covered by this notice the Commission will not institute proceedings either upon application or on its own initiative. Where undertakings assume in good faith that an agreement is covered by this notice, the Commission will not impose fines. Although not binding on them, this notice also intends to give guidance to the courts and authorities of the Member States in their application of Article 81.

5.   This notice also applies to decisions by associations of undertakings and to concerted practices.

6.   This notice is without prejudice to any interpretation of Article 81 which may be given by the Court of Justice or the Court of First Instance of the European Communities.

---

[1]   EDITOR'S NOTE: As of 1 June 2010 this Commission Notice has not been reissued following the adoption of the Treaty of Lisbon. It includes references to the old Treaty article numbers. Reference should be made to the Tables of Equivalences accompanying the consolidated Treaties in Part II of this edition for the conversion of old Treaty article numbers to new ones.

II

7.   The Commission holds the view that agreements between undertakings which affect trade between Member States do not appreciably restrict competition within the meaning of Article 81(1):

(a) if the aggregate market share held by the parties to the agreement does not exceed 10% on any of the relevant markets affected by the agreement, where the agreement is made between undertakings which are actual or potential competitors on any of these markets (agreements between competitors)(4); or

(b) if the market share held by each of the parties to the agreement does not exceed 15% on any of the relevant markets affected by the agreement, where the agreement is made between undertakings which are not actual or potential competitors on any of these markets (agreements between non-competitors).

In cases where it is difficult to classify the agreement as either an agreement between competitors or an agreement between non-competitors the 10% threshold is applicable.

8.   Where in a relevant market competition is restricted by the cumulative effect of agreements for the sale of goods or services entered into by different suppliers or distributors (cumulative foreclosure effect of parallel networks of agreements having similar effects on the market), the market share thresholds under point 7 are reduced to 5%, both for agreements between competitors and for agreements between non-competitors. Individual suppliers or distributors with a market share not exceeding 5% are in general not considered to contribute significantly to a cumulative foreclosure effect(5). A cumulative foreclosure effect is unlikely to exist if less than 30% of the relevant market is covered by parallel (networks of) agreements having similar effects.

9.   The Commission also holds the view that agreements are not restrictive of competition if the market shares do not exceed the thresholds of respectively 10%, 15% and 5% set out in point 7 and 8 during two successive calendar years by more than 2 percentage points.

10.   In order to calculate the market share, it is necessary to determine the relevant market. This consists of the relevant product market and the relevant geographic market. When defining the relevant market, reference should be had to the notice on the definition of the relevant market for the purposes of Community competition law(6). The market shares are to be calculated on the basis of sales value data or, where appropriate, purchase value data. If value data are not available, estimates based on other reliable market information, including volume data, may be used.

11.   Points 7, 8 and 9 do not apply to agreements containing any of the following hardcore restrictions:

(1) as regards agreements between competitors as defined in point 7, restrictions which, directly or indirectly, in isolation or in combination with other factors under the control of the parties, have as their object(7):

(a) the fixing of prices when selling the products to third parties;

(b) the limitation of output or sales;

(c) the allocation of markets or customers;

(2) as regards agreements between non-competitors as defined in point 7, restrictions which, directly or indirectly, in isolation or in combination with other factors under the control of the parties, have as their object:

(a) the restriction of the buyer's ability to determine its sale price, without prejudice to the possibility of the supplier imposing a maximum sale price or recommending a sale price, provided that they do not amount to a fixed or minimum sale price as a result of pressure from, or incentives offered by, any of the parties;

(b) the restriction of the territory into which, or of the customers to whom, the buyer may sell the contract goods or services, except the following restrictions which are not hardcore:
  — the restriction of active sales into the exclusive territory or to an exclusive customer group reserved to the supplier or allocated by the supplier to another buyer, where such a restriction does not limit sales by the customers of the buyer,
  — the restriction of sales to end users by a buyer operating at the wholesale level of trade,
  — the restriction of sales to unauthorised distributors by the members of a selective distribution system, and
  — the restriction of the buyer's ability to sell components, supplied for the purposes of incorporation, to customers who would use them to manufacture the same type of goods as those produced by the supplier;

(c) the restriction of active or passive sales to end users by members of a selective distribution system operating at the retail level of trade, without prejudice to the possibility of prohibiting a member of the system from operating out of an unauthorised place of establishment;

(d) the restriction of cross-supplies between distributors within a selective distribution system, including between distributors operating at different levels of trade;

(e) the restriction agreed between a supplier of components and a buyer who incorporates those components, which limits the supplier's ability to sell the components as spare parts to end users or to repairers or other service providers not entrusted by the buyer with the repair or servicing of its goods;

(3) as regards agreements between competitors as defined in point 7, where the competitors operate, for the purposes of the agreement, at a different level of the production or distribution chain, any of the hardcore restrictions listed in paragraph (1) and (2) above.

12. (1) For the purposes of this notice, the terms "undertaking", "party to the agreement", "distributor", "supplier" and "buyer" shall include their respective connected undertakings.

(2) "Connected undertakings" are:
  (a) undertakings in which a party to the agreement, directly or indirectly:
    — has the power to exercise more than half the voting rights, or
    — has the power to appoint more than half the members of the supervisory board, board of management or bodies legally representing the undertaking, or
    — has the right to manage the undertaking's affairs;
  (b) undertakings which directly or indirectly have, over a party to the agreement, the rights or powers listed in (a);
  (c) undertakings in which an undertaking referred to in (b) has, directly or indirectly, the rights or powers listed in (a);
  (d) undertakings in which a party to the agreement together with one or more of the undertakings referred to in (a), (b) or (c), or in which two or more of the latter undertakings, jointly have the rights or powers listed in (a);
  (e) undertakings in which the rights or the powers listed in (a) are jointly held by:
    — parties to the agreement or their respective connected undertakings referred to in (a) to (d), or
    — one or more of the parties to the agreement or one or more of their connected undertakings referred to in (a) to (d) and one or more third parties.

(3) For the purposes of paragraph 2(e), the market share held by these jointly held undertakings shall be apportioned equally to each undertaking having the rights or the powers listed in paragraph 2(a).

(1) This notice replaces the notice on agreements of minor importance published in OJ C 372, 9.12.1997.
(2) See, for instance, the judgment of the Court of Justice in Joined Cases C-215/96 and C-216/96 Bagnasco (Carlos) v Banca Popolare di Novara and Casa di Risparmio di Genova e Imperia (1999) ECR I-135, points 34–35. This notice is also without prejudice to the principles for assessment under Article 81(1) as expressed in the Commission notice "Guidelines on the applicability of Article 81 of the EC Treaty to horizontal cooperation agreements", OJ C 3, 6.1.2001, in particular points 17–31 inclusive, and in the Commission notice "Guidelines on vertical restraints", OJ C 291, 13.10.2000, in particular points 5–20 inclusive.
(3) OJ L 107, 30.4.1996, p. 4. This recommendation will be revised. It is envisaged to increase the annual turnover threshold from EUR 40 million to EUR 50 million and the annual balance-sheet total threshold from EUR 27 million to EUR 43 million.
(4) On what are actual or potential competitors, see the Commission notice "Guidelines on the applicability of Article 81 of the EC Treaty to horizontal cooperation agreements", OJ C 3, 6.1.2001, paragraph 9. A firm is treated as an actual competitor if it is either active on the same relevant market or if, in the absence of the agreement, it is able to switch production to the relevant products and market them in the short term without incurring significant additional costs or risks in response to a small and permanent increase in relative prices (immediate supply-side substitutability). A firm is treated as a potential competitor if there is evidence that, absent the agreement, this firm could and would be likely to undertake the necessary additional investments or other necessary switching costs so that it could enter the relevant market in response to a small and permanent increase in relative prices.
(5) See also the Commission notice "Guidelines on vertical restraints", OJ C 291, 13.10.2000, in particular paragraphs 73, 142, 143 and 189. While in the guidelines on vertical restraints in relation to certain restrictions reference is made not only to the total but also to the tied market share of a particular supplier or buyer, in this notice all market share thresholds refer to total market shares.
(6) OJ C 372, 9.12.1997, p. 5.
(7) Without prejudice to situations of joint production with or without joint distribution as defined in Article 5, paragraph 2, of Commission Regulation (EC) No 2658/2000 and Article 5, paragraph 2, of Commission Regulation (EC) No 2659/2000, OJ L 304, 5.12.2000, pp. 3 and 7 respectively.

COMMISSION REGULATION (EC) No 1400/2002 OF 31 JULY 2002

on the application of Article 81(3) of the Treaty to categories of vertical agreements and concerted practices in the motor vehicle sector

OJ L 203, 1.8.2002, p. 30*

(*As amended by the Act concerning the conditions of accession of the Czech Republic, the Republic of Estonia, the Republic of Cyprus, the Republic of Latvia, the Republic of Lithuania, the Republic of Hungary, the Republic of Malta, the Republic of Poland, the Republic of Slovenia and the Slovak Republic and the adjustments to the Treaties on which the European Union is founded, OJ L 236, 23.9.2003, p. 33)[1]

(footnotes omitted)

THE COMMISSION OF THE EUROPEAN COMMUNITIES,

Having regard to the Treaty establishing the European Community,

[1] EDITOR'S NOTE: As of 1 June 2010 this Regulation has not been amended following the adoption of the Treaty of Lisbon. It includes references to the old Treaty article numbers. Reference should be made to the Tables of Equivalences accompanying the consolidated Treaties in Part II of this edition for the conversion of old Treaty article numbers to new ones.

Having regard to Council Regulation No 19/65/EEC of 2 March 1965 on the application of Article 85(3) of the Treaty to certain categories of agreements and concerted practices, as last amended by Regulation (EC) No 1215/1999, and in particular Article 1 thereof,

Having published a draft of this Regulation,

Having consulted the Advisory Committee on Restrictive Practices and Dominant Positions,

Whereas:

(1)   Experience acquired in the motor vehicle sector regarding the distribution of new motor vehicles, spare parts and after sales services makes it possible to define categories of vertical agreements which can be regarded as normally satisfying the conditions laid down in Article 81(3).

(2)   This experience leads to the conclusion that rules stricter than those provided for by Commission Regulation (EC) No 2790/1999 of 22 December 1999 on the application of Article 81(3) of the Treaty to categories of vertical agreements and concerted practices are necessary in this sector.

(3)   These stricter rules for exemption by category (the exemption) should apply to vertical agreements for the purchase or sale of new motor vehicles, vertical agreements for the purchase or sale of spare parts for motor vehicles and vertical agreements for the purchase or sale of repair and maintenance services for such vehicles where these agreements are concluded between non-competing undertakings, between certain competitors, or by certain associations of retailers or repairers. This includes vertical agreements concluded between a distributor acting at the retail level or an authorised repairer and a (sub) distributor or repairer. This Regulation should also apply to these vertical agreements when they contain ancillary provisions on the assignment or use of intellectual property rights. The term "vertical agreements" should be defined accordingly to include both such agreements and the corresponding concerted practices.

(4)   The benefit of the exemption should be limited to vertical agreements for which it can be assumed with sufficient certainty that they satisfy the conditions of Article 81(3).

(5)   Vertical agreements falling within the categories defined in this Regulation can improve economic efficiency within a chain of production or distribution by facilitating better coordination between the participating undertakings. In particular, they can lead to a reduction in the transaction and distribution costs of the parties and to an optimisation of their sales and investment levels.

(6)   The likelihood that such efficiency-enhancing effects will outweigh any anti-competitive effects due to restrictions contained in vertical agreements depends on the degree of market power held by the undertakings concerned and therefore on the extent to which those undertakings face competition from other suppliers of goods or services regarded by the buyer as interchangeable or substitutable for one another, by reason of the products' characteristics, prices or intended use.

(7)   Thresholds based on market share should be fixed in order to reflect suppliers' market power. Furthermore, this sector-specific Regulation should contain stricter rules than those provided for by Regulation (EC) No 2790/1999, in particular for selective distribution. The thresholds below which it can be presumed that the advantages secured by vertical agreements outweigh their restrictive effects should vary with the characteristics of different types of vertical agreement. It can therefore be presumed that in general, vertical agreements have such advantages where the supplier concerned has a market share of up

to 30% on the markets for the distribution of new motor vehicles or spare parts, or of up to 40% where quantitative selective distribution is used for the sale of new motor vehicles. As regards after sales services it can be presumed that, in general, vertical agreements by which the supplier sets criteria on how its authorised repairers have to provide repair or maintenance services for the motor vehicles of the relevant make and provides them with equipment and training for the provision of such services have such advantages where the network of authorised repairers of the supplier concerned has a market share of up to 30%. However, in the case of vertical agreements containing exclusive supply obligations, it is the market share of the buyer which is relevant for determining the overall effects of such vertical agreements on the market.

(8) Above those market share thresholds, there can be no presumption that vertical agreements falling within the scope of Article 81(1) will usually give rise to objective advantages of such a character and magnitude as to compensate for the disadvantages which they create for competition. However, such advantages can be anticipated in the case of qualitative selective distribution, irrespective of the supplier's market share.

(9) In order to prevent a supplier from terminating an agreement because a distributor or a repairer engages in pro-competitive behaviour, such as active or passive sales to foreign consumers, multi-branding or subcontracting of repair and maintenance services, every notice of termination must clearly set out in writing the reasons, which must be objective and transparent. Furthermore, in order to strengthen the independence of distributors and repairers from their suppliers, minimum periods of notice should be provided for the non-renewal of agreements concluded for a limited duration and for the termination of agreements of unlimited duration.

(10) In order to foster market integration and to allow distributors or authorised repairers to seize additional business opportunities, distributors or authorised repairers have to be allowed to purchase other undertakings of the same type that sell or repair the same brand of motor vehicles within the distribution system. To this end, any vertical agreement between a supplier and a distributor or authorised repairer has to provide for the latter to have the right to transfer all of its rights and obligations to any other undertaking of its choice of the same type that sell or repairs the same brand of motor vehicles within the distribution system.

(11) In order to favour the quick resolution of disputes which arise between the parties to a distribution agreement and which might otherwise hamper effective competition, agreements should only benefit from exemption if they provide for each party to have a right of recourse to an independent expert or arbitrator, in particular where notice is given to terminate an agreement.

(12) Irrespective of the market share of the undertakings concerned, this Regulation does not cover vertical agreements containing certain types of severely anti-competitive restraints (hardcore restrictions) which in general appreciably restrict competition even at low market shares and which are not indispensable to the attainment of the positive effects mentioned above. This concerns in particular vertical agreements containing restraints such as minimum or fixed resale prices and, with certain exceptions, restrictions of the territory into which, or of the customers to whom, a distributor or repairer may sell the contract goods or services. Such agreements should not benefit from the exemption.

(13) It is necessary to ensure that effective competition within the common market and between distributors located in different Member States is not restricted if a supplier uses

selective distribution in some markets and other forms of distribution in others. In particular selective distribution agreements which restrict passive sales to any end user or unauthorised distributor located in markets where exclusive territories have been allocated should be excluded from the benefit of the exemption, as should those selective distribution agreements which restrict passive sales to customer groups which have been allocated exclusively to other distributors. The benefit of the exemption should also be withheld from exclusive distribution agreements if active or passive sales to any end user or unauthorised distributor located in markets where selective distribution is used are restricted.

(14) The right of any distributor to sell new motor vehicles passively or, where relevant, actively to end users should include the right to sell such vehicles to end users who have given authorisation to an intermediary or purchasing agent to purchase, take delivery of, transport or store a new motor vehicle on their behalf.

(15) The right of any distributor to sell new motor vehicles or spare parts or of any authorised repairer to sell repair and maintenance services to any end user passively or, where relevant, actively should include the right to use the Internet or Internet referral sites.

(16) Limits placed by suppliers on their distributors' sales to any end user in other Member States, for instance where distributor remuneration or the purchase price is made dependent on the destination of the vehicles or on the place of residence of the end users, amount to an indirect restriction on sales. Other examples of indirect restrictions on sales include supply quotas based on a sales territory other than the common market, whether or not these are combined with sales targets. Bonus systems based on the destination of the vehicles or any form of discriminatory product supply to distributors, whether in the case of product shortage or otherwise, also amount to an indirect restriction on sales.

(17) Vertical agreements that do not oblige the authorised repairers within a supplier's distribution system to honour warranties, perform free servicing and carry out recall work in respect of any motor vehicle of the relevant make sold in the common market amount to an indirect restriction of sales and should not benefit from the exemption. This obligation is without prejudice to the right of a motor vehicle supplier to oblige a distributor to make sure as regards the new motor vehicles that he has sold that the warranties are honoured and that free servicing and recall work is carried out, either by the distributor itself or, in case of subcontracting, by the authorised repairer(s) to whom these services have been subcontracted. Therefore consumers should in these cases be able to turn to the distributor if the above obligations have not been properly fulfilled by the authorised repairer to whom the distributor has subcontracted these services. Furthermore, in order to allow sales by motor vehicle distributors to end users throughout the common market, the exemption should apply only to distribution agreements which require the repairers within the supplier's network to carry out repair and maintenance services for the contract goods and corresponding goods irrespective of where these goods are sold in the common market.

(18) In markets where selective distribution is used, the exemption should apply in respect of a prohibition on a distributor from operating out of an additional place of establishment where he is a distributor of vehicles other than passenger cars or light commercial vehicles. However, this prohibition should not be exempted if it limits the expansion of the distributor's business at the authorised place of establishment by, for instance, restricting the development or acquisition of the infrastructure necessary to allow increases in sales volumes, including increases brought about by Internet sales.

(19) It would be inappropriate to exempt any vertical agreement that restricts the sale of original spare parts or spare parts of matching quality by members of the distribution system to independent repairers which use them for the provision of repair or maintenance services. Without access to such spare parts, these independent repairers would not be able to compete effectively with authorised repairers, since they could not provide consumers with good quality services which contribute to the safe and reliable functioning of motor vehicles.

(20) In order to give end users the right to purchase new motor vehicles with specifications identical to those sold in any other Member State, from any distributor selling corresponding models and established in the common market, the exemption should apply only to vertical agreements which enable a distributor to order, stock and sell any such vehicle which corresponds to a model within its contract range. Discriminatory or objectively unjustified supply conditions, in particular those regarding delivery times or prices, applied by the supplier to corresponding vehicles, are to be considered a restriction on the ability of the distributor to sell such vehicles.

(21) Motor vehicles are expensive and technically complex mobile goods which require repair and maintenance at regular and irregular intervals. However, it is not indispensable for distributors of new motor vehicles also to carry out repair and maintenance. The legitimate interests of suppliers and end users can be fully satisfied if the distributor subcontracts these services, including the honouring of warranties, free servicing and recall work, to a repairer or to a number of repairers within the supplier's distribution system. It is nevertheless appropriate to facilitate access to repair and maintenance services. Therefore, a supplier may require distributors who have subcontracted repair and maintenance services to one or more authorised repairers to give end users the name and address of the repair shop or shops in question. If any of these authorised repairers is not established in the vicinity of the sales outlet, the supplier may also require the distributor to tell end users how far the repair shop or shops in question are from the sales outlet. However, a supplier can only impose such obligations if he also imposes similar obligations on distributors whose own repair shop is not on the same premises as their sales outlet.

(22) Furthermore, it is not necessary, in order to adequately provide for repair and maintenance services, for authorised repairers to also sell new motor vehicles. The exemption should therefore not cover vertical agreements containing any direct or indirect obligation or incentive which leads to the linking of sales and servicing activities or which makes the performance of one of these activities dependent on the performance of the other; this is in particular the case where the remuneration of distributors or authorised repairers relating to the purchase or sale of goods or services necessary for one activity is made dependent on the purchase or sale of goods or services relating to the other activity, or where all such goods or services are indistinctly aggregated into a single remuneration or discount system.

(23) In order to ensure effective competition on the repair and maintenance markets and to allow repairers to offer end users competing spare parts such as original spare parts and spare parts of matching quality, the exemption should not cover vertical agreements which restrict the ability of authorised repairers within the distribution system of a vehicle manufacturer, independent distributors of spare parts, independent repairers or end users to source spare parts from the manufacturer of such spare parts or from another third party of their choice. This does not affect spare part manufacturers' liability under civil law.

(24) Furthermore, in order to allow authorised and independent repairers and end users to identify the manufacturer of motor vehicle components or of spare parts and to choose between competing spare parts, the exemption should not cover agreements by which a manufacturer of motor vehicles limits the ability of a manufacturer of components or original spare parts to place its trade mark or logo on these parts effectively and in a visible manner. Moreover, in order to facilitate this choice and the sale of spare parts, which have been manufactured according to the specifications and production and quality standards provided by the vehicle manufacturer for the production of components or spare parts, it is presumed that spare parts constitute original spare parts, if the spare part producer issues a certificate that the parts are of the same quality as the components used for the assembly of a motor vehicle and have been manufactured according to these specifications and standards. Other spare parts for which the spare part producer can issue a certificate at any moment attesting that they match the quality of the components used for the assembly of a certain motor vehicle, may be sold as spare parts of matching quality.

(25) The exemption should not cover vertical agreements which restrict authorised repairers from using spare parts of matching quality for the repair or maintenance of a motor vehicle. However, in view of the vehicle manufacturers' direct contractual involvement in repairs under warranty, free servicing, and recall operations, agreements containing obligations on authorised repairers to use original spare parts supplied by the vehicle manufacturer for these repairs should be covered by the exemption.

(26) In order to protect effective competition on the market for repair and maintenance services and to prevent foreclosure of independent repairers, motor vehicle manufacturers must allow all interested independent operators to have full access to all technical information, diagnostic and other equipment, tools, including all relevant software, and training required for the repair and maintenance of motor vehicles. Independent operators who must be allowed such access include in particular independent repairers, manufacturers of repair equipment or tools, publishers of technical information, automobile clubs, roadside assistance operators, operators offering inspection and testing services and operators offering training for repairers. In particular, the conditions of access must not discriminate between authorised and independent operators, access must be given upon request and without undue delay, and the price charged for the information should not discourage access to it by failing to take into account the extent to which the independent operator uses it. A supplier of motor vehicles should be required to give independent operators access to technical information on new motor vehicles at the same time as such access is given to its authorised repairers and must not oblige independent operators to purchase more than the information necessary to carry out the work in question. Suppliers should be obliged to give access to the technical information necessary for re-programming electronic devices in a motor vehicle. It is, however, legitimate and proper for them to withhold access to technical information which might allow a third party to bypass or disarm on-board anti-theft devices, to recalibrate electronic devices or to tamper with devices which for instance limit the speed of a motor vehicle, unless protection against theft, re-calibration or tampering can be attained by other less restrictive means. Intellectual property rights and rights regarding know-how including those which relate to the aforementioned devices must be exercised in a manner which avoids any type of abuse.

(27) In order to ensure access to and to prevent collusion on the relevant markets and to give distributors opportunities to sell vehicles of brands from two or more manufacturers that are not connected undertakings, certain specific conditions are attached to the exemption. To this end, the exemption should not be accorded to non-compete obligations. In

particular, without prejudice to the ability of the supplier to require the distributor to display the vehicles in brand-specific areas of the showroom in order to avoid brand confusion, any prohibition on sales of competing makes should not be exempted. The same applies to an obligation to display the full range of motor vehicles if it makes the sale or display of vehicles manufactured by undertakings which are not connected impossible or unreasonably difficult. Furthermore, an obligation to have brand-specific sales personnel is considered to be an indirect non-compete obligation and therefore should not be covered by the exemption, unless the distributor decides to have brand-specific sales personnel and the supplier pays all the additional costs involved.

(28) In order to ensure that repairers are able to carry out repairs or maintenance on all motor vehicles, the exemption should not apply to any obligation limiting the ability of repairers of motor vehicles to provide repair or maintenance services for brands of competing suppliers.

(29) In addition, specific conditions are required to exclude certain restrictions, sometimes imposed in the context of a selective distribution system, from the scope of the exemption. This applies in particular to obligations which have the effect of preventing the members of a selective distribution system from selling the brands of particular competing suppliers, which could easily lead to foreclosure of certain brands. Additional conditions are necessary in order to foster intra-brand competition and market integration within the common market, to create opportunities for distributors and authorised repairers who wish to seize business opportunities outside their place of establishment, and to create conditions which allow the development of multi-brand distributors. In particular a restriction on operating out of an unauthorised place of establishment for the distribution of passenger cars and light commercial vehicles or the provision of repair and maintenance services should not be exempted. The supplier may require additional sales or delivery outlets for passenger cars and light commercial vehicles or repair shops to comply with the relevant qualitative criteria applicable for similar outlets located in the same geographic area.

(30) The exemption should not apply to restrictions limiting the ability of a distributor to sell leasing services for motor vehicles.

(31) The market share limitations, the fact that certain vertical agreements are not covered, and the conditions provided for in this Regulation, should normally ensure that the agreements to which the exemption applies do not enable the participating undertakings to eliminate competition in respect of a substantial part of the goods or services in question.

(32) In particular cases in which agreements which would otherwise benefit from the exemption nevertheless have effects incompatible with Article 81(3), the Commission is empowered to withdraw the benefit of the exemption; this may occur in particular where the buyer has significant market power on the relevant market on which it resells the goods or provides the services or where parallel networks of vertical agreements have similar effects which significantly restrict access to a relevant market or competition thereon; such cumulative effects may for example arise in the case of selective distribution. The Commission may also withdraw the benefit of the exemption if competition is significantly restricted on a market due to the presence of a supplier with market power or if prices and conditions of supply to motor vehicle distributors differ substantially between geographic markets. It may also withdraw the benefit of the exemption if discriminatory prices or sales conditions, or unjustifiably high supplements, such as those charged for right hand drive vehicles, are applied for the supply of goods corresponding to the contract range.

(33) Regulation No 19/65/EEC empowers the national authorities of Member States to withdraw the benefit of the exemption in respect of vertical agreements having effects incompatible with the conditions laid down in Article 81(3), where such effects are felt in their territory, or in a part thereof, and where such territory has the characteristics of a distinct geographic market; the exercise of this national power of withdrawal should not prejudice the uniform application throughout the common market of the Community competition rules or the full effect of the measures adopted in implementation of those rules.

(34) In order to allow for better supervision of parallel networks of vertical agreements which have similar restrictive effects and which cover more than 50% of a given market, the Commission should be permitted to declare the exemption inapplicable to vertical agreements containing specific restraints relating to the market concerned, thereby restoring the full application of Article 81(1) to such agreements.

(35) The exemption should be granted without prejudice to the application of the provisions of Article 82 of the Treaty on the abuse by an undertaking of a dominant position.

(36) Commission Regulation (EC) N° 1475/95 of 28 June 1995 on the application of Article 85(3) of the Treaty to certain categories of motor vehicle distribution and servicing agreements is applicable until 30 September 2002. In order to allow all operators time to adapt vertical agreements which are compatible with that regulation and which are still in force when the exemption provided for therein expires, it is appropriate for such agreements to benefit from a transition period until 1 October 2003, during which time they should be exempted from the prohibition laid down in Article 81(1) under this Regulation.

(37) In order to allow all operators within a quantitative selective distribution system for new passenger cars and light commercial vehicles to adapt their business strategies to the non-application of the exemption to location clauses, it is appropriate to stipulate that the condition set out in Article 5(2)(b) shall enter into force on 1 October 2005.

(38) The Commission should monitor the operation of this Regulation on a regular basis, with particular regard to its effects on competition in motor vehicle retailing and in after sales servicing in the common market or relevant parts of it. This should include monitoring the effects of this Regulation on the structure and level of concentration of motor vehicle distribution and any resulting effects on competition. The Commission should also carry out an evaluation of the operation of this Regulation and draw up a report not later than 31 May 2008.

HAS ADOPTED THIS REGULATION:

Article 1 Definitions

1.   For the purposes of this Regulation:

(a) "competing undertakings" means actual or potential suppliers on the same product market; the product market includes goods or services which are regarded by the buyer as interchangeable with or substitutable for the contract goods or services, by reason of the products' characteristics, their prices and their intended use;

(b) "non-compete obligation" means any direct or indirect obligation causing the buyer not to manufacture, purchase, sell or resell goods or services which compete with the contract goods or services, or any direct or indirect obligation on the buyer to purchase from the supplier or from another undertaking designated by the supplier more than 30% of the buyer's total purchases of the contract goods, corresponding goods or services and their substitutes on the relevant market, calculated on the basis of the value of its purchases in the preceding calendar year. An obligation that the distributor sell motor vehicles from other suppliers in separate areas of the showroom in order to avoid confusion between the makes does not constitute a non-compete obligation for the purposes of this Regulation. An obligation that the distributor have brand-specific sales personnel for different brands of motor vehicles constitutes a non-compete obligation for the purposes of this Regulation, unless the distributor decides to have brand-specific sales personnel and the supplier pays all the additional costs involved;

(c) "vertical agreements" means agreements or concerted practices entered into by two or more undertakings, each of which operates, for the purposes of the agreement, at a different level of the production or distribution chain;

(d) "vertical restraints" means restrictions of competition falling within the scope of Article 81(1), when such restrictions are contained in a vertical agreement;

(e) "exclusive supply obligation" means any direct or indirect obligation causing the supplier to sell the contract goods or services only to one buyer inside the common market for the purposes of a specific use or for resale;

(f) "selective distribution system" means a distribution system where the supplier undertakes to sell the contract goods or services, either directly or indirectly, only to distributors or repairers selected on the basis of specified criteria and where these distributors or repairers undertake not to sell such goods or services to unauthorised distributors or independent repairers, without prejudice to the ability to sell spare parts to independent repairers or the obligation to provide independent operators with all technical information, diagnostic equipment, tools and training required for the repair and maintenance of motor vehicles or for the implementation of environmental protection measures;

(g) "quantitative selective distribution system" means a selective distribution system where the supplier uses criteria for the selection of distributors or repairers which directly limit their number;

(h) "qualitative selective distribution system" means a selective distribution system where the supplier uses criteria for the selection of distributors or repairers which are only qualitative in nature, are required by the nature of the contract goods or services, are laid down uniformly for all distributors or repairers applying to join the distribution system, are not applied in a discriminatory manner, and do not directly limit the number of distributors or repairers;

(i) "intellectual property rights" includes industrial property rights, copyright and neighbouring rights;

(j) "know-how" means a package of non-patented practical information, derived from experience and testing by the supplier, which is secret, substantial and identified; in this context, "secret" means that the know-how, as a body or in the precise configuration and assembly of its components, is not generally known or easily accessible; "substantial" means that the know-how includes information which is indispensable to the buyer for the use, sale or resale of the contract goods or services; "identified" means that the know-how must be described in a sufficiently comprehensive manner so as to make it possible to verify that it fulfils the criteria of secrecy and substantiality;

(k) "buyer", whether distributor or repairer, includes an undertaking which sells goods or services on behalf of another undertaking;

(l) "authorised repairer" means a provider of repair and maintenance services for motor vehicles operating within the distribution system set up by a supplier of motor vehicles;

(m) "independent repairer" means a provider of repair and maintenance services for motor vehicles not operating within the distribution system set up by the supplier of the motor vehicles for which it provides repair or maintenance. An authorised repairer within the distribution system of a given supplier shall be deemed to be an independent repairer for the purposes of this Regulation to the extent that he provides repair or maintenance services for motor vehicles in respect of which he is not a member of the respective supplier's distribution system;

(n) "motor vehicle" means a self propelled vehicle intended for use on public roads and having three or more road wheels;

(o) "passenger car" means a motor vehicle intended for the carriage of passengers and comprising no more than eight seats in addition to the driver's seat;

(p) "light commercial vehicle" means a motor vehicle intended for the transport of goods or passengers with a maximum mass not exceeding 3,5 tonnes; if a certain light commercial vehicle is also sold in a version with a maximum mass above 3,5 tonnes, all versions of that vehicle are considered to be light commercial vehicles;

(q) the "contract range" means all the different models of motor vehicles available for purchase by the distributor from the supplier;

(r) a "motor vehicle which corresponds to a model within the contract range" means a vehicle which is the subject of a distribution agreement with another undertaking within the distribution system set up by the manufacturer or with his consent and which is:
— manufactured or assembled in volume by the manufacturer, and
— identical as to body style, drive-line, chassis, and type of motor to a vehicle within the contract range;

(s) "spare parts" means goods which are to be installed in or upon a motor vehicle so as to replace components of that vehicle, including goods such as lubricants which are necessary for the use of a motor vehicle, with the exception of fuel;

(t) "original spare parts" means spare parts which are of the same quality as the components used for the assembly of a motor vehicle and which are manufactured according to the specifications and production standards provided by the vehicle manufacturer for the production of components or spare parts for the motor vehicle in question. This includes spare parts which are manufactured on the same production line as these components. It is presumed, unless the contrary is proven, that parts constitute original spare parts if the part manufacturer certifies that the parts match the quality of the components used for the assembly of the vehicle in question and have been manufactured according to the specifications and production standards of the vehicle manufacturer;

(u) "spare parts of matching quality" means exclusively spare parts made by any undertaking which can certify at any moment that the parts in question match the quality of the components which are or were used for the assembly of the motor vehicles in question;

(v) "undertakings within the distribution system" means the manufacturer and undertakings which are entrusted by the manufacturer or with the manufacturer's consent with the distribution or repair or maintenance of contract goods or corresponding goods;

(w) "end user" includes leasing companies unless the leasing contracts used provide for a transfer of ownership or an option to purchase the vehicle prior to the expiry of the contract.

2. The terms "undertaking", "supplier", "buyer", "distributor" and "repairer" shall include their respective connected undertakings.

"Connected undertakings" are:

(a) undertakings in which a party to the agreement, directly or indirectly:
  (i) has the power to exercise more than half the voting rights, or
  (ii) has the power to appoint more than half the members of the supervisory board, board of management or bodies legally representing the undertaking, or
  (iii) has the right to manage the undertaking's affairs;
(b) undertakings which directly or indirectly have, over a party to the agreement, the rights or powers listed in (a);
(c) undertakings in which an undertaking referred to in (b) has, directly or indirectly, the rights or powers listed in (a);
(d) undertakings in which a party to the agreement together with one or more of the undertakings referred to in (a), (b) or (c), or in which two or more of the latter undertakings, jointly have the rights or powers listed in (a);
(e) undertakings in which the rights or the powers listed in (a) are jointly held by:
  (i) parties to the agreement or their respective connected undertakings referred to in (a) to (d), or
  (ii) one or more of the parties to the agreement or one or more of their connected undertakings referred to in (a) to (d) and one or more third parties.

Article 2 Scope

1.   Pursuant to Article 81(3) of the Treaty and subject to the provisions of this Regulation, it is hereby declared that the provisions of Article 81(1) shall not apply to vertical agreements where they relate to the conditions under which the parties may purchase, sell or resell new motor vehicles, spare parts for motor vehicles or repair and maintenance services for motor vehicles.

The first subparagraph shall apply to the extent that such vertical agreements contain vertical restraints.

The exemption declared by this paragraph shall be known for the purposes of this Regulation as "the exemption".

2.   The exemption shall also apply to the following categories of vertical agreements:
(a) Vertical agreements entered into between an association of undertakings and its members, or between such an association and its suppliers, only if all its members are distributors of motor vehicles or spare parts for motor vehicles or repairers and if no individual member of the association, together with its connected undertakings, has a total annual turnover exceeding EUR 50 million; vertical agreements entered into by such associations shall be covered by this Regulation without prejudice to the application of Article 81 to horizontal agreements concluded between the members of the association or decisions adopted by the association;
(b) vertical agreements containing provisions which relate to the assignment to the buyer or use by the buyer of intellectual property rights, provided that those provisions do not constitute the primary object of such agreements and are directly related to the use, sale or resale of goods or services by the buyer or its customers. The exemption shall apply on condition that those provisions do not contain restrictions of competition relating to the contract goods or services which have the same object or effect as vertical restraints which are not exempted under this Regulation.

3.   The exemption shall not apply to vertical agreements entered into between competing undertakings.

However, it shall apply where competing undertakings enter into a non-reciprocal vertical agreement and:
(a) the buyer has a total annual turnover not exceeding EUR 100 million, or

(b) the supplier is a manufacturer and a distributor of goods, while the buyer is a distributor not manufacturing goods competing with the contract goods, or

(c) the supplier is a provider of services at several levels of trade, while the buyer does not provide competing services at the level of trade where it purchases the contract services.

Article 3 General conditions

1. Subject to paragraphs 2, 3, 4, 5, 6 and 7, the exemption shall apply on condition that the supplier's market share on the relevant market on which it sells the new motor vehicles, spare parts for motor vehicles or repair and maintenance services does not exceed 30%.

    However, the market share threshold for the application of the exemption shall be 40% for agreements establishing quantitative selective distribution systems for the sale of new motor vehicles.

    Those thresholds shall not apply to agreements establishing qualitative selective distribution systems.

2. In the case of vertical agreements containing exclusive supply obligations, the exemption shall apply on condition that the market share held by the buyer does not exceed 30% of the relevant market on which it purchases the contract goods or services.

3. The exemption shall apply on condition that the vertical agreement concluded with a distributor or repairer provides that the supplier agrees to the transfer of the rights and obligations resulting from the vertical agreement to another distributor or repairer within the distribution system and chosen by the former distributor or repairer.

4. The exemption shall apply on condition that the vertical agreement concluded with a distributor or repairer provides that a supplier who wishes to give notice of termination of an agreement must give such notice in writing and must include detailed, objective and transparent reasons for the termination, in order to prevent a supplier from ending a vertical agreement with a distributor or repairer because of practices which may not be restricted under this Regulation.

5. The exemption shall apply on condition that the vertical agreement concluded by the supplier of new motor vehicles with a distributor or authorised repairer provides

    (a) that the agreement is concluded for a period of at least five years; in this case each party has to undertake to give the other party at least six months' prior notice of its intention not to renew the agreement;

    (b) or that the agreement is concluded for an indefinite period; in this case the period of notice for regular termination of the agreement has to be at least two years for both parties; this period is reduced to at least one year where:

        (i) the supplier is obliged by law or by special agreement to pay appropriate compensation on termination of the agreement, or

        (ii) the supplier terminates the agreement where it is necessary to re-organise the whole or a substantial part of the network.

6. The exemption shall apply on condition that the vertical agreement provides for each of the parties the right to refer disputes concerning the fulfilment of their contractual obligations to an independent expert or arbitrator. Such disputes may relate, inter alia, to any of the following:

    (a) supply obligations;

    (b) the setting or attainment of sales targets;

    (c) the implementation of stock requirements;

    (d) the implementation of an obligation to provide or use demonstration vehicles;

    (e) the conditions for the sale of different brands;

(f) the issue whether the prohibition to operate out of an unauthorised place of establishment limits the ability of the distributor of motor vehicles other than passenger cars or light commercial vehicles to expand its business, or

(g) the issue whether the termination of an agreement is justified by the reasons given in the notice.

The right referred to in the first sentence is without prejudice to each party's right to make an application to a national court.

7. For the purposes of this Article, the market share held by the undertakings referred to in Article 1(2)(e) shall be apportioned equally to each undertaking having the rights or the powers listed in Article 1(2)(a).

Article 4 Hardcore restrictions

(Hardcore restrictions concerning the sale of new motor vehicles, repair and maintenance services or spare parts)

1. The exemption shall not apply to vertical agreements which, directly or indirectly, in isolation or in combination with other factors under the control of the parties, have as their object:

(a) the restriction of the distributor's or repairer's ability to determine its sale price, without prejudice to the supplier's ability to impose a maximum sale price or to recommend a sale price, provided that this does not amount to a fixed or minimum sale price as a result of pressure from, or incentives offered by, any of the parties;

(b) the restriction of the territory into which, or of the customers to whom, the distributor or repairer may sell the contract goods or services; however, the exemption shall apply to:

(i) the restriction of active sales into the exclusive territory or to an exclusive customer group reserved to the supplier or allocated by the supplier to another distributor or repairer, where such a restriction does not limit sales by the customers of the distributor or repairer;

(ii) the restriction of sales to end users by a distributor operating at the wholesale level of trade;

(iii) the restriction of sales of new motor vehicles and spare parts to unauthorised distributors by the members of a selective distribution system in markets where selective distribution is applied, subject to the provisions of point (i);

(iv) the restriction of the buyer's ability to sell components, supplied for the purposes of incorporation, to customers who would use them to manufacture the same type of goods as those produced by the supplier;

(c) the restriction of cross-supplies between distributors or repairers within a selective distribution system, including between distributors or repairers operating at different levels of trade;

(d) the restriction of active or passive sales of new passenger cars or light commercial vehicles, spare parts for any motor vehicle or repair and maintenance services for any motor vehicle to end users by members of a selective distribution system operating at the retail level of trade in markets where selective distribution is used. The exemption shall apply to agreements containing a prohibition on a member of a selective distribution system from operating out of an unauthorised place of establishment. However, the application of the exemption to such a prohibition is subject to Article 5(2)(b);

(e) the restriction of active or passive sales of new motor vehicles other than passenger cars or light commercial vehicles to end users by members of a selective distribution system operating at the retail level of trade in markets where selective distribution is used, without prejudice to the ability of the supplier to prohibit a member of that system from operating out of an unauthorised place of establishment;

(Hardcore restrictions only concerning the sale of new motor vehicles)

(f) the restriction of the distributor's ability to sell any new motor vehicle which corresponds to a model within its contract range;

(g) the restriction of the distributor's ability to subcontract the provision of repair and maintenance services to authorised repairers, without prejudice to the ability of the supplier to require the distributor to give end users the name and address of the authorised repairer or repairers in question before the conclusion of a sales contract and, if any of these authorised repairers is not in the vicinity of the sales outlet, to also tell end users how far the repair shop or repair shops in question are from the sales outlet; however, such obligations may only be imposed provided that similar obligations are imposed on distributors whose repair shop is not on the same premises as their sales outlet;

(Hardcore restrictions only concerning the sale of repair and maintenance services and of spare parts)

(h) the restriction of the authorised repairer's ability to limit its activities to the provision of repair and maintenance services and the distribution of spare parts;

(i) the restriction of the sales of spare parts for motor vehicles by members of a selective distribution system to independent repairers which use these parts for the repair and maintenance of a motor vehicle;

(j) the restriction agreed between a supplier of original spare parts or spare parts of matching quality, repair tools or diagnostic or other equipment and a manufacturer of motor vehicles, which limits the supplier's ability to sell these goods or services to authorised or independent distributors or to authorised or independent repairers or end users;

(k) the restriction of a distributor's or authorised repairer's ability to obtain original spare parts or spare parts of matching quality from a third undertaking of its choice and to use them for the repair or maintenance of motor vehicles, without prejudice to the ability of a supplier of new motor vehicles to require the use of original spare parts supplied by it for repairs carried out under warranty, free servicing and vehicle recall work;

(l) the restriction agreed between a manufacturer of motor vehicles which uses components for the initial assembly of motor vehicles and the supplier of such components which limits the latter's ability to place its trade mark or logo effectively and in an easily visible manner on the components supplied or on spare parts.

2. The exemption shall not apply where the supplier of motor vehicles refuses to give independent operators access to any technical information, diagnostic and other equipment, tools, including any relevant software, or training required for the repair and maintenance of these motor vehicles or for the implementation of environmental protection measures.

Such access must include in particular the unrestricted use of the electronic control and diagnostic systems of a motor vehicle, the programming of these systems in accordance with the supplier's standard procedures, the repair and training instructions and the information required for the use of diagnostic and servicing tools and equipment.

Access must be given to independent operators in a non-discriminatory, prompt and proportionate way, and the information must be provided in a usable form. If the relevant item is covered by an intellectual property right or constitutes know-how, access shall not be withheld in any abusive manner.

For the purposes of this paragraph "independent operator" shall mean undertakings which are directly or indirectly involved in the repair and maintenance of motor vehicles, in particular independent repairers, manufacturers of repair equipment or tools, independent distributors of spare parts, publishers of technical information, automobile clubs, roadside assistance operators, operators offering inspection and testing services and operators offering training for repairers.

Article 5 Specific conditions

1. As regards the sale of new motor vehicles, repair and maintenance services or spare parts, the exemption shall not apply to any of the following obligations contained in vertical agreements:

    (a) any direct or indirect non-compete obligation;

    (b) any direct or indirect obligation limiting the ability of an authorised repairer to provide repair and maintenance services for vehicles from competing suppliers;

    (c) any direct or indirect obligation causing the members of a distribution system not to sell motor vehicles or spare parts of particular competing suppliers or not to provide repair and maintenance services for motor vehicles of particular competing suppliers;

    (d) any direct or indirect obligation causing the distributor or authorised repairer, after termination of the agreement, not to manufacture, purchase, sell or resell motor vehicles or not to provide repair or maintenance services.

2. As regards the sale of new motor vehicles, the exemption shall not apply to any of the following obligations contained in vertical agreements:

    (a) any direct or indirect obligation causing the retailer not to sell leasing services relating to contract goods or corresponding goods;

    (b) any direct or indirect obligation on any distributor of passenger cars or light commercial vehicles within a selective distribution system, which limits its ability to establish additional sales or delivery outlets at other locations within the common market where selective distribution is applied.

3. As regards repair and maintenance services or the sale of spare parts, the exemption shall not apply to any direct or indirect obligation as to the place of establishment of an authorised repairer where selective distribution is applied.

Article 6 Withdrawal of the benefit of the Regulation

1. The Commission may withdraw the benefit of this Regulation, pursuant to Article 7(1) of Regulation No 19/65/EEC, where it finds in any particular case that vertical agreements to which this Regulation applies nevertheless have effects which are incompatible with the conditions laid down in Article 81(3) of the Treaty, and in particular:

    (a) where access to the relevant market or competition therein is significantly restricted by the cumulative effect of parallel networks of similar vertical restraints implemented by competing suppliers or buyers, or

    (b) where competition is restricted on a market where one supplier is not exposed to effective competition from other suppliers, or

    (c) where prices or conditions of supply for contract goods or for corresponding goods differ substantially between geographic markets, or

    (d) where discriminatory prices or sales conditions are applied within a geographic market.

2. Where in any particular case vertical agreements to which the exemption applies have effects incompatible with the conditions laid down in Article 81(3) of the Treaty in the territory of a Member State, or in a part thereof, which has all the characteristics of a distinct geographic market, the relevant authority of that Member State may withdraw the benefit of application of this Regulation in respect of that territory, under the same conditions as those provided in paragraph 1.

Article 7 Non-application of the Regulation

1.   Pursuant to Article 1a of Regulation No 19/65/EEC, the Commission may by regulation declare that, where parallel networks of similar vertical restraints cover more than 50% of a relevant market, this Regulation shall not apply to vertical agreements containing specific restraints relating to that market.

2.   A regulation pursuant to paragraph 1 shall not become applicable earlier than one year following its adoption.

Article 8 Market share calculation

1.   The market shares provided for in this Regulation shall be calculated

(a) for the distribution of new motor vehicles on the basis of the volume of the contract goods and corresponding goods sold by the supplier, together with any other goods sold by the supplier which are regarded as interchangeable or substitutable by the buyer, by reason of the products' characteristics, prices and intended use;

(b) for the distribution of spare parts on the basis of the value of the contract goods and other goods sold by the supplier, together with any other goods sold by the supplier which are regarded as interchangeable or substitutable by the buyer, by reason of the products' characteristics, prices and intended use;

(c) for the provision of repair and maintenance services on the basis of the value of the contract services sold by the members of the supplier's distribution network together with any other services sold by these members which are regarded as interchangeable or substitutable by the buyer, by reason of their characteristics, prices and intended use.

If the volume data required for those calculations are not available, value data may be used or vice versa. If such information is not available, estimates based on other reliable market information may be used. For the purposes of Article 3(2), the market purchase volume or the market purchase value respectively, or estimates thereof shall be used to calculate the market share.

2.   For the purposes of applying the market share thresholds of 30% and 40% provided for in this Regulation the following rules shall apply:

(a) the market share shall be calculated on the basis of data relating to the preceding calendar year;

(b) the market share shall include any goods or services supplied to integrated distributors for the purposes of sale;

(c) if the market share is initially not more than 30% or 40% respectively but subsequently rises above that level without exceeding 35% or 45% respectively, the exemption shall continue to apply for a period of two consecutive calendar years following the year in which the market share threshold of 30% or 40% respectively was first exceeded;

(d) if the market share is initially not more than 30% or 40% respectively but subsequently rises above 35% or 45% respectively, the exemption shall continue to apply for one calendar year following the year in which the level of 30% or 40% respectively was first exceeded;

(e) the benefit of points (c) and (d) may not be combined so as to exceed a period of two calendar years.

Article 9 Turnover calculation

1.   For the purposes of calculating total annual turnover figures referred to in Article 2(2)(a) and 2(3)(a) respectively, the turnover achieved during the previous financial year by the relevant party to the vertical agreement and the turnover achieved by its connected undertakings in respect of all goods and services, excluding all taxes and other duties, shall be added together. For this purpose, no account shall be taken of dealings between the party to the vertical agreement and its connected undertakings or between its connected undertakings.

2.   The exemption shall remain applicable where, for any period of two consecutive financial years, the total annual turnover threshold is exceeded by no more than 10%.

Article 10   Transitional period

1.   The prohibition laid down in Article 81(1) shall not apply during the period from 1 October 2002 to 30 September 2003 in respect of agreements already in force on 30 September 2002 which do not satisfy the conditions for exemption provided for in this Regulation but which satisfy the conditions for exemption provided for in Regulation (EC) No 1475/95.

2.   The prohibition laid down in Article 81(1) shall not apply to agreements existing at the date of accession for the Czech Republic, Estonia, Cyprus, Latvia, Lithuania, Hungary, Malta, Poland, Slovenia and Slovakia and which, by reason of accession, fall within the scope of Article 81(1) if, within six months from the date of accession, they are amended and thereby comply with the conditions laid down in this Regulation.

Article 11   Monitoring and evaluation report

1.   The Commission shall monitor the operation of this Regulation on a regular basis, with particular regard to its effects on:
   (a)   competition in motor vehicle retailing and in after sales servicing in the common market or relevant parts of it;
   (b)   the structure and level of concentration of motor vehicle distribution and any resulting effects on competition.

2.   The Commission shall draw up a report on this Regulation not later than 31 May 2008 having regard in particular to the conditions set out in Article 81(3).

Article 12   Entry into force and expiry

1.   This Regulation shall enter into force on 1 October 2002.

2.   Article 5(2)(b) shall apply from 1 October 2005.

3.   This Regulation shall expire on 31 May 2010.

This Regulation shall be binding in its entirety and directly applicable in all Member States.

(date of signing and signatory omitted)

COUNCIL REGULATION (EC) NO 1/2003 OF 16 DECEMBER 2002

on the implementation of the rules on competition laid down in Articles 81 and 82 of the Treaty
OJ L 1, 4.1.2003, p. 1*[1]

....

....

[1]   EDITOR'S NOTE: On 1 May 2004, the date of its implementation, Regulation 1/2003 replaced and repealed the original implementing measure, Council Regulation No 17/62, OJ Special Edition 1962, No. 204/62, p. 87, subject to transitional provisions in Art. 34(2) concerning procedural steps already taken under that Regulation, and Art. 43(1), under which Art. 8(3) of the original Regulation is retained so as to enable the Commission to revoke or amend its decisions or prohibit specified acts by the parties, where those decisions were adopted pursuant to Article 81(3) EC prior to the date of application of Regulation 1/2003 until the date of expiration of those decisions.

(*As amended by Council Regulation (EC) No 411/2004 of 26 February 2004, L 68, 6.3.2004, p. 1 and Council Regulation (EC) No 1419/2006 of 25 September 2006, L 269, 28.9.2006, p. 1).[2]

THE COUNCIL OF THE EUROPEAN UNION,

Having regard to the Treaty establishing the European Community, and in particular Article 83 thereof,

Having regard to the proposal from the Commission(1),

Having regard to the opinion of the European Parliament(2),

Having regard to the opinion of the European Economic and Social Committee(3),

Whereas:

(1)   In order to establish a system which ensures that competition in the common market is not distorted, Articles 81 and 82 of the Treaty must be applied effectively and uniformly in the Community. Council Regulation No 17 of 6 February 1962, First Regulation implementing Articles 81 and 82(4) of the Treaty(5), has allowed a Community competition policy to develop that has helped to disseminate a competition culture within the Community. In the light of experience, however, that Regulation should now be replaced by legislation designed to meet the challenges of an integrated market and a future enlargement of the Community.

(2)   In particular, there is a need to rethink the arrangements for applying the exception from the prohibition on agreements, which restrict competition, laid down in Article 81(3) of the Treaty. Under Article 83(2)(b) of the Treaty, account must be taken in this regard of the need to ensure effective supervision, on the one hand, and to simplify administration to the greatest possible extent, on the other.

(3)   The centralised scheme set up by Regulation No 17 no longer secures a balance between those two objectives. It hampers application of the Community competition rules by the courts and competition authorities of the Member States, and the system of notification it involves prevents the Commission from concentrating its resources on curbing the most serious infringements. It also imposes considerable costs on undertakings.

(4)   The present system should therefore be replaced by a directly applicable exception system in which the competition authorities and courts of the Member States have the power to apply not only Article 81(1) and Article 82 of the Treaty, which have direct applicability by virtue of the case-law of the Court of Justice of the European Communities, but also Article 81(3) of the Treaty.

(5)   In order to ensure an effective enforcement of the Community competition rules and at the same time the respect of fundamental rights of defence, this Regulation should regulate the burden of proof under Articles 81 and 82 of the Treaty. It should be for the party or the authority alleging an infringement of Article 81(1) and Article 82 of the Treaty to prove the existence thereof to the required legal standard. It should be for the undertaking or association of undertakings invoking the benefit of a defence against a finding of an infringement to demonstrate to the required legal standard that the conditions for applying such defence are satisfied. This Regulation affects neither national rules on the standard of proof nor obligations of competition authorities and courts of the

....

[2]   EDITOR'S NOTE: As of 1 June 2010 this Regulation has not been amended following the adoption of the Treaty of Lisbon. It includes references to the old Treaty article numbers. Reference should be made to the Tables of Equivalences accompanying the consolidated Treaties in Part II of this edition for the conversion of old Treaty article numbers to new ones.

Member States to ascertain the relevant facts of a case, provided that such rules and obligations are compatible with general principles of Community law.

(6)   In order to ensure that the Community competition rules are applied effectively, the competition authorities of the Member States should be associated more closely with their application. To this end, they should be empowered to apply Community law.

(7)   National courts have an essential part to play in applying the Community competition rules. When deciding disputes between private individuals, they protect the subjective rights under Community law, for example by awarding damages to the victims of infringements. The role of the national courts here complements that of the competition authorities of the Member States. They should therefore be allowed to apply Articles 81 and 82 of the Treaty in full.

(8)   In order to ensure the effective enforcement of the Community competition rules and the proper functioning of the cooperation mechanisms contained in this Regulation, it is necessary to oblige the competition authorities and courts of the Member States to also apply Articles 81 and 82 of the Treaty where they apply national competition law to agreements and practices which may affect trade between Member States. In order to create a level playing field for agreements, decisions by associations of undertakings and concerted practices within the internal market, it is also necessary to determine pursuant to Article 83(2)(e) of the Treaty the relationship between national laws and Community competition law. To that effect it is necessary to provide that the application of national competition laws to agreements, decisions or concerted practices within the meaning of Article 81(1) of the Treaty may not lead to the prohibition of such agreements, decisions and concerted practices if they are not also prohibited under Community competition law. The notions of agreements, decisions and concerted practices are autonomous concepts of Community competition law covering the coordination of behaviour of undertakings on the market as interpreted by the Community Courts. Member States should not under this Regulation be precluded from adopting and applying on their territory stricter national competition laws which prohibit or impose sanctions on unilateral conduct engaged in by undertakings. These stricter national laws may include provisions which prohibit or impose sanctions on abusive behaviour toward economically dependent undertakings. Furthermore, this Regulation does not apply to national laws which impose criminal sanctions on natural persons except to the extent that such sanctions are the means whereby competition rules applying to undertakings are enforced.

(9)   Articles 81 and 82 of the Treaty have as their objective the protection of competition on the market. This Regulation, which is adopted for the implementation of these Treaty provisions, does not preclude Member States from implementing on their territory national legislation, which protects other legitimate interests provided that such legislation is compatible with general principles and other provisions of Community law. In so far as such national legislation pursues predominantly an objective different from that of protecting competition on the market, the competition authorities and courts of the Member States may apply such legislation on their territory. Accordingly, Member States may under this Regulation implement on their territory national legislation that prohibits or imposes sanctions on acts of unfair trading practice, be they unilateral or contractual. Such legislation pursues a specific objective, irrespective of the actual or presumed effects of such acts on competition on the market. This is particularly the case of legislation which prohibits undertakings from imposing on their trading partners, obtaining or attempting to obtain from them terms and conditions that are unjustified, disproportionate or without consideration.

(10) Regulations such as 19/65/EEC(6), (EEC) No 2821/71(7), (EEC) No 3976/87(8), (EEC) No 1534/91(9), or (EEC) No 479/92(10) empower the Commission to apply Article 81(3) of the Treaty by Regulation to certain categories of agreements, decisions by associations of undertakings and concerted practices. In the areas defined by such Regulations, the Commission has adopted and may continue to adopt so called "block" exemption Regulations by which it declares Article 81(1) of the Treaty inapplicable to categories of agreements, decisions and concerted practices. Where agreements, decisions and concerted practices to which such Regulations apply nonetheless have effects that are incompatible with Article 81(3) of the Treaty, the Commission and the competition authorities of the Member States should have the power to withdraw in a particular case the benefit of the block exemption Regulation.

(11) For it to ensure that the provisions of the Treaty are applied, the Commission should be able to address decisions to undertakings or associations of undertakings for the purpose of bringing to an end infringements of Articles 81 and 82 of the Treaty. Provided there is a legitimate interest in doing so, the Commission should also be able to adopt decisions which find that an infringement has been committed in the past even if it does not impose a fine. This Regulation should also make explicit provision for the Commission's power to adopt decisions ordering interim measures, which has been acknowledged by the Court of Justice.

(12) This Regulation should make explicit provision for the Commission's power to impose any remedy, whether behavioural or structural, which is necessary to bring the infringement effectively to an end, having regard to the principle of proportionality. Structural remedies should only be imposed either where there is no equally effective behavioural remedy or where any equally effective behavioural remedy would be more burdensome for the undertaking concerned than the structural remedy. Changes to the structure of an undertaking as it existed before the infringement was committed would only be proportionate where there is a substantial risk of a lasting or repeated infringement that derives from the very structure of the undertaking.

(13) Where, in the course of proceedings which might lead to an agreement or practice being prohibited, undertakings offer the Commission commitments such as to meet its concerns, the Commission should be able to adopt decisions which make those commitments binding on the undertakings concerned. Commitment decisions should find that there are no longer grounds for action by the Commission without concluding whether or not there has been or still is an infringement. Commitment decisions are without prejudice to the powers of competition authorities and courts of the Member States to make such a finding and decide upon the case. Commitment decisions are not appropriate in cases where the Commission intends to impose a fine.

(14) In exceptional cases where the public interest of the Community so requires, it may also be expedient for the Commission to adopt a decision of a declaratory nature finding that the prohibition in Article 81 or Article 82 of the Treaty does not apply, with a view to clarifying the law and ensuring its consistent application throughout the Community, in particular with regard to new types of agreements or practices that have not been settled in the existing case-law and administrative practice.

(15) The Commission and the competition authorities of the Member States should form together a network of public authorities applying the Community competition rules in close cooperation. For that purpose it is necessary to set up arrangements for information and consultation. Further modalities for the cooperation within the network will be laid down and revised by the Commission, in close cooperation with the Member States.

(16) Notwithstanding any national provision to the contrary, the exchange of information and the use of such information in evidence should be allowed between the members of the network even where the information is confidential. This information may be used for the application of Articles 81 and 82 of the Treaty as well as for the parallel application of national competition law, provided that the latter application relates to the same case and does not lead to a different outcome. When the information exchanged is used by the receiving authority to impose sanctions on undertakings, there should be no other limit to the use of the information than the obligation to use it for the purpose for which it was collected given the fact that the sanctions imposed on undertakings are of the same type in all systems. The rights of defence enjoyed by undertakings in the various systems can be considered as sufficiently equivalent. However, as regards natural persons, they may be subject to substantially different types of sanctions across the various systems. Where that is the case, it is necessary to ensure that information can only be used if it has been collected in a way which respects the same level of protection of the rights of defence of natural persons as provided for under the national rules of the receiving authority.

(17) If the competition rules are to be applied consistently and, at the same time, the network is to be managed in the best possible way, it is essential to retain the rule that the competition authorities of the Member States are automatically relieved of their competence if the Commission initiates its own proceedings. Where a competition authority of a Member State is already acting on a case and the Commission intends to initiate proceedings, it should endeavour to do so as soon as possible. Before initiating proceedings, the Commission should consult the national authority concerned.

(18) To ensure that cases are dealt with by the most appropriate authorities within the network, a general provision should be laid down allowing a competition authority to suspend or close a case on the ground that another authority is dealing with it or has already dealt with it, the objective being that each case should be handled by a single authority. This provision should not prevent the Commission from rejecting a complaint for lack of Community interest, as the case-law of the Court of Justice has acknowledged it may do, even if no other competition authority has indicated its intention of dealing with the case.

(19) The Advisory Committee on Restrictive Practices and Dominant Positions set up by Regulation No 17 has functioned in a very satisfactory manner. It will fit well into the new system of decentralised application. It is necessary, therefore, to build upon the rules laid down by Regulation No 17, while improving the effectiveness of the organisational arrangements. To this end, it would be expedient to allow opinions to be delivered by written procedure. The Advisory Committee should also be able to act as a forum for discussing cases that are being handled by the competition authorities of the Member States, so as to help safeguard the consistent application of the Community competition rules.

(20) The Advisory Committee should be composed of representatives of the competition authorities of the Member States. For meetings in which general issues are being discussed, Member States should be able to appoint an additional representative. This is without prejudice to members of the Committee being assisted by other experts from the Member States.

(21) Consistency in the application of the competition rules also requires that arrangements be established for cooperation between the courts of the Member States and the Commission. This is relevant for all courts of the Member States that apply Articles 81

and 82 of the Treaty, whether applying these rules in lawsuits between private parties, acting as public enforcers or as review courts. In particular, national courts should be able to ask the Commission for information or for its opinion on points concerning the application of Community competition law. The Commission and the competition authorities of the Member States should also be able to submit written or oral observations to courts called upon to apply Article 81 or Article 82 of the Treaty. These observations should be submitted within the framework of national procedural rules and practices including those safeguarding the rights of the parties. Steps should therefore be taken to ensure that the Commission and the competition authorities of the Member States are kept sufficiently well informed of proceedings before national courts.

(22)   In order to ensure compliance with the principles of legal certainty and the uniform application of the Community competition rules in a system of parallel powers, conflicting decisions must be avoided. It is therefore necessary to clarify, in accordance with the case-law of the Court of Justice, the effects of Commission decisions and proceedings on courts and competition authorities of the Member States. Commitment decisions adopted by the Commission do not affect the power of the courts and the competition authorities of the Member States to apply Articles 81 and 82 of the Treaty.

(23)   The Commission should be empowered throughout the Community to require such information to be supplied as is necessary to detect any agreement, decision or concerted practice prohibited by Article 81 of the Treaty or any abuse of a dominant position prohibited by Article 82 of the Treaty. When complying with a decision of the Commission, undertakings cannot be forced to admit that they have committed an infringement, but they are in any event obliged to answer factual questions and to provide documents, even if this information may be used to establish against them or against another undertaking the existence of an infringement.

(24)   The Commission should also be empowered to undertake such inspections as are necessary to detect any agreement, decision or concerted practice prohibited by Article 81 of the Treaty or any abuse of a dominant position prohibited by Article 82 of the Treaty. The competition authorities of the Member States should cooperate actively in the exercise of these powers.

(25)   The detection of infringements of the competition rules is growing ever more difficult, and, in order to protect competition effectively, the Commission's powers of investigation need to be supplemented. The Commission should in particular be empowered to interview any persons who may be in possession of useful information and to record the statements made. In the course of an inspection, officials authorised by the Commission should be empowered to affix seals for the period of time necessary for the inspection. Seals should normally not be affixed for more than 72 hours. Officials authorised by the Commission should also be empowered to ask for any information relevant to the subject matter and purpose of the inspection.

(26)   Experience has shown that there are cases where business records are kept in the homes of directors or other people working for an undertaking. In order to safeguard the effectiveness of inspections, therefore, officials and other persons authorised by the Commission should be empowered to enter any premises where business records may be kept, including private homes. However, the exercise of this latter power should be subject to the authorisation of the judicial authority.

(27)   Without prejudice to the case-law of the Court of Justice, it is useful to set out the scope of the control that the national judicial authority may carry out when it authorises, as foreseen by national law including as a precautionary measure, assistance from law

enforcement authorities in order to overcome possible opposition on the part of the undertaking or the execution of the decision to carry out inspections in non-business premises. It results from the case-law that the national judicial authority may in particular ask the Commission for further information which it needs to carry out its control and in the absence of which it could refuse the authorisation. The case-law also confirms the competence of the national courts to control the application of national rules governing the implementation of coercive measures.

(28) In order to help the competition authorities of the Member States to apply Articles 81 and 82 of the Treaty effectively, it is expedient to enable them to assist one another by carrying out inspections and other fact-finding measures.

(29) Compliance with Articles 81 and 82 of the Treaty and the fulfilment of the obligations imposed on undertakings and associations of undertakings under this Regulation should be enforceable by means of fines and periodic penalty payments. To that end, appropriate levels of fine should also be laid down for infringements of the procedural rules.

(30) In order to ensure effective recovery of fines imposed on associations of undertakings for infringements that they have committed, it is necessary to lay down the conditions on which the Commission may require payment of the fine from the members of the association where the association is not solvent. In doing so, the Commission should have regard to the relative size of the undertakings belonging to the association and in particular to the situation of small and medium-sized enterprises. Payment of the fine by one or several members of an association is without prejudice to rules of national law that provide for recovery of the amount paid from other members of the association.

(31) The rules on periods of limitation for the imposition of fines and periodic penalty payments were laid down in Council Regulation (EEC) No 2988/74(11), which also concerns penalties in the field of transport. In a system of parallel powers, the acts, which may interrupt a limitation period, should include procedural steps taken independently by the competition authority of a Member State. To clarify the legal framework, Regulation (EEC) No 2988/74 should therefore be amended to prevent it applying to matters covered by this Regulation, and this Regulation should include provisions on periods of limitation.

(32) The undertakings concerned should be accorded the right to be heard by the Commission, third parties whose interests may be affected by a decision should be given the opportunity of submitting their observations beforehand, and the decisions taken should be widely publicised. While ensuring the rights of defence of the undertakings concerned, in particular, the right of access to the file, it is essential that business secrets be protected. The confidentiality of information exchanged in the network should likewise be safeguarded.

(33) Since all decisions taken by the Commission under this Regulation are subject to review by the Court of Justice in accordance with the Treaty, the Court of Justice should, in accordance with Article 229 thereof be given unlimited jurisdiction in respect of decisions by which the Commission imposes fines or periodic penalty payments.

(34) The principles laid down in Articles 81 and 82 of the Treaty, as they have been applied by Regulation No 17, have given a central role to the Community bodies. This central role should be retained, whilst associating the Member States more closely with the application of the Community competition rules. In accordance with the principles of subsidiarity and proportionality as set out in Article 5 of the Treaty, this Regulation does not go beyond

what is necessary in order to achieve its objective, which is to allow the Community competition rules to be applied effectively.

(35) In order to attain a proper enforcement of Community competition law, Member States should designate and empower authorities to apply Articles 81 and 82 of the Treaty as public enforcers. They should be able to designate administrative as well as judicial authorities to carry out the various functions conferred upon competition authorities in this Regulation. This Regulation recognises the wide variation which exists in the public enforcement systems of Member States. The effects of Article 11(6) of this Regulation should apply to all competition authorities. As an exception to this general rule, where a prosecuting authority brings a case before a separate judicial authority, Article 11(6) should apply to the prosecuting authority subject to the conditions in Article 35(4) of this Regulation. Where these conditions are not fulfilled, the general rule should apply. In any case, Article 11(6) should not apply to courts insofar as they are acting as review courts.

(36) As the case-law has made it clear that the competition rules apply to transport, that sector should be made subject to the procedural provisions of this Regulation. Council Regulation No 141 of 26 November 1962 exempting transport from the application of Regulation No 17(12) should therefore be repealed and Regulations (EEC) No 1017/68(13), (EEC) No 4056/86(14) and (EEC) No 3975/87(15) should be amended in order to delete the specific procedural provisions they contain.

(37) This Regulation respects the fundamental rights and observes the principles recognised in particular by the Charter of Fundamental Rights of the European Union. Accordingly, this Regulation should be interpreted and applied with respect to those rights and principles.

(38) Legal certainty for undertakings operating under the Community competition rules contributes to the promotion of innovation and investment. Where cases give rise to genuine uncertainty because they present novel or unresolved questions for the application of these rules, individual undertakings may wish to seek informal guidance from the Commission. This Regulation is without prejudice to the ability of the Commission to issue such informal guidance,

HAS ADOPTED THIS REGULATION:

Chapter I PRINCIPLES

Article 1 Application of Articles 81 and 82 of the Treaty

1. Agreements, decisions and concerted practices caught by Article 81(1) of the Treaty which do not satisfy the conditions of Article 81(3) of the Treaty shall be prohibited, no prior decision to that effect being required.

2. Agreements, decisions and concerted practices caught by Article 81(1) of the Treaty which satisfy the conditions of Article 81(3) of the Treaty shall not be prohibited, no prior decision to that effect being required.

3. The abuse of a dominant position referred to in Article 82 of the Treaty shall be prohibited, no prior decision to that effect being required.

Article 2 Burden of proof

In any national or Community proceedings for the application of Articles 81 and 82 of the Treaty, the burden of proving an infringement of Article 81(1) or of Article 82 of the Treaty shall rest on the party or the authority alleging the infringement. The undertaking or association of undertakings claiming the benefit of Article 81(3) of the Treaty shall bear the burden of proving that the conditions of that paragraph are fulfilled.

Article 3 Relationship between Articles 81 and 82 of the Treaty and national competition laws

1. Where the competition authorities of the Member States or national courts apply national competition law to agreements, decisions by associations of undertakings or concerted practices within the meaning of Article 81(1) of the Treaty which may affect trade between Member States within the meaning of that provision, they shall also apply Article 81 of the Treaty to such agreements, decisions or concerted practices. Where the competition authorities of the Member States or national courts apply national competition law to any abuse prohibited by Article 82 of the Treaty, they shall also apply Article 82 of the Treaty.

2. The application of national competition law may not lead to the prohibition of agreements, decisions by associations of undertakings or concerted practices which may affect trade between Member States but which do not restrict competition within the meaning of Article 81(1) of the Treaty, or which fulfil the conditions of Article 81(3) of the Treaty or which are covered by a Regulation for the application of Article 81(3) of the Treaty. Member States shall not under this Regulation be precluded from adopting and applying on their territory stricter national laws which prohibit or sanction unilateral conduct engaged in by undertakings.

3. Without prejudice to general principles and other provisions of Community law, paragraphs 1 and 2 do not apply when the competition authorities and the courts of the Member States apply national merger control laws nor do they preclude the application of provisions of national law that predominantly pursue an objective different from that pursued by Articles 81 and 82 of the Treaty.

Chapter II POWERS

Article 4 Powers of the Commission

For the purpose of applying Articles 81 and 82 of the Treaty, the Commission shall have the powers provided for by this Regulation.

Article 5 Powers of the competition authorities of the Member States

The competition authorities of the Member States shall have the power to apply Articles 81 and 82 of the Treaty in individual cases. For this purpose, acting on their own initiative or on a complaint, they may take the following decisions:

— requiring that an infringement be brought to an end,

— ordering interim measures,

— accepting commitments,

— imposing fines, periodic penalty payments or any other penalty provided for in their national law.

Where on the basis of the information in their possession the conditions for prohibition are not met they may likewise decide that there are no grounds for action on their part.

Article 6 Powers of the national courts

National courts shall have the power to apply Articles 81 and 82 of the Treaty.

Chapter III COMMISSION DECISIONS

Article 7 Finding and termination of infringement

1. Where the Commission, acting on a complaint or on its own initiative, finds that there is an infringement of Article 81 or of Article 82 of the Treaty, it may by decision require the undertakings and associations of undertakings concerned to bring such infringement to an

end. For this purpose, it may impose on them any behavioural or structural remedies which are proportionate to the infringement committed and necessary to bring the infringement effectively to an end. Structural remedies can only be imposed either where there is no equally effective behavioural remedy or where any equally effective behavioural remedy would be more burdensome for the undertaking concerned than the structural remedy. If the Commission has a legitimate interest in doing so, it may also find that an infringement has been committed in the past.

2.   Those entitled to lodge a complaint for the purposes of paragraph 1 are natural or legal persons who can show a legitimate interest and Member States.

Article 8 Interim measures

1.   In cases of urgency due to the risk of serious and irreparable damage to competition, the Commission, acting on its own initiative may by decision, on the basis of a prima facie finding of infringement, order interim measures.

2.   A decision under paragraph 1 shall apply for a specified period of time and may be renewed in so far this is necessary and appropriate.

Article 9 Commitments

1.   Where the Commission intends to adopt a decision requiring that an infringement be brought to an end and the undertakings concerned offer commitments to meet the concerns expressed to them by the Commission in its preliminary assessment, the Commission may by decision make those commitments binding on the undertakings. Such a decision may be adopted for a specified period and shall conclude that there are no longer grounds for action by the Commission.

2.   The Commission may, upon request or on its own initiative, reopen the proceedings:
    (a) where there has been a material change in any of the facts on which the decision was based;
    (b) where the undertakings concerned act contrary to their commitments; or
    (c) where the decision was based on incomplete, incorrect or misleading information provided by the parties.

Article 10 Finding of inapplicability

Where the Community public interest relating to the application of Articles 81 and 82 of the Treaty so requires, the Commission, acting on its own initiative, may by decision find that Article 81 of the Treaty is not applicable to an agreement, a decision by an association of undertakings or a concerted practice, either because the conditions of Article 81(1) of the Treaty are not fulfilled, or because the conditions of Article 81(3) of the Treaty are satisfied.
The Commission may likewise make such a finding with reference to Article 82 of the Treaty.

Chapter IV COOPERATION

Article 11 Cooperation between the Commission and the competition authorities of the Member States

1.   The Commission and the competition authorities of the Member States shall apply the Community competition rules in close cooperation.

2.   The Commission shall transmit to the competition authorities of the Member States copies of the most important documents it has collected with a view to applying Articles 7, 8, 9, 10 and Article 29(1). At the request of the competition authority of a Member State, the Commission shall provide it with a copy of other existing documents necessary for the assessment of the case.

3.   The competition authorities of the Member States shall, when acting under Article 81 or Article 82 of the Treaty, inform the Commission in writing before or without delay after commencing the first formal investigative measure. This information may also be made available to the competition authorities of the other Member States.

4.   No later than 30 days before the adoption of a decision requiring that an infringement be brought to an end, accepting commitments or withdrawing the benefit of a block exemption Regulation, the competition authorities of the Member States shall inform the Commission. To that effect, they shall provide the Commission with a summary of the case, the envisaged decision or, in the absence thereof, any other document indicating the proposed course of action. This information may also be made available to the competition authorities of the other Member States. At the request of the Commission, the acting competition authority shall make available to the Commission other documents it holds which are necessary for the assessment of the case. The information supplied to the Commission may be made available to the competition authorities of the other Member States. National competition authorities may also exchange between themselves information necessary for the assessment of a case that they are dealing with under Article 81 or Article 82 of the Treaty.

5.   The competition authorities of the Member States may consult the Commission on any case involving the application of Community law.

6.   The initiation by the Commission of proceedings for the adoption of a decision under Chapter III shall relieve the competition authorities of the Member States of their competence to apply Articles 81 and 82 of the Treaty. If a competition authority of a Member State is already acting on a case, the Commission shall only initiate proceedings after consulting with that national competition authority.

Article 12 Exchange of information

1.   For the purpose of applying Articles 81 and 82 of the Treaty the Commission and the competition authorities of the Member States shall have the power to provide one another with and use in evidence any matter of fact or of law, including confidential information.

2.   Information exchanged shall only be used in evidence for the purpose of applying Article 81 or Article 82 of the Treaty and in respect of the subject-matter for which it was collected by the transmitting authority. However, where national competition law is applied in the same case and in parallel to Community competition law and does not lead to a different outcome, information exchanged under this Article may also be used for the application of national competition law.

3.   Information exchanged pursuant to paragraph 1 can only be used in evidence to impose sanctions on natural persons where:
        — the law of the transmitting authority foresees sanctions of a similar kind in relation to an infringement of Article 81 or Article 82 of the Treaty or, in the absence thereof,
        — the information has been collected in a way which respects the same level of protection of the rights of defence of natural persons as provided for under the national rules of the receiving authority. However, in this case, the information exchanged cannot be used by the receiving authority to impose custodial sanctions.

Article 13 Suspension or termination of proceedings

1.   Where competition authorities of two or more Member States have received a complaint or are acting on their own initiative under Article 81 or Article 82 of the Treaty against the same agreement, decision of an association or practice, the fact that one authority is dealing with the case shall be sufficient grounds for the others to suspend the proceedings

before them or to reject the complaint. The Commission may likewise reject a complaint on the ground that a competition authority of a Member State is dealing with the case.

2.   Where a competition authority of a Member State or the Commission has received a complaint against an agreement, decision of an association or practice which has already been dealt with by another competition authority, it may reject it.

Article 14 Advisory Committee

1.   The Commission shall consult an Advisory Committee on Restrictive Practices and Dominant Positions prior to the taking of any decision under Articles 7, 8, 9, 10, 23, Article 24(2) and Article 29(1).

2.   For the discussion of individual cases, the Advisory Committee shall be composed of representatives of the competition authorities of the Member States. For meetings in which issues other than individual cases are being discussed, an additional Member State representative competent in competition matters may be appointed. Representatives may, if unable to attend, be replaced by other representatives.

3.   The consultation may take place at a meeting convened and chaired by the Commission, held not earlier than 14 days after dispatch of the notice convening it, together with a summary of the case, an indication of the most important documents and a preliminary draft decision. In respect of decisions pursuant to Article 8, the meeting may be held seven days after the dispatch of the operative part of a draft decision. Where the Commission dispatches a notice convening the meeting which gives a shorter period of notice than those specified above, the meeting may take place on the proposed date in the absence of an objection by any Member State. The Advisory Committee shall deliver a written opinion on the Commission's preliminary draft decision. It may deliver an opinion even if some members are absent and are not represented. At the request of one or several members, the positions stated in the opinion shall be reasoned.

4.   Consultation may also take place by written procedure. However, if any Member State so requests, the Commission shall convene a meeting. In case of written procedure, the Commission shall determine a time-limit of not less than 14 days within which the Member States are to put forward their observations for circulation to all other Member States. In case of decisions to be taken pursuant to Article 8, the time-limit of 14 days is replaced by seven days. Where the Commission determines a time-limit for the written procedure which is shorter than those specified above, the proposed time-limit shall be applicable in the absence of an objection by any Member State.

5.   The Commission shall take the utmost account of the opinion delivered by the Advisory Committee. It shall inform the Committee of the manner in which its opinion has been taken into account.

6.   Where the Advisory Committee delivers a written opinion, this opinion shall be appended to the draft decision. If the Advisory Committee recommends publication of the opinion, the Commission shall carry out such publication taking into account the legitimate interest of undertakings in the protection of their business secrets.

7.   At the request of a competition authority of a Member State, the Commission shall include on the agenda of the Advisory Committee cases that are being dealt with by a competition authority of a Member State under Article 81 or Article 82 of the Treaty. The Commission may also do so on its own initiative. In either case, the Commission shall inform the competition authority concerned.

A request may in particular be made by a competition authority of a Member State in respect of a case where the Commission intends to initiate proceedings with the effect of Article 11(6).

The Advisory Committee shall not issue opinions on cases dealt with by competition authorities of the Member States. The Advisory Committee may also discuss general issues of Community competition law.

Article 15 Cooperation with national courts

1. In proceedings for the application of Article 81 or Article 82 of the Treaty, courts of the Member States may ask the Commission to transmit to them information in its possession or its opinion on questions concerning the application of the Community competition rules.

2. Member States shall forward to the Commission a copy of any written judgment of national courts deciding on the application of Article 81 or Article 82 of the Treaty. Such copy shall be forwarded without delay after the full written judgment is notified to the parties.

3. Competition authorities of the Member States, acting on their own initiative, may submit written observations to the national courts of their Member State on issues relating to the application of Article 81 or Article 82 of the Treaty. With the permission of the court in question, they may also submit oral observations to the national courts of their Member State. Where the coherent application of Article 81 or Article 82 of the Treaty so requires, the Commission, acting on its own initiative, may submit written observations to courts of the Member States. With the permission of the court in question, it may also make oral observations.

   For the purpose of the preparation of their observations only, the competition authorities of the Member States and the Commission may request the relevant court of the Member State to transmit or ensure the transmission to them of any documents necessary for the assessment of the case.

4. This Article is without prejudice to wider powers to make observations before courts conferred on competition authorities of the Member States under the law of their Member State.

Article 16 Uniform application of Community competition law

1. When national courts rule on agreements, decisions or practices under Article 81 or Article 82 of the Treaty which are already the subject of a Commission decision, they cannot take decisions running counter to the decision adopted by the Commission. They must also avoid giving decisions which would conflict with a decision contemplated by the Commission in proceedings it has initiated. To that effect, the national court may assess whether it is necessary to stay its proceedings. This obligation is without prejudice to the rights and obligations under Article 234 of the Treaty.

2. When competition authorities of the Member States rule on agreements, decisions or practices under Article 81 or Article 82 of the Treaty which are already the subject of a Commission decision, they cannot take decisions which would run counter to the decision adopted by the Commission.

Chapter V POWERS OF INVESTIGATION

Article 17 Investigations into sectors of the economy and into types of agreements

1. Where the trend of trade between Member States, the rigidity of prices or other circumstances suggest that competition may be restricted or distorted within the common

market, the Commission may conduct its inquiry into a particular sector of the economy or into a particular type of agreements across various sectors. In the course of that inquiry, the Commission may request the undertakings or associations of undertakings concerned to supply the information necessary for giving effect to Articles 81 and 82 of the Treaty and may carry out any inspections necessary for that purpose.

The Commission may in particular request the undertakings or associations of undertakings concerned to communicate to it all agreements, decisions and concerted practices.

The Commission may publish a report on the results of its inquiry into particular sectors of the economy or particular types of agreements across various sectors and invite comments from interested parties.

2.   Articles 14, 18, 19, 20, 22, 23 and 24 shall apply mutatis mutandis.

Article 18 Requests for information

1.   In order to carry out the duties assigned to it by this Regulation, the Commission may, by simple request or by decision, require undertakings and associations of undertakings to provide all necessary information.

2.   When sending a simple request for information to an undertaking or association of undertakings, the Commission shall state the legal basis and the purpose of the request, specify what information is required and fix the time-limit within which the information is to be provided, and the penalties provided for in Article 23 for supplying incorrect or misleading information.

3.   Where the Commission requires undertakings and associations of undertakings to supply information by decision, it shall state the legal basis and the purpose of the request, specify what information is required and fix the time-limit within which it is to be provided. It shall also indicate the penalties provided for in Article 23 and indicate or impose the penalties provided for in Article 24. It shall further indicate the right to have the decision reviewed by the Court of Justice.

4.   The owners of the undertakings or their representatives and, in the case of legal persons, companies or firms, or associations having no legal personality, the persons authorised to represent them by law or by their constitution shall supply the information requested on behalf of the undertaking or the association of undertakings concerned. Lawyers duly authorised to act may supply the information on behalf of their clients. The latter shall remain fully responsible if the information supplied is incomplete, incorrect or misleading.

5.   The Commission shall without delay forward a copy of the simple request or of the decision to the competition authority of the Member State in whose territory the seat of the undertaking or association of undertakings is situated and the competition authority of the Member State whose territory is affected.

6.   At the request of the Commission the governments and competition authorities of the Member States shall provide the Commission with all necessary information to carry out the duties assigned to it by this Regulation.

Article 19 Power to take statements

1.   In order to carry out the duties assigned to it by this Regulation, the Commission may interview any natural or legal person who consents to be interviewed for the purpose of collecting information relating to the subject-matter of an investigation.

2.   Where an interview pursuant to paragraph 1 is conducted in the premises of an undertaking, the Commission shall inform the competition authority of the Member State in whose territory the interview takes place. If so requested by the competition authority of that Member State, its officials may assist the officials and other accompanying persons authorised by the Commission to conduct the interview.

Article 20   The Commission's powers of inspection

1.   In order to carry out the duties assigned to it by this Regulation, the Commission may conduct all necessary inspections of undertakings and associations of undertakings.

2.   The officials and other accompanying persons authorised by the Commission to conduct an inspection are empowered:
     (a)   to enter any premises, land and means of transport of undertakings and associations of undertakings;
     (b)   to examine the books and other records related to the business, irrespective of the medium on which they are stored;
     (c)   to take or obtain in any form copies of or extracts from such books or records;
     (d)   to seal any business premises and books or records for the period and to the extent necessary for the inspection;
     (e)   to ask any representative or member of staff of the undertaking or association of undertakings for explanations on facts or documents relating to the subject-matter and purpose of the inspection and to record the answers.

3.   The officials and other accompanying persons authorised by the Commission to conduct an inspection shall exercise their powers upon production of a written authorisation specifying the subject matter and purpose of the inspection and the penalties provided for in Article 23 in case the production of the required books or other records related to the business is incomplete or where the answers to questions asked under paragraph 2 of the present Article are incorrect or misleading. In good time before the inspection, the Commission shall give notice of the inspection to the competition authority of the Member State in whose territory it is to be conducted.

4.   Undertakings and associations of undertakings are required to submit to inspections ordered by decision of the Commission. The decision shall specify the subject matter and purpose of the inspection, appoint the date on which it is to begin and indicate the penalties provided for in Articles 23 and 24 and the right to have the decision reviewed by the Court of Justice. The Commission shall take such decisions after consulting the competition authority of the Member State in whose territory the inspection is to be conducted.

5.   Officials of as well as those authorised or appointed by the competition authority of the Member State in whose territory the inspection is to be conducted shall, at the request of that authority or of the Commission, actively assist the officials and other accompanying persons authorised by the Commission. To this end, they shall enjoy the powers specified in paragraph 2.

6.   Where the officials and other accompanying persons authorised by the Commission find that an undertaking opposes an inspection ordered pursuant to this Article, the Member State concerned shall afford them the necessary assistance, requesting where appropriate the assistance of the police or of an equivalent enforcement authority, so as to enable them to conduct their inspection.

7.   If the assistance provided for in paragraph 6 requires authorisation from a judicial authority according to national rules, such authorisation shall be applied for. Such authorisation may also be applied for as a precautionary measure.

8.   Where authorisation as referred to in paragraph 7 is applied for, the national judicial authority shall control that the Commission decision is authentic and that the coercive measures envisaged are neither arbitrary nor excessive having regard to the subject matter of the inspection. In its control of the proportionality of the coercive measures, the national judicial authority may ask the Commission, directly or through the Member State competition authority, for detailed explanations in particular on the grounds the Commission has for suspecting infringement of Articles 81 and 82 of the Treaty, as well as on the seriousness of the suspected infringement and on the nature of the involvement of the undertaking concerned. However, the national judicial authority may not call into question the necessity for the inspection nor demand that it be provided with the information in the Commission's file. The lawfulness of the Commission decision shall be subject to review only by the Court of Justice.

Article 21 Inspection of other premises

1.   If a reasonable suspicion exists that books or other records related to the business and to the subject-matter of the inspection, which may be relevant to prove a serious violation of Article 81 or Article 82 of the Treaty, are being kept in any other premises, land and means of transport, including the homes of directors, managers and other members of staff of the undertakings and associations of undertakings concerned, the Commission can by decision order an inspection to be conducted in such other premises, land and means of transport.

2.   The decision shall specify the subject matter and purpose of the inspection, appoint the date on which it is to begin and indicate the right to have the decision reviewed by the Court of Justice. It shall in particular state the reasons that have led the Commission to conclude that a suspicion in the sense of paragraph 1 exists. The Commission shall take such decisions after consulting the competition authority of the Member State in whose territory the inspection is to be conducted.

3.   A decision adopted pursuant to paragraph 1 cannot be executed without prior authorisation from the national judicial authority of the Member State concerned. The national judicial authority shall control that the Commission decision is authentic and that the coercive measures envisaged are neither arbitrary nor excessive having regard in particular to the seriousness of the suspected infringement, to the importance of the evidence sought, to the involvement of the undertaking concerned and to the reasonable likelihood that business books and records relating to the subject matter of the inspection are kept in the premises for which the authorisation is requested. The national judicial authority may ask the Commission, directly or through the Member State competition authority, for detailed explanations on those elements which are necessary to allow its control of the proportionality of the coercive measures envisaged.

      However, the national judicial authority may not call into question the necessity for the inspection nor demand that it be provided with information in the Commission's file. The lawfulness of the Commission decision shall be subject to review only by the Court of Justice.

4.   The officials and other accompanying persons authorised by the Commission to conduct an inspection ordered in accordance with paragraph 1 of this Article shall have the powers set out in Article 20(2)(a), (b) and (c). Article 20(5) and (6) shall apply mutatis mutandis.

Article 22 Investigations by competition authorities of Member States

1.   The competition authority of a Member State may in its own territory carry out any inspection or other fact-finding measure under its national law on behalf and for the account of the competition authority of another Member State in order to establish

whether there has been an infringement of Article 81 or Article 82 of the Treaty. Any exchange and use of the information collected shall be carried out in accordance with Article 12.

2.   At the request of the Commission, the competition authorities of the Member States shall undertake the inspections which the Commission considers to be necessary under Article 20(1) or which it has ordered by decision pursuant to Article 20(4). The officials of the competition authorities of the Member States who are responsible for conducting these inspections as well as those authorised or appointed by them shall exercise their powers in accordance with their national law.

If so requested by the Commission or by the competition authority of the Member State in whose territory the inspection is to be conducted, officials and other accompanying persons authorised by the Commission may assist the officials of the authority concerned.

Chapter VI PENALTIES

Article 23 Fines

1.   The Commission may by decision impose on undertakings and associations of undertakings fines not exceeding 1% of the total turnover in the preceding business year where, intentionally or negligently:
   (a)   they supply incorrect or misleading information in response to a request made pursuant to Article 17 or Article 18(2);
   (b)   in response to a request made by decision adopted pursuant to Article 17 or Article 18(3), they supply incorrect, incomplete or misleading information or do not supply information within the required time-limit;
   (c)   they produce the required books or other records related to the business in incomplete form during inspections under Article 20 or refuse to submit to inspections ordered by a decision adopted pursuant to Article 20(4);
   (d)   in response to a question asked in accordance with Article 20(2)(e),
      — they give an incorrect or misleading answer,
      — they fail to rectify within a time-limit set by the Commission an incorrect, incomplete or misleading answer given by a member of staff, or
      — they fail or refuse to provide a complete answer on facts relating to the subject-matter and purpose of an inspection ordered by a decision adopted pursuant to Article 20(4);
   (e)   seals affixed in accordance with Article 20(2)(d) by officials or other accompanying persons authorised by the Commission have been broken.

2.   The Commission may by decision impose fines on undertakings and associations of undertakings where, either intentionally or negligently:
   (a)   they infringe Article 81 or Article 82 of the Treaty; or
   (b)   they contravene a decision ordering interim measures under Article 8; or
   (c)   they fail to comply with a commitment made binding by a decision pursuant to Article 9.
For each undertaking and association of undertakings participating in the infringement, the fine shall not exceed 10% of its total turnover in the preceding business year.

Where the infringement of an association relates to the activities of its members, the fine shall not exceed 10% of the sum of the total turnover of each member active on the market affected by the infringement of the association.

3.   In fixing the amount of the fine, regard shall be had both to the gravity and to the duration of the infringement.

4.   When a fine is imposed on an association of undertakings taking account of the turnover of its members and the association is not solvent, the association is obliged to call for contributions from its members to cover the amount of the fine.

Where such contributions have not been made to the association within a time-limit fixed by the Commission, the Commission may require payment of the fine directly by any of the undertakings whose representatives were members of the decision-making bodies concerned of the association.

After the Commission has required payment under the second subparagraph, where necessary to ensure full payment of the fine, the Commission may require payment of the balance by any of the members of the association which were active on the market on which the infringement occurred.

However, the Commission shall not require payment under the second or the third subparagraph from undertakings which show that they have not implemented the infringing decision of the association and either were not aware of its existence or have actively distanced themselves from it before the Commission started investigating the case.

The financial liability of each undertaking in respect of the payment of the fine shall not exceed 10% of its total turnover in the preceding business year.

5.   Decisions taken pursuant to paragraphs 1 and 2 shall not be of a criminal law nature.

Article 24 Periodic penalty payments

1.   The Commission may, by decision, impose on undertakings or associations of undertakings periodic penalty payments not exceeding 5% of the average daily turnover in the preceding business year per day and calculated from the date appointed by the decision, in order to compel them:
   (a) to put an end to an infringement of Article 81 or Article 82 of the Treaty, in accordance with a decision taken pursuant to Article 7;
   (b) to comply with a decision ordering interim measures taken pursuant to Article 8;
   (c) to comply with a commitment made binding by a decision pursuant to Article 9;
   (d) to supply complete and correct information which it has requested by decision taken pursuant to Article 17 or Article 18(3);
   (e) to submit to an inspection which it has ordered by decision taken pursuant to Article 20(4).

2.   Where the undertakings or associations of undertakings have satisfied the obligation which the periodic penalty payment was intended to enforce, the Commission may fix the definitive amount of the periodic penalty payment at a figure lower than that which would arise under the original decision. Article 23(4) shall apply correspondingly.

Chapter VII LIMITATION PERIODS

Article 25 Limitation periods for the imposition of penalties

1.   The powers conferred on the Commission by Articles 23 and 24 shall be subject to the following limitation periods:
   (a) three years in the case of infringements of provisions concerning requests for information or the conduct of inspections;
   (b) five years in the case of all other infringements.

2.   Time shall begin to run on the day on which the infringement is committed. However, in the case of continuing or repeated infringements, time shall begin to run on the day on which the infringement ceases.

3.   Any action taken by the Commission or by the competition authority of a Member State for the purpose of the investigation or proceedings in respect of an infringement shall interrupt the limitation period for the imposition of fines or periodic penalty payments. The limitation period shall be interrupted with effect from the date on which the action is notified to at least one undertaking or association of undertakings which has participated in the infringement. Actions which interrupt the running of the period shall include in particular the following:

(a)   written requests for information by the Commission or by the competition authority of a Member State;

(b)   written authorisations to conduct inspections issued to its officials by the Commission or by the competition authority of a Member State;

(c)   the initiation of proceedings by the Commission or by the competition authority of a Member State;

(d)   notification of the statement of objections of the Commission or of the competition authority of a Member State.

4.   The interruption of the limitation period shall apply for all the undertakings or associations of undertakings which have participated in the infringement.

5.   Each interruption shall start time running afresh. However, the limitation period shall expire at the latest on the day on which a period equal to twice the limitation period has elapsed without the Commission having imposed a fine or a periodic penalty payment. That period shall be extended by the time during which limitation is suspended pursuant to paragraph 6.

6.   The limitation period for the imposition of fines or periodic penalty payments shall be suspended for as long as the decision of the Commission is the subject of proceedings pending before the Court of Justice.

Article 26 Limitation period for the enforcement of penalties

1.   The power of the Commission to enforce decisions taken pursuant to Articles 23 and 24 shall be subject to a limitation period of five years.

2.   Time shall begin to run on the day on which the decision becomes final.

3.   The limitation period for the enforcement of penalties shall be interrupted:

(a)   by notification of a decision varying the original amount of the fine or periodic penalty payment or refusing an application for variation;

(b)   by any action of the Commission or of a Member State, acting at the request of the Commission, designed to enforce payment of the fine or periodic penalty payment.

4.   Each interruption shall start time running afresh.

5.   The limitation period for the enforcement of penalties shall be suspended for so long as:

(a)   time to pay is allowed;

(b)   enforcement of payment is suspended pursuant to a decision of the Court of Justice.

Chapter VIII HEARINGS AND PROFESSIONAL SECRECY

Article 27 Hearing of the parties, complainants and others

1.   Before taking decisions as provided for in Articles 7, 8, 23 and Article 24(2), the Commission shall give the undertakings or associations of undertakings which are the subject of the proceedings conducted by the Commission the opportunity of being heard on the matters to which the Commission has taken objection. The Commission shall base its decisions only on objections on which the parties concerned have been able to comment. Complainants shall be associated closely with the proceedings.

2.   The rights of defence of the parties concerned shall be fully respected in the proceedings. They shall be entitled to have access to the Commission's file, subject to the legitimate interest of undertakings in the protection of their business secrets. The right of access to the file shall not extend to confidential information and internal documents of the Commission or the competition authorities of the Member States. In particular, the right of access shall not extend to correspondence between the Commission and the competition authorities of the Member States, or between the latter, including documents drawn up pursuant to Articles 11 and 14. Nothing in this paragraph shall prevent the Commission from disclosing and using information necessary to prove an infringement.

3.   If the Commission considers it necessary, it may also hear other natural or legal persons. Applications to be heard on the part of such persons shall, where they show a sufficient interest, be granted. The competition authorities of the Member States may also ask the Commission to hear other natural or legal persons.

4.   Where the Commission intends to adopt a decision pursuant to Article 9 or Article 10, it shall publish a concise summary of the case and the main content of the commitments or of the proposed course of action. Interested third parties may submit their observations within a time limit which is fixed by the Commission in its publication and which may not be less than one month. Publication shall have regard to the legitimate interest of undertakings in the protection of their business secrets.

Article 28 Professional secrecy

1.   Without prejudice to Articles 12 and 15, information collected pursuant to Articles 17 to 22 shall be used only for the purpose for which it was acquired.

2.   Without prejudice to the exchange and to the use of information foreseen in Articles 11, 12, 14, 15 and 27, the Commission and the competition authorities of the Member States, their officials, servants and other persons working under the supervision of these authorities as well as officials and civil servants of other authorities of the Member States shall not disclose information acquired or exchanged by them pursuant to this Regulation and of the kind covered by the obligation of professional secrecy. This obligation also applies to all representatives and experts of Member States attending meetings of the Advisory Committee pursuant to Article 14.

Chapter IX EXEMPTION REGULATIONS

Article 29 Withdrawal in individual cases

1.   Where the Commission, empowered by a Council Regulation, such as Regulations 19/65/EEC, (EEC) No 2821/71, (EEC) No 3976/87, (EEC) No 1534/91 or (EEC) No 479/92, to apply Article 81(3) of the Treaty by regulation, has declared Article 81(1) of the Treaty inapplicable to certain categories of agreements, decisions by associations of undertakings or concerted practices, it may, acting on its own initiative or on a complaint, withdraw the benefit of such an exemption Regulation when it finds that in any particular case an agreement, decision or concerted practice to which the exemption Regulation applies has certain effects which are incompatible with Article 81(3) of the Treaty.

2.   Where, in any particular case, agreements, decisions by associations of undertakings or concerted practices to which a Commission Regulation referred to in paragraph 1 applies have effects which are incompatible with Article 81(3) of the Treaty in the territory of a Member State, or in a part thereof, which has all the characteristics of a distinct geographic market, the competition authority of that Member State may withdraw the benefit of the Regulation in question in respect of that territory.

Chapter X GENERAL PROVISIONS

Article 30 Publication of decisions

1. The Commission shall publish the decisions, which it takes pursuant to Articles 7 to 10, 23 and 24.

2. The publication shall state the names of the parties and the main content of the decision, including any penalties imposed. It shall have regard to the legitimate interest of undertakings in the protection of their business secrets.

Article 31 Review by the Court of Justice

The Court of Justice shall have unlimited jurisdiction to review decisions whereby the Commission has fixed a fine or periodic penalty payment. It may cancel, reduce or increase the fine or periodic penalty payment imposed.

Article 32 (*deleted* by Regulation 1419/2006, OJ L269, 28.09.2006, p. 1)

Article 33 Implementing provisions

1. The Commission shall be authorised to take such measures as may be appropriate in order to apply this Regulation. The measures may concern, inter alia:
   (a) the form, content and other details of complaints lodged pursuant to Article 7 and the procedure for rejecting complaints;
   (b) the practical arrangements for the exchange of information and consultations provided for in Article 11;
   (c) the practical arrangements for the hearings provided for in Article 27.

2. Before the adoption of any measures pursuant to paragraph 1, the Commission shall publish a draft thereof and invite all interested parties to submit their comments within the time-limit it lays down, which may not be less than one month. Before publishing a draft measure and before adopting it, the Commission shall consult the Advisory Committee on Restrictive Practices and Dominant Positions.

Chapter XI TRANSITIONAL, AMENDING AND FINAL PROVISIONS

Article 34 Transitional provisions

1. Applications made to the Commission under Article 2 of Regulation No 17, notifications made under Articles 4 and 5 of that Regulation and the corresponding applications and notifications made under Regulations (EEC) No 1017/68, (EEC) No 4056/86 and (EEC) No 3975/87 shall lapse as from the date of application of this Regulation.

2. Procedural steps taken under Regulation No 17 and Regulations (EEC) No 1017/68, (EEC) No 4056/86 and (EEC) No 3975/87 shall continue to have effect for the purposes of applying this Regulation.

Article 35 Designation of competition authorities of Member States

1. The Member States shall designate the competition authority or authorities responsible for the application of Articles 81 and 82 of the Treaty in such a way that the provisions of this regulation are effectively complied with. The measures necessary to empower those authorities to apply those Articles shall be taken before 1 May 2004. The authorities designated may include courts.

2. When enforcement of Community competition law is entrusted to national administrative and judicial authorities, the Member States may allocate different powers and functions to those different national authorities, whether administrative or judicial.

3. The effects of Article 11(6) apply to the authorities designated by the Member States including courts that exercise functions regarding the preparation and the adoption of the types of decisions foreseen in Article 5. The effects of Article 11(6) do not extend to courts insofar as they act as review courts in respect of the types of decisions foreseen in Article 5.

4. Notwithstanding paragraph 3, in the Member States where, for the adoption of certain types of decisions foreseen in Article 5, an authority brings an action before a judicial authority that is separate and different from the prosecuting authority and provided that the terms of this paragraph are complied with, the effects of Article 11(6) shall be limited to the authority prosecuting the case which shall withdraw its claim before the judicial authority when the Commission opens proceedings and this withdrawal shall bring the national proceedings effectively to an end.

Article 36 Amendment of Regulation (EEC) No 1017/68
Regulation (EEC) No 1017/68 is amended as follows:

1. Article 2 is repealed;

2. in Article 3(1), the words "The prohibition laid down in Article 2" are replaced by the words "The prohibition in Article 81(1) of the Treaty";

3. Article 4 is amended as follows:
   (a) In paragraph 1, the words "The agreements, decisions and concerted practices referred to in Article 2" are replaced by the words "Agreements, decisions and concerted practices pursuant to Article 81(1) of the Treaty";
   (b) Paragraph 2 is replaced by the following:
   "2. If the implementation of any agreement, decision or concerted practice covered by paragraph 1 has, in a given case, effects which are incompatible with the requirements of Article 81(3) of the Treaty, undertakings or associations of undertakings may be required to make such effects cease."

4. Articles 5 to 29 are repealed with the exception of Article 13(3) which continues to apply to decisions adopted pursuant to Article 5 of Regulation (EEC) No 1017/68 prior to the date of application of this Regulation until the date of expiration of those decisions;

5. in Article 30, paragraphs 2, 3 and 4 are deleted.

Article 37 Amendment of Regulation (EEC) No 2988/74
In Regulation (EEC) No 2988/74, the following Article is inserted:

"Article 7a

Exclusion

This Regulation shall not apply to measures taken under Council Regulation (EC) No 1/2003 of 16 December 2002 on the implementation of the rules on competition laid down in Articles 81 and 82 of the Treaty(16)."

Article 38 Amendment of Regulation (EEC) No 4056/86
Regulation (EEC) No 4056/86 is amended as follows:

1. Article 7 is amended as follows:
   (a) Paragraph 1 is replaced by the following:
   "1. Breach of an obligation
   Where the persons concerned are in breach of an obligation which, pursuant to Article 5, attaches to the exemption provided for in Article 3, the Commission may, in order to put an end to such breach and under the conditions laid down in

Council Regulation (EC) No 1/2003 of 16 December 2002 on the implementation of the rules on competition laid down in Articles 81 and 82 of the Treaty(17) adopt a decision that either prohibits them from carrying out or requires them to perform certain specific acts, or withdraws the benefit of the block exemption which they enjoyed."

   (b) Paragraph 2 is amended as follows:

      (i) In point (a), the words "under the conditions laid down in Section II" are replaced by the words "under the conditions laid down in Regulation (EC) No 1/2003";

      (ii) The second sentence of the second subparagraph of point (c)(i) is replaced by the following:

"At the same time it shall decide, in accordance with Article 9 of Regulation (EC) No 1/2003, whether to accept commitments offered by the undertakings concerned with a view, inter alia, to obtaining access to the market for non-conference lines."

2.   Article 8 is amended as follows:

   (a) Paragraph 1 is deleted.

   (b) In paragraph 2 the words "pursuant to Article 10" are replaced by the words "pursuant to Regulation (EC) No 1/2003".

   (c) Paragraph 3 is deleted;

3.   Article 9 is amended as follows:

   (a) In paragraph 1, the words "Advisory Committee referred to in Article 15" are replaced by the words "Advisory Committee referred to in Article 14 of Regulation (EC) No 1/2003";

   (b) In paragraph 2, the words "Advisory Committee as referred to in Article 15" are replaced by the words "Advisory Committee referred to in Article 14 of Regulation (EC) No 1/2003";

4.   Articles 10 to 25 are repealed with the exception of Article 13(3) which continues to apply to decisions adopted pursuant to Article 81(3) of the Treaty prior to the date of application of this Regulation until the date of expiration of those decisions;

5.   in Article 26, the words "the form, content and other details of complaints pursuant to Article 10, applications pursuant to Article 12 and the hearings provided for in Article 23(1) and (2)" are deleted.

Article 39 Amendment of Regulation (EEC) No 3975/87
Articles 3 to 19 of Regulation (EEC) No 3975/87 are repealed with the exception of Article 6(3) which continues to apply to decisions adopted pursuant to Article 81(3) of the Treaty prior to the date of application of this Regulation until the date of expiration of those decisions.

Article 40 Amendment of Regulations No 19/65/EEC, (EEC) No 2821/71 and (EEC) No 1534/91
Article 7 of Regulation No 19/65/EEC, Article 7 of Regulation (EEC) No 2821/71 and Article 7 of Regulation (EEC) No 1534/91 are repealed.

Article 41 Amendment of Regulation (EEC) No 3976/87
Regulation (EEC) No 3976/87 is amended as follows:
1.   Article 6 is replaced by the following:

   "Article 6

   The Commission shall consult the Advisory Committee referred to in Article 14 of Council Regulation (EC) No 1/2003 of 16 December 2002 on the implementation of the rules on competition laid down in Articles 81 and 82 of the Treaty(18) before publishing a draft Regulation and before adopting a Regulation."

2.   Article 7 is repealed.

Article 42   Amendment of Regulation (EEC) No 479/92
Regulation (EEC) No 479/92 is amended as follows:
1.   Article 5 is replaced by the following:

"Article 5

Before publishing the draft Regulation and before adopting the Regulation, the Commission shall consult the Advisory Committee referred to in Article 14 of Council Regulation (EC) No 1/2003 of 16 December 2002 on the implementation of the rules on competition laid down in Articles 81 and 82 of the Treaty(19)."

2.   Article 6 is repealed.

Article 43   Repeal of Regulations No 17 and No 141
1.   Regulation No 17 is repealed with the exception of Article 8(3) which continues to apply to decisions adopted pursuant to Article 81(3) of the Treaty prior to the date of application of this Regulation until the date of expiration of those decisions.

2.   Regulation No 141 is repealed.

3.   References to the repealed Regulations shall be construed as references to this Regulation.

Article 44   Report on the application of the present Regulation
Five years from the date of application of this Regulation, the Commission shall report to the European Parliament and the Council on the functioning of this Regulation, in particular on the application of Article 11(6) and Article 17.

On the basis of this report, the Commission shall assess whether it is appropriate to propose to the Council a revision of this Regulation.

Article 45   Entry into force
This Regulation shall enter into force on the 20th day following that of its publication in the *Official Journal of the European Communities*.

It shall apply from 1 May 2004.

This Regulation shall be binding in its entirety and directly applicable in all Member States.

(date of signing and signatory omitted)

(1)   OJ C 365 E, 19.12.2000, p. 284.
(2)   OJ C 72 E, 21.3.2002, p. 305.
(3)   OJ C 155, 29.5.2001, p. 73.
(4)   The title of Regulation No 17 has been adjusted to take account of the renumbering of the Articles of the EC Treaty, in accordance with Article 12 of the Treaty of Amsterdam; the original reference was to Articles 85 and 86 of the Treaty.
(5)   OJ 13, 21.2.1962, p. 204/62. Regulation as last amended by Regulation (EC) No 1216/1999 (OJ L 148, 15.6.1999, p. 5).
(6)   Council Regulation No 19/65/EEC of 2 March 1965 on the application of Article 81(3) (The titles of the Regulations have been adjusted to take account of the renumbering of the Articles of the EC Treaty, in accordance with Article 12 of the Treaty of Amsterdam; the original reference was to Article 85(3) of the Treaty) of the Treaty to certain categories of agreements and concerted practices (OJ 36, 6.3.1965, p. 533). Regulation as last amended by Regulation (EC) No 1215/1999 (OJ L 148, 15.6.1999, p. 1).

(7)   Council Regulation (EEC) No 2821/71 of 20 December 1971 on the application of Article 81(3) (The titles of the Regulations have been adjusted to take account of the renumbering of the Articles of the EC Treaty, in accordance with Article 12 of the Treaty of Amsterdam; the original reference was to Article 85(3) of the Treaty) of the Treaty to categories of agreements, decisions and concerted practices (OJ L 285, 29.12.1971, p. 46). Regulation as last amended by the Act of Accession of 1994.

(8)   Council Regulation (EEC) No 3976/87 of 14 December 1987 on the application of Article 81(3) (The titles of the Regulations have been adjusted to take account of the renumbering of the Articles of the EC Treaty, in accordance with Article 12 of the Treaty of Amsterdam; the original reference was to Article 85(3) of the Treaty) of the Treaty to certain categories of agreements and concerted practices in the air transport sector (OJ L 374, 31.12.1987, p. 9). Regulation as last amended by the Act of Accession of 1994.

(9)   Council Regulation (EEC) No 1534/91 of 31 May 1991 on the application of Article 81(3) (The titles of the Regulations have been adjusted to take account of the renumbering of the Articles of the EC Treaty, in accordance with Article 12 of the Treaty of Amsterdam; the original reference was to Article 85(3) of the Treaty) of the Treaty to certain categories of agreements, decisions and concerted practices in the insurance sector (OJ L 143, 7.6.1991, p. 1).

(10)   Council Regulation (EEC) No 479/92 of 25 February 1992 on the application of Article 81(3) (The titles of the Regulations have been adjusted to take account of the renumbering of the Articles of the EC Treaty, in accordance with Article 12 of the Treaty of Amsterdam; the original reference was to Article 85(3) of the Treaty) of the Treaty to certain categories of agreements, decisions and concerted practices between liner shipping companies (Consortia) (OJ L 55, 29.2.1992, p. 3). Regulation amended by the Act of Accession of 1994.

(11)   Council Regulation (EEC) No 2988/74 of 26 November 1974 concerning limitation periods in proceedings and the enforcement of sanctions under the rules of the European Economic Community relating to transport and competition (OJ L 319, 29.11.1974, p. 1).

(12)   OJ 124, 28.11.1962, p. 2751/62; Regulation as last amended by Regulation No 1002/67/EEC (OJ 306, 16.12.1967, p. 1).

(13)   Council Regulation (EEC) No 1017/68 of 19 July 1968 applying rules of competition to transport by rail, road and inland waterway (OJ L 175, 23.7.1968, p. 1). Regulation as last amended by the Act of Accession of 1994.

(14)   Council Regulation (EEC) No 4056/86 of 22 December 1986 laying down detailed rules for the application of Articles 81 and 82 (The title of the Regulation has been adjusted to take account of the renumbering of the Articles of the EC Treaty, in accordance with Article 12 of the Treaty of Amsterdam; the original reference was to Articles 85 and 86 of the Treaty) of the Treaty to maritime transport (OJ L 378, 31.12.1986, p. 4). Regulation as last amended by the Act of Accession of 1994.

(15)   Council Regulation (EEC) No 3975/87 of 14 December 1987 laying down the procedure for the application of the rules on competition to undertakings in the air transport sector (OJ L 374, 31.12.1987, p. 1). Regulation as last amended by Regulation (EEC) No 2410/92 (OJ L 240, 24.8.1992, p. 18).

(16)   OJ L 1, 4.1.2003, p. 1.

(17)   OJ L 1, 4.1.2003, p. 1.

(18)   OJ L 1, 4.1.2003, p. 1.

(19)   OJ L 1, 4.1.2003, p. 1.

COUNCIL REGULATION (EC) NO 139/2004 OF 20 JANUARY 2004

on the control of concentrations between undertakings

(the EC Merger Regulation)

OJ L 24, 29.1.2004, p. 1[1]

....

(*footnotes omitted*)

THE COUNCIL OF THE EUROPEAN UNION,

Having regard to the Treaty establishing the European Community, and in particular Articles 83 and 308 thereof,

....

[1]   EDITOR'S NOTE: Regulation 139/2004 repeals and replaces the previous Merger Regulation 4064/89 with effect from 1 May 2004. See the Correlation Table in the Annex below to convert article numbers from the previous Regulation. As of 1 June 2010 this Regulation has not been amended following the adoption of the Treaty of Lisbon. It includes references to the old Treaty article numbers. Reference should be made to the Tables of Equivalences accompanying the consolidated Treaties in Part II of this edition for the conversion of old Treaty article numbers to new ones.

Having regard to the proposal from the Commission,

Having regard to the opinion of the European Parliament,

Having regard to the opinion of the European Economic and Social Committee,

Whereas:

(1)   Council Regulation (EEC) No 4064/89 of 21 December 1989 on the control of concentrations between undertakings has been substantially amended. Since further amendments are to be made, it should be recast in the interest of clarity.

(2)   For the achievement of the aims of the Treaty, Article 3(1)(g) gives the Community the objective of instituting a system ensuring that competition in the internal market is not distorted. Article 4(1) of the Treaty provides that the activities of the Member States and the Community are to be conducted in accordance with the principle of an open market economy with free competition. These principles are essential for the further development of the internal market.

(3)   The completion of the internal market and of economic and monetary union, the enlargement of the European Union and the lowering of international barriers to trade and investment will continue to result in major corporate reorganisations, particularly in the form of concentrations.

(4)   Such reorganisations are to be welcomed to the extent that they are in line with the requirements of dynamic competition and capable of increasing the competitiveness of European industry, improving the conditions of growth and raising the standard of living in the Community.

(5)   However, it should be ensured that the process of reorganisation does not result in lasting damage to competition; Community law must therefore include provisions governing those concentrations which may significantly impede effective competition in the common market or in a substantial part of it.

(6)   A specific legal instrument is therefore necessary to permit effective control of all concentrations in terms of their effect on the structure of competition in the Community and to be the only instrument applicable to such concentrations. Regulation (EEC) No 4064/89 has allowed a Community policy to develop in this field. In the light of experience, however, that Regulation should now be recast into legislation designed to meet the challenges of a more integrated market and the future enlargement of the European Union. In accordance with the principles of subsidiarity and of proportionality as set out in Article 5 of the Treaty, this Regulation does not go beyond what is necessary in order to achieve the objective of ensuring that competition in the common market is not distorted, in accordance with the principle of an open market economy with free competition.

(7)   Articles 81 and 82, while applicable, according to the case-law of the Court of Justice, to certain concentrations, are not sufficient to control all operations which may prove to be incompatible with the system of undistorted competition envisaged in the Treaty. This Regulation should therefore be based not only on Article 83 but, principally, on Article 308 of the Treaty, under which the Community may give itself the additional powers of action necessary for the attainment of its objectives, and also powers of action with regard to concentrations on the markets for agricultural products listed in Annex I to the Treaty.

(8)   The provisions to be adopted in this Regulation should apply to significant structural changes, the impact of which on the market goes beyond the national borders of any one

Member State. Such concentrations should, as a general rule, be reviewed exclusively at Community level, in application of a "one-stop shop" system and in compliance with the principle of subsidiarity. Concentrations not covered by this Regulation come, in principle, within the jurisdiction of the Member States.

(9)   The scope of application of this Regulation should be defined according to the geographical area of activity of the undertakings concerned and be limited by quantitative thresholds in order to cover those concentrations which have a Community dimension. The Commission should report to the Council on the implementation of the applicable thresholds and criteria so that the Council, acting in accordance with Article 202 of the Treaty, is in a position to review them regularly, as well as the rules regarding pre-notification referral, in the light of the experience gained; this requires statistical data to be provided by the Member States to the Commission to enable it to prepare such reports and possible proposals for amendments. The Commission's reports and proposals should be based on relevant information regularly provided by the Member States.

(10) A concentration with a Community dimension should be deemed to exist where the aggregate turnover of the undertakings concerned exceeds given thresholds; that is the case irrespective of whether or not the undertakings effecting the concentration have their seat or their principal fields of activity in the Community, provided they have substantial operations there.

(11) The rules governing the referral of concentrations from the Commission to Member States and from Member States to the Commission should operate as an effective corrective mechanism in the light of the principle of subsidiarity; these rules protect the competition interests of the Member States in an adequate manner and take due account of legal certainty and the "one-stop shop" principle.

(12) Concentrations may qualify for examination under a number of national merger control systems if they fall below the turnover thresholds referred to in this Regulation. Multiple notification of the same transaction increases legal uncertainty, effort and cost for undertakings and may lead to conflicting assessments. The system whereby concentrations may be referred to the Commission by the Member States concerned should therefore be further developed.

(13) The Commission should act in close and constant liaison with the competent authorities of the Member States from which it obtains comments and information.

(14) The Commission and the competent authorities of the Member States should together form a network of public authorities, applying their respective competences in close cooperation, using efficient arrangements for information-sharing and consultation, with a view to ensuring that a case is dealt with by the most appropriate authority, in the light of the principle of subsidiarity and with a view to ensuring that multiple notifications of a given concentration are avoided to the greatest extent possible. Referrals of concentrations from the Commission to Member States and from Member States to the Commission should be made in an efficient manner avoiding, to the greatest extent possible, situations where a concentration is subject to a referral both before and after its notification.

(15) The Commission should be able to refer to a Member State notified concentrations with a Community dimension which threaten significantly to affect competition in a market within that Member State presenting all the characteristics of a distinct market. Where the concentration affects competition on such a market, which does not constitute a substantial part of the common market, the Commission should be obliged, upon request,

to refer the whole or part of the case to the Member State concerned. A Member State should be able to refer to the Commission a concentration which does not have a Community dimension but which affects trade between Member States and threatens to significantly affect competition within its territory. Other Member States which are also competent to review the concentration should be able to join the request. In such a situation, in order to ensure the efficiency and predictability of the system, national time limits should be suspended until a decision has been reached as to the referral of the case. The Commission should have the power to examine and deal with a concentration on behalf of a requesting Member State or requesting Member States.

(16) The undertakings concerned should be granted the possibility of requesting referrals to or from the Commission before a concentration is notified so as to further improve the efficiency of the system for the control of concentrations within the Community. In such situations, the Commission and national competition authorities should decide within short, clearly defined time limits whether a referral to or from the Commission ought to be made, thereby ensuring the efficiency of the system. Upon request by the undertakings concerned, the Commission should be able to refer to a Member State a concentration with a Community dimension which may significantly affect competition in a market within that Member State presenting all the characteristics of a distinct market; the undertakings concerned should not, however, be required to demonstrate that the effects of the concentration would be detrimental to competition. A concentration should not be referred from the Commission to a Member State which has expressed its disagreement to such a referral. Before notification to national authorities, the undertakings concerned should also be able to request that a concentration without a Community dimension which is capable of being reviewed under the national competition laws of at least three Member States be referred to the Commission. Such requests for pre-notification referrals to the Commission would be particularly pertinent in situations where the concentration would affect competition beyond the territory of one Member State. Where a concentration capable of being reviewed under the competition laws of three or more Member States is referred to the Commission prior to any national notification, and no Member State competent to review the case expresses its disagreement, the Commission should acquire exclusive competence to review the concentration and such a concentration should be deemed to have a Community dimension. Such pre-notification referrals from Member States to the Commission should not, however, be made where at least one Member State competent to review the case has expressed its disagreement with such a referral.

(17) The Commission should be given exclusive competence to apply this Regulation, subject to review by the Court of Justice.

(18) The Member States should not be permitted to apply their national legislation on competition to concentrations with a Community dimension, unless this Regulation makes provision therefor. The relevant powers of national authorities should be limited to cases where, failing intervention by the Commission, effective competition is likely to be significantly impeded within the territory of a Member State and where the competition interests of that Member State cannot be sufficiently protected otherwise by this Regulation. The Member States concerned must act promptly in such cases; this Regulation cannot, because of the diversity of national law, fix a single time limit for the adoption of final decisions under national law.

(19) Furthermore, the exclusive application of this Regulation to concentrations with a Community dimension is without prejudice to Article 296 of the Treaty, and does not prevent the Member States from taking appropriate measures to protect legitimate

interests other than those pursued by this Regulation, provided that such measures are compatible with the general principles and other provisions of Community law.

(20) It is expedient to define the concept of concentration in such a manner as to cover operations bringing about a lasting change in the control of the undertakings concerned and therefore in the structure of the market. It is therefore appropriate to include, within the scope of this Regulation, all joint ventures performing on a lasting basis all the functions of an autonomous economic entity. It is moreover appropriate to treat as a single concentration transactions that are closely connected in that they are linked by condition or take the form of a series of transactions in securities taking place within a reasonably short period of time.

(21) This Regulation should also apply where the undertakings concerned accept restrictions directly related to, and necessary for, the implementation of the concentration. Commission decisions declaring concentrations compatible with the common market in application of this Regulation should automatically cover such restrictions, without the Commission having to assess such restrictions in individual cases. At the request of the undertakings concerned, however, the Commission should, in cases presenting novel or unresolved questions giving rise to genuine uncertainty, expressly assess whether or not any restriction is directly related to, and necessary for, the implementation of the concentration. A case presents a novel or unresolved question giving rise to genuine uncertainty if the question is not covered by the relevant Commission notice in force or a published Commission decision.

(22) The arrangements to be introduced for the control of concentrations should, without prejudice to Article 86(2) of the Treaty, respect the principle of non-discrimination between the public and the private sectors. In the public sector, calculation of the turnover of an undertaking concerned in a concentration needs, therefore, to take account of undertakings making up an economic unit with an independent power of decision, irrespective of the way in which their capital is held or of the rules of administrative supervision applicable to them.

(23) It is necessary to establish whether or not concentrations with a Community dimension are compatible with the common market in terms of the need to maintain and develop effective competition in the common market. In so doing, the Commission must place its appraisal within the general framework of the achievement of the fundamental objectives referred to in Article 2 of the Treaty establishing the European Community and Article 2 of the Treaty on European Union.

(24) In order to ensure a system of undistorted competition in the common market, in furtherance of a policy conducted in accordance with the principle of an open market economy with free competition, this Regulation must permit effective control of all concentrations from the point of view of their effect on competition in the Community. Accordingly, Regulation (EEC) No 4064/89 established the principle that a concentration with a Community dimension which creates or strengthens a dominant position as a result of which effective competition in the common market or in a substantial part of it would be significantly impeded should be declared incompatible with the common market.

(25) In view of the consequences that concentrations in oligopolistic market structures may have, it is all the more necessary to maintain effective competition in such markets. Many oligopolistic markets exhibit a healthy degree of competition. However, under certain circumstances, concentrations involving the elimination of important competitive constraints that the merging parties had exerted upon each other, as well as a reduction of

competitive pressure on the remaining competitors, may, even in the absence of a likelihood of coordination between the members of the oligopoly, result in a significant impediment to effective competition. The Community courts have, however, not to date expressly interpreted Regulation (EEC) No 4064/89 as requiring concentrations giving rise to such non-coordinated effects to be declared incompatible with the common market. Therefore, in the interests of legal certainty, it should be made clear that this Regulation permits effective control of all such concentrations by providing that any concentration which would significantly impede effective competition, in the common market or in a substantial part of it, should be declared incompatible with the common market. The notion of "significant impediment to effective competition" in Article 2(2) and (3) should be interpreted as extending, beyond the concept of dominance, only to the anti-competitive effects of a concentration resulting from the non-coordinated behaviour of undertakings which would not have a dominant position on the market concerned.

(26) A significant impediment to effective competition generally results from the creation or strengthening of a dominant position. With a view to preserving the guidance that may be drawn from past judgments of the European courts and Commission decisions pursuant to Regulation (EEC) No 4064/89, while at the same time maintaining consistency with the standards of competitive harm which have been applied by the Commission and the Community courts regarding the compatibility of a concentration with the common market, this Regulation should accordingly establish the principle that a concentration with a Community dimension which would significantly impede effective competition, in the common market or in a substantial part thereof, in particular as a result of the creation or strengthening of a dominant position, is to be declared incompatible with the common market.

(27) In addition, the criteria of Article 81(1) and (3) of the Treaty should be applied to joint ventures performing, on a lasting basis, all the functions of autonomous economic entities, to the extent that their creation has as its consequence an appreciable restriction of competition between undertakings that remain independent.

(28) In order to clarify and explain the Commission's appraisal of concentrations under this Regulation, it is appropriate for the Commission to publish guidance which should provide a sound economic framework for the assessment of concentrations with a view to determining whether or not they may be declared compatible with the common market.

(29) In order to determine the impact of a concentration on competition in the common market, it is appropriate to take account of any substantiated and likely efficiencies put forward by the undertakings concerned. It is possible that the efficiencies brought about by the concentration counteract the effects on competition, and in particular the potential harm to consumers, that it might otherwise have and that, as a consequence, the concentration would not significantly impede effective competition, in the common market or in a substantial part of it, in particular as a result of the creation or strengthening of a dominant position. The Commission should publish guidance on the conditions under which it may take efficiencies into account in the assessment of a concentration.

(30) Where the undertakings concerned modify a notified concentration, in particular by offering commitments with a view to rendering the concentration compatible with the common market, the Commission should be able to declare the concentration, as modified, compatible with the common market. Such commitments should be proportionate to the competition problem and entirely eliminate it. It is also appropriate

to accept commitments before the initiation of proceedings where the competition problem is readily identifiable and can easily be remedied. It should be expressly provided that the Commission may attach to its decision conditions and obligations in order to ensure that the undertakings concerned comply with their commitments in a timely and effective manner so as to render the concentration compatible with the common market. Transparency and effective consultation of Member States as well as of interested third parties should be ensured throughout the procedure.

(31) The Commission should have at its disposal appropriate instruments to ensure the enforcement of commitments and to deal with situations where they are not fulfilled. In cases of failure to fulfil a condition attached to the decision declaring a concentration compatible with the common market, the situation rendering the concentration compatible with the common market does not materialise and the concentration, as implemented, is therefore not authorised by the Commission. As a consequence, if the concentration is implemented, it should be treated in the same way as a non-notified concentration implemented without authorisation. Furthermore, where the Commission has already found that, in the absence of the condition, the concentration would be incompatible with the common market, it should have the power to directly order the dissolution of the concentration, so as to restore the situation prevailing prior to the implementation of the concentration. Where an obligation attached to a decision declaring the concentration compatible with the common market is not fulfilled, the Commission should be able to revoke its decision. Moreover, the Commission should be able to impose appropriate financial sanctions where conditions or obligations are not fulfilled.

(32) Concentrations which, by reason of the limited market share of the undertakings concerned, are not liable to impede effective competition may be presumed to be compatible with the common market. Without prejudice to Articles 81 and 82 of the Treaty, an indication to this effect exists, in particular, where the market share of the undertakings concerned does not exceed 25% either in the common market or in a substantial part of it.

(33) The Commission should have the task of taking all the decisions necessary to establish whether or not concentrations with a Community dimension are compatible with the common market, as well as decisions designed to restore the situation prevailing prior to the implementation of a concentration which has been declared incompatible with the common market.

(34) To ensure effective control, undertakings should be obliged to give prior notification of concentrations with a Community dimension following the conclusion of the agreement, the announcement of the public bid or the acquisition of a controlling interest. Notification should also be possible where the undertakings concerned satisfy the Commission of their intention to enter into an agreement for a proposed concentration and demonstrate to the Commission that their plan for that proposed concentration is sufficiently concrete, for example on the basis of an agreement in principle, a memorandum of understanding, or a letter of intent signed by all undertakings concerned, or, in the case of a public bid, where they have publicly announced an intention to make such a bid, provided that the intended agreement or bid would result in a concentration with a Community dimension. The implementation of concentrations should be suspended until a final decision of the Commission has been taken. However, it should be possible to derogate from this suspension at the request of the undertakings concerned, where appropriate. In deciding whether or not to grant a derogation, the Commission should take account of all pertinent factors, such as the nature and gravity of damage to the undertakings concerned or to third parties, and the threat to competition posed by the

concentration. In the interest of legal certainty, the validity of transactions must nevertheless be protected as much as necessary.

(35) A period within which the Commission must initiate proceedings in respect of a notified concentration and a period within which it must take a final decision on the compatibility or incompatibility with the common market of that concentration should be laid down. These periods should be extended whenever the undertakings concerned offer commitments with a view to rendering the concentration compatible with the common market, in order to allow for sufficient time for the analysis and market testing of such commitment offers and for the consultation of Member States as well as interested third parties. A limited extension of the period within which the Commission must take a final decision should also be possible in order to allow sufficient time for the investigation of the case and the verification of the facts and arguments submitted to the Commission.

(36) The Community respects the fundamental rights and observes the principles recognised in particular by the Charter of Fundamental Rights of the European Union. Accordingly, this Regulation should be interpreted and applied with respect to those rights and principles.

(37) The undertakings concerned must be afforded the right to be heard by the Commission when proceedings have been initiated; the members of the management and supervisory bodies and the recognised representatives of the employees of the undertakings concerned, and interested third parties, must also be given the opportunity to be heard.

(38) In order properly to appraise concentrations, the Commission should have the right to request all necessary information and to conduct all necessary inspections throughout the Community. To that end, and with a view to protecting competition effectively, the Commission's powers of investigation need to be expanded. The Commission should, in particular, have the right to interview any persons who may be in possession of useful information and to record the statements made.

(39) In the course of an inspection, officials authorised by the Commission should have the right to ask for any information relevant to the subject matter and purpose of the inspection; they should also have the right to affix seals during inspections, particularly in circumstances where there are reasonable grounds to suspect that a concentration has been implemented without being notified; that incorrect, incomplete or misleading information has been supplied to the Commission; or that the undertakings or persons concerned have failed to comply with a condition or obligation imposed by decision of the Commission. In any event, seals should only be used in exceptional circumstances, for the period of time strictly necessary for the inspection, normally not for more than 48 hours.

(40) Without prejudice to the case-law of the Court of Justice, it is also useful to set out the scope of the control that the national judicial authority may exercise when it authorises, as provided by national law and as a precautionary measure, assistance from law enforcement authorities in order to overcome possible opposition on the part of the undertaking against an inspection, including the affixing of seals, ordered by Commission decision. It results from the case-law that the national judicial authority may in particular ask of the Commission further information which it needs to carry out its control and in the absence of which it could refuse the authorisation. The case-law also confirms the competence of the national courts to control the application of national rules governing the implementation of coercive measures. The competent authorities of the

Member States should cooperate actively in the exercise of the Commission's investigative powers.

(41) When complying with decisions of the Commission, the undertakings and persons concerned cannot be forced to admit that they have committed infringements, but they are in any event obliged to answer factual questions and to provide documents, even if this information may be used to establish against themselves or against others the existence of such infringements.

(42) For the sake of transparency, all decisions of the Commission which are not of a merely procedural nature should be widely publicised. While ensuring preservation of the rights of defence of the undertakings concerned, in particular the right of access to the file, it is essential that business secrets be protected. The confidentiality of information exchanged in the network and with the competent authorities of third countries should likewise be safeguarded.

(43) Compliance with this Regulation should be enforceable, as appropriate, by means of fines and periodic penalty payments. The Court of Justice should be given unlimited jurisdiction in that regard pursuant to Article 229 of the Treaty.

(44) The conditions in which concentrations, involving undertakings having their seat or their principal fields of activity in the Community, are carried out in third countries should be observed, and provision should be made for the possibility of the Council giving the Commission an appropriate mandate for negotiation with a view to obtaining non-discriminatory treatment for such undertakings.

(45) This Regulation in no way detracts from the collective rights of employees, as recognised in the undertakings concerned, notably with regard to any obligation to inform or consult their recognised representatives under Community and national law.

(46) The Commission should be able to lay down detailed rules concerning the implementation of this Regulation in accordance with the procedures for the exercise of implementing powers conferred on the Commission. For the adoption of such implementing provisions, the Commission should be assisted by an Advisory Committee composed of the representatives of the Member States as specified in Article 23,

HAS ADOPTED THIS REGULATION:

Article 1 Scope

1. Without prejudice to Article 4(5) and Article 22, this Regulation shall apply to all concentrations with a Community dimension as defined in this Article.

2. A concentration has a Community dimension where:
   (a) the combined aggregate worldwide turnover of all the undertakings concerned is more than EUR 5000 million; and
   (b) the aggregate Community-wide turnover of each of at least two of the undertakings concerned is more than EUR 250 million,
   unless each of the undertakings concerned achieves more than two-thirds of its aggregate Community-wide turnover within one and the same Member State.

3. A concentration that does not meet the thresholds laid down in paragraph 2 has a Community dimension where:
   (a) the combined aggregate worldwide turnover of all the undertakings concerned is more than EUR 2500 million;
   (b) in each of at least three Member States, the combined aggregate turnover of all the undertakings concerned is more than EUR 100 million;

(c) in each of at least three Member States included for the purpose of point (b), the aggregate turnover of each of at least two of the undertakings concerned is more than EUR 25 million; and

(d) the aggregate Community-wide turnover of each of at least two of the undertakings concerned is more than EUR 100 million,

unless each of the undertakings concerned achieves more than two-thirds of its aggregate Community-wide turnover within one and the same Member State.

4. On the basis of statistical data that may be regularly provided by the Member States, the Commission shall report to the Council on the operation of the thresholds and criteria set out in paragraphs 2 and 3 by 1 July 2009 and may present proposals pursuant to paragraph 5.

5. Following the report referred to in paragraph 4 and on a proposal from the Commission, the Council, acting by a qualified majority, may revise the thresholds and criteria mentioned in paragraph 3.

Article 2 Appraisal of concentrations

1. Concentrations within the scope of this Regulation shall be appraised in accordance with the objectives of this Regulation and the following provisions with a view to establishing whether or not they are compatible with the common market.

In making this appraisal, the Commission shall take into account:

(a) the need to maintain and develop effective competition within the common market in view of, among other things, the structure of all the markets concerned and the actual or potential competition from undertakings located either within or outwith the Community;

(b) the market position of the undertakings concerned and their economic and financial power, the alternatives available to suppliers and users, their access to supplies or markets, any legal or other barriers to entry, supply and demand trends for the relevant goods and services, the interests of the intermediate and ultimate consumers, and the development of technical and economic progress provided that it is to consumers' advantage and does not form an obstacle to competition.

2. A concentration which would not significantly impede effective competition in the common market or in a substantial part of it, in particular as a result of the creation or strengthening of a dominant position, shall be declared compatible with the common market.

3. A concentration which would significantly impede effective competition, in the common market or in a substantial part of it, in particular as a result of the creation or strengthening of a dominant position, shall be declared incompatible with the common market.

4. To the extent that the creation of a joint venture constituting a concentration pursuant to Article 3 has as its object or effect the coordination of the competitive behaviour of undertakings that remain independent, such coordination shall be appraised in accordance with the criteria of Article 81(1) and (3) of the Treaty, with a view to establishing whether or not the operation is compatible with the common market.

5. In making this appraisal, the Commission shall take into account in particular:
   — whether two or more parent companies retain, to a significant extent, activities in the same market as the joint venture or in a market which is downstream or upstream

from that of the joint venture or in a neighbouring market closely related to this market,

— whether the coordination which is the direct consequence of the creation of the joint venture affords the undertakings concerned the possibility of eliminating competition in respect of a substantial part of the products or services in question.

Article 3 Definition of concentration

1. A concentration shall be deemed to arise where a change of control on a lasting basis results from:

    (a) the merger of two or more previously independent undertakings or parts of undertakings, or

    (b) the acquisition, by one or more persons already controlling at least one undertaking, or by one or more undertakings, whether by purchase of securities or assets, by contract or by any other means, of direct or indirect control of the whole or parts of one or more other undertakings.

2. Control shall be constituted by rights, contracts or any other means which, either separately or in combination and having regard to the considerations of fact or law involved, confer the possibility of exercising decisive influence on an undertaking, in particular by:

    (a) ownership or the right to use all or part of the assets of an undertaking;

    (b) rights or contracts which confer decisive influence on the composition, voting or decisions of the organs of an undertaking.

3. Control is acquired by persons or undertakings which:

    (a) are holders of the rights or entitled to rights under the contracts concerned; or

    (b) while not being holders of such rights or entitled to rights under such contracts, have the power to exercise the rights deriving therefrom.

4. The creation of a joint venture performing on a lasting basis all the functions of an autonomous economic entity shall constitute a concentration within the meaning of paragraph 1(b).

5. A concentration shall not be deemed to arise where:

    (a) credit institutions or other financial institutions or insurance companies, the normal activities of which include transactions and dealing in securities for their own account or for the account of others, hold on a temporary basis securities which they have acquired in an undertaking with a view to reselling them, provided that they do not exercise voting rights in respect of those securities with a view to determining the competitive behaviour of that undertaking or provided that they exercise such voting rights only with a view to preparing the disposal of all or part of that undertaking or of its assets or the disposal of those securities and that any such disposal takes place within one year of the date of acquisition; that period may be extended by the Commission on request where such institutions or companies can show that the disposal was not reasonably possible within the period set;

    (b) control is acquired by an office-holder according to the law of a Member State relating to liquidation, winding up, insolvency, cessation of payments, compositions or analogous proceedings;

    (c) the operations referred to in paragraph 1(b) are carried out by the financial holding companies referred to in Article 5(3) of Fourth Council Directive 78/660/EEC of 25 July 1978 based on Article 54(3)(g) of the Treaty on the annual accounts of certain types of companies provided however that the voting rights in respect of the holding are exercised, in particular in relation to the appointment of members of the management and supervisory bodies of the undertakings in which they have holdings, only to maintain the full value of those investments and not to determine directly or indirectly the competitive conduct of those undertakings.

Article 4 Prior notification of concentrations and pre-notification referral at the request of the notifying parties

1. Concentrations with a Community dimension defined in this Regulation shall be notified to the Commission prior to their implementation and following the conclusion of the agreement, the announcement of the public bid, or the acquisition of a controlling interest.

   Notification may also be made where the undertakings concerned demonstrate to the Commission a good faith intention to conclude an agreement or, in the case of a public bid, where they have publicly announced an intention to make such a bid, provided that the intended agreement or bid would result in a concentration with a Community dimension.

   For the purposes of this Regulation, the term "notified concentration" shall also cover intended concentrations notified pursuant to the second subparagraph. For the purposes of paragraphs 4 and 5 of this Article, the term "concentration" includes intended concentrations within the meaning of the second subparagraph.

2. A concentration which consists of a merger within the meaning of Article 3(1)(a) or in the acquisition of joint control within the meaning of Article 3(1)(b) shall be notified jointly by the parties to the merger or by those acquiring joint control as the case may be. In all other cases, the notification shall be effected by the person or undertaking acquiring control of the whole or parts of one or more undertakings.

3. Where the Commission finds that a notified concentration falls within the scope of this Regulation, it shall publish the fact of the notification, at the same time indicating the names of the undertakings concerned, their country of origin, the nature of the concentration and the economic sectors involved. The Commission shall take account of the legitimate interest of undertakings in the protection of their business secrets.

4. Prior to the notification of a concentration within the meaning of paragraph 1, the persons or undertakings referred to in paragraph 2 may inform the Commission, by means of a reasoned submission, that the concentration may significantly affect competition in a market within a Member State which presents all the characteristics of a distinct market and should therefore be examined, in whole or in part, by that Member State.

   The Commission shall transmit this submission to all Member States without delay. The Member State referred to in the reasoned submission shall, within 15 working days of receiving the submission, express its agreement or disagreement as regards the request to refer the case. Where that Member State takes no such decision within this period, it shall be deemed to have agreed.

   Unless that Member State disagrees, the Commission, where it considers that such a distinct market exists, and that competition in that market may be significantly affected by the concentration, may decide to refer the whole or part of the case to the competent authorities of that Member State with a view to the application of that State's national competition law.

   The decision whether or not to refer the case in accordance with the third subparagraph shall be taken within 25 working days starting from the receipt of the reasoned submission by the Commission. The Commission shall inform the other Member States and the persons or undertakings concerned of its decision. If the Commission does not take a decision within this period, it shall be deemed to have adopted a decision to refer the case in accordance with the submission made by the persons or undertakings concerned.

If the Commission decides, or is deemed to have decided, pursuant to the third and fourth subparagraphs, to refer the whole of the case, no notification shall be made pursuant to paragraph 1 and national competition law shall apply. Article 9(6) to (9) shall apply mutatis mutandis.

5. With regard to a concentration as defined in Article 3 which does not have a Community dimension within the meaning of Article 1 and which is capable of being reviewed under the national competition laws of at least three Member States, the persons or undertakings referred to in paragraph 2 may, before any notification to the competent authorities, inform the Commission by means of a reasoned submission that the concentration should be examined by the Commission.

The Commission shall transmit this submission to all Member States without delay.

Any Member State competent to examine the concentration under its national competition law may, within 15 working days of receiving the reasoned submission, express its disagreement as regards the request to refer the case.

Where at least one such Member State has expressed its disagreement in accordance with the third subparagraph within the period of 15 working days, the case shall not be referred. The Commission shall, without delay, inform all Member States and the persons or undertakings concerned of any such expression of disagreement.

Where no Member State has expressed its disagreement in accordance with the third subparagraph within the period of 15 working days, the concentration shall be deemed to have a Community dimension and shall be notified to the Commission in accordance with paragraphs 1 and 2. In such situations, no Member State shall apply its national competition law to the concentration.

6. The Commission shall report to the Council on the operation of paragraphs 4 and 5 by 1 July 2009. Following this report and on a proposal from the Commission, the Council, acting by a qualified majority, may revise paragraphs 4 and 5.

Article 5 Calculation of turnover

1. Aggregate turnover within the meaning of this Regulation shall comprise the amounts derived by the undertakings concerned in the preceding financial year from the sale of products and the provision of services falling within the undertakings' ordinary activities after deduction of sales rebates and of value added tax and other taxes directly related to turnover. The aggregate turnover of an undertaking concerned shall not include the sale of products or the provision of services between any of the undertakings referred to in paragraph 4.

Turnover, in the Community or in a Member State, shall comprise products sold and services provided to undertakings or consumers, in the Community or in that Member State as the case may be.

2. By way of derogation from paragraph 1, where the concentration consists of the acquisition of parts, whether or not constituted as legal entities, of one or more undertakings, only the turnover relating to the parts which are the subject of the concentration shall be taken into account with regard to the seller or sellers.

However, two or more transactions within the meaning of the first subparagraph which take place within a two-year period between the same persons or undertakings shall be treated as one and the same concentration arising on the date of the last transaction.

3.   In place of turnover the following shall be used:
    (a) for credit institutions and other financial institutions, the sum of the following income items as defined in Council Directive 86/635/EEC, after deduction of value added tax and other taxes directly related to those items, where appropriate:
        (i)   interest income and similar income;
        (ii) income from securities:
            — income from shares and other variable yield securities,
            — income from participating interests,
            — income from shares in affiliated undertakings;
        (iii) commissions receivable;
        (iv) net profit on financial operations;
        (v)   other operating income.
    The turnover of a credit or financial institution in the Community or in a Member State shall comprise the income items, as defined above, which are received by the branch or division of that institution established in the Community or in the Member State in question, as the case may be;
    (b) for insurance undertakings, the value of gross premiums written which shall comprise all amounts received and receivable in respect of insurance contracts issued by or on behalf of the insurance undertakings, including also outgoing reinsurance premiums, and after deduction of taxes and parafiscal contributions or levies charged by reference to the amounts of individual premiums or the total volume of premiums; as regards Article 1(2)(b) and (3)(b), (c) and (d) and the final part of Article 1(2) and (3), gross premiums received from Community residents and from residents of one Member State respectively shall be taken into account.

4.   Without prejudice to paragraph 2, the aggregate turnover of an undertaking concerned within the meaning of this Regulation shall be calculated by adding together the respective turnovers of the following:
    (a) the undertaking concerned;
    (b) those undertakings in which the undertaking concerned, directly or indirectly:
        (i)   owns more than half the capital or business assets, or
        (ii) has the power to exercise more than half the voting rights, or
        (iii) has the power to appoint more than half the members of the supervisory board, the administrative board or bodies legally representing the undertakings, or
        (iv) has the right to manage the undertakings' affairs;
    (c) those undertakings which have in the undertaking concerned the rights or powers listed in (b);
    (d) those undertakings in which an undertaking as referred to in (c) has the rights or powers listed in (b);
    (e) those undertakings in which two or more undertakings as referred to in (a) to (d) jointly have the rights or powers listed in (b).

5.   Where undertakings concerned by the concentration jointly have the rights or powers listed in paragraph 4(b), in calculating the aggregate turnover of the undertakings concerned for the purposes of this Regulation:
    (a) no account shall be taken of the turnover resulting from the sale of products or the provision of services between the joint undertaking and each of the undertakings

concerned or any other undertaking connected with any one of them, as set out in paragraph 4(b) to (e);

(b) account shall be taken of the turnover resulting from the sale of products and the provision of services between the joint undertaking and any third undertakings. This turnover shall be apportioned equally amongst the undertakings concerned.

Article 6 Examination of the notification and initiation of proceedings

1. The Commission shall examine the notification as soon as it is received.

(a) Where it concludes that the concentration notified does not fall within the scope of this Regulation, it shall record that finding by means of a decision.

(b) Where it finds that the concentration notified, although falling within the scope of this Regulation, does not raise serious doubts as to its compatibility with the common market, it shall decide not to oppose it and shall declare that it is compatible with the common market.

A decision declaring a concentration compatible shall be deemed to cover restrictions directly related and necessary to the implementation of the concentration.

(c) Without prejudice to paragraph 2, where the Commission finds that the concentration notified falls within the scope of this Regulation and raises serious doubts as to its compatibility with the common market, it shall decide to initiate proceedings. Without prejudice to Article 9, such proceedings shall be closed by means of a decision as provided for in Article 8(1) to (4), unless the undertakings concerned have demonstrated to the satisfaction of the Commission that they have abandoned the concentration.

2. Where the Commission finds that, following modification by the undertakings concerned, a notified concentration no longer raises serious doubts within the meaning of paragraph 1(c), it shall declare the concentration compatible with the common market pursuant to paragraph 1(b).

The Commission may attach to its decision under paragraph 1(b) conditions and obligations intended to ensure that the undertakings concerned comply with the commitments they have entered into vis-à-vis the Commission with a view to rendering the concentration compatible with the common market.

3. The Commission may revoke the decision it took pursuant to paragraph 1(a) or (b) where:

(a) the decision is based on incorrect information for which one of the undertakings is responsible or where it has been obtained by deceit,

or

(b) the undertakings concerned commit a breach of an obligation attached to the decision.

4. In the cases referred to in paragraph 3, the Commission may take a decision under paragraph 1, without being bound by the time limits referred to in Article 10(1).

5. The Commission shall notify its decision to the undertakings concerned and the competent authorities of the Member States without delay.

Article 7 Suspension of concentrations

1. A concentration with a Community dimension as defined in Article 1, or which is to be examined by the Commission pursuant to Article 4(5), shall not be implemented either before its notification or until it has been declared compatible with the common market pursuant to a decision under Articles 6(1)(b), 8(1) or 8(2), or on the basis of a presumption according to Article 10(6).

2. Paragraph 1 shall not prevent the implementation of a public bid or of a series of transactions in securities including those convertible into other securities admitted to trading on a market such as a stock exchange, by which control within the meaning of Article 3 is acquired from various sellers, provided that:
    (a) the concentration is notified to the Commission pursuant to Article 4 without delay; and
    (b) the acquirer does not exercise the voting rights attached to the securities in question or does so only to maintain the full value of its investments based on a derogation granted by the Commission under paragraph 3.

3. The Commission may, on request, grant a derogation from the obligations imposed in paragraphs 1 or 2. The request to grant a derogation must be reasoned. In deciding on the request, the Commission shall take into account inter alia the effects of the suspension on one or more undertakings concerned by the concentration or on a third party and the threat to competition posed by the concentration. Such a derogation may be made subject to conditions and obligations in order to ensure conditions of effective competition. A derogation may be applied for and granted at any time, be it before notification or after the transaction.

4. The validity of any transaction carried out in contravention of paragraph 1 shall be dependent on a decision pursuant to Article 6(1)(b) or Article 8(1), (2) or (3) or on a presumption pursuant to Article 10(6).

    This Article shall, however, have no effect on the validity of transactions in securities including those convertible into other securities admitted to trading on a market such as a stock exchange, unless the buyer and seller knew or ought to have known that the transaction was carried out in contravention of paragraph 1.

Article 8 Powers of decision of the Commission

1. Where the Commission finds that a notified concentration fulfils the criterion laid down in Article 2(2) and, in the cases referred to in Article 2(4), the criteria laid down in Article 81(3) of the Treaty, it shall issue a decision declaring the concentration compatible with the common market.

    A decision declaring a concentration compatible shall be deemed to cover restrictions directly related and necessary to the implementation of the concentration.

2. Where the Commission finds that, following modification by the undertakings concerned, a notified concentration fulfils the criterion laid down in Article 2(2) and, in the cases referred to in Article 2(4), the criteria laid down in Article 81(3) of the Treaty, it shall issue a decision declaring the concentration compatible with the common market.

    The Commission may attach to its decision conditions and obligations intended to ensure that the undertakings concerned comply with the commitments they have entered into vis-à-vis the Commission with a view to rendering the concentration compatible with the common market.

    A decision declaring a concentration compatible shall be deemed to cover restrictions directly related and necessary to the implementation of the concentration.

3. Where the Commission finds that a concentration fulfils the criterion defined in Article 2(3) or, in the cases referred to in Article 2(4), does not fulfil the criteria laid down in Article 81(3) of the Treaty, it shall issue a decision declaring that the concentration is incompatible with the common market.

4.   Where the Commission finds that a concentration:
  (a) has already been implemented and that concentration has been declared incompatible
       with the common market, or
  (b) has been implemented in contravention of a condition attached to a decision taken
       under paragraph 2, which has found that, in the absence of the condition, the
       concentration would fulfil the criterion laid down in Article 2(3) or, in the cases
       referred to in Article 2(4), would not fulfil the criteria laid down in Article 81(3) of
       the Treaty,

  the Commission may:

  — require the undertakings concerned to dissolve the concentration, in particular
     through the dissolution of the merger or the disposal of all the shares or assets
     acquired, so as to restore the situation prevailing prior to the implementation of the
     concentration; in circumstances where restoration of the situation prevailing before
     the implementation of the concentration is not possible through dissolution of the
     concentration, the Commission may take any other measure appropriate to achieve
     such restoration as far as possible,
  — order any other appropriate measure to ensure that the undertakings concerned
     dissolve the concentration or take other restorative measures as required in its
     decision.

  In cases falling within point (a) of the first subparagraph, the measures referred to in that
  subparagraph may be imposed either in a decision pursuant to paragraph 3 or by separate
  decision.

5.   The Commission may take interim measures appropriate to restore or maintain conditions
      of effective competition where a concentration:
  (a) has been implemented in contravention of Article 7, and a decision as to the
       compatibility of the concentration with the common market has not yet
       been taken;
  (b) has been implemented in contravention of a condition attached to a decision under
       Article 6(1)(b) or paragraph 2 of this Article;
  (c) has already been implemented and is declared incompatible with the common market.

6.   The Commission may revoke the decision it has taken pursuant to paragraphs 1 or 2
      where:
  (a) the declaration of compatibility is based on incorrect information for which one
       of the undertakings is responsible or where it has been obtained by deceit; or
  (b) the undertakings concerned commit a breach of an obligation attached to the
       decision.

7.   The Commission may take a decision pursuant to paragraphs 1 to 3 without being bound
      by the time limits referred to in Article 10(3), in cases where:
  (a) it finds that a concentration has been implemented
       (i)   in contravention of a condition attached to a decision under Article 6(1)(b), or
       (ii) in contravention of a condition attached to a decision taken under paragraph 2
             and in accordance with Article 10(2), which has found that, in the absence of the
             condition, the concentration would raise serious doubts as to its compatibility
             with the common market; or
  (b) a decision has been revoked pursuant to paragraph 6.

8.   The Commission shall notify its decision to the undertakings concerned and the
      competent authorities of the Member States without delay.

Article 9 Referral to the competent authorities of the Member States

1. The Commission may, by means of a decision notified without delay to the undertakings concerned and the competent authorities of the other Member States, refer a notified concentration to the competent authorities of the Member State concerned in the following circumstances.

2. Within 15 working days of the date of receipt of the copy of the notification, a Member State, on its own initiative or upon the invitation of the Commission, may inform the Commission, which shall inform the undertakings concerned, that:

    (a) a concentration threatens to affect significantly competition in a market within that Member State, which presents all the characteristics of a distinct market, or

    (b) a concentration affects competition in a market within that Member State, which presents all the characteristics of a distinct market and which does not constitute a substantial part of the common market.

3. If the Commission considers that, having regard to the market for the products or services in question and the geographical reference market within the meaning of paragraph 7, there is such a distinct market and that such a threat exists, either:

    (a) it shall itself deal with the case in accordance with this Regulation; or

    (b) it shall refer the whole or part of the case to the competent authorities of the Member State concerned with a view to the application of that State's national competition law.

    If, however, the Commission considers that such a distinct market or threat does not exist, it shall adopt a decision to that effect which it shall address to the Member State concerned, and shall itself deal with the case in accordance with this Regulation.

    In cases where a Member State informs the Commission pursuant to paragraph 2(b) that a concentration affects competition in a distinct market within its territory that does not form a substantial part of the common market, the Commission shall refer the whole or part of the case relating to the distinct market concerned, if it considers that such a distinct market is affected.

4. A decision to refer or not to refer pursuant to paragraph 3 shall be taken:

    (a) as a general rule within the period provided for in Article 10(1), second subparagraph, where the Commission, pursuant to Article 6(1)(b), has not initiated proceedings; or

    (b) within 65 working days at most of the notification of the concentration concerned where the Commission has initiated proceedings under Article 6(1)(c), without taking the preparatory steps in order to adopt the necessary measures under Article 8(2), (3) or (4) to maintain or restore effective competition on the market concerned.

5. If within the 65 working days referred to in paragraph 4(b) the Commission, despite a reminder from the Member State concerned, has not taken a decision on referral in accordance with paragraph 3 nor has taken the preparatory steps referred to in paragraph 4(b), it shall be deemed to have taken a decision to refer the case to the Member State concerned in accordance with paragraph 3(b).

6. The competent authority of the Member State concerned shall decide upon the case without undue delay.

    Within 45 working days after the Commission's referral, the competent authority of the Member State concerned shall inform the undertakings concerned of the result of the preliminary competition assessment and what further action, if any, it proposes to take.

The Member State concerned may exceptionally suspend this time limit where necessary information has not been provided to it by the undertakings concerned as provided for by its national competition law.

Where a notification is requested under national law, the period of 45 working days shall begin on the working day following that of the receipt of a complete notification by the competent authority of that Member State.

7. The geographical reference market shall consist of the area in which the undertakings concerned are involved in the supply and demand of products or services, in which the conditions of competition are sufficiently homogeneous and which can be distinguished from neighbouring areas because, in particular, conditions of competition are appreciably different in those areas. This assessment should take account in particular of the nature and characteristics of the products or services concerned, of the existence of entry barriers or of consumer preferences, of appreciable differences of the undertakings' market shares between the area concerned and neighbouring areas or of substantial price differences.

8. In applying the provisions of this Article, the Member State concerned may take only the measures strictly necessary to safeguard or restore effective competition on the market concerned.

9. In accordance with the relevant provisions of the Treaty, any Member State may appeal to the Court of Justice, and in particular request the application of Article 243 of the Treaty, for the purpose of applying its national competition law.

Article 10 Time limits for initiating proceedings and for decisions
1. Without prejudice to Article 6(4), the decisions referred to in Article 6(1) shall be taken within 25 working days at most. That period shall begin on the working day following that of the receipt of a notification or, if the information to be supplied with the notification is incomplete, on the working day following that of the receipt of the complete information.

That period shall be increased to 35 working days where the Commission receives a request from a Member State in accordance with Article 9(2)or where, the undertakings concerned offer commitments pursuant to Article 6(2) with a view to rendering the concentration compatible with the common market.

2. Decisions pursuant to Article 8(1) or (2) concerning notified concentrations shall be taken as soon as it appears that the serious doubts referred to in Article 6(1)(c) have been removed, particularly as a result of modifications made by the undertakings concerned, and at the latest by the time limit laid down in paragraph 3.

3. Without prejudice to Article 8(7), decisions pursuant to Article 8(1) to (3) concerning notified concentrations shall be taken within not more than 90 working days of the date on which the proceedings are initiated. That period shall be increased to 105 working days where the undertakings concerned offer commitments pursuant to Article 8(2), second subparagraph, with a view to rendering the concentration compatible with the common market, unless these commitments have been offered less than 55 working days after the initiation of proceedings.

The periods set by the first subparagraph shall likewise be extended if the notifying parties make a request to that effect not later than 15 working days after the initiation of proceedings pursuant to Article 6(1)(c). The notifying parties may make only one such request. Likewise, at any time following the initiation of proceedings, the periods set by the first subparagraph may be extended by the Commission with the agreement of the notifying parties. The total duration of any extension or extensions effected pursuant to this subparagraph shall not exceed 20 working days.

4. The periods set by paragraphs 1 and 3 shall exceptionally be suspended where, owing to circumstances for which one of the undertakings involved in the concentration is responsible, the Commission has had to request information by decision pursuant to Article 11 or to order an inspection by decision pursuant to Article 13.

    The first subparagraph shall also apply to the period referred to in Article 9(4)(b).

5. Where the Court of Justice gives a judgment which annuls the whole or part of a Commission decision which is subject to a time limit set by this Article, the concentration shall be re-examined by the Commission with a view to adopting a decision pursuant to Article 6(1).

    The concentration shall be re-examined in the light of current market conditions.

    The notifying parties shall submit a new notification or supplement the original notification, without delay, where the original notification becomes incomplete by reason of intervening changes in market conditions or in the information provided. Where there are no such changes, the parties shall certify this fact without delay.

    The periods laid down in paragraph 1 shall start on the working day following that of the receipt of complete information in a new notification, a supplemented notification, or a certification within the meaning of the third subparagraph.

    The second and third subparagraphs shall also apply in the cases referred to in Article 6(4) and Article 8(7).

6. Where the Commission has not taken a decision in accordance with Article 6(1)(b), (c), 8(1), (2) or (3) within the time limits set in paragraphs 1 and 3 respectively, the concentration shall be deemed to have been declared compatible with the common market, without prejudice to Article 9.

Article 11 Requests for information

1. In order to carry out the duties assigned to it by this Regulation, the Commission may, by simple request or by decision, require the persons referred to in Article 3(1)(b), as well as undertakings and associations of undertakings, to provide all necessary information.

2. When sending a simple request for information to a person, an undertaking or an association of undertakings, the Commission shall state the legal basis and the purpose of the request, specify what information is required and fix the time limit within which the information is to be provided, as well as the penalties provided for in Article 14 for supplying incorrect or misleading information.

3. Where the Commission requires a person, an undertaking or an association of undertakings to supply information by decision, it shall state the legal basis and the purpose of the request, specify what information is required and fix the time limit within which it is to be provided. It shall also indicate the penalties provided for in Article 14 and indicate or impose the penalties provided for in Article 15. It shall further indicate the right to have the decision reviewed by the Court of Justice.

4. The owners of the undertakings or their representatives and, in the case of legal persons, companies or firms, or associations having no legal personality, the persons authorised to

represent them by law or by their constitution, shall supply the information requested on behalf of the undertaking concerned. Persons duly authorised to act may supply the information on behalf of their clients. The latter shall remain fully responsible if the information supplied is incomplete, incorrect or misleading.

5. The Commission shall without delay forward a copy of any decision taken pursuant to paragraph 3 to the competent authorities of the Member State in whose territory the residence of the person or the seat of the undertaking or association of undertakings is situated, and to the competent authority of the Member State whose territory is affected. At the specific request of the competent authority of a Member State, the Commission shall also forward to that authority copies of simple requests for information relating to a notified concentration.

6. At the request of the Commission, the governments and competent authorities of the Member States shall provide the Commission with all necessary information to carry out the duties assigned to it by this Regulation.

7. In order to carry out the duties assigned to it by this Regulation, the Commission may interview any natural or legal person who consents to be interviewed for the purpose of collecting information relating to the subject matter of an investigation. At the beginning of the interview, which may be conducted by telephone or other electronic means, the Commission shall state the legal basis and the purpose of the interview.

Where an interview is not conducted on the premises of the Commission or by telephone or other electronic means, the Commission shall inform in advance the competent authority of the Member State in whose territory the interview takes place. If the competent authority of that Member State so requests, officials of that authority may assist the officials and other persons authorised by the Commission to conduct the interview.

Article 12 Inspections by the authorities of the Member States

1. At the request of the Commission, the competent authorities of the Member States shall undertake the inspections which the Commission considers to be necessary under Article 13(1), or which it has ordered by decision pursuant to Article 13(4). The officials of the competent authorities of the Member States who are responsible for conducting these inspections as well as those authorised or appointed by them shall exercise their powers in accordance with their national law.

2. If so requested by the Commission or by the competent authority of the Member State within whose territory the inspection is to be conducted, officials and other accompanying persons authorised by the Commission may assist the officials of the authority concerned.

Article 13 The Commission's powers of inspection

1. In order to carry out the duties assigned to it by this Regulation, the Commission may conduct all necessary inspections of undertakings and associations of undertakings.

2. The officials and other accompanying persons authorised by the Commission to conduct an inspection shall have the power:
    (a) to enter any premises, land and means of transport of undertakings and associations of undertakings;
    (b) to examine the books and other records related to the business, irrespective of the medium on which they are stored;
    (c) to take or obtain in any form copies of or extracts from such books or records;

(d) to seal any business premises and books or records for the period and to the extent necessary for the inspection;

(e) to ask any representative or member of staff of the undertaking or association of undertakings for explanations on facts or documents relating to the subject matter and purpose of the inspection and to record the answers.

3. Officials and other accompanying persons authorised by the Commission to conduct an inspection shall exercise their powers upon production of a written authorisation specifying the subject matter and purpose of the inspection and the penalties provided for in Article 14, in the production of the required books or other records related to the business which is incomplete or where answers to questions asked under paragraph 2 of this Article are incorrect or misleading. In good time before the inspection, the Commission shall give notice of the inspection to the competent authority of the Member State in whose territory the inspection is to be conducted.

4. Undertakings and associations of undertakings are required to submit to inspections ordered by decision of the Commission. The decision shall specify the subject matter and purpose of the inspection, appoint the date on which it is to begin and indicate the penalties provided for in Articles 14 and 15 and the right to have the decision reviewed by the Court of Justice. The Commission shall take such decisions after consulting the competent authority of the Member State in whose territory the inspection is to be conducted.

5. Officials of, and those authorised or appointed by, the competent authority of the Member State in whose territory the inspection is to be conducted shall, at the request of that authority or of the Commission, actively assist the officials and other accompanying persons authorised by the Commission. To this end, they shall enjoy the powers specified in paragraph 2.

6. Where the officials and other accompanying persons authorised by the Commission find that an undertaking opposes an inspection, including the sealing of business premises, books or records, ordered pursuant to this Article, the Member State concerned shall afford them the necessary assistance, requesting where appropriate the assistance of the police or of an equivalent enforcement authority, so as to enable them to conduct their inspection.

7. If the assistance provided for in paragraph 6 requires authorisation from a judicial authority according to national rules, such authorisation shall be applied for. Such authorisation may also be applied for as a precautionary measure.

8. Where authorisation as referred to in paragraph 7 is applied for, the national judicial authority shall ensure that the Commission decision is authentic and that the coercive measures envisaged are neither arbitrary nor excessive having regard to the subject matter of the inspection. In its control of proportionality of the coercive measures, the national judicial authority may ask the Commission, directly or through the competent authority of that Member State, for detailed explanations relating to the subject matter of the inspection. However, the national judicial authority may not call into question the necessity for the inspection nor demand that it be provided with the information in the Commission's file. The lawfulness of the Commission's decision shall be subject to review only by the Court of Justice.

Article 14 Fines

1. The Commission may by decision impose on the persons referred to in Article 3(1)b, undertakings or associations of undertakings, fines not exceeding 1% of the aggregate turnover of the undertaking or association of undertakings concerned within the meaning of Article 5 where, intentionally or negligently:

(a) they supply incorrect or misleading information in a submission, certification, notification or supplement thereto, pursuant to Article 4, Article 10(5) or Article 22(3);

(b) they supply incorrect or misleading information in response to a request made pursuant to Article 11(2);

(c) in response to a request made by decision adopted pursuant to Article 11(3), they supply incorrect, incomplete or misleading information or do not supply information within the required time limit;

(d) they produce the required books or other records related to the business in incomplete form during inspections under Article 13, or refuse to submit to an inspection ordered by decision taken pursuant to Article 13(4);

(e) in response to a question asked in accordance with Article 13(2)(e),
   — they give an incorrect or misleading answer,
   — they fail to rectify within a time limit set by the Commission an incorrect, incomplete or misleading answer given by a member of staff, or
   — they fail or refuse to provide a complete answer on facts relating to the subject matter and purpose of an inspection ordered by a decision adopted pursuant to Article 13(4);

(f) seals affixed by officials or other accompanying persons authorised by the Commission in accordance with Article 13(2)(d) have been broken.

2. The Commission may by decision impose fines not exceeding 10% of the aggregate turnover of the undertaking concerned within the meaning of Article 5 on the persons referred to in Article 3(1)b or the undertakings concerned where, either intentionally or negligently, they:

(a) fail to notify a concentration in accordance with Articles 4 or 22(3) prior to its implementation, unless they are expressly authorised to do so by Article 7(2) or by a decision taken pursuant to Article 7(3);

(b) implement a concentration in breach of Article 7;

(c) implement a concentration declared incompatible with the common market by decision pursuant to Article 8(3) or do not comply with any measure ordered by decision pursuant to Article 8(4) or (5);

(d) fail to comply with a condition or an obligation imposed by decision pursuant to Articles 6(1)(b), Article 7(3) or Article 8(2), second subparagraph.

3. In fixing the amount of the fine, regard shall be had to the nature, gravity and duration of the infringement.

4. Decisions taken pursuant to paragraphs 1, 2 and 3 shall not be of a criminal law nature.

Article 15 Periodic penalty payments

1. The Commission may by decision impose on the persons referred to in Article 3(1)b, undertakings or associations of undertakings, periodic penalty payments not exceeding 5% of the average daily aggregate turnover of the undertaking or association of undertakings concerned within the meaning of Article 5 for each working day of delay, calculated from the date set in the decision, in order to compel them:

(a) to supply complete and correct information which it has requested by decision taken pursuant to Article 11(3);

(b) to submit to an inspection which it has ordered by decision taken pursuant to Article 13(4);

(c) to comply with an obligation imposed by decision pursuant to Article 6(1)(b), Article 7(3) or Article 8(2), second subparagraph; or;

(d) to comply with any measures ordered by decision pursuant to Article 8(4) or (5).

2.   Where the persons referred to in Article 3(1)(b), undertakings or associations of undertakings have satisfied the obligation which the periodic penalty payment was intended to enforce, the Commission may fix the definitive amount of the periodic penalty payments at a figure lower than that which would arise under the original decision.

Article 16 Review by the Court of Justice
The Court of Justice shall have unlimited jurisdiction within the meaning of Article 229 of the Treaty to review decisions whereby the Commission has fixed a fine or periodic penalty payments; it may cancel, reduce or increase the fine or periodic penalty payment imposed.

Article 17 Professional secrecy
1.   Information acquired as a result of the application of this Regulation shall be used only for the purposes of the relevant request, investigation or hearing.

2.   Without prejudice to Article 4(3), Articles 18 and 20, the Commission and the competent authorities of the Member States, their officials and other servants and other persons working under the supervision of these authorities as well as officials and civil servants of other authorities of the Member States shall not disclose information they have acquired through the application of this Regulation of the kind covered by the obligation of professional secrecy.

3.   Paragraphs 1 and 2 shall not prevent publication of general information or of surveys which do not contain information relating to particular undertakings or associations of undertakings.

Article 18 Hearing of the parties and of third persons
1.   Before taking any decision provided for in Article 6(3), Article 7(3), Article 8(2) to (6), and Articles 14 and 15, the Commission shall give the persons, undertakings and associations of undertakings concerned the opportunity, at every stage of the procedure up to the consultation of the Advisory Committee, of making known their views on the objections against them.

2.   By way of derogation from paragraph 1, a decision pursuant to Articles 7(3) and 8(5) may be taken provisionally, without the persons, undertakings or associations of undertakings concerned being given the opportunity to make known their views beforehand, provided that the Commission gives them that opportunity as soon as possible after having taken its decision.

3.   The Commission shall base its decision only on objections on which the parties have been able to submit their observations. The rights of the defence shall be fully respected in the proceedings. Access to the file shall be open at least to the parties directly involved, subject to the legitimate interest of undertakings in the protection of their business secrets.

4.   In so far as the Commission or the competent authorities of the Member States deem it necessary, they may also hear other natural or legal persons. Natural or legal persons showing a sufficient interest and especially members of the administrative or management bodies of the undertakings concerned or the recognised representatives of their employees shall be entitled, upon application, to be heard.

Article 19 Liaison with the authorities of the Member States
1.   The Commission shall transmit to the competent authorities of the Member States copies of notifications within three working days and, as soon as possible, copies of the most important documents lodged with or issued by the Commission pursuant to this Regulation. Such documents shall include commitments offered by the undertakings

concerned vis-à-vis the Commission with a view to rendering the concentration compatible with the common market pursuant to Article 6(2) or Article 8(2), second subparagraph.

2.   The Commission shall carry out the procedures set out in this Regulation in close and constant liaison with the competent authorities of the Member States, which may express their views upon those procedures. For the purposes of Article 9 it shall obtain information from the competent authority of the Member State as referred to in paragraph 2 of that Article and give it the opportunity to make known its views at every stage of the procedure up to the adoption of a decision pursuant to paragraph 3 of that Article; to that end it shall give it access to the file.

3.   An Advisory Committee on concentrations shall be consulted before any decision is taken pursuant to Article 8(1) to (6), Articles 14 or 15 with the exception of provisional decisions taken in accordance with Article 18(2).

4.   The Advisory Committee shall consist of representatives of the competent authorities of the Member States. Each Member State shall appoint one or two representatives; if unable to attend, they may be replaced by other representatives. At least one of the representatives of a Member State shall be competent in matters of restrictive practices and dominant positions.

5.   Consultation shall take place at a joint meeting convened at the invitation of and chaired by the Commission. A summary of the case, together with an indication of the most important documents and a preliminary draft of the decision to be taken for each case considered, shall be sent with the invitation. The meeting shall take place not less than 10 working days after the invitation has been sent. The Commission may in exceptional cases shorten that period as appropriate in order to avoid serious harm to one or more of the undertakings concerned by a concentration.

6.   The Advisory Committee shall deliver an opinion on the Commission's draft decision, if necessary by taking a vote. The Advisory Committee may deliver an opinion even if some members are absent and unrepresented. The opinion shall be delivered in writing and appended to the draft decision. The Commission shall take the utmost account of the opinion delivered by the Committee. It shall inform the Committee of the manner in which its opinion has been taken into account.

7.   The Commission shall communicate the opinion of the Advisory Committee, together with the decision, to the addressees of the decision. It shall make the opinion public together with the decision, having regard to the legitimate interest of undertakings in the protection of their business secrets.

Article 20 Publication of decisions

1.   The Commission shall publish the decisions which it takes pursuant to Article 8(1) to (6), Articles 14 and 15 with the exception of provisional decisions taken in accordance with Article 18(2) together with the opinion of the Advisory Committee in the Official Journal of the European Union.

2.   The publication shall state the names of the parties and the main content of the decision; it shall have regard to the legitimate interest of undertakings in the protection of their business secrets.

Article 21 Application of the Regulation and jurisdiction

1.   This Regulation alone shall apply to concentrations as defined in Article 3, and Council Regulations (EC) No 1/2003, (EEC) No 1017/68, (EEC) No 4056/86 and (EEC) No

3975/87 shall not apply, except in relation to joint ventures that do not have a Community dimension and which have as their object or effect the coordination of the competitive behaviour of undertakings that remain independent.

2.   Subject to review by the Court of Justice, the Commission shall have sole jurisdiction to take the decisions provided for in this Regulation.

3.   No Member State shall apply its national legislation on competition to any concentration that has a Community dimension.

The first subparagraph shall be without prejudice to any Member State's power to carry out any enquiries necessary for the application of Articles 4(4), 9(2) or after referral, pursuant to Article 9(3), first subparagraph, indent (b), or Article 9(5), to take the measures strictly necessary for the application of Article 9(8).

4.   Notwithstanding paragraphs 2 and 3, Member States may take appropriate measures to protect legitimate interests other than those taken into consideration by this Regulation and compatible with the general principles and other provisions of Community law.

Public security, plurality of the media and prudential rules shall be regarded as legitimate interests within the meaning of the first subparagraph.

Any other public interest must be communicated to the Commission by the Member State concerned and shall be recognised by the Commission after an assessment of its compatibility with the general principles and other provisions of Community law before the measures referred to above may be taken. The Commission shall inform the Member State concerned of its decision within 25 working days of that communication.

Article 22 Referral to the Commission

1.   One or more Member States may request the Commission to examine any concentration as defined in Article 3 that does not have a Community dimension within the meaning of Article 1 but affects trade between Member States and threatens to significantly affect competition within the territory of the Member State or States making the request.

Such a request shall be made at most within 15 working days of the date on which the concentration was notified, or if no notification is required, otherwise made known to the Member State concerned.

2.   The Commission shall inform the competent authorities of the Member States and the undertakings concerned of any request received pursuant to paragraph 1 without delay.

Any other Member State shall have the right to join the initial request within a period of 15 working days of being informed by the Commission of the initial request.

All national time limits relating to the concentration shall be suspended until, in accordance with the procedure set out in this Article, it has been decided where the concentration shall be examined. As soon as a Member State has informed the Commission and the undertakings concerned that it does not wish to join the request, the suspension of its national time limits shall end.

3.   The Commission may, at the latest 10 working days after the expiry of the period set in paragraph 2, decide to examine, the concentration where it considers that it affects trade between Member States and threatens to significantly affect competition within the territory of the Member State or States making the request. If the Commission does not take a decision within this period, it shall be deemed to have adopted a decision to examine the concentration in accordance with the request.

The Commission shall inform all Member States and the undertakings concerned of its decision. It may request the submission of a notification pursuant to Article 4.

The Member State or States having made the request shall no longer apply their national legislation on competition to the concentration.

4. Article 2, Article 4(2) to (3), Articles 5, 6, and 8 to 21 shall apply where the Commission examines a concentration pursuant to paragraph 3. Article 7 shall apply to the extent that the concentration has not been implemented on the date on which the Commission informs the undertakings concerned that a request has been made.

Where a notification pursuant to Article 4 is not required, the period set in Article 10(1) within which proceedings may be initiated shall begin on the working day following that on which the Commission informs the undertakings concerned that it has decided to examine the concentration pursuant to paragraph 3.

5. The Commission may inform one or several Member States that it considers a concentration fulfils the criteria in paragraph 1. In such cases, the Commission may invite that Member State or those Member States to make a request pursuant to paragraph 1.

Article 23 Implementing provisions
1. The Commission shall have the power to lay down in accordance with the procedure referred to in paragraph 2:
   (a) implementing provisions concerning the form, content and other details of notifications and submissions pursuant to Article 4;
   (b) implementing provisions concerning time limits pursuant to Article 4(4), (5) Articles 7, 9, 10 and 22;
   (c) the procedure and time limits for the submission and implementation of commitments pursuant to Article 6(2) and Article 8(2);
   (d) implementing provisions concerning hearings pursuant to Article 18.

2. The Commission shall be assisted by an Advisory Committee, composed of representatives of the Member States.
   (a) Before publishing draft implementing provisions and before adopting such provisions, the Commission shall consult the Advisory Committee.
   (b) Consultation shall take place at a meeting convened at the invitation of and chaired by the Commission. A draft of the implementing provisions to be taken shall be sent with the invitation. The meeting shall take place not less than 10 working days after the invitation has been sent.
   (c) The Advisory Committee shall deliver an opinion on the draft implementing provisions, if necessary by taking a vote. The Commission shall take the utmost account of the opinion delivered by the Committee.

Article 24 Relations with third countries
1. The Member States shall inform the Commission of any general difficulties encountered by their undertakings with concentrations as defined in Article 3 in a third country.

2. Initially not more than one year after the entry into force of this Regulation and, thereafter periodically, the Commission shall draw up a report examining the treatment accorded to undertakings having their seat or their principal fields of activity in the Community, in the terms referred to in paragraphs 3 and 4, as regards concentrations in third countries. The Commission shall submit those reports to the Council, together with any recommendations.

3. Whenever it appears to the Commission, either on the basis of the reports referred to in paragraph 2 or on the basis of other information, that a third country does not grant

undertakings having their seat or their principal fields of activity in the Community, treatment comparable to that granted by the Community to undertakings from that country, the Commission may submit proposals to the Council for an appropriate mandate for negotiation with a view to obtaining comparable treatment for undertakings having their seat or their principal fields of activity in the Community.

4.   Measures taken under this Article shall comply with the obligations of the Community or of the Member States, without prejudice to Article 307 of the Treaty, under international agreements, whether bilateral or multilateral.

Article 25 Repeal

1.   Without prejudice to Article 26(2), Regulations (EEC) No 4064/89 and (EC) No 1310/97 shall be repealed with effect from 1 May 2004.

2.   References to the repealed Regulations shall be construed as references to this Regulation and shall be read in accordance with the correlation table in the Annex.

Article 26 Entry into force and transitional provisions

1.   This Regulation shall enter into force on the 20th day following that of its publication in the Official Journal of the European Union.

It shall apply from 1 May 2004.

2.   Regulation (EEC) No 4064/89 shall continue to apply to any concentration which was the subject of an agreement or announcement or where control was acquired within the meaning of Article 4(1) of that Regulation before the date of application of this Regulation, subject, in particular, to the provisions governing applicability set out in Article 25(2) and (3) of Regulation (EEC) No 4064/89 and Article 2 of Regulation (EEC) No 1310/97.

3.   As regards concentrations to which this Regulation applies by virtue of accession, the date of accession shall be substituted for the date of application of this Regulation.

This Regulation shall be binding in its entirety and directly applicable in all Member States.

(*date of signing and signatory omitted*)

ANNEX

CORRELATION TABLE

Regulation (EEC) No 4064/89	This Regulation
Article 1(1), (2) and (3)	Article 1(1), (2) and (3)
Article 1(4)	Article 1(4)
Article 1(5)	Article 1(5)
Article 2(1)	Article 2(1)
—	Article 2(2)
Article 2(2)	Article 2(3)
Article 2(3)	Article 2(4)
Article 2(4)	Article 2(5)
Article 3(1)	Article 3(1)
Article 3(2)	Article 3(4)
Article 3(3)	Article 3(2)
Article 3(4)	Article 3(3)

Regulation (EEC) No 4064/89	This Regulation
—	Article 3(4)
Article 3(5)	Article 3(5)
Article 4(1) first sentence	Article 4(1) first subpara.
Article 4(1) second sentence	—
—	Article 4(1) second and third subpara.
Article 4(2) and (3)	Article 4(2) and (3)
—	Article 4(4) to (6)
Article 5(1) to (3)	Article 5(1) to (3)
Article 5(4) introductory words	Article 5(4) introductory words
Article 5(4) point (a)	Article 5(4) point (a)
Article 5(4) point (b), introductory words	Article 5(4) point (b), introductory words
Article 5(4) point (b), first indent	Article 5(4) point (b)(i)
Article 5(4) point (b), second indent	Article 5(4) point (b)(ii)
Article 5(4) point (b), third indent	Article 5(4) point (b)(iii)
Article 5(4) point (b), fourth indent	Article 5(4) point (b)(iv)
Article 5(4) points (c), (d) and (e)	Article 5(4) points (c), (d) and (e)
Article 5(5)	Article 5(5)
Article 6(1) introductory words	Article 6(1) introductory words
Article 6(1) points (a) and (b)	Article 6(1) points (a) and (b)
Article 6(1) point (c)	Article 6(1) point (c), first sentence
Article 6(2) to (5)	Article 6(2) to (5)
Article 7(1)	Article 7(1)
Article 7(3)	Article 7(2)
Article 7(4)	Article 7(3)
Article 7(5)	Article 7(4)
Article 8(1)	Article 6(1) point (c), second sentence
Article 8(2)	Article 8(1) and (2)
Article 8(3)	Article 8(3)
Article 8(4)	Article 8(4)
—	Article 8(5)
Article 8(5)	Article 8(6)
Article 8(6)	Article 8(7)
—	Article 8(8)
Article 9(1) to (9)	Article 9(1) to (9)
Article 9(10)	—
Article 10(1) and (2)	Article 10(1) and (2)
Article 10(3)	Article 10(3) first subpara., first sentence
—	Article 10(3) first subpara., second sentence
—	Article 10(3) second subpara.
Article 10(4)	Article 10(4) first subpara.
—	Article 10(4) second subpara.
Article 10(5)	Article 10(5) first and fourth subparas.
—	Article 10(5) second, third & fifth subparas.
Article 10(6)	Article 10(6)
Article 11(1)	Article 11(1)
Article 11(2)	—
Article 11(3)	Article 11(2)
Article 11(4)	Article 11(4) first sentence

Regulation (EEC) No 4064/89	This Regulation
—	Article 11(4) second and third sentences
Article 11(5) first sentence	—
Article 11(5) second sentence	Article 11(3)
Article 11(6)	Article 11(5)
—	Article 11(6) and (7)
Article 12	Article 12
Article 13(1) first subpara.	Article 13(1)
Article 13(1) second subpara.	Article 13(2) introductory words
	introductory words
Article 13(1) second subpara. point (a)	Article 13(2) point (b)
Article 13(1) second subpara. point (b)	Article 13(2) point (c)
Article 13(1) second subpara. point (c)	Article 13(2) point (e)
Article 13(1) second subpara. point (d)	Article 13(2) point (a)
—	Article 13(2) point (d)
Article 13(2)	Article 13(3)
Article 13(3)	Article 13(4) first and second sentences
Article 13(4)	Article 13(4) third sentence
Article 13(5)	Article 13(5) first sentence
	Article 13(5) second sentence
—	Article 13(6)
Article 13(6) first sentence	
Article 13(6) second sentence	
—	Article 13(7) and (8)
Article 14(1) introductory words	Article 14(1) introductory words
Article 14(1) point (a)	Article 14(2) point (a)
Article 14(1) point (b)	Article 14(1) point (a)
Article 14(1) point (c)	Article 14(1) points (b) and (c)
Article 14(1) point (d)	Article 14(1) point (d)
—	Article 14(1) points (e) and (f)
Article 14(2) introductory words	Article 14(2) introductory words
Article 14(2) point (a)	Article 14(2) point (d)
Article 14(2) points (b) and (c)	Article 14(2) points (b) and (c)
Article 14(3)	Article 14(3)
Article 14(4)	Article 14(4)
Article 15(1) introductory words	Article 15(1) introductory words
Article 15(1) points (a) and (b)	Article 15(1) points (a) and (b)
Article 15(2) introductory words	Article 15(1) introductory words
Article 15(2) point (a)	Article 15(1) point (c)
Article 15(2) point (b)	Article 15(1) point (d)
Article 15(3)	Article 15(2)
Articles 16 to 20	Articles 16 to 20
Article 21(1)	Article 21(2)
Article 21(2)	Article 21(3)
Article 21(3)	Article 21(4)
Article 22(1)	Article 21(1)
Article 22(3)	—
—	Article 22(1) to (3)
Article 22(4)	Article 22(4)
Article 22(5)	—

Regulation (EEC) No 4064/89	This Regulation
—	Article 22(5)
Article 23	Article 23(1)
—	Article 23(2)
Article 24	Article 24
—	Article 25
Article 25(1)	Article 26(1), first subpara.
—	Article 26(1), second subpara.
Article 25(2)	Article 26(2)
Article 25(3)	Article 26(3)
—	Annex

COMMISSION REGULATION (EC) No 772/2004 OF 27 APRIL 2004

on the application of Article 81(3) of the Treaty to categories of technology transfer agreements
OJ L 123, 24.4.2004, p. 11[1]

(footnotes omitted)

THE COMMISSION OF THE EUROPEAN COMMUNITIES,

Having regard to the Treaty establishing the European Community,

Having regard to Council Regulation No 19/65/EEC of 2 March 1965 on application of Article 85(3) of the Treaty to certain categories of agreements and concerted practices, and in particular Article 1 thereof,

Having published a draft of this Regulation,

After consulting the Advisory Committee on Restrictive Practices and Dominant Positions,

Whereas:

(1)   Regulation No 19/65/EEC empowers the Commission to apply Article 81(3) of the Treaty by Regulation to certain categories of technology transfer agreements and corresponding concerted practices to which only two undertakings are party which fall within Article 81(1).

(2)   Pursuant to Regulation No 19/65/EEC, the Commission has, in particular, adopted Regulation (EC) No 240/96 of 31 January 1996 on the application of Article 85(3) of the Treaty to certain categories of technology transfer agreements.

(3)   On 20 December 2001 the Commission published an evaluation report on the transfer of technology block exemption Regulation (EC) No 240/96 This generated a public debate on the application of Regulation (EC) No 240/96 and on the application in general of Article 81(1) and (3) of the Treaty to technology transfer agreements. The response to the evaluation report from Member States and third parties has been generally in favour of reform of Community competition policy on technology transfer agreements. It is therefore appropriate to repeal Regulation (EC) No 240/96.

[1]   EDITOR'S NOTE: As of 1 June 2010 this Regulation has not been amended following the adoption of the Treaty of Lisbon. It includes references to the old Treaty article numbers. Reference should be made to the Tables of Equivalences accompanying the consolidated Treaties in Part II of this edition for the conversion of old Treaty article numbers to new ones.

(4)   This Regulation should meet the two requirements of ensuring effective competition and providing adequate legal security for undertakings. The pursuit of these objectives should take account of the need to simplify the regulatory framework and its application. It is appropriate to move away from the approach of listing exempted clauses and to place greater emphasis on defining the categories of agreements which are exempted up to a certain level of market power and on specifying the restrictions or clauses which are not to be contained in such agreements. This is consistent with an economics-based approach which assesses the impact of agreements on the relevant market. It is also consistent with such an approach to make a distinction between agreements between competitors and agreements between non-competitors.

(5)   Technology transfer agreements concern the licensing of technology. Such agreements will usually improve economic efficiency and be pro-competitive as they can reduce duplication of research and development, strengthen the incentive for the initial research and development, spur incremental innovation, facilitate diffusion and generate product market competition.

(6)   The likelihood that such efficiency-enhancing and pro-competitive effects will outweigh any anti-competitive effects due to restrictions contained in technology transfer agreements depends on the degree of market power of the undertakings concerned and, therefore, on the extent to which those undertakings face competition from undertakings owning substitute technologies or undertakings producing substitute products.

(7)   This Regulation should only deal with agreements where the licensor permits the licensee to exploit the licensed technology, possibly after further research and development by the licensee, for the production of goods or services. It should not deal with licensing agreements for the purpose of subcontracting research and development. It should also not deal with licensing agreements to set up technology pools, that is to say, agreements for the pooling of technologies with the purpose of licensing the created package of intellectual property rights to third parties.

(8)   For the application of Article 81(3) by regulation, it is not necessary to define those technology transfer agreements that are capable of falling within Article 81(1). In the individual assessment of agreements pursuant to Article 81(1), account has to be taken of several factors, and in particular the structure and the dynamics of the relevant technology and product markets.

(9)   The benefit of the block exemption established by this Regulation should be limited to those agreements which can be assumed with sufficient certainty to satisfy the conditions of Article 81(3). In order to attain the benefits and objectives of technology transfer, the benefit of this Regulation should also apply to provisions contained in technology transfer agreements that do not constitute the primary object of such agreements, but are directly related to the application of the licensed technology.

(10)   For technology transfer agreements between competitors it can be presumed that, where the combined share of the relevant markets accounted for by the parties does not exceed 20% and the agreements do not contain certain severely anti-competitive restraints, they generally lead to an improvement in production or distribution and allow consumers a fair share of the resulting benefits.

(11)   For technology transfer agreements between non-competitors it can be presumed that, where the individual share of the relevant markets accounted for by each of the parties does not exceed 30% and the agreements do not contain certain severely anti-competitive restraints, they generally lead to an improvement in production or distribution and allow consumers a fair share of the resulting benefits.

(12) There can be no presumption that above these market-share thresholds technology transfer agreements do fall within the scope of Article 81(1). For instance, an exclusive licensing agreement between non-competing undertakings does often not fall within the scope of Article 81(1). There can also be no presumption that, above these market-share thresholds, technology transfer agreements falling within the scope of Article 81(1) will not satisfy the conditions for exemption. However, it can also not be presumed that they will usually give rise to objective advantages of such a character and size as to compensate for the disadvantages which they create for competition.

(13) This Regulation should not exempt technology transfer agreements containing restrictions which are not indispensable to the improvement of production or distribution. In particular, technology transfer agreements containing certain severely anti-competitive restraints such as the fixing of prices charged to third parties should be excluded from the benefit of the block exemption established by this Regulation irrespective of the market shares of the undertakings concerned. In the case of such hardcore restrictions the whole agreement should be excluded from the benefit of the block exemption.

(14) In order to protect incentives to innovate and the appropriate application of intellectual property rights, certain restrictions should be excluded from the block exemption. In particular exclusive grant back obligations for severable improvements should be excluded. Where such a restriction is included in a licence agreement only the restriction in question should be excluded from the benefit of the block exemption.

(15) The market-share thresholds, the non-exemption of technology transfer agreements containing severely anti-competitive restraints and the excluded restrictions provided for in this Regulation will normally ensure that the agreements to which the block exemption applies do not enable the participating undertakings to eliminate competition in respect of a substantial part of the products in question.

(16) In particular cases in which the agreements falling under this Regulation nevertheless have effects incompatible with Article 81(3), the Commission should be able to withdraw the benefit of the block exemption. This may occur in particular where the incentives to innovate are reduced or where access to markets is hindered.

(17) Council Regulation (EC) No 1/2003 of 16 December 2002 on the implementation of the rules on competition laid down in Articles 81 and 82 of the Treaty empowers the competent authorities of Member States to withdraw the benefit of the block exemption in respect of technology transfer agreements having effects incompatible with Article 81(3), where such effects are felt in their respective territory, or in a part thereof, and where such territory has the characteristics of a distinct geographic market. Member States must ensure that the exercise of this power of withdrawal does not prejudice the uniform application throughout the common market of the Community competition rules or the full effect of the measures adopted in implementation of those rules.

(18) In order to strengthen supervision of parallel networks of technology transfer agreements which have similar restrictive effects and which cover more than 50% of a given market, the Commission should be able to declare this Regulation inapplicable to technology transfer agreements containing specific restraints relating to the market concerned, thereby restoring the full application of Article 81 to such agreements.

(19) This Regulation should cover only technology transfer agreements between a licensor and a licensee. It should cover such agreements even if conditions are stipulated for more than

one level of trade, by, for instance, requiring the licensee to set up a particular distribution system and specifying the obligations the licensee must or may impose on resellers of the products produced under the licence. However, such conditions and obligations should comply with the competition rules applicable to supply and distribution agreements. Supply and distribution agreements concluded between a licensee and its buyers should not be exempted by this Regulation.

(20)   This Regulation is without prejudice to the application of Article 82 of the Treaty,

HAS ADOPTED THIS REGULATION:

Article 1 Definitions

1.   For the purposes of this Regulation, the following definitions shall apply:

(a) "agreement" means an agreement, a decision of an association of undertakings or a concerted practice;

(b) "technology transfer agreement" means a patent licensing agreement, a know-how licensing agreement, a software copyright licensing agreement or a mixed patent, know-how or software copyright licensing agreement, including any such agreement containing provisions which relate to the sale and purchase of products or which relate to the licensing of other intellectual property rights or the assignment of intellectual property rights, provided that those provisions do not constitute the primary object of the agreement and are directly related to the production of the contract products; assignments of patents, know-how, software copyright or a combination thereof where part of the risk associated with the exploitation of the technology remains with the assignor, in particular where the sum payable in consideration of the assignment is dependent on the turnover obtained by the assignee in respect of products produced with the assigned technology, the quantity of such products produced or the number of operations carried out employing the technology, shall also be deemed to be technology transfer agreements;

(c) "reciprocal agreement" means a technology transfer agreement where two undertakings grant each other, in the same or separate contracts, a patent licence, a know-how licence, a software copyright licence or a mixed patent, know-how or software copyright licence and where these licences concern competing technologies or can be used for the production of competing products;

(d) "non-reciprocal agreement" means a technology transfer agreement where one undertaking grants another undertaking a patent licence, a know-how licence, a software copyright licence or a mixed patent, know-how or software copyright licence, or where two undertakings grant each other such a licence but where these licences do not concern competing technologies and cannot be used for the production of competing products;

(e) "product" means a good or a service, including both intermediary goods and services and final goods and services;

(f) "contract products" means products produced with the licensed technology;

(g) "intellectual property rights" includes industrial property rights, know-how, copyright and neighbouring rights;

(h) "patents" means patents, patent applications, utility models, applications for registration of utility models, designs, topographies of semiconductor products, supplementary protection certificates for medicinal products or other products for which such supplementary protection certificates may be obtained and plant breeder's certificates;

(i) "know-how" means a package of non-patented practical information, resulting from experience and testing, which is:

(i)   secret, that is to say, not generally known or easily accessible,

(ii) substantial, that is to say, significant and useful for the production of the contract products, and

(iii) identified, that is to say, described in a sufficiently comprehensive manner so as to make it possible to verify that it fulfils the criteria of secrecy and substantiality;

(j)   "competing undertakings" means undertakings which compete on the relevant technology market and/or the relevant product market, that is to say:

   (i)   competing undertakings on the relevant technology market, being undertakings which license out competing technologies without infringing each others' intellectual property rights (actual competitors on the technology market); the relevant technology market includes technologies which are regarded by the licensees as interchangeable with or substitutable for the licensed technology, by reason of the technologies' characteristics, their royalties and their intended use,

   (ii) competing undertakings on the relevant product market, being undertakings which, in the absence of the technology transfer agreement, are both active on the relevant product and geographic market(s) on which the contract products are sold without infringing each others' intellectual property rights (actual competitors on the product market) or would, on realistic grounds, undertake the necessary additional investments or other necessary switching costs so that they could timely enter, without infringing each others' intellectual property rights, the(se) relevant product and geographic market(s) in response to a small and permanent increase in relative prices (potential competitors on the product market); the relevant product market comprises products which are regarded by the buyers as interchangeable with or substitutable for the contract products, by reason of the products' characteristics, their prices and their intended use;

(k)   "selective distribution system" means a distribution system where the licensor undertakes to license the production of the contract products only to licensees selected on the basis of specified criteria and where these licensees undertake not to sell the contract products to unauthorised distributors;

(l)   "exclusive territory" means a territory in which only one undertaking is allowed to produce the contract products with the licensed technology, without prejudice to the possibility of allowing within that territory another licensee to produce the contract products only for a particular customer where this second licence was granted in order to create an alternative source of supply for that customer;

(m)   "exclusive customer group" means a group of customers to which only one undertaking is allowed actively to sell the contract products produced with the licensed technology;

(n)   "severable improvement" means an improvement that can be exploited without infringing the licensed technology.

2.   The terms "undertaking", "licensor" and "licensee" shall include their respective connected undertakings.

"Connected undertakings" means:

(a)   undertakings in which a party to the agreement, directly or indirectly:

   (i)   has the power to exercise more than half the voting rights, or

   (ii) has the power to appoint more than half the members of the supervisory board, board of management or bodies legally representing the undertaking, or

   (iii) has the right to manage the undertaking's affairs;

(b)   undertakings which directly or indirectly have, over a party to the agreement, the rights or powers listed in (a);

(c)   undertakings in which an undertaking referred to in (b) has, directly or indirectly, the rights or powers listed in (a);

(d) undertakings in which a party to the agreement together with one or more of the undertakings referred to in (a), (b) or (c), or in which two or more of the latter undertakings, jointly have the rights or powers listed in (a);

(e) undertakings in which the rights or the powers listed in (a) are jointly held by:
    (i) parties to the agreement or their respective connected undertakings referred to in (a) to (d), or
    (ii) one or more of the parties to the agreement or one or more of their connected undertakings referred to in (a) to (d) and one or more third parties.

Article 2 Exemption

Pursuant to Article 81(3) of the Treaty and subject to the provisions of this Regulation, it is hereby declared that Article 81(1) of the Treaty shall not apply to technology transfer agreements entered into between two undertakings permitting the production of contract products.

This exemption shall apply to the extent that such agreements contain restrictions of competition falling within the scope of Article 81(1). The exemption shall apply for as long as the intellectual property right in the licensed technology has not expired, lapsed or been declared invalid or, in the case of know-how, for as long as the know-how remains secret, except in the event where the know-how becomes publicly known as a result of action by the licensee, in which case the exemption shall apply for the duration of the agreement.

Article 3 Market-share thresholds

1. Where the undertakings party to the agreement are competing undertakings, the exemption provided for in Article 2 shall apply on condition that the combined market share of the parties does not exceed 20% on the affected relevant technology and product market.

2. Where the undertakings party to the agreement are not competing undertakings, the exemption provided for in Article 2 shall apply on condition that the market share of each of the parties does not exceed 30% on the affected relevant technology and product market.

3. For the purposes of paragraphs 1 and 2, the market share of a party on the relevant technology market(s) is defined in terms of the presence of the licensed technology on the relevant product market(s). A licensor's market share on the relevant technology market shall be the combined market share on the relevant product market of the contract products produced by the licensor and its licensees.

Article 4 Hardcore restrictions

1. Where the undertakings party to the agreement are competing undertakings, the exemption provided for in Article 2 shall not apply to agreements which, directly or indirectly, in isolation or in combination with other factors under the control of the parties, have as their object:
    (a) the restriction of a party's ability to determine its prices when selling products to third parties;
    (b) the limitation of output, except limitations on the output of contract products imposed on the licensee in a non-reciprocal agreement or imposed on only one of the licensees in a reciprocal agreement;
    (c) the allocation of markets or customers except:
        (i) the obligation on the licensee(s) to produce with the licensed technology only within one or more technical fields of use or one or more product markets,

(ii) the obligation on the licensor and/or the licensee, in a non-reciprocal agreement, not to produce with the licensed technology within one or more technical fields of use or one or more product markets or one or more exclusive territories reserved for the other party,

(iii) the obligation on the licensor not to license the technology to another licensee in a particular territory,

(iv) the restriction, in a non-reciprocal agreement, of active and/or passive sales by the licensee and/or the licensor into the exclusive territory or to the exclusive customer group reserved for the other party,

(v) the restriction, in a non-reciprocal agreement, of active sales by the licensee into the exclusive territory or to the exclusive customer group allocated by the licensor to another licensee provided the latter was not a competing undertaking of the licensor at the time of the conclusion of its own licence,

(vi) the obligation on the licensee to produce the contract products only for its own use provided that the licensee is not restricted in selling the contract products actively and passively as spare parts for its own products,

(vii) the obligation on the licensee, in a non-reciprocal agreement, to produce the contract products only for a particular customer, where the licence was granted in order to create an alternative source of supply for that customer;

(d) the restriction of the licensee's ability to exploit its own technology or the restriction of the ability of any of the parties to the agreement to carry out research and development, unless such latter restriction is indispensable to prevent the disclosure of the licensed know-how to third parties.

2.   Where the undertakings party to the agreement are not competing undertakings, the exemption provided for in Article 2 shall not apply to agreements which, directly or indirectly, in isolation or in combination with other factors under the control of the parties, have as their object:

(a) the restriction of a party's ability to determine its prices when selling products to third parties, without prejudice to the possibility of imposing a maximum sale price or recommending a sale price, provided that it does not amount to a fixed or minimum sale price as a result of pressure from, or incentives offered by, any of the parties;

(b) the restriction of the territory into which, or of the customers to whom, the licensee may passively sell the contract products, except:

(i)   the restriction of passive sales into an exclusive territory or to an exclusive customer group reserved for the licensor,

(ii) the restriction of passive sales into an exclusive territory or to an exclusive customer group allocated by the licensor to another licensee during the first two years that this other licensee is selling the contract products in that territory or to that customer group,

(iii) the obligation to produce the contract products only for its own use provided that the licensee is not restricted in selling the contract products actively and passively as spare parts for its own products,

(iv) the obligation to produce the contract products only for a particular customer, where the licence was granted in order to create an alternative source of supply for that customer,

(v) the restriction of sales to end-users by a licensee operating at the wholesale level of trade,

(vi) the restriction of sales to unauthorised distributors by the members of a selective distribution system;

(c) the restriction of active or passive sales to end-users by a licensee which is a member of a selective distribution system and which operates at the retail level, without prejudice to the possibility of prohibiting a member of the system from operating out of an unauthorised place of establishment.

3.   Where the undertakings party to the agreement are not competing undertakings at the time of the conclusion of the agreement but become competing undertakings afterwards, paragraph 2 and not paragraph 1 shall apply for the full life of the agreement unless the agreement is subsequently amended in any material respect.

Article 5 Excluded restrictions
1.   The exemption provided for in Article 2 shall not apply to any of the following obligations contained in technology transfer agreements:
   (a) any direct or indirect obligation on the licensee to grant an exclusive licence to the licensor or to a third party designated by the licensor in respect of its own severable improvements to or its own new applications of the licensed technology;
   (b) any direct or indirect obligation on the licensee to assign, in whole or in part, to the licensor or to a third party designated by the licensor, rights to its own severable improvements to or its own new applications of the licensed technology;
   (c) any direct or indirect obligation on the licensee not to challenge the validity of intellectual property rights which the licensor holds in the common market, without prejudice to the possibility of providing for termination of the technology transfer agreement in the event that the licensee challenges the validity of one or more of the licensed intellectual property rights.

2.   Where the undertakings party to the agreement are not competing undertakings, the exemption provided for in Article 2 shall not apply to any direct or indirect obligation limiting the licensee's ability to exploit its own technology or limiting the ability of any of the parties to the agreement to carry out research and development, unless such latter restriction is indispensable to prevent the disclosure of the licensed know-how to third parties.

Article 6 Withdrawal in individual cases
1.   The Commission may withdraw the benefit of this Regulation, pursuant to Article 29(1) of Regulation (EC) No 1/2003, where it finds in any particular case that a technology transfer agreement to which the exemption provided for in Article 2 applies nevertheless has effects which are incompatible with Article 81(3) of the Treaty, and in particular where:
   (a) access of third parties' technologies to the market is restricted, for instance by the cumulative effect of parallel networks of similar restrictive agreements prohibiting licensees from using third parties' technologies;
   (b) access of potential licensees to the market is restricted, for instance by the cumulative effect of parallel networks of similar restrictive agreements prohibiting licensors from licensing to other licensees;
   (c) without any objectively valid reason, the parties do not exploit the licensed technology.

2.   Where, in any particular case, a technology transfer agreement to which the exemption provided for in Article 2 applies has effects which are incompatible with Article 81(3) of the Treaty in the territory of a Member State, or in a part thereof, which has all the characteristics of a distinct geographic market, the competition authority of that Member State may withdraw the benefit of this Regulation, pursuant to Article 29(2) of Regulation (EC) No 1/2003, in respect of that territory, under the same circumstances as those set out in paragraph 1 of this Article.

Article 7 Non-application of this Regulation

1. Pursuant to Article 1a of Regulation No 19/65/EEC, the Commission may by regulation declare that, where parallel networks of similar technology transfer agreements cover more than 50% of a relevant market, this Regulation is not to apply to technology transfer agreements containing specific restraints relating to that market.

2. A regulation pursuant to paragraph 1 shall not become applicable earlier than six months following its adoption.

Article 8 Application of the market-share thresholds

1. For the purposes of applying the market-share thresholds provided for in Article 3 the rules set out in this paragraph shall apply.

   The market share shall be calculated on the basis of market sales value data. If market sales value data are not available, estimates based on other reliable market information, including market sales volumes, may be used to establish the market share of the undertaking concerned.

   The market share shall be calculated on the basis of data relating to the preceding calendar year.

   The market share held by the undertakings referred to in point (e) of the second subparagraph of Article 1(2) shall be apportioned equally to each undertaking having the rights or the powers listed in point (a) of the second subparagraph of Article 1(2).

2. If the market share referred to in Article 3(1) or (2) is initially not more than 20% respectively 30% but subsequently rises above those levels, the exemption provided for in Article 2 shall continue to apply for a period of two consecutive calendar years following the year in which the 20% threshold or 30% threshold was first exceeded.

Article 9 Repeal

Regulation (EC) No 240/96 is repealed.

References to the repealed Regulation shall be construed as references to this Regulation.

Article 10 Transitional period

The prohibition laid down in Article 81(1) of the Treaty shall not apply during the period from 1 May 2004 to 31 March 2006 in respect of agreements already in force on 30 April 2004 which do not satisfy the conditions for exemption provided for in this Regulation but which, on 30 April 2004, satisfied the conditions for exemption provided for in Regulation (EC) No 240/96.

Article 11 Period of validity

This Regulation shall enter into force on 1 May 2004.

It shall expire on 30 April 2014.

This Regulation shall be binding in its entirety and directly applicable in all Member States.

(*date of signing and signatory omitted*)

COMMISSION REGULATION (EC) NO 773/2004 OF 7 APRIL 2004

relating to the conduct of proceedings by the Commission pursuant to Articles 81 and 82 of the EC Treaty

OJ L 123, 27.4.2004, p. 18*

....

(*As amended by Commission Regulation (EC) No 1792/2006 of 23 October 2006, OJ L 362, 20.12.2006, p. 1 and Commission Regulation (EC) No 622/2008 of 30 June 2008, OJ L 171, 1.7.2008, p. 3)[1]

(footnotes omitted)

THE COMMISSION OF THE EUROPEAN COMMUNITIES,

Having regard to the Treaty establishing the European Community,

Having regard to the Agreement on the European Economic Area,

Having regard to Council Regulation (EC) No 1/2003 of 16 December 2002 on the implementation of the rules on competition laid down in Articles 81 and 82 of the Treaty, and in particular Article 33 thereof,

After consulting the Advisory Committee on Restrictive Practices and Dominant Positions,

Whereas:

(1)   Regulation (EC) No 1/2003 empowers the Commission to regulate certain aspects of proceedings for the application of Articles 81 and 82 of the Treaty. It is necessary to lay down rules concerning the initiation of proceedings by the Commission as well as the handling of complaints and the hearing of the parties concerned.

(2)   According to Regulation (EC) No 1/2003, national courts are under an obligation to avoid taking decisions which could run counter to decisions envisaged by the Commission in the same case. According to Article 11(6) of that Regulation, national competition authorities are relieved from their competence once the Commission has initiated proceedings for the adoption of a decision under Chapter III of Regulation (EC) No 1/2003. In this context, it is important that courts and competition authorities of the Member States are aware of the initiation of proceedings by the Commission. The Commission should therefore be able to make public its decisions to initiate proceedings.

(3)   Before taking oral statements from natural or legal persons who consent to be interviewed, the Commission should inform those persons of the legal basis of the interview and its voluntary nature. The persons interviewed should also be informed of the purpose of the interview and of any record which may be made.

In order to enhance the accuracy of the statements, the persons interviewed should also be given an opportunity to correct the statements recorded. Where information gathered from oral statements is exchanged pursuant to Article 12 of Regulation (EC) No 1/2003,

....

[1]   EDITOR'S NOTE: As of 1 June 2010 this Regulation has not been amended following the adoption of the Treaty of Lisbon. It includes references to the old Treaty article numbers. Reference should be made to the Tables of Equivalences accompanying the consolidated Treaties in Part II of this edition for the conversion of old Treaty article numbers to new ones.

that information should only be used in evidence to impose sanctions on natural persons where the conditions set out in that Article are fulfilled.

(4) Pursuant to Article 23(1)(d) of Regulation (EC) No 1/2003 fines may be imposed on undertakings and associations of undertakings where they fail to rectify within the time limit fixed by the Commission an incorrect, incomplete or misleading answer given by a member of their staff to questions in the course of inspections. It is therefore necessary to provide the undertaking concerned with a record of any explanations given and to establish a procedure enabling it to add any rectification, amendment or supplement to the explanations given by the member of staff who is not or was not authorised to provide explanations on behalf of the undertaking. The explanations given by a member of staff should remain in the Commission file as recorded during the inspection.

(5) Complaints are an essential source of information for detecting infringements of competition rules. It is important to define clear and efficient procedures for handling complaints lodged with the Commission.

(6) In order to be admissible for the purposes of Article 7 of Regulation (EC) No 1/2003, a complaint must contain certain specified information.

(7) In order to assist complainants in submitting the necessary facts to the Commission, a form should be drawn up. The submission of the information listed in that form should be a condition for a complaint to be treated as a complaint as referred to in Article 7 of Regulation (EC) No 1/2003.

(8) Natural or legal persons having chosen to lodge a complaint should be given the possibility to be associated closely with the proceedings initiated by the Commission with a view to finding an infringement. However, they should not have access to business secrets or other confidential information belonging to other parties involved in the proceedings.

(9) Complainants should be granted the opportunity of expressing their views if the Commission considers that there are insufficient grounds for acting on the complaint. Where the Commission rejects a complaint on the grounds that a competition authority of a Member State is dealing with it or has already done so, it should inform the complainant of the identity of that authority.

(10) In order to respect the rights of defence of undertakings, the Commission should give the parties concerned the right to be heard before it takes a decision.

(11) Provision should also be made for the hearing of persons who have not submitted a complaint as referred to in Article 7 of Regulation (EC) No 1/2003 and who are not parties to whom a statement of objections has been addressed but who can nevertheless show a sufficient interest. Consumer associations that apply to be heard should generally be regarded as having a sufficient interest, where the proceedings concern products or services used by the end-consumer or products or services that constitute a direct input into such products or services. Where it considers this to be useful for the proceedings, the Commission should also be able to invite other persons to express their views in writing and to attend the oral hearing of the parties to whom a statement of objections has been addressed. Where appropriate, it should also be able to invite such persons to express their views at that oral hearing.

(12) To improve the effectiveness of oral hearings, the Hearing Officer should have the power to allow the parties concerned, complainants, other persons invited to the hearing, the Commission services and the authorities of the Member States to ask questions during the hearing.

(13)   When granting access to the file, the Commission should ensure the protection of business secrets and other confidential information. The category of "other confidential information" includes information other than business secrets, which may be considered as confidential, insofar as its disclosure would significantly harm an undertaking or person. The Commission should be able to request undertakings or associations of undertakings that submit or have submitted documents or statements to identify confidential information.

(14)   Where business secrets or other confidential information are necessary to prove an infringement, the Commission should assess for each individual document whether the need to disclose is greater than the harm which might result from disclosure.

(15)   In the interest of legal certainty, a minimum time-limit for the various submissions provided for in this Regulation should be laid down.

(16)   This Regulation replaces Commission Regulation (EC) No 2842/98 of 22 December 1998 on the hearing of parties in certain proceedings under Articles 85 and 86 of the EC Treaty (1), which should therefore be repealed.

(17)   This Regulation aligns the procedural rules in the transport sector with the general rules of procedure in all sectors. Commission Regulation (EC) No 2843/98 of 22 December 1998 on the form, content and other details of applications and notifications provided for in Council Regulations (EEC) No 1017/68, (EEC) No 4056/86 and (EEC) No 3975/87 applying the rules on competition to the transport sector should therefore be repealed.

(18)   Regulation (EC) No 1/2003 abolishes the notification and authorisation system. Commission Regulation (EC) No 3385/94 of 21 December 1994 on the form, content and other details of applications and notifications provided for in Council Regulation No 17 should therefore be repealed,

HAS ADOPTED THIS REGULATION:

Chapter I SCOPE

Article 1 Subject-matter and scope
This regulation applies to proceedings conducted by the Commission for the application of Articles 81 and 82 of the Treaty.

Chapter II INITIATION OF PROCEEDINGS

Article 2 Initiation of proceedings
1.   The Commission may decide to initiate proceedings with a view to adopting a decision pursuant to Chapter III of Regulation (EC) No 1/2003 at any point in time, but no later than the date on which it issues a preliminary assessment as referred to in Article 9(1) of that Regulation, a statement of objections or a request for the parties to express their interest in engaging in settlement discussions, or the date on which a notice pursuant to Article 27(4) of that Regulation is published, whichever is the earlier.

2.   The Commission may make public the initiation of proceedings, in any appropriate way. Before doing so, it shall inform the parties concerned.

3.   The Commission may exercise its powers of investigation pursuant to Chapter V of Regulation (EC) No 1/2003 before initiating proceedings.

4. The Commission may reject a complaint pursuant to Article 7 of Regulation (EC) No 1/2003 without initiating proceedings.

Chapter III INVESTIGATIONS BY THE COMMISSION

Article 3 Power to take statements

1. Where the Commission interviews a person with his consent in accordance with Article 19 of Regulation (EC) No 1/2003, it shall, at the beginning of the interview, state the legal basis and the purpose of the interview, and recall its voluntary nature. It shall also inform the person interviewed of its intention to make a record of the interview.

2. The interview may be conducted by any means including by telephone or electronic means.

3. The Commission may record the statements made by the persons interviewed in any form. A copy of any recording shall be made available to the person interviewed for approval. Where necessary, the Commission shall set a time-limit within which the person interviewed may communicate to it any correction to be made to the statement.

Article 4 Oral questions during inspections

1. When, pursuant to Article 20(2)(e) of Regulation (EC) No 1/2003, officials or other accompanying persons authorised by the Commission ask representatives or members of staff of an undertaking or of an association of undertakings for explanations, the explanations given may be recorded in any form.

2. A copy of any recording made pursuant to paragraph 1 shall be made available to the undertaking or association of undertakings concerned after the inspection.

3. In cases where a member of staff of an undertaking or of an association of undertakings who is not or was not authorised by the undertaking or by the association of undertakings to provide explanations on behalf of the undertaking or association of undertakings has been asked for explanations, the Commission shall set a time-limit within which the undertaking or the association of undertakings may communicate to the Commission any rectification, amendment or supplement to the explanations given by such member of staff. The rectification, amendment or supplement shall be added to the explanations as recorded pursuant to paragraph 1.

Chapter IV HANDLING OF COMPLAINTS

Article 5 Admissibility of complaints

1. Natural and legal persons shall show a legitimate interest in order to be entitled to lodge a complaint for the purposes of Article 7 of Regulation (EC) No 1/2003.

    Such complaints shall contain the information required by Form C, as set out in the Annex. The Commission may dispense with this obligation as regards part of the information, including documents, required by Form C.

2. Three paper copies as well as, if possible, an electronic copy of the complaint shall be submitted to the Commission. The complainant shall also submit a non-confidential version of the complaint, if confidentiality is claimed for any part of the complaint.

3. Complaints shall be submitted in one of the official languages of the Community.

Article 6 Participation of complainants in proceedings

1. Where the Commission issues a statement of objections relating to a matter in respect of which it has received a complaint, it shall provide the complainant with a copy of the non-confidential version of the statement of objections, except in cases where the settlement

procedure applies, where it shall inform the complainant in writing of the nature and subject matter of the procedure. The Commission shall also set a time limit within which the complainant may make known its views in writing.

2.   The Commission may, where appropriate, afford complainants the opportunity of expressing their views at the oral hearing of the parties to which a statement of objections has been issued, if complainants so request in their written comments.

Article 7 Rejection of complaints

1.   Where the Commission considers that on the basis of the information in its possession there are insufficient grounds for acting on a complaint, it shall inform the complainant of its reasons and set a time-limit within which the complainant may make known its views in writing. The Commission shall not be obliged to take into account any further written submission received after the expiry of that time-limit.

2.   If the complainant makes known its views within the time-limit set by the Commission and the written submissions made by the complainant do not lead to a different assessment of the complaint, the Commission shall reject the complaint by decision.

3.   If the complainant fails to make known its views within the time-limit set by the Commission, the complaint shall be deemed to have been withdrawn.

Article 8 Access to information

1.   Where the Commission has informed the complainant of its intention to reject a complaint pursuant to Article 7(1) the complainant may request access to the documents on which the Commission bases its provisional assessment. For this purpose, the complainant may however not have access to business secrets and other confidential information belonging to other parties involved in the proceedings.

2.   The documents to which the complainant has had access in the context of proceedings conducted by the Commission under Articles 81 and 82 of the Treaty may only be used by the complainant for the purposes of judicial or administrative proceedings for the application of those Treaty provisions.

Article 9 Rejections of complaints pursuant to Article 13 of Regulation (EC) No 1/2003

Where the Commission rejects a complaint pursuant to Article 13 of Regulation (EC) No 1/2003, it shall inform the complainant without delay of the national competition authority which is dealing or has already dealt with the case.

Chapter V EXERCISE OF THE RIGHT TO BE HEARD

Article 10 Statement of objections and reply

1.   The Commission shall inform the parties concerned of the objections raised against them. The statement of objections shall be notified in writing to each of the parties against whom objections are raised.

2.   The Commission shall, when notifying the statement of objections to the parties concerned, set a time-limit within which these parties may inform it in writing of their views. The Commission shall not be obliged to take into account written submissions received after the expiry of that time-limit.

3.   The parties may, in their written submissions, set out all facts known to them which are relevant to their defence against the objections raised by the Commission. They shall attach any relevant documents as proof of the facts set out. They shall provide a paper original as well as an electronic copy or, where they do not provide an electronic copy, 30 paper copies of their submission and of the documents attached to it. They may propose

that the Commission hear persons who may corroborate the facts set out in their submission.

Article 10a Settlement procedure in cartel cases

1. After the initiation of proceedings pursuant to Article 11(6) of Regulation (EC) No 1/2003, the Commission may set a time limit within which the parties may indicate in writing that they are prepared to engage in settlement discussions with a view to possibly introducing settlement submissions. The Commission shall not be obliged to take into account replies received after the expiry of that time limit.

   If two or more parties within the same undertaking indicate their willingness to engage in settlement discussions pursuant to the first subparagraph, they shall appoint a joint representation to engage in discussions with the Commission on their behalf. When setting the time limit referred to in the first subparagraph, the Commission shall indicate to the relevant parties that they are identified within the same undertaking, for the sole purpose of enabling them to comply with this provision.

2. Parties taking part in settlement discussions may be informed by the Commission of:
   (a) the objections it envisages to raise against them;
   (b) the evidence used to determine the envisaged objections;
   (c) non-confidential versions of any specified accessible document listed in the case file at that point in time, in so far as a request by the party is justified for the purpose of enabling the party to ascertain its position regarding a time period or any other particular aspect of the cartel; and
   (d) the range of potential fines.
   This information shall be confidential vis-à-vis third parties, save where the Commission has given a prior explicit authorisation for disclosure.

   Should settlement discussions progress, the Commission may set a time limit within which the parties may commit to follow the settlement procedure by introducing settlement submissions reflecting the results of the settlement discussions and acknowledging their participation in an infringement of Article 81 of the Treaty as well as their liability. Before the Commission sets a time limit to introduce their settlement submissions, the parties concerned shall be entitled to have the information specified in Article 10a(2), first subparagraph disclosed to them, upon request, in a timely manner. The Commission shall not be obliged to take into account settlement submissions received after the expiry of that time limit.

3. When the statement of objections notified to the parties reflects the contents of their settlement submissions, the written reply to the statement of objections by the parties concerned shall, within a time limit set by the Commission, confirm that the statement of objections addressed to them reflects the contents of their settlement submissions.

   The Commission may then proceed to the adoption of a Decision pursuant to Article 7 and Article 23 of Regulation (EC) No 1/2003 after consultation of the Advisory Committee on Restrictive Practices and Dominant Positions pursuant to Article 14 of Regulation (EC) No 1/2003.

4. The Commission may decide at any time during the procedure to discontinue settlement discussions altogether in a specific case or with respect to one or more of the parties involved, if it considers that procedural efficiencies are not likely to be achieved.

Article 11 Right to be heard

1. The Commission shall give the parties to whom it addresses a statement of objections the opportunity to be heard before consulting the Advisory Committee referred to in Article 14(1) of Regulation (EC) No 1/2003.

2. The Commission shall, in its decisions, deal only with objections in respect of which the parties referred to in paragraph 1 have been able to comment.

Article 12

1. The Commission shall give the parties to whom it addresses a statement of objections the opportunity to develop their arguments at an oral hearing, if they so request in their written submissions.

2. However, when introducing their settlement submissions the parties shall confirm to the Commission that they would only require having the opportunity to develop their arguments at an oral hearing, if the statement of objections does not reflect the contents of their settlement submissions.

Article 13 Hearing of other persons

1. If natural or legal persons other than those referred to in Articles 5 and 11 apply to be heard and show a sufficient interest, the Commission shall inform them in writing of the nature and subject matter of the procedure and shall set a time-limit within which they may make known their views in writing.

2. The Commission may, where appropriate, invite persons referred to in paragraph 1 to develop their arguments at the oral hearing of the parties to whom a statement of objections has been addressed, if the persons referred to in paragraph 1 so request in their written comments.

3. The Commission may invite any other person to express its views in writing and to attend the oral hearing of the parties to whom a statement of objections has been addressed. The Commission may also invite such persons to express their views at that oral hearing.

Article 14 Conduct of oral hearings

1. Hearings shall be conducted by a Hearing Officer in full independence.

2. The Commission shall invite the persons to be heard to attend the oral hearing on such date as it shall determine.

3. The Commission shall invite the competition authorities of the Member States to take part in the oral hearing. It may likewise invite officials and civil servants of other authorities of the Member States.

4. Persons invited to attend shall either appear in person or be represented by legal representatives or by representatives authorised by their constitution as appropriate. Undertakings and associations of undertakings may also be represented by a duly authorised agent appointed from among their permanent staff.

5. Persons heard by the Commission may be assisted by their lawyers or other qualified persons admitted by the Hearing Officer.

6. Oral hearings shall not be public. Each person may be heard separately or in the presence of other persons invited to attend, having regard to the legitimate interest of the undertakings in the protection of their business secrets and other confidential information.

7. The Hearing Officer may allow the parties to whom a statement of objections has been addressed, the complainants, other persons invited to the hearing, the Commission services and the authorities of the Member States to ask questions during the hearing.

8. The statements made by each person heard shall be recorded. Upon request, the recording of the hearing shall be made available to the persons who attended the hearing. Regard

shall be had to the legitimate interest of the parties in the protection of their business secrets and other confidential information.

Chapter VI ACCESS TO THE FILE AND TREATMENT OF CONFIDENTIAL INFORMATION

Article 15 Access to the file and use of documents

1. If so requested, the Commission shall grant access to the file to the parties to whom it has addressed a statement of objections. Access shall be granted after the notification of the statement of objections.

1a. After the initiation of proceedings pursuant to Article 11(6) of Regulation (EC) No 1/2003 and in order to enable the parties willing to introduce settlement submissions to do so, the Commission shall disclose to them the evidence and documents described in Article 10a(2) upon request and subject to the conditions established in the relevant subparagraphs. In view thereof, when introducing their settlement submissions, the parties shall confirm to the Commission that they will only require access to the file after the receipt of the statement of objections, if the statement of objections does not reflect the contents of their settlement submissions.

2. The right of access to the file shall not extend to business secrets, other confidential information and internal documents of the Commission or of the competition authorities of the Member States.

   The right of access to the file shall also not extend to correspondence between the Commission and the competition authorities of the Member States or between the latter where such correspondence is contained in the file of the Commission.

3. Nothing in this Regulation prevents the Commission from disclosing and using information necessary to prove an infringement of Articles 81 or 82 of the Treaty.

4. Documents obtained through access to the file pursuant to this Article shall only be used for the purposes of judicial or administrative proceedings for the application of Articles 81 and 82 of the Treaty.

Article 16 Identification and protection of confidential information

1. Information, including documents, shall not be communicated or made accessible by the Commission in so far as it contains business secrets or other confidential information of any person.

2. Any person which makes known its views pursuant to Article 6(1), Article 7(1), Article 10(2) and Article 13(1) and (3) or subsequently submits further information to the Commission in the course of the same procedure, shall clearly identify any material which it considers to be confidential, giving reasons, and provide a separate non-confidential version by the date set by the Commission for making its views known.

3. Without prejudice to paragraph 2 of this Article, the Commission may require undertakings and associations of undertakings which produce documents or statements pursuant to Regulation (EC) No 1/2003 to identify the documents or parts of documents which they consider to contain business secrets or other confidential information belonging to them and to identify the undertakings with regard to which such documents are to be considered confidential. The Commission may likewise require undertakings or associations of undertakings to identify any part of a statement of objections, a case summary drawn up pursuant to Article 27(4) of Regulation (EC) No 1/2003 or a decision adopted by the Commission which in their view contains business secrets.

The Commission may set a time-limit within which the undertakings and associations of undertakings are to:
(a) substantiate their claim for confidentiality with regard to each individual document or part of document, statement or part of statement;
(b) provide the Commission with a non-confidential version of the documents or statements, in which the confidential passages are deleted;
(c) provide a concise description of each piece of deleted information.

4.   If undertakings or associations of undertakings fail to comply with paragraphs 2 and 3, the Commission may assume that the documents or statements concerned do not contain confidential information.

Chapter VII GENERAL AND FINAL PROVISIONS

Article 17 Time-limits
1.   In setting the time limits provided for in Article 3(3), Article 4(3), Article 6(1), Article 7(1), Article 10(2), Article 10a(1), Article 10a(2), Article 10a(3) and Article 16(3), the Commission shall have regard both to the time required for preparation of the submission and to the urgency of the case.

2.   The time-limits referred to in Article 6(1), Article 7(1) and Article 10(2) shall be at least four weeks. However, for proceedings initiated with a view to adopting interim measures pursuant to Article 8 of Regulation (EC) No 1/2003, the time-limit may be shortened to one week.

3.   The time limits referred to in Article 4(3), Article 10a(1), Article 10a(2) and Article 16(3) shall be at least two weeks. The time limit referred to in Article 3(3) shall be at least two weeks, except for settlement submissions, for which corrections shall be made within one week. The time limit referred to in Article 10a(3) shall be at least two weeks.

4.   Where appropriate and upon reasoned request made before the expiry of the original time-limit, time-limits may be extended.

Article 18 Repeals
Regulations (EC) No 2842/98, (EC) No 2843/98 and (EC) No 3385/94 are repealed. References to the repealed regulations shall be construed as references to this regulation.

Article 19 Transitional provisions
Procedural steps taken under Regulations (EC) No 2842/98 and (EC) No 2843/98 shall continue to have effect for the purpose of applying this Regulation.

Article 20 Entry into force
This Regulation shall enter into force on 1 May 2004.

This Regulation shall be binding in its entirety and directly applicable in all Member States.

ANNEX

FORM C COMPLAINT PURSUANT TO ARTICLE 7 OF REGULATION (EC) No 1/2003

I Information regarding the complainant and the undertaking(s) or association of undertakings giving rise to the complaint
1.   Give full details on the identity of the legal or natural person submitting the complaint. Where the complainant is an undertaking, identify the corporate group to which it

belongs and provide a concise overview of the nature and scope of its business activities. Provide a contact person (with telephone number, postal and e-mail-address) from which supplementary explanations can be obtained.

2. Identify the undertaking(s) or association of undertakings whose conduct the complaint relates to, including, where applicable, all available information on the corporate group to which the undertaking(s) complained of belong and the nature and scope of the business activities pursued by them. Indicate the position of the complainant vis-à-vis the undertaking(s) or association of undertakings complained of (e.g. customer, competitor).

II Details of the alleged infringement and evidence

3. Set out in detail the facts from which, in your opinion, it appears that there exists an infringement of Article 81 or 82 of the Treaty and/or Article 53 or 54 of the EEA agreement. Indicate in particular the nature of the products (goods or services) affected by the alleged infringements and explain, where necessary, the commercial relationships concerning these products. Provide all available details on the agreements or practices of the undertakings or associations of undertakings to which this complaint relates. Indicate, to the extent possible, the relative market positions of the undertakings concerned by the complaint.

4. Submit all documentation in your possession relating to or directly connected with the facts set out in the complaint (for example, texts of agreements, minutes of negotiations or meetings, terms of transactions, business documents, circulars, correspondence, notes of telephone conversations . . .). State the names and address of the persons able to testify to the facts set out in the complaint, and in particular of persons affected by the alleged infringement. Submit statistics or other data in your possession which relate to the facts set out, in particular where they show developments in the marketplace (for example information relating to prices and price trends, barriers to entry to the market for new suppliers etc.).

5. Set out your view about the geographical scope of the alleged infringement and explain, where that is not obvious, to what extent trade between Member States or between the Community and one or more EFTA States that are contracting parties of the EEA Agreement may be affected by the conduct complained of.

III Finding sought from the Commission and legitimate interest

6. Explain what finding or action you are seeking as a result of proceedings brought by the Commission.

7. Set out the grounds on which you claim a legitimate interest as complainant pursuant to Article 7 of Regulation (EC) No 1/2003. State in particular how the conduct complained of affects you and explain how, in your view, intervention by the Commission would be liable to remedy the alleged grievance.

IV Proceedings before national competition authorities or national courts

8. Provide full information about whether you have approached, concerning the same or closely related subject-matters, any other competition authority and/or whether a lawsuit has been brought before a national court. If so, provide full details about the administrative or judicial authority contacted and your submissions to such authority.

Declaration that the information given in this form and in the Annexes thereto is given entirely in good faith.

Date and signature.

COMMISSION REGULATION (EU) No 267/2010 OF 24 MARCH 2010

on the application of Article 101(3) of the Treaty on the Functioning of the European Union to certain categories of agreements, decisions and concerted practices in the insurance sector

OJ L 83, 30.3.2010, p. 1

(footnotes omitted)

THE EUROPEAN COMMISSION,

Having regard to the Treaty on the Functioning of the European Union,

Having regard to Council Regulation (EEC) No 1534/91 of 31 May 1991 on the application of Article 85(3) of the Treaty to certain categories of agreements, decisions and concerted practices in the insurance sector, and in particular Article 1(1)(a), (b), (c) and (e) thereof,

Having published a draft of this Regulation,

After consulting the Advisory Committee on Restrictive Practices and Dominant Positions,

Whereas:

(1) Regulation (EEC) No 1534/91 empowers the Commission to apply Article 101(3) of the Treaty on the Functioning of the European Union by regulation to certain categories of agreements, decisions and concerted practices in the insurance sector which have as their object cooperation with respect to:
 — the establishment of common risk premium tariffs based on collectively ascertained statistics or the number of claims,
 — the establishment of common standard policy conditions,
 — the common coverage of certain types of risks,
 — the settlement of claims,
 — the testing and acceptance of security devices,
 — registers of, and information on, aggravated risks.

(2) Pursuant to Regulation (EEC) No 1534/91, the Commission adopted Regulation (EC) No 358/2003 of 27 February 2003 on the application of Article 81(3) of the Treaty to certain categories of agreements, decisions and concerted practices in the insurance sector. Regulation (EC) No 358/2003 expires on 31 March 2010.

(3) Regulation (EC) No 358/2003 does not grant an exemption to agreements concerning the settlement of claims and registers of, and information on, aggravated risks. The Commission considered that it lacked sufficient experience in handling individual cases to make use of the power conferred by Regulation (EEC) No 1534/91 in those fields. That situation has not changed. Furthermore, although Regulation (EC) No 358/2003 granted an exemption for the establishment of standard policy conditions and the testing and acceptance of security devices, this Regulation should not do so since the Commission's review of the functioning of Regulation (EC) No 358/2003 revealed that it was no longer necessary to include such agreements in a sector specific block exemption regulation. In the context where those two categories of agreements are not specific to the insurance sector and, as the review showed, can also give rise to certain competition concerns, it is more appropriate that they be subject to self-assessment.

(4) Following a public consultation launched on 17 April 2008, the Commission adopted a report to the European Parliament and the Council on the functioning of Regulation (EC)

No 358/2003 (the Report) on 24 March 2009. In the Report and its accompanying Working Document (the Working Document) preliminary amendments of Regulation (EC) No 358/2003 were proposed. On 2 June 2009, the Commission held a public meeting with interested parties, including representatives of the insurance sector, consumer organisations and national competition authorities, on the findings and proposals in the Report and Working Document.

(5) This Regulation should ensure effective protection of competition while providing benefits to consumers and adequate legal security for undertakings. The pursuit of those objectives should take account of the Commission's experience in this field, and the results of the consultations leading up to the adoption of this Regulation.

(6) Regulation (EEC) No 1534/91 requires the exempting regulation of the Commission to define the categories of agreements, decisions and concerted practices to which it applies, to specify the restrictions or clauses which may, or may not, appear in the agreements, decisions and concerted practices, and to specify the clauses which must be contained in the agreements, decisions and concerted practices or the other conditions which must be satisfied.

(7) Nevertheless, it is appropriate to continue the approach taken in Regulation (EC) No 358/2003 of placing the emphasis on defining categories of agreements which are exempted up to a certain level of market share and on specifying the restrictions or clauses which are not to be contained in such agreements.

(8) The benefit of the block exemption established by this Regulation should be limited to those agreements which can be assumed with sufficient certainty to satisfy the conditions of Article 101(3) of the Treaty. For the application of Article 101(3) of the Treaty by regulation, it is not necessary to define those agreements which are capable of falling within Article 101(1) of the Treaty. At the same time, there is no presumption that agreements which do not benefit from this Regulation are either caught by Article 101(1) of the Treaty or that they fail to satisfy the conditions of Article 101(3) of the Treaty. In the individual assessment of agreements under Article 101(1) of the Treaty, account must be taken of several factors, and in particular the market structure on the relevant market.

(9) Collaboration between insurance undertakings or within associations of undertakings in the compilation of information (which may also involve some statistical calculations) allowing the calculation of the average cost of covering a specified risk in the past or, for life insurance, tables of mortality rates or of the frequency of illness, accident and invalidity, makes it possible to improve the knowledge of risks and facilitates the rating of risks for individual companies. This can in turn facilitate market entry and thus benefit consumers. The same applies to joint studies on the probable impact of extraneous circumstances that may influence the frequency or scale of claims, or the yield of different types of investments. It is, however, necessary to ensure that such collaboration is only exempted to the extent to which it is necessary to attain these objectives. It is therefore appropriate to stipulate in particular that agreements on commercial premiums are not exempted. Indeed, commercial premiums may be lower than the amounts indicated by the compilations, tables or study results in question, since insurers can use the revenues from their investments in order to reduce their premiums. Moreover, the compilations, tables or studies in question should be non-binding and serve only for reference purposes. The exchange of information not necessary to attain the objectives set out in this recital should not be covered by this Regulation.

(10) Moreover, the narrower the categories into which statistics on the cost of covering a specified risk in the past are grouped, the more leeway insurance undertakings have to differentiate

their commercial premiums when they calculate them. It is therefore appropriate to exempt joint compilations of the past cost of risks on condition that the available statistics are provided with as much detail and differentiation as is actuarially adequate.

(11) Furthermore, access to the joint compilations, tables and study results is necessary both for insurance undertakings active on the geographic or product market in question and for those considering entering that market. Similarly access to such compilations, tables and study results may be of value to consumer organisations or customer organisations. Insurance undertakings not yet active on the market in question and consumer or customer organisations must be granted access to such compilations, tables and study results on reasonable, affordable and non-discriminatory terms, as compared with insurance undertakings already present on that market. Such terms might for example include a commitment from an insurance undertaking not yet present on the market to provide statistical information on claims, should it ever enter the market and might also include membership of the association of insurers responsible for producing the compilations. An exception to the requirement to grant access to consumer organisations and customer organisations should be possible on the grounds of public security, for example where the information relates to the security systems of nuclear plants or the weakness of flood prevention systems.

(12) The reliability of joint compilations, tables and studies becomes greater as the amount of statistics on which they are based is increased. Insurers with high market shares may generate sufficient statistics internally to be able to make reliable compilations, but those with small market shares may not be able to do so, and new entrants are even less likely to be able to generate such statistics. The inclusion in such joint compilations, tables and studies of information from all insurers on a market, including large ones, in principle promotes competition by helping smaller insurers, and facilitates market entry. Given this specificity of the insurance sector, it is not appropriate to subject any exemption for such joint compilations, tables and studies to market share thresholds.

(13) Co-insurance or co-reinsurance pools can, in certain limited circumstances, be necessary to allow the participating undertakings of a pool to provide insurance or reinsurance for risks for which they might only offer insufficient cover in the absence of the pool. Those types of pools do not generally give rise to a restriction of competition under Article 101(1) of the Treaty and are thus not prohibited by it.

(14) Co-insurance or co-reinsurance pools can allow insurers and reinsurers to provide insurance or reinsurance for risks even if pooling goes beyond what is necessary to ensure that such a risk is covered. However, such pools can involve restrictions of competition, such as the standardisation of policy conditions and even of amounts of cover and premiums. It is therefore appropriate to lay down the circumstances in which such pools can benefit from exemption.

(15) For genuinely new risks it is not possible to know in advance what subscription capacity is necessary to cover the risk, nor whether two or more pools could co-exist for the purposes of providing the specific type of insurance concerned. A pooling arrangement offering the co-insurance or co-reinsurance of such new risks can therefore be exempted for a limited period of time without a market share threshold. Three years should constitute an adequate period for the constitution of sufficient historical information on claims to assess the necessity or otherwise of a pool.

(16) Risks which did not previously exist should be considered as new risks. However, in exceptional circumstances, a risk may be considered as a new risk where an objective

analysis indicates that the nature of the risk has changed so materially that it is not possible to know in advance what subscription capacity is necessary in order to cover such a risk.

(17) For risks which are not new, co-insurance and co-reinsurance pools which involve a restriction of competition may, in certain limited circumstances, involve benefits so as to justify an exemption under Article 101(3) of the Treaty, even if they could be replaced by two or more competing insurance entities. They may, for example, allow their participating undertakings to gain the necessary experience of the sector of insurance involved, or they may allow cost savings, or reduction of commercial premiums through joint reinsurance on advantageous terms. However, any exemption should be limited to agreements which do not afford the undertakings involved the possibility of eliminating competition in respect of a substantial part of the products in question. Consumers can benefit effectively from pools only if there is sufficient competition in the relevant markets in which the pools operate. This condition should be regarded as being met when the market share of a pool remains below a given threshold and can therefore be presumed to be subject to actual or potential competition from undertakings which are not participating in that pool.

(18) This Regulation should therefore grant an exemption to any such co-insurance or co-reinsurance pool which has existed for more than three years, or which is not created in order to cover a new risk, on condition that the combined market share held by the participating undertakings does not exceed certain thresholds. The threshold for co-insurance pools should be lower because co- insurance pools may involve uniform policy conditions and commercial premiums. For the assessment of whether a pool fulfils the market share condition, the overall market share of the participating undertakings should be aggregated. The market share of each participating undertaking is based on the overall gross premium income of that participating undertaking both within and outside that pool in the same relevant market. These exemptions however should only apply if the pool in question meets the further conditions laid down in this Regulation, which are intended to keep to a minimum the restrictions of competition between the participating undertakings of the pool. An individual analysis would be necessary in such cases, in order to determine whether or not the conditions set out in this Regulation are fulfilled.

(19) In order to facilitate the conclusion of agreements, some of which can involve significant investment decisions, the period of validity of this Regulation should be fixed at seven years.

(20) The Commission may withdraw the benefit of this Regulation, pursuant to Article 29(1) of Council Regulation (EC) No 1/2003 of 16 December 2002 on the implementation of the rules on competition laid down in Articles 81 and 82 of the Treaty, where it finds in a particular case that an agreement to which the exemptions provided for in this Regulation apply nevertheless has effects which are incompatible with Article 101(3) of the Treaty.

(21) The competition authority of a Member State may withdraw the benefit of this Regulation pursuant to Article 29(2) of Regulation (EC) No 1/2003 in respect of the territory of that Member State, or a part thereof where, in a particular case, an agreement to which the exemptions provided for in this Regulation apply nevertheless has effects which are incompatible with Article 101(3) of the Treaty in the territory of that Member State, or in a part thereof, and where such territory has all the characteristics of a distinct geographic market.

(22) In determining whether the benefit of this Regulation should be withdrawn pursuant to Article 29 of Regulation (EC) No 1/2003, the anti-competitive effects that may derive from the existence of links between a co-insurance or co-reinsurance pool and/or its

participating undertakings and other pools and/or their participating undertakings on the same relevant market are of particular importance, HAS ADOPTED THIS REGULATION:

Chapter I DEFINITIONS

Article 1 Definitions

For the purposes of this Regulation, the following definitions shall apply:

1. "agreement" means an agreement, a decision of an association of undertakings or a concerted practice;

2. "participating undertakings" means undertakings party to the agreement and their respective connected undertakings;

3. "connected undertakings" means:
    (a) undertakings in which a party to the agreement, directly or indirectly:
        (i) has the power to exercise more than half the voting rights; or
        (ii) has the power to appoint more than half the members of the supervisory board, board of management or bodies legally representing the undertaking; or
        (iii) has the right to manage the undertaking's affairs;
    (b) undertakings which directly or indirectly have, over a party to the agreement, the rights or powers listed in point (a);
    (c) undertakings in which an undertaking referred to in point (b) has, directly or indirectly, the rights or powers listed in point (a);
    (d) undertakings in which a party to the agreement together with one or more of the undertakings referred to in points (a), (b) or (c), or in which two or more of the latter undertakings, jointly have the rights or powers listed in point (a);
    (e) undertakings in which the rights or powers listed in point (a) are jointly held by:
        (i) parties to the agreement or their respective connected undertakings referred to in points (a) to (d); or
        (ii) one or more of the parties to the agreement or one or more of their connected undertakings referred to in points (a) to (d) and one or more third parties;

4. "co-insurance pools" means groups set up by insurance undertakings either directly or through brokers or authorised agents, with the exception of ad-hoc co-insurance agreements on the subscription market, whereby a certain part of a given risk is covered by a lead insurer and the remaining part of the risk is covered by follow insurers who are invited to cover that remainder, which:
    (a) agree to underwrite, in the name and for the account of all the participants, the insurance of a specified risk category; or
    (b) entrust the underwriting and management of the insurance of a specified risk category, in their name and on their behalf, to one of the insurance undertakings, to a common broker or to a common body set up for this purpose;

5. "co-reinsurance pools" means groups set up by insurance undertakings either directly or through broker or authorised agents, possibly with the assistance of one or more reinsurance undertakings, with the exception of ad-hoc co-reinsurance agreements on the subscription market, whereby a certain part of a given risk is covered by a lead insurer and the remaining part of this risk is covered by follow insurers who are then invited to cover that remainder in order to:
    (a) reinsure mutually all or part of their liabilities in respect of a specified risk category;
    (b) incidentally accept, in the name and on behalf of all the participants, the reinsurance of the same category of risks;

6. "new risks" means:

(a) risks which did not previously exist, and for which insurance cover requires the development of an entirely new insurance product, not involving an extension, improvement or replacement of an existing insurance product; or

(b) in exceptional cases, risks the nature of which has, on the basis of an objective analysis, changed so materially that it is not possible to know in advance what subscription capacity is necessary in order to cover such a risk;

7. "commercial premium" means the price which is charged to the purchaser of an insurance policy.

Chapter II JOINT COMPILATIONS, TABLES, AND STUDIES

Article 2 Exemption

Pursuant to Article 101(3) of the Treaty and subject to the provisions of this Regulation, Article 101(1) of the Treaty shall not apply to agreements entered into between two or more undertakings in the insurance sector with respect to:

(a) the joint compilation and distribution of information necessary for the following purposes:

    (i) calculation of the average cost of covering a specified risk in the past (hereinafter compilations);

    (ii) construction of mortality tables, and tables showing the frequency of illness, accident and invalidity in connection with insurance involving an element of capitalisation (hereinafter tables);

(b) the joint carrying-out of studies on the probable impact of general circumstances external to the interested undertakings, either on the frequency or scale of future claims for a given risk or risk category or on the profitability of different types of investment (hereinafter studies), and the distribution of the results of such studies.

Article 3 Conditions for exemption

1. The exemption provided for in Article 2(a) shall apply on condition that the compilations or tables:

    (a) are based on the assembly of data, spread over a number of risk years chosen as an observation period, which relate to identical or comparable risks in sufficient numbers to constitute a base which can be handled statistically and which will yield figures on the following, amongst others:

        (i) the number of claims during the said period;

        (ii) the number of individual risks insured in each risk year of the chosen observation period;

        (iii) the total amounts paid or payable in respect of claims that have arisen during the said period;

        (iv) the total amount of capital insured for each risk year during the chosen observation period;

    (b) include as detailed a breakdown of the available statistics as is actuarially adequate;

    (c) do not include in any way elements for contingencies, income deriving from reserves, administrative or commercial costs or fiscal or parafiscal contributions, and take into account neither revenues from investments nor anticipated profits.

2. The exemptions provided for in Article 2 shall apply on condition that the compilations, tables or study results:

    (a) do not identify the insurance undertakings concerned or any insured party;

    (b) when compiled and distributed, include a statement that they are non-binding;

    (c) do not contain any indication of the level of commercial premiums;

(d)   are made available on reasonable, affordable and non- discriminatory terms, to any insurance undertaking which requests a copy of them, including insurance undertakings which are not active on the geographic or product market to which those compilations, tables or study results refer;

(e)   except where non-disclosure is objectively justified on grounds of public security, are made available on reasonable, affordable and non-discriminatory terms, to consumer organisations or customer organisations which request access to them in specific and precise terms for a duly justified reason.

Article 4 Agreements not covered by the exemption

The exemptions provided for in Article 2 shall not apply where participating undertakings enter into an undertaking or commitment among themselves, or oblige other undertakings, not to use compilations or tables that differ from those referred to in Article 2(a), or not to depart from the results of the studies referred to in Article 2(b).

Chapter III COMMON COVERAGE OF CERTAIN TYPES OF RISKS

Article 5 Exemption

Pursuant to Article 101(3) of the Treaty and subject to the provisions of this Regulation, Article 101(1) of the Treaty shall not apply to agreements entered into between two or more undertakings in the insurance sector with respect to the setting-up and operation of pools of insurance undertakings or of insurance undertakings and reinsurance undertakings for the common coverage of a specific category of risks in the form of co-insurance or co-reinsurance.

Article 6 Application of exemption and market share thresholds

1.   As concerns co-insurance or co-reinsurance pools which are created in order exclusively to cover new risks, the exemption provided for in Article 5 shall apply for a period of three years from the date of the first establishment of the pool, regardless of the market share of the pool.

2.   As concerns co-insurance or co-reinsurance pools which do not fall within the scope of paragraph 1, the exemption provided for in Article 5 shall apply as long as this Regulation remains in force, on condition that the combined market share held by the participating undertakings does not exceed:
(a)   in the case of co-insurance pools, 20% of any relevant market;
(b)   in the case of co-reinsurance pools, 25% of any relevant market.

3.   In calculating the market share of a participating undertaking on the relevant market, account shall be taken of:
(a)   the market share of the participating undertaking within the pool in question;
(b)   the market share of the participating undertaking within another pool on the same relevant market as the pool in question, to which the participating undertaking is a party; and
(c)   the market share of the participating undertaking on the same relevant market as the pool in question, outside any pool.

4.   For the purposes of applying the market share thresholds provided for in paragraph 2, the following rules shall apply:
(a)   the market share shall be calculated on the basis of gross premium income; if gross premium income data are not available, estimates based on other reliable market information, including insurance cover provided or insured risk value, may be used to establish the market share of the undertaking concerned;
(b)   the market share shall be calculated on the basis of data relating to the preceding calendar year.

5.   Where the market share referred to in paragraph 2(a) is initially not more than 20% but subsequently rises above that level without exceeding 25%, the exemption provided for in Article 5 shall continue to apply for a period of two consecutive calendar years following the year in which the 20% threshold was first exceeded.

6.   Where the market share referred to in paragraph 2(a) is initially not more than 20% but subsequently rises above 25%, the exemption provided for in Article 5 shall continue to apply for a period of one calendar year following the year in which the level of 25% was first exceeded.

7.   The benefit of paragraphs 5 and 6 may not be combined so as to exceed a period of two calendar years.

8.   Where the market share referred to in paragraph 2(b) is initially not more than 25% but subsequently rises above that level without exceeding 30%, the exemption provided for in Article 5 shall continue to apply for a period of two consecutive calendar years following the year in which the 25% threshold was first exceeded.

9.   Where the market share referred to in paragraph 2(b) is initially not more than 25% but subsequently rises above 30%, the exemption provided for in Article 5 shall continue to apply for a period of one calendar year following the year in which the level of 30% was first exceeded.

10.   The benefit of paragraphs 8 and 9 may not be combined so as to exceed a period of two calendar years.

Article 7 Conditions for exemption

The exemption provided for in Article 5 shall apply on condition that:

(a)   each participating undertaking having given a reasonable period of notice has the right to withdraw from the pool, without incurring any sanctions;

(b)   the rules of the pool do not oblige any participating undertaking of the pool to insure or reinsure through the pool and do not restrict any participating undertaking of the pool from insuring or reinsuring outside the pool, in whole or in part, any risk of the type covered by the pool;

(c)   the rules of the pool do not restrict the activity of the pool or its participating undertakings to the insurance or reinsurance of risks located in any particular geographical part of the Union;

(d)   the agreement does not limit output or sales;

(e)   the agreement does not allocate markets or customers; and

(f)   the participating undertakings of a co-reinsurance pool do not agree on the commercial premiums which they charge for direct insurance.

Chapter IV FINAL PROVISIONS

Article 8 Transitional period

The prohibition laid down in Article 101(1) of the Treaty shall not apply during the period from 1 April 2010 to 30 September 2010 in respect of agreements already in force on 31 March 2010 which do not satisfy the conditions for exemption provided for in this Regulation but which satisfy the conditions for exemption provided for in Regulation (EC) No 358/2003.

Article 9 Period of validity

This Regulation shall enter into force on 1 April 2010.

It shall expire on 31 March 2017.

This Regulation shall be binding in its entirety and directly applicable in all Member States.

(date of signing and signatory omitted).

COMMISSION REGULATION (EU) NO 330/2010 OF 20 APRIL 2010

on the application of Article 101(3) of the Treaty on the Functioning of the European Union to categories of vertical agreements and concerted practices

OJ L102, 23.4.2010, p. 1

....

(footnotes omitted)

THE EUROPEAN COMMISSION,

Having regard to the Treaty on the Functioning of the European Union,

Having regard to Regulation No 19/65/EEC of the Council of 2 March 1965 on the application of Article 85(3) of the Treaty to certain categories of agreements and concerted practices, and in particular Article 1 thereof,

Having published a draft of this Regulation,

After consulting the Advisory Committee on Restrictive Practices and Dominant Positions,

Whereas:

(1)   Regulation No 19/65/EEC empowers the Commission to apply Article 101(3) of the Treaty on the Functioning of the European Union by regulation to certain categories of vertical agreements and corresponding concerted practices falling within Article 101(1) of the Treaty.

(2)   Commission Regulation (EC) No 2790/1999 of 22 December 1999 on the application of Article 81(3) of the Treaty to categories of vertical agreements and concerted practices defines a category of vertical agreements which the Commission regarded as normally satisfying the conditions laid down in Article 101(3) of the Treaty. In view of the overall positive experience with the application of that Regulation, which expires on 31 May 2010, and taking into account further experience acquired since its adoption, it is appropriate to adopt a new block exemption regulation.

(3)   The category of agreements which can be regarded as normally satisfying the conditions laid down in Article 101(3) of the Treaty includes vertical agreements for the purchase or sale of goods or services where those agreements are concluded between non-competing undertakings, between certain competitors or by certain associations of retailers of goods. It also includes vertical agreements containing ancillary provisions on the assignment or use of intellectual property rights. The term 'vertical agreements' should include the corresponding concerted practices.

(4)   For the application of Article 101(3) of the Treaty by regulation, it is not necessary to define those vertical agreements which are capable of falling within Article 101(1) of the Treaty. In the individual assessment of agreements under Article 101(1) of the Treaty, account has to be taken of several factors, and in particular the market structure on the supply and purchase side.

(5)   The benefit of the block exemption established by this Regulation should be limited to vertical agreements for which it can be assumed with sufficient certainty that they satisfy the conditions of Article 101(3) of the Treaty.

(6)   Certain types of vertical agreements can improve economic efficiency within a chain of production or distribution by facilitating better coordination between the participating undertakings. In particular, they can lead to a reduction in the transaction and distribution costs of the parties and to an optimisation of their sales and investment levels.

(7)   The likelihood that such efficiency-enhancing effects will outweigh any anti-competitive effects due to restrictions contained in vertical agreements depends on the degree of market power of the parties to the agreement and, therefore, on the extent to which those undertakings face competition from other suppliers of goods or services regarded by their customers as interchangeable or substitutable for one another, by reason of the products' characteristics, their prices and their intended use.

(8)   It can be presumed that, where the market share held by each of the undertakings party to the agreement on the relevant market does not exceed 30%, vertical agreements which do not contain certain types of severe restrictions of competition generally lead to an improvement in production or distribution and allow consumers a fair share of the resulting benefits.

(9)   Above the market share threshold of 30%, there can be no presumption that vertical agreements falling within the scope of Article 101(1) of the Treaty will usually give rise to objective advantages of such a character and size as to compensate for the disadvantages which they create for competition. At the same time, there is no presumption that those vertical agreements are either caught by Article 101(1) of the Treaty or that they fail to satisfy the conditions of Article 101(3) of the Treaty.

(10)   This Regulation should not exempt vertical agreements containing restrictions which are likely to restrict competition and harm consumers or which are not indispensable to the attainment of the efficiency-enhancing effects. In particular, vertical agreements containing certain types of severe restrictions of competition such as minimum and fixed resale-prices, as well as certain types of territorial protection, should be excluded from the benefit of the block exemption established by this Regulation irrespective of the market share of the undertakings concerned.

(11)   In order to ensure access to or to prevent collusion on the relevant market, certain conditions should be attached to the block exemption. To this end, the exemption of non-compete obligations should be limited to obligations which do not exceed a defined duration. For the same reasons, any direct or indirect obligation causing the members of a selective distribution system not to sell the brands of particular competing suppliers should be excluded from the benefit of this Regulation.

(12)   The market-share limitation, the non-exemption of certain vertical agreements and the conditions provided for in this Regulation normally ensure that the agreements to which the block exemption applies do not enable the participating undertakings to eliminate competition in respect of a substantial part of the products in question.

(13)   The Commission may withdraw the benefit of this Regulation, pursuant to Article 29(1) of Council Regulation (EC) No 1/2003 of 16 December 2002 on the implementation of the rules on competition laid down in Articles 81 and 82 of the Treaty, where it finds in a particular case that an agreement to which the exemption provided for in this Regulation applies nevertheless has effects which are incompatible with Article 101(3) of the Treaty.

(14)   The competition authority of a Member State may withdraw the benefit of this Regulation pursuant to Article 29(2) of Regulation (EC) No 1/2003 in respect of the territory of that Member State, or a part thereof where, in a particular case, an agreement to which the exemption provided for in this Regulation applies nevertheless has effects which are incompatible with Article 101(3) of the Treaty in the territory of that Member State, or in a part thereof, and where such territory has all the characteristics of a distinct geographic market.

(15)   In determining whether the benefit of this Regulation should be withdrawn pursuant to Article 29 of Regulation (EC) No 1/2003, the anti-competitive effects that may derive from the existence of parallel networks of vertical agreements that have similar effects which significantly restrict access to a relevant market or competition therein are of particular importance. Such cumulative effects may for example arise in the case of selective distribution or non compete obligations.

(16)   In order to strengthen supervision of parallel networks of vertical agreements which have similar anti-competitive effects and which cover more than 50% of a given market, the Commission may by regulation declare this Regulation inapplicable to vertical agreements containing specific restraints relating to the market concerned, thereby restoring the full application of Article 101 of the Treaty to such agreements,

HAS ADOPTED THIS REGULATION:

Article 1 Definitions

1.   For the purposes of this Regulation, the following definitions shall apply:

   (a)   "vertical agreement" means an agreement or concerted practice entered into between two or more undertakings each of which operates, for the purposes of the agreement or the concerted practice, at a different level of the production or distribution chain, and relating to the conditions under which the parties may purchase, sell or resell certain goods or services;

   (b)   "vertical restraint" means a restriction of competition in a vertical agreement falling within the scope of Article 101(1) of the Treaty;

   (c)   "competing undertaking" means an actual or potential competitor; "actual competitor" means an undertaking that is active on the same relevant market; "potential competitor" means an undertaking that, in the absence of the vertical agreement, would, on realistic grounds and not just as a mere theoretical possibility, in case of a small but permanent increase in relative prices be likely to undertake, within a short period of time, the necessary additional investments or other necessary switching costs to enter the relevant market;

   (d)   "non-compete obligation" means any direct or indirect obligation causing the buyer not to manufacture, purchase, sell or resell goods or services which compete with the contract goods or services, or any direct or indirect obligation on the buyer to purchase from the supplier or from another undertaking designated by the supplier more than 80% of the buyer's total purchases of the contract goods or services and their substitutes on the relevant market, calculated on the basis of the value or, where such is standard industry practice, the volume of its purchases in the preceding calendar year;

   (e)   "selective distribution system" means a distribution system where the supplier undertakes to sell the contract goods or services, either directly or indirectly, only to distributors selected on the basis of specified criteria and where these distributors undertake not to sell such goods or services to unauthorised distributors within the territory reserved by the supplier to operate that system;

   (f)   "intellectual property rights" includes industrial property rights, know how, copyright and neighbouring rights;

(g) "know-how" means a package of non-patented practical information, resulting from experience and testing by the supplier, which is secret, substantial and identified: in this context, "secret" means that the know-how is not generally known or easily accessible; "substantial" means that the know-how is significant and useful to the buyer for the use, sale or resale of the contract goods or services; "identified" means that the know-how is described in a sufficiently comprehensive manner so as to make it possible to verify that it fulfils the criteria of secrecy and substantiality;

(h) "buyer" includes an undertaking which, under an agreement falling within Article 101(1) of the Treaty, sells goods or services on behalf of another undertaking;

(i) "customer of the buyer" means an undertaking not party to the agreement which purchases the contract goods or services from a buyer which is party to the agreement.

2. For the purposes of this Regulation, the terms "undertaking", "supplier" and "buyer" shall include their respective connected undertakings.

'Connected undertakings' means:

(a) undertakings in which a party to the agreement, directly or indirectly:
   (i) has the power to exercise more than half the voting rights, or
   (ii) has the power to appoint more than half the members of the supervisory board, board of management or bodies legally representing the undertaking, or
   (iii) has the right to manage the undertaking's affairs;

(b) undertakings which directly or indirectly have, over a party to the agreement, the rights or powers listed in point (a);

(c) undertakings in which an undertaking referred to in point (b) has, directly or indirectly, the rights or powers listed in point (a);

(d) undertakings in which a party to the agreement together with one or more of the undertakings referred to in points (a), (b) or (c), or in which two or more of the latter undertakings, jointly have the rights or powers listed in point (a);

(e) undertakings in which the rights or the powers listed in point (a) are jointly held by:
   (i) parties to the agreement or their respective connected undertakings referred to in points (a) to (d), or
   (ii) one or more of the parties to the agreement or one or more of their connected undertakings referred to in points (a) to (d) and one or more third parties.

Article 2 Exemption

1. Pursuant to Article 101(3) of the Treaty and subject to the provisions of this Regulation, it is hereby declared that Article 101(1) of the Treaty shall not apply to vertical agreements.

   This exemption shall apply to the extent that such agreements contain vertical restraints.

2. The exemption provided for in paragraph 1 shall apply to vertical agreements entered into between an association of undertakings and its members, or between such an association and its suppliers, only if all its members are retailers of goods and if no individual member of the association, together with its connected undertakings, has a total annual turnover exceeding EUR 50 million. Vertical agreements entered into by such associations shall be covered by this Regulation without prejudice to the application of Article 101 of the Treaty to horizontal agreements concluded between the members of the association or decisions adopted by the association.

3. The exemption provided for in paragraph 1 shall apply to vertical agreements containing provisions which relate to the assignment to the buyer or use by the buyer of intellectual property rights, provided that those provisions do not constitute the primary object of such agreements and are directly related to the use, sale or resale of goods or services by the buyer or its customers. The exemption applies on condition that, in relation to the contract

goods or services, those provisions do not contain restrictions of competition having the same object as vertical restraints which are not exempted under this Regulation.

4.   The exemption provided for in paragraph 1 shall not apply to vertical agreements entered into between competing undertakings. However, it shall apply where competing undertakings enter into a non-reciprocal vertical agreement and:
   (a) the supplier is a manufacturer and a distributor of goods, while the buyer is a distributor and not a competing undertaking at the manufacturing level; or
   (b) the supplier is a provider of services at several levels of trade, while the buyer provides its goods or services at the retail level and is not a competing undertaking at the level of trade where it purchases the contract services.

5.   This Regulation shall not apply to vertical agreements the subject matter of which falls within the scope of any other block exemption regulation, unless otherwise provided for in such a regulation.

Article 3 Market share threshold

1.   The exemption provided for in Article 2 shall apply on condition that the market share held by the supplier does not exceed 30% of the relevant market on which it sells the contract goods or services and the market share held by the buyer does not exceed 30% of the relevant market on which it purchases the contract goods or services.

2.   For the purposes of paragraph 1, where in a multi party agreement an undertaking buys the contract goods or services from one undertaking party to the agreement and sells the contract goods or services to another undertaking party to the agreement, the market share of the first undertaking must respect the market share threshold provided for in that paragraph both as a buyer and a supplier in order for the exemption provided for in Article 2 to apply.

Article 4 Restrictions that remove the benefit of the block exemption — hardcore restrictions

The exemption provided for in Article 2 shall not apply to vertical agreements which, directly or indirectly, in isolation or in combination with other factors under the control of the parties, have as their object:
(a) the restriction of the buyer's ability to determine its sale price, without prejudice to the possibility of the supplier to impose a maximum sale price or recommend a sale price, provided that they do not amount to a fixed or minimum sale price as a result of pressure from, or incentives offered by, any of the parties;

(b) the restriction of the territory into which, or of the customers to whom, a buyer party to the agreement, without prejudice to a restriction on its place of establishment, may sell the contract goods or services, except:
   (i)   the restriction of active sales into the exclusive territory or to an exclusive customer group reserved to the supplier or allocated by the supplier to another buyer, where such a restriction does not limit sales by the customers of the buyer,
   (ii) the restriction of sales to end users by a buyer operating at the wholesale level of trade,
   (iii) the restriction of sales by the members of a selective distribution system to unauthorised distributors within the territory reserved by the supplier to operate that system, and
   (iv) the restriction of the buyer's ability to sell components, supplied for the purposes of incorporation, to customers who would use them to manufacture the same type of goods as those produced by the supplier;

(c) the restriction of active or passive sales to end users by members of a selective distribution system operating at the retail level of trade, without prejudice to the possibility of prohibiting a member of the system from operating out of an unauthorised place of establishment;

(d) the restriction of cross-supplies between distributors within a selective distribution system, including between distributors operating at different level of trade;

(e) the restriction, agreed between a supplier of components and a buyer who incorporates those components, of the supplier's ability to sell the components as spare parts to end-users or to repairers or other service providers not entrusted by the buyer with the repair or servicing of its goods.

Article 5 Excluded restrictions

1. The exemption provided for in Article 2 shall not apply to the following obligations contained in vertical agreements:

   (a) any direct or indirect non-compete obligation, the duration of which is indefinite or exceeds five years;

   (b) any direct or indirect obligation causing the buyer, after termination of the agreement, not to manufacture, purchase, sell or resell goods or services;

   (c) any direct or indirect obligation causing the members of a selective distribution system not to sell the brands of particular competing suppliers.

   For the purposes of point (a) of the first subparagraph, a non- compete obligation which is tacitly renewable beyond a period of five years shall be deemed to have been concluded for an indefinite duration.

2. By way of derogation from paragraph 1(a), the time limitation of five years shall not apply where the contract goods or services are sold by the buyer from premises and land owned by the supplier or leased by the supplier from third parties not connected with the buyer, provided that the duration of the non-compete obligation does not exceed the period of occupancy of the premises and land by the buyer.

3. By way of derogation from paragraph 1(b), the exemption provided for in Article 2 shall apply to any direct or indirect obligation causing the buyer, after termination of the agreement, not to manufacture, purchase, sell or resell goods or services where the following conditions are fulfilled:

   (a) the obligation relates to goods or services which compete with the contract goods or services;

   (b) the obligation is limited to the premises and land from which the buyer has operated during the contract period;

   (c) the obligation is indispensable to protect know-how transferred by the supplier to the buyer;

   (d) the duration of the obligation is limited to a period of one year after termination of the agreement.

   Paragraph 1(b) is without prejudice to the possibility of imposing a restriction which is unlimited in time on the use and disclosure of know-how which has not entered the public domain.

Article 6 Non-application of this Regulation

Pursuant to Article 1a of Regulation No 19/65/EEC, the Commission may by regulation declare that, where parallel networks of similar vertical restraints cover more than 50% of a relevant market, this Regulation shall not apply to vertical agreements containing specific restraints relating to that market.

Article 7 Application of the market share threshold

For the purposes of applying the market share thresholds provided for in Article 3 the following rules shall apply:

(a) the market share of the supplier shall be calculated on the basis of market sales value data and the market share of the buyer shall be calculated on the basis of market purchase value data. If market sales value or market purchase value data are not available, estimates based on other reliable market information, including market sales and purchase volumes, may be used to establish the market share of the undertaking concerned;

(b)   the market shares shall be calculated on the basis of data relating to the preceding calendar year;

(c)   the market share of the supplier shall include any goods or services supplied to vertically integrated distributors for the purposes of sale;

(d)   if a market share is initially not more than 30% but subsequently rises above that level without exceeding 35%, the exemption provided for in Article 2 shall continue to apply for a period of two consecutive calendar years following the year in which the 30% market share threshold was first exceeded;

(e)   if a market share is initially not more than 30% but subsequently rises above 35 %, the exemption provided for in Article 2 shall continue to apply for one calendar year following the year in which the level of 35% was first exceeded;

(f)   the benefit of points (d) and (e) may not be combined so as to exceed a period of two calendar years;

(g)   the market share held by the undertakings referred to in point (e) of the second subparagraph of Article 1(2) shall be apportioned equally to each undertaking having the rights or the powers listed in point (a) of the second subparagraph of Article 1(2).

Article 8 Application of the turnover threshold

1.   For the purpose of calculating total annual turnover within the meaning of Article 2(2), the turnover achieved during the previous financial year by the relevant party to the vertical agreement and the turnover achieved by its connected undertakings in respect of all goods and services, excluding all taxes and other duties, shall be added together. For this purpose, no account shall be taken of dealings between the party to the vertical agreement and its connected undertakings or between its connected undertakings.

2.   The exemption provided for in Article 2 shall remain applicable where, for any period of two consecutive financial years, the total annual turnover threshold is exceeded by no more than 10%.

Article 9 Transitional period

The prohibition laid down in Article 101(1) of the Treaty shall not apply during the period from 1 June 2010 to 31 May 2011 in respect of agreements already in force on 31 May 2010 which do not satisfy the conditions for exemption provided for in this Regulation but which, on 31 May 2010, satisfied the conditions for exemption provided for in Regulation (EC) No 2790/1999.

Article 10 Period of validity

This Regulation shall enter into force on 1 June 2010.

It shall expire on 31 May 2022.

This Regulation shall be binding in its entirety and directly applicable in all Member States.

(date of signing and signatory omitted)

VII Social Policy

A) EQUALITIES LAW

COUNCIL DIRECTIVE 2000/43/EC OF 29 JUNE 2000

implementing the principle of equal treatment between persons irrespective of racial or ethnic origin

OJ L 180, 19.7.2000, p. 22[1]

(footnotes omitted)

THE COUNCIL OF THE EUROPEAN UNION,

Having regard to the Treaty establishing the European Community and in particular Article 13 thereof,

Having regard to the proposal from the Commission,

Having regard to the opinion of the European Parliament,

Having regard to the opinion of the Economic and Social Committee,

Having regard to the opinion of the Committee of the Regions,

Whereas:

(1)   The Treaty on European Union marks a new stage in the process of creating an ever closer union among the peoples of Europe.

(2)   In accordance with Article 6 of the Treaty on European Union, the European Union is founded on the principles of liberty, democracy, respect for human rights and fundamental freedoms, and the rule of law, principles which are common to the Member States, and should respect fundamental rights as guaranteed by the European Convention for the protection of Human Rights and Fundamental Freedoms and as they result from the constitutional traditions common to the Member States, as general principles of Community Law.

(3)   The right to equality before the law and protection against discrimination for all persons

[1]   EDITOR'S NOTE: As of 1 June 2010 this Directive has not been amended following the adoption of the Treaty of Lisbon. It includes references to the old Treaty article numbers. Reference should be made to the Tables of Equivalences accompanying the consolidated Treaties in Part II of this edition for the conversion of old Treaty article numbers to new ones.

constitutes a universal right recognised by the Universal Declaration of Human Rights, the United Nations Convention on the Elimination of all forms of Discrimination Against Women, the International Convention on the Elimination of all forms of Racial Discrimination and the United Nations Covenants on Civil and Political Rights and on Economic, Social and Cultural Rights and by the European Convention for the Protection of Human Rights and Fundamental Freedoms, to which all Member States are signatories.

(4) It is important to respect such fundamental rights and freedoms, including the right to freedom of association. It is also important, in the context of the access to and provision of goods and services, to respect the protection of private and family life and transactions carried out in this context.

(5) The European Parliament has adopted a number of Resolutions on the fight against racism in the European Union.

(6) The European Union rejects theories which attempt to determine the existence of separate human races. The use of the term "racial origin" in this Directive does not imply an acceptance of such theories.

(7) The European Council in Tampere, on 15 and 16 October 1999, invited the Commission to come forward as soon as possible with proposals implementing Article 13 of the EC Treaty as regards the fight against racism and xenophobia.

(8) The Employment Guidelines 2000 agreed by the European Council in Helsinki, on 10 and 11 December 1999, stress the need to foster conditions for a socially inclusive labour market by formulating a coherent set of policies aimed at combating discrimination against groups such as ethnic minorities.

(9) Discrimination based on racial or ethnic origin may undermine the achievement of the objectives of the EC Treaty, in particular the attainment of a high level of employment and of social protection, the raising of the standard of living and quality of life, economic and social cohesion and solidarity. It may also undermine the objective of developing the European Union as an area of freedom, security and justice.

(10) The Commission presented a communication on racism, xenophobia and anti-Semitism in December 1995.

(11) The Council adopted on 15 July 1996 Joint Action (96/443/JHA) concerning action to combat racism and xenophobia under which the Member States undertake to ensure effective judicial cooperation in respect of offences based on racist or xenophobic behaviour.

(12) To ensure the development of democratic and tolerant societies which allow the participation of all persons irrespective of racial or ethnic origin, specific action in the field of discrimination based on racial or ethnic origin should go beyond access to employed and self-employed activities and cover areas such as education, social protection including social security and healthcare, social advantages and access to and supply of goods and services.

(13) To this end, any direct or indirect discrimination based on racial or ethnic origin as regards the areas covered by this Directive should be prohibited throughout the Community. This prohibition of discrimination should also apply to nationals of third countries, but does not cover differences of treatment based on nationality and is without prejudice to provisions governing the entry and residence of third-country nationals and their access to employment and to occupation.

(14) In implementing the principle of equal treatment irrespective of racial or ethnic origin, the Community should, in accordance with Article 3(2) of the EC Treaty, aim to eliminate inequalities, and to promote equality between men and women, especially since women are often the victims of multiple discrimination.

(15) The appreciation of the facts from which it may be inferred that there has been direct or indirect discrimination is a matter for national judicial or other competent bodies, in accordance with rules of national law or practice. Such rules may provide in particular for indirect discrimination to be established by any means including on the basis of statistical evidence.

(16) It is important to protect all natural persons against discrimination on grounds of racial or ethnic origin. Member States should also provide, where appropriate and in accordance with their national traditions and practice, protection for legal persons where they suffer discrimination on grounds of the racial or ethnic origin of their members.

(17) The prohibition of discrimination should be without prejudice to the maintenance or adoption of measures intended to prevent or compensate for disadvantages suffered by a group of persons of a particular racial or ethnic origin, and such measures may permit organisations of persons of a particular racial or ethnic origin where their main object is the promotion of the special needs of those persons.

(18) In very limited circumstances, a difference of treatment may be justified where a characteristic related to racial or ethnic origin constitutes a genuine and determining occupational requirement, when the objective is legitimate and the requirement is proportionate. Such circumstances should be included in the information provided by the Member States to the Commission.

(19) Persons who have been subject to discrimination based on racial and ethnic origin should have adequate means of legal protection. To provide a more effective level of protection, associations or legal entities should also be empowered to engage, as the Member States so determine, either on behalf or in support of any victim, in proceedings, without prejudice to national rules of procedure concerning representation and defence before the courts.

(20) The effective implementation of the principle of equality requires adequate judicial protection against victimisation.

(21) The rules on the burden of proof must be adapted when there is a prima facie case of discrimination and, for the principle of equal treatment to be applied effectively, the burden of proof must shift back to the respondent when evidence of such discrimination is brought.

(22) Member States need not apply the rules on the burden of proof to proceedings in which it is for the court or other competent body to investigate the facts of the case. The procedures thus referred to are those in which the plaintiff is not required to prove the facts, which it is for the court or competent body to investigate.

(23) Member States should promote dialogue between the social partners and with non-governmental organisations to address different forms of discrimination and to combat them.

(24) Protection against discrimination based on racial or ethnic origin would itself be strengthened by the existence of a body or bodies in each Member State, with competence to analyse the problems involved, to study possible solutions and to provide concrete assistance for the victims.

(25) This Directive lays down minimum requirements, thus giving the Member States the option of introducing or maintaining more favourable provisions. The implementation of this Directive should not serve to justify any regression in relation to the situation which already prevails in each Member State.

(26) Member States should provide for effective, proportionate and dissuasive sanctions in case of breaches of the obligations under this Directive.

(27) The Member States may entrust management and labour, at their joint request, with the implementation of this Directive as regards provisions falling within the scope of collective agreements, provided that the Member States take all the necessary steps to ensure that they can at all times guarantee the results imposed by this Directive.

(28) In accordance with the principles of subsidiarity and proportionality as set out in Article 5 of the EC Treaty, the objective of this Directive, namely ensuring a common high level of protection against discrimination in all the Member States, cannot be sufficiently achieved by the Member States and can therefore, by reason of the scale and impact of the proposed action, be better achieved by the Community. This Directive does not go beyond what is necessary in order to achieve those objectives,

HAS ADOPTED THIS DIRECTIVE:

Chapter I **GENERAL PROVISIONS**

Article 1 Purpose
The purpose of this Directive is to lay down a framework for combating discrimination on the grounds of racial or ethnic origin, with a view to putting into effect in the Member States the principle of equal treatment.

Article 2 Concept of discrimination
1.   For the purposes of this Directive, the principle of equal treatment shall mean that there shall be no direct or indirect discrimination based on racial or ethnic origin.

2.   For the purposes of paragraph 1:
      (a) direct discrimination shall be taken to occur where one person is treated less favourably than another is, has been or would be treated in a comparable situation on grounds of racial or ethnic origin;
      (b) indirect discrimination shall be taken to occur where an apparently neutral provision, criterion or practice would put persons of a racial or ethnic origin at a particular disadvantage compared with other persons, unless that provision, criterion or practice is objectively justified by a legitimate aim and the means of achieving that aim are appropriate and necessary.

3.   Harassment shall be deemed to be discrimination within the meaning of paragraph 1, when an unwanted conduct related to racial or ethnic origin takes place with the purpose or effect of violating the dignity of a person and of creating an intimidating, hostile, degrading, humiliating or offensive environment. In this context, the concept of harassment may be defined in accordance with the national laws and practice of the Member States.

4.   An instruction to discriminate against persons on grounds of racial or ethnic origin shall be deemed to be discrimination within the meaning of paragraph 1.

Article 3 Scope
1.   Within the limits of the powers conferred upon the Community, this Directive shall apply to all persons, as regards both the public and private sectors, including public bodies, in relation to:

(a) conditions for access to employment, to self-employment and to occupation, including selection criteria and recruitment conditions, whatever the branch of activity and at all levels of the professional hierarchy, including promotion;

(b) access to all types and to all levels of vocational guidance, vocational training, advanced vocational training and retraining, including practical work experience;

(c) employment and working conditions, including dismissals and pay;

(d) membership of and involvement in an organisation of workers or employers, or any organisation whose members carry on a particular profession, including the benefits provided for by such organisations;

(e) social protection, including social security and healthcare;

(f) social advantages;

(g) education;

(h) access to and supply of goods and services which are available to the public, including housing.

2. This Directive does not cover difference of treatment based on nationality and is without prejudice to provisions and conditions relating to the entry into and residence of third-country nationals and stateless persons on the territory of Member States, and to any treatment which arises from the legal status of the third-country nationals and stateless persons concerned.

Article 4 Genuine and determining occupational requirements

Notwithstanding Article 2(1) and (2), Member States may provide that a difference of treatment which is based on a characteristic related to racial or ethnic origin shall not constitute discrimination where, by reason of the nature of the particular occupational activities concerned or of the context in which they are carried out, such a characteristic constitutes a genuine and determining occupational requirement, provided that the objective is legitimate and the requirement is proportionate.

Article 5 Positive action

With a view to ensuring full equality in practice, the principle of equal treatment shall not prevent any Member State from maintaining or adopting specific measures to prevent or compensate for disadvantages linked to racial or ethnic origin.

Article 6 Minimum requirements

1. Member States may introduce or maintain provisions which are more favourable to the protection of the principle of equal treatment than those laid down in this Directive.

2. The implementation of this Directive shall under no circumstances constitute grounds for a reduction in the level of protection against discrimination already afforded by Member States in the fields covered by this Directive.

Chapter II REMEDIES AND ENFORCEMENT

Article 7 Defence of rights

1. Member States shall ensure that judicial and/or administrative procedures, including where they deem it appropriate conciliation procedures, for the enforcement of obligations under this Directive are available to all persons who consider themselves wronged by failure to apply the principle of equal treatment to them, even after the relationship in which the discrimination is alleged to have occurred has ended.

2. Member States shall ensure that associations, organisations or other legal entities, which have, in accordance with the criteria laid down by their national law, a legitimate interest in ensuring that the provisions of this Directive are complied with, may engage, either on

behalf or in support of the complainant, with his or her approval, in any judicial and/or administrative procedure provided for the enforcement of obligations under this Directive.

3.   Paragraphs 1 and 2 are without prejudice to national rules relating to time limits for bringing actions as regards the principle of equality of treatment.

Article 8 Burden of proof

1.   Member States shall take such measures as are necessary, in accordance with their national judicial systems, to ensure that, when persons who consider themselves wronged because the principle of equal treatment has not been applied to them establish, before a court or other competent authority, facts from which it may be presumed that there has been direct or indirect discrimination, it shall be for the respondent to prove that there has been no breach of the principle of equal treatment.

2.   Paragraph 1 shall not prevent Member States from introducing rules of evidence which are more favourable to plaintiffs.

3.   Paragraph 1 shall not apply to criminal procedures.

4.   Paragraphs 1, 2 and 3 shall also apply to any proceedings brought in accordance with Article 7(2).

5.   Member States need not apply paragraph 1 to proceedings in which it is for the court or competent body to investigate the facts of the case.

Article 9 Victimisation

Member States shall introduce into their national legal systems such measures as are necessary to protect individuals from any adverse treatment or adverse consequence as a reaction to a complaint or to proceedings aimed at enforcing compliance with the principle of equal treatment.

Article 10 Dissemination of information

Member States shall take care that the provisions adopted pursuant to this Directive, together with the relevant provisions already in force, are brought to the attention of the persons concerned by all appropriate means throughout their territory.

Article 11 Social dialogue

1.   Member States shall, in accordance with national traditions and practice, take adequate measures to promote the social dialogue between the two sides of industry with a view to fostering equal treatment, including through the monitoring of workplace practices, collective agreements, codes of conduct, research or exchange of experiences and good practices.

2.   Where consistent with national traditions and practice, Member States shall encourage the two sides of the industry without prejudice to their autonomy to conclude, at the appropriate level, agreements laying down anti-discrimination rules in the fields referred to in Article 3 which fall within the scope of collective bargaining. These agreements shall respect the minimum requirements laid down by this Directive and the relevant national implementing measures.

Article 12 Dialogue with non-governmental organisations

Member States shall encourage dialogue with appropriate non-governmental organisations which have, in accordance with their national law and practice, a legitimate interest in contributing to the fight against discrimination on grounds of racial and ethnic origin with a view to promoting the principle of equal treatment.

Chapter III BODIES FOR THE PROMOTION OF EQUAL TREATMENT

Article 13

1.   Member States shall designate a body or bodies for the promotion of equal treatment of all persons without discrimination on the grounds of racial or ethnic origin. These bodies may form part of agencies charged at national level with the defence of human rights or the safeguard of individuals' rights.

2.   Member States shall ensure that the competences of these bodies include:
   — without prejudice to the right of victims and of associations, organisations or other legal entities referred to in Article 7(2), providing independent assistance to victims of discrimination in pursuing their complaints about discrimination,
   — conducting independent surveys concerning discrimination,
   — publishing independent reports and making recommendations on any issue relating to such discrimination.

Chapter IV FINAL PROVISIONS

Article 14 Compliance

Member States shall take the necessary measures to ensure that:
(a)   any laws, regulations and administrative provisions contrary to the principle of equal treatment are abolished;

(b)   any provisions contrary to the principle of equal treatment which are included in individual or collective contracts or agreements, internal rules of undertakings, rules governing profit-making or non-profit-making associations, and rules governing the independent professions and workers' and employers' organisations, are or may be declared, null and void or are amended.

Article 15 Sanctions

Member States shall lay down the rules on sanctions applicable to infringements of the national provisions adopted pursuant to this Directive and shall take all measures necessary to ensure that they are applied. The sanctions, which may comprise the payment of compensation to the victim, must be effective, proportionate and dissuasive. The Member States shall notify those provisions to the Commission by 19 July 2003 at the latest and shall notify it without delay of any subsequent amendment affecting them.

Article 16 Implementation

Member States shall adopt the laws, regulations and administrative provisions necessary to comply with this Directive by 19 July 2003 or may entrust management and labour, at their joint request, with the implementation of this Directive as regards provisions falling within the scope of collective agreements. In such cases, Member States shall ensure that by 19 July 2003, management and labour introduce the necessary measures by agreement, Member States being required to take any necessary measures to enable them at any time to be in a position to guarantee the results imposed by this Directive. They shall forthwith inform the Commission thereof.

When Member States adopt these measures, they shall contain a reference to this Directive or be accompanied by such a reference on the occasion of their official publication. The methods of making such a reference shall be laid down by the Member States.

Article 17 Report

1. Member States shall communicate to the Commission by 19 July 2005, and every five years thereafter, all the information necessary for the Commission to draw up a report to the European Parliament and the Council on the application of this Directive.

2. The Commission's report shall take into account, as appropriate, the views of the European Monitoring Centre on Racism and Xenophobia, as well as the viewpoints of the social partners and relevant non-governmental organisations. In accordance with the principle of gender mainstreaming, this report shall, inter alia, provide an assessment of the impact of the measures taken on women and men. In the light of the information received, this report shall include, if necessary, proposals to revise and update this Directive.

Article 18 Entry into force

This Directive shall enter into force on the day of its publication in the *Official Journal of the European Communities*.

Article 19 Addressees

This Directive is addressed to the Member States.

(date of signing and signatory omitted)

Council Directive 2000/78/EC of 27 November 2000

establishing a general framework for equal treatment in employment and occupation

OJ L 303, 2.12.2000, p. 16[1]

....

(footnotes omitted)

THE COUNCIL OF THE EUROPEAN UNION,

Having regard to the Treaty establishing the European Community, and in particular Article 13 thereof,

Having regard to the proposal from the Commission,

Having regard to the Opinion of the European Parliament,

Having regard to the Opinion of the Economic and Social Committee,

Having regard to the Opinion of the Committee of the Regions,

Whereas:

(1) In accordance with Article 6 of the Treaty on European Union, the European Union is founded on the principles of liberty, democracy, respect for human rights and fundamental freedoms, and the rule of law, principles which are common to all Member States and it

....

[1] EDITOR'S NOTE: As of 1 June 2010 this Directive has not been amended following the adoption of the Treaty of Lisbon. It includes references to the old Treaty article numbers. Reference should be made to the Tables of Equivalences accompanying the consolidated Treaties in Part II of this edition for the conversion of old Treaty article numbers to new ones.

respects fundamental rights, as guaranteed by the European Convention for the Protection of Human Rights and Fundamental Freedoms and as they result from the constitutional traditions common to the Member States, as general principles of Community law.

(2)   The principle of equal treatment between women and men is well established by an important body of Community law, in particular in Council Directive 76/207/EEC of 9 February 1976 on the implementation of the principle of equal treatment for men and women as regards access to employment, vocational training and promotion, and working conditions.

(3)   In implementing the principle of equal treatment, the Community should, in accordance with Article 3(2) of the EC Treaty, aim to eliminate inequalities, and to promote equality between men and women, especially since women are often the victims of multiple discrimination.

(4)   The right of all persons to equality before the law and protection against discrimination constitutes a universal right recognised by the Universal Declaration of Human Rights, the United Nations Convention on the Elimination of All Forms of Discrimination against Women, United Nations Covenants on Civil and Political Rights and on Economic, Social and Cultural Rights and by the European Convention for the Protection of Human Rights and Fundamental Freedoms, to which all Member States are signatories. Convention No 111 of the International Labour Organisation (ILO) prohibits discrimination in the field of employment and occupation.

(5)   It is important to respect such fundamental rights and freedoms. This Directive does not prejudice freedom of association, including the right to establish unions with others and to join unions to defend one's interests.

(6)   The Community Charter of the Fundamental Social Rights of Workers recognises the importance of combating every form of discrimination, including the need to take appropriate action for the social and economic integration of elderly and disabled people.

(7)   The EC Treaty includes among its objectives the promotion of coordination between employment policies of the Member States. To this end, a new employment chapter was incorporated in the EC Treaty as a means of developing a coordinated European strategy for employment to promote a skilled, trained and adaptable workforce.

(8)   The Employment Guidelines for 2000 agreed by the European Council at Helsinki on 10 and 11 December 1999 stress the need to foster a labour market favourable to social integration by formulating a coherent set of policies aimed at combating discrimination against groups such as persons with disability. They also emphasise the need to pay particular attention to supporting older workers, in order to increase their participation in the labour force.

(9)   Employment and occupation are key elements in guaranteeing equal opportunities for all and contribute strongly to the full participation of citizens in economic, cultural and social life and to realising their potential.

(10)   On 29 June 2000 the Council adopted Directive 2000/43/EC implementing the principle of equal treatment between persons irrespective of racial or ethnic origin. That Directive already provides protection against such discrimination in the field of employment and occupation.

(11)   Discrimination based on religion or belief, disability, age or sexual orientation may undermine the achievement of the objectives of the EC Treaty, in particular the attainment

of a high level of employment and social protection, raising the standard of living and the quality of life, economic and social cohesion and solidarity, and the free movement of persons.

(12) To this end, any direct or indirect discrimination based on religion or belief, disability, age or sexual orientation as regards the areas covered by this Directive should be prohibited throughout the Community. This prohibition of discrimination should also apply to nationals of third countries but does not cover differences of treatment based on nationality and is without prejudice to provisions governing the entry and residence of third-country nationals and their access to employment and occupation.

(13) This Directive does not apply to social security and social protection schemes whose benefits are not treated as income within the meaning given to that term for the purpose of applying Article 141 of the EC Treaty, nor to any kind of payment by the State aimed at providing access to employment or maintaining employment.

(14) This Directive shall be without prejudice to national provisions laying down retirement ages.

(15) The appreciation of the facts from which it may be inferred that there has been direct or indirect discrimination is a matter for national judicial or other competent bodies, in accordance with rules of national law or practice. Such rules may provide, in particular, for indirect discrimination to be established by any means including on the basis of statistical evidence.

(16) The provision of measures to accommodate the needs of disabled people at the workplace plays an important role in combating discrimination on grounds of disability.

(17) This Directive does not require the recruitment, promotion, maintenance in employment or training of an individual who is not competent, capable and available to perform the essential functions of the post concerned or to undergo the relevant training, without prejudice to the obligation to provide reasonable accommodation for people with disabilities.

(18) This Directive does not require, in particular, the armed forces and the police, prison or emergency services to recruit or maintain in employment persons who do not have the required capacity to carry out the range of functions that they may be called upon to perform with regard to the legitimate objective of preserving the operational capacity of those services.

(19) Moreover, in order that the Member States may continue to safeguard the combat effectiveness of their armed forces, they may choose not to apply the provisions of this Directive concerning disability and age to all or part of their armed forces. The Member States which make that choice must define the scope of that derogation.

(20) Appropriate measures should be provided, i.e. effective and practical measures to adapt the workplace to the disability, for example adapting premises and equipment, patterns of working time, the distribution of tasks or the provision of training or integration resources.

(21) To determine whether the measures in question give rise to a disproportionate burden, account should be taken in particular of the financial and other costs entailed, the scale and financial resources of the organisation or undertaking and the possibility of obtaining public funding or any other assistance.

(22) This Directive is without prejudice to national laws on marital status and the benefits dependent thereon.

(23) In very limited circumstances, a difference of treatment may be justified where a characteristic related to religion or belief, disability, age or sexual orientation constitutes a genuine and determining occupational requirement, when the objective is legitimate and the requirement is proportionate. Such circumstances should be included in the information provided by the Member States to the Commission.

(24) The European Union in its Declaration No 11 on the status of churches and non-confessional organisations, annexed to the Final Act of the Amsterdam Treaty, has explicitly recognised that it respects and does not prejudice the status under national law of churches and religious associations or communities in the Member States and that it equally respects the status of philosophical and non-confessional organisations. With this in view, Member States may maintain or lay down specific provisions on genuine, legitimate and justified occupational requirements which might be required for carrying out an occupational activity.

(25) The prohibition of age discrimination is an essential part of meeting the aims set out in the Employment Guidelines and encouraging diversity in the workforce. However, differences in treatment in connection with age may be justified under certain circumstances and therefore require specific provisions which may vary in accordance with the situation in Member States. It is therefore essential to distinguish between differences in treatment which are justified, in particular by legitimate employment policy, labour market and vocational training objectives, and discrimination which must be prohibited.

(26) The prohibition of discrimination should be without prejudice to the maintenance or adoption of measures intended to prevent or compensate for disadvantages suffered by a group of persons of a particular religion or belief, disability, age or sexual orientation, and such measures may permit organisations of persons of a particular religion or belief, disability, age or sexual orientation where their main object is the promotion of the special needs of those persons.

(27) In its Recommendation 86/379/EEC of 24 July 1986 on the employment of disabled people in the Community, the Council established a guideline framework setting out examples of positive action to promote the employment and training of disabled people, and in its Resolution of 17 June 1999 on equal employment opportunities for people with disabilities, affirmed the importance of giving specific attention inter alia to recruitment, retention, training and lifelong learning with regard to disabled persons.

(28) This Directive lays down minimum requirements, thus giving the Member States the option of introducing or maintaining more favourable provisions. The implementation of this Directive should not serve to justify any regression in relation to the situation which already prevails in each Member State.

(29) Persons who have been subject to discrimination based on religion or belief, disability, age or sexual orientation should have adequate means of legal protection. To provide a more effective level of protection, associations or legal entities should also be empowered to engage in proceedings, as the Member States so determine, either on behalf or in support of any victim, without prejudice to national rules of procedure concerning representation and defence before the courts.

(30) The effective implementation of the principle of equality requires adequate judicial protection against victimisation.

(31) The rules on the burden of proof must be adapted when there is a prima facie case of discrimination and, for the principle of equal treatment to be applied effectively, the burden of proof must shift back to the respondent when evidence of such discrimination is brought. However, it is not for the respondent to prove that the plaintiff adheres to a particular religion or belief, has a particular disability, is of a particular age or has a particular sexual orientation.

(32) Member States need not apply the rules on the burden of proof to proceedings in which it is for the court or other competent body to investigate the facts of the case. The procedures thus referred to are those in which the plaintiff is not required to prove the facts, which it is for the court or competent body to investigate.

(33) Member States should promote dialogue between the social partners and, within the framework of national practice, with non-governmental organisations to address different forms of discrimination at the workplace and to combat them.

(34) The need to promote peace and reconciliation between the major communities in Northern Ireland necessitates the incorporation of particular provisions into this Directive.

(35) Member States should provide for effective, proportionate and dissuasive sanctions in case of breaches of the obligations under this Directive.

(36) Member States may entrust the social partners, at their joint request, with the implementation of this Directive, as regards the provisions concerning collective agreements, provided they take any necessary steps to ensure that they are at all times able to guarantee the results required by this Directive.

(37) In accordance with the principle of subsidiarity set out in Article 5 of the EC Treaty, the objective of this Directive, namely the creation within the Community of a level playing-field as regards equality in employment and occupation, cannot be sufficiently achieved by the Member States and can therefore, by reason of the scale and impact of the action, be better achieved at Community level. In accordance with the principle of proportionality, as set out in that Article, this Directive does not go beyond what is necessary in order to achieve that objective,

HAS ADOPTED THIS DIRECTIVE:

Chapter I GENERAL PROVISIONS

Article 1 Purpose
The purpose of this Directive is to lay down a general framework for combating discrimination on the grounds of religion or belief, disability, age or sexual orientation as regards employment and occupation, with a view to putting into effect in the Member States the principle of equal treatment.

Article 2 Concept of discrimination
1. For the purposes of this Directive, the "principle of equal treatment" shall mean that there shall be no direct or indirect discrimination whatsoever on any of the grounds referred to in Article 1.

2. For the purposes of paragraph 1:
    (a) direct discrimination shall be taken to occur where one person is treated less favourably than another is, has been or would be treated in a comparable situation, on any of the grounds referred to in Article 1;
    (b) indirect discrimination shall be taken to occur where an apparently neutral provision, criterion or practice would put persons having a particular religion or belief, a

particular disability, a particular age, or a particular sexual orientation at a particular disadvantage compared with other persons unless:

(i)   that provision, criterion or practice is objectively justified by a legitimate aim and the means of achieving that aim are appropriate and necessary, or

(ii) as regards persons with a particular disability, the employer or any person or organisation to whom this Directive applies, is obliged, under national legislation, to take appropriate measures in line with the principles contained in Article 5 in order to eliminate disadvantages entailed by such provision, criterion or practice.

3.   Harassment shall be deemed to be a form of discrimination within the meaning of paragraph 1, when unwanted conduct related to any of the grounds referred to in Article 1 takes place with the purpose or effect of violating the dignity of a person and of creating an intimidating, hostile, degrading, humiliating or offensive environment. In this context, the concept of harassment may be defined in accordance with the national laws and practice of the Member States.

4.   An instruction to discriminate against persons on any of the grounds referred to in Article 1 shall be deemed to be discrimination within the meaning of paragraph 1.

5.   This Directive shall be without prejudice to measures laid down by national law which, in a democratic society, are necessary for public security, for the maintenance of public order and the prevention of criminal offences, for the protection of health and for the protection of the rights and freedoms of others.

Article 3 Scope

1.   Within the limits of the areas of competence conferred on the Community, this Directive shall apply to all persons, as regards both the public and private sectors, including public bodies, in relation to:

(a)   conditions for access to employment, to self-employment or to occupation, including selection criteria and recruitment conditions, whatever the branch of activity and at all levels of the professional hierarchy, including promotion;

(b)   access to all types and to all levels of vocational guidance, vocational training, advanced vocational training and retraining, including practical work experience;

(c)   employment and working conditions, including dismissals and pay;

(d)   membership of, and involvement in, an organisation of workers or employers, or any organisation whose members carry on a particular profession, including the benefits provided for by such organisations.

2.   This Directive does not cover differences of treatment based on nationality and is without prejudice to provisions and conditions relating to the entry into and residence of third-country nationals and stateless persons in the territory of Member States, and to any treatment which arises from the legal status of the third-country nationals and stateless persons concerned.

3.   This Directive does not apply to payments of any kind made by state schemes or similar, including state social security or social protection schemes.

4.   Member States may provide that this Directive, in so far as it relates to discrimination on the grounds of disability and age, shall not apply to the armed forces.

Article 4 Occupational requirements

1.   Notwithstanding Article 2(1) and (2), Member States may provide that a difference of treatment which is based on a characteristic related to any of the grounds referred to in Article 1 shall not constitute discrimination where, by reason of the nature of the

particular occupational activities concerned or of the context in which they are carried out, such a characteristic constitutes a genuine and determining occupational requirement, provided that the objective is legitimate and the requirement is proportionate.

2.   Member States may maintain national legislation in force at the date of adoption of this Directive or provide for future legislation incorporating national practices existing at the date of adoption of this Directive pursuant to which, in the case of occupational activities within churches and other public or private organisations the ethos of which is based on religion or belief, a difference of treatment based on a person's religion or belief shall not constitute discrimination where, by reason of the nature of these activities or of the context in which they are carried out, a person's religion or belief constitute a genuine, legitimate and justified occupational requirement, having regard to the organisation's ethos. This difference of treatment shall be implemented taking account of Member States' constitutional provisions and principles, as well as the general principles of Community law, and should not justify discrimination on another ground.

Provided that its provisions are otherwise complied with, this Directive shall thus not prejudice the right of churches and other public or private organisations, the ethos of which is based on religion or belief, acting in conformity with national constitutions and laws, to require individuals working for them to act in good faith and with loyalty to the organisation's ethos.

Article 5 Reasonable accommodation for disabled persons
In order to guarantee compliance with the principle of equal treatment in relation to persons with disabilities, reasonable accommodation shall be provided. This means that employers shall take appropriate measures, where needed in a particular case, to enable a person with a disability to have access to, participate in, or advance in employment, or to undergo training, unless such measures would impose a disproportionate burden on the employer. This burden shall not be disproportionate when it is sufficiently remedied by measures existing within the framework of the disability policy of the Member State concerned.

Article 6 Justification of differences of treatment on grounds of age
1.   Notwithstanding Article 2(2), Member States may provide that differences of treatment on grounds of age shall not constitute discrimination, if, within the context of national law, they are objectively and reasonably justified by a legitimate aim, including legitimate employment policy, labour market and vocational training objectives, and if the means of achieving that aim are appropriate and necessary.

Such differences of treatment may include, among others:
(a) the setting of special conditions on access to employment and vocational training, employment and occupation, including dismissal and remuneration conditions, for young people, older workers and persons with caring responsibilities in order to promote their vocational integration or ensure their protection;
(b) the fixing of minimum conditions of age, professional experience or seniority in service for access to employment or to certain advantages linked to employment;
(c) the fixing of a maximum age for recruitment which is based on the training requirements of the post in question or the need for a reasonable period of employment before retirement.

2.   Notwithstanding Article 2(2), Member States may provide that the fixing for occupational social security schemes of ages for admission or entitlement to retirement or invalidity benefits, including the fixing under those schemes of different ages for employees or groups or categories of employees, and the use, in the context of such schemes, of age

criteria in actuarial calculations, does not constitute discrimination on the grounds of age, provided this does not result in discrimination on the grounds of sex.

Article 7 Positive action

1. With a view to ensuring full equality in practice, the principle of equal treatment shall not prevent any Member State from maintaining or adopting specific measures to prevent or compensate for disadvantages linked to any of the grounds referred to in Article 1.

2. With regard to disabled persons, the principle of equal treatment shall be without prejudice to the right of Member States to maintain or adopt provisions on the protection of health and safety at work or to measures aimed at creating or maintaining provisions or facilities for safeguarding or promoting their integration into the working environment.

Article 8 Minimum requirements

1. Member States may introduce or maintain provisions which are more favourable to the protection of the principle of equal treatment than those laid down in this Directive.

2. The implementation of this Directive shall under no circumstances constitute grounds for a reduction in the level of protection against discrimination already afforded by Member States in the fields covered by this Directive.

Chapter II REMEDIES AND ENFORCEMENT

Article 9 Defence of rights

1. Member States shall ensure that judicial and/or administrative procedures, including where they deem it appropriate conciliation procedures, for the enforcement of obligations under this Directive are available to all persons who consider themselves wronged by failure to apply the principle of equal treatment to them, even after the relationship in which the discrimination is alleged to have occurred has ended.

2. Member States shall ensure that associations, organisations or other legal entities which have, in accordance with the criteria laid down by their national law, a legitimate interest in ensuring that the provisions of this Directive are complied with, may engage, either on behalf or in support of the complainant, with his or her approval, in any judicial and/or administrative procedure provided for the enforcement of obligations under this Directive.

3. Paragraphs 1 and 2 are without prejudice to national rules relating to time limits for bringing actions as regards the principle of equality of treatment.

Article 10 Burden of proof

1. Member States shall take such measures as are necessary, in accordance with their national judicial systems, to ensure that, when persons who consider themselves wronged because the principle of equal treatment has not been applied to them establish, before a court or other competent authority, facts from which it may be presumed that there has been direct or indirect discrimination, it shall be for the respondent to prove that there has been no breach of the principle of equal treatment.

2. Paragraph 1 shall not prevent Member States from introducing rules of evidence which are more favourable to plaintiffs.

3. Paragraph 1 shall not apply to criminal procedures.

4. Paragraphs 1, 2 and 3 shall also apply to any legal proceedings commenced in accordance with Article 9(2).

5.   Member States need not apply paragraph 1 to proceedings in which it is for the court or competent body to investigate the facts of the case.

Article 11 Victimisation
Member States shall introduce into their national legal systems such measures as are necessary to protect employees against dismissal or other adverse treatment by the employer as a reaction to a complaint within the undertaking or to any legal proceedings aimed at enforcing compliance with the principle of equal treatment.

Article 12 Dissemination of information
Member States shall take care that the provisions adopted pursuant to this Directive, together with the relevant provisions already in force in this field, are brought to the attention of the persons concerned by all appropriate means, for example at the workplace, throughout their territory.

Article 13 Social dialogue
1.   Member States shall, in accordance with their national traditions and practice, take adequate measures to promote dialogue between the social partners with a view to fostering equal treatment, including through the monitoring of workplace practices, collective agreements, codes of conduct and through research or exchange of experiences and good practices.

2.   Where consistent with their national traditions and practice, Member States shall encourage the social partners, without prejudice to their autonomy, to conclude at the appropriate level agreements laying down anti-discrimination rules in the fields referred to in Article 3 which fall within the scope of collective bargaining. These agreements shall respect the minimum requirements laid down by this Directive and by the relevant national implementing measures.

Article 14 Dialogue with non-governmental organisations
Member States shall encourage dialogue with appropriate non-governmental organisations which have, in accordance with their national law and practice, a legitimate interest in contributing to the fight against discrimination on any of the grounds referred to in Article 1 with a view to promoting the principle of equal treatment.

Chapter III PARTICULAR PROVISIONS

Article 15 Northern Ireland
1.   In order to tackle the under-representation of one of the major religious communities in the police service of Northern Ireland, differences in treatment regarding recruitment into that service, including its support staff, shall not constitute discrimination insofar as those differences in treatment are expressly authorised by national legislation.

2.   In order to maintain a balance of opportunity in employment for teachers in Northern Ireland while furthering the reconciliation of historical divisions between the major religious communities there, the provisions on religion or belief in this Directive shall not apply to the recruitment of teachers in schools in Northern Ireland in so far as this is expressly authorised by national legislation.

Chapter IV FINAL PROVISIONS

Article 16 Compliance
Member States shall take the necessary measures to ensure that:
(a)   any laws, regulations and administrative provisions contrary to the principle of equal treatment are abolished;

(b)   any provisions contrary to the principle of equal treatment which are included in contracts or collective agreements, internal rules of undertakings or rules governing the independent occupations and professions and workers' and employers' organisations are, or may be, declared null and void or are amended.

Article 17 Sanctions

Member States shall lay down the rules on sanctions applicable to infringements of the national provisions adopted pursuant to this Directive and shall take all measures necessary to ensure that they are applied. The sanctions, which may comprise the payment of compensation to the victim, must be effective, proportionate and dissuasive. Member States shall notify those provisions to the Commission by 2 December 2003 at the latest and shall notify it without delay of any subsequent amendment affecting them.

Article 18 Implementation

Member States shall adopt the laws, regulations and administrative provisions necessary to comply with this Directive by 2 December 2003 at the latest or may entrust the social partners, at their joint request, with the implementation of this Directive as regards provisions concerning collective agreements. In such cases, Member States shall ensure that, no later than 2 December 2003, the social partners introduce the necessary measures by agreement, the Member States concerned being required to take any necessary measures to enable them at any time to be in a position to guarantee the results imposed by this Directive. They shall forthwith inform the Commission thereof.

In order to take account of particular conditions, Member States may, if necessary, have an additional period of 3 years from 2 December 2003, that is to say a total of 6 years, to implement the provisions of this Directive on age and disability discrimination. In that event they shall inform the Commission forthwith. Any Member State which chooses to use this additional period shall report annually to the Commission on the steps it is taking to tackle age and disability discrimination and on the progress it is making towards implementation. The Commission shall report annually to the Council.

When Member States adopt these measures, they shall contain a reference to this Directive or be accompanied by such reference on the occasion of their official publication. The methods of making such reference shall be laid down by Member States.

Article 19 Report

1.   Member States shall communicate to the Commission, by 2 December 2005 at the latest and every five years thereafter, all the information necessary for the Commission to draw up a report to the European Parliament and the Council on the application of this Directive.

2.   The Commission's report shall take into account, as appropriate, the viewpoints of the social partners and relevant non-governmental organisations. In accordance with the principle of gender mainstreaming, this report shall, inter alia, provide an assessment of the impact of the measures taken on women and men. In the light of the information received, this report shall include, if necessary, proposals to revise and update this Directive.

Article 20 Entry into force

This Directive shall enter into force on the day of its publication in the *Official Journal of the European Communities*.

Article 21 Addressees
This Directive is addressed to the Member States.

(date of signing and signatory omitted)

Council Directive 2004/113/EC of 13 December 2004

implementing the principle of equal treatment between men and women in the access to and supply of goods and services

OJ L 373, 21.12.2004, p. 37[1]

(footnotes and preamble omitted)

Chapter I GENERAL PROVISIONS

Article 1 Purpose
The purpose of this Directive is to lay down a framework for combating discrimination based on sex in access to and supply of goods and services, with a view to putting into effect in the Member States the principle of equal treatment between men and women.

Article 2 Definitions
For the purposes of this Directive, the following definitions shall apply:

(a)   direct discrimination: where one person is treated less favourably, on grounds of sex, than another is, has been or would be treated in a comparable situation;

(b)   indirect discrimination: where an apparently neutral provision, criterion or practice would put persons of one sex at a particular disadvantage compared with persons of the other sex, unless that provision, criterion or practice is objectively justified by a legitimate aim and the means of achieving that aim are appropriate and necessary;

(c)   harassment: where an unwanted conduct related to the sex of a person occurs with the purpose or effect of violating the dignity of a person and of creating an intimidating, hostile, degrading, humiliating or offensive environment;

(d)   sexual harassment: where any form of unwanted physical, verbal, non-verbal or physical conduct of a sexual nature occurs, with the purpose or effect of violating the dignity of a person, in particular when creating an intimidating, hostile, degrading, humiliating or offensive environment.

Article 3 Scope
1.   Within the limits of the powers conferred upon the Community, this Directive shall apply to all persons who provide goods and services, which are available to the public irrespective of the person concerned as regards both the public and private sectors, including public bodies, and which are offered outside the area of private and family life and the transactions carried out in this context.

2.   This Directive does not prejudice the individual's freedom to choose a contractual partner as long as an individual's choice of contractual partner is not based on that person's sex.

---

[1]   EDITOR'S NOTE: As of 1 June 2010 this Directive has not been amended following the adoption of the Treaty of Lisbon. It includes references to the old Treaty article numbers. Reference should be made to the Tables of Equivalences accompanying the consolidated Treaties in Part II of this edition for the conversion of old Treaty article numbers to new ones.

3.   This Directive shall not apply to the content of media and advertising nor to education.

4.   This Directive shall not apply to matters of employment and occupation. This Directive shall not apply to matters of selfemployment, insofar as these matters are covered by other Community legislative acts.

Article 4 Principle of equal treatment

1.   For the purposes of this Directive, the principle of equal treatment between men and women shall mean that
     (a) there shall be no direct discrimination based on sex, including less favourable treatment of women for reasons of pregnancy and maternity;
     (b) there shall be no indirect discrimination based on sex.

2.   This Directive shall be without prejudice to more favourable provisions concerning the protection of women as regards pregnancy and maternity.

3.   Harassment and sexual harassment within the meaning of this Directive shall be deemed to be discrimination on the grounds of sex and therefore prohibited. A person's rejection of, or submission to, such conduct may not be used as a basis for a decision affecting that person.

4.   Instruction to direct or indirect discrimination on the grounds of sex shall be deemed to be discrimination within the meaning of this Directive.

5.   This Directive shall not preclude differences in treatment, if the provision of the goods and services exclusively or primarily to members of one sex is justified by a legitimate aim and the means of achieving that aim are appropriate and necessary.

Article 5 Actuarial factors

1.   Member States shall ensure that in all new contracts concluded after 21 December 2007 at the latest, the use of sex as a factor in the calculation of premiums and benefits for the purposes of insurance and related financial services shall not result in differences in individuals' premiums and benefits.

2.   Notwithstanding paragraph 1, Member States may decide before 21 December 2007 to permit proportionate differences in individuals' premiums and benefits where the use of sex is a determining factor in the assessment of risk based on relevant and accurate actuarial and statistical data. The Member States concerned shall inform the Commission and ensure that accurate data relevant to the use of sex as a determining actuarial factor are compiled, published and regularly updated. These Member States shall review their decision five years after 21 December 2007, taking into account the Commission report referred to in Article 16, and shall forward the results of this review to the Commission.

3.   In any event, costs related to pregnancy and maternity shall not result in differences in individuals' premiums and benefits. Member States may defer implementation of the measures necessary to comply with this paragraph until two years after 21 December 2007 at the latest. In that case the Member States concerned shall immediately inform the Commission.

Article 6 Positive action

With a view to ensuring full equality in practice between men and women, the principle of equal treatment shall not prevent any Member State from maintaining or adopting specific measures to prevent or compensate for disadvantages linked to sex.

Article 7 Minimum requirements

1.   Member States may introduce or maintain provisions which are more favourable to the protection of the principle of equal treatment between men and women than those laid down in this Directive.

2.   The implementation of this Directive shall in no circumstances constitute grounds for a reduction in the level of protection against discrimination already afforded by Member States in the fields covered by this Directive.

Chapter II REMEDIES AND ENFORCEMENT

Article 8 Defence of rights

1.   Member States shall ensure that judicial and/or administrative procedures, including where they deem it appropriate conciliation procedures, for the enforcement of the obligations under this Directive are available to all persons who consider themselves wronged by failure to apply the principle of equal treatment to them, even after the relationship in which the discrimination is alleged to have occurred has ended.

2.   Member States shall introduce into their national legal systems such measures as are necessary to ensure real and effective compensation or reparation, as the Member States so determine, for the loss and damage sustained by a person injured as a result of discrimination within the meaning of this Directive, in a way which is dissuasive and proportionate to the damage suffered. The fixing of a prior upper limit shall not restrict such compensation or reparation.

3.   Member States shall ensure that associations, organisations or other legal entities, which have, in accordance with the criteria laid down by their national law, a legitimate interest in ensuring that the provisions of this Directive are complied with, may engage, on behalf or in support of the complainant, with his or her approval, in any judicial and/or administrative procedure provided for the enforcement of obligations under this Directive.

4.   Paragraphs 1 and 3 shall be without prejudice to national rules on time limits for bringing actions relating to the principle of equal treatment.

Article 9 Burden of proof

1.   Member States shall take such measures as are necessary, in accordance with their national judicial systems, to ensure that, when persons who consider themselves wronged because the principle of equal treatment has not been applied to them establish, before a court or other competent authority, facts from which it may be presumed that there has been direct or indirect discrimination, it shall be for the respondent to prove that there has been no breach of the principle of equal treatment.

2.   Paragraph 1 shall not prevent Member States from introducing rules of evidence, which are more favourable to plaintiffs.

3.   Paragraph 1 shall not apply to criminal procedures.

4.   Paragraphs 1, 2 and 3 shall also apply to any proceedings brought in accordance with Article 8(3).

5.   Member States need not apply paragraph 1 to proceedings in which it is for the court or other competent authority to investigate the facts of the case.

Article 10 Victimisation

Member States shall introduce into their national legal systems such measures as are necessary to protect persons from any adverse treatment or adverse consequence as a reaction to a complaint or to legal proceedings aimed at enforcing compliance with the principle of equal treatment.

Article 11 Dialogue with relevant stakeholders

With a view to promoting the principle of equal treatment, Member States shall encourage dialogue with relevant stakeholders which have, in accordance with national law and practice, a legitimate interest in contributing to the fight against discrimination on grounds of sex in the area of access to and supply of goods and services.

Chapter III BODIES FOR THE PROMOTION OF EQUAL TREATMENT

Article 12

1. Member States shall designate and make the necessary arrangements for a body or bodies for the promotion, analysis, monitoring and support of equal treatment of all persons without discrimination on the grounds of sex. These bodies may form part of agencies charged at national level with the defence of human rights or the safeguard of individuals' rights, or the implementation of the principle of equal treatment.

2. Member States shall ensure that the competencies of the bodies referred to in paragraph 1 include:

    (a) without prejudice to the rights of victims and of associations, organisations or other legal entities referred to in Article 8(3), providing independent assistance to victims of discrimination in pursuing their complaints about discrimination;

    (b) conducting independent surveys concerning discrimination;

    (c) publishing independent reports and making recommendations on any issue relating to such discrimination.

Chapter IV FINAL PROVISIONS

Article 13 Compliance

Member States shall take the necessary measures to ensure that the principle of equal treatment is respected in relation to the access to and supply of goods and services within the scope of this Directive, and in particular that:

(a) any laws, regulations and administrative provisions contrary to the principle of equal treatment are abolished;

(b) any contractual provisions, internal rules of undertakings, and rules governing profit-making or non-profit-making associations contrary to the principle of equal treatment are, or may be, declared null and void or are amended.

Article 14 Penalties

Member States shall lay down the rules on penalties applicable to infringements of the national provisions adopted pursuant to this Directive and shall take all measures necessary to ensure that they are applied. The penalties, which may comprise the payment of compensation to the victim, shall be effective, proportionate and dissuasive. Member States shall notify those provisions to the Commission by 21 December 2007 at the latest and shall notify it without delay of any subsequent amendment affecting them.

Article 15 Dissemination of information

Member States shall take care that the provisions adopted pursuant to this Directive, together with the relevant provisions already in force, are brought to the attention of the persons concerned by all appropriate means throughout their territory.

Article 16 Reports

1.   Member States shall communicate all available information concerning the application of this Directive to the Commission, by 21 December 2009, and every five years thereafter.

The Commission shall draw up a summary report, which shall include a review of the current practices of Member States in relation to Article 5 with regard to the use of sex as a factor in the calculation of premiums and benefits. It shall submit this report to the European Parliament and to the Council no later 21 December 2010. Where appropriate, the Commission shall accompany its report with proposals to modify the Directive.

2.   The Commission's report shall take into account the viewpoints of relevant stakeholders.

Article 17 Transposition

1.   Member States shall bring into force the laws, regulations and administrative provisions necessary to comply with this Directive by 21 December 2007 at the latest. They shall forthwith communicate to the Commission the text of those provisions.

When Member States adopt these measures, they shall contain a reference to this Directive or be accompanied by such a reference on the occasion of their official publication. The methods of making such publication of reference shall be laid down by the Member States.

2.   Member States shall communicate to the Commission the text of the main provisions of national law which they adopt in the field covered by this Directive.

Article 18 Entry into force

This Directive shall enter into force on the day of its publication in the *Official Journal of the European Union*.

Article 19 Addressees

This Directive is addressed to the Member States.

(Date of signing and signatory omitted).

DIRECTIVE 2006/54/EC OF THE EUROPEAN PARLIAMENT AND OF THE COUNCIL OF 5 JULY 2006

on the implementation of the principle of equal opportunities and equal treatment of men and women in matters of employment and occupation (recast)[1]

OJ L 204, 26.7.2006, p. 23[2]

....

THE EUROPEAN PARLIAMENT AND THE COUNCIL OF THE EUROPEAN UNION,

Having regard to the Treaty establishing the European Community, and in particular Article 141(3) thereof,

Having regard to the proposal from the Commission,

....

[1]   EDITOR'S NOTE: Directive 2006/54 repeals and replaces the following directives on gender equality: Directives 75/117/EEC; 76/207/EEC; 86/378/EEC; and 97/80/EC, with effect from 15 August 2009. See the Correlation Table in Annex II below to convert article numbers from the previous directives.

[2]   EDITOR'S NOTE: As of 1 June 2010 this Directive has not been amended following the adoption of the Treaty of Lisbon. It includes references to the old Treaty article numbers. Reference should be made to the Tables of Equivalences accompanying the consolidated Treaties in Part II of this edition for the conversion of old Treaty article numbers to new ones.

Having regard to the opinion of the European Economic and Social Committee [1],

Acting in accordance with the procedure laid down in Article 251 of the Treaty [2],

Whereas:

(1)   Council Directive 76/207/EEC of 9 February 1976 on the implementation of the principle of equal treatment for men and women as regards access to employment, vocational training and promotion, and working conditions [3] and Council Directive 86/378/EEC of 24 July 1986 on the implementation of the principle of equal treatment for men and women in occupational social security schemes [4] have been significantly amended [5]. Council Directive 75/117/EEC of 10 February 1975 on the approximation of the laws of the Member States relating to the application of the principle of equal pay for men and women [6] and Council Directive 97/80/EC of 15 December 1997 on the burden of proof in cases of discrimination based on sex [7] also contain provisions which have as their purpose the implementation of the principle of equal treatment between men and women. Now that new amendments are being made to the said Directives, it is desirable, for reasons of clarity, that the provisions in question should be recast by bringing together in a single text the main provisions existing in this field as well as certain developments arising out of the case-law of the Court of Justice of the European Communities (hereinafter referred to as the Court of Justice).

(2)   Equality between men and women is a fundamental principle of Community law under Article 2 and Article 3(2) of the Treaty and the case-law of the Court of Justice. Those Treaty provisions proclaim equality between men and women as a "task" and an "aim" of the Community and impose a positive obligation to promote it in all its activities.

(3)   The Court of Justice has held that the scope of the principle of equal treatment for men and women cannot be confined to the prohibition of discrimination based on the fact that a person is of one or other sex. In view of its purpose and the nature of the rights which it seeks to safeguard, it also applies to discrimination arising from the gender reassignment of a person.

(4)   Article 141(3) of the Treaty now provides a specific legal basis for the adoption of Community measures to ensure the application of the principle of equal opportunities and equal treatment in matters of employment and occupation, including the principle of equal pay for equal work or work of equal value.

(5)   Articles 21 and 23 of the Charter of Fundamental Rights of the European Union also prohibit any discrimination on grounds of sex and enshrine the right to equal treatment between men and women in all areas, including employment, work and pay.

(6)   Harassment and sexual harassment are contrary to the principle of equal treatment between men and women and constitute discrimination on grounds of sex for the purposes of this Directive. These forms of discrimination occur not only in the workplace, but also in the context of access to employment, vocational training and promotion. They should therefore be prohibited and should be subject to effective, proportionate and dissuasive penalties.

(7)   In this context, employers and those responsible for vocational training should be encouraged to take measures to combat all forms of discrimination on grounds of sex and, in particular, to take preventive measures against harassment and sexual harassment in the workplace and in access to employment, vocational training and promotion, in accordance with national law and practice.

(8)   The principle of equal pay for equal work or work of equal value as laid down by Article 141 of the Treaty and consistently upheld in the case-law of the Court of Justice constitutes an important aspect of the principle of equal treatment between men and women and an essential and indispensable part of the *acquis communautaire*, including the case-law of the Court concerning sex discrimination. It is therefore appropriate to make further provision for its implementation.

(9)   In accordance with settled case-law of the Court of Justice, in order to assess whether workers are performing the same work or work of equal value, it should be determined whether, having regard to a range of factors including the nature of the work and training and working conditions, those workers may be considered to be in a comparable situation.

(10) The Court of Justice has established that, in certain circumstances, the principle of equal pay is not limited to situations in which men and women work for the same employer.

(11) The Member States, in collaboration with the social partners, should continue to address the problem of the continuing gender-based wage differentials and marked gender segregation on the labour market by means such as flexible working time arrangements which enable both men and women to combine family and work commitments more successfully. This could also include appropriate parental leave arrangements which could be taken up by either parent as well as the provision of accessible and affordable child-care facilities and care for dependent persons.

(12) Specific measures should be adopted to ensure the implementation of the principle of equal treatment in occupational social security schemes and to define its scope more clearly.

(13) In its judgment of 17 May 1990 in Case C-262/88 [8], the Court of Justice determined that all forms of occupational pension constitute an element of pay within the meaning of Article 141 of the Treaty.

(14) Although the concept of pay within the meaning of Article 141 of the Treaty does not encompass social security benefits, it is now clearly established that a pension scheme for public servants falls within the scope of the principle of equal pay if the benefits payable under the scheme are paid to the worker by reason of his/her employment relationship with the public employer, notwithstanding the fact that such scheme forms part of a general statutory scheme. According to the judgments of the Court of Justice in Cases C-7/93 [9] and C-351/00 [10], that condition will be satisfied if the pension scheme concerns a particular category of workers and its benefits are directly related to the period of service and calculated by reference to the public servant's final salary. For reasons of clarity, it is therefore appropriate to make specific provision to that effect.

(15) The Court of Justice has confirmed that whilst the contributions of male and female workers to a defined-benefit pension scheme are covered by Article 141 of the Treaty, any inequality in employers' contributions paid under funded defined-benefit schemes which is due to the use of actuarial factors differing according to sex is not to be assessed in the light of that same provision.

(16) By way of example, in the case of funded defined-benefit schemes, certain elements, such as conversion into a capital sum of part of a periodic pension, transfer of pension rights, a reversionary pension payable to a dependant in return for the surrender of part of a pension or a reduced pension where the worker opts to take earlier retirement, may be unequal where the inequality of the amounts results from the effects of the use of actuarial factors differing according to sex at the time when the scheme's funding is implemented.

(17) It is well established that benefits payable under occupational social security schemes are not to be considered as remuneration insofar as they are attributable to periods of employment prior to 17 May 1990, except in the case of workers or those claiming under them who initiated legal proceedings or brought an equivalent claim under the applicable national law before that date. It is therefore necessary to limit the implementation of the principle of equal treatment accordingly.

(18) The Court of Justice has consistently held that the Barber Protocol [11] does not affect the right to join an occupational pension scheme and that the limitation of the effects in time of the judgment in Case C-262/88 does not apply to the right to join an occupational pension scheme. The Court of Justice also ruled that the national rules relating to time limits for bringing actions under national law may be relied on against workers who assert their right to join an occupational pension scheme, provided that they are not less favourable for that type of action than for similar actions of a domestic nature and that they do not render the exercise of rights conferred by Community law impossible in practice. The Court of Justice has also pointed out that the fact that a worker can claim retroactively to join an occupational pension scheme does not allow the worker to avoid paying the contributions relating to the period of membership concerned.

(19) Ensuring equal access to employment and the vocational training leading thereto is fundamental to the application of the principle of equal treatment of men and women in matters of employment and occupation. Any exception to this principle should therefore be limited to those occupational activities which necessitate the employment of a person of a particular sex by reason of their nature or the context in which they are carried out, provided that the objective sought is legitimate and complies with the principle of proportionality.

(20) This Directive does not prejudice freedom of association, including the right to establish unions with others and to join unions to defend one's interests. Measures within the meaning of Article 141(4) of the Treaty may include membership or the continuation of the activity of organisations or unions whose main objective is the promotion, in practice, of the principle of equal treatment between men and women.

(21) The prohibition of discrimination should be without prejudice to the maintenance or adoption of measures intended to prevent or compensate for disadvantages suffered by a group of persons of one sex. Such measures permit organisations of persons of one sex where their main object is the promotion of the special needs of those persons and the promotion of equality between men and women.

(22) In accordance with Article 141(4) of the Treaty, with a view to ensuring full equality in practice between men and women in working life, the principle of equal treatment does not prevent Member States from maintaining or adopting measures providing for specific advantages in order to make it easier for the under-represented sex to pursue a vocational activity or to prevent or compensate for disadvantages in professional careers. Given the current situation and bearing in mind Declaration No 28 to the Amsterdam Treaty, Member States should, in the first instance, aim at improving the situation of women in working life.

(23) It is clear from the case-law of the Court of Justice that unfavourable treatment of a woman related to pregnancy or maternity constitutes direct discrimination on grounds of sex. Such treatment should therefore be expressly covered by this Directive.

(24) The Court of Justice has consistently recognised the legitimacy, as regards the principle of equal treatment, of protecting a woman's biological condition during pregnancy and maternity and of introducing maternity protection measures as a means to achieve

substantive equality. This Directive should therefore be without prejudice to Council Directive 92/85/EEC of 19 October 1992 on the introduction of measures to encourage improvements in the safety and health at work of pregnant workers and workers who have recently given birth or are breastfeeding [12]. This Directive should further be without prejudice to Council Directive 96/34/EC of 3 June 1996 on the framework agreement on parental leave concluded by UNICE, CEEP and the ETUC [13].

(25) For reasons of clarity, it is also appropriate to make express provision for the protection of the employment rights of women on maternity leave and in particular their right to return to the same or an equivalent post, to suffer no detriment in their terms and conditions as a result of taking such leave and to benefit from any improvement in working conditions to which they would have been entitled during their absence.

(26) In the Resolution of the Council and of the Ministers for Employment and Social Policy, meeting within the Council, of 29 June 2000 on the balanced participation of women and men in family and working life [14], Member States were encouraged to consider examining the scope for their respective legal systems to grant working men an individual and non-transferable right to paternity leave, while maintaining their rights relating to employment.

(27) Similar considerations apply to the granting by Member States to men and women of an individual and non-transferable right to leave subsequent to the adoption of a child. It is for the Member States to determine whether or not to grant such a right to paternity and/ or adoption leave and also to determine any conditions, other than dismissal and return to work, which are outside the scope of this Directive.

(28) The effective implementation of the principle of equal treatment requires appropriate procedures to be put in place by the Member States.

(29) The provision of adequate judicial or administrative procedures for the enforcement of the obligations imposed by this Directive is essential to the effective implementation of the principle of equal treatment.

(30) The adoption of rules on the burden of proof plays a significant role in ensuring that the principle of equal treatment can be effectively enforced. As the Court of Justice has held, provision should therefore be made to ensure that the burden of proof shifts to the respondent when there is a prima facie case of discrimination, except in relation to proceedings in which it is for the court or other competent national body to investigate the facts. It is however necessary to clarify that the appreciation of the facts from which it may be presumed that there has been direct or indirect discrimination remains a matter for the relevant national body in accordance with national law or practice. Further, it is for the Member States to introduce, at any appropriate stage of the proceedings, rules of evidence which are more favourable to plaintiffs.

(31) With a view to further improving the level of protection offered by this Directive, associations, organisations and other legal entities should also be empowered to engage in proceedings, as the Member States so determine, either on behalf or in support of a complainant, without prejudice to national rules of procedure concerning representation and defence.

(32) Having regard to the fundamental nature of the right to effective legal protection, it is appropriate to ensure that workers continue to enjoy such protection even after the relationship giving rise to an alleged breach of the principle of equal treatment has ended. An employee defending or giving evidence on behalf of a person protected under this Directive should be entitled to the same protection.

(33) It has been clearly established by the Court of Justice that in order to be effective, the principle of equal treatment implies that the compensation awarded for any breach must be adequate in relation to the damage sustained. It is therefore appropriate to exclude the fixing of any prior upper limit for such compensation, except where the employer can prove that the only damage suffered by an applicant as a result of discrimination within the meaning of this Directive was the refusal to take his/her job application into consideration.

(34) In order to enhance the effective implementation of the principle of equal treatment, Member States should promote dialogue between the social partners and, within the framework of national practice, with non-governmental organisations.

(35) Member States should provide for effective, proportionate and dissuasive penalties for breaches of the obligations under this Directive.

(36) Since the objectives of this Directive cannot be sufficiently achieved by the Member States and can therefore be better achieved at Community level, the Community may adopt measures in accordance with the principle of subsidiarity as set out in Article 5 of the Treaty. In accordance with the principle of proportionality, as set out in that Article, this Directive does not go beyond what is necessary in order to achieve those objectives.

(37) For the sake of a better understanding of the different treatment of men and women in matters of employment and occupation, comparable statistics disaggregated by sex should continue to be developed, analysed and made available at the appropriate levels.

(38) Equal treatment of men and women in matters of employment and occupation cannot be restricted to legislative measures. Instead, the European Union and the Member States should continue to promote the raising of public awareness of wage discrimination and the changing of public attitudes, involving all parties concerned at public and private level to the greatest possible extent. The dialogue between the social partners could play an important role in this process.

(39) The obligation to transpose this Directive into national law should be confined to those provisions which represent a substantive change as compared with the earlier Directives. The obligation to transpose the provisions which are substantially unchanged arises under the earlier Directives.

(40) This Directive should be without prejudice to the obligations of the Member States relating to the time limits for transposition into national law and application of the Directives set out in Annex I, Part B.

(41) In accordance with paragraph 34 of the Interinstitutional agreement on better law-making [15], Member States are encouraged to draw up, for themselves and in the interest of the Community, their own tables, which will, as far as possible, illustrate the correlation between this Directive and the transposition measures and to make them public,

HAVE ADOPTED THIS DIRECTIVE:

TITLE I
GENERAL PROVISIONS

Article 1 Purpose
The purpose of this Directive is to ensure the implementation of the principle of equal opportunities and equal treatment of men and women in matters of employment and occupation.

To that end, it contains provisions to implement the principle of equal treatment in relation to:

(a)   access to employment, including promotion, and to vocational training;

(b)   working conditions, including pay;

(c)   occupational social security schemes.

It also contains provisions to ensure that such implementation is made more effective by the establishment of appropriate procedures.

Article 2 Definitions
1.   For the purposes of this Directive, the following definitions shall apply:
   (a) "direct discrimination": where one person is treated less favourably on grounds of sex than another is, has been or would be treated in a comparable situation;
   (b) "indirect discrimination": where an apparently neutral provision, criterion or practice would put persons of one sex at a particular disadvantage compared with persons of the other sex, unless that provision, criterion or practice is objectively justified by a legitimate aim, and the means of achieving that aim are appropriate and necessary;
   (c) "harassment": where unwanted conduct related to the sex of a person occurs with the purpose or effect of violating the dignity of a person, and of creating an intimidating, hostile, degrading, humiliating or offensive environment;
   (d) "sexual harassment": where any form of unwanted verbal, non-verbal or physical conduct of a sexual nature occurs, with the purpose or effect of violating the dignity of a person, in particular when creating an intimidating, hostile, degrading, humiliating or offensive environment;
   (e) "pay": the ordinary basic or minimum wage or salary and any other consideration, whether in cash or in kind, which the worker receives directly or indirectly, in respect of his/her employment from his/her employer;
   (f) "occupational social security schemes": schemes not governed by Council Directive 79/7/EEC of 19 December 1978 on the progressive implementation of the principle of equal treatment for men and women in matters of social security [16] whose purpose is to provide workers, whether employees or self-employed, in an undertaking or group of undertakings, area of economic activity, occupational sector or group of sectors with benefits intended to supplement the benefits provided by statutory social security schemes or to replace them, whether membership of such schemes is compulsory or optional.

2.   For the purposes of this Directive, discrimination includes:
   (a) harassment and sexual harassment, as well as any less favourable treatment based on a person's rejection of or submission to such conduct;
   (b) instruction to discriminate against persons on grounds of sex;
   (c) any less favourable treatment of a woman related to pregnancy or maternity leave within the meaning of Directive 92/85/EEC.

Article 3 Positive action
Member States may maintain or adopt measures within the meaning of Article 141(4) of the Treaty with a view to ensuring full equality in practice between men and women in working life.

TITLE II
SPECIFIC PROVISIONS

Chapter 1 EQUAL PAY

Article 4 Prohibition of discrimination
For the same work or for work to which equal value is attributed, direct and indirect discrimination on grounds of sex with regard to all aspects and conditions of remuneration shall be eliminated.

In particular, where a job classification system is used for determining pay, it shall be based on the same criteria for both men and women and so drawn up as to exclude any discrimination on grounds of sex.

Chapter 2 EQUAL TREATMENT IN OCCUPATIONAL SOCIAL SECURITY SCHEMES

Article 5 Prohibition of discrimination

Without prejudice to Article 4, there shall be no direct or indirect discrimination on grounds of sex in occupational social security schemes, in particular as regards:

(a)   the scope of such schemes and the conditions of access to them;

(b)   the obligation to contribute and the calculation of contributions;

(c)   the calculation of benefits, including supplementary benefits due in respect of a spouse or dependants, and the conditions governing the duration and retention of entitlement to benefits.

Article 6 Personal scope

This Chapter shall apply to members of the working population, including self-employed persons, persons whose activity is interrupted by illness, maternity, accident or involuntary unemployment and persons seeking employment and to retired and disabled workers, and to those claiming under them, in accordance with national law and/or practice.

Article 7 Material scope

1.   This Chapter applies to:
   (a)   occupational social security schemes which provide protection against the following risks:
      (i)   sickness,
      (ii)   invalidity,
      (iii)   old age, including early retirement,
      (iv)   industrial accidents and occupational diseases,
      (v)   unemployment;
   (b)   occupational social security schemes which provide for other social benefits, in cash or in kind, and in particular survivors' benefits and family allowances, if such benefits constitute a consideration paid by the employer to the worker by reason of the latter's employment.

2.   This Chapter also applies to pension schemes for a particular category of worker such as that of public servants if the benefits payable under the scheme are paid by reason of the employment relationship with the public employer. The fact that such a scheme forms part of a general statutory scheme shall be without prejudice in that respect.

Article 8 Exclusions from the material scope

1.   This Chapter does not apply to:
   (a)   individual contracts for self-employed persons;
   (b)   single-member schemes for self-employed persons;
   (c)   insurance contracts to which the employer is not a party, in the case of workers;
   (d)   optional provisions of occupational social security schemes offered to participants individually to guarantee them:
      (i)   either additional benefits,
      (ii)   or a choice of date on which the normal benefits for self-employed persons will start, or a choice between several benefits;
   (e)   occupational social security schemes in so far as benefits are financed by contributions paid by workers on a voluntary basis.

2.   This Chapter does not preclude an employer granting to persons who have already reached the retirement age for the purposes of granting a pension by virtue of an occupational social security scheme, but who have not yet reached the retirement age for the purposes of granting a statutory retirement pension, a pension supplement, the aim of which is to make equal or more nearly equal the overall amount of benefit paid to these persons in relation to the amount paid to persons of the other sex in the same situation who have already reached the statutory retirement age, until the persons benefiting from the supplement reach the statutory retirement age.

Article 9 Examples of discrimination
1.   Provisions contrary to the principle of equal treatment shall include those based on sex, either directly or indirectly, for:
 (a) determining the persons who may participate in an occupational social security scheme;
 (b) fixing the compulsory or optional nature of participation in an occupational social security scheme;
 (c) laying down different rules as regards the age of entry into the scheme or the minimum period of employment or membership of the scheme required to obtain the benefits thereof;
 (d) laying down different rules, except as provided for in points (h) and (j), for the reimbursement of contributions when a worker leaves a scheme without having fulfilled the conditions guaranteeing a deferred right to long-term benefits;
 (e) setting different conditions for the granting of benefits or restricting such benefits to workers of one or other of the sexes;
 (f) fixing different retirement ages;
 (g) suspending the retention or acquisition of rights during periods of maternity leave or leave for family reasons which are granted by law or agreement and are paid by the employer;
 (h) setting different levels of benefit, except in so far as may be necessary to take account of actuarial calculation factors which differ according to sex in the case of defined-contribution schemes; in the case of funded defined-benefit schemes, certain elements may be unequal where the inequality of the amounts results from the effects of the use of actuarial factors differing according to sex at the time when the scheme's funding is implemented;
 (i) setting different levels for workers' contributions;
 (j) setting different levels for employers' contributions, except:
   (i) in the case of defined-contribution schemes if the aim is to equalise the amount of the final benefits or to make them more nearly equal for both sexes,
   (ii) in the case of funded defined-benefit schemes where the employer's contributions are intended to ensure the adequacy of the funds necessary to cover the cost of the benefits defined;
 (k) laying down different standards or standards applicable only to workers of a specified sex, except as provided for in points (h) and (j), as regards the guarantee or retention of entitlement to deferred benefits when a worker leaves a scheme.

2.   Where the granting of benefits within the scope of this Chapter is left to the discretion of the scheme's management bodies, the latter shall comply with the principle of equal treatment.

Article 10 Implementation as regards self-employed persons
1.   Member States shall take the necessary steps to ensure that the provisions of occupational social security schemes for self-employed persons contrary to the principle of equal treatment are revised with effect from 1 January 1993 at the latest or for Member States

whose accession took place after that date, at the date that Directive 86/378/EEC became applicable in their territory.

2.   This Chapter shall not preclude rights and obligations relating to a period of membership of an occupational social security scheme for self-employed persons prior to revision of that scheme from remaining subject to the provisions of the scheme in force during that period.

Article 11 Possibility of deferral as regards self-employed persons

As regards occupational social security schemes for self-employed persons, Member States may defer compulsory application of the principle of equal treatment with regard to:

(a)   determination of pensionable age for the granting of old-age or retirement pensions, and the possible implications for other benefits:
   (i)   either until the date on which such equality is achieved in statutory schemes,
   (ii) or, at the latest, until such equality is prescribed by a directive;

(b)   survivors' pensions until Community law establishes the principle of equal treatment in statutory social security schemes in that regard;

(c)   the application of Article 9(1)(i) in relation to the use of actuarial calculation factors, until 1 January 1999 or for Member States whose accession took place after that date until the date that Directive 86/378/EEC became applicable in their territory.

Article 12 Retroactive effect

1.   Any measure implementing this Chapter, as regards workers, shall cover all benefits under occupational social security schemes derived from periods of employment subsequent to 17 May 1990 and shall apply retroactively to that date, without prejudice to workers or those claiming under them who have, before that date, initiated legal proceedings or raised an equivalent claim under national law. In that event, the implementation measures shall apply retroactively to 8 April 1976 and shall cover all the benefits derived from periods of employment after that date. For Member States which acceded to the Community after 8 April 1976, and before 17 May 1990, that date shall be replaced by the date on which Article 141 of the Treaty became applicable in their territory.

2.   The second sentence of paragraph 1 shall not prevent national rules relating to time limits for bringing actions under national law from being relied on against workers or those claiming under them who initiated legal proceedings or raised an equivalent claim under national law before 17 May 1990, provided that they are not less favourable for that type of action than for similar actions of a domestic nature and that they do not render the exercise of rights conferred by Community law impossible in practice.

3.   For Member States whose accession took place after 17 May 1990 and which were on 1 January 1994 Contracting Parties to the Agreement on the European Economic Area, the date of 17 May 1990 in the first sentence of paragraph 1 shall be replaced by 1 January 1994.

4.   For other Member States whose accession took place after 17 May 1990, the date of 17 May 1990 in paragraphs 1 and 2 shall be replaced by the date on which Article 141 of the Treaty became applicable in their territory.

Article 13 Flexible pensionable age

Where men and women may claim a flexible pensionable age under the same conditions, this shall not be deemed to be incompatible with this Chapter.

Chapter 3 EQUAL TREATMENT AS REGARDS ACCESS TO EMPLOYMENT, VOCATIONAL TRAINING AND PROMOTION AND WORKING CONDITIONS

Article 14 Prohibition of discrimination

1. There shall be no direct or indirect discrimination on grounds of sex in the public or private sectors, including public bodies, in relation to:

    (a) conditions for access to employment, to self-employment or to occupation, including selection criteria and recruitment conditions, whatever the branch of activity and at all levels of the professional hierarchy, including promotion;

    (b) access to all types and to all levels of vocational guidance, vocational training, advanced vocational training and retraining, including practical work experience;

    (c) employment and working conditions, including dismissals, as well as pay as provided for in Article 141 of the Treaty;

    (d) membership of, and involvement in, an organisation of workers or employers, or any organisation whose members carry on a particular profession, including the benefits provided for by such organisations.

2. Member States may provide, as regards access to employment including the training leading thereto, that a difference of treatment which is based on a characteristic related to sex shall not constitute discrimination where, by reason of the nature of the particular occupational activities concerned or of the context in which they are carried out, such a characteristic constitutes a genuine and determining occupational requirement, provided that its objective is legitimate and the requirement is proportionate.

Article 15 Return from maternity leave

A woman on maternity leave shall be entitled, after the end of her period of maternity leave, to return to her job or to an equivalent post on terms and conditions which are no less favourable to her and to benefit from any improvement in working conditions to which she would have been entitled during her absence.

Article 16 Paternity and adoption leave

This Directive is without prejudice to the right of Member States to recognise distinct rights to paternity and/or adoption leave. Those Member States which recognise such rights shall take the necessary measures to protect working men and women against dismissal due to exercising those rights and ensure that, at the end of such leave, they are entitled to return to their jobs or to equivalent posts on terms and conditions which are no less favourable to them, and to benefit from any improvement in working conditions to which they would have been entitled during their absence.

TITLE III
HORIZONTAL PROVISIONS

Chapter 1 REMEDIES AND ENFORCEMENT

SECTION 1 REMEDIES

Article 17 Defence of rights

1. Member States shall ensure that, after possible recourse to other competent authorities including where they deem it appropriate conciliation procedures, judicial procedures for the enforcement of obligations under this Directive are available to all persons who consider themselves wronged by failure to apply the principle of equal treatment to them, even after the relationship in which the discrimination is alleged to have occurred has ended.

2. Member States shall ensure that associations, organisations or other legal entities which have, in accordance with the criteria laid down by their national law, a legitimate interest

in ensuring that the provisions of this Directive are complied with, may engage, either on behalf or in support of the complainant, with his/her approval, in any judicial and/or administrative procedure provided for the enforcement of obligations under this Directive.

3.   Paragraphs 1 and 2 are without prejudice to national rules relating to time limits for bringing actions as regards the principle of equal treatment.

Article 18 Compensation or reparation

Member States shall introduce into their national legal systems such measures as are necessary to ensure real and effective compensation or reparation as the Member States so determine for the loss and damage sustained by a person injured as a result of discrimination on grounds of sex, in a way which is dissuasive and proportionate to the damage suffered. Such compensation or reparation may not be restricted by the fixing of a prior upper limit, except in cases where the employer can prove that the only damage suffered by an applicant as a result of discrimination within the meaning of this Directive is the refusal to take his/her job application into consideration.

SECTION 2 BURDEN OF PROOF

Article 19 Burden of proof

1.   Member States shall take such measures as are necessary, in accordance with their national judicial systems, to ensure that, when persons who consider themselves wronged because the principle of equal treatment has not been applied to them establish, before a court or other competent authority, facts from which it may be presumed that there has been direct or indirect discrimination, it shall be for the respondent to prove that there has been no breach of the principle of equal treatment.

2.   Paragraph 1 shall not prevent Member States from introducing rules of evidence which are more favourable to plaintiffs.

3.   Member States need not apply paragraph 1 to proceedings in which it is for the court or competent body to investigate the facts of the case.

4.   Paragraphs 1, 2 and 3 shall also apply to:
    (a) the situations covered by Article 141 of the Treaty and, insofar as discrimination based on sex is concerned, by Directives 92/85/EEC and 96/34/EC;
    (b) any civil or administrative procedure concerning the public or private sector which provides for means of redress under national law pursuant to the measures referred to in (a) with the exception of out-of-court procedures of a voluntary nature or provided for in national law.

5.   This Article shall not apply to criminal procedures, unless otherwise provided by the Member States.

Chapter 2 PROMOTION OF EQUAL TREATMENT—DIALOGUE

Article 20 Equality bodies

1.   Member States shall designate and make the necessary arrangements for a body or bodies for the promotion, analysis, monitoring and support of equal treatment of all persons without discrimination on grounds of sex. These bodies may form part of agencies with responsibility at national level for the defence of human rights or the safeguard of individuals' rights.

2.   Member States shall ensure that the competences of these bodies include:
    (a) without prejudice to the right of victims and of associations, organisations or other legal entities referred to in Article 17(2), providing independent assistance to victims of discrimination in pursuing their complaints about discrimination;

    (b) conducting independent surveys concerning discrimination;

    (c) publishing independent reports and making recommendations on any issue relating to such discrimination;

    (d) at the appropriate level exchanging available information with corresponding European bodies such as any future European Institute for Gender Equality.

Article 21 Social dialogue

1.   Member States shall, in accordance with national traditions and practice, take adequate measures to promote social dialogue between the social partners with a view to fostering equal treatment, including, for example, through the monitoring of practices in the workplace, in access to employment, vocational training and promotion, as well as through the monitoring of collective agreements, codes of conduct, research or exchange of experience and good practice.

2.   Where consistent with national traditions and practice, Member States shall encourage the social partners, without prejudice to their autonomy, to promote equality between men and women, and flexible working arrangements, with the aim of facilitating the reconciliation of work and private life, and to conclude, at the appropriate level, agreements laying down anti-discrimination rules in the fields referred to in Article 1 which fall within the scope of collective bargaining. These agreements shall respect the provisions of this Directive and the relevant national implementing measures.

3.   Member States shall, in accordance with national law, collective agreements or practice, encourage employers to promote equal treatment for men and women in a planned and systematic way in the workplace, in access to employment, vocational training and promotion.

4.   To this end, employers shall be encouraged to provide at appropriate regular intervals employees and/or their representatives with appropriate information on equal treatment for men and women in the undertaking.

    Such information may include an overview of the proportions of men and women at different levels of the organisation; their pay and pay differentials; and possible measures to improve the situation in cooperation with employees' representatives.

Article 22 Dialogue with non-governmental organisations

Member States shall encourage dialogue with appropriate non-governmental organisations which have, in accordance with their national law and practice, a legitimate interest in contributing to the fight against discrimination on grounds of sex with a view to promoting the principle of equal treatment.

Chapter 3 GENERAL HORIZONTAL PROVISIONS

Article 23 Compliance

Member States shall take all necessary measures to ensure that:

(a) any laws, regulations and administrative provisions contrary to the principle of equal treatment are abolished;

(b) provisions contrary to the principle of equal treatment in individual or collective contracts or agreements, internal rules of undertakings or rules governing the independent occupations and professions and workers' and employers' organisations or any other arrangements shall be, or may be, declared null and void or are amended;

(c) occupational social security schemes containing such provisions may not be approved or extended by administrative measures.

Article 24 Victimisation

Member States shall introduce into their national legal systems such measures as are necessary to protect employees, including those who are employees' representatives provided for by national laws and/or practices, against dismissal or other adverse treatment by the employer as a reaction to a complaint within the undertaking or to any legal proceedings aimed at enforcing compliance with the principle of equal treatment.

Article 25 Penalties

Member States shall lay down the rules on penalties applicable to infringements of the national provisions adopted pursuant to this Directive, and shall take all measures necessary to ensure that they are applied. The penalties, which may comprise the payment of compensation to the victim, must be effective, proportionate and dissuasive. The Member States shall notify those provisions to the Commission by 5 October 2005 at the latest and shall notify it without delay of any subsequent amendment affecting them.

Article 26 Prevention of discrimination

Member States shall encourage, in accordance with national law, collective agreements or practice, employers and those responsible for access to vocational training to take effective measures to prevent all forms of discrimination on grounds of sex, in particular harassment and sexual harassment in the workplace, in access to employment, vocational training and promotion.

Article 27 Minimum requirements

1. Member States may introduce or maintain provisions which are more favourable to the protection of the principle of equal treatment than those laid down in this Directive.

2. Implementation of this Directive shall under no circumstances be sufficient grounds for a reduction in the level of protection of workers in the areas to which it applies, without prejudice to the Member States' right to respond to changes in the situation by introducing laws, regulations and administrative provisions which differ from those in force on the notification of this Directive, provided that the provisions of this Directive are complied with.

Article 28 Relationship to Community and national provisions

1. This Directive shall be without prejudice to provisions concerning the protection of women, particularly as regards pregnancy and maternity.

2. This Directive shall be without prejudice to the provisions of Directive 96/34/EC and Directive 92/85/EEC.

Article 29 Gender mainstreaming

Member States shall actively take into account the objective of equality between men and women when formulating and implementing laws, regulations, administrative provisions, policies and activities in the areas referred to in this Directive.

Article 30 Dissemination of information

Member States shall ensure that measures taken pursuant to this Directive, together with the provisions already in force, are brought to the attention of all the persons concerned by all suitable means and, where appropriate, at the workplace.

TITLE IV
FINAL PROVISIONS

Article 31 Reports

1. By 15 February 2011, the Member States shall communicate to the Commission all the information necessary for the Commission to draw up a report to the European Parliament and the Council on the application of this Directive.

2. Without prejudice to paragraph 1, Member States shall communicate to the Commission, every four years, the texts of any measures adopted pursuant to Article 141(4) of the Treaty, as well as reports on these measures and their implementation. On the basis of that information, the Commission will adopt and publish every four years a report establishing a comparative assessment of any measures in the light of Declaration No 28 annexed to the Final Act of the Treaty of Amsterdam.

3. Member States shall assess the occupational activities referred to in Article 14(2), in order to decide, in the light of social developments, whether there is justification for maintaining the exclusions concerned. They shall notify the Commission of the results of this assessment periodically, but at least every 8 years.

Article 32 Review

By 15 February 2011 at the latest, the Commission shall review the operation of this Directive and if appropriate, propose any amendments it deems necessary.

Article 33 Implementation

Member States shall bring into force the laws, regulations and administrative provisions necessary to comply with this Directive by 15 August 2008 at the latest or shall ensure, by that date, that management and labour introduce the requisite provisions by way of agreement. Member States may, if necessary to take account of particular difficulties, have up to one additional year to comply with this Directive. Member States shall take all necessary steps to be able to guarantee the results imposed by this Directive. They shall forthwith communicate to the Commission the texts of those measures.

When Member States adopt these measures, they shall contain a reference to this Directive or be accompanied by such reference on the occasion of their official publication. They shall also include a statement that references in existing laws, regulations and administrative provisions to the Directives repealed by this Directive shall be construed as references to this Directive. Member States shall determine how such reference is to be made and how that statement is to be formulated.

The obligation to transpose this Directive into national law shall be confined to those provisions which represent a substantive change as compared with the earlier Directives. The obligation to transpose the provisions which are substantially unchanged arises under the earlier Directives.

Member States shall communicate to the Commission the text of the main provisions of national law which they adopt in the field covered by this Directive.

Article 34 Repeal

1. With effect from 15 August 2009 Directives 75/117/EEC, 76/207/EEC, 86/378/EEC and 97/80/EC shall be repealed without prejudice to the obligations of the Member States relating to the time-limits for transposition into national law and application of the Directives set out in Annex I, Part B.

2.   References made to the repealed Directives shall be construed as being made to this Directive and should be read in accordance with the correlation table in Annex II.

Article 35 Entry into force

This Directive shall enter into force on the 20th day following its publication in the *Official Journal of the European Union*.

Article 36 Addressees

This Directive is addressed to the Member States.

(date of signing and signatories omitted)

[1]   OJ C 157, 28.6.2005, p. 83.
[2]   Opinion of the European Parliament of 6 July 2005 (not yet published in the Official Journal), Council Common Position of 10 March 2006 (OJ C 126 E, 30.5.2006, p. 33) and Position of the European Parliament of 1 June 2006 (not yet published in the Official Journal).
[3]   OJ L 39, 14.2.1976, p. 40. Directive as amended by Directive 2002/73/EC of the European Parliament and of the Council (OJ L 269, 5.10.2002, p. 15).
[4]   OJ L 225, 12.8.1986, p. 40. Directive as amended by Directive 96/97/EC (OJ L 46, 17.2.1997, p. 20).
[5]   See Annex I Part A.
[6]   OJ L 45, 19.2.1975, p. 19.
[7]   OJ L 14, 20.1.1998, p. 6. Directive as amended by Directive 98/52/EC (OJ L 205, 22.7.1998, p. 66).
[8]   C-262/88: Barber v Guardian Royal Exchange Assurance Group (1990 ECR I-1889).
[9]   C-7/93: Bestuur van het Algemeen Burgerlijk Pensioenfonds v G. A. Beune (1994 ECR I-4471).
[10]   C-351/00: Pirkko Niemi (2002 ECR I-7007).
[11]   Protocol 17 concerning Article 141 of the Treaty establishing the European Community (1992).
[12]   OJ L 348, 28.11.1992, p. 1.
[13]   OJ L 145, 19.6.1996, p. 4. Directive as amended by Directive 97/75/EC (OJ L 10, 16.1.1998, p. 24).
[14]   OJ C 218, 31.7.2000, p. 5.
[15]   OJ C 321, 31.12.2003, p. 1.
[16]   OJ L 6, 10.1.1979, p. 24.

ANNEX I *(omitted)*

ANNEX II CORRELATION TABLE

Dir. 75/117	Dir. 76/207	Dir. 86/378	Dir. 97/80	This Directive
—	Art. 1(1)	Art. 1	Art. 1	Art. 1
—	Art. 1(2)	—	—	—
—	Art. 2(2), first indent	—	Art. 2(1), (a)	—
—	Art. 2(2), second indent	—	Art. 2(2)	Art. 2(1),(b)
—	Art. 2(2), third and fourth indents	—	—	Art. 2(1),(c) & (d)
—	—	—	—	Art. 2(1), (e)
—	—	Art. 2(1)	—	Art. 2(1), (f)
—	Art. 2(3),(4) & (7) third subpara.	—	—	Art. 2(2)
—	Art. 2(8)	—	—	Art. 3
Art. 1	—	—	—	Art. 4
—	—	Art. 5(1)	—	Art. 5
—	—	Art. 3	—	Art. 6
—	—	Art. 4	—	Art. 7(1)
—	—	—	—	Art. 7(2)
		Art. 2(2)		Art. 8(1)

Dir. 75/117	Dir. 76/207	Dir. 86/378	Dir. 97/80	This Directive
—	—	Art. 2(3)	—	Art. 8(2)
—	—	Art. 6	—	Art. 9
—	—	Art. 8	—	Art. 10
—	—	Art. 9	—	Art. 11
—	—	(Art. 2 of Dir. 96/97)	—	Art. 12
—	—	Art. 9a	—	Art. 13
—	Arts. 2(1) & 3(1)	—	Art. 2(1)	Art. 14(1)
—	Art. 2(6)	—	—	Art. 14(2)
—	Art. 2(7), second subpara.	—	—	Art. 15
—	Art. 2(7), fourth subpara., second & third sentence	—	—	Art. 16
Art. 2	Art. 6(1)	Art. 10	—	Art. 17(1)
—	Art. 6(3)	—	—	Art. 17(2)
—	Art. 6(4)	—	—	Art. 17(3)
—	Art. 6(2)	—	—	Art. 18
—	—	—	Arts. 3 & 4	Art. 19
—	Art. 8a	—	—	Art. 20
—	Art. 8b	—	—	Art. 21
—	Art. 8c	—	—	Art. 22
Arts. 3 & 6	Art. 3 (2)(a)	—	—	Art. 23(a)
Art. 4	Art. 3(2)(b)	Art. 7(a)	—	Art. 23(b)
—	—	Art. 7(b)	—	Art. 23(c)
Art. 5	Art. 7	Art. 11	—	Art. 24
Art. 6	—	—	—	—
—	Art. 8d	—	—	Art. 25
	Art. 2(5)			Art. 26
—	Art. 8e(1)	—	Art. 4(2)	Art. 27(1)
—	Art. 8e(2)	—	Art. 6	Art. 27(2)
—	Art. 2(7) first subpara.	Art. 5(2)	—	Art. 28(1)
—	Art. 2(7) fourth subpara. first sentence			Art. 28(2)
—	Art. 1(1a)			Art. 29
Art. 7	Art. 8	—	Art. 5	Art. 30
Art. 9	Art. 10	Art. 12(2)	Art. 7, fourth Subpara.	Art. 31(1) & (2)
—	Art. 9(2)	—	—	Art. 31(3)
—	—	—	—	Art. 32
Art. 8	Art. 9(1), first subpara. & 9 (2) & (3)	Art. 12(1)	Art. 7, first, second & third subparas.	Art. 33
—	Art. 9(1), second subpara.	—	—	—
—	—	—	—	Art. 34
—	—	—	—	Art. 35
—	—	—	—	Art. 36
—	—	Annex	—	—

B) Working Conditions

Council Directive 89/391/EEC of 12 June 1989

on the introduction of measures to encourage improvements in the safety and health of workers at work*

OJ L 183, 29.6.1989, p. 1[1]

....

(*As amended by Regulation (EC) No 1882/2003 of the European Parliament and of the Council of 29 September 2003, OJ L 284, 31.10.2003, p. 1, Directive 2007/30/EC of the European Parliament and of the Council of 20 June 2007, OJ L 165, 27.6.2007, p. 21, Regulation (EC) No 1137/2008 of the European Parliament and of the Council of 22 October 2008, OJ L 311, 21.11.2008, p. 1, and corrected by Corrigendum, OJ L 275, 5.10.1990, p. 42)

(footnotes omitted)

THE COUNCIL OF THE EUROPEAN COMMUNITIES,

Having regard to the Treaty establishing the European Economic Community, and in particular Article 118a thereof [Article 153 TFEU],

Having regard to the proposal from the Commission, drawn up after consultation with the Advisory Committee on Safety, Hygiene and Health Protection at Work,

In cooperation with the European Parliament,

Having regard to the opinion of the Economic and Social Committee,

Whereas Article 118a of the Treaty [Article 153 TFEU] provides that the Council shall adopt, by means of Directives, minimum requirements for encouraging improvements, especially in the working environment, to guarantee a better level of protection of the safety and health of workers;

Whereas this Directive does not justify any reduction in levels of protection already achieved in individual Member States, the Member State being committed, under the Treaty, to encouraging improvements in conditions in this area and to harmonizing conditions while maintaining the improvements made;

Whereas it is known that workers can be exposed to the effects of dangerous environmental factors at the work place during the course of their working life;

Whereas, pursuant to Article 118a of the Treaty [Article 153 TFEU], such Directives must avoid imposing administrative, financial and legal constraints which would hold back the creation and development of small and medium-sized undertakings;

Whereas the communication from the Commission on its programme concerning safety, hygiene and health at work provides for the adoption of Directives designed to guarantee the safety and health of workers;

....

[1]   EDITOR'S NOTE: This Directive refers to the original European Economic Community (EEC) Treaty numbers in force at the time of its publication. In this edition the replacement article numbers contained in the Treaty on the Functioning of the European Union (TFEU) have been inserted in closed brackets after each Treaty reference for ease of conversion.

Whereas the Council, in its resolution of 21 December 1987 on safety, hygiene and health at work, took note of the Commission's intention to submit to the Council in the near future a Directive on the organization of the safety and health of workers at the work place;

Whereas in February 1988 the European Parliament adopted four resolutions following the debate on the internal market and worker protection; whereas these resolutions specifically invited the Commission to draw up a framework Directive to serve as a basis for more specific Directives covering all the risks connected with safety and health at the work place;

Whereas Member States have a responsibility to encourage improvements in the safety and health of workers on their territory; whereas taking measures to protect the health and safety of workers at work also helps, in certain cases, to preserve the health and possibly the safety of persons residing with them;

Whereas Member States' legislative systems covering safety and health at the work place differ widely and need to be improved; whereas national provisions on the subject, which often include technical specifications and/or self-regulatory standards, may result in different levels of safety and health protection and allow competition at the expense of safety and health;

Whereas the incidence of accidents at work and occupational diseases is still too high; whereas preventive measures must be introduced or improved without delay in order to safeguard the safety and health of workers and ensure a higher degree of protection;

Whereas, in order to ensure an improved degree of protection, workers and/or their representatives must be informed of the risks to their safety and health and of the measures required to reduce or eliminate these risks; whereas they must also be in a position to contribute, by means of balanced participation in accordance with national laws and/or practices, to seeing that the necessary protective measures are taken;

Whereas information, dialogue and balanced participation on safety and health at work must be developed between employers and workers and/or their representatives by means of appropriate procedures and instruments, in accordance with national laws and/or practices;

Whereas the improvement of workers' safety, hygiene and health at work is an objective which should not be subordinated to purely economic considerations;

Whereas employers shall be obliged to keep themselves informed of the latest advances in technology and scientific findings concerning work-place design, account being taken of the inherent dangers in their undertaking, and to inform accordingly the workers' representatives exercising participation rights under this Directive, so as to be able to guarantee a better level of protection of workers' health and safety;

Whereas the provisions of this Directive apply, without prejudice to more stringent present or future Community provisions, to all risks, and in particular to those arising from the use at work of chemical, physical and biological agents covered by Directive 80/1107/EEC, as last amended by Directive 88/642/EEC;

Whereas, pursuant to Decision 74/325/EEC, the Advisory Committee on Safety, Hygiene and Health Protection at Work is consulted by the Commission on the drafting of proposals in this field;

Whereas a Committee composed of members nominated by the Member States needs to be set up to assist the Commission in making the technical adaptations to the individual Directives provided for in this Directive.

HAS ADOPTED THIS DIRECTIVE:

SECTION I GENERAL PROVISIONS

Article 1 Object

1. The object of this Directive is to introduce measures to encourage improvements in the safety and health of workers at work.

2. To that end it contains general principles concerning the prevention of occupational risks, the protection of safety and health, the elimination of risk and accident factors, the informing, consultation, balanced participation in accordance with national laws and/or practices and training of workers and their representatives, as well as general guidelines for the implementation of the said principles.

3. This Directive shall be without prejudice to existing or future national and Community provisions which are more favourable to protection of the safety and health of workers at work.

Article 2 Scope

1. This Directive shall apply to all sectors of activity, both public and private (industrial, agricultural, commercial, administrative, service, educational, cultural, leisure, etc.).

2. This Directive shall not be applicable where characteristics peculiar to certain specific public service activities, such as the armed forces or the police, or to certain specific activities in the civil protection services inevitably conflict with it.

    In that event, the safety and health of workers must be ensured as far as possible in the light of the objectives of this Directive.

Article 3 Definitions

For the purposes of this Directive, the following terms shall have the following meanings:

(a) worker: any person employed by an employer, including trainees and apprentices but excluding domestic servants;

(b) employer: any natural or legal person who has an employment relationship with the worker and has responsibility for the undertaking and/or establishment;

(c) workers' representative with specific responsibility for the safety and health of workers: any person elected, chosen or designated in accordance with national laws and/or practices to represent workers where problems arise relating to the safety and health protection of workers at work;

(d) prevention: all the steps or measures taken or planned at all stages of work in the undertaking to prevent or reduce occupational risks.

Article 4

1. Member States shall take the necessary steps to ensure that employers, workers and workers' representatives are subject to the legal provisions necessary for the implementation of this Directive.

2. In particular, Member States shall ensure adequate controls and supervision.

SECTION II EMPLOYERS' OBLIGATIONS

Article 5 General provision

1. The employer shall have a duty to ensure the safety and health of workers in every aspect related to the work.

2. Where, pursuant to Article 7 (3), an employer enlists competent external services or persons, this shall not discharge him from his responsibilities in this area.

3. The workers' obligations in the field of safety and health at work shall not affect the principle of the responsibility of the employer.

4. This Directive shall not restrict the option of Member States to provide for the exclusion or the limitation of employers' responsibility where occurrences are due to unusual and unforeseeable circumstances, beyond the employers' control, or to exceptional events, the consequences of which could not have been avoided despite the exercise of all due care.

    Member States need not exercise the option referred to in the first subparagraph.

Article 6 General obligations on employers

1. Within the context of his responsibilities, the employer shall take the measures necessary for the safety and health protection of workers, including prevention of occupational risks and provision of information and training, as well as provision of the necessary organization and means.

    The employer shall be alert to the need to adjust these measures to take account of changing circumstances and aim to improve existing situations.

2. The employer shall implement the measures referred to in the first subparagraph of paragraph 1 on the basis of the following general principles of prevention:
    (a) avoiding risks;
    (b) evaluating the risks which cannot be avoided:
    (c) combating the risks at source;
    (d) adapting the work to the individual, especially as regards the design of work places, the choice of work equipment and the choice of working and production methods, with a view, in particular, to alleviating monotonous work and work at a predetermined work-rate and to reducing their effect on health.
    (e) adapting to technical progress;
    (f) replacing the dangerous by the non-dangerous or the less dangerous;
    (g) developing a coherent overall prevention policy which covers technology, organization of work, working conditions, social relationships and the influence of factors related to the working environment;
    (h) giving collective protective measures priority over individual protective measures;
    (i) giving appropriate instructions to the workers.

3. Without prejudice to the other provisions of this Directive, the employer shall, taking into account the nature of the activities of the enterprise and/or establishment:
    (a) evaluate the risks to the safety and health of workers, inter alia in the choice of work equipment, the chemical substances or preparations used, and the fitting-out of work places.
    Subsequent to this evaluation and as necessary, the preventive measures and the working and production methods implemented by the employer must:
    — assure an improvement in the level of protection afforded to workers with regard to safety and health,

— be integrated into all the activities of the undertaking and/or establishment and at all hierarchical levels;

(b) where he entrusts tasks to a worker, take into consideration the worker's capabilities as regards health and safety;

(c) ensure that the planning and introduction of new technologies are the subject of consultation with the workers and/or their representatives, as regards the consequences of the choice of equipment, the working conditions and the working environment for the safety and health of workers;

(d) take appropriate steps to ensure that only workers who have received adequate instructions may have access to areas where there is serious and specific danger.

4.   Without prejudice to the other provisions of this Directive, where several undertakings share a work place, the employers shall cooperate in implementing the safety, health and occupational hygiene provisions and, taking into account the nature of the activities, shall coordinate their actions in matters of the protection and prevention of occupational risks, and shall inform one another and their respective workers and/or workers' representatives of these risks.

5.   Measures related to safety, hygiene and health at work may in no circumstances involve the workers in financial cost.

Article 7 Protective and preventive services

1.   Without prejudice to the obligations referred to in Articles 5 and 6, the employer shall designate one or more workers to carry out activities related to the protection and prevention of occupational risks for the undertaking and/or establishment.

2.   Designated workers may not be placed at any disadvantage because of their activities related to the protection and prevention of occupational risks.

Designated workers shall be allowed adequate time to enable them to fulfil their obligations arising from this Directive.

3.   If such protective and preventive measures cannot be organized for lack of competent personnel in the undertaking

and/or establishment, the employer shall enlist competent external services or persons.

4.   Where the employer enlists such services or persons, he shall inform them of the factors known to affect, or suspected of affecting, the safety and health of the workers and they must have access to the information referred to in Article 10 (2).

5.   In all cases:
— the workers designated must have the necessary capabilities and the necessary means,
— the external services or persons consulted must have the necessary aptitudes and the necessary personal and professional means, and
— the workers designated and the external services or persons consulted must be sufficient in number to deal with the organization of protective and preventive measures, taking into account the size of the undertaking and/or establishment and/or the hazards to which the workers are exposed and their distribution throughout the entire undertaking and/or establishment.

6.   The protection from, and prevention of, the health and safety risks which form the subject of this Article shall be the responsibility of one or more workers, of one service or of separate services whether from inside or outside the undertaking and/or establishment.

The worker(s) and/or agency(ies) must work together whenever necessary.

7.   Member States may define, in the light of the nature of the activities and size of the undertakings, the categories of undertakings in which the employer, provided he is competent, may himself take responsibility for the measures referred to in paragraph 1.

8.   Member States shall define the necessary capabilities and aptitudes referred to in paragraph 5.

They may determine the sufficient number referred to in paragraph 5.

Article 8 First aid, fire-fighting and evacuation of workers, serious and imminent danger

1.   The employer shall:
   — take the necessary measures for first aid, fire-fighting and evacuation of workers, adapted to the nature of the activities and the size of the undertaking and/or establishment and taking into account other persons present,
   — arrange any necessary contacts with external services, particularly as regards first aid, emergency medical care, rescue work and fire-fighting.

2.   Pursuant to paragraph 1, the employer shall, inter alia, for first aid, fire-fighting and the evacuation of workers, designate the workers required to implement such measures.

The number of such workers, their training and the equipment available to them shall be adequate, taking account of the size and/or specific hazards of the undertaking and/or establishment.

3.   The employer shall:
   (a) as soon as possible, inform all workers who are, or may be, exposed to serious and imminent danger of the risk involved and of the steps taken or to be taken as regards protection;
   (b) take action and give instructions to enable workers in the event of serious, imminent and unavoidable danger to stop work and/or immediately to leave the work place and proceed to a place of safety;
   (c) save in exceptional cases for reasons duly substantiated, refrain from asking workers to resume work in a working situation where there is still a serious and imminent danger.

4.   Workers who, in the event of serious, imminent and unavoidable danger, leave their workstation and/or a dangerous area may not be placed at any disadvantage because of their action and must be protected against any harmful and unjustified consequences, in accordance with national laws and/or practices.

5.   The employer shall ensure that all workers are able, in the event of serious and imminent danger to their own safety and/or that of other persons, and where the immediate superior responsible cannot be contacted, to take the appropriate steps in the light of their knowledge and the technical means at their disposal, to avoid the consequences of such danger.

Their actions shall not place them at any disadvantage, unless they acted carelessly or there was negligence on their part.

Article 9 Various obligations on employers

1.   The employer shall:
   (a) be in possession of an assessment of the risks to safety and health at work, including those facing groups of workers exposed to particular risks;

(b) decide on the protective measures to be taken and, if necessary, the protective equipment to be used;

(c) keep a list of occupational accidents resulting in a worker being unfit for work for more than three working days;

(d) draw up, for the responsible authorities and in accordance with national laws and/or practices, reports on occupational accidents suffered by his workers.

2. Member States shall define, in the light of the nature of the activities and size of the undertakings, the obligations to be met by the different categories of undertakings in respect of the drawing-up of the documents provided for in paragraph 1 (a) and (b) and when preparing the documents provided for in paragraph 1 (c) and (d).

Article 10 Worker information

1. The employer shall take appropriate measures so that workers and/or their representatives in the undertaking and/or establishment receive, in accordance with national laws and/or practices which may take account, inter alia, of the size of the undertaking and/or establishment, all the necessary information concerning:

(a) the safety and health risks and protective and preventive measures and activities in respect of both the undertaking and/or establishment in general and each type of workstation and/or job;

(b) the measures taken pursuant to Article 8 (2).

2. The employer shall take appropriate measures so that employers of workers from any outside undertakings and/or establishments engaged in work in his undertaking and/or establishment receive, in accordance with national laws and/or practices, adequate information concerning the points referred to in paragraph 1 (a) and (b) which is to be provided to the workers in question.

3. The employer shall take appropriate measures so that workers with specific functions in protecting the safety and health of workers, or workers' representatives with specific responsibility for the safety and health of workers shall have access, to carry out their functions and in accordance with national laws and/or practices, to:

(a) the risk assessment and protective measures referred to in Article 9 (1) (a) and (b);

(b) the list and reports referred to in Article 9 (1) (c) and (d);

(c) the information yielded by protective and preventive measures, inspection agencies and bodies responsible for safety and health.

Article 11 Consultation and participation of workers

1. Employers shall consult workers and/or their representatives and allow them to take part in discussions on all questions relating to safety and health at work.

This presupposes:
— the consultation of workers,
— the right of workers and/or their representatives to make proposals,
— balanced participation in accordance with national laws and/or practices.

2. Workers or workers' representatives with specific responsibility for the safety and health of workers shall take part in a balanced way, in accordance with national laws and/or practices, or shall be consulted in advance and in good time by the employer with regard to:

(a) any measure which may substantially affect safety and health;

(b) the designation of workers referred to in Articles 7 (1) and 8 (2) and the activities referred to in Article 7 (1);

(c) the information referred to in Articles 9 (1) and 10;
(d) the enlistment, where appropriate, of the competent services or persons outside the undertaking and/or establishment, as referred to in Article 7 (3);
(e) the planning and organization of the training referred to in Article 12.

3.   Workers' representatives with specific responsibility for the safety and health of workers shall have the right to ask the employer to take appropriate measures and to submit proposals to him to that end to mitigate hazards for workers and/or to remove sources of danger.

4.   The workers referred to in paragraph 2 and the workers' representatives referred to in paragraphs 2 and 3 may not be placed at a disadvantage because of their respective activities referred to in paragraphs 2 and 3.

5.   Employers must allow workers' representatives with specific responsibility for the safety and health of workers adequate time off work, without loss of pay, and provide them with the necessary means to enable such representatives to exercise their rights and functions deriving from this Directive.

6.   Workers and/or their representatives are entitled to appeal, in accordance with national law and/or practice, to the authority responsible for safety and health protection at work if they consider that the measures taken and the means employed by the employer are inadequate for the purposes of ensuring safety and health at work.

Workers' representatives must be given the opportunity to submit their observations during inspection visits by the competent authority.

Article 12 Training of workers
1.   The employer shall ensure that each worker receives adequate safety and health training, in particular in the form of information and instructions specific to his workstation or job:
— on recruitment,
— in the event of a transfer or a change of job,
— in the event of the introduction of new work equipment or a change in equipment,
— in the event of the introduction of any new technology.
      The training shall be:
— adapted to take account of new or changed risks, and
— repeated periodically if necessary.

2.   The employer shall ensure that workers from outside undertakings and/or establishments engaged in work in his undertaking and/or establishment have in fact received appropriate instructions regarding health and safety risks during their activities in his undertaking and/or establishment.

3.   Workers' representatives with a specific role in protecting the safety and health of workers shall be entitled to appropriate training.

4.   The training referred to in paragraphs 1 and 3 may not be at the workers' expense or at that of the workers' representatives.

The training referred to in paragraph 1 must take place during working hours.

The training referred to in paragraph 3 must take place during working hours or in accordance with national practice either within or outside the undertaking and/or the establishment.

SECTION III WORKERS' OBLIGATIONS

Article 13

1. It shall be the responsibility of each worker to take care as far as possible of his own safety and health and that of other persons affected by his acts or omissions at work in accordance with his training and the instructions given by his employer.

2. To this end, workers must in particular, in accordance with their training and the instructions given by their employer:
   (a) make correct use of machinery, apparatus, tools, dangerous substances, transport equipment and other means of production;
   (b) make correct use of the personal protective equipment supplied to them and, after use, return it to its proper place;
   (c) refrain from disconnecting, changing or removing arbitrarily safety devices fitted, e.g. to machinery, apparatus, tools, plant and buildings, and use such safety devices correctly;
   (d) immediately inform the employer and/or the workers with specific responsibility for the safety and health of workers of any work situation they have reasonable grounds for considering represents a serious and immediate danger to safety and health and of any shortcomings in the protection arrangements;
   (e) cooperate, in accordance with national practice, with the employer and/or workers with specific responsibility for the safety and health of workers, for as long as may be necessary to enable any tasks or requirements imposed by the competent authority to protect the safety and health of workers at work to be carried out;
   (f) cooperate, in accordance with national practice, with the employer and/or workers with specific responsibility for the safety and health of workers, for as long as may be necessary to enable the employer to ensure that the working environment and working conditions are safe and pose no risk to safety and health within their field of activity.

SECTION IV MISCELLANEOUS PROVISIONS

Article 14 Health surveillance

1. To ensure that workers receive health surveillance appropriate to the health and safety risks they incur at work, measures shall be introduced in accordance with national law and/or practices.

2. The measures referred to in paragraph 1 shall be such that each worker, if he so wishes, may receive health surveillance at regular intervals.

3. Health surveillance may be provided as part of a national health system.

Article 15 Risk groups
Particularly sensitive risk groups must be protected against the dangers which specifically affect them.

Article 16 Individual Directives – Amendments – General scope of this Directive

1. The Council, acting on a proposal from the Commission based on Article 118a of the Treaty [Article 153 TFEU], shall adopt individual Directives, inter alia, in the areas listed in the Annex.

2. This Directive and, without prejudice to the procedure referred to in Article 17 concerning technical adjustments, the individual Directives may be amended in accordance with the procedure provided for in Article 118a of the Treaty [Article 153 TFEU].

3.   The provisions of this Directive shall apply in full to all the areas covered by the individual Directives, without prejudice to more stringent and/or specific provisions contained in these individual Directives.

Article 17 Committee procedure

1.   The Commission shall be assisted by a committee to make purely technical adjustments to the individual directives provided for in Article 16(1) in order to take account of:

(a) the adoption of directives in the field of technical harmonisation and standardisation;

(b) technical progress, changes in international regulations or specifications and new findings.

Those measures, designed to amend non-essential elements of the individual directives, shall be adopted in accordance with the regulatory procedure with scrutiny referred to in paragraph 2. On imperative grounds of urgency, the Commission may have recourse to the urgency procedure referred to in paragraph 3.

2.   Where reference is made to this paragraph, Article 5a(1) to (4) and Article 7 of Decision 1999/468/EC shall apply, having regard to the provisions of Article 8 thereof.

3.   Where reference is made to this paragraph, Article 5a(1), (2), (4) and (6) and Article 7 of Decision 1999/468/EC shall apply, having regard to the provisions of Article 8 thereof.

Article 17a Implementation reports

1.   Every five years, the Member States shall submit a single report to the Commission on the practical implementation of this Directive and individual Directives within the meaning of Article 16(1), indicating the points of view of the social partners. The report shall assess the various points related to the practical implementation of the different Directives and, where appropriate and available, provide data disaggregated by gender.

2.   The structure of the report, together with a questionnaire specifying its content, shall be defined by the Commission, in cooperation with the Advisory Committee on Safety and Health at Work.

The report shall include a general part on the provisions of this Directive relating to the common principles and points applicable to all of the Directives referred to in paragraph 1.

To complement the general part, specific chapters shall deal with implementation of the particular aspects of each Directive, including specific indicators, where available.

3.   The Commission shall submit the structure of the report, together with the above-mentioned questionnaire specifying its content, to the Member States at least six months before the end of the period covered by the report. The report shall be transmitted to the Commission within 12 months of the end of the five-year period that it covers.

4.   Using these reports as a basis, the Commission shall evaluate the implementation of the Directives concerned in terms of their relevance, of research and of new scientific knowledge in the various fields in question. It shall, within 36 months of the end of the five-year period, inform the European Parliament, the Council, the European Economic and Social Committee and the Advisory Committee on Safety and Health at Work of the results of this evaluation and, if necessary, of any initiatives to improve the operation of the regulatory framework.

5.   The first report shall cover the period 2007 to 2012.

Article 18 Final provisions

1. Member States shall bring into force the laws, regulations and administrative provisions necessary to comply with this Directive by 31 December 1992.

    They shall forthwith inform the Commission thereof.

2. Member States shall communicate to the Commission the texts of the provisions of national law which they have already adopted or adopt in the field covered by this Directive.

Article 19

This Directive is addressed to the Member States.

(*date of signing and signatory omitted*)

ANNEX

LIST OF AREAS REFERRED TO IN ARTICLE 16 (1) – WORK PLACES

— Work equipment

— Personal protective equipment

— Work with visual display units

— Handling of heavy loads involving risk of back injury

— Temporary or mobile work sites

— Fisheries and agriculture

COUNCIL DIRECTIVE 92/85/EEC OF 19 OCTOBER 1992

on the introduction of measures to encourage improvements in the safety and health at work of pregnant workers and workers who have recently given birth or are breastfeeding (tenth individual Directive within the meaning of Article 16 (1) of Directive 89/391/EEC)*

OJ L 348, 28.11.1992, p. 1

....

(*As amended by Directive 2007/30/EC of the European Parliament and of the Council of 20 June 2007, OJ L 165, 27.6.2007, p. 21)[1]

(*footnotes omitted*)

THE COUNCIL OF THE EUROPEAN COMMUNITIES,

Having regard to the Treaty establishing the European Economic Community, and in particular Article 118a thereof [Article 153 TFEU],

Having regard to the proposal from the Commission, drawn up after consultation with the Advisory Committee on Safety, Hygiene and Health Protection at work,

In cooperation with the European Parliament,

---

[1] EDITOR'S NOTE: This Directive refers to the original European Economic Community (EEC) Treaty numbers in force at the time of its publication. In this edition the replacement article numbers contained in the Treaty on the Functioning of the European Union (TFEU) have been inserted in closed brackets after each Treaty reference for ease of conversion.

Having regard to the opinion of the Economic and Social Committee,

Whereas Article 118a of the Treaty [Article 153 TFEU] provides that the Council shall adopt, by means of directives, minimum requirements for encouraging improvements, especially in the working environment, to protect the safety and health of workers;

Whereas this Directive does not justify any reduction in levels of protection already achieved in individual Member States, the Member States being committed, under the Treaty, to encouraging improvements in conditions in this area and to harmonizing conditions while maintaining the improvements made;

Whereas, under the terms of Article 118a of the Treaty [Article 153 TFEU], the said directives are to avoid imposing administrative, financial and legal constraints in a way which would hold back the creation and development of small and medium-sized undertakings;

Whereas, pursuant to Decision 74/325/EEC, as last amended by the 1985 Act of Accession, the Advisory Committee on Safety, Hygiene and Health protection at Work is consulted by the Commission on the drafting of proposals in this field;

Whereas the Community Charter of the fundamental social rights of workers, adopted at the Strasbourg European Council on 9 December 1989 by the Heads of State or Government of 11 Member States, lays down, in paragraph 19 in particular, that:

'Every worker must enjoy satisfactory health and safety conditions in his working environment. Appropriate measures must be taken in order to achieve further harmonization of conditions in this area while maintaining the improvements made';

Whereas the Commission, in its action programme for the implementation of the Community Charter of the fundamental social rights of workers, has included among its aims the adoption by the Council of a Directive on the protection of pregnant women at work;

Whereas Article 15 of Council Directive 89/391/EEC of 12 June 1989 on the introduction of measures to encourage improvements in the safety and health of workers at work provides that particularly sensitive risk groups must be protected against the dangers which specifically affect them;

Whereas pregnant workers, workers who have recently given birth or who are breastfeeding must be considered a specific risk group in many respects, and measures must be taken with regard to their safety and health;

Whereas the protection of the safety and health of pregnant workers, workers who have recently given birth or workers who are breastfeeding should not treat women on the labour market unfavourably nor work to the detriment of directives concerning equal treatment for men and women;

Whereas some types of activities may pose a specific risk, for pregnant workers, workers who have recently given birth or workers who are breastfeeding, of exposure to dangerous agents, processes or working conditions; whereas such risks must therefore be assessed and the result of such assessment communicated to female workers and/or their representatives;

Whereas, further, should the result of this assessment reveal the existence of a risk to the safety or health of the female worker, provision must be made for such worker to be protected;

Whereas pregnant workers and workers who are breastfeeding must not engage in activities which have been assessed as revealing a risk of exposure, jeopardizing safety and health, to certain particularly dangerous agents or working conditions;

Whereas provision should be made for pregnant workers, workers who have recently given birth or workers who are breastfeeding not to be required to work at night where such provision is necessary from the point of view of their safety and health;

Whereas the vulnerability of pregnant workers, workers who have recently given birth or who are breastfeeding makes it necessary for them to be granted the right to maternity leave of at least 14 continuous weeks, allocated before and/or after confinement, and renders necessary the compulsory nature of maternity leave of at least two weeks, allocated before and/or after confinement;

Whereas the risk of dismissal for reasons associated with their condition may have harmful effects on the physical and mental state of pregnant workers, workers who have recently given birth or who are breastfeeding; whereas provision should be made for such dismissal to be prohibited;

Whereas measures for the organization of work concerning the protection of the health of pregnant workers, workers who have recently given birth or workers who are breastfeeding would serve no purpose unless accompanied by the maintenance of rights linked to the employment contract, including maintenance of payment and/or entitlement to an adequate allowance;

Whereas, moreover, provision concerning maternity leave would also serve no purpose unless accompanied by the maintenance of rights linked to the employment contract and or entitlement to an adequate allowance;

Whereas the concept of an adequate allowance in the case of maternity leave must be regarded as a technical point of reference with a view to fixing the minimum level of protection and should in no circumstances be interpreted as suggesting an analogy between pregnancy and illness,

HAS ADOPTED THIS DIRECTIVE

SECTION I PURPOSE AND DEFINITIONS

Article 1 Purpose
1. The purpose of this Directive, which is the tenth individual Directive within the meaning of Article 16 (1) of Directive 89/391/EEC, is to implement measures to encourage improvements in the safety and health at work of pregnant workers and workers who have recently given birth or who are breastfeeding.

2. The provisions of Directive 89/391/EEC, except for Article 2 (2) thereof, shall apply in full to the whole area covered by paragraph 1, without prejudice to any more stringent and/or specific provisions contained in this Directive.

3. This Directive may not have the effect of reducing the level of protection afforded to pregnant workers, workers who have recently given birth or who are breastfeeding as compared with the situation which exists in each Member State on the date on which this Directive is adopted.

Article 2 Definitions
For the purposes of this Directive:
(a) pregnant worker shall mean a pregnant worker who informs her employer of her condition, in accordance with national legislation and/or national practice;

(b) worker who has recently given birth shall mean a worker who has recently given birth within the meaning of national legislation and/or national practice and who informs her employer of her condition, in accordance with that legislation and/or practice;

(c)   worker who is breastfeeding shall mean a worker who is breastfeeding within the meaning of national legislation and/or national practice and who informs her employer of her condition, in accordance with that legislation and/or practice.

SECTION II GENERAL PROVISIONS

Article 3 Guidelines

1.   In consultation with the Member States and assisted by the Advisory Committee on Safety, Hygiene and Health Protection at Work, the Commission shall draw up guidelines on the assessment of the chemical, physical and biological agents and industrial processes considered hazardous for the safety or health of workers within the meaning of Article 2.

The guidelines referred to in the first subparagraph shall also cover movements and postures, mental and physical fatigue and other types of physical and mental stress connected with the work done by workers within the meaning of Article 2.

2.   The purpose of the guidelines referred to in paragraph 1 is to serve as a basis for the assessment referred to in Article 4 (1).

To this end, Member States shall bring these guidelines to the attention of all employers and all female workers and/or their representatives in the respective Member State.

Article 4 Assessment and information

1.   For all activities liable to involve a specific risk of exposure to the agents, processes or working conditions of which a non-exhaustive list is given in Annex I, the employer shall assess the nature, degree and duration of exposure, in the undertaking and/or establishment concerned, of workers within the meaning of Article 2, either directly or by way of the protective and preventive services referred to in Article 7 of Directive 89/391/EEC, in order to:
— assess any risks to the safety or health and any possible effect on the pregnancy or breastfeeding of workers within the meaning of Article 2,
— decide what measures should be taken.

2.   Without prejudice to Article 10 of Directive 89/391/EEC, workers within the meaning of Article 2 and workers likely to be in one of the situations referred to in Article 2 in the undertaking and/or establishment concerned and/or their representatives shall be informed of the results of the assessment referred to in paragraph 1 and of all measures to be taken concerning health and safety at work.

Article 5 Action further to the results of the assessment

1.   Without prejudice to Article 6 of Directive 89/391/EEC, if the results of the assessment referred to in Article 4 (1) reveal a risk to the safety or health or an effect on the pregnancy or breastfeeding of a worker within the meaning of Article 2, the employer shall take the necessary measures to ensure that, by temporarily adjusting the working conditions and/or the working hours of the worker concerned, the exposure of that worker to such risks is avoided.

2.   If the adjustment of her working conditions and/or working hours is not technically and/or objectively feasible, or cannot reasonably be required on duly substantiated grounds, the employer shall take the necessary measures to move the worker concerned to another job.

3.   If moving her to another job is not technically and/or objectively feasible or cannot reasonably be required on duly substantiated grounds, the worker concerned shall be

granted leave in accordance with national legislation and/or national practice for the whole of the period necessary to protect her safety or health.

4. The provisions of this Article shall apply mutatis mutandis to the case where a worker pursuing an activity which is forbidden pursuant to Article 6 becomes pregnant or starts breastfeeding and informs her employer thereof.

Article 6 Cases in which exposure is prohibited

In addition to the general provisions concerning the protection of workers, in particular those relating to the limit values for occupational exposure:

1. pregnant workers within the meaning of Article 2 (a) may under no circumstances be obliged to perform duties for which the assessment has revealed a risk of exposure, which would jeopardize safety or health, to the agents and working conditions listed in Annex II, Section A;

2. workers who are breastfeeding, within the meaning of Article 2 (c), may under no circumstances be obliged to perform duties for which the assessment has revealed a risk of exposure, which would jeopardize safety or health, to the agents and working conditions listed in Annex II, Section B.

Article 7 Night work

1. Member States shall take the necessary measures to ensure that workers referred to in Article 2 are not obliged to perform night work during their pregnancy and for a period following childbirth which shall be determined by the national authority competent for safety and health, subject to submission, in accordance with the procedures laid down by the Member States, of a medical certificate stating that this is necessary for the safety or health of the worker concerned.

2. The measures referred to in paragraph 1 must entail the possibility, in accordance with national legislation and/or national practice, of:
   (a) transfer to daytime work; or
   (b) leave from work or extension of maternity leave where such a transfer is not technically and/or objectively feasible or cannot reasonably by required on duly substantiated grounds.

Article 8 Maternity leave

1. Member States shall take the necessary measures to ensure that workers within the meaning of Article 2 are entitled to a continuous period of maternity leave of a least 14 weeks allocated before and/or after confinement in accordance with national legislation and/or practice.

2. The maternity leave stipulated in paragraph 1 must include compulsory maternity leave of at least two weeks allocated before and/or after confinement in accordance with national legislation and/or practice.

Article 9 Time off for ante-natal examinations

Member States shall take the necessary measures to ensure that pregnant workers within the meaning of Article 2 (a) are entitled to, in accordance with national legislation and/or practice, time off, without loss of pay, in order to attend ante-natal examinations, if such examinations have to take place during working hours.

Article 10 Prohibition of dismissal

In order to guarantee workers, within the meaning of Article 2, the exercise of their health and safety protection rights as recognized under this Article, it shall be provided that:

1.   Member States shall take the necessary measures to prohibit the dismissal of workers, within the meaning of Article 2, during the period from the beginning of their pregnancy to the end of the maternity leave referred to in Article 8 (1), save in exceptional cases not connected with their condition which are permitted under national legislation and/or practice and, where applicable, provided that the competent authority has given its consent;

2.   if a worker, within the meaning of Article 2, is dismissed during the period referred to in point 1, the employer must cite duly substantiated grounds for her dismissal in writing;

3.   Member States shall take the necessary measures to protect workers, within the meaning of Article 2, from consequences of dismissal which is unlawful by virtue of point 1.

Article 11 Employment rights

In order to guarantee workers within the meaning of Article 2 the exercise of their health and safety protection rights as recognized in this Article, it shall be provided that:

1.   in the cases referred to in Articles 5, 6 and 7, the employment rights relating to the employment contract, including the maintenance of a payment to, and/or entitlement to an adequate allowance for, workers within the meaning of Article 2, must be ensured in accordance with national legislation and/or national practice;

2.   in the case referred to in Article 8, the following must be ensured:
    (a) the rights connected with the employment contract of workers within the meaning of Article 2, other than those referred to in point (b) below;
    (b) maintenance of a payment to, and/or entitlement to an adequate allowance for, workers within the meaning of Article 2;

3.   the allowance referred to in point 2 (b) shall be deemed adequate if it guarantees income at least equivalent to that which the worker concerned would receive in the event of a break in her activities on grounds connected with her state of health, subject to any ceiling laid down under national legislation;

4.   Member States may make entitlement to pay or the allowance referred to in points 1 and 2 (b) conditional upon the worker concerned fulfilling the conditions of eligibility for such benefits laid down under national legislation.

    These conditions may under no circumstances provide for periods of previous employment in excess of 12 months immediately prior to the presumed date of confinement.

Article 12 Defence of rights

Member States shall introduce into their national legal systems such measures as are necessary to enable all workers who should themselves wronged by failure to comply with the obligations arising from this Directive to pursue their claims by judicial process (and/or, in accordance with national laws and/or practices) by recourse to other competent authorities.

Article 13 Amendments to the Annexes

1.   Strictly technical adjustments to Annex I as a result of technical progress, changes in international regulations or specifications and new findings in the area covered by this Directive shall be adopted in accordance with the procedure laid down in Article 17 of Directive 89/391/EEC.

2.   Annex II may be amended only in accordance with the procedure laid down in Article 118a of the Treaty [Article 153 TFEU].

Article 14 Final provisions

1. Member States shall bring into force the laws, regulations and administrative provisions necessary to comply with this Directive not later than two years after the adoption thereof or ensure, at the latest two years after adoption of this Directive, that the two sides of industry introduce the requisite provisions by means of collective agreements, with Member States being required to make all the necessary provisions to enable them at all times to guarantee the results laid down by this Directive. They shall forthwith inform the Commission thereof.

2. When Member States adopt the measures referred to in paragraph 1, they shall contain a reference of this Directive or shall be accompanied by such reference on the occasion of their official publication. The methods of making such a reference shall be laid down by the Member States.

3. Member States shall communicate to the Commission the texts of the essential provisions of national law which they have already adopted or adopt in the field governed by this Directive.

Article 15

This Directive is addressed to the Member States.

(*date of signing and signatory omitted*)

ANNEXES (*omitted*)

COUNCIL DIRECTIVE 94/33/EC OF 22 JUNE 1994

on the protection of young people at work

OJ L 216, 20.8.1994, p. 12*

(*As amended by Directive 2007/30/EC of the European Parliament and of the Council of 20 June 2007, OJ L 165, 27.6.2007, p. 21)

(*footnotes and preamble omitted*)

SECTION I

Article 1 Purpose

1. Member States shall take the necessary measures to prohibit work by children.

    They shall ensure, under the conditions laid down by this Directive, that the minimum working or employment age is not lower than the minimum age at which compulsory full-time schooling as imposed by national law ends or 15 years in any event.

2. Member States ensure that work by adolescents is strictly regulated and protected under the conditions laid down in this Directive.

3. Member States shall ensure in general that employers guarantee that young people have working conditions which suit their age.

    They shall ensure that young people are protected against economic exploitation and against any work likely to harm their safety, health or physical, mental, moral or social development or to jeopardize their education.

Article 2 Scope

1.   This Directive shall apply to any person under 18 years of age having an employment contract or an employment relationship defined by the law in force in a Member State and/or governed by the law in force in a Member State.

2.   Member States may make legislative or regulatory provision for this Directive not to apply, within the limits and under the conditions which they set by legislative or regulatory provision, to occasional work or short-term work involving:
     (a) domestic service in a private household, or
     (b) work regarded as not being harmful, damaging or dangerous to young people in a family undertaking.

Article 3 Definitions

For the purposes of this Directive:

(a) 'young person' shall mean any person under 18 years of age referred to in Article 2 (1);

(b) 'child' shall mean any young person of less than 15 years of age or who is still subject to compulsory full-time schooling under national law;

(c) 'adolescent' shall mean any young person of at least 15 years of age but less than 18 years of age who is no longer subject to compulsory full-time schooling under national law;

(d) 'light work' shall mean all work which, on account of the inherent nature of the tasks which it involves and the particular conditions under which they are performed:
     (i)   is not likely to be harmful to the safety, health or development of children, and
     (ii) is not such as to be harmful to their attendance at school, their participation in vocational guidance or training programmes approved by the competent authority or their capacity to benefit from the instruction received;

(e) 'working time' shall mean any period during which the young person is at work, at the employer's disposal and carrying out his activity or duties in accordance with national legislation and/or practice;

(f) 'rest period' shall mean any period which is not working time.

Article 4 Prohibition of work by children

1.   Member States shall adopt the measures necessary to prohibit work by children.

2.   Taking into account the objectives set out in Article 1, Member States may make legislative or regulatory provision for the prohibition of work by children not to apply to:
     (a) children pursuing the activities set out in Article 5;
     (b) children of at least 14 years of age working under a combined work/training scheme or an in-plant work-experience scheme, provided that such work is done in accordance with the conditions laid down by the competent authority;
     (c) children of at least 14 years of age performing light work other than that covered by Article 5; light work other than that covered by Article 5 may, however, be performed by children of 13 years of age for a limited number of hours per week in the case of categories of work determined by national legislation.

3.   Member States that make use of the opinion referred to in paragraph 2 (c) shall determine, subject to the provisions of this Directive, the working conditions relating to the light work in question.

Article 5 Cultural or similar activities

1. The employment of children for the purposes of performance in cultural, artistic, sports or advertising activities shall be subject to prior authorization to be given by the competent authority in individual cases.

2. Member States shall by legislative or regulatory provision lay down the working conditions for children in the cases referred to in paragraph 1 and the details of the prior authorization procedure, on condition that the activities:
    (i) are not likely to be harmful to the safety, health or development of children, and
    (ii) are not such as to be harmful to their attendance at school, their participation in vocational guidance or training programmes approved by the competent authority or their capacity to benefit from the instruction received.

3. By way of derogation from the procedure laid down in paragraph 1, in the case of children of at least 13 years of age, Member States may authorize, by legislative or regulatory provision, in accordance with conditions which they shall determine, the employment of children for the purposes of performance in cultural, artistic, sports or advertising activities.

4. The Member States which have a specific authorization system for modelling agencies with regard to the activities of children may retain that system.

SECTION II

Article 6 General obligations on employers

1. Without prejudice to Article 4 (1), the employer shall adopt the measures necessary to protect the safety and health of young people, taking particular account of the specific risks referred to in Article 7 (1).

2. The employer shall implement the measures provided for in paragraph 1 on the basis of an assessment of the hazards to young people in connection with their work.

    The assessment must be made before young people begin work and when there is any major change in working conditions and must pay particular attention to the following points:
    (a) the fitting-out and layout of the workplace and the workstation;
    (b) the nature, degree and duration of exposure to physical, biological and chemical agents;
    (c) the form, range and use of work equipment, in particular agents, machines, apparatus and devices, and the way in which they are handled;
    (d) the arrangement of work processes and operations and the way in which these are combined (organization of work);
    (e) the level of training and instruction given to young people.
    Where this assessment shows that there is a risk to the safety, the physical or mental health or development of young people, an appropriate free assessment and monitoring of their health shall be provided at regular intervals without prejudice to Directive 89/391/EEC.

    The free health assessment and monitoring may form part of a national health system.

3. The employer shall inform young people of possible risks and of all measures adopted concerning their safety and health.

    Furthermore, he shall inform the legal representatives of children of possible risks and of all measures adopted concerning children's safety and health.

4.   The employer shall involve the protective and preventive services referred to in Article 7 of Directive 89/391/EEC in the planning, implementation and monitoring of the safety and health conditions applicable to young people.

Article 7 Vulnerability of young people – Prohibition of work

1.   Member States shall ensure that young people are protected from any specific risks to their safety, health and development which are a consequence of their lack of experience, of absence of awareness of existing or potential risks or of the fact that young people have not yet fully matured.

2.   Without prejudice to Article 4 (1), Member States shall to this end prohibit the employment of young people for:
   (a) work which is objectively beyond their physical or psychological capacity;
   (b) work involving harmful exposure to agents which are toxic, carcinogenic, cause heritable genetic damage, or harm to the unborn child or which in any other way chronically affect human health;
   (c) work involving harmful exposure to radiation;
   (d) work involving the risk of accidents which it may be assumed cannot be recognized or avoided by young persons owing to their insufficient attention to safety or lack of experience or training; or
   (e) work in which there is a risk to health from extreme cold or heat, or from noise or vibration.
   Work which is likely to entail specific risks for young people within the meaning of paragraph 1 includes:
   —   work involving harmful exposure to the physical, biological and chemical agents referred to in point I of the Annex, and
   —   processes and work referred to in point II of the Annex.

3.   Member States may, by legislative or regulatory provision, authorize derogations from paragraph 2 in the case of adolescents where such derogations are indispensable for their vocational training, provided that protection of their safety and health is ensured by the fact that the work is performed under the supervision of a competent person within the meaning of Article 7 of Directive 89/391/EEC and provided that the protection afforded by that Directive is guaranteed.

SECTION III

Article 8 Working time

1.   Member States which make use of the option in Article 4 (2) (b) or (c) shall adopt the measures necessary to limit the working time of children to:
   (a) eight hours a day and 40 hours a week for work performed under a combined work/ training scheme or an in-plant work-experience scheme;
   (b) two hours on a school day and 12 hours a week for work performed in term-time outside the hours fixed for school attendance, provided that this is not prohibited by national legislation and/or practice;
   in no circumstances may the daily working time exceed seven hours; this limit may be raised to eight hours in the case of children who have reached the age of 15;

   (c) seven hours a day and 35 hours a week for work performed during a period of at least a week when school is not operating; these limits may be raised to eight hours a day and 40 hours a week in the case of children who have reached the age of 15;
   (d) seven hours a day and 35 hours a week for light work performed by children no longer subject to compulsory full-time schooling under national law.

2. Member States shall adopt the measures necessary to limit the working time of adolescents to eight hours a day and 40 hours a week.

3. The time spent on training by a young person working under a theoretical and/or practical combined work/training scheme or an in-plant work-experience scheme shall be counted as working time.

4. Where a young person is employed by more than one employer, working days and working time shall be cumulative.

5. Member States may, by legislative or regulatory provision, authorize derogations from paragraph 1 (a) and paragraph 2 either by way of exception or where there are objective grounds for so doing.

    Member States shall, by legislative or regulatory provision, determine the conditions, limits and procedure for implementing such derogations.

Article 9 Night work

1. (a) Member States which make use of the option in Article 4 (2) (b) or (c) shall a dopt the measures necessary to prohibit work by children between 8 p.m. and 6 a.m.

    (b) Member States shall adopt the measures necessary to prohibit work by adolescents either between 10 p.m. and 6 a.m. or between 11 p.m. and 7 a.m.

2. (a) Member States may, by legislative or regulatory provision, authorize work by adolescents in specific areas of activity during the period in which night work is prohibited as referred to in paragraph 1 (b).

    In that event, Member States shall take appropriate measures to ensure that the adolescent is supervised by an adult where such supervision is necessary for the adolescent's protection.

    (b) If point (a) is applied, work shall continue to be prohibited between midnight and 4 a.m.

    However, Member States may, by legislative or regulatory provision, authorize work by adolescents during the period in which night work is prohibited in the following cases, where there are objective grounds for so doing and provided that adolescents are allowed suitable compensatory rest time and that the objectives set out in Article 1 are not called into question:

    — work performed in the shipping or fisheries sectors;
    — work performed in the context of the armed forces or the police;
    — work performed in hospitals or similar establishments;
    — cultural, artistic, sports or advertising activities.

3. Prior to any assignment to night work and at regular intervals thereafter, adolescents shall be entitled to a free assessment of their health and capacities, unless the work they do during the period during which work is prohibited is of an exceptional nature.

Article 10 Rest period

1. (a) Member States which make use of the option in Article 4 (2) (b) or (c) shall adopt the measures necessary to ensure that, for each 24-hour period, children are entitled to a minimum rest period of 14 consecutive hours.

    (b) Member States shall adopt the measures necessary to ensure that, for each 24-hour period, adolescents are entitled to a minimum rest period of 12 consecutive hours.

2. Member States shall adopt the measures necessary to ensure that, for each seven-day period:
    — children in respect of whom they have made use of the option in Article 4 (2) (b) or (c), and
    — adolescents are entitled to a minimum rest period of two days, which shall be consecutive if possible.
    Where justified by technical or organization reasons, the minimum rest period may be reduced, but may in no circumstances be less than 36 consecutive hours.

    The minimum rest period referred to in the first and second subparagraphs shall in principle include Sunday.

3. Member States may, by legislative or regulatory provision, provide for the minimum rest periods referred to in paragraphs 1 and 2 to be interrupted in the case of activities involving periods of work that are split up over the day or are of short duration.

4. Member States may make legislative or regulatory provision for derogations from paragraph 1 (b) and paragraph 2 in respect of adolescents in the following cases, where there are objective grounds for so doing and provided that they are granted appropriate compensatory rest time and that the objectives set out in Article 1 are not called into question:
    (a) work performed in the shipping or fisheries sectors;
    (b) work performed in the context of the armed forces or the police;
    (c) work performed in hospitals or similar establishments;
    (d) work performed in agriculture;
    (e) work performed in the tourism industry or in the hotel, restaurant and café sector;
    (f) activities involving periods of work split up over the day.

Article 11 Annual rest
Member States which make use of the option referred to in Article 4 (2) (b) or (c) shall see to it that a period free of any work is included, as far as possible, in the school holidays of children subject to compulsory full-time schooling under national law.

Article 12 Breaks
Member States shall adopt the measures necessary to ensure that, where daily working time is more than four and a half hours, young people are entitled to a break of at least 30 minutes, which shall be consecutive if possible.

Article 13 Work by adolescents in the event of force majeure
Member States may, by legislative or regulatory provision, authorize derogations from Article 8 (2), Article 9 (1) (b), Article 10 (1) (b) and, in the case of adolescents, Article 12, for work in the circumstances referred to in Article 5 (4) of Directive 89/391/EEC, provided that such work is of a temporary nature and must be performed immediately, that adult workers are not available and that the adolescents are allowed equivalent compensatory rest time within the following three weeks.

SECTION IV

Article 14 Measures
Each Member State shall lay down any necessary measures to be applied in the event of failure to comply with the provisions adopted in order to implement this Directive; such measures must be effective and proportionate.

Article 15 Adaptation of the Annex

Adaptations of a strictly technical nature to the Annex in the light of technical progress, changes in international rules or specifications and advances in knowledge in the field covered by this Directive shall be adopted in accordance with the procedure provided for in Article 17 of Directive 89/391/EEC.

Article 16 Non-reducing clause

Without prejudice to the right of Member States to develop, in the light of changing circumstances, different provisions on the protection of young people, as long as the minimum requirements provided for by this Directive are complied with, the implementation of this Directive shall not constitute valid grounds for reducing the general level of protection afforded to young people.

Article 17 Final provisions

1. (a) Member States shall bring into force the laws, regulations and administrative provisions necessary to comply with this Directive not later than 22 June 1996 or ensure, by that date at the latest, that the two sides of industry introduce the requisite provisions by means of collective agreements, with Member States being required to make all the necessary provisions to enable them at all times to guarantee the results laid down by this Directive.
    (b) The United Kingdom may refrain from implementing the first subparagraph of Article 8 (1) (b) with regard to the provision relating to the maximum weekly working time, and also Article 8(2) and Article 9 (1) (b) and (2) for a period of four years from the date specified in subparagraph (a).

    The Commission shall submit a report on the effects of this provision.

    The Council, acting in accordance with the conditions laid down by the Treaty, shall decide whether this period should be extended.
    (c) Member States shall forthwith inform the Commission thereof.

2. When Member States adopt the measures referred to in paragraph 1, such measures shall contain a reference to this Directive or shall be accompanied by such reference on the occasion of their official publication. The methods of making such reference shall be laid down by Member States.

3. Member States shall communicate to the Commission the texts of the main provisions of national law which they have already adopted or adopt in the field governed by this Directive.

4. Member States shall report to the Commission every five years on the practical implementation of the provisions of this Directive, indicating the viewpoints of the two sides of industry.

    The Commission shall inform the European Parliament, the Council and the Economic and Social Committee thereof.

5. The Commission shall periodically submit to the European Parliament, the Council and the Economic and Social Committee a report on the application of this Directive taking into account paragraphs 1, 2, 3 and 4.

Article 17a Implementation report

Every five years, the Member States shall submit to the Commission a report on the practical implementation of this Directive in the form of a specific chapter of the single report referred to in Article 17a(1), (2) and (3) of Directive 89/391/EEC, which serves as a basis for the Commission's evaluation, in accordance with Article 17a(4) of that Directive.

Article 18
This Directive is addressed to the Member States.

(*Date of signing and signatory omitted*)

ANNEX (*omitted*)

DIRECTIVE 2003/88/EC OF THE EUROPEAN PARLIAMENT AND OF THE COUNCIL OF 4 NOVEMBER 2003

concerning certain aspects of the organisation of working time
OJ L 299, 18.11.2003, p. 9[1]

....

(*footnotes omitted*)

THE EUROPEAN PARLIAMENT AND THE COUNCIL OF THE EUROPEAN UNION,

Having regard to the Treaty establishing the European Community, and in particular Article 137(2) thereof,

Having regard to the proposal from the Commission,

Having regard to the opinion of the European Economic and Social Committee,

Having consulted the Committee of the Regions,

Acting in accordance with the procedure referred to in Article 251 of the Treaty,

Whereas:
(1)   Council Directive 93/104/EC of 23 November 1993, concerning certain aspects of the organisation of working time, which lays down minimum safety and health requirements for the organisation of working time, in respect of periods of daily rest, breaks, weekly rest, maximum weekly working time, annual leave and aspects of night work, shift work and patterns of work, has been significantly amended. In order to clarify matters, a codification of the provisions in question should be drawn up.

(2)   Article 137 of the Treaty provides that the Community is to support and complement the activities of the Member States with a view to improving the working environment to protect workers' health and safety. Directives adopted on the basis of that Article are to avoid imposing administrative, financial and legal constraints in a way which would hold back the creation and development of small and medium-sized undertakings.

(3)   The provisions of Council Directive 89/391/EEC of 12 June 1989 on the introduction of measures to encourage improvements in the safety and health of workers at work remain fully applicable to the areas covered by this Directive without prejudice to more stringent and/or specific provisions contained herein.

....

1   EDITOR'S NOTE: Directive 2003/88 repealed and replaced Directive 93/104/EC and its amendment, Directive 2000/34/EC. See the Correlation Table in Annex II below to convert article numbers from the original Directive. For conversion of the Treaty numbers from the EC Treaty to the Treaty on the Functioning of the European Union (TFEU) refer to the Table of Equivalences for the TFEU in Part II of this edition.

(4)   The improvement of workers' safety, hygiene and health at work is an objective which should not be subordinated to purely economic considerations.

(5)   All workers should have adequate rest periods. The concept of "rest" must be expressed in units of time, i.e. in days, hours and/or fractions thereof. Community workers must be granted minimum daily, weekly and annual periods of rest and adequate breaks. It is also necessary in this context to place a maximum limit on weekly working hours.

(6)   Account should be taken of the principles of the International Labour Organisation with regard to the organisation of working time, including those relating to night work.

(7)   Research has shown that the human body is more sensitive at night to environmental disturbances and also to certain burdensome forms of work organisation and that long periods of night work can be detrimental to the health of workers and can endanger safety at the workplace.

(8)   There is a need to limit the duration of periods of night work, including overtime, and to provide for employers who regularly use night workers to bring this information to the attention of the competent authorities if they so request.

(9)   It is important that night workers should be entitled to a free health assessment prior to their assignment and thereafter at regular intervals and that whenever possible they should be transferred to day work for which they are suited if they suffer from health problems.

(10) The situation of night and shift workers requires that the level of safety and health protection should be adapted to the nature of their work and that the organisation and functioning of protection and prevention services and resources should be efficient.

(11) Specific working conditions may have detrimental effects on the safety and health of workers. The organisation of work according to a certain pattern must take account of the general principle of adapting work to the worker.

(12) A European Agreement in respect of the working time of seafarers has been put into effect by means of Council Directive 1999/63/EC of 21 June 1999 concerning the Agreement on the organisation of working time of seafarers concluded by the European Community Shipowners' Association (ECSA) and the Federation of Transport Workers' Unions in the European Union (FST) based on Article 139(2) of the Treaty. Accordingly, the provisions of this Directive should not apply to seafarers.

(13) In the case of those "share-fishermen" who are employees, it is for the Member States to determine, pursuant to this Directive, the conditions for entitlement to, and granting of, annual leave, including the arrangements for payments.

(14) Specific standards laid down in other Community instruments relating, for example, to rest periods, working time, annual leave and night work for certain categories of workers should take precedence over the provisions of this Directive.

(15) In view of the question likely to be raised by the organisation of working time within an undertaking, it appears desirable to provide for flexibility in the application of certain provisions of this Directive, whilst ensuring compliance with the principles of protecting the safety and health of workers.

(16) It is necessary to provide that certain provisions may be subject to derogations implemented, according to the case, by the Member States or the two sides of industry. As a general rule, in the event of a derogation, the workers concerned must be given equivalent compensatory rest periods.

(17) This Directive should not affect the obligations of the Member States concerning the deadlines for transposition of the Directives set out in Annex I, part B,

HAVE ADOPTED THIS DIRECTIVE:

Chapter 1 SCOPE AND DEFINITIONS

Article 1 Purpose and scope

1. This Directive lays down minimum safety and health requirements for the organisation of working time.

2. This Directive applies to:
    (a) minimum periods of daily rest, weekly rest and annual leave, to breaks and maximum weekly working time; and
    (b) certain aspects of night work, shift work and patterns of work.

3. This Directive shall apply to all sectors of activity, both public and private, within the meaning of Article 2 of Directive 89/391/EEC, without prejudice to Articles 14, 17, 18 and 19 of this Directive.

    This Directive shall not apply to seafarers, as defined in Directive 1999/63/EC without prejudice to Article 2(8) of this Directive.

4. The provisions of Directive 89/391/EEC are fully applicable to the matters referred to in paragraph 2, without prejudice to more stringent and/or specific provisions contained in this Directive.

Article 2 Definitions

For the purposes of this Directive, the following definitions shall apply:

1. "working time" means any period during which the worker is working, at the employer's disposal and carrying out his activity or duties, in accordance with national laws and/or practice;

2. "rest period" means any period which is not working time;

3. "night time" means any period of not less than seven hours, as defined by national law, and which must include, in any case, the period between midnight and 5.00;

4. "night worker" means:
    (a) on the one hand, any worker, who, during night time, works at least three hours of his daily working time as a normal course; and
    (b) on the other hand, any worker who is likely during night time to work a certain proportion of his annual working time, as defined at the choice of the Member State concerned:
        (i) by national legislation, following consultation with the two sides of industry; or
        (ii) by collective agreements or agreements concluded between the two sides of industry at national or regional level;

5. "shift work" means any method of organising work in shifts whereby workers succeed each other at the same work stations according to a certain pattern, including a rotating pattern, and which may be continuous or discontinuous, entailing the need for workers to work at different times over a given period of days or weeks;

6. "shift worker" means any worker whose work schedule is part of shift work;

7. "mobile worker" means any worker employed as a member of travelling or flying personnel by an undertaking which operates transport services for passengers or goods by road, air or inland waterway;

8. "offshore work" means work performed mainly on or from offshore installations (including drilling rigs), directly or indirectly in connection with the exploration, extraction or exploitation of mineral resources, including hydrocarbons, and diving in connection with such activities, whether performed from an offshore installation or a vessel;

9. "adequate rest" means that workers have regular rest periods, the duration of which is expressed in units of time and which are sufficiently long and continuous to ensure that, as a result of fatigue or other irregular working patterns, they do not cause injury to themselves, to fellow workers or to others and that they do not damage their health, either in the short term or in the longer term.

Chapter 2 MINIMUM REST PERIODS – OTHER ASPECTS OF THE ORGANISATION OF WORKING TIME

Article 3 Daily rest
Member States shall take the measures necessary to ensure that every worker is entitled to a minimum daily rest period of 11 consecutive hours per 24-hour period.

Article 4 Breaks
Member States shall take the measures necessary to ensure that, where the working day is longer than six hours, every worker is entitled to a rest break, the details of which, including duration and the terms on which it is granted, shall be laid down in collective agreements or agreements between the two sides of industry or, failing that, by national legislation.

Article 5 Weekly rest period
Member States shall take the measures necessary to ensure that, per each seven-day period, every worker is entitled to a minimum uninterrupted rest period of 24 hours plus the 11 hours' daily rest referred to in Article 3.

If objective, technical or work organisation conditions so justify, a minimum rest period of 24 hours may be applied.

Article 6 Maximum weekly working time
Member States shall take the measures necessary to ensure that, in keeping with the need to protect the safety and health of workers:
(a) the period of weekly working time is limited by means of laws, regulations or administrative provisions or by collective agreements or agreements between the two sides of industry;
(b) the average working time for each seven-day period, including overtime, does not exceed 48 hours.

Article 7 Annual leave
1. Member States shall take the measures necessary to ensure that every worker is entitled to paid annual leave of at least four weeks in accordance with the conditions for entitlement to, and granting of, such leave laid down by national legislation and/or practice.

2. The minimum period of paid annual leave may not be replaced by an allowance in lieu, except where the employment relationship is terminated.

Chapter 3 NIGHT WORK – SHIFT WORK – PATTERNS OF WORK

Article 8 Length of night work
Member States shall take the measures necessary to ensure that:

(a)   normal hours of work for night workers do not exceed an average of eight hours in any 24-hour period;

(b)   night workers whose work involves special hazards or heavy physical or mental strain do not work more than eight hours in any period of 24 hours during which they perform night work.

For the purposes of point (b), work involving special hazards or heavy physical or mental strain shall be defined by national legislation and/or practice or by collective agreements or agreements concluded between the two sides of industry, taking account of the specific effects and hazards of night work.

Article 9 Health assessment and transfer of night workers to day work
1.   Member States shall take the measures necessary to ensure that:
    (a)   night workers are entitled to a free health assessment before their assignment and thereafter at regular intervals;
    (b)   night workers suffering from health problems recognised as being connected with the fact that they perform night work are transferred whenever possible to day work to which they are suited.

2.   The free health assessment referred to in paragraph 1(a) must comply with medical confidentiality.

3.   The free health assessment referred to in paragraph 1(a) may be conducted within the national health system.

Article 10 Guarantees for night-time working
Member States may make the work of certain categories of night workers subject to certain guarantees, under conditions laid down by national legislation and/or practice, in the case of workers who incur risks to their safety or health linked to night-time working.

Article 11 Notification of regular use of night workers
Member States shall take the measures necessary to ensure that an employer who regularly uses night workers brings this information to the attention of the competent authorities if they so request.

Article 12 Safety and health protection
Member States shall take the measures necessary to ensure that:
(a)   night workers and shift workers have safety and health protection appropriate to the nature of their work;

(b)   appropriate protection and prevention services or facilities with regard to the safety and health of night workers and shift workers are equivalent to those applicable to other workers and are available at all times.

Article 13 Pattern of work
Member States shall take the measures necessary to ensure that an employer who intends to organise work according to a certain pattern takes account of the general principle of adapting work to the worker, with a view, in particular, to alleviating monotonous work and work at a predetermined work-rate, depending on the type of activity, and of safety and health requirements, especially as regards breaks during working time.

Chapter 4 MISCELLANEOUS PROVISIONS

Article 14 More specific Community provisions
This Directive shall not apply where other Community instruments contain more specific requirements relating to the organisation of working time for certain occupations or occupational activities.

Article 15 More favourable provisions
This Directive shall not affect Member States' right to apply or introduce laws, regulations or administrative provisions more favourable to the protection of the safety and health of workers or to facilitate or permit the application of collective agreements or agreements concluded between the two sides of industry which are more favourable to the protection of the safety and health of workers.

Article 16 Reference periods
Member States may lay down:
(a)   for the application of Article 5 (weekly rest period), a reference period not exceeding 14 days;

(b)   for the application of Article 6 (maximum weekly working time), a reference period not exceeding four months.

    The periods of paid annual leave, granted in accordance with Article 7, and the periods of sick leave shall not be included or shall be neutral in the calculation of the average;

(c)   for the application of Article 8 (length of night work), a reference period defined after consultation of the two sides of industry or by collective agreements or agreements concluded between the two sides of industry at national or regional level.

If the minimum weekly rest period of 24 hours required by Article 5 falls within that reference period, it shall not be included in the calculation of the average.

Chapter 5 DEROGATIONS AND EXCEPTIONS

Article 17 Derogations
1.   With due regard for the general principles of the protection of the safety and health of workers, Member States may derogate from Articles 3 to 6, 8 and 16 when, on account of the specific characteristics of the activity concerned, the duration of the working time is not measured and/or predetermined or can be determined by the workers themselves, and particularly in the case of:
    (a) managing executives or other persons with autonomous decision-taking powers;
    (b) family workers; or
    (c) workers officiating at religious ceremonies in churches and religious communities.

2.   Derogations provided for in paragraphs 3, 4 and 5 may be adopted by means of laws, regulations or administrative provisions or by means of collective agreements or agreements between the two sides of industry provided that the workers concerned are afforded equivalent periods of compensatory rest or that, in exceptional cases in which it is not possible, for objective reasons, to grant such equivalent periods of compensatory rest, the workers concerned are afforded appropriate protection.

3.   In accordance with paragraph 2 of this Article derogations may be made from Articles 3, 4, 5, 8 and 16:
    (a) in the case of activities where the worker's place of work and his place of residence are distant from one another, including offshore work, or where the worker's different places of work are distant from one another;

    (b) in the case of security and surveillance activities requiring a permanent presence in order to protect property and persons, particularly security guards and caretakers or security firms;

    (c) in the case of activities involving the need for continuity of service or production, particularly:

        (i)   services relating to the reception, treatment and/or care provided by hospitals or similar establishments, including the activities of doctors in training, residential institutions and prisons;

        (ii) dock or airport workers;

        (iii) press, radio, television, cinematographic production, postal and telecommunications services, ambulance, fire and civil protection services;

        (iv) gas, water and electricity production, transmission and distribution, household refuse collection and incineration plants;

        (v) industries in which work cannot be interrupted on technical grounds;

        (vi) research and development activities;

        (vii) agriculture;

        (viii) workers concerned with the carriage of passengers on regular urban transport services;

    (d) where there is a foreseeable surge of activity, particularly in:

        (i)   agriculture;

        (ii) tourism;

        (iii) postal services;

    (e) in the case of persons working in railway transport:

        (i)   whose activities are intermittent;

        (ii) who spend their working time on board trains; or

        (iii) whose activities are linked to transport timetables and to ensuring the continuity and regularity of traffic;

    (f) in the circumstances described in Article 5(4) of Directive 89/391/EEC;

    (g) in cases of accident or imminent risk of accident.

4.   In accordance with paragraph 2 of this Article derogations may be made from Articles 3 and 5:

    (a) in the case of shift work activities, each time the worker changes shift and cannot take daily and/or weekly rest periods between the end of one shift and the start of the next one;

    (b) in the case of activities involving periods of work split up over the day, particularly those of cleaning staff.

5.   In accordance with paragraph 2 of this Article, derogations may be made from Article 6 and Article 16(b), in the case of doctors in training, in accordance with the provisions set out in the second to the seventh subparagraphs of this paragraph.

With respect to Article 6 derogations referred to in the first subparagraph shall be permitted for a transitional period of five years from 1 August 2004.

Member States may have up to two more years, if necessary, to take account of difficulties in meeting the working time provisions with respect to their responsibilities for the organisation and delivery of health services and medical care. At least six months before the end of the transitional period, the Member State concerned shall inform the Commission giving its reasons, so that the Commission can give an opinion, after appropriate consultations, within the three months following receipt of such information. If the Member State does not follow the opinion of the Commission, it will justify its decision. The notification and justification of the Member State and the opinion of the

Commission shall be published in the *Official Journal of the European Union* and forwarded to the European Parliament.

Member States may have an additional period of up to one year, if necessary, to take account of special difficulties in meeting the responsibilities referred to in the third subparagraph. They shall follow the procedure set out in that subparagraph.

Member States shall ensure that in no case will the number of weekly working hours exceed an average of 58 during the first three years of the transitional period, an average of 56 for the following two years and an average of 52 for any remaining period.

The employer shall consult the representatives of the employees in good time with a view to reaching an agreement, wherever possible, on the arrangements applying to the transitional period. Within the limits set out in the fifth subparagraph, such an agreement may cover:
(a) the average number of weekly hours of work during the transitional period; and
(b) the measures to be adopted to reduce weekly working hours to an average of 48 by the end of the transitional period.

With respect to Article 16(b) derogations referred to in the first subparagraph shall be permitted provided that the reference period does not exceed 12 months, during the first part of the transitional period specified in the fifth subparagraph, and six months thereafter.

Article 18 Derogations by collective agreements

Derogations may be made from Articles 3, 4, 5, 8 and 16 by means of collective agreements or agreements concluded between the two sides of industry at national or regional level or, in conformity with the rules laid down by them, by means of collective agreements or agreements concluded between the two sides of industry at a lower level.

Member States in which there is no statutory system ensuring the conclusion of collective agreements or agreements concluded between the two sides of industry at national or regional level, on the matters covered by this Directive, or those Member States in which there is a specific legislative framework for this purpose and within the limits thereof, may, in accordance with national legislation and/or practice, allow derogations from Articles 3, 4, 5, 8 and 16 by way of collective agreements or agreements concluded between the two sides of industry at the appropriate collective level.

The derogations provided for in the first and second subparagraphs shall be allowed on condition that equivalent compensating rest periods are granted to the workers concerned or, in exceptional cases where it is not possible for objective reasons to grant such periods, the workers concerned are afforded appropriate protection.

Member States may lay down rules:
(a) for the application of this Article by the two sides of industry; and

(b) for the extension of the provisions of collective agreements or agreements concluded in conformity with this Article to other workers in accordance with national legislation and/ or practice.

Article 19 Limitations to derogations from reference periods

The option to derogate from Article 16(b), provided for in Article 17(3) and in Article 18, may not result in the establishment of a reference period exceeding six months.

However, Member States shall have the option, subject to compliance with the general principles relating to the protection of the safety and health of workers, of allowing, for objective or technical reasons or reasons concerning the organisation of work, collective agreements or agreements concluded between the two sides of industry to set reference periods in no event exceeding 12 months.

Before 23 November 2003, the Council shall, on the basis of a Commission proposal accompanied by an appraisal report, re-examine the provisions of this Article and decide what action to take.

Article 20   Mobile workers and offshore work

1. Articles 3, 4, 5 and 8 shall not apply to mobile workers.

    Member States shall, however, take the necessary measures to ensure that such mobile workers are entitled to adequate rest, except in the circumstances laid down in Article 17(3)(f) and (g).

2. Subject to compliance with the general principles relating to the protection of the safety and health of workers, and provided that there is consultation of representatives of the employer and employees concerned and efforts to encourage all relevant forms of social dialogue, including negotiation if the parties so wish, Member States may, for objective or technical reasons or reasons concerning the organisation of work, extend the reference period referred to in Article 16(b) to 12 months in respect of workers who mainly perform offshore work.

3. Not later than 1 August 2005 the Commission shall, after consulting the Member States and management and labour at European level, review the operation of the provisions with regard to offshore workers from a health and safety perspective with a view to presenting, if need be, the appropriate modifications.

Article 21   Workers on board seagoing fishing vessels

1. Articles 3 to 6 and 8 shall not apply to any worker on board a seagoing fishing vessel flying the flag of a Member State.

    Member States shall, however, take the necessary measures to ensure that any worker on board a seagoing fishing vessel flying the flag of a Member State is entitled to adequate rest and to limit the number of hours of work to 48 hours a week on average calculated over a reference period not exceeding 12 months.

2. Within the limits set out in paragraph 1, second subparagraph, and paragraphs 3 and 4 Member States shall take the necessary measures to ensure that, in keeping with the need to protect the safety and health of such workers:
    (a) the working hours are limited to a maximum number of hours which shall not be exceeded in a given period of time; or
    (b) a minimum number of hours of rest are provided within a given period of time.
    The maximum number of hours of work or minimum number of hours of rest shall be specified by law, regulations, administrative provisions or by collective agreements or agreements between the two sides of the industry.

3. The limits on hours of work or rest shall be either:
    (a) maximum hours of work which shall not exceed:
        (i)   14 hours in any 24-hour period; and
        (ii) 72 hours in any seven-day period; or
    (b) minimum hours of rest which shall not be less than:
        (i)   10 hours in any 24-hour period; and
        (ii) 77 hours in any seven-day period.

4.   Hours of rest may be divided into no more than two periods, one of which shall be at least six hours in length, and the interval between consecutive periods of rest shall not exceed 14 hours.

5.   In accordance with the general principles of the protection of the health and safety of workers, and for objective or technical reasons or reasons concerning the organisation of work, Member States may allow exceptions, including the establishment of reference periods, to the limits laid down in paragraph 1, second subparagraph, and paragraphs 3 and 4. Such exceptions shall, as far as possible, comply with the standards laid down but may take account of more frequent or longer leave periods or the granting of compensatory leave for the workers. These exceptions may be laid down by means of:
(a)   laws, regulations or administrative provisions provided there is consultation, where possible, of the representatives of the employers and workers concerned and efforts are made to encourage all relevant forms of social dialogue; or
(b)   collective agreements or agreements between the two sides of industry.

6.   The master of a seagoing fishing vessel shall have the right to require workers on board to perform any hours of work necessary for the immediate safety of the vessel, persons on board or cargo, or for the purpose of giving assistance to other vessels or persons in distress at sea.

7.   Members States may provide that workers on board seagoing fishing vessels for which national legislation or practice determines that these vessels are not allowed to operate in a specific period of the calendar year exceeding one month, shall take annual leave in accordance with Article 7 within that period.

Article 22   Miscellaneous provisions
1.   A Member State shall have the option not to apply Article 6, while respecting the general principles of the protection of the safety and health of workers, and provided it takes the necessary measures to ensure that:
(a)   no employer requires a worker to work more than 48 hours over a seven-day period, calculated as an average for the reference period referred to in Article 16(b), unless he has first obtained the worker's agreement to perform such work;
(b)   no worker is subjected to any detriment by his employer because he is not willing to give his agreement to perform such work;
(c)   the employer keeps up-to-date records of all workers who carry out such work;
(d)   the records are placed at the disposal of the competent authorities, which may, for reasons connected with the safety and/or health of workers, prohibit or restrict the possibility of exceeding the maximum weekly working hours;
(e)   the employer provides the competent authorities at their request with information on cases in which agreement has been given by workers to perform work exceeding 48 hours over a period of seven days, calculated as an average for the reference period referred to in Article 16(b).
Before 23 November 2003, the Council shall, on the basis of a Commission proposal accompanied by an appraisal report, re-examine the provisions of this paragraph and decide on what action to take.

2.   Member States shall have the option, as regards the application of Article 7, of making use of a transitional period of not more than three years from 23 November 1996, provided that during that transitional period:
(a)   every worker receives three weeks' paid annual leave in accordance with the conditions for the entitlement to, and granting of, such leave laid down by national legislation and/or practice; and

(b) the three-week period of paid annual leave may not be replaced by an allowance in lieu, except where the employment relationship is terminated.

3. If Member States avail themselves of the options provided for in this Article, they shall forthwith inform the Commission thereof.

Chapter 6 FINAL PROVISIONS

Article 23 Level of Protection
Without prejudice to the right of Member States to develop, in the light of changing circumstances, different legislative, regulatory or contractual provisions in the field of working time, as long as the minimum requirements provided for in this Directive are complied with, implementation of this Directive shall not constitute valid grounds for reducing the general level of protection afforded to workers.

Article 24 Reports
1. Member States shall communicate to the Commission the texts of the provisions of national law already adopted or being adopted in the field governed by this Directive.

2. Member States shall report to the Commission every five years on the practical implementation of the provisions of this Directive, indicating the viewpoints of the two sides of industry.

    The Commission shall inform the European Parliament, the Council, the European Economic and Social Committee and the Advisory Committee on Safety, Hygiene and Health Protection at Work thereof.

3. Every five years from 23 November 1996 the Commission shall submit to the European Parliament, the Council and the European Economic and Social Committee a report on the application of this Directive taking into account Articles 22 and 23 and paragraphs 1 and 2 of this Article.

Article 25 Review of the operation of the provisions with regard to workers on board seagoing fishing vessels
Not later than 1 August 2009 the Commission shall, after consulting the Member States and management and labour at European level, review the operation of the provisions with regard to workers on board seagoing fishing vessels, and, in particular examine whether these provisions remain appropriate, in particular, as far as health and safety are concerned with a view to proposing suitable amendments, if necessary.

Article 26 Review of the operation of the provisions with regard to workers concerned with the carriage of passengers
Not later than 1 August 2005 the Commission shall, after consulting the Member States and management and labour at European level, review the operation of the provisions with regard to workers concerned with the carriage of passengers on regular urban transport services, with a view to presenting, if need be, the appropriate modifications to ensure a coherent and suitable approach in the sector.

Article 27 Repeal
1. Directive 93/104/EC, as amended by the Directive referred to in Annex I, part A, shall be repealed, without prejudice to the obligations of the Member States in respect of the deadlines for transposition laid down in Annex I, part B.

2. The references made to the said repealed Directive shall be construed as references to this Directive and shall be read in accordance with the correlation table set out in Annex II.

Article 28 Entry into force
This Directive shall enter into force on 2 August 2004.

Article 29 Addressees
This Directive is addressed to the Member States.

(*Date of signing and signatories omitted*)

ANNEX I (*omitted*)

ANNEX II

CORRELATION TABLE

Directive 93/104/EC	This Directive
Articles 1 to 5	Articles 1 to 5
Article 6, introductory words	Article 6, introductory words
Article 6(1)	Article 6(a)
Article 6(2)	Article 6(b)
Article 7	Article 7
Article 8, introductory words	Article 8, introductory words
Article 8(1)	Article 8(a)
Article 8(2)	Article 8(b)
Articles 9, 10 and 11	Articles 9, 10 and 11
Article 12, introductory words	Article 12, introductory words
Article 12(1)	Article 12(a)
Article 12(2)	Article 12(b)
Articles 13, 14 and 15	Articles 13, 14 and 15
Article 16, introductory words	Article 16, introductory words
Article 16(1)	Article 16(a)
Article 16(2)	Article 16(b)
Article 16(3)	Article 16(c)
Article 17(1)	Article 17(1)
Article 17(2), introductory words	Article 17(2)
Article 17(2)(1)	Article 17(3)(a) to (e)
Article 17(2)(2)	Article 17(3)(f) to (g)
Article 17(2)(3)	Article 17(4)
Article 17(2)(4)	Article 17(5)
Article 17(3)	Article 18
Article 17(4)	Article 19
Article 17a(1)	Article 20(1), first subpara.
Article 17a(2)	Article 20(1), second subpara.
Article 17a(3)	Article 20(2)
Article 17a(4)	Article 20(3)
Article 17b(1)	Article 21(1), first subparagraph
Article 17b(2)	Article 21(1), second subparagraph
Article 17b(3)	Article 21(2)
Article 17b(4)	Article 21(3)
Article 17b(5)	Article 21(4)
Article 17b(6)	Article 21(5)

Directive 93/104/EC	This Directive
Article 17b(7)	Article 21(6)
Article 17b(8)	Article 21(7)
Article 18(1)(a)	—
Article 18(1)(b)(i)	Article 22(1)
Article 18(1)(b)(ii)	Article 22(2)
Article 18(1)(c)	Article 22(3)
Article 18(2)	—
Article 18(3)	Article 23
Article 18(4)	Article 24(1)
Article 18(5)	Article 24(2)
Article 18(6)	Article 24(3)
—	Article 25 (1)
—	Article 26 (2)
—	Article 27
—	Article 28
Article 19	Article 29
—	Annex I
—	Annex II

Chronological Index*

---

* Ordered by publication date in the *Official Journal of the European Union* unless otherwise stated

Thematic Index

THE CONFIDENCE BOOSTER WORKBOOK

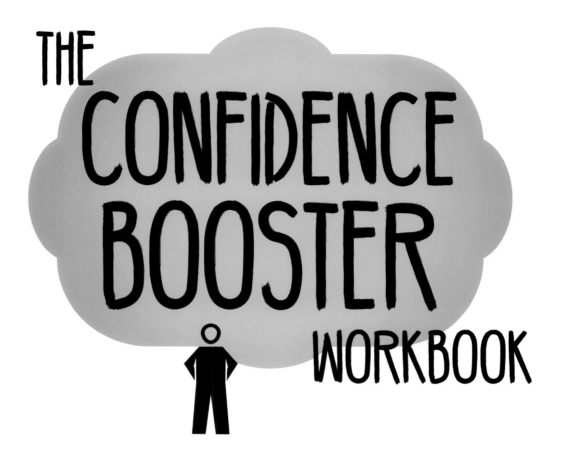

THE CONFIDENCE BOOSTER WORKBOOK

TIPS, TRICKS AND TESTS TO IMPROVE YOUR CONFIDENCE

MARTIN PERRY

hamlyn

An Hachette UK Company
www.hachette.co.uk

First published in Great Britain in 2005 as *Confidence Boosters* by Hamlyn,
an imprint of Octopus Publishing Group Ltd
Carmelite House, 50 Victoria Embankment, London EC4Y 0DZ
www.octopusbooks.co.uk

Published in 2009 by Pyramid, an imprint of Octopus Publishing Group Ltd

This edition published in 2018 by Pyramid for Hamlyn,
a division of Octopus Publishing Group Ltd

ISBN 978-0-7537-3337-0

A CIP catalogue record for this book is available from the British Library

Printed and bound in China

10 9 8 7 6 5 4 3 2 1

For the Pyramid edition
Publisher: Lucy Pessell
Design: Lisa Layton
Illustrations, back cover and interior: David Beswick at 'ome design
Editor: Sarah Vaughan
Production Controller: Katie Jarvis
Person icon credit, front cover and interior: Created by Pyetro Rapp from the Noun Project

CONTENTS

INTRODUCTION

Having confidence can be the vital passport to success in your personal and professional life. Confidence enables you to take on new challenges, to trust yourself in difficult situations, to go beyond your perceived limits, to tackle things you have never done before and to make full use of your natural talent and capability. Confidence gives you the courage not to worry about the consequences of failure. The hallmark of all truly confident people is that they focus on what they can do, and about the positive outcomes they will achieve, rather than worrying about what they can't do, and what might go wrong. Without confidence, life's challenges can seem insurmountable. Confidence provides the vigour to tackle these challenges.

LOSS OF CONFIDENCE

Once confidence has been lost, doubt and uncertainty prevail. The unconfident person gets into a cycle of behaviour that becomes increasingly difficult to break. Fear of failure leads to indecision, which leads to further self-doubt. Lost confidence can cause you, for example, to:

• Avoid calling someone for a date, in case you are rejected.
• Blame others when things go wrong, rather than learning from your mistakes.
• Struggle to make clear-cut decisions in case you get them wrong.
• Avoid applying for jobs you want, because of the fear of being interviewed.

The good news is that lost confidence is not lost for ever – it has simply been overlaid by self-doubt.

Your natural confidence is there inside you at all times.

REGAINING YOUR CONFIDENCE

The aim of this book is to help you break out of the negative cycle of self-doubt and enter into a positive cycle of increased confidence, success and happiness. The book provides key insights into why we lose confidence, in order to provide better understanding of why your confidence has disappeared, and these are supported by simple, practical exercises that will enable you to start rebuilding your confidence straight away.

The exercises are drawn from the work I have done as a Confidence Coach with clients over the last five years. Many of these people had forgotten what it felt like to be confident. For them self-doubt had become a way of life. However the majority have now got their confidence back and are taking on new challenges with a renewed belief in themselves. They are living testimony to the motto: 'It doesn't have to be this way.'

PHONE A FRIEND

Why not get a friend or relative to work with you on some of the exercises? This is the next best thing to having a professional coach. Choose someone you can trust and will enjoy working with. It will make the process more enjoyable if they also want to build up their confidence. Using this system means that you have someone who you are accountable to other than yourself.

Agree to call each other on a weekly basis to check on each other's progress. This will keep the confidence-building process moving. In your conversations, you can ask such questions as:

• What success have you had in the last week?
• What setbacks have you suffered?
• What did you learn from those setbacks?
• What would you like to achieve this week?
• What support do you need to make good that achievement?

To have confidence is as natural as being able to walk or talk. Those who regain their confidence after having lost it value it even more than those who have always had it. To rebuild confidence takes courage and desire. I hope that this book will make this journey much easier for you.

Before you can start to improve your levels of self-confidence, it is important for you to determine how confident you are now, and to learn about what confidence is and how it manifests itself in everyday life. This chapter will help you assess your initial level of confidence and give you an appreciation of how the techniques outlined in this book could help you.

EXERCISE

How confident are you?

To assess your current state of confidence, for each of the 10 statements below rate yourself on a scale of 1–10 (where 1 means you agree strongly with the statement, and 10 means you disagree strongly with it).

1. I am scared of saying no to others in case they dislike me.

2. I feel the need to be accepted by agreeing with everyone, regardless of whether I actually agree with them or not.

3. I don't give myself the allowance and freedom to get things wrong and make mistakes.

4. I don't forgive myself for the mistakes I make.

5. I often think 'I am not good enough'.

6. I often compare myself unfavourably with others.

7. I feel riddled with guilt when I am tempted to do things that I want to do.

8. I am frightened of achieving success.

9. I find it difficult to make clear-cut decisions.

10. I am often too hard on myself.

Your score

Under 30: lack of confidence is really holding you back.

30–70: you need to work on your confidence using the exercises in this book.

Over 70: you are well on your way to having the confidence you need to succeed.

What is confidence?

Being confident means feeling positive about what you can do, and not worrying about what you can't do, but having the will to learn. Self-confidence is the oil that smoothly turns the wheels of the relationship between you, your capability – that is, your natural talents, skills and potential – and your ability to make good that capability.

Outer or 'enforced' confidence

There is a preconception that confident people are loud, bold, extrovert types who can handle any personal and professional situation that they face with the minimum of fuss and the maximum of certainty. The truth, however, is that those people who are the greatest self-promoters about who they are and what they do are often wearing a 'mask' of confidence. This is the outer expression of the person's behaviour, which may hide an inner fear or uncertainty from which they are trying to escape.

This is not real confidence. It is 'enforced' confidence, and they are 'confidence enforcers'. They wear the mask of confidence to ensure that they remain in control of situations, and this is born out of the fear of not being in control. They have discovered that the more control they have over others the greater respect they are afforded. A confidence enforcer's need for control over people and situations arises from the fact that they were at one time or another made to feel small inside by other people. They realize that the feeling of being small will not get them very far in the world, so they have developed an over-inflated self-view, so that they can feel big and make others feel small.

Why is such behaviour perceived as confidence?

The answer is simply because confidence enforcers don't give off a hint of self-doubt. They seem so sure of themselves. 'How could I possibly be wrong?', they seem to suggest. They don't want to be seen to be wrong or not in control, because they feed off others' perceptions of them as someone who is always right and in control.

People with low amounts of confidence can often be intimidated by a confidence enforcer, since the enforcer appears hard to stand up to because of the amount of power and control they seem to have at their disposal. They haven't got enough inner strength at their disposal to handle the confidence enforcer. The enforcer feeds off this fear, because it is a way for them to get some recognition and find a place and role in the world. School bullies and tyrannical bosses are good examples of this.

INNER OR 'TRUE' CONFIDENCE

True confidence is different; it is a 'quiet' state and begins on the inside. In this context, 'quiet' means that there is no interference upon a natural state of affairs. No background noise, no doubts, no comparison with others, no fear of failure, no worry about what others are thinking – this is the inner state of confidence. There is the 'golden triangle' between the person, their capability and the moment.

Have you ever observed a leading professional – perhaps a dancer, musician, athlete or surgeon – at work? You will notice that, when they are performing or operating at their very peak, they exude a sense of quietness and authority. What we are witnessing is the state of no interference between the person and their capability; this allows them to perform at the peak of their ability, because there is nothing preventing them from doing so.

In the presence of confidence, doubt can't exist.

The cycle of confidence

In the presence of such people you have complete confidence that they will do what they say they will do. For example, if you love to watch great dancers in action, you will pay to see a leading ballet company, because the individuals in that company are dedicated to the art of dance. They are confident dancers. They dance with confidence. When they dance, their confidence in themselves causes the audience to have complete confidence in them, which adds to the confidence of the dancers...and thus the cycle of confidence flows.

If your boss asks you to lock up the office when you finish work, and you do this job in a complete way on a regular basis, then your boss will have increased confidence in you. Knowing this, you will complete the task with increased confidence, which further cements the boss's confidence in you, and so the confidence cycle flows. If a garage does excellent work on your car, you are inclined to recommend them to others, because you have complete confidence in their ability to fix cars. They are mechanics of confidence and thus you have confidence in them because of the confidence they

YOU ARE
CONFIDENT

PEOPLE HAVE
CONFIDENCE IN YOU

YOUR
CONFIDENCE
IS INCREASED

have in what they do; as a result others have confidence in the mechanics because of your confidence in them and the others having confidence in you.

So you can cause other people to have confidence in you, as well as you having confidence in yourself and confidence in others. You can give others good reason to have confidence in you.

ZERO INTERFERENCE REQUIRES:

- No doubts
- No comparison with others
- No fear of failure
- No worry about what others are thinking

The nature of confidence

To understand more about the inner nature of confidence, think about some similar words and expressions. The word confidence is related to the terms 'confide' and 'confidential'. When you confide in someone, you permit them to know information that you trust they will not pass on to others. That person becomes a 'confidant', because you have confidence in their ability to keep a confidence. Again, when information is deemed to be confidential, or something is told 'in confidence', it indicates that it remains secret and its contents are not to be disclosed. If the confidant were to break that trust, they would betray your confidence.

So a state of confidence is one of being able to trust your own capability. You have been gifted this capability of confidence.

Zero interference means that nothing comes between the person and their capability.

THE CONFIDENCE SPECTRUM

People vary in their self-view and outward manner, ranging from arrogance, at one end of the spectrum, through the well-balanced state of confidence, to low self-esteem at the other extreme. In addition, there are a couple of intermediate states, namely supreme confidence and self-doubt. You need to know about all of these before you can start to improve your own confidence levels.

Arrogance

I ALWAYS WIN

Arrogant people assume that they will succeed at a given task. They have had success before. It is natural for them to think that success will continue to come their way. Arrogant people are disliked because they believe that they have a divine right to continued success. When a politician or business magnate falls from grace, it can very often cause great delight in others because their assumption of continued power has been shattered. The assumption is in fact a belief that what was before will always be.

Arrogance, or the bloated self-view that success is permanent, means that the person often becomes so consumed with their own self-importance that they are no longer able to attract continued success. With every success their ego grows until there is no living space for anything else except themselves.

supreme confidence + assumption = arrogance

Arrogance is at the top end of the confidence spectrum.

Supreme confidence

I WILL WIN

Supremely confident people have no doubts that they will succeed. They focus on their strengths and have a keen sense of what they want, but allied to this is a powerful will – a hunger and desire to succeed 'come what may'. Each success that they attract confirms their self-worth. Their hunger and desire prevent them from becoming assumptive about success. These are the people who set the trends and break the records for others to follow. The supremely confident person believes with every cell of their being that they will succeed, but if for some reason they don't it rarely diminishes their strong and powerful self-view that they will succeed next time.

This type of person invariably learns wisely from their failures, and it will take a major shock and reverse to sever their line of trust between themselves and their capability. Such supremely confident people might, for example, be millionaires who for some reason lose their personal fortune and become bankrupt, only to rebuild their personal wealth through a new venture. There is a very fine line, however, between supreme confidence and arrogance. Sometimes when a person becomes too familiar with success they cross this thin dividing line. Too much success can lead to arrogance, because the person has become so used to success that they take it for granted that success will continue to occur.

The test for the supremely confident person is: can they keep renewing their relationship with success and remaining hungry for success? It is the absence of familiarity with success that keeps the supremely confident person on the right side of the line.

confidence + belief = supreme confidence

Confidence

I SHOULD WIN

Confident people prepare to attract the outcome they seek. They focus on the strengths that they will bring to any given situation. They have had success before, and draw on those previous successes to inform them that they can attract success again. Their well of success is deep and their line of trust between themselves and their capability is strong.

natural capability + trust = confidence

Self-doubt

I'LL PROBABLY LOSE

Self-doubters tend to focus on all the things that will or could go wrong. They worry about the potential negative outcomes, because past evidence suggests that they will have a negative outcome. They focus on their own doubts rather than their own strengths. Their self-doubts are stronger than their ability to focus on their strengths, because of the impact that 'failure' has had on them before. They feel the pain of previous failure and are worried of having more 'failure' to experience. They know that they have the ability to take on the situation they face, but nevertheless these doubts hold sway. The line of trust between themselves and their capability has been disconnected.

capability - trust = self-doubt

Low self-esteem

NO POINT BOTHERING

Self-esteem means the value that a person places upon who they are and what they do. People with low self-esteem feel that it is not worth even trying to succeed, because they will fail anyway. Their opinion of themselves is low because they have resigned themselves to playing the role of the loser or the victim. They believe that, in life, others win and succeed, but they don't. They become trapped in this cycle.

Where there is low self-esteem, confidence needs careful rebuilding. This can be achieved through the person sampling small, achievable successes, so that they begin to have a relationship with success and thus with the self-confidence that says 'I can succeed'.

natural capability - trust - self-worth = low self-esteem

FIND CONFIDENCE IN EVERYDAY LIFE

A very simple way to begin to gain confidence is to think about examples of where confidence exists in everyday life. The purpose of this is that you become a confidence 'researcher', and thereby start to think in a more positive way than maybe you have been used to.

The confidence magnet

To attract confidence you must have confidence. If you don't have confidence, you must go and 'collect' some, thus becoming a confidence 'magnet'. Here are some examples to get you started.

SUCCESS
WEALTH
PROMOTION

- The confidence that a tightrope walker has in their ability to stay on the rope.
- The confidence that reliable people inspire in others that the job will get done.
- The confidence we have that the sun will rise and set tomorrow.
- The confidence we have in our bodies' ability to do those things that we generally don't have to think much about, such as breathing.
- The confidence we have that we will heal when we cut ourselves.
- The confidence a pilot has in the mechanics of his plane.
- The confidence of a child in the presence of his or her parents.

EXERCISE # Collect examples of confidence

Collect some examples from everyday life of where you can see confidence in action. Either write the examples down in a notebook, or collect examples in picture form and create a collage. In this collage, place a picture of yourself to associate yourself with confidence. The purpose of this exercise is that, by collecting examples, you begin to become attracted to confidence by virtue of the fact that you are looking for it.

HOW TO COMBAT NEGATIVE INFLUENCES

We are all born with a degree of natural confidence. This gives us the ability to do without even thinking all those things that we might now think of as automatic – breathing, smiling, sleeping, seeing, hearing, walking, talking, laughing and crying. It is only when we fear we might lose one of these 'innate' abilities that we realize how much they mean to us in our everyday living. Our natural confidence, however, is soon affected by negative influences.

SEVEN MAJOR NEGATIVE INFLUENCES

In this chapter, each of the seven major negative influences is covered in turn, first giving you an insight into their nature and possible sources, and then pointing you towards positive ways of countering their effects.

NEGATIVE INFLUENCES

- Blame and criticism
- Conformity
- Exclusion
- Competition
- Disappointment
- Perfectionism
- Dominance

Blame and criticism

The twin influences of blame and criticism gradually eat away at your natural confidence. They can come from a number of different sources.

Your parents

Perhaps you always received criticism from your parents, which can happen for the most unexpected reasons, for example the fact that you were born a girl and they had set their hearts on a boy, or vice versa, so that you will never meet their expectations of who they wanted you to be. Maybe as a child you were clumsy, and so your parents constantly berated you for your clumsiness, which then put you under even greater pressure not to be clumsy, which of course made you even more clumsy.

mistakes + blame = low confidence

Perhaps your parents held very high expectations for you, to compensate for what they were not able to achieve in their own lives. If you were unable to meet these high expectations, their disappointment in you turned to criticism. In the presence of criticism, it becomes very difficult to feel confident.

TOP 5 SYMPTOMS OF BLAME AND CRITICISM

1. You think that everything is your fault.
2. You become highly sensitive to criticism.
3. You expect to be told off whatever you do.
4. You blame yourself when things don't work out.
5. You dare not take risks in case you fail.

The workplace

Maybe you work for a boss or manager who never says an encouraging word to you, even when you do good work, so that you expect them to find fault with everything you do. Whenever you are called into their office, you presume it is because you have done something wrong. You work in an atmosphere of uncertainty, never sure if you are doing a good job, and with one eye over your shoulder for another negative comment about what you are doing.

Some companies believe that this way of working keeps staff on their toes. The thinking is that when the staff feel insecure they work harder to make sure they keep their jobs. It certainly does make the staff feel insecure, but there is little evidence to show that it makes them more confident and therefore more accomplished in their work.

If they want to retain a happy and confident workforce, good managers will always praise their staff for the things they have done well in the workplace, rather than always focusing on what they have not done well. They will call their staff into the office, sit them down and point out their successes. This gives the staff confidence in their bosses, as well as more confidence in themselves.

good work + encouragement = self-confidence

Partners
Being constantly criticized by a partner can have very negative consequences on your confidence. Criticism eats away at your natural confidence, especially since you are more open and susceptible to those people who are close to you, and therefore are more deeply affected by their negative words. It may be that your partner has a 'perfect' view of what they want you to be like, and you don't fit this identikit picture. The gap between their 'perfect' partner imagery and the real you causes them to be critical of the things that you do that don't fit their image.

This state of affairs is very unsettling and creates a deep feeling of unease that will make you think that whatever you do won't be good enough. All you ever hear about yourself are negative messages, and gradually these negative messages take root and you start to believe them. Eventually, you may even feel that you deserve the criticism.

Conformity

Have you ever been in a room full of people and known the answer to a question, asked by a teacher or work colleague, but kept quiet in case you were wrong? This is probably because the last time you gave a wrong answer you were laughed at. If you are a sensitive person, the pain of this feeling of being laughed at may have been so great that you will make sure it never happens again.

Alternatively, your classmates or colleagues may have criticized you for always being right. It was not your fault that you knew the answer, but this reaction made you not want to be right, because of the criticism that would invite. You don't want to be excluded from your friends' circle, so you rein in your desire to participate fully in the class or meeting to avoid being regarded as either too bright or an idiot. The significance of this is that it damages the intimate feeling of trust between you and yourself.

opportunity - trust = remorse

You know the answer but you dare not say it. This leads to a state of contradiction in yourself, where you end up ignoring your instincts because they are not what everyone else is saying, feeling or thinking. Therefore you must be wrong. You ignore your gut feelings in case you are wrong, even though they often turn out to be right. This can lead to much regret and remorse, meaning that you dare not go out and do the things that you want to do in case you fail.

Another problem may be that we think it is too late to do the things that we want to do, such as learning to play a musical instrument, leaving our partners, sailing around the world or starting a new career. Our decision-making becomes influenced by what others do, rather than what our instincts and gut feelings are telling us to do.

TOP 5 SYMPTOMS OF CONFORMITY

1. You put off making decisions in case you are wrong.
2. You are timid and don't accept opportunities when they arise.
3. You judge yourself ('I'm stupid').
4. You try too hard to please others.
5. You make decisions because you think you should, rather than because you want to.

Exclusion

You may have been overlooked for promotion at work, even though you were well qualified. Perhaps you were not allowed into a group or gang of friends, without explanation, even though you had done nothing wrong. Exclusion has a very powerful impact upon confidence, because it creates a strong feeling of loneliness and the sense that you are not good enough. You presume that there must be something wrong with you, because frequently this exclusion comes without explanation or reason. The impact of the loneliness causes you to reflect inwardly and presume that you are at fault, since others have clearly found reason not to include you. This is an early symptom of self-sabotage, which will be fully explained later in the book (see page 58).

TOP 5 SYMPTOMS OF EXCLUSION

1. You constantly 'suck up' to the decision-maker, so that you can be included.
2. Your confidence state is one of uncertainty, because you don't know where you stand with others.
3. You constantly experience the feeling that you are not good enough.
4. You feel resentment and jealousy that others get the opportunities and you don't.
5. You make unfortunate comparisons with those that are included.

Competition

From a very early age, we are introduced to the notion of competition. At school, we learn how to play competitive sports, and our academic performance is assessed and often compared with that of others. In adult life, we often encounter the same kind of thinking in our working environment.

If you compete and don't win on a regular basis, you can develop the mindset that you will never achieve what you want. It is the mindset that says that someone else gets there first. You become accustomed to disappointment. This affects your confidence because of the contradiction between trying your best and not being rewarded for your efforts. You then expect not to win and develop a 'what's the point?' attitude.

TOP 5 SYMPTOMS OF COMPETITION

1. You compare yourself with others.
2. You start to doubt your own ability.
3. You put yourself under stress and pressure to succeed, when you are already trying as hard as you can.
4. You find yourself wanting to impress and get approval and confirmation from others.
5. In extreme examples, you may even use stealing, deception, lying and cheating to get what you want, because the way that you usually do things does not achieve the desired result.

Disappointment

Imagine that your boss has indicated you are in line for the next promotion that becomes available. You begin to imagine what this new job would be like – increased salary, responsibility commensurate with your capability, increased benefits. Then, when the job does become available, for no apparent reason, and without explanation, your boss overlooks you and offers the job to another candidate. All the expectancy that has been building up in you over the months turns to disappointment.

Disappointment can also materialize in personal relationships. Maybe you were due to marry the person you really loved, when your partner broke off the relationship because they had fallen for someone else. Think how this major disappointment might affect your confidence.

If you have experienced much disappointment in your life, this will eventually cause you to mistrust both others and yourself. Thus, you become wary of committing yourself in case disappointment happens again. You become cynical and don't believe what people tell you. Broken promises can have a major impact upon your ability to trust.

TOP 5 SYMPTOMS OF DISAPPOINTMENT

1. You expect things to go wrong, so you don't even bother trying.
2. You feel that you are not good enough for something good to happen to you.
3. You grow to fear hope, in case of being let down.
4. You mistrust when things go well, feeling that something is bound to go wrong.
5. You don't commit to relationships, for fear of being let down.

promises + disappointment = mistrust

Perfectionism

The problem of perfectionism often stems from your parents, who may have set very high standards for you to live up to. This causes you to have extremely high standards and expectations for yourself and your own children, because your parents wanted you to do better. You may have received the message from this that other people value you for how much you have accomplished or achieved rather than for who you are. You may then measure yourself against what your parents were able to achieve. Perfectionism becomes a dominant influence rather than a liberating one, because you are not free to make mistakes. This affects your confidence, because you feel that you must do everything perfectly first time round.

TOP 5 SYMPTOMS OF PERFECTIONISM

1. You think that failure is unacceptable.
2. You won't let others see your mistakes.
3. You anticipate and fear disapproval.
4. You have a constant need for reassurance.
5. You criticize yourself for not being perfect.

Dominance

Being bullied, at school or in the workplace, can have devastating and long-lasting effects on your confidence. This bullying can take the form of being undermined in front of others, singled out and treated differently, ridiculed or subjected to excessive monitoring or supervision. There are many other ways, too, in which you can be made to feel victimized.

The moment you show that you are sensitive about, or can be hurt by something – it could be a physical imperfection, your accent, your background, your gender or your age – you become a target for a bully. You become more and more self-conscious about it, and you then mentally attack yourself because of it.

This process diminishes your self-confidence, because you perceive that people can take from you at will and you haven't developed the mental muscle to resist. You become a compulsive giver to others, before they even ask, just to spare yourself the possibility of being bullied. Giving becomes a safety measure to prevent bullying. Those who undercharge for their professional services have often been on the receiving end of bullying. They are scared to charge the going rate for their services for fear of rejection.

TOP 5 SYMPTOMS OF DOMINANCE

1. You take on the role of 'the victim' and accept the blame for everything that goes wrong.
2. You give too much of yourself to others, because you think that is what they expect of you.
3. You let others walk all over you at great emotional cost to yourself.
4. You find it difficult to say no.
5. You find it difficult to value yourself, while attributing great importance to other people's opinions of you.

Don't allow others to walk all over you – build your mental muscle and resist them.

CONFIDENCE ECOLOGY

Just as a plant thrives in the presence of the right stimuli, such as light, nutrients and water, so confidence feeds on positive messages. Once you have learned how to combat all the negative messages that are thrown your way, you can start to focus on the positive ones instead, and these will gradually help your confidence to grow and flourish. Other people can have a significant bearing on this, however, depending on what sorts of people they are, how much influence they have over you and how they treat you.

Cold qualities

Have you ever worked for someone who had a cold disposition? You never felt able to take a problem to them, they criticized you whenever you made a mistake, and they were cynical when you showed enthusiasm. It is very difficult to feel confident in the presence of people who are critical, judgemental, cynical and dominant. Their negativity creates a very cold working atmosphere, which is simply not conducive to the growth of confidence.

cynicism   criticism

arrogance   judgement

superiority   bullying

Warm qualities

On the other hand, have you noticed how confident you feel in the presence of managers who are naturally warm, encouraging and supportive? They say good things to you when you do good work, show you how to improve and help you when you are down.

encouragement

trust

understanding

compassion

belief

recognition

CASE STUDY

Tony was a hugely talented professional footballer tipped by many critics to play the sport at international level. However, after a big-money transfer, Tony completely lost his form. He was still a talented footballer, but he had lost confidence in his ability.

It transpired that the root of Tony's problems lay in his relationship with his manager. Tony's manager had created a culture of fear at the club. Players were only ever told when they had done something wrong, and were never encouraged or acknowledged when they did something well. Some players responded to this fear culture and performed at their best, but Tony was not one of them.

He thrived on warmth and support. He needed the manager to put an arm around him, to tell him what he had done well and what he needed to work on to improve. In the absence of this support, Tony's game became riddled with anxiety and he found himself dropped from the team.

Six months later, his manager left to take up the reins at another club and a new boss was appointed. The new boss was exactly what Tony needed and Tony rejoined the team. The new manager was supportive and encouraging, he believed in Tony and he gave him the responsibility of the club captaincy. As a result of this support, Tony rediscovered his love of the game and went on to win many international caps. Tony's emotional needs were being met and his confidence was able to grow.

The fear of failure can have a debilitating impact upon a person's natural confidence. The consequences of suffering from this fear mean that we stay permanently in our personal comfort zone. We only do what we know it is safe to do. Fear of failure prevents us from ever taking any risks in case we fail. Thus, when challenges and new opportunities present themselves to us, we don't meet them for fear of failing. This chapter of the book helps you assess your own level of fear of failure, works through the possible causes of this fear, and finally offers positive solutions to help you overcome it.

 EXERCISE

Are you afraid of failure?

To assess your current fear of failure, for each of the 10 statements below, rate yourself on a scale of 1–10 (where 1 means you agree strongly with the statement, and 10 means you disagree strongly with it).

1. I worry about what others will think of me if I fail.
2. I think of myself as a failure if I try to do something and fail.
3. I feel under pressure to succeed.
4. I would prefer to stay in my comfort zone and not try rather than fail.
5. I resist taking on new challenges and opportunities in case I fail.
6. I fear success in case others think I am better than they are.
7. I am afraid of success in case I have to live up to new expectations.
8. My ego prevents me from taking risks in case I fail.
9. I ignore my instincts and gut feelings when they suggest I try something new.
10. I constantly think about my previous failures.

Your score

Under 30: the fear of failure is really holding you back.

30–70: you need to work on overcoming your fear of failure using the exercises in this book.

Over 70: fear of failure is not really having a dangerous impact on your confidence.

FIVE MAJOR INFLUENCES OF DEVELOPING FEAR

These are the most common reasons for people developing a strong fear of failure, and they are covered in turn on the following pages.

COMMON CAUSES

- Over-protective parents
- Fear of the unknown
- High expectancy
- Egotism
- Previous failures

Over-protective parents

Parents who are over-protective impose strong boundaries that limit what you can and can't do. These boundaries are for the purposes of your safety, but serve to limit your ability to take risks and discover your own potential.

The over-protective parents genuinely want to help, because they can't bear to see you get hurt. They want the best for you and will do anything for you, so much so that you come to rely on them, and when the going gets tough you know that they will bail you out. A good example of this occurs when young people are travelling the world; when they run out of money, they simply call their parents to ask for money to be sent to the city where they are stranded, rather than working out a solution that will resolve the problem in which they find themselves.

All of this leads the individual to the stage where they do not want to get into any situation that involves an element of risk, because they automatically wait for their parents to support them before they do anything. This then has a negative impact on their self-confidence, because they are unused to handling challenges and thus back down when things do get difficult.

You need to take risks to discover your potential.

Fear of the unknown

Frequently, fear of failure is induced by fear of the unknown. Perhaps we are attempting to do something that we have never done before, and therefore we cannot be sure what the outcome of our efforts is going to be. So we stick with the safety and security of what we know, which means that no risks need to be taken and there is no chance of failure. This might mean that we ignore our instincts, which might be telling us to take a particular course of action.

For example, someone might have a great idea for a new business, but is put off initiating the idea because no one else has tried it, so therefore they think there must be something flawed in the idea. The reality is that they might very well have been the first person to have had the idea, but they don't trust themselves enough to take it further.

A person's instincts are designed to provide them with information that will be useful for their survival and success. A confident person will listen to this quiet inner voice and try to respond to it, whereas a person who is low on confidence will be loath to trust their instincts in case they are wrong.

instinct - confidence = mistrust

CASE STUDY

Melanie, who was 48 years old, felt trapped in her life and desperately wanted freedom. She was in a marriage of 24 years' standing, but was in love with a young man she had met while on a business trip abroad. She was deeply torn.

She had a desperate fear of making a move abroad into something new, in case it didn't work. Her heart said: 'Yes, this is the happiness that I seek.' Something else, however, said: 'No, it's too risky. What if it doesn't work? I've been 20 years in this relationship – it's steady, it's stable, it's comfortable, yet I'm unhappy.'

The question for her to answer was: 'Do I stay as I am, take no risks and be unhappy and live to regret not trying, or do I do what my heart desires, trust myself that it's the right thing to do and move into the unknown?'

She opted for the latter, since she knew that if she didn't she would not be able to live with herself. Her instincts were telling her to go, but it had been so long since she last listened to her instincts that she had lost the habit of responding to them. She chose to leave her unhappy marriage and Melanie is now living very happily with the man of her dreams and has no regrets about her decision.

High expectancy

The term 'high expectancy' means the anticipation or demand of a certain, very positive result. This level of expectancy is very often prevalent in the world of business and work, where the demand for results can stifle creativity for the following reasons:

• To meet shareholder demand.
• Because jobs are on the line.
• Because you are paid to get results.

The pressure is on for you to perform, and you dare not fail. So you remain in the comfort zone of what you know will work in order to prevent any chance of failure. This means that you may have to stifle your instinctive urges, which may be telling you to pursue an idea that has the potential to be very successful, but you dare not in case you are somehow wrong.

Blame Culture

Perhaps you fear for your job if you fail, or you fear the wrath of your boss, who may have to take the responsibility and consequences for your failure. In other words, you are working in a blame culture. In a blame culture, those involved always look on the negative side of things, and fall into the following traps.

1. Looking to point the finger when things go wrong.
2. Indulging in politics, backbiting and gossip.
3. Hiding problems so that they fester.
4. Having a fear of initiating new ideas.
5. Dismissing the merits of what has been achieved.
6. Failing to analyse the reasons why defeat occurred, meaning that the same problems will arise again.
7. Exploiting each other's weaknesses.
8. Failing to encourage or give praise when good things are achieved.
9. Expecting the worst in adversity.
10. Lacking self-discipline.

Success Culture

A good manager will create a workplace atmosphere that encourages the creative staff to try new ideas, without worrying about being blamed and criticized if things don't work out. This is the hallmark of a success culture. In contrast to the blame culture, the success culture fosters only positive thinking, manifested in the following.

1. No pointing the finger when things go wrong.
2. Providing unconditional support for each member of the team.
3. Dealing with problems in an upfront and honest manner.
4. Giving permission to try new ideas.
5. Celebrating success.
6. Learning quickly from defeat.
7. Focusing on each person's strengths.
8. Each person knowing the part they play in achieving success.
9. Having no doubts in adversity.
10. Having good self-discipline and a positive attitude.

A STORY OF FEAR

In a village, the children were told by their parents: 'Whatever you do, don't go near the top of the mountain. It's where the monster lives.' All the previous generations of children had heeded this warning and not gone near the top of the mountain.

One day, some brave young men in the village decided that they had to go and see the monster – to see what it was really like and to defeat it. So they loaded their packs with provisions and set off up the mountain. Halfway up, they were stopped in their tracks by a huge roar and a terrible stench. Half the men ran down the mountain screaming. The other half of the group continued on their journey. As they got further up the mountain, they noticed that the monster was smaller than they had expected – but it continued to roar and emit the stench that had all but one of the men running for their lives back down the mountain into the village.

'I am going to get the monster,' the one remaining man said to himself, and took another step forward. As he did so, the monster shrank until it was the same size as the man. As he took another step towards the monster, it shrank again. It was still hideously ugly and continued to emit the stench, but the man was so close to the monster now that he could actually pick it up and hold it in the palm of his hand.

As he looked at it, he said to the monster: 'Well, then, who are you?'

In a tiny, high-pitched voice, the monster squeaked: 'My name is fear.'

Egotism

Sometimes people with big egos, who think that they are above average, have a strong fear of failure. The greater the personal ego, the greater the sense of loss can be should the unthinkable happen. This is a loss of status in the eyes of others, who will suddenly perceive that the egotistical person is not as powerful as they previously thought. Therefore egotists often make excuses for not doing something, so that they don't have to fail and lose face.

A CONVERSATION WITH FEAR OF FAILURE

It's fairly easy to recognize when we are subject to the fear of failure. In our minds we provide ourselves with the perfect reasons why we shouldn't do something. Does this sort of self talk sound familiar?

'I want to take a walk on a hill behind my house, but I remember how difficult it was last time, so I won't go.'

'I'd like to learn Spanish in time for my holidays, but what if no one understands me and laughs at my feeble attempts to speak the language?'

'Maybe I should write a book, but what if the publishers reject it?'

'I think I'll apply for a new job, but what if I can't think of anything to ask the employers at the interview?'

'Maybe I should visit a friend, but what if she's not at home?'

'I'd really like to invite a girl out for a drink, but what if she says no?'

'I'd love to learn a musical instrument, but what if it's too hard?'

'I want spend a day away from the family, but what if they think I'm being selfish?'

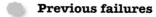
Previous failures

If we have tried and failed before and been heavily criticized for it, this criticism and feeling of hurt can have a detrimental effect upon our subsequent attempts. We simply don't want to experience the pain again, so we don't try. Any thoughts of trying something new or experimenting with an idea are immediately linked to the pain of previous failed attempts.

FEAR OF SUCCESS

As well as experiencing fear of failure, we can also suffer from the fear of success. We don't want to succeed and stand out from the crowd, because this would mean that we have to step outside our personal comfort zone. People would suddenly notice us and we might have to live up to new expectations. People can experience fear of success because they don't want others to think less of them, or suspect that they have become big-headed or have got ideas beyond their station. Peer-group pressure can disable a person's desire to get ahead, simply because they are afraid of the reaction if they leave their friends behind.

CASE STUDY

The Swedish champion golfer Anika Sorensom is a great example of someone who had a fear of success.
In the early part of what was to become a hugely successful career, Anika would sometimes miss sinkable putts when she was in championship-winning positions, in order to avoid winning and thus having to make speeches, which she absolutely dreaded. It was only when she came to terms with making acceptance speeches that she began to make those championship-winning putts.

CONQUERING FEAR OF FAILURE

Did you stand up and walk the first time that you tried? Did you form perfectly constructed sentences the first time that you tried to speak? Did you sing in harmony the first time you tried to sing? Did you balance perfectly the first time you tried to ride a bike? Were you able to swim the length of the pool the first time you tried to swim? Children learn quickly because they are not afraid to fail. Imagine the absurdity of a child who falls after they take their first step and says: 'I give up. I'm a failure at walking!'

The pressure to get things right first time inhibits the ability to learn. If you put yourself under pressure to be perfect, ease off and stop trying to aspire to mastership in a discipline that you are still learning.

 Successful people who overcame failure

Sir Edmund Hillary

Sir Edmund Hillary failed on his first attempt to conquer Mount Everest, but he refused to give up. After his first unsuccessful attempt, he famously said, 'Mount Everest, you have defeated me once and you might defeat me again. But I'm coming back again and again, and I'm going to win because you've grown all that you are going to grow and I'm still growing.' On 29 May 1953, with the Sherpa Tenzing Norgay, he successfully set foot on the highest point on Earth and became the first mountaineer to conquer the legendary Mount Everest.

Joan Jett

In 1980, Joan Jett sent a tape to all the major and minor record companies. Despite receiving a mailbox full of rejection letters, she believed in herself and her song so strongly that she finally found a record company who shared her belief. Her classic 1980s anthem, 'I Love Rock 'n' Roll', is now estimated to be worth a cool $20 million.

Sir Winston Churchill

Churchill failed in his first two attempts to gain admittance to army school. He was tutored for the entry exam and passed – barely – on his third attempt. His father was not impressed by his son's average marks and wrote a scathing letter predicting Churchill's future to be that of a 'wastrel' leading a futile life. However, Winston Churchill went on to become British Prime Minister and, in further testimony to his strong will, he overcame a severe speech impediment to become one of the most powerful orators in world history.

If these people had given in at the first set-back they would never have achieved such phenomenal success.

INTERPRETING FAILURE

Failure is only a problem if you interpret it as such. There may be an extremely good reason why you failed in a particular situation. This may or may not have been within your control. If it wasn't, why worry? If it was, however, use the experience in a positive way to improve yourself.

The self-doubting approach

Self-doubters use failure as proof of their inadequacy. When a person who suffers from self-doubt 'fails', they perceive themselves to be a failure. In other words, they take the failure very personally, since it simply confirms their self-view of themselves as someone who doesn't succeed. They associate themselves with the failure rather than being able to see the failure as an opportunity to learn. Often they will give up and retreat back into their comfort zone because of their desire not to repeat the failure experience again.

This can happen after a person has been for a job interview and has been rejected. They would prefer to remain in a job that they don't like rather than subject themselves to the possibility of failure again. The wise person does not take the rejection personally, and learns how to be a better interviewee next time.

Self-doubters use blame and excuses to explain the unfortunate outcome:

'I can't do it.'
'I didn't work hard enough.'
'It was too hard for me.'
'It was someone else's fault.'
'I had bad luck.'

The confident approach

Confident people, on the other hand, see failure as an opportunity to learn and improve. They never blame themselves when they fail, but look to see what went wrong, why it went wrong and how they can learn from the experience. Confident people give themselves permission to fail. If we do this, we free ourselves from the restraints and anxiety about failing.

You may take on a personal challenge and fail. The question to ask yourself is: can you handle the consequences if you do fail? Confident people do this all the time. What separates the best in their chosen professions from the rest is their ability to handle failure. They follow the dictum:

'We will not have failure – only success and new learning.'

Confident people use failure as a source of feedback:

'I learned what never to do again.'

In summary, if you fail, look for the reason and find a solution to the problem. List possible opportunities. Ask yourself 'What have I learned?' and try again.

CONFIDENCE CHECKLIST

Ask the following questions:	Tell Yourself
• Have I really failed?	✓ I'll do better next time. ✓ I'll learn from my mistakes. ✓ I can do it.
• What have I learned?	

OVERCOMING BARRIERS TO SUCCESS

On any journey towards achieving your goals, it is natural to expect that some difficulties or barriers will present themselves for you to overcome. If it were any other way, being successful would be far too simple.

Success is not easily gained. You may or may not be worthy of wearing the 'crown' of success. This is why challenges or difficulties occur along the way – to see how serious you are about accomplishing success. The successful person never takes their mind off the goal they are trying to achieve. They know that the time of the greatest difficulty is very often the signal that success is not far away.

So, in overcoming obstacles, successful people are driven by a goal or a sense of mission and purpose that keeps them going forward. In their darkest hour, they remind themselves of why they are pursuing that particular goal, and this reconnects them to the desire to succeed. The goal must be desirable, or the pain of failure will be stronger than the desire to succeed.

Focus on your goal.

Dealing with failure

If you have experienced previous failures, and the negative impact of these is inhibiting you from trying something new, it is important to 'resolve' your failures. When things happen that seriously affect your confidence, the imagery from those negative moments influences your behaviour.

The mind/body connection is a very powerful one. For everything that you think in your mind, your body has a reaction, regardless of whether it is real or imagined. For example, have you ever had a bad dream? Usually, you will wake up and your heart is racing and you are sweating and agitated, even though all you were doing was sleeping. In your mind, however, there was something bad going on and your body was reacting to it.

If you are alone at home and you hear a noise and interpret it as the wind, you are fine; if you interpret it as a prowler, however, your fight-or-flight response takes over, your heart starts beating very fast, your eyes dilate and you are scared.

These are just two examples of how strong the connection is between your mind and your body. So, if you have negative imagery stored in your mind from the past, it can very easily have an adverse effect on your confidence.

EXERCISE

Imagine that success, or the fulfilment of a goal, is like running 100 metres. On the way to reaching the finishing line, you have to negotiate several problems or potential failures in the form of hurdles that get progressively higher.

At 10 metres comes the first, fairly low hurdle. If you are a weak-willed person, or have very low self-esteem, you may give up at this point, saying 'Oh it's too difficult', and not bother trying again. If you are more determined, however, you will find a way to get over the hurdle and continue the run.

When you reach the next hurdle, your attitude will again determine whether you give up or continue. So the run continues until you meet the highest hurdle just before the end. This is the big test. Will you be able to summon up the strength of will and energy required to clear the hurdle and claim the prize of success?

EXERCISE

This meditative exercise is designed to help you find any negative
images stored in your mind, and 'rewrite' them as positive ones.
Find a quiet place where you will not be disturbed for 20 minutes. Sit in
a comfortable chair, or lie on the floor. Close your eyes, bring your focus
inward and centre on your breathing. Breathe in steadily and deeply, then
exhale slowly, three times altogether.
Begin to relax your body, starting with your shoulders and neck, then the
muscles in your face, then your arms and hands, then your lower body, and
finally your legs, feet and ankles.
Now imagine a path leading out from your house, and that you are walking
down this path away from your house to a special place, a place where you
feel safe and free, a place where you feel confident and powerful. It can
be a real place or an imaginary one – a meadow, a beach, a mountaintop,
a waterfall, in fact any place that is your place, somewhere you feel good.
Find somewhere to sit down and make yourself comfortable. As you sit
here, wrap yourself in a bubble of light in the colour of your choice.
Think about what happened to you. Re-create the event or story
in your mind that had such a negative effect upon your
confidence or self-belief. Answer these questions:

- How old are you?
- What is the weather like?
- Who is around?
- What time of day is it?
- What time of year is it?
- What does it smell like?
- Who is speaking? What are they saying or doing to you?
- How does this make you feel?

Now imagine all the negative feeling caused by this event escaping out
of you through a blue tube that is connected to your feet. Allow that
negativity to run down the blue tube and out into a lake or sea that
you can visualize.
Finally, rewrite the negative scene in your mind with a different outcome
or ending. This is your opportunity to create the ending that you
would like to have happened in that scene.

CASE STUDY

Julia had never felt comfortable singing, even though she loved music. Her insecurity about the sound of her own voice was so bad that she did not even dare sing in the comfort of her own home. She was able to trace this insecurity back to when she was young, and in particular a day when she returned home filled with excitement having had a success in the school music exam.

Julia was delighted and ran all the way home to tell the news to her parents. She got home and ran excitedly into the garden, where she saw her father. She ran up to him, and told him in a delighted voice that she had got full marks in the singing exam. Instead of sharing in her delight, he looked at his daughter in a serious way and said gravely: 'I am surprised. Your voice has some faults in it, and doesn't really merit that sort of mark, I'm sure.'

His daughter was flattened by this news, and the incident made such an impression on her that it took her a very long time to overcome this lack of fatherly support. She felt very awkward about her singing, initially not wanting to sing in the presence of others, then not wanting to sing even to herself.

Thirty years later, Julia decided to rewrite this moment from her past: instead of her father ignoring her, he lifts her off the floor and swings her around excitedly, exclaiming 'Well done, my girl, well done!' He continues to show exuberance and excitement until they both collapse on the ground exhausted. Thus Julia was able to overcome her feeling of self-consciousness and awkwardness when she sang because she had successfully rewritten a moment from her negative past.

WHAT WILL HAPPEN IF YOU FAIL?

Think about what might happen if you tried something that was outside your comfort zone and you failed. The reason for doing this is to help you recognize that the consequences of failing are never as shameful as you think they might be. If you happen to fail:

- What would you say?
- What would others say?
- What would your boss say?
- What would your friends say?
- What would your family say?
- What would your colleagues say?

Make a note of how you presume each of the above would react. If you believe they would be supportive, then you have nothing to fear. If you suspect that your friends, for example, would criticize you, then speak directly to them and address the matter. Ask them if they can be more supportive of you, since you want to do your best.

FRIEND   YOU   BOSS

Maybe the biggest critic of failure will be you.

CASE STUDY

Jake was a young tennis player who regularly criticized himself for making mistakes and not being good enough. He saw players of a similar age and capability getting ahead of him and so put himself under tremendous pressure to do better than them. Whenever he made a mistake on the court, for example, missing an easy volley, he would indulge in tirades of personal abuse. He felt that he should not be making any mistakes at all, when in reality he was still learning the game. To overcome this self-defeating habit, he took the pressure off by telling himself that he was a student of the game and did not have to be perfect. After every game he kept a log of his performance, in which he wrote down:

- aspects of his game that he did well and was proud of;
- aspects of his game that he would like to improve on, with details of how he would incorporate these into training.

By doing this, he had a clear plan he could follow to improve his game without yelling at himself for not being perfect.

What would you do if you knew you couldn't fail?

Consider what you would actually do if you were guaranteed not to fail.

What is my first step?
Write down the next action step that you need to take in order to further matters.

When will I take this step?
Write down the day that you will take this step. It is important that you commit a specific time to do this, otherwise the task will be forgotten.

Who can I tell that I am going to do this?
It is important that you become accountable to someone other than yourself when you determine to break out of your comfort zone. You will then have someone to check on your progress and to help you if you get intimidated.

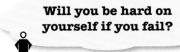

Will you be hard on yourself if you fail?

Many of us find it extremely difficult to say no to other people when they ask us to do something, even if doing it will cause us great inconvenience. We believe that a refusal will seem unfriendly or even hostile, and that people will not like us if we say no to them. Yet this is quite untrue – saying no in the right situation may not only alleviate stress on you but also command respect from other people. This chapter will help you discover how good you are at saying no, and then if necessary provide you with the ammunition you need to take a positive stand for your own good.

EXERCISE

Test: Can you say no?

For each of the 10 statements below, rate yourself on a scale of 1–10 (where 1 means you agree strongly with the statement, and 10 means you disagree strongly with it).

1. I worry about hurting others' feelings.

2. I say yes when I really mean no.

3. I dare not speak the truth to others.

4. I want to be liked and approved of.

5. People treat me like a doormat and walk all over me.

6. I worry what others will think of me.

7. I agree to do things because I think that is what others expect of me.

8. I fear saying no to others in case they dislike me.

9. I have to build up my confidence before I can say no to someone.

10. I think that people will get mad with me if I say no.

Your score

Under 30: you need to work through this chapter thoroughly to develop the confidence to say no.

30–70: you need to continue to work on your ability to say no using the exercises in this book.

Over 70: the ability to say no is not a problem for you.

Learning to say no is a natural part of development.

Understanding no

Many people have a fear of saying no to others, but no is an influence that you can use to your advantage. It is nothing to be afraid of. No exists to be used for the purposes of enabling a human to have choice. This is one of the features and beauties of being human. Without this choice we become like robots, with no will, and this is not the nature of the human design or purpose. No is a valuable tool that enables us to exercise this choice.

This power exists so that we do not become subject to influences that will take us away from our natural course of development and growth. However, we have to win this power, as part of our development, as part of the struggle to exercise our choice about what we will have and won't have.

People who say no are perceived as being cold. This is because the nature of the no influence is cold. No anaesthetizes things. It is like a cold shaft of power that prevents things from growing. No is a vital ally.

Use 'no' to stop things that you don't want.

WHY IS IT DIFFICULT TO SAY NO?

If you find it difficult to say no, you are not alone. It is probably the most common reason behind the fact that many people have difficulty in rebuilding their confidence. Those who find it hard to say no often do so because they don't want to hurt other people's feelings. They worry that if they say no the other person will take offence and a friendship will be lost. There are several reasons why this might happen.

Being perceived as cold

If you are a warm-hearted, generous and giving person, you will probably worry that others will perceive you as being cold if you say no. Warm-hearted people can find it difficult to say no simply because to be able to say no effectively means that you have to become a little bit cool. The quality of no by nature is a cold influence, because the function of an effective no is to be able to neutralize those things that you personally do not want to process.

Playing the victim

If you have a history of being bullied or victimized, it is possible that you will find it difficult to say no to others. The reason for this is that bullying causes you to take on the role of the victim. You become someone who accepts the blame for everything. Bullying leaves a lot of wounds and scars in the victim; if these wounds have not healed, it becomes difficult to say no because of the fear of being wounded by the person you are rejecting. Your assumed role is the victim, so that people walk all over you. You expect others to have more power than you do, or you simply don't use the power that you have at your disposal because it is not in your role to do so.

victim + bullying = low self-esteem

Being sensitive to others' needs

If you are sensitive and a friend asks you to do something for them that you don't want to do, your sensitivity will make you aware of your friend's need and also your own need. So you feel both, which means that you become caught in an emotional tug-of-war between ensuring that your needs are met and trying to help your friend. It is very difficult to say no when you are caught in this situation.

Yearning for inclusion

One of the psychological anxieties that comes with the struggle to say no is the uncertainty of what will come back to us from others when we do. How will the person to whom we are saying no react?

- Will they explode?
- Will they get angry?
- Will they make us feel bad?
- Will they make us feel a lesser person?

If we are sensitive in some way, we will not want to hurt another's feelings, while at the same time we do not want to do things that are not right for us. This psychological uncertainty is born from the potential hurt and pain that may come our way from rejecting others, and if we have been hurt before this may be something that we certainly want to avoid. So we end up saying yes to avoid this potential conflict and confrontation. This yes means that the gate remains open for this other person to include us in their world, even if it is on their terms rather than our own. We want to be included in their world, because it represents an inclusion of sorts. As we seek security in our lives, we will often seek it from whatever source is available, even to our own detriment.

WHY DO PEOPLE FIND IT DIFFICULT TO SAY NO?

warm-hearted people	are afraid of seeming cold
victims	don't believe they can say no
sensitive people	are worried about how others feel

SAYING NO ASSERTIVELY

If you wish your no to be taken seriously, the method of delivering it is very important. First of all, you need to believe it yourself, and to do this you will need to overcome all the common fallacies that usually get in the way and concentrate on your own rights instead.

Don't think...	Think...
• If I refuse, others will feel hurt or angry. • If I refuse, others won't like or love me. • It's rude or selfish to refuse. • If I refuse, I won't be able to make any requests of others. • Their needs are more important than mine.	• I have the right to say yes or no for myself. • I have the right to set my own priorities. • I have the right to state the difficulties that others' requests of me will cause.

Don't forget that other people have the right to make requests of you, so you should not just respond aggressively when they do.

EXERCISE

Be assertive
If the other person repeats their request or persists in assuming that you will comply, calmly employ the following techniques.

1. Breathe deeply

2. Be firm in your vocal tone and body language

3. Start your answer with the word no

4. Keep the reply short and clear, but not abrupt

5. Give the real reason for refusing; don't invent excuses

6. Avoid 'I can't' phrases; use 'I'd prefer not' or 'I'd rather not'

7. Don't apologize profusely, if at all (one 'I'm sorry, but...' will suffice)

8. Acknowledge the requester by name

9. Ask for more information if needed

10. Ask for more time if needed

11. Repeat your refusal

12. Slow down and emphasize the words you are repeating

13. State your reason, if you did not state it the first time

14. Don't search for better reasons

SAYING NO IN YOUR PERSONAL AND PROFESSIONAL LIFE

It becomes more difficult to say no when the stakes are perceived to be higher. For example, it is not difficult to say no to someone who asks you if you want sauce on your pie, but when job security or a friendship is seen to be on the line, then you need to be mentally and emotionally stronger. Sometimes a little courage is called for in order to help you to change the dynamic of a situation.

Remember that courage can be found within you at all times, and this courage is simply waiting to be called upon. In the presence of your courage, others will afford you greater respect. Courage is a very powerful quality and serves those who decide to stand up for whatever they believe is just and right. Here are four typical scenarios in everyday life that you might find difficult.

1. Saying no to taking on more work
2. Saying no to friends
3. Taking defective goods back to a shop
4. Saying no to voluntary work

1. Saying no to taking on more work

If you lack confidence in being able to say no, this area can cause a lot of problems. You may find it difficult to say no to your boss for fear of upsetting them, creating an awkward atmosphere in the workplace and losing a possible promotion. In addition, you may feel that saying no jeopardizes your long-term job security; so you end up saying yes, taking on more work and increasing the pressure on yourself. Your social and work life balances suffer and you stop enjoying your work.

Don't let your personal life suffer because you can't say no.

Your employer may not be happy about you not staying to do overtime, but it is totally reasonable to refuse when it is inconvenient for you. If you agree to do something you don't want to do, you will probably feel dissatisfied with yourself. You may also feel angry and resentful at your boss. In this case, the no may come across non-verbally, in missing deadlines, being silent and sullen, thinking of other things when in the presence of the other person.

Self-denying behaviour and attitudes will probably reinforce the unwanted behaviour and demands of others and encourage them to keep making unreasonable requests of you. In some workplaces, you are seen to be slacking if you take lunch, for example, or if you choose to leave the office at the agreed hour of closing. This brings an unseen pressure which suggests that you are not a team player totally committed to the success of the organization. Of course, you may be the most efficient and effective member of the workforce and you get your job done, plus more, in the time agreed, but somehow that is never seen as enough.

CASE STUDY

Helen was expected to work late. No one asked her to. It was simply expected in the culture that had been created in the high-pressure PR company where she was employed. She wanted to go to a black-tie function with her partner one Friday evening. She was dreading telling her boss that she would be leaving on time that day, since the firm was busy with a new account. Her boss would not like it. Yet she plucked up the courage to tell them. She said, respectfully but firmly: 'I understand you prefer me to work late, but today I will be leaving work on time because I have an engagement that means a lot to me. I trust that will be OK with you.' This statement achieves three things.

1. It shows that she understands her boss's needs.
2. It states what she will be doing.
3. It checks that this is OK with the boss.

Remember that for some managers, their jobs are their lives. Invariably, they are paid to handle greater responsibility. You are personally responsible for your work/life balances. If you take the position that you won't stay late to do extra work, then you may begin to educate your boss that working long hours is not necessarily conducive to extra efficiency.

2. Saying no to friends

Saying no to your friends is made especially difficult because of the fear of losing their friendship and the worry about what they will say to others about you. Here is a story (opposite) to demonstrate the problem.

Use understanding when saying no to friends

In order for your no to be received well and not thrown back in your face, you will need to nurture the right feelings in the other person. The way to do this is to enable the other person to feel understood. In the case study opposite, Suzanne told her friend that she appreciated her situation, and often this feeling of being understood is actually more important than the outcome of the dealing.

Once the person to whom you are saying no feels that they are understood, this makes it much easier for them to receive your no. Their inner systems are warmed by being understood, and this warmth allows them to understand you. This leads to agreement, because you have understanding meeting understanding.

The first task is to let the person know that you understand their situation. Then you can tell them no. Then ask them if all is clear as a result.

understanding + no = agreement

This should leave matters clear with nothing left over. In understanding another, try using expressions like these:

'This isn't the answer that you want to hear, but...'
'I know you may not like this, but...'
'I really appreciate you asking me to help, but...'
'I understand your situation, but...'
'I would dearly love to help, but...'

CASE STUDY

Suzanne often took phone calls throughout the evening, in the privacy of her own home, from friends who used her as a free counsellor regarding their relationship problems. Suzanne was not a professional counsellor, but others had become used to her resolving their personal problems. Suzanne's whole evenings were often spent receiving such calls, since the more calls she took the more people presumed it was OK to call her. Often her friends did not even have the courtesy to ask if Suzanne was 'open' to this kind of conversation. They called her on the presumption that she was available to hear their problems. Suzanne was getting more and more drained, and her husband began to complain that they never spent any time together. Suzanne took the calls because she was a generous person who did not want to let her friends down. She wanted to stop these 'free counselling' sessions, but she did not know what to say to her friends. She decided to seek professional advice. When her friends called, she was advised to take the call if she really had to, but not to let it run past five minutes in length. After a maximum of five minutes, she was instructed to end the call.

Suzanne was quite nervous about doing this, as she imagined her friends would think 'What's the matter with Suzanne?' and she was worried that she would be thought of in a negative light, particularly since calls had previously lasted up to two hours. Her fear was that she might lose her friends when she took this position, but she was advised: 'If they are your friends, they will want what is right for you. If they are not truly your friends and are simply using you for free counselling, it is better that you know this. The people who are truly your friends want the best for you. If there are those who might resent you saying no, why do they think that way?'

Suzanne took this advice, and found that she could say no and not feel guilty about it. She was very honest when saying no. Before the conversation developed, she would say: 'It's great to hear from you, and, as you know, I would love to help, but the truth is that I want to spend time with my husband. I appreciate that you have really urgent matters to get off your chest, but this isn't the best time for me. Is that OK?' This approach worked well, and Suzanne was truly relieved that at last she could create some time and space for herself and her husband.

3. Taking defective goods back to a shop

People who have less confidence than they would like often accept what they are given and don't want to make a fuss. They doubt their ability to change things. An example of this can be seen when a person goes to a shop and buys something that turns out to be unsuitable.

The unconfident person feels timid about returning it. They recognize that taking goods back requires more effort, so it becomes easier to let the matter drop. Unconfident people are intimidated by shop assistants and suspect that the assistant will take it personally if goods are returned. Remember, though, that you are not rejecting the person. You are making sure that you get what you paid for. If you accept damaged goods, you accept less. By returning the goods, you are making a stand for yourself.

Many people worry about being thought of as a nuisance. Confidence in this situation comes from the fact that you won't pay good money for shoddy work; so you are being a nuisance, but you are doing so in the interests of fairness.

THE STORY OF NO

NO, I WANT TO SEE THE MANAGER.

A woman bought a leather jacket from a reputable shop. After only two weeks, the jacket fell apart. She took it back to the shop, but the staff said that she could not have her money back. Knowing that she was in the right, she refused to leave the shop until her money was refunded. She demanded to see the manager, who again tried to 'fob her off'. She still did not yield, and eventually the manager gave her a full refund. The strength of her no was stronger than the no of the shop.

4. Saying no to voluntary work

Have you ever found yourself dealing with a person who would like you to volunteer for something when you do not actually want to? You find yourself agreeing, and later you kick yourself for doing so. This is probably not the first time this has happened either. Saying no to others who ask for your help, information or resources is often difficult. Saying no may conflict with your genuine desire to help and be seen as a team player.

You may worry that a refusal will make you sound unfriendly; however, saying no is one of the things you must do to honour your prior commitments and manage your time well. Keep in mind that saying yes to everyone else results in saying no to your own priorities. No is not synonymous with being rude, unfriendly or nasty. It simply means that at this time you will not be able to accommodate the request.

Evaluate the situation

Resist the tendency to agree automatically; give yourself time to evaluate your energy and ability to accommodate a particular request and decide whether you truly want to be involved. This applies to situations that are truly voluntary, and not to job assignments couched as requests.

Explore your motives in continually saying yes. Do you have a strong need to feel useful? Many people encourage others to ask for their help. Being constantly called upon is a real boost to the ego. The down side is that your desire to be needed can be taken advantage of by others who know that they can always count on you.

Give a positive refusal

Be polite, and be understanding, but say no. Help others find other ways to solve their problems. Search for a way to be useful without doing the entire project. Offer referrals or suggestions about how they can handle the situation. Encourage them to come to you if there are problems for which there are no other solutions, but also encourage self-reliance.

MAKING RULES

All nightclubs have bouncers on the door – strong, fit, aggressive people who have the power to decide who can and who can't enter the club. For example, some clubs have a 'no jeans' rule. If anyone wearing jeans tries to get in, the bouncers stop them. Other club bouncers may say 'no trainers' or 'nobody under 30'. This is to give the club distinction, or to attract a particular crowd. Without such rules, the club becomes general. Anybody can go in.

It is the same for you. If you have no rules, people can walk all over you. When you have rules, people know exactly where they stand, and they can be educated in what to ask and what not to ask. Thus you take on the role of the educator. This allows you to change the way people react to you. When you take clear, strong positions about the things that you value, the radiation from this position will invariably be stronger than the desire of the person to criticize you, judge you or put you down. In this way, you can change the balance of power. Give people a chance to change how they react to you. When they meet your security about yourself, they will also feel secure.

With rules you become a stronger person. You will be much clearer about what you are saying no to, and why you are saying no, because you are the defender of the things you value.

Enjoy saying no.

Decide what you want and say no to the rest.

Employ the confidence 'bouncers'

This exercise helps you put in place a strategy that will enable you to say no with greater confidence, and to understand why you are saying no. Imagine you have just bought a nightclub that represents your confidence.

The first thing to do is give it a name, such as:
The Happiness Club or Club Confidence.

Then think about the different rooms that you would like to have in it. All these rooms should reflect some of the qualities of the owner, for example:

The Champions' Room – where the best in others is celebrated.
The Party Room – with non-stop music and dancing.
The Dwelling Room – a place of quiet and contemplation.
The Inspiration Room – where people go to think original thoughts.

Lastly, and most importantly, create the rules of the club: Which instructions will you give to your confidence 'bouncers'? Which 'undesirables' do you want to prevent from entering the club? These could be self-doubt, unfortunate comparison with others, putting yourself down, or fear of speaking the truth.

Then, when you hear a little voice inside you saying:

'I'll never succeed as a...'
'I'm not as good as...'
'I can't tell them what I want to say'
'I dare not...'

it is the time for the confidence bouncers to get to work.

They will tell the little voice:
'I'm sorry, self-doubt/comparison/fear, you are not a member of this club. You are refused entry and cannot come in.'

BUILD YOUR NO-MUSCLE

If you have trouble saying no, the best way to gain confidence is to build up your 'no-muscle'. You can do this by practising saying no in situations that do not have a lot of emotional charge to them. Once you become comfortable, build up to saying no to the things that have more emotional impact. You will become more confident and self-assertive as you practise.

The 'no' mantra

Try to commit this little saying to memory. The more you say it to yourself the stronger your no-power will become.

**When I say no I mean no.
No means no.**

EXERCISE

Develop no-power

To help build up your no-muscle, over a period of one month make a mark (such as a blue circle) on your middle finger to remind you to practise saying no. In addition, every time you say no make a small mark or signal to yourself, such as tapping yourself on the knee three times, or stroking your nose. Then say quietly to yourself: 'I like saying no. I want to say no again.' These will become your no-power signal and phrase. When you do this for about six months, your no-muscle will develop extra power, and you will get no-power simply from making your no-signal. This works by creating an 'anchor' for the essence of no. So through the repetitive act of making the same signal to yourself every time you say no, the signal will start to have an internal connection for you to the power of no. The following are simple examples of how you could start to build up your no-muscle.

• Don't answer the phone if doing so would interrupt your work.
• Delete all e-mails that you know are not of any value.
• Say no firmly to the telemarketer who interrupts your evening meal.

BUILD YOUR MENTAL POWER

One of the common problems with saying no is that we have to say it out loud – but what about the art of saying no mentally? This is where it is possible to access plenty of no-power.

Make a decision

This kind of no begins with a decision – you decide that you are not going to have something, or are not going to be subject to something that you no longer want in your life. Without this initial decision, your no has nothing to gravitate around. A decision about which you are clear in your mind acts like a pathfinder: it removes the fog and shifts the doubt about which direction you should be going in. Habits and patterns can get ingrained in the system and can be difficult to change. A clear decision makes this change possible, creating definite leadership for yes and no to follow. Decisions come from knowing what you want (see the exercise on page 55).

Picture it

Once you have decided what you don't want, imagine yourself rejecting it. Do this just before you go to sleep, and then again first thing in the morning. These are the best times to programme your system. To do this, consider a situation that you might find yourself in the next day – perhaps facing the tyrannical boss, or getting involved in unpleasant gossip with friends. While picturing this scenario, imagine that you are there in this situation, saying no, maybe to a demand from your boss to work late or to gossiping with your friends, even though you feel uncomfortable doing so. This no you are saying is happening in your mind. You are deciding mentally: 'No, I won't have that.' Do this before sleep and again when you wake up. Imagine the scenario that you will be facing and mentally see yourself saying no.

Make it real

You will arrive at work or meet your friends the next day having already prepared the ground by living through the situation once before in your mind. This makes it much easier for you to act it out physically. When the situation arises that you don't want, it will be simple to say no because you have prepared yourself mentally to do so. You have accessed the no-power that you need in your preparation. This is the key – to say no physically, you need to have the mental no-power in the first place.

Many people possess the ability to 'shoot themselves in the foot', often when they are on the verge of success or when something good is about to happen in their life. This chapter explains what self-sabotage is and where it comes from, and gives you a five-stage plan in how to counteract it effectively. This plan includes developing neutralizers, receiving confidence messages, learning to complete things, becoming a success magnet and developing willpower.

EXERCISE

Are you prone to self-sabotage?

For each of the 10 statements below, rate yourself on a scale of 1–10 (where 1 means you agree strongly with the statement, and 10 means you disagree strongly with it).

1. Success isn't for me, it's for someone else.
2. I worry that others will be jealous of me if I succeed.
3. Everyone else is right when they blame me.
4. I usually stop just 10 per cent this side of success.
5. When I receive positive messages about myself, I think 'You can't be talking about me'.
6. I start projects and I don't finish them.
7. I am addicted to struggle.
8. I do things that destroy the relationships with the people I love.

9. I expect something to go wrong when things are going well.
10. I do things that jeopardize my job and financial stability.

Your score

Under 30: self-sabotage is seriously affecting your ability to succeed.

30–70: you need to work on overcoming self-sabotage using the exercises in this book.

Over 70: you are not letting self-sabotage bring you down.

WHAT IS SELF-SABOTAGE?

Self-sabotage is caused by incidents in your life that affect the way you think about success, so much so that you develop an identity, or persona, as someone who does not succeed. This means that whenever you have opportunities to succeed, in your personal or professional life, you find yourself sabotaging the opportunity.

Often this is not deliberate – you simply cannot help yourself. Self-sabotage is not something that you do consciously. It is a power or influence that resides in your subconscious self, and results from the combustible mix of success and failure 'exploding' inside you.

Sometimes people will self-sabotage to confirm their self-image as someone who does not succeed, which may have been created by incidents in their past. This is how they choose to be seen at a subconscious level. People can become very comfortable with not succeeding. It confirms their view of themselves that success is for someone else and not for them.

How did this self-view get there? Self-sabotage can build up from a whole range of experiences and disappointments. Here are some examples.

• Being stood up on an important date.
• Being regularly passed over for promotion at work by others less talented than you.
• Being mocked and put down by others, thereby constantly being given negative messages.
• Making a mistake that has a negative impact on your team, company or circle of friends.

SELF-PROGRAMMING

You have been invited out on a date. You begin to look forward to it keenly, because you have been invited by someone you find really attractive. So you make sure you are looking your best. You put on your favourite outfit and arrive at the venue in good time. You then begin to wait for your date.

The appointed hour arrives and there is no sign of the date. Maybe 20 minutes pass, and there is still no sign. After an hour of waiting, you realize that the person is not going to come, so you make your way back home.

At this point you are very likely to be experiencing disappointment. This means that you have invested energy in the date. You have prepared, anticipated and waited. You have built, within yourself, 'hot-date energy'. Now, when your date does not show up, all that energy that you built in yourself for the date simply becomes unused. So, instead of you returning home happy and fulfilled that the date has worked out, with the energy all used up, you return home with the unused energy.

This is where potential trouble begins. If you return home and think to yourself 'They didn't show up because I am not attractive', you begin to programme yourself with the self-view that you are not attractive. Because this self-programming takes place at a time when you are most hurt and disappointed, it becomes more powerful. So the next time you are invited out on a date you turn it down because you can't stand the thought of being stood up and disappointed again – you make sure that does not happen by rejecting the date. This is self-sabotaging behaviour in action.

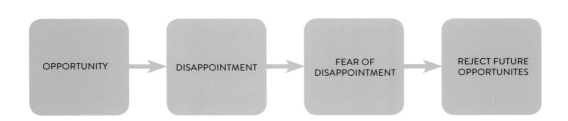

OPPORTUNITY → DISAPPOINTMENT → FEAR OF DISAPPOINTMENT → REJECT FUTURE OPPORTUNITES

Here are some common examples of the ways you could self-sabotage your happiness:

Relationships
You finally attract someone who is right for you, but you somehow make it go wrong. You don't believe you deserve the right person.

Financial
You finally make some money, but then you go and make an investment that you know is unwise. You don't believe that you deserve to have that money.

Well-being
You lose your partner or job, so you go on a heavy drinking binge, even though you know it is harmful. You don't believe that you are a person of standing.

Five stages to overcoming self-sabotage

The good news is that you can beat self-sabotage by working through five stages, which are described in detail over the following pages.
Stage 1: Develop neutralizers
Stage 2: Receive confidence messages
Stage 3: Learn to complete things
Stage 4: Become a success magnet
Stage 5: Develop willpower

STAGE 1:
DEVELOP NEUTRALIZERS

To prevent self-sabotage being able to take hold whenever a negative outcome occurs in our personal and professional lives, we have to be able to develop 'neutralizers'. Neutralizers are mindsets that enable negative experiences to be effectively defused.

For example, in the case of a date not turning up, you could react in four different ways.

1. You tell yourself 'It wasn't meant to be'.
2. You go to a bar and pick up someone else.
3. You acknowledge how miserable, annoyed and let down you feel, and move on.
4. You tell yourself you are unattractive, and that you can't blame someone for standing you up for that reason.

The last approach is perfect for creating a self-sabotage mindset. You have taken the blame for what went wrong. The first three approaches, however, can all act as neutralizers. Number 1 takes a philosophical approach to the situation and attaches no blame to yourself for what happened. Number 2 is the most pro-active approach, and means that you can return home having had a date; the 'hot-date energy' has been used, leaving no sense of regret or remorse. Number 3 is recommended, because if you give expression to your feelings they are less likely to fester and simmer in quiet resentment.

> **Be philosophical. Take control of the situation. Express your feelings and move on.**

STAGE 2:
RECEIVE CONFIDENCE MESSAGES

CASE STUDY

> Seven-times Wimbledon champion 'Pistol' Pete Sampras knows the benefit of the positive motivational message. During a difficult period in his career, Sampras often carried with him onto the court a letter from his wife, to help him through testing moments of self-doubt and uncertainty. The letter was supportive and reminded Sampras that he was a multiple champion and that he was possibly the best player ever to pick up a tennis racket.

Your message

What is the message you would like to receive in moments of doubts and difficulty? Is there someone who could give you this message? Why not ask a person close to you if they would write a motivational message for you that captures the qualities and excellence that they see in you? If there is no one who can give you this message, then simply write your own.

Many people have never thought of asking someone else to provide them with such a positive message. 'Surely,' they say, 'if I want it, they will give it to me naturally?' The problem is that often the people who are closest to us don't always know what we need until we tell them. The purpose of a message like this is that it reminds us of the best of ourselves at times when we face doubt and difficulty. A motivational message carries the emotional support we need to help us through the difficult times. It gives us the strength to keep going and reach our goals.

STAGE 3:
LEARN TO COMPLETE THINGS

Self-saboteurs are notorious for not being able to complete things. They get bored easily and stop short of success, rather than having the discipline to see things through to the end. This means that there are many loose ends, or incompletions, in their lives that need tidying up if they are to overcome the self-sabotage habit.

What are incompletions?

Incompletions are those things in your personal and professional life that you have simply left unfinished because you became distracted or bored, or forgot about them. The impact of incompletions on confidence is that they build the internal pattern of never finishing things, which means that you tend to give up before the finishing line.

If you set yourself a goal or challenge that seems inviting when you set it, the chances are that, if you are a person who never completes things or sees them through, you will move on to another goal before this one has been completed.

Things that fall into this category include:

- A dent on your car that you have been meaning to get fixed for the last six months.
- A work qualification that you have stopped short of completing.
- A piece of artwork that you started, but is now sitting untouched in the garage.
- A Spanish class you enrolled for, but stopped attending after four weeks.
- A gym membership you took out, but have not used for three months.

Making excuses

Incompleters tend to be inspired at the beginning of a project, but that early inspiration evaporates as soon as they find reasons why the project is not such a good idea. The original inspiration gets overlaid by their habits and established patterns. So the person has a new initiative that feels bright and inspiring, but this new feeling is not strong enough to survive the pressure of the old habits, and eventually it withers. They then find themselves making excuses to avoid completing the project, such as:

- I don't want to get the dent in the car repaired since I'm bound to get another dent sometime.
- There's no point in finishing the work qualification since I won't get promoted anyway.
- There's no point in continuing Spanish because I'll never live in Spain.
- There's no point going to the gym, because no one will ever fancy me.

Start to complete

From now on, don't start another project until you have completed all outstanding ones. The purpose of this is to rebuild the trust and discipline in yourself to finish what you started. This will help overcome self-sabotage, because you will build the muscle to cross the finishing line in what you do rather than giving up before completion. A good way of doing this is to find positive reasons to finish each task. So, in the examples given above:

- You get the dent in your car repaired so that you feel good whenever you look at the car.
- You complete the work qualification because you want to give yourself the best possible chance of being promoted.
- You complete the Spanish programme to develop your versatility in languages and because you never know when it will come in handy.
- You start going to the gym again so that you will have more energy to complete more things.

STAGE 4:
BECOME A SUCCESS MAGNET

Get used to the notion that you can attract success. Why shouldn't you be successful? The key to becoming successful is to develop successful habits. Self-saboteurs tend to believe that success is for others, not themselves, and are embarrassed at the thought of success, while desperately craving it. Their self-sabotage has driven success away before, and therefore it is essential that they get back on good terms with success.

Start small

The key to becoming a 'success magnet' is to attract success a little bit at a time, so that you get accustomed to having success in your life. When actions match intentions, success occurs. When success occurs, more success occurs, because success attracts success. Lots of small successes lead to one big success, and hence to a state of great confidence and belief.

So your task is to reduce your goals into simple, manageable chunks that you can achieve effortlessly. Notice the weight that this takes off your shoulders, and how much more enjoyment you have as you work towards your goals. Beware of over-intending, putting too much pressure on yourself to succeed, or setting yourself impossible targets.

In the sport of horse racing, English trainer Martin Pipe became champion National Hunt trainer for many years running, by sending his young horses to races where they were certain to win. He thus bred confidence in his horses by setting them simple, 'can't fail' challenges, so that they became accustomed to success. He gradually made the targets harder for his horses, but they had become so used to winning that when the major races came along they simply carried on winning.

SET YOURSELF SMALL GOALS

Imagine that Z is your target and you are currently standing at point A. From there, Z can seem a very long way away, and this in itself can cause inertia. The best way to handle this challenge is to set yourself a target, which you could call B, that represents a very simple and achievable next step forward. Look no further than reaching B. When you have reached B, set yourself the task of reaching C. This is a great formula for overcoming self-sabotage, because you look no further than the next simple goal, and on the way to the big final goal you gather a series of small successes.

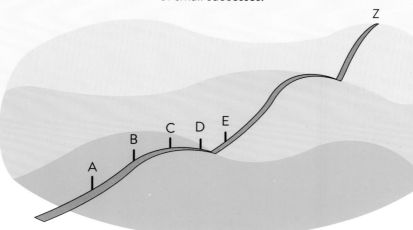

Mark your successes

Make sure you acknowledge each success that you have along the way. When you set yourself a small goal and achieve it, give yourself a pat on the back and tell yourself that you have had a success. Perhaps mark it by giving yourself a small gift or present, to confirm the success and to send yourself the message that success is good.

STAGE 5:
DEVELOP WILLPOWER

One of the undoubted characteristics of those people who overcome self-sabotage is the quality of will. These people have all developed an abundance of willpower.

• The will to keep persevering in the face of adversity.
• The will not to accept no for an answer.
• The will to believe in their own capability despite what others may say or think.
• The will never to let go of their dream.
• The will to overcome odds.

Every human being has a certain amount of willpower and everyone has the capacity to build up or strengthen their willpower. Just as lifting weights develops muscles, exercising your willpower makes it stronger.

Each time you use your willpower to accomplish something it becomes stronger. Each time you turn away from weakness and accomplish something difficult you are building up the power of your will, the power to choose your own course of action.

Willpower is cultivated in simple ways. For example, a man wakes up in the middle of the night, hears the rain falling and remembers that he has left his toolbox in the garden. He has a choice – he can forget about it, go back to sleep and collect it in the morning, or he can get up out of bed, get dressed, go to the garden, get the toolbox and return to bed.

Which action he takes will depend upon the value he has for his tools. The greater the value he has for the tools the stronger the will and desire to look after them. The question is: can he settle and go to sleep knowing that something is not right?

Willpower is the refusal to accept the limitations of a given situation and the desire to change it.

> **Give yourself the opportunity to do things you didn't know you could achieve.**

 Exercise your will

Will is built slowly, a bit at a time. Here are some ways to develop your will:

- Do a sponsored walk or run that enables you to go beyond your comfort zone and surprise yourself.
- Read stories about people who never gave up and still succeeded, such as Helen Keller, Gandhi or Mother Theresa. You will find that their capacity to continue in the face of adversity was forged by a strong and unbreakable will.
- Don't leave the dishes in the sink overnight, do all the washing-up straight away and come down to a clean kitchen and a fresh start in the morning. This means that you develop a habit of completing things, not putting things off, which will leave you more energized – not less.
- When working out in the gym, do a few extra repetitions past your targets, to develop the mental muscle of going the extra distance. The capability to do the extra repetitions is there within you. It's down to you whether you tap into that resource or not.
- If you always clean your teeth with your toothbrush in your right hand, try using your left hand instead. This will break your habitual pattern and help you develop versatility. Breaking old habits and patterns ensures that you are better prepared for new situations.

CASE STUDY

Mike became the manager of a football club who were experiencing difficult times. The club had developed a strong and very negative blame culture. Every time they conceded a goal the players' heads went down. Their body language was negative and full of self-pity. They simply expected to lose. Mike's first task was to change that negative culture. Whenever they conceded a goal Mike taught them to see it as an opportunity to demonstrate their strength in adversity. Rather than feeling sorry for themselves they used the reverse to show their strength of character. By changing the players' mindset, Mike was able to turn the negative culture into a positive one and the players very quickly began to achieve better results.

A strong feeling that you are being overwhelmed by demands from your work, family, social life or other sources may mean that you find it hard to cope with everyday life. This can be very hard to admit, either to yourself or to other people, but admitting it is the first stage in finding a solution to the problem. This chapter takes you through five stages in a process that will help you learn to cope. The other four stages are reducing other people's expectations, overcoming procrastination, avoiding distractions, and remaining energized and relaxed.

EXERCISE

How well are you coping?

To find out how well you are coping with everyday life, for each of the 10 statements below rate yourself on a scale of 1-10 (where 1 means you agree strongly with the statement, and 10 means you disagree strongly with it).

1. I don't set myself any goals because I don't want to be disappointed if I fail.
2. I can't currently see the wood for the trees.
3. I feel snowed under and can't make a decision.
4. I am never really satisfied with work that I have completed.
5. I believe that, if I don't do a perfect job, I am less of a person.
6. I find it hard to delegate because I don't trust others to do the job.
7. At the end of the day, I feel drained and exhausted and wonder: 'Just exactly what did I do today?'
8. However hard I work, the workload does not seem to get any less.

9. I dare not tell anyone that I can't cope, in case they think I am inefficient.
10. I take on too much in my life because I dare not say no, in case others think less of me.

Your score

Under 30: you are feeling overwhelmed and unable to cope.

30–70: you need to learn more about coping by using the exercises in this book.

Over 70: you are coping well.

Feeling overwhelmed

When the amount of energy that you have to give in any situation is not equal to the amount of energy being demanded, you will feel out of your depth, overwhelmed and unable to cope. This applies not just to a desk overcrowded with paper, unopened mail and so on – it could occur when making a decision, when attempting to reach a goal or target you have set for yourself, or when thinking about a deadline you are facing.

Brain 'flooding'

This occurs when we take in more information than we can effectively process. The brain loses its focus because of the volume of the incoming flood, and you consequently feel as if you are drowning. For example, you intend to spend the day working on a report, but when you get into the office your phone keeps ringing, the computer system crashes and your boss wants to see you for an important meeting, so the report gets forgotten, causing more stress. When this happens on a regular and continuous basis, your reserves of energy run out and you can't take any more demands upon you. At this point, burnout occurs, and you may need to take a holiday. In summary, the demands upon you have become greater than your ability to meet those demands.

This feeling of being overwhelmed has a negative effect on your confidence, because confidence comes from the simple ability to be able to do something. It is as if you simply have not got enough mental, physical and emotional resources to be able to handle the incoming traffic. What then happens is that your personal tolerances begin to become stretched.

Five stages in learning to cope

The feeling of being overwhelmed is like being caught in an avalanche, buried under a weight of tasks. How do you deal with it, when your energy is completely sapped by the amount that you have to do? Again, there are five stages:

Stage 1: Admit that you can't cope
Stage 2: Reduce other people's expectations
Stage 3: Overcome procrastination
Stage 4: Avoid distractions
Stage 5: Remain energized and relaxed

STAGE 1:
ADMIT THAT YOU CAN'T COPE

Don't be ashamed of the fact that you are overwhelmed. Many people, especially those in positions of authority, consider it to be a sign of weakness to admit to others that they are experiencing this feeling of not being able to cope. It is tantamount to saying that you are not the right person for the job, because, surely, the right person for the job would be able to cope. This is not usually true – there are many perfectly logical and legitimate reasons why you might be feeling like this.

Admit it to yourself

In the same way that an alcoholic makes the first step to overcoming the addiction by accepting that they have a drink problem, admitting to yourself that you are out of your depth is a vital first step. There may be people in your network who would be only too happy to help you cope with your situation, but you simply have not even thought to ask them.

Admit it to others

Once you have accepted the truth, you can begin to tell people you trust that you are struggling to cope. Your ego and pride may not easily allow you to do this, because to admit to not being able to cope will shatter the view that you want others to have of you as someone who is near-perfect and can handle any personal and professional situation that is thrown at them. This image-shattering may actually be a good thing, however. If you no longer have the stress of having an image to live up to, you can start to be who you really are, and not as you want others to see you.

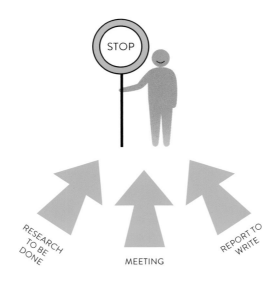

STAGE 2:
REDUCE OTHER PEOPLE'S EXPECTATIONS

If people are imposing unrealistic deadlines on you, try to renegotiate them. When you reach the point of being overwhelmed, you need to stop any new items coming into the system so that you can deal with what is already there. When you have caught up, you can then begin to reopen the systems to incoming 'traffic'.

Remember that you have both the power and permission to do whatever is necessary in order to do the best job that you can. Sometimes others don't know what your situation is, and when they do they will happily help you do a more effective job.

Relieve the pressure

Sometimes others have an attachment and draw mental and emotional energy from us when we give to them all the time. We provide power for them at our personal expense. We give, they receive, and they don't give back. We become attached to giving to them, and they expect to receive from us. They won't let us change, because they are reliant on us.

As described in How to Say No, page 42, when you say no you are often helping both yourself and others. By relieving the pressure on yourself, you will find that you can cope much better with your workload, for example, and as a consequence will have more energy, strength and independence. Others will find that they are not as reliant on you as they thought, and saying no to them may even cause them to have greater respect for you.

Be honest with yourself.

STAGE 3:
OVERCOME PROCRASTINATION

When we experience a sense of being overwhelmed, procrastination can easily take hold. Procrastination – putting things off – includes not starting things and not finishing things. We find it hard to start either because the task we are facing seems so overwhelming we think we cannot possibly finish it, or because we have developed a highly critical picture about the form the completion will take. So we delay the completion in the hope of avoiding self-criticism.

When you become a serious procrastinator, you rehearse over and over in your mind how you are going to do something, and then, when you do nothing, it does not disturb your perfect vision. A little voice inside you says things like:

• What if I make the wrong decision?
• I'd like to go to the seaside, but, there again, I'd like to stay in.
• I know that I really should dump him, but I keep having second thoughts.
• I would really like to move house, but I can't face the hassle of house-hunting.

Dealing with your tolerations

We all have a number of things in our lives that we are putting up with, which have a negative effect upon us, contributing to a decline in our confidence levels. These are known as tolerations or energy drains. They can range from small things such as a missing shirt button that you never get round to replacing to more important factors such as a tyrannical boss who is making life a misery for you in the workplace.

In the course of a life we will never reach a point where we have no tolerations whatsoever, but you can reduce the number of things that you are currently actively tolerating. People sometimes forget that they can take control over the things that are bothering them. When you become adept at dealing with your tolerations, you develop the self-discipline and confidence to deal with things at the time they need dealing with, whether you like dealing with them or not. This enables you to develop a 'can do' mentality.

Move forward

Make a list of five things that you are currently tolerating in each of the following situations and determine whether you can see a solution to each item or not. It does not matter whether they are big or small items. Each category has some examples to give you some ideas:

Your home

- It is messy.
- The carpets need cleaning.
- The walls need painting.
- The furniture is old and worn.
- The attic needs clearing out.

Your work

- I am working too many hours.
- I am undercharging for my services.
- I am in the wrong line of work.
- The future is unpredictable.
- I have had inadequate training.

Your well-being

- I am overweight.
- I am drinking too much.
- I am eating a poor diet.
- I am physically unfit.
- I am smoking too heavily.

Your finances

- I am constantly living beyond my budget.
- I have no idea how much I spend on a monthly basis.
- I am weighed down with debt.
- I am owed money that is long overdue.
- I am being seriously underpaid.

Your life balances

- It's all work and no play.
- I haven't had a holiday for a long time.
- I never treat myself to things I would like.
- I am taking life too seriously.
- I can't switch off.

Using the five separate lists of things you are tolerating, make a positive decision to do something about at least one item from each list. When you have achieved this first stage, move on to the next set of five tasks, and so on. Eventually, your list of tolerations will be much reduced, and you will have changed your mindset to one of getting things done rather than putting them off. This will improve your confidence, since it will prove to you that things are not always as difficult as you imagine them to be, and you will not feel so daunted by challenges – large or small – in future.

STAGE 4:
AVOID DISTRACTIONS

It is important to keep your self-discipline in the face of everyday distractions. For example, it can be very tempting to absorb yourself in the internet, particularly if you are working in an office environment or are self-employed and do not have the discipline of others to keep you focused.

Another thing that can happen when we feel overwhelmed is that we allow ourselves to become distracted as a way of not having to face the fact that we cannot cope. This makes us feel that we are doing something, which we justify to ourselves by saying 'As soon as I have just surfed the net, I'll crack on with...'.

STAGE 5:
REMAIN ENERGIZED AND RELAXED

Develop escape valves to provide an outlet for the pressure that builds up in you during periods of feeling overwhelmed, otherwise the pressure will take all of your energy. At such times, there are more demands on your energy than at most other times, so it is essential that you are fit in body and mind. Here are some good ways of keeping your energy levels up:

- Go to the gym.

- Go dancing.

- Take energizing walks.

- Play sport.

- Have interests outside the workplace.

- Practise relaxation and meditation techniques.

Many of us find it difficult to talk to new people in a social situation, because we lack the confidence to chat to 'strangers' and perceive ourselves as 'shy'. Making 'small talk' is easier than you might think, and this chapter will show you how to develop your social skills and overcome any shyness you might have, by taking you through eight simple stages.

EXERCISE

How good are you at small talk?

To assess how good you are at small talk, for each of the 10 statements below rate yourself on a scale of 1–10 (where 1 means you agree strongly with the statement, and 10 means you disagree strongly with it).

1. I dry up in social situations.

2. I forget people's names easily.

3. I find it hard to initiate conversations.

4. I find small talk superficial.

5. I worry that people will find me intrusive if I ask them questions.

6. I worry what others will think of me.

7. I feel awkward in the presence of people that I don't know.

8. I have lost my sense of curiosity about people.

9. I feel awkward about sharing my interests with others.

10. I have stopped keeping abreast of current affairs.

Your score

Under 30: inability to make small talk is really holding you back.

30–70: you need to work on overcoming fear of small talk using the exercises in this book.

Over 70: fear of small talk is not really having a detrimental effect on your confidence.

Small talk

It is called 'small talk' because it focuses on the small details of life rather than the bigger picture. It is noticeable that those people who excel at making small talk generally have a keen sense of curiosity about people and life. The ability to make good small talk comes from having an 'overspill' of references, facts and information. This means that you are filled to overflowing with references, facts and information that you want to share with others.

The roots of shyness

The inability to make effective small talk can cripple the social lives of many people. It can prevent business people 'networking' effectively. Poor social skills can prevent shy people from being able to ask someone out for a date, and can also make the workplace a misery for new members of staff who find it hard to make acquaintances. The inability to make small talk has its roots in our early conditioning.

'Don't talk to strangers'

This warning is given to us from an early age. It is an understandable warning to a child to keep them from harm, but can become a permanent mindset, meaning that an adult does not talk to strangers because these are still regarded as people to avoid. The adult will only initiate conversations with someone they already know and trust.

'Don't pry'

Children are educated, in the best interests of respect, not to pry into other people's business, because this is considered rude. Again, we take this attitude forward into our adult years, meaning that we dare not ask people questions in case they think we are prying into their personal lives or are being intrusive.

'Curiosity killed the cat'

If, as children, we ask genuine questions of our parents or teachers out of a natural curiosity to learn and discover, then, if the parent or teacher is too busy or simply does not know the answer, we are told not to ask so many questions. This educates us not to be inquisitive and to stifle our natural curiosity.

'Don't interrupt'

When, as children, in our enthusiasm to speak and make ourselves heard, we are admonished and told to not interrupt, or to speak only when we are spoken to, again this builds a mindset that makes it difficult to be spontaneous in conversation. It introduces a formal code of behaviour based on 'don't' rather than 'do', so that you end up needing permission to speak. All this conditioning can have a negative impact on our ability to make effective small talk. When faced with people that we have never met before, these psychologies can take a firm and decisive grip, and we mentally freeze.

Eight stages to effective small talk

To improve your ability to talk to new people in social situations, there are eight stages for you to work through.

Top 5 traits of people who find small talk difficult	Top 5 traits of people who find small talk easy
1. They worry about what other people will think of them. 2. They don't want to seem intrusive. 3. They feel awkward and self-conscious in the presence of people they don't know. 4. They worry about what they should say next in conversation. 5. They have lost some of their sense of curiosity about people and life.	1. They are happy to initiate conversations. 2. They have a way of making others feel at ease in uncomfortable situations. 3. They have a genuine interest in other people and their lives. 4. They are good listeners. 5. They are constantly updating their references.

STAGE 1:
IMPROVE YOUR REFERENCE BASE

If you find small talk difficult, then set out to improve your cultural reference base. For example, try to learn and discover something new each week about any of these different areas:

- World events
- Sport
- Trends in fashion
- The state of the financial markets
- Innovations
- New developments in science
- Business trends
- Recent films and books
- Developments in health and well-being
- Celebrity behaviour

What you are looking for when starting a conversation are points of connection. In order to be conversant, you must be well informed. In order to be well informed, you must be well read.

> **The more you know, the more you will have to talk about with other people.**

STAGE 2:
START A CONVERSATION

The best way to start a conversation is with simple, non-controversial observations. You could, for example:

- Comment on the news headlines.
- Discuss the local traffic situations.
- Point out peculiarities and trends in the weather.
- Mention the new colour scheme in the office.
- Talk about how your children are wearing the same fashions you once did.

When you share your opinions and observations, other people are more inclined to do the same. When all else fails, try giving a compliment.

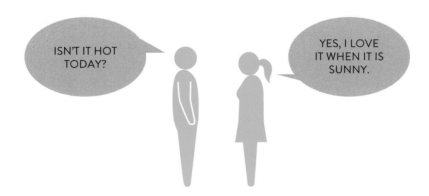

Don't wait for someone to
approach you, start
a conversation yourself.

STAGE 3:
ASKING QUESTIONS

Many people believe that the best way to keep a conversation going is to ask questions. Try asking someone:

• Whether they like going to the movies or the theatre.
• What they thought about last night's big sports game or soap episode.
• Where they grew up.
• How long they have been in their profession.

The key, however, is learning how to use questions to start a conversation, not to control it. Don't ask too many questions and avoid those that sound too probing, personal or aggressive.

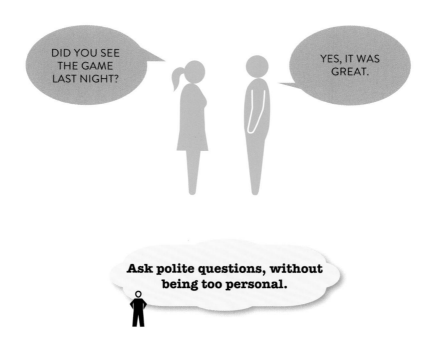

DID YOU SEE THE GAME LAST NIGHT?

YES, IT WAS GREAT.

Ask polite questions, without
being too personal.

STAGE 4:
REVEAL SOMETHING OF YOURSELF

Although it is risky, when you reveal something about yourself the level of conversation can become deeper. Once you start sharing more with other people, they will start sharing more with you.

Obviously, you don't want to air your 'dirty laundry' or give people more information than they can handle. If your instinct tells you a subject is inappropriate, it probably is. Appropriate topics might be:

- Your opinion on a recent movie.
- Where you went to college or university.
- What pets you have.
- Your favourite sports team.
- Your experiences at a new restaurant.

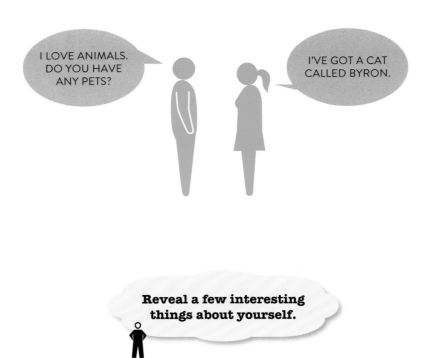

Reveal a few interesting things about yourself.

STAGE 5:
DEAL WITH AWKWARD SILENCES

One of the fears that many people have about making small talk is the awkward silence – that moment when conversation dries up and neither of you is able to find anything with which to restart the chat. The awkwardness seems to last for ever, until one of you makes a suitable excuse and the agony is over.

What can you do to prevent that occasional awkward silence when the conversation just runs out of steam? The worst time to come up with something to talk about is at the very moment when conversation has dried up, so try thinking in advance of two or three things to bring up during a lull. They could involve current events, sports or music, for example.

STAGE 6:
REMEMBER NAMES

Many people forget the names of new people to whom they are introduced, because either they are not listening properly or there is too much background noise for the information to be properly processed.

When you are introduced to someone, listen carefully. If it seems appropriate, you can say: 'Would you say your name again? I'm not sure I got it'; 'That's a nice name. Would you pronounce it again?'; or 'How do you spell your name?' You could also repeat the person's name once or twice in the conversation; this will help you remember the name as well as letting the other person know that you know it. For example:

- Thanks, Gerald, for that information.
- Charlene, I really appreciate your sharing that.
- Helen, that was a charming story.
- Good to meet you, Will.

Be careful, however, not to overdo this, since constant repetition of someone's name can be seen as a sign of over-familiarity and become irritating.

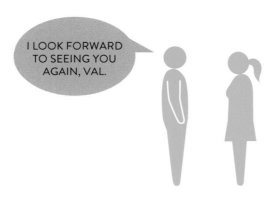

Use your listening skills to remember names and to make the other person feel appreciated and understood.

STAGE 7:
MAKE AN IMPRESSION

What you say accounts for about 20 per cent of the first impression you create. The sound of your voice accounts for about 30 per cent, and 50 per cent is related to non-verbal messages, such as body language. Here are eight ways to create a good first impression.

Pretend you are meeting an old friend

Imagine that the person you are meeting for the first time, or are trying to impress, is an old friend you have not seen for many years. You are pleased and excited to see that person again. Adopt this attitude and the rest will come naturally.

Mirror body language

When the person you are meeting folds their arms, do the same. If they lightly touch your arm, do the same to them. If you are sitting down, cross your legs in the same direction as theirs. These actions may seem obvious to you, but are rarely noticed by the other person, who will subconsciously feel that you are sympathetic towards them. When you do this, the conversation becomes more like a dance than a war.

Use positive body language to make a good first impression.

Echo their language

If the person calls their newborn son their 'boy', don't call it a baby, child or infant. Call it a 'boy'. If the person refers to their work as a profession, don't call it their job. Using their special language is a form of verbal mirroring. It tells the person you are on the same wavelength.

Lean forward

A slight forward lean indicates that you are interested in what the person is saying, are listening intently and don't want to miss a word. Leaning back says that you want to be somewhere else and are halfway there.

Make eye contact

Letting the other person know that they are the most important person in the room begins with how you think about them. Tell yourself that they are the most important person in the room. Give them your full attention, because that is how you would want others to treat you. Don't look vaguely into space, or keep looking over their shoulder to see if someone more important has just arrived. Make frequent eye contact, lasting no more than two or three seconds each time. Never stare continuously and intensely into the other person's eyes, however, since this will make them feel very uncomfortable.

Use touch and body language

A firm handshake on meeting someone can work wonders. To assist in developing a positive handshake, try imagining when you meet someone that you are a powerful and successful business person. The former US President Bill Clinton always radiates positive body language and one of his hallmarks is the two-arm handshake. This is accomplished by shaking the other person's right hand, while lightly grabbing their arm with your left hand. The higher up their arm you place your left hand the greater the warmth you are felt to be radiating towards them. Another of his tricks is biting his lip to indicate sympathy for another's pain or suffering. For example, if a person is telling you a hard-luck story, gently bite your lip to let them know that you feel for them.

Vary your tone of voice

Make sure your voice is not a monotonous drone. Vary the pitch of your voice to accentuate key points. Also try to vary your speeds; a quicker speed is useful if you want to create some excitement in the conversation, and a slower speed helps if you want to create some calm and reflection. If you want to create some intimacy, speak in a quiet voice, almost a whisper.

Involve your listener

Some people try to cover up their nerves by talking continuously. They fear that their audience will not find them interesting, so don't risk leaving a pause in the conversation in case people make their excuses and leave. So try to break up your conversation. Check that the listener is still with you by asking them what they think about what you are saying, or whether they have any points of view. Invite them into the conversation rather than excluding them.

STAGE 8:
DEVELOP YOUR LISTENING SKILLS

If you have a poor attention or listening span, then small talk is probably hard work for you. The ability to create space for others is as important a skill in small talk as asking starter questions.

It can be difficult being quiet enough inside oneself to be able to listen. When we listen, conversation is easy. When our heads are full of wondering what to say next, then we miss the flow of the conversation, and it does not get out of first gear. To develop your listening skills, spend one minute per day doing nothing but listening. Listen to the sounds around you.

• How many sounds do you hear?
• Which are close to you and which are far away?
• Are the sounds deep or shrill?
• Are they harsh sounds or soft sounds?

In other words, listen properly and learn to analyse what you hear. Become a sounds connoisseur. This will lead to increased stillness and enable you to hear the words of others much better

PUTTING THE THEORY INTO ACTION

Remember that small talk is anything but trivial. People do business with people they know, like and trust. There is no better way for people to get to know you than by you talking to them. Although engaging a person you don't know in conversation may be difficult, don't give up. The art of small talk takes practice, as the eight stages above have demonstrated.

Fear of public speaking – whether it be a small private presentation at school, college or work, or a full-blown formal after-dinner or wedding speech – is reported to be one of the greatest fears in adults across the world. Even those people who are normally quite confident in other areas of life can be reduced to a nervous wreck just by the thought of it. This chapter will help you conquer your fear and become a successful public speaker.

 EXERCISE

How confident are you at public speaking?

To assess your current state of confidence in public speaking, for each of the 10 statements below rate yourself on a scale of 1–10 (where 1 means you agree strongly with the statement, and 10 means you disagree strongly with it).

1. I feel anxious when I learn that I will perform in front of others.

2. I attempt to avoid giving presentations if I can get out of doing them.

3. I suffer from a lot of anxiety about my presentations ahead of time.

4. I feel uncomfortable being in the spotlight when speaking in front of others.

5. I worry about embarrassing myself in front of others.

6. I worry that others will criticize me when I make presentations.

7. I am afraid to let others see that I feel fear and vulnerability.

8. I worry that I will dry up when I make a speech.

9. I feel that I will lose credibility if I make an ineffective speech.

10. I worry that others will ask me a question that I can't answer.

Your score

Under 30: you really do fear public speaking.

30–70: you need to work on your public speaking skills using the exercises in this book.

Over 70: you have the confidence to speak in public.

Top 5 traits of people who excel at making speeches
1. They want to share what they know.
2. They enjoy building a rapport with people.
3. They don't feel under pressure to be perfect.
4. They trust in their own ability to handle a difficult audience.
5. They learn quickly from their mistakes.

Why do we fear public speaking?

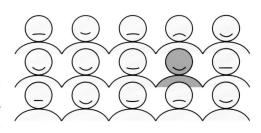

Without doubt, this is an area that can cripple a person's confidence. The thought of having to make a speech or presentation is often greater than making the speech itself. For many under-confident speakers, the fear arises because, suddenly, you are the centre of attention. Everyone is looking at you, waiting to hear what you have to say. You feel that people will laugh at you if you make any mistakes or 'dry up' through sheer weight of nerves.

In truth, however, this is probably not the case at all. Your audience, collectively, may appear daunting, but is made up of individuals who are most likely very interested in what you have to say, and will accord you the respect you deserve if you only give them a chance to do so.

Four stages to successful public speaking

Overcoming your fear can be tackled by working through the following stages:

Stage 1: Win over the audience
Stage 2: Identify your key message
Stage 3: Learn presentation skills
Stage 4: Interact with the audience

STAGE 1:
WIN OVER THE AUDIENCE

The biggest single anxiety that people have when it comes to making speeches and presentations relates to the audience. What is the relationship between the speaker and the audience? Perhaps you feel self-conscious and the attention that you are suddenly receiving becomes a pressure to perform to meet the expectations of the audience. You feel that you will be judged by the audience and made to feel a fool, and that in the spotlight your personal world is suddenly open to scrutiny. Thus, the speaker in an act of self-protection becomes defensive about making the speech so that previous wounds don't get reopened.

In a one-on-one or small-group situation, a speaker can adjust what they are saying to meet the responses of the individual or group and make sure their needs are addressed. In a speech, you can't neutralize the individual quite so easily, and often this is the unspoken fear of the unconfident speaker. In an audience situation everything gets amplified; so, if one person starts to become unsettled and argumentative, you worry that this will spread like a virus to the rest of the audience.

This can produce a very great internal pressure and the performer can become highly sensitive to potential audience reaction.

• Will they judge me?
• Will they criticize me?
• What if they don't listen?

These questions dominate the unconfident speaker's thoughts, eat away at their confidence and make the speech or performance an exercise in personal torture.

the messenger + the message = the mission

Sharing your wisdom

A good way to think when making a speech or presentation is that you are there to share your wisdom. Talk to one person at a time. Literally, look directly into the eyes of one listener at a time, just as you normally do in one-on-one conversation. This will be difficult at first if you are used to scanning or avoiding eye contact, but it is worth the effort to acquire this basic habit of effective speech.

CASE STUDY

Tony was a very successful and famous concert pianist. The number one lesson that he had learned after 15 years in his career as a professional musician was that the role of the audience is to witness the musician's attempt to connect to and transfer the essence of music.
This means that the musician's first dedication is to music.
Each performance provides the musician with an opportunity to build their living connection to music. Without this connection, the audience will feel nothing from the performer. When the musician connects to the essence of music, the audience can have an unforgettable experience. Thus the role of the musician is to be a messenger, and the role of the audience is to be witness to that message.
A performer who believes this is much less subject to the vagaries of the audience. Even if there are only five people in the audience, the performer can still see it as another chance to connect to the thing they love to do the most and share this with others.

WHO HAS THE POWER?

A girl works in a medical research laboratory. She has to make presentations about her research, but lacks confidence in doing so. These presentations are for colleagues who are there to provide tips and objective criticism. This makes her very tense because she feels sensitive to this potential criticism and worries that she is going to be judged by the audience. She is sensitive to any potential criticism because she takes it personally, having been hurt and wounded before by criticism.
This takes her away from her key messages and focus. She has made the fatal speaker mistake of becoming subject to the perceived power of the audience. The audience is unaware that it has such power. In her mind, the role of the audience has become magnified beyond its real power.

STAGE 2:
IDENTIFY YOUR KEY MESSAGE

The next task is to be clear about the key message or messages that you want to present. Your task is to be a messenger on behalf of those key messages. This enables you to be neutral with regard to whether the audience likes you or not. It is not really about you – it is about the message. The audience either gets the message or it doesn't. Being a messenger on behalf of the message allows you to become very clear in your role.

Developing 'overspill'

When making a speech or presentation, it is important to have 'overspill' – in other words, to be overflowing with content, ideas and thoughts about your chosen subject. If you can, spend every available moment before your speech thinking about it, collecting examples, researching and talking to others. Live it and breathe it. This is the way to generate overspill. It means that you have something to give and therefore need an audience to give it to.

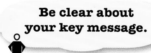

Be clear about your key message.

Studying the great speakers

To develop your communication skills, why not listen to recordings of the speeches of some of the best speakers who have taken to the world's stages? The following are excellent examples.

Winston Churchill 'We will fight them on the beaches' (1940)
Malcolm X 'The ballot or the bullet' (1964)
John F. Kennedy 'Ask not what your country can do for you' (1961)
Martin Luther King 'I have a dream' (1963)
Franklin D. Roosevelt 'A date which will live in infamy' (1941)

Stay relaxed

It is important to stay relaxed when you are making a presentation, especially if you suffer from nerves. Here is a simple tip to help you settle your nerves. Take a slow, steady in-breath. Now imagine you have a tiny feather on the end of your nose and, as you exhale, do so as gently as possible, so that the feather is not dislodged. Concentrate only on the feather. This deep-breathing technique will calm you down.

Stay relaxed by breathing slowly and steadily.

STAGE 3:
LEARN PRESENTATION SKILLS

Delivering an effective presentation begins well before you get on stage. It begins with the preparation that you have done beforehand. Here are some tips and exercises to help you improve your preparation. The following exercises will enable you to take greater control of your presentation.

Improve your mental agility

The purpose of this exercise is to help you develop a greater mental agility and versatility, excellent for when you may need to think on your feet.
This exercise is best done with a partner.
Stand facing your partner, about a metre (3 feet) away. Ask your partner a question, such as: 'Give me four girls' names beginning with the letter C.'
Your partner might reply: 'Charlotte, Clara, Cathy, Chloe.'
Your partner then asks you a question, such as: 'Give me the names of four countries beginning with the letter S.' You might reply: 'South Korea, Suriname, Scotland, Sweden.'
Take turns asking each other simple questions like this. Don't make it too difficult. The aim is to develop accuracy and speed. Do this exercise at a fast pace for 10 minutes. When you have finished, you should feel mentally bright, quick and sharp.

Project your voice

This exercise will help you when you are addressing a large audience.
While reading out loud, imagine that the words are like arrows shooting out of your mouth towards your intended target. Start with a fairly close target, and then progress to ones that are further away:
• Project the words 1 metre (3 feet);
• Project them to the end of the room;
• Project them out of the house and across the street.

EXERCISE

Balance the two halves of the brain

This exercise helps to balance the left (the logical side) and the right (the creative side) of the brain, and to get them working in harmony. Most individuals have a distinct preference for one of these styles of thinking; some are more 'whole-brained' and are equally adept at both modes. Left-brain people focus on logical thinking, order, structure, analysis and accuracy. Right-brained subjects focus on aesthetics, feeling and creativity. Take two juggling balls, or other soft balls, one in each hand, and gently throw them to your partner, who is standing about a metre (3 feet) away, ensuring that they land in your partner's hands. Your partner throws them back to you. Throw the balls back and forth for at least five minutes. Again, don't make it difficult. Try to develop a nice gentle rhythm as you do this. When you finish this exercise, you should feel steady, cool and balanced.

EXERCISE

Vary your speed of delivery

Practise reading at different speeds. Take a piece of writing and try reading out loud:

- very slowly;
- very quickly;
- very steadily and methodically.

After this exercise, you will feel that you can make a presentation at your own preferred speed, rather than rushing it because you are nervous or worried about the reaction of the audience.

EXERCISE

Develop versatility
This exercise will help you develop versatility in your presentation skills.
Imagine that you are reading out loud to:
• a child;
• a grandparent;
• a head of state;
• an audience of 10,000.

How is your speed of delivery different when reading to a child, as distinct from a head of state? How is your tone of voice different when you are delivering to an audience of 10,000, as compared with when you are reading to a grandparent?

STAGE 4:
INTERACT WITH THE AUDIENCE

The way in which you interact with your audience will determine how effective your presentation will be. Poor communicators often put their audience to sleep by hiding behind slides or other visual aids. These are useful for putting key information across, but too many means that you lose eye contact with your audience.

Don't be frightened to speak from the heart. If you feel passionately about your subject, let the audience feel that passion. Passion helps make a talk memorable, because it increases the rate of knowledge transfer between the speaker and audience.

If you are using a podium, remember that you can walk out from behind it. Sometimes speakers get attached to the power the podium implies. Former US President Bill Clinton gave a good example of how to do this during the 1992 presidential debate with George Bush and Ross Perot. Clinton walked out in front of his podium and addressed individual people in the audience while his opponents stayed behind their podiums. This gave the impression that they were hiding while Clinton was being honest and open.

Share your wisdom.
Talk to one person at a time.
Be passionate about your subject.

Answering difficult questions

Many unconfident speakers have a great deal of fear about being asked a difficult question. They fear that their limitations will somehow be exposed, the audience will no longer take them seriously and they will lose face. The problem arises when the speaker assumes the role of expert – the person who has all the answers to all the questions.

This adopted role places an enormous amount of pressure on the speaker to be perfect. So how you position yourself in the eyes of the audience is vital. An ideal way to begin the talk is to let the audience know your background and expertise, and the reason why you are making this presentation. Let them know about the areas that you excel in, so that they feel confidence in who you are and what you can do. This will settle the audience. Let them know that you may not have all the answers, but that they are welcome to ask you questions. Tell them that, if they ask you a question to which you don't have an immediate answer, you will promise to get back to them within seven days. Ask them if this is OK. When you set up your presentation in this way, you let the audience know the rules by which you will both proceed. You have taken the pressure off yourself by not pretending to be the expert.

I'LL GET BACK TO YOU ON THAT NEXT WEEK.

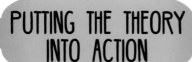

Answer questions if you can, or promise an answer within a set time limit.

PUTTING THE THEORY INTO ACTION

In summary, when faced with making a speech or presentation, remember to:

- Practise your oratorical skills.
- Learn from great speakers.
- Stay relaxed by breathing slowly and steadily.
- Be clear about your key message.
- Be passionate about your subject.

- Share your wisdom.
- Talk to one person at a time.
- Interact with the audience.
- Answer questions if you can, or promise an answer within a set time limit.

Our confidence levels may be lower than they ideally should be merely because we are constantly comparing ourselves unfavourably with other people who appear to be happier or more successful than we are. This chapter explains why we are so quick to make comparisons, and then gives advice on how we can minimize this tendency by appreciating what we have got – after all, there are many other people who are in worse situations than us – and by learning to enjoy the success of others as well as our own.

EXERCISE

Are you comparing yourself with others?

To assess how much you compare yourself with others, for each of the 10 statements below rate yourself on a scale of 1–10 (where 1 means you agree strongly with the statement, and 10 means you disagree strongly with it).

1. I look at others and envy what they have got.
2. I resent others for their success.
3. I think I should have done more with my life.
4. I tell myself that I am not as good as...
5. When I have a success, I tell myself that someone else would have done it better.
6. I think the grass is greener on the other side.
7. I forget about my own strengths and qualities.
8. I look at others and think 'I will never be where they are'.

9. I feel insecure about who others are and what they do.
10. I don't enjoy seeing others succeed.

Your score

Under 30: unfortunate comparison is draining your confidence.

30–70: you need to work on overcoming comparison using the exercises in this book.

Over 70: unfortunate comparison is not a serious flaw.

Top 10 messages of unfortunate comparison
1. The neighbours are making more money than we are.
2. My sister attracts more intelligent guys than I do.
3. The boss drives a faster car than I do.
4. My brother has a bigger house than I do.
5. Others in the gym are fitter than I am.
6. I'm not good enough to work for the best companies.
7. My friends are more attractive than I am.
8. My work colleagues are more effective presenters than I am.
9. My mates are better socializers than I am.
10. My father was more successful than I will ever be.

WHAT IS UNFORTUNATE COMPARISON?

One common, yet unconscious, way in which we reduce our confidence is by comparing ourselves to others, especially to people who are further up the wealth/career/looks/skills ladder than we are. Inevitably, our confidence plummets. Very often the person we compare ourselves with, or are jealous of, has something we want or are searching for.

For example, they may be where you want to be in your company or profession. In this instance, it's not the person that you are jealous of but the fact that they have achieved the thing you want. It may be that they have looks that you are envious of. Perhaps you are a person who always discounts yourself and thinks that you are not important, and that others are more important than you are.

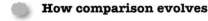 **How comparison evolves**

Comparison begins with competition when we lose our first running race and realize that someone else is faster than us. It continues through school exams, when someone else gets a better grade than us. It affects us as teenagers when our boyfriend or girlfriend leaves us for someone else. It carries on into our careers when we are passed over for a promotion in favour of someone else. It is there in our later years when we see people with less talent than us succeeding.

THE INFLUENCES THAT CAUSE US TO COMPARE

Advertising suggests to us that there is the perfect car to drive, the perfect figure to have, the perfect house to own, the perfect lifestyle to aspire to and so on. The pressure to look perfect is huge. In Hollywood, for example, it is no longer acceptable just to be a great actor. To succeed in the cut-throat movie business, you need either to be a superb character actor or to have stunning looks. Now men and women all over the world want to look like film, television or pop stars. When people go for cosmetic surgery today, 75 per cent of them describe a celebrity feature that captures the look they are trying to achieve.

Body image

Do you think to yourself: 'I'm too fat. I'm too skinny. Is there something wrong with me?'

Although self-esteem applies to every aspect of how you see yourself, it is often mentioned in terms of appearance or body image. Body image is how you see yourself, and how you feel about your physical appearance. We tend to relate self-esteem to body image for several reasons.

Most people care about how other people see them. Unfortunately, many people judge others by things like the clothes they wear, the shape of their body, or the way they wear their hair. If a person feels that he or she looks different from others, then body image and self-esteem may be affected negatively. Some people think they need to change how they look or act in order to feel good about themselves; but if you can train yourself to reprogramme the way you look at your body, you can defend yourself from negative comments – both those that come from others and those that come from you.

The first thing to do is recognize that your body is your own, no matter what shape, size or colour it comes in. Remember that it is no one's business but your own what your body is like – ultimately, you have to be happy with yourself. Remember, too, that there are things about yourself you can't change, such as your height and shoe size, and you should accept and love these things about yourself. If, however, there are things about yourself that you do want to change, make clear goals for yourself. For example, if you want to lose weight commit yourself to exercising three to four times a week and eating nutritiously. Accomplishing the goals you set for yourself can help to improve your self-esteem.

Would you really be happier if you looked taller or shorter, had curly hair rather than straight hair?

CASE STUDY

One of the last people you would expect to find mentioned in a study of unfortunate comparison would be the American tennis champion André Agassi. However, at the French Open Championships in 2001 an extraordinary thing happened to André. He was playing Sebastian Grosjean and was winning easily, when two games into the second set, former US President Bill Clinton arrived, to a massive ovation. Agassi was totally thrown, as if his world had been usurped. He stopped playing his normal game and for the next two sets his opponent swept him away. Then Clinton, clearly shocked by what he was seeing, left. Agassi immediately improved. Clinton then returned and Agassi fell apart again. Agassi lost. His confidence was destroyed by the arrival of a personality greater than his own.

Five stages to beat unfortunate comparison

There are five stages to work through:

Stage 1: Think about others
Stage 2: Develop appreciation
Stage 3: Be self-encouraging
Stage 4: Learn the language of confidence
Stage 5: Be the very best you can be

STAGE 1:
THINK ABOUT OTHERS

It is so easy to be jealous of someone else's success. Jealousy is a very draining quality to have and it has a negative impact on confidence, because it leads to the view that others are better than you and that what you do is not significant.

Sometimes, supposedly 'superior' rivals or colleagues derive energy from knowing that others are looking at them and thinking: 'You are so much better than I am.' Try to resist feeding their egos in this way. The message you are sending to yourself is: 'I can't achieve what they have achieved.'

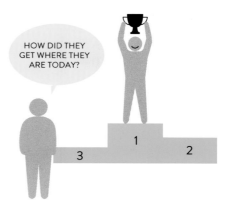

HOW DID THEY GET WHERE THEY ARE TODAY?

There is another view, however, that you can have of someone who appears to be more successful than you are. Why not use their success to inspire you rather than to drag you down? For example, try asking yourself:

• What can I learn from them?
• What is it about them that I am jealous of?
• What is it they are doing that, if I did it, would enable me to reach their level of success?

STAGE 2:
DEVELOP APPRECIATION

When people suffer from unfortunate comparison with others, they often overlook the good things that they have in their own lives. It is an excellent idea to take stock of your own life from time to time, as a reminder of all the positive things that you have, rather than worrying about what you don't have.

Many of us fail to notice the little things that make life so sweet. In a culture that promotes the idea that 'bigger is better', it is easy to forget to take time to appreciate the simple joys, the little gifts that life gives to us each day. Simple joys are around us at every moment – all we need to do is be aware of them.

Gratitude moments

Try to make some time in your life for gratitude moments. These are moments when you can express simple appreciation for the good things in your life. For example:

- I appreciate my supportive and loving family.
- I appreciate my work and the people I work with.

Top 5 traits of people who compare themselves with others	Top 5 traits of people who don't compare themselves with others
1. They think the grass is greener on the other side.	1. They feel secure about who they are and what they do.
2. They forget about their own strengths and positive qualities.	2. They learn from the best of others.
3. They look at others and think 'I will never be where they are'.	3. They see others as partners, not competitors.
4. They are jealous of other people's success.	4. They enjoy seeing others succeed.
5. They use others as ideals.	5. They have an intimate sense of personal trust about who they are and what they do.

STAGE 3: BE SELF-ENCOURAGING

Another way that insecurity leading to comparison can occur is when we don't get confirmation and encouragement from others after we do good work. If this happens on a regular basis, it creates a feeling of uncertainty that can be alleviated by self-confirmation. The following exercise gives an example of how self-confirmation works.

EXERCISE

Self confirmation

If you are always comparing yourself unfavourably with others at work, try practising this exercise in self-confirmation.
Make a list of the qualities that you bring to the workplace and remind yourself of them before you begin work each day. Rather than thinking too much about how good others are, what about how good you are?

What am I good at?

✓ I'm patient.

✓ I'm well organized.

✓ I'm really good at listening to people.

✓ I'm good at solving difficult problems.

STAGE 4:
LEARN THE LANGUAGE OF CONFIDENCE

Fragile confidence can be very easily undermined by the way in which we speak to ourselves. We may do something slightly wrong and call ourselves 'stupid'. We drop something and we accuse ourselves of being 'clumsy'. Most people carry on a silent conversation with themselves during much of the day. This 'self-talk' has a direct effect on our thoughts and behaviour.

Research shows that approximately 87 per cent of the things we say to ourselves about ourselves are negative, self-destructive and undermining. You have probably heard the term 'self-fulfilling prophecy'. Self-talk is very much like a self-fulfilling prophecy – something you think about so much you can actually make it happen. When your self-talk is positive ('things will work out', 'I know I can do the job'), you are giving yourself permission to succeed and so you probably will. When your self-talk is negative ('I know I'll have a terrible time', 'I'm not good enough to be a manager'), you are giving up on yourself, and therefore you will probably not even try to succeed. Often your self-talk reflects the values and behaviour you learned as a child, and the self-esteem you now have as an adult.

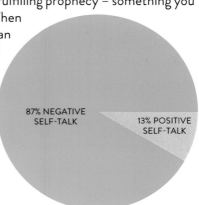

87% NEGATIVE SELF-TALK

13% POSITIVE SELF-TALK

Thoughts and behaviours

Self-talk can direct your thoughts and behaviour. If you think 'I know I can do the job', you will be more willing to apply for it. During the interview, you will be more likely to exhibit confidence in yourself and your abilities, and have a better chance at success. If, however, you say to yourself 'I'll never get hired for the position', you may not even apply for it, guaranteeing that you will not get the job.

Physical and mental effects

Negative self-talk can increase your distress and can make effects such as headaches or stomach pain much worse. It can also encourage you to behave in self-destructive ways, further distressing your body ('No one cares, so why shouldn't I have another drink?'). Fortunately, positive self-talk can have the opposite effect, leading to a confident, positive attitude.

New self-talk

For example, imagine that a new, difficult assignment is given to you at work. You could think: 'I can't do this. It's too difficult. I don't know how to do this job.' However, why not talk to yourself differently about the task? For example, you could say to yourself: 'Look at the challenge. This task, regardless of how difficult it may seem, gives me an opportunity to learn new skills.' Here are some examples of negative and positive self-talk.

Problem	Negative message	Positive message
Rejection	'What if they say no?'	'What if they say yes?'
Comparison	'I'm not as good as...'	'What can I learn from...?'
Obstacles	'It's a problem.'	'There is a way around this.'
Perfectionism	'I did OK but...'	'I'm satisfied I did my best.'
Others	'What will others think of me?'	'I'm my own person.'
Results	'What if i make a mistake?'	'I wonder what that experience will be like?'
Age	'I'm too old to do that.'	'I may be in my later year but I'd love to try.'
Defeatism	'I can't do it.'	'I don't have to do it perfectly.'

Using power words

Positive affirmations have been utilized by the self-development industry for a long time, as a surefire way of programming your mind to help you attract to yourself the things that you want. For example, if you wanted to pursue wealth, the affirmation might be: 'I am wealthy.' The problem with this is that, if you are not wealthy, the subconscious mind can easily dismiss the suggestion, as it is not your current reality. It is rather like affirming that you are 2 metres tall, when you are in fact 1.85 metres. When you use the words 'I am' to yourself, then you open yourself up to dismissal from the subconscious.

A more effective way to programme yourself is with the use of power words. Say, for example, that you wish to acquire wealth. You may have been using the affirmation: 'I am wealthy.' When using power words, however, the word to use is 'wealth'. In quiet consideration, think about the concepts of wealth and what it means to you. What kind of lifestyle changes would you have to make to attract wealth?

If I had £1 million what would I do?
Where would I live?
What car would I drive?
To what cause would I donate part of my wealth?

By thinking about the concept of wealth, you are instructing your conscious mind to tell your subconscious mind to personalize what the word means to you. You create in your subconscious your reality of the word. You leave no doubt as to what the word encompasses, without having to try to fool your subconscious mind into believing that you already have it.

Practise the concept of power words. Choose a new word each week and during quiet time, contemplate what the word means to you. Here are some examples:

• Wealth
• Inspiration
• Health
• Energy
• Wisdom
• Intelligence
• Strength
• Belief

STAGE 5:
BE THE VERY BEST YOU CAN BE

Whenever we undermine our confidence by comparing ourselves unfortunately with others, we also undermine our own sense of uniqueness. Of course, we may not be perfect at what we do, but the reality is that we are not meant to be. Of course, there are others who can do what we do better, but there are also others who are not as good as we are.

From those who are better than us, what can we learn? For those who are not as accomplished as we are, what can we teach them? Understanding one's place and purpose in the world has occupied the minds of some of the world's greatest thinkers over the ages. So what is the true position where you are concerned?

When confidence is low, it becomes easy to be self-discounting, or to have the view that who you are and what you do does not matter. Confident people see that what they do does matter, and they always attach significance and importance to their activities. For example, a schoolteacher who teaches their class with care and respect is significant in the lives of their pupils. Thus, this schoolteacher is the best schoolteacher that they can be. A sales professional who works to ensure their clients receive the best possible customer service is significant in the lives of their clients. Thus, this sales professional is the best sales professional that they can be. The trend in these examples is that the individual is endeavouring to be the very best they can be at whatever they have chosen to do. They all have a significant part to play in the world. The schoolteacher and the sales professional are only two of the very many roles that it is possible to play. Each role constitutes a small picture in the stained-glass window of life.

To make this significance conscious, it helps to have a personal mission statement. Mission statements have got a bad name in business, simply because they tend to be very wordy and are created by consensus. A good mission statement, however, can be invaluable in providing a sense of focus, direction and purpose to your life.

Creating your personal mission statement

Begin this process by brainstorming. Write down everything that is important to you. Think about all the different aspects of your life: family, career, friends, love relationships, spirituality, moral values, dreams and goals. You could create a personal mission statement from the answers you give to these questions.

- What kind of world do you want to live in?
- What part do you want to play in shaping that world?
- Why do you do this? What is your motive behind it?
- How will others benefit from what you do?
- If you did not do this, what would be missing from the world?
- What makes you sparkle and feel alive? What are the activities that you love to do?

REASONS FOR HAVING A PERSONAL MISSION STATEMENT

- A clear and concise mission statement gives you a compass to guide you through life.
- A mission statement can act as a lantern, an anchor, at times a conscience.
- It should reflect your core values. It is like your personal constitution, the supreme law from which you make all your decisions.
- It enables you to represent and reflect the deepest and best from within you.
- A mission statement is drawn out from the quality of your inner life and has a deep connection to your values. (For example, Harley-Davidson's values are: 'Tell the truth; be fair; keep your promises; respect the individual; encourage intellectual curiosity.')
- A good mission statement is there to inspire and propel you.

- What is the most exciting and fulfilling part of your life?
- If you were going to be recognized by others as a success, what would you want to be known for?

All of the above should begin to give you a better sense of who you are and what you stand for. Your mission statement is designed to convey this. Once you have brainstormed, look for connections between the ideas, and decide what will be included in your statement. The purpose is to have something to use as a guide, to keep you focused on what is truly important.

Write your statement in a format that makes sense for you. You can write one flowing statement or break it down into the different aspects of your life. Beware of writing that is too long, however, as you need to be able to recall your mission statement easily. Also remember to revise your personal mission statement – as you grow and expand, allow your statement to do the same. A mental conception of your personal mission statement is not enough. You must write it down on paper and put it up on your wall – ideally, where you can see it every day.

This chapter focuses on developing confidence in situations that can often cause self-doubt and anxiety to flare: attracting the opposite sex, asking for a pay rise, making 'cold' telephone calls and competitive confidence. The emotional stakes are raised in these situations because rejection or a negative outcome can have powerful consequences upon a person's self-worth when money, competition or relationships are involved.

Having confidence becomes vital in increasing your chances of success, because the greater the confidence you have in yourself, the greater the confidence you will cause others to have in you, thus increasing your chances of a successful outcome.

Going into these four areas with self-doubt and anxiety to the fore is akin to trying to cross the border into another country without the correct currency. Confidence enables you to be well prepared for the experience ahead.

I deserve success.
I believe that I will succeed.
I am confident and
courageous.

ATTRACTING THE OPPOSITE SEX

It may be difficult for you to relax in the presence of members of the opposite sex, because you feel vulnerable and have a lack of confidence caused by the fear of rejection. Perhaps you are attracted to a person because they have something you need, so you perceive them to be in a position of power and you in a position of need. For example, you might perceive a potential partner as being a strong provider, having excellent social skills, or being a good home-maker.

The more attractive the person is to you, the more that is at stake, because their approval rating scores much higher. That is, your need of approval and acceptance by them increases in direct proportion to how attractive you find them. If they reject you, the more attractive the person is the greater the fall will be.

their attractiveness + your need for approval = anxiety

Feeling good about yourself

The key to having confidence in this social situation is to feel attractive yourself. When you feel good about yourself, others will feel good about being around you, and you will become an 'attraction magnet'. Feeling attractive comes from engaging in what are known as 'flow' activities.

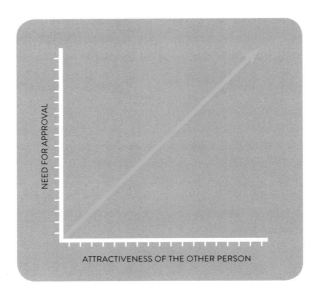

Flow activities
What are the activities that make you feel good about yourself? Some examples might be:

- Going to the gym
- Doing yoga
- Playing sport
- Going for energizing walks
- Going dancing
- Soaking in the bath
- Having weekend breaks
- Meditating
- Singing
- Making someone feel special

Sometimes people stop doing the things they love to do because of external pressures, or because they don't want to appear selfish. For example, if you have a demanding job, it is essential that you engage in flow activities to provide you with the energy to handle the demands of the job. Without the flow activity, eventually the job will use up all your energy; few people who are slaves to their jobs find it easy to attract relationships.

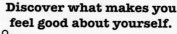

Discover what makes you feel good about yourself.

So make sure that you pencil into your diary at least one flow activity a week, and schedule your other activities around your flow engagements. By doing this, you will guarantee that some time in the week is dedicated to you alone, a vital first step in becoming attractive first to yourself and then to the opposite gender.

Initiating the first date

The key to initiating the first date is to discover what the other person's interests are, and then plan a suitable activity. For the busy professional, meeting for a first date over coffee or a drink is a good way to start. A nice, clean restaurant bar, a coffee or juice café with a pleasant atmosphere gives you a chance to converse and possibly plan another date. If the other person likes the unusual, then try rooftop views. Bringing your date to the highest point in the city can be exhilarating for both of you. Some hotels, restaurants or buildings have rooftop terraces for people to enjoy, especially at night.

The first date

Lots of people worry so much about the first date that they do whatever they can to avoid having one. However, once you have conquered a few first-date nerves you will find that the first date can be terrific fun. You are meeting each other for the first time and there is so much to discover.

The most terrifying barrier to developing relationships is learning to communicate. What do you talk about? Should you tell him or her about your childhood, your therapist, your plans for the future, your history of failed relationships?

'What if I can't think of anything to say?'
The first thing to remember is that people frequently make the mistake of talking too much on the first date. They often monopolize conversations, droning on and on about topics that bore their date to tears. Very often, this conversational over-compensation comes from being nervous and the fear of the long awkward silence.

Talk about subjects of interest to you both.

Keep in mind that if your date likes you, or would like to get to know you better, they will give you a lot of information to follow up on. If they are not attracted to you, they will not give you much of anything, and it will be very difficult to maintain a decent conversation. No matter how charming you are, if they don't help you out you will eventually have to admit defeat and walk away. So be sure to listen for the topics they would like to discuss. Listening is an interactive activity.

As you learn how to communicate, the rest begins to come more and more easily. For example, as you are listening to someone, try to understand not just what they are saying but also why they are saying it. In order to converse for maximum attraction, you need to keep two other things in mind:

• You need to tell them about yourself.
• You need to maintain a proper talk/listen ratio.

The important thing is to show the other person that you are willing to drop all outside distractions and to focus on their needs for a while, and they will return the favour when appropriate.

Initiating the second date

Before the date draws to a close, if you would like to see the person again this is the best time to initiate the second date. However, you need to determine the signals your date is giving you. From their response, judge whether it is feasible to invite them out again.

Warm response
If the date has enjoyed your company and feels warmly towards you, you can register this warmth in their constant eye contact, smiles, an easy rapport between you, the light touching of arms and hands, ready laughter and the sense of time passing easily. Tell them how much you have enjoyed the date, and ask whether they would like to meet up again. Keep the tone light and pleasant.

Cool response
If the date has been cool, this does not mean that they don't want to see you again. Don't be put off, as the person may be reserved and may want to spend more time in getting to know you. They may have recently left a relationship and may want time to find their relationship feet again.

Don't be overly pushy for the next meeting, as they might feel crowded. Give them space. It may work best to arrange to call them. Make sure you have each other's numbers for a call or text message. You can send them a message after the date to tell them how much you appreciated their company. Their response will give you further clues as to your next step.

If they reply saying how much they enjoyed the evening, you can set up another date. If they don't reply, leave it a few days and then call them for a chat to see how they are. If the conversation flows on the call, invite them out on a second date.

Cold response

You can say the date has been cold if the dealings were formal and stiff, with very little natural flow and rapport. Eye contact is minimal and conversation is forced with the distinct feeling of not having very much in common.

Ask yourself why the date was cold. Were you or the other person feeling under the weather, or did you really have nothing in common? Did you struggle to make conversation and bring them out of themselves? Was the venue less than perfect? If the date has not worked out, whatever you do don't be hard on yourself. Learn from it.

 Second date rejected

If they reject the idea of a second date, don't take it personally. Every date that you go on is fantastic experience in learning to develop rapport with the opposite gender. The rejection may simply be a sign that they were not right for you. From every date, something good comes. Capture the learning from the date and apply it to the next date.

What could you do better on the next date? For example:

• Talk less about yourself.
• Be more relaxed.
• Ask your date more questions.
• Pay your date more compliments.

If you are inexperienced in the dating game, it may take you a few dates to develop the right balance of confidence and relaxation. The date is the opportunity for you to show who you really are and to create an opportunity for the other person to do the same. With practice, you will be able to be yourself on a date and thus attract into your life someone else who likes you just for who you are.

To be successful at initiating a relationship, remember to:

- Discover what makes you feel good about yourself.
- Try to understand how other people think and feel.
- Tailor your first date to the other person's interests.
- Talk on subjects of interest to you both.
- Listen to your date.
- Be sensitive to their response to the first date when deciding how to follow it up.
- Learn from any unsuccessful date.

ASKING FOR A PAY RISE

Many of us fear approaching our boss to ask for a pay rise, because he or she is perceived as the person in authority and is seen to be more powerful than we are. Imagine that you have decided you are not receiving remuneration that is commensurate with your contribution, and that to address this problem you need to go directly to your boss to make your case for a pay rise. How do you build up your confidence enough to do this?

Build up your confidence

Start by thinking about your contribution to the company or organization that you work for:

- The qualities you bring to the workplace.
- The success you have had in your current job.
- The pride you have in your work.

Get your timing right

First think carefully about when the best time to approach your boss might be. You don't want to ask for money the day after your company has made some workers redundant. Ideally, wait for good news. If you have recently had an argument with your boss for one reason or another, now is not the right time either. You should ask for a pay rise when conditions are right, both for your particular situation and for the situation of your company. Try to make your move at a time when profits are up, or just after you have finished a major project that made your department look good.

The greater the value you place upon what you do, the greater the value of the return to you.

EXERCISE

Think success

Add up the contribution that you make to the success of your company or organization, and decide what amount of money you think would be commensurate with this contribution.

Now imagine that pay cheque coming into your bank account on a monthly basis. How does it feel when you think about this?

Savour the feeling of seeing this amount of money coming into your account. Enjoy the additional financial power this will give you. Delight in the treats you will enjoy with this extra, well-earned money. When you have fully savoured the feeling of this experience, make a small movement or gesture, such as clicking your fingers or scratching your nose. This gesture becomes your link to the desired state or feeling of being rewarded appropriately for your efforts.

Do this exercise twice a day in the period before you go to see your boss. Just before you go into their office to ask for the pay increase, make, to yourself, the link or gesture that connects you to the feeling of receiving a healthy monthly pay cheque.

You are now emotionally prepared to set foot in their office, feeling a strong sense of value for who you are and what you do.

Do your research

Research salary information by finding out how much other people in your position would or do receive. Know how much you should be paid. If you can take any kind of documentation or maybe even a quote in with you when you approach your boss for a rise, that may prove helpful. Check newspaper advertisements or the internet, as well as simply talking to people, to find out how much you deserve to be earning.

Decide what to ask for

Ask for more than you expect. This shows that you mean business and makes sure you are much more likely to get what you want. Say what you want to receive, but don't turn the discussion into a demand for money.

Don't be afraid to ask about benefits, such as company cars, as part of your negotiation.

Body language

Body language is crucial. Maintain eye contact with your boss, not with the ceiling, window or your fingernails. Don't fiddle with anything, so tie back your hair or leave off jewellery if you have fiddling tendencies. Sit up and smile. Clothes also play a part in the impression you make. Dress as you want to be perceived. Sexy is not advisable, but businesslike is. Dress for your next position.

Approach the subject

Have a basic plan ready. Focus on all your accomplishments, any new business that you have brought to the company, how you have made your department and, consequently, your boss, shine. Have you, for instance, put in a lot of overtime over an extended period?

Don't sound desperate

You are asking for a pay rise, so you obviously think you deserve one. Whatever you do, however, don't sound desperate. When you talk with your boss about a salary increase, talk as if you deserve the rise. Above all, never talk about any debts that you have, since this will make you come across as unprofessional.

I'LL LOSE MY CAR IF YOU DON'T GIVE ME A PAY RISE.

PUTTING THE THEORY INTO ACTION

To successfully ask for a pay rise, remember to:

• Think positively about the contribution you make to the company.
• Time your approach to the boss accurately.
• Research and know how much your position is worth.
• Ask for more than you expect to receive.
• Talk as if you deserve the rise – don't be needy or desperate.
• Do the think success exercise.

MAKING 'COLD' TELEPHONE CALLS

Many people in business have a tremendous fear of the cold call, particularly those who are new to running a small business and feel that they have to make cold calls to attract new clients. If you are a sensitive person, you don't want to offend or disturb the other person on the line. Perhaps you also fear being emotionally wounded by their potential rejection of your services. Maybe the receiver of the call will slam the phone down or speak to you abusively. When you are 'needy' for business, these rejections hurt, simply because you are desperate and very desirous of a 'yes' from the potential client.

Confidence in this situation comes from the belief that you are going to succeed, whatever the opposition. It helps to stand up when you make cold calls, and have the attitude 'It's a great day – this conversation is going to be a success.'

Preparing for the call

Before you engage in a session of cold calling, prepare to build mental and emotional strength with this daily exercise. The well of strength is built by asking yourself certain questions that enable you to focus on the strengths and qualities you possess, so that when you make cold calls you have a reservoir or well of strength to draw power from. Typical questions would be:

• What are the qualities that I bring to the job?
• What success have I had in my job?
• What positive things do clients/colleagues say about me?
• What benefits will the work that I do, or the services that I provide, have on the person I am calling?

GIVE YOURSELF A NICKNAME

Think also about what name or nickname you could give yourself to describe the motivation or reason why you do what you do. Here are some examples.

Nickname	Motivation
The Achiever	You make things happen.
The Leader	You provide direction for others.
The Winner	You take on all challenges that come your way.
The Avenger	You want to prove a point to those who said you would not succeed.
The Provider	You want to support your family.
The Trailblazer	You want to push back the limits in your field of work.
The Team Player	You want to enjoy the camaraderie of others.
The Wealth Gatherer	You are working to gather financial rewards.
The Giver	You provide an outstanding level of service for others.
The Warrior	You want to be better than anyone else.
The Impresser	You want to live up to the expectations of other people.
The Inspirer	You want to make the world a better place.

Telephone techniques

The first 15 seconds of any telephone call are crucial. One key to telephone success is knowing how to make your voice convey a professional tone. Here are some suggestions.

- Use your natural voice pitch. Unconsciously 'switching' your voice to create another image is not only artificial but also harmful to your voice over time.
- Stand up when making the call, as this increases your power and assertiveness. Smile as you talk – this releases endorphins into the body. Endorphins are the 'feelgood' hormone. You feel better and the person on the other end of the line will feel better.
- Notice the responses of your callers. Do people often misunderstand your name or ask you to repeat yourself? Do they hesitate when you expect them to speak? It is possible that they may not be able to hear or understand you very well.
- Listen actively. Let the person on the other end know you are listening. Use responses such as 'Yes', 'I understand' and 'Certainly'.
- Know exactly why you are calling. This is essential. Be able to articulate your motivations clearly and concisely. This sounds obvious, but plenty of people don't handle this well and thus make a less than confident first impression.
- Know as much as possible about the company or person you are calling.
- Try to get a connection within any company before you call. If you can't make a connection, determine whom you are trying to reach (such as a human resources person, a senior staff member or a particular manager).
- Be courteous and enthusiastic. If you connect with the person you were hoping to reach, ask if he or she is available to talk at that time or whether it would be better to schedule a later time to talk.
- Keep your responses short and to the point.
- Be friendly yet professional.
- Take notes (especially names).
- Be sure to follow up, sending any materials they request. Ask whether they prefer that you follow up by phone, e-mail etc.
- Be sure to send thank-you notes after any substantial phone conversation (interview, information sharing etc.).

COMPETITIVE CONFIDENCE

This section is applicable to both sporting and professional situations where you are measured by your performance. The problem with this outward measuring system is that it can be highly damaging to confidence. It can lead to self-pressure and a feeling of 'I'm not good enough' or 'I'm not as good as they are'. Almost every day we are required to respond to this way of measuring our performance. Confidence can plummet quickly, even though we may be trying our very best, so it is doubly important to retain a positive focus.

Sporting performance

If you play any kind of sport, you may often find yourself in a situation where somebody asks you, in all innocence, 'Did you win?' or 'How did you do?' when you have finished playing. If your reply is 'No, I lost' or 'I was seven over par', then the tendency in these moments is to feel a sense of shortfall. You probably feel that in another person's eyes you have failed. Perhaps you worry about what they will think of you. Maybe they exude an air of superiority that they did better than you, which serves to compound your anxiety.

Professional performance

The 'outcome question' constantly asked of sales professionals is 'How many sales have you made?' If you run workshops, the outcome question will be 'How many people attended the workshop?' If you are a teacher, your pupils' exam results may be judged. There are countless ways in which all kinds of workers are assessed on their professional performance.

Positive reminders

It is at these moments that we need a reminder that we are confident, and the exercise opposite is designed to enable you to connect to the 'already confident' you. When we are without confidence, we are afraid to try. Fear and anxiety impose themselves upon us. To be able to hold on to your confidence in the face of self-doubt, consider all the many moments in your life when you have felt proud, when you have had a go, when you have given your best without knowing the consequences or outcome of your actions. These could include passing your driving test, performing a concert or making a difficult phone call. The fact is that we must have been confident in those situations to have even tried to do these things – confident and courageous.

EXERCISE

The confidence book

Buy yourself a new notebook and begin to write down in it some moments in your life when you tried to do something new. It does not matter whether you succeeded or failed, it is the fact that you had the confidence to try that counts. Focus on the fact that you feel proud of who you are and what you did. Your confidence lives in the ability to do. Here are some examples.

- 1970. School running race. Ran as fast as I could.
- 1988. Gave a seminar to business people on body language. Really did a thorough job.
- 1999. Overcame food allergy. Required great self-discipline.

At the end of the week, read these moments aloud to yourself. Better still, ask someone to read them to you, ideally with a favourite piece of music playing in the background. The music creates the conditions that allow the emotions to be open, and therefore better permits you to receive the messages about yourself. Use the same piece of music each time that you do this exercise. The more you do the exercise, the stronger the link you will have between the feelings of confidence when you felt good about yourself and this music. After six months, you will be able to play the music without doing the exercise and it will cause you to feel confident and courageous.

Try to do this exercise every week for a few months. Confidence underpins each of the moments when you feel proud of yourself, but self-doubt and criticism fragment this line of confidence. When this exercise works, it will reconnect the natural line of confidence that lives in you, and you will start to feel the natural, untainted confidence that you had when you were three or four years old.

You have had hundreds of confident moments.

The daily exercises, tips and techniques provided in this chapter are designed to allow you to implement all the ideas that have been discussed in this book. The purpose of engaging in this programme is to ensure that you turn the ideas into real confidence in your personal life.

THE 17-DAY PROGRAMME

Day 1:	Mental confidence	Day 10:	Trust
Day 2:	Physical confidence	Day 11:	Small talk
Day 3:	Say no	Day 12:	Be in the present
Day 4:	Tolerations	Day 13:	Show appreciation
Day 5:	Flow activities	Day 14:	Reduce dispersion
Day 6:	The language of confidence	Day 15:	Ask for what you want
Day 7:	Self-encouragement	Day 16:	Accept compliments
Day 8:	Develop willpower	Day 17:	Celebrate
Day 9:	Practise forgiveness		

Using the programme

For real confidence to build and grow, you will need to implement these ideas on a daily basis until the new confidence habits and patterns become permanent. Don't do more than one exercise per day, to give space for the new habits and patterns to grow. Give yourself around three months to work through the entire programme. You may be tempted to stop the programme after a few weeks, once you start to have some success, but keep going, building your confidence foundations. The stronger the foundations that you build the more secure your confidence will be when it is tested.

Day 1: Mental confidence

How much of your time do you spend thinking about things that you can do nothing about? Unnecessary worry can be very draining on natural confidence. Worry invariably leads to self-doubt, procrastination and inaction. Excessive worry causes the mental focus to be on what will go wrong rather than what will go right. A lot of worry is often about things that we can do nothing about anyway, or about things that are never going to happen.

EXERCISE

Record your thoughts

This simple exercise is designed to help you get the mental clutter out of your head and free up your thinking for more confident decision-making. On a blank sheet of paper, write down all your thoughts for 30 minutes. Don't censor these thoughts. Put down your darkest thoughts if they arise. Put down on paper the thoughts as they come into your head. Make sure that you complete the full 30 minutes. Write down everything that you think, then throw the piece of paper away. If you genuinely find it hard to clear a 30-minute space in your day, start with five minutes to get the process moving, and then gradually try to increase the time you spend on the exercise.

bathroom needs cleaning

that tv presenter is really annoying

why are planets round?

Day 2: Physical confidence

Absence of confidence manifests itself in the way we walk and the way we carry ourselves physically. Naturally confident people carry themselves in a confident way. So it makes sense, if you want to increase your confidence, to carry yourself confidently. This sends a confident message both to yourself and to others. Observe the way that you walk.

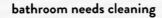

2

EXERCISE

Walk with confidence

A confident walk does not necessarily have to be fast. It needs to suit you and your physical body type. A confident walk could be relaxed and loose, or it could be brisk and upright with military precision. Experiment with both kinds of walk. The point of the exercise is to find a walk that gives you a feeling of increased confidence and purpose.

Day 3: Say no

This day is for developing the habit of saying no with more confidence and less fear. To begin with, observe all the things that you say yes to that you would rather say no to. For example:

• Letting people walk all over you.
• Not complaining when you have received poor service at a shop or restaurant.
• Allowing others to put you down.
• Accepting second best from yourself when you know that you could do better.
• Getting drawn into criticism, judgement and gossip about others that you would prefer to avoid.

Determine to say no next time

In your notebook, make a note of those things that you have said yes to that you want to say no to next time. So, for example, if you have just let someone walk all over you, decide what you want to do next time this happens. Utilize the tips from the chapter How to Say No, page 42, as you do this.

Day 4: Tolerations

This is the day to catch up with those annoying little things in your life that you have been putting off. When you deal with your tolerations, you develop the muscle to deal with things at the time they need dealing with, whether you like dealing with them or not.

Putting things off causes energy stagnation. For example, if you just vaguely think 'I must clean the rust from the car sometime', you will probably never find the impetus to actually do it. Instead, say to yourself that you will do it on Tuesday. When Tuesday comes, because you have told yourself that you will do this job, you will be able to summon up the necessary energy and willpower.

Dealing with tolerations builds the habit of nipping problems in the bud before they grow. Whatever the situation, take charge and deal with it. If you don't, it will become more and more difficult to handle. The more tasks you don't do – after having said you will do them – the greater will be the build-up of unused energy within you, and this can lead to laziness, false promises and other problems. So dealing with your tolerations enables you to tidy up many loose ends in the background of your life.

EXERCISE

Deal with tolerations

Make a list of those things in your life that you are tolerating from:
• your home
• your work
• your well-being
• your life balances
• your finances

Home – change lightbulb in kitchen

Work – request payrise

Well-being – join gym

Finance – work out budget

From your list, choose to:
• do one thing about the house
• do one business/work item
• improve one aspect of your well-being
• deal with one financial item
• do one thing just for you

Day 5: Flow activities

5

For building confidence today, engage in flow activities. Flow activities, as described on page 114, are those things that you truly enjoy doing. They are things you really want to do, rather than just feeling that you should do them. They are activities that leave you feeling energized and buoyant.

Many people fall into the trap of feeling guilty about doing things that they want to, for fear of being seen to be selfish. They have got into the habit of giving to others before they give to themselves. They may worry: 'What will others think of me if I do something for myself?' However, true friends will support you when you spend time on yourself.

EXERCISE

Enjoy a flow activity

Choose one flow activity to engage in today, and set aside time for doing it.

Day 6: The language of confidence

Today is the day to choose a power word to use. A power word is a word that powers a quality that you want to build. In quiet moments during the day, for example, in a traffic jam, or in a queue, you can also consider confidence by thinking about the following.

- Who are confident people?
- Look around – where can you see confidence in action right now?
- Where might you find confidence in daily life?
- What does it mean to talk to someone in confidence?
- What does confidence feel like when you have it?
- What does confidence enable you to do that you could not do before?
- Can you act in confidence, even if you don't have it?

EXERCISE

Use a power word

CONFIDENCE

If the quality you are searching for is confidence, then your power word today is 'confidence'. Write your power word down on a small card so that you will remember it throughout the day. Say the word to yourself. 'Confidence. Confidence. Confidence.' Savour its resonance. Using this method, you send a message to yourself that you are interested in developing this vital quality and are wanting to attract more of it into your life.

Day 7: Self-encouragement

Self-encouragement is an invaluable ally in building confidence, because it is a way of sending positive messages to yourself, rather than either sending yourself negative messages or waiting for others to tell you how well you have done at something. The best time to do this is before you begin work. Remind yourself of some of the qualities that you will be bringing to the workplace today.

If you don't know of any, or put yourself down so much that you don't think you bring anything to the workplace, then try asking four or five friends or colleagues what they see are the qualities that you bring to your job. Ask them to write them down anonymously on a piece of paper for you.

EXERCISE

Encourage yourself

When you are clear about the qualities that you will be bringing to the workplace today, say them to yourself before work and at various times throughout the day, such as mid-morning, lunch and mid-afternoon. For example: 'Today I will be bringing the qualities of good organization, punctuality, support for others and customer service skills to the workplace.' When you have finished your day's work, remind yourself of the qualities that you brought to the workplace today.

Day 8: Develop willpower

Developing willpower is invaluable for confidence-building, as it puts more power and positive energy in the personal vitality tank for whenever you might need it. The absence of willpower leads to giving up easily, being put off by difficulty and not believing that you can succeed.

EXERCISE

Go one step further	
Today's task is to choose one activity that you do regularly that you would like to go the extra mile with, as a way of increasing your willpower. Here are some examples:	
Don't be put off	When someone rejects an idea that you have, don't accept the first no, but use that no as an opportunity to discover more about what they really need.
Don't wait	If you see something that is not right, don't wait for someone else to act, do something about it yourself. You may be the catalyst for change.
Try new things	Do a sponsored walk or activity that enables you to go beyond your perceived boundaries of what you believe is possible.
Seek inspiration	Read stories of people who never gave up and still succeeded.
Do it now	Rather than leave the dishes in the sink overnight to soak, do all the washing-up tonight and come down to a clean kitchen and a fresh start in the morning.
Set new targets	When working out, do a few extra repetitions past your targets, to develop the mental muscle of going one extra step.

Day 9: Practise forgiveness

Today you will focus on practising forgiveness. Being able to forgive will help you overcome the negative habit of attaching blame to others and yourself.

EXERCISE

Forgive someone

The task today is to forgive yourself at least once and one other person or group of people. Try one of the following:

- Forgive the driver who cut you up in traffic.
- Forgive yourself when you make a mistake.
- Forgive the waiter who spilled juice on your jacket.
- Forgive the person who turned up late for an appointment with you.

Day 10: Trust

Building trust between yourself and your instinct is an invaluable investment. Trust is a vital ally in building confidence, because the more trust that you have in yourself the greater will be your ability to make difficult decisions and to do things that you have never attempted before.

EXERCISE

Trust your instincts

This simple and fun exercise should be performed for about 20 minutes. All you need is a matchbox and some floor space.

Take a matchbox and throw it out onto the floor a short distance in front of you. Now close your eyes. With your eyes still closed, walk over to the matchbox and pick it up in your hand. Don't be hesitant when you do this. Practise being confident and trust yourself. At the same time, don't rush or get impatient if you don't pick the matchbox up the first time – keep trying. When you have mastered this, close your eyes before you throw the matchbox. This time, you will not have seen it land. With your eyes still closed, walk over to the matchbox and pick it up. This is obviously harder, but persevere and practise throwing the box further away from yourself and enjoy walking with confidence towards the box. Don't worry so much about where the box is. Let your instincts direct you there.

Day 11: Small talk

Today you will concentrate on increasing your confidence in making small talk.

Starting a Conversation

Initiate a conversation with someone you have never spoken to before, then see if you can keep it going for at least a minute by responding to the other person's statements with comments and further questions of your own. Any of the following general subjects could be used:

- the weather
- world events
- trends in fashion
- office news
- sports headlines
- popular music
- popular TV programmes
- local transport

Other ways of starting a conversation might be:

- asking for directions   • asking the time
- making observations about an incident you have both witnessed
- making a positive comment about something the other person is wearing
- remarking on the view
- talking about health, if at the doctor's or dentist's
- making comments in the movie queue about the forthcoming film
- if sitting in a café, commenting on the other person's choice of food and drink

Day 12: Be in the present

Today the task for you is to slow down and try to allow yourself to become more present in each moment. When you are present and in the moment then you are not able to worry about the past or future. When you are caught up in a fast-paced, results-driven life, it is very easy to fall into the trap of focusing on the future. Being in the present means just that. All your senses are tuned in to each moment of your life as you live it.

One of the major obstacles to being in the present is the background noise that can go on in a person's life. Negative self-talk, worrying about the past and fretting about the future can all take us away from the moment, the present, where life is lived. The state of confidence is a quiet state, with no background noise.

EXERCISE

Focus on here and now

To assist in reducing background noise, here is a very simple 30-second exercise that you can do anywhere.

Stage 1: Pay attention to your external focus
Focus on something outside yourself. For example, spend 10 seconds focusing on something that you can see, such as an object in the room, movement outside the window or the pattern of the clouds.

Stage 2: Pay attention to your breathing
Focus on your breathing for 10 seconds. Take a nice deep, steady breath in, and then exhale slowly and steadily. Repeat this exercise a couple of times.

Stage 3: Listen
Focus on what you can hear for 10 seconds. Listen to the sounds around you.
• How many do you hear?
• Are they close in or far away?
• Are the sounds deep or shrill?

Day 13: Show appreciation

Today you will develop a positive outlook on life. Confident people are naturally able to see the advantages and opportunities in any given situation. Negative people tend to focus on how gloomy everything is.

13

EXERCISE

Find the positive

If, for example, you are at the dentist's, rather than having a negative mindset about the experience you could use the time to reach any number of new insights.

• 'I'm lucky to have teeth. A toothless life would be much less pleasurable.'

• 'Without the pain of the drill, my teeth would fall out. Perhaps some other difficulties in life also help me accomplish good things.'

Try to apply this positive approach today to a situation about which you normally have negative feelings.

Day 14: Reduce dispersion

Dispersion and disruption are a constant feature of our daily lives. Our concentration is constantly being interrupted by requests from others, by the telephone ringing, by e-mails arriving on our desktops or by somebody wanting something now. All of these interruptions lead to weaker and weaker concentration and less completion. This means that we are always trying to catch ourselves up, leading to self-doubt and the feeling that we can't cope.

EXERCISE

Focus on the concentration

Set aside a certain time during the day for concentrating on one activity, and try to block everything else out. Make up your mind: 'I am going to do X for 15 minutes straight.' For an entire 15 minutes, don't stop for anything that is not life-threatening. You can practise this while riding on a bus or waiting for an appointment. Set yourself a goal of 15 minutes to focus exclusively on one subject. It may be a problem you are having at work, a personal goal or an issue in a relationship. The following week, increase this to 20 minutes, and after that week increase it by five-minute intervals on a weekly basis.

Day 15: Ask for what you want

Unconfident people often find it daunting to ask for what they want. They fear being rejected and being perceived as greedy and selfish. Another common mistake is to expect others to know what you need and want, which, of course, they don't. Take a moment to reflect on the past week. Note how many times you have said what you did not want instead of what you wanted. 'I don't want to continue worrying about this.' 'I don't want to do this work any more.' 'I don't want to have to tell you again.' 'I don't like what is going on here.'

Not asking for what you want results in living a less effective life than you are already living. People who learn to ask for what they want tend to get better jobs, more money, less depression and less anxiety, and generally report feeling happier about their lives.

Asking for what you want does not mean you will get everything you ask for. It means you will get more out of life, and surprisingly more than you ever expected to get. When you ask for what you want, you actually tell others you are OK. Asking for what you want may get you some of the following:

• A promotion at work.
• Your child knowing exactly what you want, instead of guessing at what is behind your request.
• Your partner no longer feeling ambiguous about what to expect from you.

When you begin to ask for what you want from others around you, you will have clear communications and people will be able to trust you. Also, you will be getting more of what you really want and a lot less of what others want you to have. The energy generated by practising this technique will be obvious and rewarding.

EXERCISE

Be very clear

Ask for what you want at least once today. State clearly: 'What I want is ...'
Invite those around you to ask for what they want as well. If something does
not make sense to you, tell the other person you are not clear about what it is
they want. When you ask for what you want, it is important to remember to
say 'I' instead of 'you', 'we' or 'they'.
Practise this exercise and you will start to notice how much more you are
getting, and how your life is becoming more and more full of activities, money
and positive results.

Day 16: Accept compliments

Many people feel awkward when they receive a compliment or someone
says something positive to them. 'You can't possibly be talking about me',
they think, and dismiss the comment by changing the direction of the
conversation. They tend to think that they are not worthy of the compliment and feel
embarrassed. If you are like this, it is very difficult for others to compliment you. It is as if
they are giving you a gift that you will not even open.

16

EXERCISE

Enjoy being complimented

Your task today is to accept compliments that come your way. Instead of
rejecting any compliment, enjoy the moment and say 'thank you'. In this way,
the compliment will be received. The giver of the compliment feels good and
you are creating an opportunity that allows them to win, too, as they don't want
the compliment thrown back in their face. Giving to yourself is as important as
giving to others, so start to develop this habit by accepting compliments.

Day 17: Celebrate

If you have had success with any of the exercises you have worked through on the previous days, today you should celebrate that success. Confident people are never slow to celebrate, because they have a natural appreciation of success and its worth. Celebrating success is a way of appreciating it and sending out the message that you want more success.

Mark your success

Celebrate success by:
- buying yourself a gift or treat
- booking a holiday
- booking yourself in for a massage or other relaxing treatment
- taking time to be alone
- hosting a party
- spending time with your friends
- going to that restaurant you've always wanted to try

The point is to make some kind of gesture from you to yourself that attaches significance to the success you have just had.

CONCLUSION

Congratulations on progressing this far! Rebuilding confidence and overcoming doubt takes no little courage and bravery. If you have completed the majority of the confidence-building exercises, you should now be a significantly more confident person from the one who first bought this book. Now you need to review the progress that you have made to date and clarify your next steps forward.

Reviewing your progress

Every month, it is a good idea to revisit some of the key insights and perceptions that you have learned from this book. Take a step back from your demanding life and remind yourself of what you want and what you need to do to achieve this.

Remember the advice given in the introduction to work through the book with a friend. Having support is invaluable when you embark on any kind of personal development journey, simply because you are attempting to build new positive habits and patterns in place of self-defeating patterns. Support enables you to feel that you are not alone on the journey. Remember that confidence grows in the presence of warmth and encouragement, so make use of all the help that is available. You are not a lesser person for asking for help.

Building confidence comes from lots of small efforts all pointing in the same direction, rather than one big effort. There may be knock-backs and minor disappointments on the way, but the key to success is for you to personally decide that you will have confidence, and that you will not allow your life to be lived in the shadow of self-doubt.

Don't just hope for increased confidence or think that maybe you would like to be more confident. Decide that you will be more confident. Once you make that decision, you become committed to achieving that goal. Remember that confidence is there inside you at all times. Sometimes it gets overlaid by doubt, but your confidence has never really left you. It now awaits the chance to serve you so that you can live the best life that you possibly can.

INDEX

INDEX

ACKNOWLEDGEMENTS

Main images Illustrator: David Beswick at 'ome
Person icon credit: Pyetro Rapp from the Noun Project

ACKNOWLEDGEMENTS

Main images Illustrator: David Beswick at 'ome
Person icon credit: Pyetro Rapp from the Noun Project